International Conferences e-Society 2022 and Mobile Learning 2022

Online
12-14 March 2022

ISBN: 978-1-7138-5790-7

Printed from e-media with permission by:

Curran Associates, Inc.
57 Morehouse Lane
Red Hook, NY 12571

Some format issues inherent in the e-media version may also appear in this print version.

Printed with permission by Curran Associates, Inc. (2022)

For permission requests, please contact International Association for Development of the Information Society (IADIS) at the address below.

International Association for Development of the Information Society (IADIS)
Rua Sao Sebastiao Da Pedreira
No. 100, 30, 1050-209
Lisbon, Portugal

Phone: 351 21 3151373
Fax: 351 21 3151244

secretariat@iadis.org

Additional copies of this publication are available from:

Curran Associates, Inc.
57 Morehouse Lane
Red Hook, NY 12571 USA
Phone: 845-758-0400
Fax: 845-758-2633
Email: curran@proceedings.com
Web: www.proceedings.com

TABLE OF CONTENTS

FULL PAPERS

SHORT PAPERS

REFLECTION

FULL
PAPERS

USABILITY AND USER EXPERIENCE IN OPEN COMMUNITY WEB PORTALS: A CASE STUDY IN SMART PORTS DOMAIN

Shabnam Kazemi, Deniz Cetinkaya, Gernot Liebchen and Reza Sahandi
Department of Computing and Informatics, Bournemouth University
Talbot Campus, Poole, United Kingdom

ABSTRACT

Open community web portals and information sharing platforms have been widely used to generate and share knowledge. Recent advances in technology and growing interest in crowdsourcing tools have helped to improve the technical competency and quality of these platforms. However, usability and user experience aspects are still challenging as satisfying the needs of different users is an open problem for such systems. This paper presents a case study of the user experience improvement of an open community web portal that facilitates information sharing in the context of smart ports domain. The case study employed data collection methods such as surveys and focus group meetings coupled with usability tests to collect feedback. User scenarios were designed and tested on the SPEED (Smart Ports Entrepreneurial Ecosystem Development) open community portal. Feedback around the user interface of the portal was mostly positive. There have been minor improvements in the navigation of the portal. Findings and lessons learnt are presented in this paper.

KEYWORDS

Usability, User Experience, Smart Posts Web Portal, Usability of Web Systems, Human Computer Interaction

1. INTRODUCTION

The constant striving towards efficiency, innovation and global competition is putting pressure on businesses and their software providers to shift from desktop software to web applications or web portals. According to Stoffel and Cunningham (2005), Web portal is "...a single-point, integrated, multi-channel, user-personalised, user customisable Internet site providing access to information, people, and processes". Web portals have been widely implemented and used for different purposes for many years (Sampson and Manouselis, 2005). This popularity of web applications and web portals to promote consistent web presences and provisions of services brings however some challenges, such as how to motivate user participation and how to engage users (Brakel, 2003, Butler et al., 2002, Faliagka et al., 2015, Li and Jiang, 2019, Ridings and Gefen, 2004, Spallek et al., 2008).

Principal ways of encouraging web portal users' interactions and influencing their behaviours are connected to characteristics such as content (contained business related information or access to external information resources), design (providing users with the pleasant, usable, and stable environment), personalisation capabilities (serving users' specific preference and needs), and formation of virtual communities (bringing together users with similar interests and needs) (Butler et al., 2010, Sampson and Manouselis, 2005, Zhou, 2003). That means that usability attributes result in increasing engagement (Nam, 2014), higher quality information (Attfield et al., 2011), richer user experiences (Li and Jiang, 2019), and improved opportunities to ask or receive clarification on resources (Arthana et al., 2019, Maligat et al., 2020, Rohayati et al., 2018, Sampson and Manouselis, 2005, Zarish et al., 2019). User experience and usability features have played a significant role in stimulating engagement and formation of users' expectations (Li and Jiang, 2019, Ekaterina, 2017, Butler et al., 2010).

As the need for usable web portals for potential and new users is still demanding (Oliha, 2020, Oliha, 2014, Frøkjær et al., 2000, Liao et al., 2011), we present an empirical study about the usability and user experience of web portals in this paper. A case study evaluating the usability and user experience of the SPEED (Smart

Ports Entrepreneurial Ecosystem Development) open community Web portal is presented. This ideation platform has been developed to build a network community connecting high-tech start-ups with large and complex ports across four European countries, namely Belgium, France, the Netherlands and the UK. Focus group meetings were applied to examine the ease of use, community focus, information benefits, and navigation of the portal. The case study provided us with important lessons learnt which will be useful for portal developers.

The remainder of the paper is organised as follows: paper continues with a brief discussion of related literature in the next section. Section 3 presents the details of the case study followed by the lessons learnt in Section 4. Finally, Section 5 presents the conclusions and recommends potential future work.

2. BACKGROUND

Sales portals, customer portals solutions, intranet portals, and all other information portals allow users to connect to one another and provide a richer user experience such as peer commenting, and social networking (Benz et al., 2020, Butler et al., 2010). Past research has shown that individuals use web portals to save time and cost when sharing information (Benz et al., 2020, Guo et al., 2018). Web portals often require users to create user profiles in order to enable users to share knowledge or to participate in social networking activities (Benz et al., 2020). Once registered, users are more encouraged to be involved if they benefit from the resources and business focus networking (Hann et al., 2007).

Usability testing on various organisational web portals have indicated that engagement is heavily influenced by a portal's context (Al-Debei, 2013), consistent user interface (Axelsson, 2012) and its associated process flow (Attfield et al., 2011). To be precise, ease of use, information benefits, accessibility to resources, content creditability, usefulness, trustworthiness, accuracy, clarity, information architecture and its integration to external content providers and easy navigation could affect an individual's decision in engaging with a portal or not (Feledi et al., 2013, Kakol et al., 2017, Maligat et al., 2020),

For instance, the usability evaluation of an Indonesian cultural heritage crowdsourcing information platform has shown that low workflow efficiency affected users' satisfaction negatively (Arthana et al., 2019). Similarly, the test plan of a multimedia platform that promotes communication and information sharing among educators, parents and children indicated a couple of usability issues, such as navigation (lack of back button), commenting and editing profiles failures, which affected its users' attitude (Laranjeiro et al., 2017).

In another study by Shayganmehr and Montazer (2019), the importance of age on using e-government websites was demonstrated that pop-up notifications and advertisements on the homepage were annoying only to elderlies. This means that care need to be taken not to take users' willingness to engage with a system for granted, and it highlights the importance of usability investigations and improvements of web portals. In this study, we identified the best practices from the literature and applied the most common principles during the early phases of the development. Then we employed usability testing and focus group methods to improve the user experience. Next section explains the case study and outcomes of the focus group meetings.

3. CASE STUDY

The SPEED portal is an open community information portal, and its main purpose has been the promotion of innovation and efficiency in the smart port domain by building an ecosystem for smart port app development. This open community platform provides services to port stakeholders (such as port authorities, customs and excises), logistic companies (including ships, road, train), technology entrepreneurs, start-ups, students and members of the public.

The information shared on the portal is divided in the following main categories:

- *Port Logistics Challenges:* Accumulate and display ideas for further development.
- *Smart Port Technologies:* Existing software and hardware technologies that help improving port logistic systems.
- *Business Profiles:* Company profiles in the seaport domain.
- *Events:* SPEED project events (e.g., seminars, webinars, and hackathons).
- *Proof-of-Concept Solutions:* Feasible software and hardware proposals and principles.
- *Ongoing Research and Additional Output:* Published and ongoing research studies.

The home page provides links to all of these categories and easy navigation to different pages such as Help or Registration pages. Figure 1 shows a screenshot of the main page below.

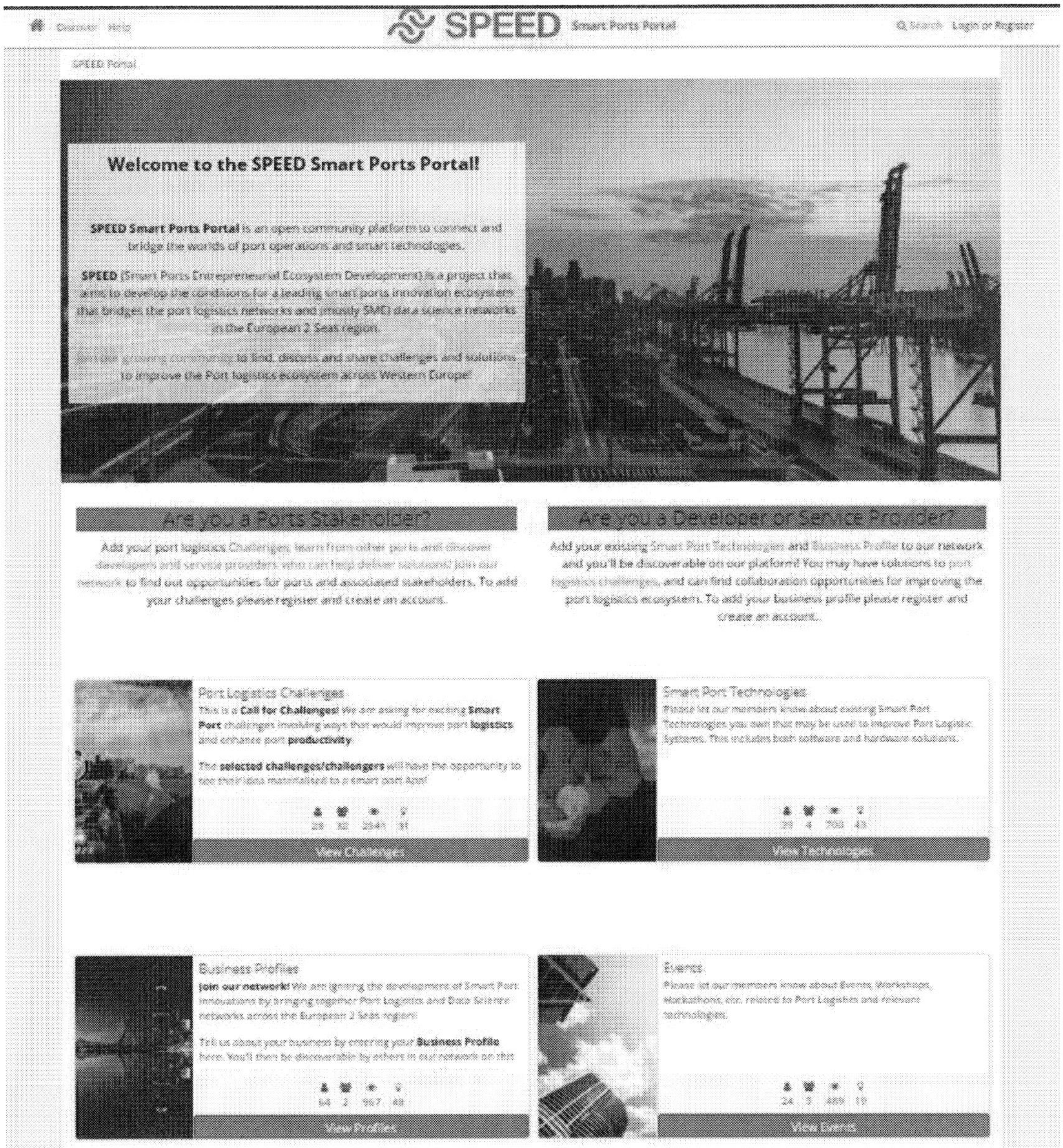

Figure 1. Screenshot of the SPEED Portal homepage

As part of the portal's development the overall quality of the portal's user experience was assessed. This assessment consisted of a survey covering various parts of the portal including portal engagement, a survey covering the general web experiences, and subsequent usability testing of the portal.

Many of the outcomes were helpful in improving the portal's user experience. There were, however, a few questions raised that resulted from the usability testing phase. For instance, the workflow that was considered for the port logistics challenges was not clear to the users. Similarly, users found the portal's navigation difficult due to the vocabulary choices; for example, users were often confused with terms like "Ideas" as they were used for all six categories (challenges, solutions, events, etc.), or "Conversation" to discover the ports connected to the portal. This terminology was result of adopting an already existing crowdsourcing providers functionality. Usability testing certainly could have helped to address some of these issues before users encountered them. However, the development was only as good as our ability to anticipate users' behaviours, and a thorough usability testing would have helped us to represent the content in a manner that was not confusing to the users.

Focus group meetings were viewed as a viable supplement to open discussion and improve user experience as it is a valuable way to engage in conversation with users in order to establish users' expectations. Conducting focus group meetings was in essence taking a step back to reassess users' expectations of the navigation of the platform. This assisted us to limit the impact of potentially biased usability task designs and clarifying underlying assumptions.

In the literature, it is often stated that using multiple methods for collecting user feedback provides a better, more complete, picture of the user experience. For example, Nielsen (1997), suggests observation to supplement focus groups and Oldham (2008) proposes focus groups, usability testing, and surveys can be used effectively together to discover both how users think and how they navigate a web site. Hence, focus groups were viewed as a unique opportunity to assess the quality of usability features of the SPEED open community portal through collecting qualitative feedback from users about their web experiences.

The focus group had eight members consisting of partners from the SPEED project from both industry and ports community as well as academics in relevant disciplines (SPEEDProject, 2021). In addition, our team from Bournemouth University (BU) and one IT support member of the crowdsourcing solution provider attended all focus group meetings. We held three sessions in April, May and June last year. All meetings were run remotely via Zoom due to the constraints posed by the Covid 19 pandemic, and since the members were based in different European countries, namely in the UK, Belgium and the Netherlands.

The focus group sessions were moderated by one of the senior software developers from our team who had experience moderating usability testing. A planning session was conducted by the BU team to formulate the questions, and to design the protocol in two parts. Part one focused on the SPEED Portal User Interface, and part two focused on the SPEED Portal Increasing Engagement Ideas.

3.1 SPEED Portal User Interface

For the first part, we shared the link of the Web portal (SPEEDPortal, 2021) with the focus group members, and we asked them to register as well as to sign a consent form. While the instructions were explained to all members in the meeting, an eight-question survey was shared via Mentimeter (https://www.mentimeter.com) to get the participants' anonymous feedback about the portal. We gave the users some pre-defined tasks and asked their opinion of the usability of the portal. Figure 2 presents the questions and the initial results for the Mentimeter survey.

3.2 SPEED Portal Increasing Engagement Ideas

In the second part, ideas for engagement and publicising were collected via Padlet (https://padlet.com). Suggestions were collected and listed under multiple categories which were shared with the members for their approval to have a consensus. Figure 3 shows a sample Padlet entry. We collected over 25 responses suggesting various improvements for better user experience.

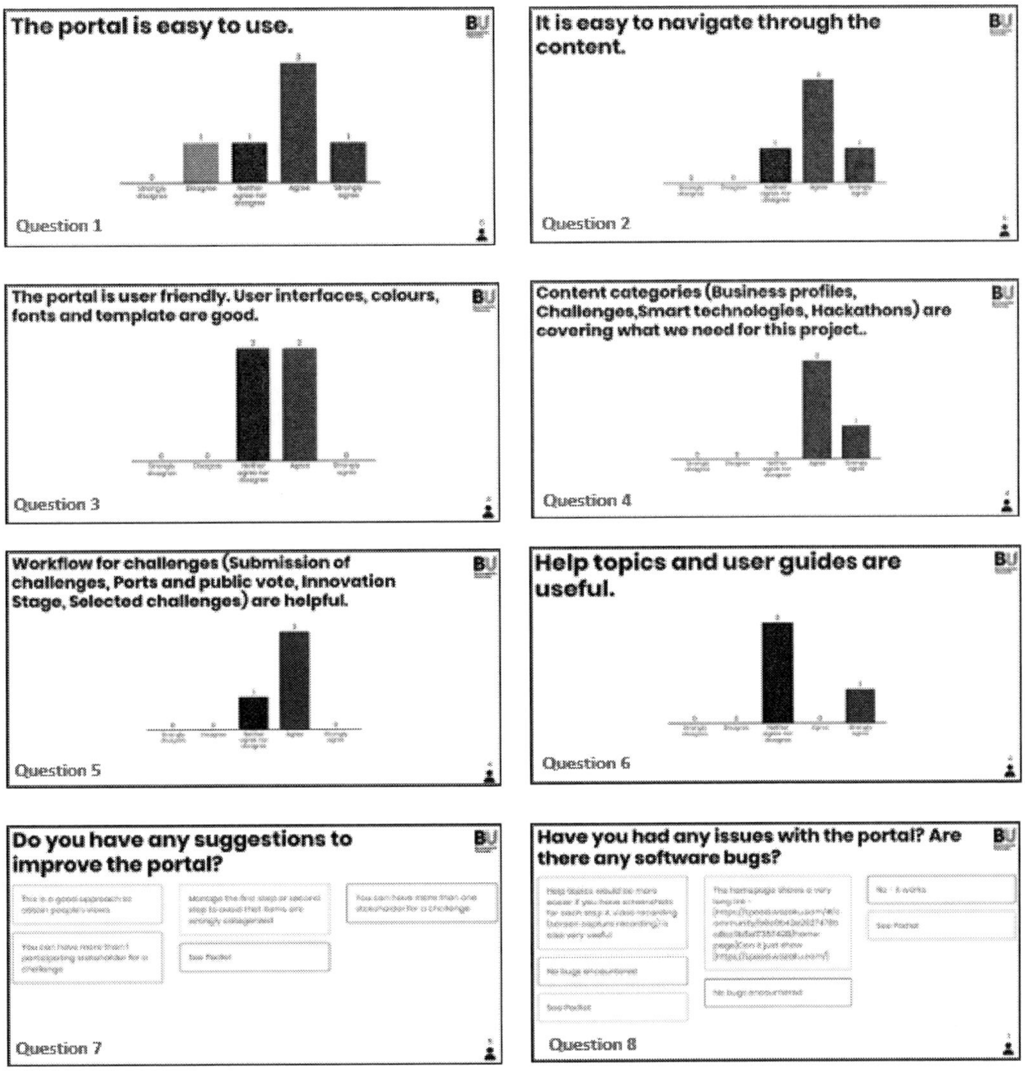

Figure 2. Mentimeter anonymous results

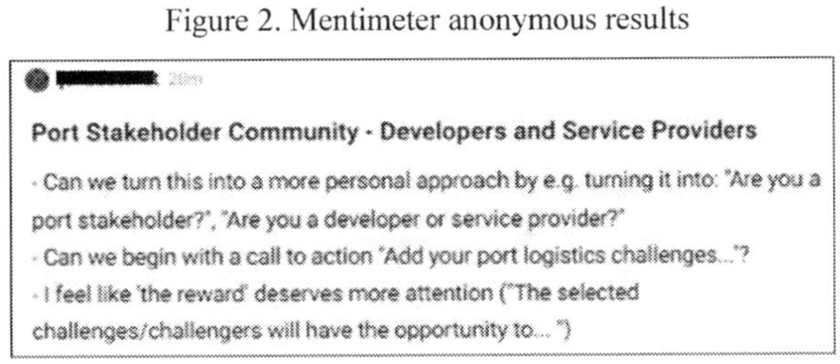

Figure 3. Sample Padlet entry

We needed to run a second short survey to agree on a few points where focus group members had different opinions. For example, while a number of users suggested an approval stage in the workflow for adding new content, some participants did not agree. Due to the platform is designed to be an open community platform we needed to clarify these points. Figure 4 shows a sample question about the workflow on the portal. As a result, a private stage is added in the workflow for automatic approval of the content but with a flexibility to be able to unpublish content by the admin.

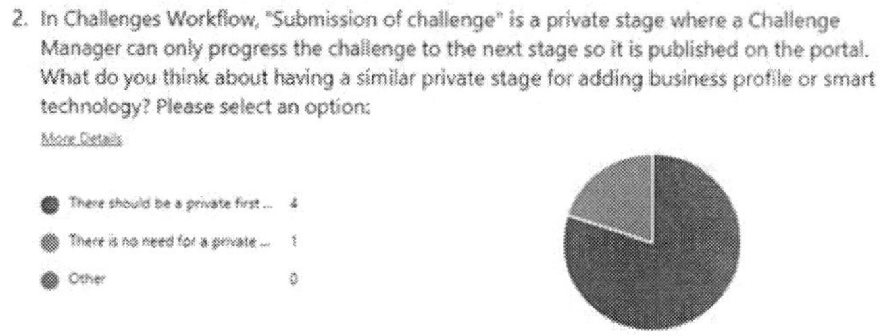

Figure 4. Sample survey question

With our experiments and focus group feedback, we could redesign different parts of the system and improve the user experience. Next section presents the lessons learnt and summarises the improvements done.

4. LESSONS LEARNT

As a result of our interactions with the different stakeholders, we included aspects in the portal which could have been neglected if we would not have sought the input of key stakeholders. The following list of changes were specifically taken on:

- Improving the Help topics and user guidelines
- Revising the workflow for adding new content
- Explaining the aim of the portal on the main page
- Revising the text and messages to be more clear
- Changing the language to call to action
- Improving the layout
- Adding an Events section for project related events
- Adding links between the submitted ideas
- Social media integration
- Getting feedback from the portal users
- Improving the navigation between pages

These can be roughly divided into overlapping lessons categories related to:

- *Content and functionality* (Adding an Events section for project related events, Adding links between the submitted ideas*, Social media integration, Getting feedback from the portal users*),
- *Visual layout and presentation* (Changing the language to call to action, Improving the layout), and
- *Understandability and navigation* (Improving the help topics and user guidelines, Revising the workflow for adding new content, Explaining the aim of the portal on the main page, Adding links between the submitted ideas*, Improving the navigation between pages).

Some of the aspects taken forward are related to two lesson categories, namely "Adding links between the submitted ideas", which can be considered as adding functionality and aiding navigation (indicated with a *). "Getting feedback from the portal user" is a functionality that can easily be integrated, but it also aids a positive feedback loop, which will hopefully ensure further user engagement.

A few suggestions were agreed to be postponed or not implemented. This was either due to the fact that it was not possible to implement given underlying platform limitations, or not needed at that time. For example, adding a calendar view for the events, and adding an idea category filter were not required. However, social media integration could not be fully implemented due to technical limitations, so considered as future work. Action items were listed and shared with the stakeholders. The BU team members and the IT support team members have implemented the changes incrementally where focus group members had a chance to check and provide feedback during the update. The overall goal throughout the implementation was to maintain some common goals of usability as much as feasible which include but are not limited to:

- Presentation of information and choices in a clear and concise way,
- Reducing ambiguity,
- Increasing consistency,
- Allowing user control over preferences,
- Aiming for minimalist design, and
- Placement of important items in relevant areas, etc.

Finally, areas of improvement were applied in response to feedback collected in both focus groups and usability testing, and invitees were given the opportunity to provide feedback as a follow-up measure to see if the changes met their expectations. The focus group members were satisfied with the portal's user interface, content, workflow and functions. Further usability tests have been carried out by inviting technology providers and challenge owners to use the portal. The portal is now stable and consistently used with continuous feedback and minor updates. The inclusion of the stakeholders clearly helped to identify issues with a portal that was created by professional developers.

5. CONCLUSION

User feedback on web portals' design and more importantly, understanding how users interact with the knowledge sharing platforms are significant to realise the issues that users may encounter when visiting a portal. In this study, data collected through focus group meetings and usability testing helped to improve the usability and user experience of the portal so that users were satisfied with the portal's context, user interface, and its associated process flow. As such, the study presents a real-world example of improving an information sharing portal. Navigation and accessibility to the portal's information were straightforward. We believe that outcomes and lessons learnt could be helpful in designing future knowledge sharing web portals. It could be argued that the use case of the portal may be a very niche one, but the ultimate purpose of the portal is to share information, and to collect feedback and contributions. That means that this ultimate purpose will be the same as the purposes of many web portals. Whilst lessons learnt about functionality may be less generally applicable, the lessons learnt about navigation, accessibility are important ones to consider. Since this may depend on the targeted user group, a similar practicable approach as taken in this case study is recommended when improving the usability of an information sharing platform, namely by employing focus group studies or similar open feedback channels. Variations may occur depending on the user group and the purpose of a portal, but the ultimate experience of a portal can only be judged by the portal's users themselves, and not by the developers even if they are experienced usability experts. As a future work, we would like to revise the content management approach to have a more flexible method. We are also planning to increase the visibility of the portal and to extend the application domain so that it has more impact.

ACKNOWLEDGEMENT

SPEED (Smart Ports Entrepreneurial Ecosystem Development) Project is funded by EU Interreg 2 Seas Mers Zeeën programme. The authors would like to thank Aikaterini Kakaounaki for her support in this project.

REFERENCES

Al-Debei, M. 2013. Developing and Implementing a Web Portal Success Model. *Jordan Journal of Business Administration*, 9, 161-190.

Arthana, I. K. R., Pradnyana, I. M. A. & Dantes, G. R. Usability testing on website wadaya based on ISO 9241-11. 2019. Institute of Physics Publishing.

Attfield, S., Kazai, G., Lalmas, M. & Piwowarski, B. 2011. Towards a science of user engagement (Position Paper), Fourth ACM International Conference on Web Search and Data Mining (WSDM).

Axelsson, C.-A. W. 2012. *Consistency in Web Design from a User Perspective.*

Benz, C., Zierau, N. & Satzger, G. Not all tasks are alike: Exploring the effect of task representation on user engagement in crowd-based idea evaluation. 2020. Association for Information Systems.

Brakel, P. 2003. Information portals: A strategy for importing external content. *The Electronic Library,* 21, 591-600.

Butler, B., Kiesler, S. & Kraut, R. 2002. Community Effort in Online Groups: Who Does the Work and Why? *Leadership at a Distance,* 54.

Butler, B. S., Sharma, N., Irwin, J. & Spallek, H. 2010. "You are not alone": Effects of highlighting social aspects on responsiveness, joining, and profile information sharing in an information portal. *Proceedings of the American Society for Information Science and Technology,* 47, 1-9.

Ekaterina, L. The role of user expectations in design and development of personalised health information websites and portals. 2017.

Faliagka, E., Lalou, E., Rigou, M. & Sirmakessis, S. 2015. Usability and aesthetics: The case of architectural websites. Springer Verlag.

Feledi, D., Fenz, S. & Lechner, L. 2013. Toward web-based information security knowledge sharing. *Information Security Technical Report.*

Frøkjær, E., Hertzum, M. & Hornbæk, K. 2000. Measuring usability: are effectiveness, efficiency, and satisfaction really correlated?

Guo, S., Chen, R., Li, H. & Liu, Y. Capability Matching and Heuristic Search for Job Assignment in Crowdsourced Web Application Testing. 2018 IEEE International Conference on Systems, Man, and Cybernetics (SMC), 7-10 Oct. 2018 2018. 4387-4392.

Hann, I.-H., Hui, K.-L., Lee, S.-Y. T. & Png, I. P. L. 2007. Overcoming Online Information Privacy Concerns: An Information-Processing Theory Approach. *Journal of Management Information Systems,* 24, 13-42.

Kakol, M., Nielek, R. & Wierzbicki, A. 2017. Understanding and predicting Web content credibility using the Content Credibility Corpus. *Information Processing & Management,* 53, 1043-1061.

Laranjeiro, D., Antunes, M. J. & Santos, P. Multimedia platform development for parental involvement in learning of children attending kindergarten: Iterative cicles of development. 2017. SciTePress, 208-219.

Li, C. F. & Jiang, Y. Q. 2019. Research on the optimization method of website based on user experience. Springer Verlag.

Liao, C., To, P.-L., Liu, C.-C., Kuo, P.-Y. & Chuang, S.-H. J. O. I. R. 2011. Factors influencing the intended use of web portals. 35, 237-254.

Maligat, D. E., Torio, J. O., Bigueras, R. T., Arispe, M. C. & Palaoag, T. D. Web-based Knowledge Management System for Camarines Norte State College. 2020. Institute of Physics Publishing.

Nam, J. 2014. Understanding the motivation to use web portals. *Computers in Human Behavior,* 36, 263–273.

Nielsen, J. 1997. The use and misuse of focus groups. *IEEE Software,* 14, 94-95.

Oldham, B. W. 2008. Focus Groups and Usability Testing in Redesigning an Academic Library's Web Site. *Journal of Web Librarianship,* 2, 219-246.

Oliha, F. Evaluating Usability of Academic Web Portals for Clearance Services. 2020.

Oliha, F. 2014. Web Portal Usability Among Nigerian University Students: A Case Study of University of Benin, Nigeria. 33, 199-206.

Ridings, C. M. & Gefen, D. 2004. Virtual Community Attraction: Why People Hang Out Online. *Journal of Computer-Mediated Communication,* 10, 00-00.

Rohayati, Y., Wulandari, S. & Sari, K. Usability Evaluation of Digital Service Company Portal Using Importance Performance Analysis. 6th International Conference on Information and Communication Technology (ICoICT), 3-5 May 2018 2018. 49-54.

Sampson, D. & Manouselis, N. 2005. A Flexible Evaluation Framework for Web Portals Based on Multi-criteria Analysis. *Web portals.*

Shayganmehr, M. & Montazer, G. A. Identifying Indexes Affecting the Quality of E-Government Websites. 2019 5th International Conference on Web Research (ICWR), 24-25 April 2019 2019. 167-171.

Spallek, H., Butler, B. S., Schleyer, T. K., Weiss, P. M., Wang, X., Thyvalikakath, T. P., Hatala, C. L. & Naderi, R. A. 2008. Supporting Emerging Disciplines with e-Communities: Needs and Benefits. *J Med Internet Res,* 10, e19.

SPEED Portal. Available via https://speed.wazoku.com/ccc/speedportal [Accessed September 2021].

SPEED Project. Available via https://www.interreg2seas.eu/nl/speed [Accessed September 2021].

Stoffel, B. & Cunningham, J. J. R. S. R. 2005. Library participation in campus web portals: an initial survey. 33, 144-160.

Zarish, S. S., Habib, S. & Islam, M. Analyzing Usability of Educational Websites Using Automated Tools. International Conference on Computer and Information Sciences (ICCIS), 3-4 April 2019 2019. 1-4.

Zhou, J. 2003. A History of Web Portals and Their Development in Libraries. *Information Technology and Libraries,* 22, 119-128.

PARENTS' VIEWS ON RISKY ONLINE BEHAVIORS AND POSITIVE TECHNOLOGICAL DEVELOPMENT AMONG HONG KONG EARLY ADOLESCENTS

Wilfred W.F. Lau[1], Morris S.Y. Jong[1], Gustavo S. Mesch[2] and Tianna T.Y. Leung[1]
[1]Department of Curriculum and Instruction, The Chinese University of Hong Kong, Hong Kong SAR, China
[2]Department of Sociology, The University of Haifa, Israel

ABSTRACT

With the increasing use of technology in the 21st century, most people must access the Internet every day, and the new generation of young people has even greater access to the Internet than previous generations had. This study investigated parents' views on risky online behaviors and positive technological development (PTD) among early adolescents in Hong Kong. Additionally, it explored the influence of parenting styles on the Internet use of early adolescents. The sample consisted of 11 parents from six families (five fathers and six mothers) whose children were 11- to 15-year-old adolescents from six secondary schools. This study used semi-structured interviews to elicit the parents' views and conducted thematic analysis to analyze the interview data. The results indicate that early adolescents participated in few risky online behaviors but exhibited significant PTD. Three relationships, which were mediated by a variety of factors, such as personal interests and peer influence, were identified between risky online behaviors and PTD. Parents limiting their children's online activity often led to their children refusing to share the Internet content they consume with their parents. When parents allowed their children to use the Internet without any restrictions, the children either indulged in or self-regulated their Internet use. The parenting styles of the parents in each family were consistent. However, the mothers generally spent more time with their children than did the fathers and were more familiar with their children's Internet use habits. Herein, we propose some specific suggestions for schools and parents to reduce adolescents' online risk-taking and promote PTD.

KEYWORDS

Parents, Early Adolescents, Risky Online Behaviors, Positive Technological Development

1. INTRODUCTION

Numerous studies have been conducted on risky online behaviors among adolescents (Chan et al., 2014; Lau & Yuen, 2013; Wong et al., 2014). However, little research has explored the positive technological development (PTD) of adolescents and how it is related to their risky online behaviors. Few studies have investigated how parenting styles affect the Internet use of youth or distinguished the influence of fathers and mothers on the Internet use of adolescents (Shek et al., 2018). Furthermore, studies have tended to investigate risky online behaviors on the basis of self-reported questionnaires completed by adolescents (Gámez-Guadix et al., 2016). To fill these gaps in the literature, this study elicited parents' views on risky online behaviors and PTD among Hong Kong early adolescents. It also explored the influence of parenting styles on the Internet use of early adolescents. The research questions were as follows: "In what risky online behaviors do early adolescents engage?", "How do early adolescents use technology positively?", "What relationships exist between risky online behaviors and PTD in early adolescents?", and "How do parenting styles affect early adolescents' Internet use?"

This study focused on early adolescents because they experience drastic physical, social, emotional, and cognitive changes as they transition from childhood to adolescence. During this transition, adolescents develop a stronger sense of individuality and a desire for self-exploration, including on the Internet, but are vulnerable to online risk-taking due to changes in brain structure and hormones (Smith et al., 2013). Guiding early adolescents in proper use of the Internet is therefore paramount.

2. LITERATURE REVIEW

2.1 Risky Online Behaviors

Risky behaviors can be defined as "behaviors that are associated with some probability of a maladaptive outcome—that is, an outcome that can impede the acquisition of culturally-accepted goals" (Defoe, 2021, p. 2) and risky online behaviors refer to such behaviors in online settings. Risk exposure and self-control are the two key predictors of risky behaviors during adolescence. The changing physical and social environment in which adolescents live can either protect them from or expose them to various risks. Risky online behaviors occur in a variety of forms, and the risks adolescents encounter online can be broadly classified into four categories: content risks (e.g., exposure to illegal and harmful content), contact risks (e.g., contact with strangers and cyberbullying), commercial risks (e.g., illegal downloading), and privacy risks (e.g., exposure of personal information and intrusion of privacy) (Livingstone & Haddon, 2008). Studies have reported that Hong Kong early adolescents engage in risky online behaviors such as committing unauthorized acts, Internet addiction, engaging in online plagiarism, consuming online pornography, and cyberbullying (Chan et al., 2014; Lau & Yuen, 2013; Wong et al., 2014).

2.2 PTD

Herein, "positive" is used to describe valuable attributes and events that contribute to the self-improvement and social development of adolescents (Bers et al., 2012). Although scholars originally postulated that six developmental assets (competence, confidence, caring, connection, character, and contribution) are associated with PTD (Bers et al., 2012), we discuss PTD from the perspective of three dimensions, which were validated in a previous study involving Hong Kong early adolescents (Lau, 2015) and are defined as follows:

1. perceived technological self-efficacy, which refers to an individual's ability to confidently use new technologies;
2. technological contribution, which refers to an individual's ideas to make meaningful contributions to the society by using technology; and
3. social uses of technology, which refers to an individual's ability to use technology to express care to or to connect and build relationships with others.

2.3 Influence of Parenting Styles on Children's Internet Use

Parenting styles have been widely categorized as authoritative, authoritarian, permissive, or neglectful (Baumrind, 1971; Maccoby & Martin, 1983). Moilanen et al. (2015) demonstrated that authoritarian and permissive parenting inhibit self-regulation among adolescents whereas authoritative parenting promotes self-regulation among adolescents. In addition, parental overprotection has been associated with problematic Internet and social media use (Koronczai et al., 2020). Lee and Chae (2007) found that parental warmth leads to greater Internet use for educational purposes and more positive Internet behaviors. Özgur (2019) reported that adolescents from families with warm, authoritative, and authoritarian parenting styles were less dependent on online games than were adolescents from families with other parenting styles.

3. METHOD

3.1 Participants and Procedure

Semi-structured interviews were conducted with 11 parents (five fathers and six mothers) from six families whose children were 11- to 15-year-old adolescents from six secondary schools in Hong Kong. Informed consent was obtained from the respective schools and parents before data collection. In view of the pandemic situation at the time of the interviews, the interviews were conducted over Zoom and transcribed for data analysis. The interviews consisted of questions in two sections. The questions in the first section were related to the demographic information and Internet use of the parents' children. The second section evaluated the parents' views concerning children's risky online behaviors and PTD and their relationships and their parenting styles in relation to their children's Internet use by using four predetermined open-ended questions corresponding to the aforementioned research questions. Prompt questions were used throughout the interviews to encourage parents to expand on their ideas if necessary. Because of the scope of the paper, we herein report only the findings related to the parents' responses to the four predetermined research questions. Both the fathers and mothers of the families involved were present for their respective interviews, with the exception of one family, the father of which could not participate due to work obligations outside Hong Kong; only the mother was interviewed.

3.2 Information about the Early Adolescents and their Internet Use

The adolescent children of the six families interviewed comprised five boys and one girl aged from 11 to 15 years. Over half (70%) of the children had used computers/the Internet for 3 years or less at the time of the interviews, and most (83%) of them considered their computer proficiency to be fair or good. All of the children possessed smartphones. Most (83%) of them spent less than 5 hours per day using computers/the Internet at home for online lessons, and most (83%) of them spent less than 3 hours per day using computers/the Internet at home for learning other than online lessons. All of the children spent less than 3 hours per day using computers/the Internet at home for entertainment and social networking.

3.3 Data Analysis

The qualitative data gathered from the semi-structured interviews were thematically analyzed, which involved (1) familiarization with the data, (2) coding, (3) theme identification, (4) theme review, (5) theme naming, and (6) write-up (Braun & Clarke, 2006). Both deductive and inductive coding were used to analyze the data. Deductive coding was appropriate for the data related to preconceived themes derived from theories, such as those concerning PTD and parenting styles. In this study, PTD was conceptualized using the three dimensions of perceived technological self-efficacy, technological contribution, and social uses of technology (Lau, 2015), and parenting styles was conceptualized through categorization as authoritative, authoritarian, permissive, or neglectful (Baumrind, 1971; Maccoby & Martin, 1983). Inductive coding was necessary for the themes that emerged naturalistically from the data without any theories.

4. RESULTS

Thematic analysis revealed the themes and subthemes presented in the following subsections. Direct quotes from the interviewed parents are provided to illustrate the identified themes and subthemes and demonstrate how the results were derived.

4.1 Few Risky Online Behaviors

Overall, the adolescents from the six families engaged in few risky online behaviors. The parents of two of the families said that their children did not engage in any risky online behaviors. However, the father of Family 4 stated that his child was a victim of cyberbullying by his classmates and had also discovered that his child had accessed inappropriate age-restricted pages to watch adult content:

"He has been bullied by others. When he was the chairman of the class committee, I don't know if his classmates did it for fun or what, but they would abuse him verbally." Father, Family 4.

"Sometimes we see him watching some adult content. He usually watches on the phone but seldom on the computer." Father, Family 4.

Some of the parents mentioned that their children relied too much on electronic devices and exhibited Internet dependency. This sparked worries about their children's ability to communicate face-to-face in the future. One parent observed that his child's body language was less expressive in everyday conversation since he used technology to communicate.
"He uses technology to do something, and he becomes overreliant on it. He cannot communicate with others through the iPad for his whole life; he must interact with others face-to-face. I think he has started using less body language. Using the iPad affects him so much. I think the main negative effect is overreliance." Father, Family 4.

4.2 Significant PTD

Regarding perceived technological self-efficacy, all the parents claimed that their children exhibited high self-efficacy when using the Internet:
"I think using technology is beneficial to him. He is confident. When he uses technology, he is faster than when he reads books." Father, Family 4.

Adolescents can explore the Internet confidently without their parents' assistance. The parents of two families said that their children were more familiar with the use of computers, smartphones, and software than they were and that they are unable to assist with their children's use of the Internet. Instead, they had to seek assistance from their children when they were faced with computer-related problems.

"Even if we want to help, our son is much better than us at using computers. In fact, we cannot help him, but he helps us. He often confidently says 'Let me handle this issue' when we encounter computer trouble." Father, Family 2.

We found that the adolescents were willing to try using different online applications and new technologies to help them develop their own interests. During the COVID-19 pandemic, young people have independently explored and determined ways to improve learning and maintain classmate relationships by using the Internet—for instance, setting up online study groups on Zoom. The daughter of Family 6 used an iPad app to create music independently as a hobby.

Regarding technological contribution, several parents said that their children recorded videos and posted them on platforms like YouTube to express themselves and share content with others. The contents of the videos include community events, cooking, scenery, and daily life.

"He records some incidents that happen in the community or makes some videos and uploads them to YouTube. He has been to Kwun Tong Promenade; he thought the scenery was beautiful. He said he wants more people to watch his videos. He said that if he can record it, then others can view it." Mother, Family 1.

"When his mother makes cakes, he takes photos and posts them on platforms like YouTube so that others can see. He wants to express that he has had this experience." Father, Family 4.

Regarding social uses of technology, adolescents maintain relationships with family through the Internet. The mother of Family 1 indicated that she and her son maintained social bonds with relatives by using the Internet. They keep in touch with the son's father and grandparents, who live in Mainland China, by using social media tools such as WeChat and through voice calls or video calls.

"He also chats with his father on video calls. His father is in the Mainland now and cannot come back to Hong Kong, and his grandparents also live in the Mainland. We always keep in contact with each other through WeChat." Mother, Family 1.

Some of the parents also said that their adolescent children used the Internet to maintain relationships with classmates and would use various social media tools to do so. The mother of Family 4 indicated that her son organized meetings with his classmates and interacted with his classmates through study and discussion groups on Google Meet and Zoom. For example, to prepare for an English examination, her son organized study sessions, during which he and his classmates expressed mutual support.

"He can use the iPad to read spontaneously. He uses it to communicate with his classmates through Zoom. Several classmates discuss what they want to discuss in a group; they learn from each other." Mother, Family 4.

Apart from using the Internet to connect with relatives and classmates, adolescents also use the Internet to connect with teachers. The son of Family 2 collected video clips of his primary school life and made a compilation video as a gift for his teacher.

4.3 Multiple Relationships between Risky Online Behaviors and PTD

Interviews with the parents of some families revealed that their children exhibited PTD more often than they engaged in negative Internet behaviors. Some of the parents reported that their children exhibited an equal degree of positive and negative online behaviors, and others reported that their children exhibited either positive or negative behaviors. Some of the parents mentioned that other factors may influence adolescents' Internet use in daily life, including the degree to which they engage risky online behaviors or exhibit PTD.

The first factor is the tendency of young people to have various interests and engage in other meaningful activities, which attract them away from risky online behaviors. The father of Family 2 expressed that because his son spent more time on his hobbies, he was more involved in extracurricular activities and was less likely to engage in online risk-taking.

"But in daily life, some factors affect his computer use. My son has many hobbies, and he cares about his academic results. He wants to achieve good performance in these endeavors, which pulls him away from the computer. This is a positive factor, and its impact is larger than when he uses the computer for other purposes." Father, Family 2.

The second factor is the influence of adolescents' peers. Some of the parents pointed out that their children's use of the Internet was influenced by their peers. Some of the parents indicated that their children were so strongly influenced by their friends that they often watched the videos recommended by their friends, even if they were not enthusiastic about doing so.

"He is largely affected by peers and is familiar with the trends. Although he is not keen on it, sometimes he shows us some Korean pop stars or funny YouTube videos. We believe that he knows about those things because of his friends." Father, Family 2.

"His friends send some links to him through WhatsApp, related to bullying at school or some bad stories in society. If others do not send it to him, he does not search for this kind of information, because he does not like it." Father, Family 5.

4.4 Internet Parenting Styles

4.4.1 Parental Control and Monitoring

The interviews revealed that some of the parents restricted how long and how often their children could use the Internet. Some of the parents set up specific rules for their children; for example, their children could only play games on their smartphones for a few hours on a holiday and must allow their parents to see the content they access on the Internet. Some of the parents even reported taking away their children's devices if their children broke any of their rules or continued playing on their phone at inappropriate times.

The mother of Family 5 said that they usually monitored their son's Internet use rather than letting him explore freely and tried their best to filter information before passing it on to their children. They claimed that although their son is mostly willing to comply with their rules, he often hides the content of his WhatsApp chats with classmates from them.

"When he finds some interesting apps or games, he asks us to help him download them because we have activated the parental control on his phone. He needs our approval before he can download any apps." Mother, Family 5

Some of the parents also mentioned that their adolescent children had become more protective of their privacy and were sometimes reluctant to tell them what content they consumed online. The parents tended to agree that they should respect their children and that checking the contents of their children's phones constituted an invasion of privacy. The father of Family 5 said that they respected their son's privacy because their son had already grown up.

"He has grown up; I have to respect his privacy. If I want to set an example and teach him to understand privacy issues, I need to show him that I respect his privacy. I need to let him know that his father respects his privacy. However, if he oversteps on some issues, I will speak to him: 'I read the chat on your phone, I did not intend to do that.'" Father, Family 5.

4.4.2 Parental Permissiveness and Negligence

Some of the parents had less parental control than others and set hardly any rules for their children's Internet use. The father of Family 4 described his parenting style as permissive and reported that he could not control his son's excessive Internet use.

"If we do not monitor him, he would seize the chance to play games . . . even if we scold him, he still does it . . . Once he comes back home, he immediately goes for the iPad. I must keep it from him and not let him touch it." Father, Family 4.

The mother of Family 3 did not impose any restrictions on her child's computer use and trusted his self-regulation. Nevertheless, he engaged in various Internet behaviors and exhibited strong self-discipline compared with the other children whose parents adopted a permissive parenting style.

"I have not needed to pay much attention to his behaviors ever since he was very young. We could not help with his homework; he relied on himself." Mother, Family 3.

4.4.3 Consistency between Maternal and Paternal Parenting Styles

In this study, the father and mother of each family exhibited consistent parenting styles and agreed on the children's education. The mothers were generally more involved in their children's Internet use than were the fathers, especially in the family in which the father traveled for work while the mother was a full-time housewife who was, therefore, responsible for childcare. In two of the six families we interviewed, the mothers reported that they spent more time with their children than did their children's fathers and were more familiar with their children's Internet use habits. In one of the families, the mother answered more questions than did the father during the second half of the interview.

5. DISCUSSION AND IMPLICATIONS

Three relationships between risky online behaviors and PTD among early adolescents were identified in the present study: some of the adolescents exhibited PTD more often than they engaged in risky online behaviors, some exhibited the same extent of PTD and risky online behaviors, and some exhibited either PTD or risky online behaviors. Furthermore, these relationships were mediated by a variety of factors, such as personal interests and peer influence. This study revealed that some of the parents restricted their children's online behaviors, which resulted in their children refusing to share the Internet content they consumed with their parents. When the parents allowed their children to use the Internet without any restrictions, the children either indulged in or self-regulated their Internet use. These findings are in line with those reported in prior studies (Moilanen et al., 2015; Özgur, 2019). The present study also indicated that fathers and mothers played distinct roles in guiding their adolescent children's' Internet use. The mothers generally spent more time with their children than did the fathers and were more familiar with their children's Internet use habits. However, each pair of parents adopted consistent parenting styles.

Online risk-taking is common among early adolescents. Schools and parents are both responsible for educating youth regarding Internet use because home and school are two critical environments for adolescent development (Smyth & Darmody, 2021). Schools should plan curricula designed to educate students on critical thinking skills and discourage risky online behaviors to enable adolescents to make proper decisions when confronted with inappropriate online content. Schools should work closely with parents to implement effective interventions for youth and organize workshops to teach parents knowledge and skills of Internet parenting.

Previous studies have reported that parental mediation strategies are effective in cultivating adolescents' self-regulation skills (Eisenberg et al., 2005). For restrictive mediation, Lin and Chen (2016) suggested that parents should adopt appropriate disciplinary methods. In a healthy family relationship, parents can openly discuss and formulate reasonable rules for Internet use, such as restricting the consumption of violent and pornographic videos and the amount of time spent on games and entertainment, with their children. The parent–child relationship and parental behaviors strongly influence adolescent behaviors (Liu et al., 2013). If parents engage in high-risk behaviors, their children may also choose to engage in those behaviors. Parents should be aware of the exemplary role that they play in the lives of their children. When enforcing Internet use rules with their children, parents should also follow their own rules. Parents should clearly communicate their expectations for Internet use with their children; for example, if parents ask their children not to use their mobile phones when eating, those parents should follow the same rule. Parents must respect the privacy of and demonstrate their trust in their adolescent children rather than interfering excessively in their children's online behaviors. However, if the parents of adolescents who exhibit poor self-discipline and high Internet dependence want to use monitoring software to guide their children's Internet use, they should focus on determining how often their children surf the Internet and talk to others rather than focus on the details of their children's content consumption and online interactions (Ghosh et al., 2018).

For active mediation, high parental responsiveness and acceptance cultivate an open, warm, and caring environment in which adolescents are more willing to disclose information to their parents (Smetana et al., 2006). This helps protect young people from risky online behaviors and enables them to navigate the digital world more safely and wisely. Rather than prohibiting negative behaviors, parents may encourage positive behaviors (Blackwell et al., 2016). Parents may discuss with their adolescent children what they can accomplish with technology, encourage them to develop technological self-efficacy, and teach them how to use the Internet to care for others and contribute to society. Furthermore, parents may adopt appropriate parental mediation strategies depending on their children's characteristics and provide opportunities for children to enhance their self-regulation and emotion regulation skills (Chen & Chng, 2016).

6. CONCLUSIONS

This study investigated risky online behavior and PTD among Hong Kong early adolescents and how parenting styles affect early adolescents' online behaviors. Schools should develop relevant curricula to educate students on positive Internet use and collaborate with parents to nurture adolescents. Parents should adopt appropriate mediation strategies to help children use the Internet positively.

The present study has some limitations that must be addressed in the future. Only one of the adolescents discussed was female; future studies should involve an equal number of boys and girls. In our sample, the fathers and mothers in each of the six families adopted the same parenting styles; therefore, we were unable to compare the views of such families with those of families that adopt inconsistent parenting styles. Future studies should include families with inconsistent parenting styles for comparison. This study relied on data from semi-structured interviews conducted with parents; ethnographic research is necessary to observe how parents and adolescents behave and interact in authentic family settings.

ACKNOWLEDGEMENT

The work described in this paper was fully supported by a grant from the Research Grants Council of the Hong Kong Special Administrative Region, China (Project No. CUHK 14608120).

REFERENCES

Baumrind, D., 1971. Current patterns of parental authority. *Developmental Psychology Monograph*, Vol. 4, pp. 1-103.

Bers, M. et al., 2012. Positive technological development: The multifaceted nature of youth technology use toward improving self and society. In B. J. Foley & C. C. Ching (Eds.), *Constructing the Self in a Digital World*, pp. 110-136. Cambridge University Press, Cambridge, United Kingdom.

Blackwell, L. et al., 2016. Managing expectations: Technology tensions among parents and teens. *Proceedings of the 19th ACM Conference on Computer-Supported Cooperative Work & Social Computing*. Michigan, USA, pp. 1390-1401.

Braun, V. and Clarke, V., 2006. Using thematic analysis in psychology. *Qualitative Research in Psychology*, Vol. 3, No. 2, pp. 77-101.

Chan, C. K. et al., 2014. A latent class analysis of adolescents' risky online behaviors. In *AECT Convention 2014*.

Chen, V. H. H. and Chng, G. S., 2016. Active and restrictive parental mediation over time: Effects on youths' self-regulatory competencies and impulsivity. *Computers & Education*, Vol. 98, pp. 206-212.

Defoe, I. N., 2021. Towards a hybrid criminological and psychological model of risk behavior: The developmental neuro-ecological risk-taking model (DNERM). *Developmental Review*, Vol. 62, 100995.

Eisenberg, N. et al., 2005. Relations among positive parenting, children's effortful control, and externalizing problems: A three-wave longitudinal study. *Child Development*, Vol. 76, No. 5, pp. 1055-1071.

Ghosh, A. K. et al., 2018. Safety vs. surveillance: What children have to say about mobile apps for parental control. *Proceedings of the 2018 CHI Conference on Human Factors in Computing Systems.* Montréal, QC, Canada, pp. 1-14.

Gámez-Guadix, M. et al., 2016. Risky online behaviors among adolescents: Longitudinal relations among problematic Internet use, cyberbullying perpetration, and meeting strangers online. *Journal of Behavioral Addictions*, Vol. 5, No. 1, pp. 100-107.

Koronczai, B. et al., 2020. Parental bonding and problematic internet or social media use among adolescents. *Psychiatria Hungarica*, Vol. 35, No. 1, pp. 73-80.

Lau, W. W. F., 2015. Positive technological development: How do students and parents perceive it? *Proceedings of EdMedia 2015-World Conference on Educational Media and Technology*. Montreal, Canada, pp. 74-78.

Lau, W. W. F. and Yuen, A. H. K., 2013. Adolescents' risky online behaviours: The influence of gender, religion, and parenting style. *Computers in Human Behavior*, Vol. 29, No. 6, pp. 2690-2696.

Lee, S.-J. and Chae, Y.-G., 2007. Children's Internet use in a family context: Influence on family relationships and parental mediation. *CyberPsychology & Behavior*, Vol. 10, No. 5, pp. 640-644.

Lin, H.-T. and Chen, H.-J., 2016. Relationships between parental internet intervention, school engagement, and risky online behaviors among adolescents: The moderating role of family cohesion. *Journal of Research in Education Sciences*, Vol. 61, No. 4, pp. 205-242.

Liu, Q.-X. et al., 2013. Perceived parent-adolescent relationship, perceived parental online behaviors and pathological internet use among adolescents: Gender-specific differences. *PLOS ONE*, Vol. 8, No. 9, e75642.

Livingstone, S. and Haddon, L., 2008. Risky experiences for children online: Charting European research on children and the Internet. *Children & Society*, Vol. 22, No. 4, pp. 314-323.

Maccoby, E. E. and Martin, J. A., 1983. Socialization in the context of the family: Parent-child interaction. In E. M. Hetherington & P. H. Mussen (Eds.), *Handbook of Child Psychology: Socialization, Personality, and Social Development*, pp. 1-101. Wiley, New York, USA.

Moilanen, K. L. et al., 2015. Bidirectional associations between self-regulation and parenting styles in early adolescence. *Journal of Research on Adolescence*, Vol. 25, No. 2, pp. 246-262.

Özgur, H., 2019. Online game addiction among Turkish adolescents: The effect of internet parenting style. *Malaysian Online Journal of Educational Technology*, Vol. 7, No. 1, pp. 47-68.

Shek, D. T. et al., 2018. The influence of parental control and parent-child relational qualities on adolescent internet addiction: A 3-year longitudinal study in Hong Kong. *Frontiers in Psychology*, Vol. 7, No. 9, pp. 642.

Smetana, J. G. et al., 2006. Disclosure and secrecy in adolescent-parent relationships. *Child Development*, Vol. 77, No. 1, pp. 201-217.

Smith, A. R. et al., 2013. Impact of socio-emotional context, brain development, and pubertal maturation on adolescent risk-taking. *Hormones and Behavior*, Vol. 64, No. 2, pp. 323-332.

Smyth, E. and Darmody, M., 2021. *Risk and protective factors in adolescent behaviour: The role of family, school and neighbourhood characteristics in (mis)behaviour among young people.* Retrieved from https://www.esri.ie/system/files/publications/RS119.pdf

Wong, D. S. W. et al., 2014. Cyberbullying perpetration and victimization among adolescents in Hong Kong. *Children and Youth Services Review*, Vol. 36, pp. 133-140.

OPPORTUNITIES, THREATS AND SOLUTION TECHNIQUES OF DEEP-FAKE TECHNOLOGY: A SYSTEMATIC REVIEW

Ahmadreza Shamsabadi[1], Hengameh Mojdeganlou[2], Alireza Barzegary[3], Amirata Fakhfouri[3], Kimia Azad[3], Mohammad Heydari[4], Zahra Pashaei[5] and Esmaeil Mehraeen[4]

[1]*Department of Health Information Technology, Esfarayen Faculty of Medical Sciences, Esfarayen, Iran*
[2]*Department of Pathology, Urmia University of Medical Sciences, Urmia, Iran*
[3]*School of Medicine, Islamic Azad University, Tehran, Iran*
[4]*Department of Health Information Technology, Khalkhal University of Medical Sciences, Khalkhal, Iran*
[5]*Iranian Research Center for HIV/AIDS, Iranian Institute for Reduction of High Risk Behaviors, Tehran University of Medical Sciences, Tehran, Iran*

ABSTRACT

Recently deepfake have become the most popular. Although it has also positive uses in many industries, it is a big threat to societies. So, concerns remain over the dark side of this technology. Since there are few studies evaluating different aspects of deep fakes& their benefits, threats, and methods to combat this technology. We tried to provide a complete overview of deepfake detection methods, the opportunities & threats of this technology. We performed a systematic search using the keywords in the online databases including PubMed, Scopus, Science Direct, and Web of Science. All the related papers and documents published in English were retrieved from 2015 through July 2021. Our search strategy included several combinations of keywords including: "Deep fake", "fake reality", "artificial intelligence", Generative Adversarial Networks (GAN), "Videos", and "programming". A review of studies showed that entertainment was the most mentioned use of deepfake technology. According to the findings, creating non-consensual pornography and threat to privacy and democracy was significant in the menace category. Also uses for malicious purposes, the spread of false information and manipulated news and, the threat to social security were the other mentioned threats in several articles. Deepfakes are new technologies and they are still developing. We have found in our added studies that deepfake has good potential for improvement and helping. Besides its various opportunities, we know that it can be pretty much harmful. It's mostly used in Virtual Reality (VR) and Augmented Reality (AR).

KEYWORDS

Deepfake, Technology, Opportunity, Threat, Solution

1. INTRODUCTION

With the advent of new cameras and smart phone technologies and increased reach on social media, large number of digital images and videos has been created and are added on the internet very fast (Li and Lyu, 2018, Yu et al., 2019). This has led to the creation of various image editing software's and technologies (Yu et al., 2019).

By the use of artificial intelligence (AI) applications, fake videos can be made. By merging or replacing images and videos, facial mapping technology and AI could help swapping the face of a person on a video into the face of another person (Westerlund, 2019, Chawla, 2019, Maras and Alexandrou, 2019).

Many popular applications including: Face app, Fake app, Snapchat, Zao and deep nude app with face swapping features are widely used. Some make it difficult to distinguish between real and fake photos or videos (Öhman, 2019). The fake videos and misinformation can quickly reach millions of people through social media and can impact millions of users and society (Figueira and Oliveira, 2017).

This technology has benefits and threats. It has positive uses in educational media, medical and social field, advertising and branding (Vaccaro et al.). In The film industry, special face editing, special effects and even new movies, starring dead actors can be made by assistance of deep fake technology (Yu et al., 2019,

Westerlund, 2019). Deep fake has also threats to political system, society and national security. by interfering in elections, and affecting on lives of public figures including celebrities, for example, by replacing their face in porn videos (Floridi, 2018, Hasan and Salah, 2019).

In recent years' deep fake have become most popular. Although it has also positive uses in many industries, it is a big threat to the societies. So, concerns remain over the dark side of this technology. Since there are few studies evaluating different aspects of deep fakes and its benefits, threats and methods to combat this technology. We tried to provide a complete overview of deepfake detection methods, the opportunities and threats of this technology.

2. METHODS

This study was a narrative review of current evidence conducted in July 2021. The authors investigated the threats and opportunities and detection methods of new deep fakes.

2.1 Data Sources

We performed a systematic search using the keywords in the online databases including PubMed, Scopus, Science Direct, and Web of Science. All the related papers and documents published in English were retrieved from 2015 through July 2021.Our search strategy included several combinations of keywords including: "Deep fake", "fake reality", "artificial intelligence", Generative Adversarial Networks (GAN), "Videos", and "programming".

2.2 Study Selection

The most relevant studies by titles and abstracts were retrieved by three independent investigators. The full content of the retrieved papers was reviewed, and the most relevant papers were selected based on the eligibility criteria. The relevant data were extracted and organized in tables. The peer-reviewed original papers published in English that meet the eligibility criteria were included in the final report. The exclusion criteria were as follows: non-English papers, unavailability of the full-text document, and duplicated results in databases.

3. RESULTS

In this study, 348 documents were gathered using a systematic search strategy. After a primary review of retrieved articles, 192 duplicates were removed, and the title and abstract of the remaining 156 resources were reviewed. After applying the selection criteria, 103articles were excluded, and only 43 articles met the inclusion criteria and were included in the final review.

These studies were conducted in USA (n=26) Italy(n=3), Switzerland(n=2), China(n=2), Taiwan(n=2), India(n=1), Spain(n=1), Germany(n=1), Malaysia(n=1), UAE(n=1), South Korea(n=1), Ethiopia(n=1), England (n=1).

A total of 43 articles from multiple databases were selected. We used the data extraction sheet to summarize the information of the authors, type of article (e.g., case series), publication date, and country of origin. Two independent investigators gathered this information and further organized them in the Tables. All the selected articles were cross-checked by other authors to ensure no duplications or overlap exists in the content. Two independent researchers evaluated the quality of articles and the risk of bias. A third independent investigator was consulted to resolve probable differences of thoughts in either case. The full text of select articles was fully read and the key findings were extracted.

Review of studies showed that entertainment was the most mentioned use of the deep fake technology. Besides that, Virtual Reality (VR) and Augmented Reality (AR), human face generation, photorealisticvscenery generation, creating Animation were also noticeably seen in the mentioned studies. According to the findings, create non-consensual pornography and Threat to privacy and democracy was significant in the menace category. Also Uses for malicious purposes, the spread of false information and manipulated news and, threat to social security were the other mentioned threats in several articles (Table 1). Studies have revealed that different techniques have been used to identify fake information content from real, each with a different solution techniques framework, such as, biometric-based forensic, large margin cosine loss function (LMCL), using inconsistent head poses and etc. However, according to the findings, the basis of most solution techniques is the use of convolution neural network (CNN).

4. DISCUSSION

Understanding this new form of media requires first understanding what deepfakes are and how they are created. As mentioned, the word is a combination of "deep (learning)" and "fake (content). It's important to know that; deep fake is not just a mixture of two videos. Instead, it is far more complex than that. It is a model of artificial intelligence (Wagner and Blewer, 2019). According to the use of artificial intelligence (AI) in this technology, it will develop daily, and also it will be more prevalent. With applications like "Face app", "Fake app", Snapchat, Zao, and etc. it is more likely that deepfakes spread worldwide. In addition, it is much easier to use deep fake for normal people.

In this study, we have evaluated this technology in three different categories, which are opportunities, threats, and diagnosis techniques of "deepfakes". The result indicates that one of the most common opportunities and usage of deepfake is producing parody videos for entertainment. Parody, to the degree, that it is perceived as a parody by its planned audience, sends the message that it is not the original, thus cannot form a false statement of fact (Gerstner, 2020). Similar to our study, Brian D. et al, suggest that deepfake can not only be used for making parody videos, but also for use in pointed attacks against individuals or institutions (Dolhansky et al., 2020b).

This analysis supports the theory that one of the other important opportunities of deepfake, is its usage in Virtual Reality (VR) and Augmented Reality (AR). In addition to our findings, Deressa W. et al, have also found that Deepfakes can be used for the creation of hyper-realistic Computer Generated Imagery (CGI), Virtual Reality (VR), Augmented Reality (AR), Education, Animation, Arts, and Cinema (Wodajo and Atnafu, 2021). Deepfakes have several other opportunities as well like, educational purposes, animation creation, etc. it has also immense potential in the health care system. For example, the technological improvements that have resulted in deepfakes are readily applicable to different aspects of plastic surgery, posing both profits and troubles to patients, providers, and future research (Crystal et al., 2020).

Deepfake is a new technology and it is still unknown, for this reason besides having opportunities it can be abused. So, it is certain that deepfake can have many unknown threats, which we indicate the most important ones. The data suggest that creating non-consensual pornography is the most mentioned threat in our added studies. It was the first use of deepfakes, and continues to pose a threat mostly to women, ranging from celebrities to journalists, and those that simply draw unwanted attention (Agarwal et al., 2020a). Another significant threat is that deepfake can be used for nefarious purposes. Andrei O. J. Kwok et al, believes that the Malicious use of this technology for fraud, falsification, and abuse created more hazards than opportunities for various investors (Kwok and Koh, 2021). We have also other threats in our added studies, like Creation and spread of false information and manipulated news, a threat to social security, a threat to privacy and democracy, etc.

In addition to opportunities and threats, we have found that several different methods for diagnosing deepfake exist. We have to diagnose deepfake, to prevent fraud and abuse of this technology. Agarwal S. et al, have found a novel way to detect deepfake. They have shown that a combination of a facial and behavioral biometric is highly efficient at detecting these face-swap deep fakes. Unlike many other methods, this approach is less susceptible to counterattack and generalizes well to previously unseen deep fakes with previously unnoticed people (Agarwal et al., 2020a). Another way to distinguish deepfake from real videos is Dynamic Prototype Network (DPNet). Loc T. et al, propose this new method (DPNet). DPNet works by first learning the typical representations of the temporal variations within the hidden space, by grouping the patch-wise representation of real video closer together while pushing those of fake videos farther away(Trinh et al., 2021). Last but not least, we should improve our methods to detect deepfakes.

Table 1. Frequency of deep fake opportunities and threats

Type of Threats	Frequency	Type of Opportunities	Frequency
Create non-consensual pornography	25	producing parody videos for entertainment	12
Threat to privacy and democracy	24	Can be used Virtual Reality (VR) and Augmented Reality(AR)	6
Used for nefarious/ malicious purposes	23	can be used to create animation	5
Creation and spread of false information and manipulated news	23	can be synthetic video generation for movies, storytelling and modern-day streaming services.	5
Threat to social security	20	can be used for education	4
Lead to misrepresentation, confusion, and erosion of trust	17	applicable to facets of plastic surgery	1
threat to the trustworthiness of digital information	15	The museum uses to recreate an immersive visitor interaction	1
Manipulate public opinions and harm society	14	realistic rendition of videos celebrity in advertisements and destination marketing, without the celebrity having actually to perform	1
Used to create political distress	14	creating voices who have lost theirs	1
Commit small to large-scale fraud	13	updating episodes of movies without reshooting those	1
Disrupt democratic elections	12	the ability to add deceased actors into new movies	1
Reduce the amount of information that videos carry to viewers	9	can be used to create realistic videos of events that happened, but that were not actually recorded.	1
Abuse created more perils than opportunities for various stakeholders	9	can be used to create extremely accurate reenactments of historical events.	1
Use for unethical purposes and defamation of people	8	content that was originally recorded in one language can be more seamlessly dubbed into another language	1
can be utilized to alter the identity of a person in a video	6	Face-swapping can be used to allow vulnerable people to speak the truth while preserving their anonymity.	1
Can lead to serious legal consequences	5	realistic video lectures can be created just using the sound recording of the lecture and a few still photographs of the lecturer	1
Creating uncertainty of video evidence to make legal verdicts	5	can enhance visitor learning engagement and experience in galleries	1
phishing	5	used for creation of hyper-realistic Computer Generated Imagery (CGI)	1
Creating serious threat to Knowledge	5	offer companies user co-innovation opportunities	1
Creation of fraudulent social media profiles	4	photorealistic scenery generation	1
Used for dating scams	4	can help in automating game design	1
Sow civil unrest	3	presents immense potential in healthcare	1
Hacking voice based authentication systems	3	has proven to offer significant diagnostic benefits	1
Used to create blackmail someone	3	In tourism, useful in advertising and marketing content creation	1
Use for act of interpreting information that mimics reality	3		
Fuel dis-information campaigns	3		
Use in targeted attacks against individuals or institutions	2		
Logical-access voice spoofing	2		
Impersonate voices	2		
Serving as authentic representations matters	1		
Disrupting in intellectual property	1		
Intentional infliction of emotional distress (IIED)	1		
Used to fake terrorism events	1		
Fake surveillance videos	1		
Create chaos in financial markets by creating fake news	1		
Threat biometric access control	1		

5. CONCLUSION

Deepfakes are new technologies and they are still developing. We have found in our added studies that deepfake has good potential for improvement and helping. Beside its various opportunities we know that it can be pretty much harmful. It's mostly used in Virtual Reality (VR) and Augmented Reality (AR). It can also be used to improve the health care system and the education system. But, it is still unknown and it can be harmful such as making non-consensual pornography. Currently, we are trying to expand our techniques to detect deepfake from reality so we can reduce its threats.

ACKNOWLEDGEMENT

The present study was conducted in collaboration with Khalkhal University of Medical Sciences, and Esfarayen University of Medical Sciences.

REFERENCES

Agarwal, S. & Farid, H. Detecting Deep-Fake Videos From Aural and Oral Dynamics. Proceedings of the IEEE/CVF Conference on Computer Vision and Pattern Recognition, 2021. 981-989.

Agarwal, S., Farid, H., El-Gaaly, T. & Lim, S.-N. Detecting deep-fake videos from appearance and behavior. 2020 IEEE International Workshop on Information Forensics and Security (WIFS), 2020a. IEEE, 1-6.

Agarwal, S., Farid, H., Fried, O. & Agrawala, M. Detecting deep-fake videos from phoneme-viseme mismatches. Proceedings of the IEEE/CVF Conference on Computer Vision and Pattern Recognition Workshops, 2020b. 660-661.

Agarwal, S., Farid, H., Gu, Y., He, M., Nagano, K. & Li, H. Protecting World Leaders Against Deep Fakes. CVPR workshops, 2019.

Agarwal, S. & Varshney, L. R. 2019. Limits of deepfake detection: A robust estimation viewpoint. *arXiv preprint arXiv:1905.03493*.

Amerini, I., Galteri, L., Caldelli, R. & Del Bimbo, A. Deepfake video detection through optical flow based cnn. Proceedings of the IEEE/CVF International Conference on Computer Vision Workshops, 2019. 0-0.

Carlini, N. & Farid, H. Evading deepfake-image detectors with white-and black-box attacks. Proceedings of the IEEE/CVF Conference on Computer Vision and Pattern Recognition Workshops, 2020. 658-659.

Chawla, R. 2019. Deepfakes: How a pervert shook the world. *International Journal of Advance Research and Development,* 4, 4-8.

Chen, H.-S., Rouhsedaghat, M., Ghani, H., Hu, S., You, S. & Kuo, C.-C. J. DefakeHop: A Light-Weight High-Performance Deepfake Detector. 2021 IEEE International Conference on Multimedia and Expo (ICME), 2021. IEEE, 1-6.

Chen, T., Kumar, A., Nagarsheth, P., Sivaraman, G. & Khoury, E. Generalization of audio deepfake detection. Proc. Odyssey 2020 The Speaker and Language Recognition Workshop, 2020. 132-137.

Crystal, D. T., Cuccolo, N. G., Ibrahim, A., Furnas, H. & Lin, S. J. 2020. Photographic and video deepfakes have arrived: how machine learning may influence plastic surgery. *Plastic and reconstructive surgery,* 145, 1079-1086.

De Lima, O., Franklin, S., Basu, S., Karwoski, B. & George, A. 2020. Deepfake detection using spatiotemporal convolutional networks. *arXiv preprint arXiv:2006.14749*.

Dolhansky, B., Bitton, J., Pflaum, B., Lu, J., Howes, R., Wang, M. & Canton Ferrer, C. 2020a. The deepfake detection challenge dataset. *arXiv e-prints*, arXiv: 2006.07397.

Dolhansky, B., Bitton, J., Pflaum, B., Lu, J., Howes, R., Wang, M. & Ferrer, C. C. 2020b. The deepfake detection challenge (dfdc) dataset. *arXiv preprint arXiv:2006.07397*.

Fallis, D. 2020. The epistemic threat of deepfakes. *Philosophy & Technology*, 1-21.

Fernandes, S., Raj, S., Ewetz, R., Pannu, J. S., Jha, S. K., Ortiz, E., Vintila, I. & Salter, M. Detecting deepfake videos using attribution-based confidence metric. Proceedings of the IEEE/CVF Conference on Computer Vision and Pattern Recognition Workshops, 2020. 308-309.

Fernandes, S., Raj, S., Ortiz, E., Vintila, I., Salter, M., Urosevic, G. & Jha, S. Predicting heart rate variations of deepfake videos using neural ode. Proceedings of the IEEE/CVF International Conference on Computer Vision Workshops, 2019. 0-0.

Figueira, Á. & Oliveira, L. 2017. The current state of fake news: challenges and opportunities. *Procedia Computer Science,* 121, 817-825.

Floridi, L. 2018. Artificial intelligence, deepfakes and a future of ectypes. *Philosophy & Technology,* 31, 317-321.

Gandhi, A. & Jain, S. Adversarial perturbations fool deepfake detectors. 2020 International Joint Conference on Neural Networks (IJCNN), 2020. IEEE, 1-8.

Gerstner, E. 2020. Face/off:" DeepFake" face swaps and privacy laws. *Def. Counsel J.,* 87, 1.

Guarnera, L., Giudice, O. & Battiato, S. Deepfake detection by analyzing convolutional traces. Proceedings of the IEEE/CVF Conference on Computer Vision and Pattern Recognition Workshops, 2020a. 666-667.

Guarnera, L., Giudice, O. & Battiato, S. 2020b. Fighting deepfake by exposing the convolutional traces on images. *IEEE Access,* 8, 165085-165098.

Güera, D. & Delp, E. J. Deepfake video detection using recurrent neural networks. 2018 15th IEEE international conference on advanced video and signal based surveillance (AVSS), 2018. IEEE, 1-6.

Hasan, H. R. & Salah, K. 2019. Combating deepfake videos using blockchain and smart contracts. *Ieee Access,* 7, 41596-41606.

Hernandez-Ortega, J., Tolosana, R., Fierrez, J. & Morales, A. 2020. Deepfakeson-phys: Deepfakes detection based on heart rate estimation. *arXiv preprint arXiv:2010.00400.*

Hsu, C.-C., Zhuang, Y.-X. & Lee, C.-Y. 2020. Deep fake image detection based on pairwise learning. *Applied Sciences,* 10, 370.

Hussain, S., Neekhara, P., Jere, M., Koushanfar, F. & Mcauley, J. Adversarial deepfakes: Evaluating vulnerability of deepfake detectors to adversarial examples. Proceedings of the IEEE/CVF Winter Conference on Applications of Computer Vision, 2021. 3348-3357.

Kaliyar, R. K., Goswami, A. & Narang, P. 2021. DeepFakE: improving fake news detection using tensor decomposition-based deep neural network. *The Journal of Supercomputing,* 77, 1015-1037.

Kim, M., Tariq, S. & Woo, S. S. FReTAL: Generalizing Deepfake Detection using Knowledge Distillation and Representation Learning. Proceedings of the IEEE/CVF Conference on Computer Vision and Pattern Recognition, 2021. 1001-1012.

Korshunov, P. & Marcel, S. 2018. Deepfakes: a new threat to face recognition? assessment and detection. *arXiv preprint arXiv:1812.08685.*

Korshunov, P. & Marcel, S. Vulnerability assessment and detection of deepfake videos. 2019 International Conference on Biometrics (ICB), 2019. IEEE, 1-6.

Kwok, A. O. & Koh, S. G. 2021. Deepfake: A social construction of technology perspective. *Current Issues in Tourism,* 24, 1798-1802.

Li, Y. & Lyu, S. 2018. Exposing deepfake videos by detecting face warping artifacts. *arXiv preprint arXiv:1811.00656.*

Li, Y., Yang, X., Sun, P., Qi, H. & Lyu, S. Celeb-df: A large-scale challenging dataset for deepfake forensics. Proceedings of the IEEE/CVF Conference on Computer Vision and Pattern Recognition, 2020. 3207-3216.

Lyu, S. Deepfake detection: Current challenges and next steps. 2020 IEEE International Conference on Multimedia & Expo Workshops (ICMEW), 2020. IEEE, 1-6.

Maras, M.-H. & Alexandrou, A. 2019. Determining authenticity of video evidence in the age of artificial intelligence and in the wake of deepfake videos. *The International Journal of Evidence & Proof,* 23, 255-262.

Mittal, T., Bhattacharya, U., Chandra, R., Bera, A. & Manocha, D. 2020. Emotions don't lie: A deepfake detection method using audio-visual affective cues. *arXiv preprint arXiv:2003.06711,* 3.

Neekhara, P., Dolhansky, B., Bitton, J. & Ferrer, C. C. Adversarial threats to deepfake detection: A practical perspective. Proceedings of the IEEE/CVF Conference on Computer Vision and Pattern Recognition, 2021. 923-932.

Öhman, C. 2019. Introducing the pervert's dilemma: a contribution to the critique of Deepfake Pornography. *Ethics and Information Technology,* 1-8.

Rössler, A., Cozzolino, D., Verdoliva, L., Riess, C., Thies, J. & Nießner, M. 2018. Faceforensics: A large-scale video dataset for forgery detection in human faces. *arXiv preprint arXiv:1803.09179.*

Trinh, L., Tsang, M., Rambhatla, S. & Liu, Y. Interpretable and trustworthy deepfake detection via dynamic prototypes. Proceedings of the IEEE/CVF Winter Conference on Applications of Computer Vision, 2021. 1973-1983.

Vaccaro, A. R., Getz, C. L., Cohen, B. E., Cole, B. J. & Donnally, C. J., 3RD 2020. Practice Management During the COVID-19 Pandemic. *The Journal of the American Academy of Orthopaedic Surgeons,* 28, 464-470.

Wagner, T. L. & Blewer, A. 2019. "The Word Real Is No Longer Real": Deepfakes, Gender, and the Challenges of AI-Altered Video. *Open Information Science,* 3, 32-46.

Wang, J., Wu, Z., Chen, J. & Jiang, Y.-G. 2021. M2TR: Multi-modal Multi-scale Transformers for Deepfake Detection. *arXiv preprint arXiv:2104.09770.*

Westerlund, M. 2019. The emergence of deepfake technology: A review. *Technology Innovation Management Review*, 9.

Wodajo, D. & Atnafu, S. 2021. Deepfake Video Detection Using Convolutional Vision Transformer. *arXiv preprint arXiv:2102.11126*.

Yang, X., Li, Y. & Lyu, S. Exposing deep fakes using inconsistent head poses. ICASSP 2019-2019 IEEE International Conference on Acoustics, Speech and Signal Processing (ICASSP), 2019. IEEE, 8261-8265.

Yu, C.-M., Chang, C.-T. & Ti, Y.-W. 2019. Detecting Deepfake-forged contents with separable convolutional neural network and image segmentation. *arXiv preprint arXiv:1912.12184*.

Zhao, H., Zhou, W., Chen, D., Wei, T., Zhang, W. & Yu, N. Multi-attentional deepfake detection. Proceedings of the IEEE/CVF Conference on Computer Vision and Pattern Recognition, 2021. 2185-2194.

FROM DEEPFAKE TO DEEP-USEFUL: RISKS AND OPPORTUNITIES THROUGH A SYSTEMATIC LITERATURE REVIEW

Nikolaos Misirlis and Harris Bin Munawar
HAN University of Applied Sciences, 6826CC, R31, Arhnem, The Netherlands

ABSTRACT

Deepfake videos are defined as a resulting media from the synthesis of different persons' images and videos – mostly faces-, replacing a real one. The easy spread of such videos leads to elevate misinformation and represents a threat to society and democracy today. The present study aims to collect and analyze the relevant literature through a systematic procedure. We present 27 articles from scientific databases revealing threats for the society, democracies, the political life but presents as well advantages of this technology in entertainment, gaming, education, and public life. The research indicates high scientific interest in deepfake detection algorithms as well as the ethical aspect of such technology. This article covers the scientific gap since, to the best of our knowledge, this is the first systematic literature review in the field.

A discussion has already started among academics and practitioners concerning the spread of fake news. The next step of fake news considers the use of artificial intelligence and machine learning algorithms that create hyper-realistic videos, called deepfake. Deepfake technology is continuously attracting the attention of scholars the last 3 years more and more. The importance on conducting research to this field derives from the necessity to understand the theory. The first contextual approach is related to the epistemological points-of-view of the concept. The second one is related to the phenomenological disadvantages of the field. Despite that, the authors will try to focus not only on the disadvantages of the field but also on the positive aspects of the technology.

KEYWORDS

Deepfake, Literature Review, Videos

1. INTRODUCTION

A discussion has already started among academics and practitioners concerning the spread of fake news (Durall et al., 2019, Korshunov and Marcel, 2018). The next step of fake news considers the use of artificial intelligence and machine learning algorithms that create hyper-realistic videos, called deepfake. Deepfake technology is continuously attracting the attention of scholars the last 3 years more and more.

Deepfake videos make their presence in almost every aspect of life. From politicians to celebrities, normal people, urban legend lovers and conspiracy theorists, all seem to be threatened or involved to the deepfake phenomenon. The vast majority of deepfake videos are related to pornography. A recent research from Deeptracelabs (deeptracelabs.com) indicated that 96% of deepfake videos are found to contain fake pornographic content with celebrities, attracting more that 134 million views. Only a smaller number of deepfake videos is related to politicians. The aforementioned research of Deeptrace found that more than 14000 deepfake videos were circulated online last year, respect to almost 8000 in 2018. The same research indicates that deepfake videos are not restricted to porn industry and politics, even if these two categories dominate the field. Together with the porn industry and the politics, criminals use artificial intelligence in order to impersonate CEOs voice and scam people (Stehouwer et al., 2019).

User-friendly apps render very easy to create and share deepfakes videos. Social media, especially content-sharing platforms, contribute to the ease in spreading these videos. Due to this fact several academics define the era we live a "post-truth" era, where the line between real and fake is extremely thin (Yatid, 2019, Neves et al., 2019, Sabir et al., 2019).

The study of deepfakes is important for both scholars and practitioners. Even though, scholarly research has only recently started to study the field with the literature to be still sparse (Öhman, 2019). The present research aims to cover this gap by reviewing the articles related only to deepfake from scholar databases. Previous research (Stehouwer et al., 2019)is conducted in the field, only by reviewing magazines' (non-academic) articles. The originality of this paper consist to the fact that this is the first systematic literature review for deepfake-only related articles from scientific-only databases.

The article is structured as follows. After the introduction, the methodology followed for the review is analyzed. Consequently, the major findings of the research are presented as well as the upcoming threats of the deepfake technology. Furthermore, the opportunities and the positive aspects from the use of deepfakes are discussed. The study concludes with future implications and limitations.

The importance on conducting research to this field derives from the necessity to understand the theory. The first contextual approach is related to the epistemological points-of-view of the concept. The second one is related to the phenomenological disadvantages of the field. Despite that, the authors will try to focus not only on the disadvantages of the field but also on the positive aspects of the technology.

2. MATERIAL AND METHODS

The Cochrane method is used for the systematic literature review and the findings are presented in accord with the PRISMA guidelines (Preferred Reporting Items for Systematic Reviews and Meta-Analyses). Google Scholar, EBSCO, Scopus and ScienceDirect were first searched, until January 2020, using a search strategy based on one single keyword and its possible combinations – Deepfake OR 'Deep fake'. The search strategy was then applied to each of the aforementioned databases, all articles were downloaded and merged into a single library in order to check for duplicate articles.

2.1 Results and Study Characteristics

The initial research returned 859 articles. After the duplicates removal, 825 articles were remained. From them, 784 articles were excluded due to several reasons, mostly irrelevance. The title of the articles were relevant to the topic discussed (deepfake), but after the first read, there was no relevance with our research.

Furthermore, articles from: Newspapers, citations, websites, blogs, vlogs, theses or dissertations, annual reports, white papers from companies, non-English journals, editorials, posters and presentations, eBooks, interviews and preprints were excluded from our research. The originality of our research is based on the fact that, to the best of our knowledge, this is the first literature review of scientific articles, therefore any other type of article should be excluded from the analysis. The topic is relatively new and academic search engines show results that should not be included to an academic literature review. As a consequence, from a vast amount of results (n=859), we finally are able to take into consideration only 3.1% of those. From the remaining 41 articles, 14 were excluded after the first screen due to irrelevance. Only 27 articles met the inclusion criteria (Figure 1).

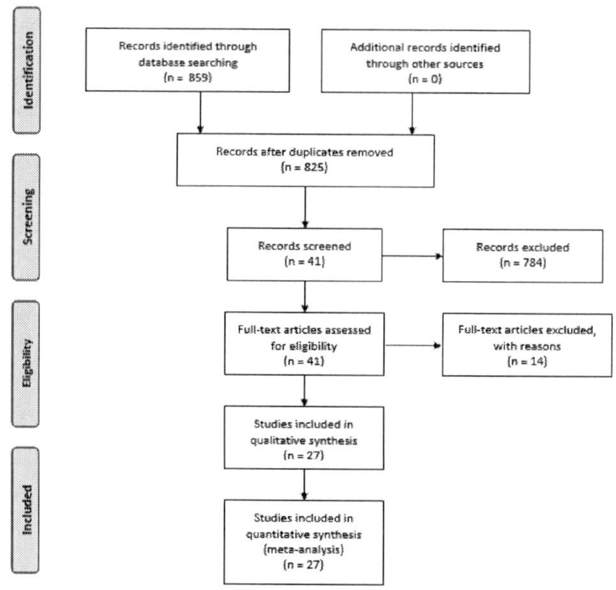

Figure 1. PRISMA flowchart depicting the study selection process

All 27 articles were published either in 2018 (n=5, 18.5%) or in 2019 (n=22, 81.5%). This metric by itself can be interpret as an index how much 'young' the topic is and explain the low number of publications. This field of science is in its infancy. Practitioners and R&Ds from companies are ahead, with Academia to follow in this case. This observation by itself enforces the fact that more research needs to be done, not only on the technological aspects of the field but also from a sociological – philosophical perspective. 59% of the articles come from American institutions (63% if we consider a UK/USA collaboration on an article). Other countries' institutions that contribute the research are Australia, Portugal together with Spain, Germany, United Arab Emirates and Taiwan with only one article for each country (3.7%) and Switzerland, The Netherlands, Italy with 2 articles (7.4%). Table 1 summarizes the 27 articles studied. For each article, the topics, the tools and the methods used are briefly explained.

Table 1. Topics covered by the articles of the review, including country of the authors' affiliation and year of publication

Author(s) & Year	Country	Topics	Tools and/ or methodology*
Akhtar and Dasgupta (2019)	USA	Comparative experimental investigation & Face authenticity	Face manipulation detection
Diakopoulos and Johnson (2019)	USA	US 2020 electoral integrity and ethical issues	Scenarios development
Westling (2019)	USA	Emerging technologies and online platform regulations	-
Hasan and Salah (2019)	UAE	Deepfake detection. Use of Ethereum smart contracts to trace and track the provenance and history of digital content to its original source	Blockchain-based
Hsu et al. (2020)	Taiwan	Forgery detection and identification.	deep learning-based approach
Chesney and Citron (2018)	USA	Risks for democracy and national security	-

Author(s) & Year	Country	Topics	Tools and/ or methodology*
Kozemczak (2019)	USA	Risks for democracy	-
Nguyen et al. (2019)	Australia	Threats to privacy, democracy and national security	Literature review on deepfake detection
Amerini et al. (2019)	Italy	Adoption of optical flow fields to exploit possible inter-frame dissimilarities	Forensic technique able to discern between fake and original videos
Güera and Delp (2018)	USA	Use of convolutional neural network (CNN) to extract frame-level features	Train a recurrent neural network (RNN)
Korshunov and Marcel (2018)	Switzerland	Deepfake detection – tampering detection	Algorithms' evaluation
Dixon Jr (2019)	USA	Effects of deepfake in political campaigns, business interests and video evidence in court rooms	-
Koopman et al. (2018)	The Netherlands	Forensic challenges Detection of deepfake manipulation through	Photo Response non Uniformity (PRNU) model
Maras and Alexandrou (2019)	USA	Pornographic images analysis	-
Farish (2019)	UK, USA	UK's legislation analysis	-
Yang et al. (2019)	USA	Exposition of AI-generated fake face images or videos	Error revealing
Li et al. (2018)	USA	Eye-blinking detection for deepfake video detection	-
Öhman (2019)	UK	Ethical aspects of deepfake. Analysis of the pervert's dilemma (deepfake vs. private sexual fantasy)	-
Stehouwer et al. (2019)	USA	Detection of digital face manipulation	Use of databases with numerous types of facial forgeries
Agarwal et al. (2019)	USA	Threats to democracy & national security	Forensic technique for facial expressions and movements
Neves et al. (2019)	Portugal, Spain	Face-synthesis detection system.	Use of free datasets
Sabir et al. (2019)	USA	Deepfake detection	Faceforensics++
Metaxas (2018)	USA	Ethical policies and epistemological education	Definition for deepfakes, classification of deepfake types and identification of risks and opportunities
Dolhansky et al. (2019)	USA	Deepfake video detection	DFDC datasets
Wagner and Blewer (2019)	USA	deepfake videos evaluation on enforcing gendered disparities within visual information	-
Durall et al. (2019)	Germany	Deepfake video detection	Classical frequency domain analysis. Image forensics and forgery detection
Korshunov and Marcel (2019)	Switzerland	Deepfake detection	VidTIMIT database

* n/a tool or methodology when the topis is self-explanatory

3. RESULTS

3.1 Major Findings and Characteristics of the Articles

Regarding the topics in each article, deepfake detection articles dominate the literature with 15 papers to be focused completely on this topic. 6 articles are focusing on the risks and threats to society and democracy and 2 consider strictly the ethical aspects of the topic. Regarding the threats, the following 4 are the most discussed in research today, namely: politics, technological skepticism, outdated legal framework, use of celebrities, and not only, to pornographic-related videos and threats for the democracy and our society. The following paragraphs will sum up the findings of the research.

3.2 Threats and Risks

The speed of disinformation spread seems to be one of the worst threats of Democracy today (Agarwal et al., 2019, Chesney and Citron, 2018, Kozemczak, 2019, Nguyen et al., 2019). Social media facilitate this process by spreading information among users who prefer to share without first verifying the content (Dekker et al., 2020, Stover, 2018, Wirth, 2019). When deepfakes are used in order to criticize and satirize public figures or politicians, it's too obvious to understand the fake content. But the line between what is real and what can harm the society is still indistinct. It is under dispute whether deepfake technology will facilitate or not the overall structure of the society. An obvious satire on politicians and parodies could be also accepted, if unharmful, but what happens when deepfake videos affect the global stock market by creating rumors or even worst, when deepfakes involve terrorist actions?

Since deepfake videos represent a rather new technology, the legal legislation is still weak. To the best of our knowledge, California is the only state in US that already signed a legislation that makes distribution of digital material related to deepfake, illegal, 60 days before elections (TÉCNICO, 2014). Maybe, more states need to follow California's paradigm, especially now that the US elections approach. The latest research of Deeptracelabs indicates that 96% of deepfake videos concern pornography, but it is easy to misuse porn for political purposes. The case of Rana Ayyub is showing clearly that the distinction between politics and pornography is difficult to define.

Another threat of deepfake is related to citizens' trust towards information, technology, journalism and even democracy. Citizens are losing trust in institutions, becoming more and more tech-skeptic and apathetic - what's called *"information apocalypse" and "reality apathy"* (Stover, 2018, Wirth, 2019). As a result of this lack of confidence in the media, citizens will perceive as fake news even those cases which are true only because they are convinced that what did not fit their opinion must be fake.

Though expected, most of the articles focus on the 'dark' side of this technology. The present study, even though it recognizes how serious the misuse of technology can be, will analyze some positive aspects of deepfake and propose future implications of this technology. The reviewed literature focused almost exclusively on the 'dark' side of this technology and systematically ignored its positive, ethical or beneficial future applications and societal implications. This result was in line with the expectations of the authors of this study. The outcome is discussed in more detail in the next section.

4. DISCUSSION

The discourse in the reviewed literature almost entirely consists of the risks, threats and challenges of deepfake technology, and ignores some beneficial ways in which it can contribute to the fields of entertainment, education, healthcare and business. The authors argue that this indicates a bias. This is especially noticeable in our study because we excluded journalistic publications from the review. A comparable review by Westerlund (2019) has a section about the benefits of deepfake technology that exclusively sites non-academic publications.

Based on examples of specific applications of deepfake and adjacent technology in academic publications, the researchers will point out some of the potential beneficial uses of such technology ignored in present academic literature.

In the entertainment sector, applications of deepfake technology are not limited to pornography. Filmmakers can also benefit from this technology with realistic depictions of actors who are not available, or even dead, such as the brief appearance of Peter Cushing in the 2016 Star Wars film Rogue One, and James Dean being featured in the 2020 film Finding Jack (Monroe, 2020). The Dali Museum in Florida features a deepfake of the iconic surrealist painter to engage its visitors (Mihailova, 2021) and is a telling example of the application of deepfake technology for education, especially history education. These examples of virtual immortality also open doors for a critical look at identity and subjectivity.

In the health sector, research has shown that Augmented and Virtual Reality simulations have significant potential benefits in the areas of mental health and pain management (for example: Riva et al. (2019). A 2020 south Korean documentary showed the gratitude of a mother who was able to meet, in virtual reality, her daughter who had died four years prior (Stein, 2021). Deepfake technology can enhance virtual reality and thus improve such interventions (Bose and Aarabi, 2019).

In the business sector, as sales move online, returns have significant financial implications for businesses and have consequences relating to the environment and logistics (Cullinane et al., 2019). Virtual try-ons help reduce such returns (Hwangbo et al., 2020) but there are limitations in the use of virtual reality technology for this purpose (Boletsis and Karahasanovic, 2020). Advancements in deepfake technology can help improve the possibility of trying on clothing and cosmetics on your own virtual image before buying. This will eventually mean lesser need for human supermodels, who usually fall in a narrow range of body types and skin tones. The use of deepfake technology to make popular footballer David Beckham speak nine languages in the Malaria Must Die campaign indicates that its use in marketing is not necessarily deceptive (de Ruiter, 2021).

5. CONCLUSION

This is the first systematic review of deepfake-related articles publish only in scientific journals. The research revealed only 27 relevant articles that fit the field of study, due to the fact that the field itself is in its infancy. All articles are related to the negative aspect of the deepfake technology, though there is still ground to pave and look for opportunities. The present literature review present a solid base for future researchers to build more complete review in the years to come. Together with this, the authors of the present study want to focus on the positive implications of deepfake technology in society that will be formed from more responsible and active citizens, in order to enforce even more the democracy around the globe. Deepfakes are only a tool, like knifes are. It is up to citizens, scientists and practitioners to transform this knife from a deadly weapon to a scalpel that will benefit the society.

REFERENCES

AgarwaL, S., Farid, H., Gu, Y., He, M., Nagano, K. & Li, H. Protecting World Leaders Against Deep Fakes. Proceedings of the IEEE Conference on Computer Vision and Pattern Recognition Workshops, 2019. 38-45.

Akhtar, Z. & Dasgupta, D. 2019. A Comparative Evaluation of Local Feature Descriptors for DeepFakes Detection.

Amerini, I., Galteri, L., Caldelli, R. & Del bimbo, A. Deepfake Video Detection through Optical Flow based CNN. Proceedings of the IEEE International Conference on Computer Vision Workshops, 2019. 0-0.

Boletsis, C. & Karahasanovic, A. Immersive Technologies in Retail: Practices of Augmented and Virtual Reality. CHIRA, 2020. 281-290.

Bose, A. J. & Aarabl, P. Virtual Fakes: DeepFakes for Virtual Reality. 2019 IEEE 21st International Workshop on Multimedia Signal Processing (MMSP), 2019. IEEE, 1-1.

Chesney, R. & Citron, D. K. 2018. Deep fakes: a looming challenge for privacy, democracy, and national security.

Cullinane, S., Browne, M., Karlsson, E. & WANG, Y. 2019. Retail clothing returns: A review of key issues. *Contemporary operations and logistics*, 301-322.

De Ruiter, A. 2021. The Distinct Wrong of Deepfakes. *Philosophy & Technology*, 1-22.

Dekker, R., Van den brink, P. & Meijer, A. 2020. Social media adoption in the police: Barriers and strategies. *Government Information Quarterly*, 101441.

Diakopoulos, N. & Johnson, D. 2019. Anticipating and Addressing the Ethical Implications of Deepfakes in the Context of Elections. *Available at SSRN 3474183*.

Dixon JR, H. B. 2019. Deepfakes: More Frightening Than Photoshop on Steroids. *The Judges' Journal,* 58, 35-37.

Dolhansky, B., Howes, R., Pflaum, B., Baram, N. & Ferrer, C. C. 2019. The Deepfake Detection Challenge (DFDC) Preview Dataset. *arXiv preprint arXiv:1910.08854*.

Durall, R., Keuper, M., Pfreundt, F.-J. & Keuper, J. 2019. Unmasking DeepFakes with simple Features. *arXiv preprint arXiv:1911.00686*.

Farish, K. 2019. Do deepfakes pose a golden opportunity? Considering whether English law should adopt California's publicity right in the age of the deepfake. *Journal of Intellectual Property Law & Practice*.

Güera, D. & Delp, E. J. Deepfake video detection using recurrent neural networks. 2018 15th IEEE International Conference on Advanced Video and Signal Based Surveillance (AVSS), 2018. IEEE, 1-6.

Hasan, H. R. & Salah, K. 2019. Combating Deepfake Videos Using Blockchain and Smart Contracts. *IEEE Access,* 7, 41596-41606.

Hsu, C.-C., Zhuang, Y.-X. & Lee, C.-Y. 2020. Deep fake image detection based on pairwise learning. *Applied Sciences,* 10, 370.

Hwangbo, H., Kim, E. H., LEE, S.-H. & JANG, Y. J. 2020. Effects of 3D Virtual "Try-On" on Online Sales and Customers' Purchasing Experiences. *IEEE Access,* 8, 189479-189489.

Koopman, M., Rodriguez, A. M. & Geradts, Z. Detection of Deepfake Video Manipulation. Conference: IMVIP, 2018.

Korshunov, P. & Marcel, S. 2018. Deepfakes: a new threat to face recognition? assessment and detection. *arXiv preprint arXiv:1812.08685*.

Korshunov, P. & Marcel, S. Vulnerability assessment and detection of deepfake videos. The 12th IAPR International Conference on Biometrics (ICB), 2019. 1-6.

Kozemczak, V. 2019. Deep Fakes: Preserving Truth & Human Rights in an Era of Truth Decay.

Li, Y., Chang, M.-C. & Lyu, S. In ictu oculi: Exposing ai created fake videos by detecting eye blinking. 2018 IEEE International Workshop on Information Forensics and Security (WIFS), 2018. IEEE, 1-7.

Maras, M.-H. & Alexandrou, A. 2019. Determining authenticity of video evidence in the age of artificial intelligence and in the wake of Deepfake videos. *The International Journal of Evidence & Proof,* 23, 255-262.

Metaxas, P. 2018. Technology, Propaganda, and the Limits of Human Intellect. *arXiv preprint arXiv:1806.09541*.

Mihailova, M. 2021. To Dally with Dalí: Deepfake (Inter) faces in the Art Museum. *Convergence,* 27, 882-898.

Monroe, D. 2020. Digital humans on the big screen. *Communications of the ACM,* 63, 12-14.

Neves, J. C., Tolosana, R., Vera-rodriguez, R., Lopes, V. & Proença, H. 2019. Real or Fake? Spoofing State-Of-The-Art Face Synthesis Detection Systems. *arXiv preprint arXiv:1911.05351*.

Nguyen, T. T., Nguyen, C. M., Nguyen, D. T., Nguyen, D. T. & Nahavandi, S. 2019. Deep Learning for Deepfakes Creation and Detection. *arXiv preprint arXiv:1909.11573*.

Öhman, C. 2019. Introducing the pervert's dilemma: a contribution to the critique of Deepfake Pornography. *Ethics and Information Technology*, 1-8.

Riva, G., Wiederhold, B. K. & Mantovani, F. 2019. Neuroscience of virtual reality: from virtual exposure to embodied medicine. *Cyberpsychology, Behavior, and Social Networking,* 22, 82-96.

Sabir, E., Cheng, J., Jaiswal, A., Abdalmageed, W., Masi, I. & Natarajan, P. 2019. Recurrent Convolutional Strategies for Face Manipulation Detection in Videos. *Interfaces (GUI),* 3, 1.

Stehouwer, J., Dang, H., Liu, F., Liu, X. & Jain, A. 2019. On the Detection of Digital Face Manipulation. *arXiv preprint arXiv:1910.01717*.

Stein, J.-P. 2021. Conjuring up the departed in virtual reality: The good, the bad, and the potentially ugly. *Psychology of Popular Media*.

Stover, D. 2018. Garlin Gilchrist: Fighting fake news and the information apocalypse. *Bulletin of the Atomic Scientists,* 74, 283-288.

Wagner, T. L. & Blewer, A. 2019. "The Word Real Is No Longer Real": Deepfakes, Gender, and the Challenges of AI-Altered Video. *Open Information Science,* 3, 32-46.

Westerlund, M. 2019. The emergence of deepfake technology: A review. *Technology Innovation Management Review,* 9.

Westling, J. 2019. Are Deep Fakes a Shallow Concern? A Critical Analysis of the Likely Societal Reaction to Deep Fakes. *A Critical Analysis of the Likely Societal Reaction to Deep Fakes (July 24, 2019)*.

Wirth, A. 2019. Cyberinsights: Artificial Intelligence: Friend and Foe. *Biomedical instrumentation & technology,* 53, 378-383.

Yang, X., Li, Y. & Lyu, S. Exposing deep fakes using inconsistent head poses. ICASSP 2019-2019 IEEE International Conference on Acoustics, Speech and Signal Processing (ICASSP), 2019. IEEE, 8261-8265.

Yatid, M. M. 2019. Truth Tampering Through Social Media: Malaysia's Approach in Fighting Disinformation & Misinformation. *IKAT: The Indonesian Journal of Southeast Asian Studies,* 2, 203-230.

SURVEYING PARENTAL MEDIATION AND DIGITAL LITERACY. WERE PARENTS READY DURING COVID-19?

Evangelia Daskalaki[1,i,*], Costas Panagiotakis[1,ii], Harris Papadakis[i] and Paraskevi Fragopoulou[1,i]
[i]Department of Electrical and Computer Engineering
[ii]Department of Management Science and Technology
Hellenic Mediterranean University, P.O Box 71500, 71410 Heraklion, Greece

ABSTRACT

The pandemic initiated an extensive and sudden digital transformation in the society. It forced parents and children to take a digital surge in their lives. The aim of our survey is to explore to what extend children's online behavior has changed during the pandemic, to study whether demographic factors and digital literacy of parents, are associated with the changes observed, and lastly to explore to what extend parents are familiar with age and content classification systems online, which will allow them to make informed decisions about media content consumed by their children. The study reveals that a significant percentage of parents (29.8%) report changes in the online habits of their children. Furthermore, our research affirms that digital literacy of parents is the key to overcome potential online risks of children, especially during the pandemic. Notably, the age group 9-12 is the age group, which shows the biggest percentage of parents noticing changes in their child's online habits. Finally, it is revealed that parents were unprepared to follow this fast transformation pace, and only a low percentages of them appears to be familiar with age (49.8%) and content classification systems (27.9%) online.

KEYWORDS

Survey, Pandemic, Covid-19, Children Online Behavior, Parental Guidance, Digital Literacy

1. INTRODUCTION

Living conditions at home have changed suddenly and profoundly by the COVID-19 outbreak causing such problems as mandatory lockdown, the need to home educate, and disparities in physical and mental health of children (Jiao, et al., 2020) (Montag & Elhai, 2020) (Vessey & Betz, 2020) (Spinelli, et al., 2020) (Dunton, et al., 2020) (Roe, et al., 2021). Moreover, the pandemic initiated an extensive, sudden and dramatic digital transformation in the society (Iivari, et al., 2020). It forced parents and children to take an extraordinary digital leap in their everyday life and practices, including children's education. Abruptly children's education was transformed from a traditional classroom procedure to a remote, digital one. An entire generation of children had to start managing and mastering with digital tools to participate in their compulsory education. This required significant adjustments not only from children and their teachers, but also from their families. According to the European survey of (Vuorikari, et al., 2020) more than two-thirds of the responding parents in all participating countries would need more guidelines on how to support children with online education activities.

Parents were not trained to embrace online learning which made them resist or event reject online education. The reasons behind this according to (Dong, et al., 2020) were the shortcomings of online learning, young children's inadequate self-regulation, and their lack of time and professional knowledge in supporting children's online training.

Additionally, certain scholars report that online learning during the pandemic failed to enhance students' motivation and attention (Wong, 2020). This is due to a lack of supervision and strategy from people closest to them, including parents, teachers, and a supportive environment, which would play an essential role in online

[1] E. Daskalaki, C. Panagiotakis and P. Fragopoulou are also with the Foundation for Research and Technology- Hellas (FORTH), Institute of Computer Science, 70013 Heraklion, Crete, Greece.
* Corresponding Author Evangelia Daskalaki eva@ics.forth.gr

learning. On top of that, the adoption of online-based learning also involved internet connections, which affected the quality of learning (Lemay, et al., 2021).

A percentage of 71.7% of the families that took part in a survey from (Eyimaya & Irmak, 2021) highlight that screen-time of children has increased during the pandemic. The latter study reported that gender, age, household income, mother's employment status, family's screen time rules, and inconsistent parenting practices emerged as significant predictors for children's screen time model.

According to a study from (Pavlenko & Pavlenko, 2020), digital literacy of family members with preschool children was found to be the key to positive experiences during COVID-19. Thus, now more than ever, digital literacy plays an important role in order to avoid and overcome online risks with the support of parental regulations for children's online involvement (Daskalaki, et al., 2020) (Livingstone & Helsper, 2008).

2. THE PRESENT STUDY

By taking into consideration all the aforementioned scholar reports, the present study aims to put another piece in the complex puzzle of the impact that the pandemic had on the online behavior of children and parents. Thus, we are primarily focused on examining to what extent children's online habits changed due to the outbreak of COVID-19, from the perspective of the parents. Apart from the fact that screen time has increased, which was inevitable due to homeschooling, we aim to understand in which ways these changes occurred, which leads us to our first research question:

Research Question 1. If and to what extent has children's online behavior changed due to the COVID-19 outbreak, according to their parents perspective.

Moreover, we seek to understand how several factors, including demographics and the digital literacy of parents, are associated with children's online behavior during the pandemic. We make the hypothesis that variables like children's age, gender, online parental control, discussion frequency about online safety, and other variables, are not necessarily associated with changes parents observed in the online behavior of their children. This leads us to our second research question:

Research Question 2. By exploring different factors, including demographics and digital literacy of parents, can we make any assumptions about the association of these factors and changes that parents observe in the online behavior of their children?

Lastly, we aim to evaluate whether parents know how to use age classification systems and associated content descriptors that would allow them to make good informed decisions about media content their children could consume without causing any harm. Accordingly, our third research question arises as follows:

Research Question 3. To what extent are parents familiar with age classification systems and content descriptors that will allow them to make a good informed decision about whether their child should watch and/or engage with the media content without posing any harm?

3. METHODS

3.1 Participants and Procedure

The responses of the survey were collected anonymously with the method of Computer-Assisted Web Interviewing, via online questionnaires. The survey took place from November 16, 2020 until January 5, 2021.

During data collection, Greece was in a lockdown state due to COVID-19, and schools (public and private) were practicing distance learning via online platforms. Greece entered lockdown for the first time early March 2020, which included Stay-at-home orders, total movement control, and the closure of schools. Until May 2021, schools opened and closed locally according to epidemiological data of the municipality they operate[2] (Hale, et al., 2021).

[2] https://ourworldindata.org/coronavirus/country/greece

The participants of the survey were clearly informed throughout the study that participation in this research was voluntary. Each participant was asked at the beginning of the questionnaire to select which of his/her children he/she would consider as the subject for the survey questions.

A total of 1750 parents completed the online survey. Table 1 presents the demographic information of the participants. The vast majority of the participants are Female (83.6%). As far as the participants' age is concerned, most of the parents are 40-49 years old (56.2%), then 30-39 years old (30.7%), followed by ages 50-59 (11.6%), ages 20-29 (1%) and lastly ages 60 and older (0.5%). Children's ages, that parents considered as the subject of the survey questions, are mostly 9-12 y.o. (40.6%), then 6-8 y.o. (22.4%), followed by 13-15 y.o. (18.5%), then children 15 y.o. and older (9.1%) and lastly children 3-5 y.o. (7.7%). Most parents declare to have over 10 years of online activity (65.9%) and a Higher Education degree (64.3%). The gender of children, which parents considered as the subject of the survey, was 46.3% Girls and 53.7% Boys.

Table 1. Demographic information of the sample

Measure	*Participants*	*N*	*%*
Age	20-29 y.o.	17	1
	30-39 y.o.	538	30.7
	40-49 y.o.	983	56.2
	50-59 y.o.	203	11.6
	60+	9	0.5
		Total 1750	100
Participants' Gender	Female	1463	1
	Male	287	30.7
		Total 1750	100
Participants' Children Age	3-5 y.o.	134	7.7
	6-8 y.o.	392	22.4
	9-12 y.o.	710	40.6
	13-15 y.o.	324	18.5
	15+	160	9.1
		Total 1720	98.3
Participants' Children Gender	Girls	811	46.3
	Boys	939	53.7
		Total 1750	100
Educational Level	Gymnasium Certificate	60	3.4
	High-school Certificate	568	32.2
	Higher Education	1126	64.3
		Total 1750	100
Years of online activity	<2	38	2.2
	2-4 years	121	6.9
	5-10	438	25.0
	>10 years	1153	65.9
		Total 1750	100
Residence	City (population>10,000)	1208	69.0
	Village (population<10,000)	542	31.0
		Total 1750	100

3.2 Questionnaire and Measures

The online questionnaire was released with specific guidelines on how to be filled. It was specially designed to derive conclusions on how online use and online behavior has shifted during the pandemic, in order to draw recommendations for various stakeholders / target groups such as:

- **Parents**: Concerning the need for improved parental supervision and possibly improved awareness raising and parental understanding, especially during the pandemic.
- **Schools**: Concerning the degree of guidance provided by educators and the level of readiness in confronting emerging risks during the pandemic. Involvement of schools in digital safety education

(cultivation of vigilance, assistance in resilience development), and digital literacy acquired by existing curricula.

- **State/Ministry of Education**: Concerning educational strategies that could be applied during the pandemic to support both parents and children.

The questionnaire contained both quantitative (close-ended) and qualitative (open-ended) questions. In total it consists of 28 questions, from which 19 where multiple choice, three Likert, one open-ended, and seven were demographic questions. By using qualitative research, we seek to explain different perspectives of parents and to uncover trends in thought. The questionnaire was divided into three thematic parts. The first part explored parental supervision, parental digital literacy, and parent-child relationship with respect to internet use. Table 2 shows all questions, measures, and frequencies for this first part of the questionnaire.

The second part of the questionnaire explored parental familiarity with audiovisual age classification systems and their knowledge on how to use tools and methods that would help them rate audiovisual media content (e.g. online gaming, audiovisual streaming content, etc.). Table 3 shows the questions, the measures, and the frequencies of the second part of the questionnaire. This part of the questionnaire also explored parental digital literacy with a focus to age classification system in media.

Finally, the third part contained demographic questions. Table 1 shows the demographic questions of the questionnaire, together with the frequencies.

It should also be noted that a specific statement "My child does not have online interaction" was added as an answer to some of the question, and denotes that the child is not left alone to interact with applications or persons online, but rather the parents choose what the child will watch or engage with, while online. In other words, the child is a passive receiver of the online content, and the parents choose and interact for the child. This is more applicable for small children, who consume online products, but have no other interactions online. Last, but not least, all the questions and answers of the questionnaire were written in Greek.

Assumptions of statistical tests were considered prior to analyses. All statistical tests were conducted using the SPSS software, version 27.0.

4. RESULTS

4.1 Results of the Evaluation of Changes Observed Since the Outbreak of the Pandemic

In the preliminary assessment of the data, the Shapiro Wilk test results rejected the null hypothesis of normality for all the variables of the dataset. This means that the distributions of our variables are statistically significantly different from a normal distributions (Sig < .001), thus non-parametric tests are applied in the main analysis. Regarding the statistical analysis of the responses of the parents, we see in Table 2 that 29.8% (N=521) of all parents have noticed changes in their child's online habits after the outbreak of the pandemic (Table 2 - Pandemic variable). We have analyzed the free text answers of the next open ended question "Would you please describe what kind of changes have you noticed during the pandemic?", only for those parents who answered positively in the previous question, and grouped the similar answers together. According to the responses 84% (N=363) say that their children have noticeable increase in the time they spend online, 8% (N=36) of parents say their children are feeling more anxious and distressed, 5% (N=22) say their children make excessive use of the internet (they refer to it as internet addiction), and 3% (N=13) say their children are playing either more online games or they started to play online games while they did not before.

Table 2. Questions and frequencies of the first part of the questionnaire

Questions	Variable name	(Grouped) Responses	N	%
Have you noticed any change in your child's online habits after the outbreak of the pandemic?	Pandemic Variable	My child doesn't have online interactions	403	23.0
		No	826	47.2
		Yes	521	29.8
If yes, would you please describe what kind of changes you have noticed during the pandemic? (open ended question)	Changes Variable	My child spends more time online	363	84
		My child is more anxious and distressed	36	8
		My child makes excessive use	22	5
		My child plays more games online	13	3
Do you feel in control of your child's online activity?	Control Variable	No	226	12.9
		Partially	848	48.5
		Yes	676	38.6
What worries you most about your child's online activity?(multiple choice)	Worries Variable	Excessive use	1119	63.9
		Personal data exposure	497	28.4
		Bad Influences from the internet	1199	68.5
		Malware	247	14.1
		Online reputation	172	9.8
		Stranger danger	561	32.1
Are you using parental control software?	Parental Control Variable	I would like to, but I don't know how	319	18.2
		No	574	32.8
		Partially	363	20.7
		Yes	494	28.2
Have you set limits on how much time your child is allowed to spend on the computer on a daily basis?	Limits Variable	No	328	18.7
		Yes	1422	81.3
At what age did your child start using the internet?	Starting age Variable	3-5	374	21.4
		6-8	657	37.5
		9-11	539	30.8
		12-14	363	9.5
		>=15	494	0.8
At what age did your child acquire its own social media profile?	SM profile Variable	I am not allowing it	976	56
		5-7	7	0
		8-10	125	7
		11-13	482	28
		14-15	131	7
		>=16	29	2
Does your child trust you with personal information about the internet (such as SM passwords or online interactions)?	Trust Variable	My child doesn't have online interactions	680	38.9
		No	196	11.2
		Yes	874	49.9
How often do you discuss with your child about online safety?	Discussion Variable	Never	51	2.9
		Rarely	229	13.1
		Occasionally	972	55.5
		Very Often	498	28.5
Do you feel you have enough knowledge to advise your child on how to stay safe online	Knowledge Variable	I don't know	407	23.3
		No	388	22.2
		Yes	955	54.6
How often do you seek information about online safety?	Awareness Variable	Rarely	412	24
		Occasionally	1080	62
		Very Often	258	15
Can you tell with whom your child is chatting online?	Chatting Variable	My child doesn't have online interactions	628	35.9
		No	196	11.2
		Yes	926	52.9

Apart from the quantitative results, we also observed that a lot of the free text answers in the question "Would you please describe what kind of changes have you noticed during the pandemic?" reveal emotional distress from parents. For instance, one mother says about her 15-year-old daughter that "Of course! Our children are required to be in front of a screen all day! Which makes it impossible for us to monitor their media use, so your questionnaire is invalid! Open the schools and then we talk again!". A father says about his 12 year-old daughter "She is glued to her cellphone since the first lockdown", and a mother says about her 15 year-old son that "Now he doesn't even go to bathroom without his cellphone". This reveals that dealing with the quarantine is a particularly stressful experience for parents who must balance personal life, work, and raising children, being left alone without other resources. According to (Spinelli, et al., 2020) this situation puts parents at a higher risk of experiencing distress, potentially impairing their ability to be supportive caregivers.

Table 3. Questions and frequencies of the second part of the questionnaire

Questions	*Variable name*	*Responses*	*N*	*%*
Are you aware of age classification systems on the internet, e.g. PEGI scale for online games?	Age Classification	No	871	49.8
		Yes	879	50.2
Are you aware of what the following descriptive content symbols from PEGI scale signify?	Content Classification	No	1262	72.1
		Yes	488	27.9
When your child watches audiovisual content online, would you like to be aware of the potential harmful content contained in this video/game?	Content Rating	I don't know	34	1.9
		No	30	1.7
		Yes	1686	96.3
When your child watches audiovisual content online, would you like to be aware of the age rating so that you make an informed decision to allow it or not?	Age Rating	I don't know	32	1.8
		No	12	0.7
		Yes	1706	7.5
Would you rather have age rating (e.g.8+) or content rating (e.g. violence) or both?	Preferences	Age Rating	114	6.5
		Content Rating	149	8.5
		Both	1487	85.0
Do you believe that age classifications provide enough information for parents to keep their children safe from potentially harmful content?	Enough Information	I don't know	196	11.2
		No	396	22.6
		Yes	1158	66.2
At what age did your child start using the internet?	Experience	Never	1586	90.6
		Rarely	122	7.0
		Regularly	35	2.0
		Often	7	0.4

Additionally, in the question "What worries you most about your child's online activity" (Table 2- Worries variable), parents mostly answer "Bad influences from the internet" (68.5%) and "Excessive use" (63.9%). On the other hand, "Stranger Danger" receives 32.1% (Table 2), which is small compared to the two aforementioned worries of the parents. All these kind of responses reveal a very difficult situation parents are positioned in, with their new roles as educators and full-time entertainers (Attavar, 2021).

Subsequently, we conducted Pearson's Chi-square test of independence to determine whether there exists association between variables. All the variables that we report meet the conditions that each observation is independent of all the others, no more than 20% of the expected counts are less than 5, and all individual expected counts are 1 or greater (Yates, et al., 1999).

Specifically, we focused on the distribution of the variable of the question "Have you noticed any changes in your child's online habits after the outbreak of the pandemic?" which we will call the "Pandemic variable" (Table *2*). Our Null Hypothesis (H_0) is that the pandemic variable is independent of all the other variables in the demographics Table 1 and Table 2. In other words, make the hypothesis (H_0) that there is no association between the pandemic variable and the other variables mentioned in Table 1 and Table 2.

What we observed from our analysis, is that the pandemic variable is indeed dependent of the participant's children age, thus we reject the Null Hypothesis between those two variables $x^2(8, 1720) = 413.740$, $p < .001$. The effect size of this finding is moderately strong (V = .347, where V stands for Cramer's V). By comparing children's ages of parents who observe changes in their child's online habits, we see that the ones who observe changes have higher percentages for children aged 9-12 (48.6%), ages 13-15 (24.5%), and ages 6-8 (16%). Thus we conclude that 6-15 year-olds have been affected from the pandemic according to the results, with the age group 9-12 being the mostly affected (Figure 1).

Results of the Spearman's rho correlation proved significant positive association (Sig. two tailed) between children's age and:

- Starting age variable $r_S = .634$, $p < .001$, C.I. 95% [.604, .663], N = 1720
- Social Media (SM) profile variable $r_S = .701$, $p < .001$, C.I. 95% [.676, .725], N = 1750
- Parent's age $r_S = .461$, $p = .000$, C.I.95% [.422, .499], N = 1750

We conducted chi-square test analysis to examine if the pandemic variable and the above mentioned variables are independent. After our analysis we reject the Null Hypothesis (H_0) for all the below mentioned variables. Namely:

- The Pandemic variable is associated with the starting age variable with moderate association between variables $x^2(8, 1750) = 145.743$, $p < .001$, V = .290
- The pandemic variable is associated with the SM profile variable with moderately strong association $x^2(10, 1750) = 357.944$, $p < .001$, V = .320

- The pandemic variable is associated with the discussions variable with small effect size $x^2(6, 1750) = 52.885$, $p < .001$, $V = .123$
- The pandemic variable is associated with the knowledge variable with small effect size $x^2(4, 1750) = 20.473$, $p < .001$, $V = .076$
- The Pandemic variable is also associated with the trust variable with strong association between variables $x^2(4, 1750) = 635.133$, $p < .001$, $V = .426$

As we observe from the cross tab statistics of the pandemic variable and the starting age variable, parents who have responded that they have noticed change in their child's online habits after the outbreak of the pandemic, are more likely to have answered that their child started to use the internet between 9-11 y.o. (35.9% vs. 33.7%) and 3-5 y.o. (17.1% vs. 15.0%), compared to parents that have not noticed change. On the other hand parents who responded that have not noticed any change during the pandemic, are more likely to have answered that their child started to use the internet between 6-8 y.o. (37.9% vs. 35.9%), 12-14 y.o. (12.2% vs. 10.7%), and 15+ y.o. (1.2% vs. 0.4%).

Moreover, comparing the percentages from the cross tab statistics of the pandemic variable and the SM profile variable, we see that parents who observe changes in their child's online habits say in high percentage that they do not allow their children to have their own social media (44.3% vs. 43.6%), they answer that they have started a social media profile at 11-13 y.o. (38.4% vs. 33.5%), then 8-10 y.o. (9.8% vs. 8.7%). Contrarily, parents who claim that their children have not been affected by the pandemic give higher percentages for ages 14-15 y.o. (11.5% vs.5.8%) and 16+ y.o. (2.2%vs. 1.3%). This observation is also inline with our previous finding that younger children seem to be more affected by the pandemic, because as we can see from Spearman's rho correlation there is a positive association between children's age and SM profile variable. This reveals that the older the child is, the older it created its own SM profile and the younger a child is the younger it created a SM profile. This also shows that the average age of children opening a profile in SM tends to decline over the years (Daskalaki, et al., 2020).

What's more, the chi-square test between the pandemic variable and the discussion variable $x^2(6, 1750) = 52.885$, $p < .001$, $V = .123$ indicates also that parents who answer that they noticed changes in their child's online habits after the outbreak of the pandemic have higher score in the answer that they rarely discuss online safety with their child compared to parents who do not notice changes after the pandemic (12.3% vs. 10.9%). On the other hand, parents who answer that they have not noticed changes have higher score in answers "Occasionally" (57.3% vs 56.2%) and "Very Often" (30.1% vs. 29.9%). Authors in (Wang, et al., 2020) also support that good parenting practices gain significance during the lockdown at home.

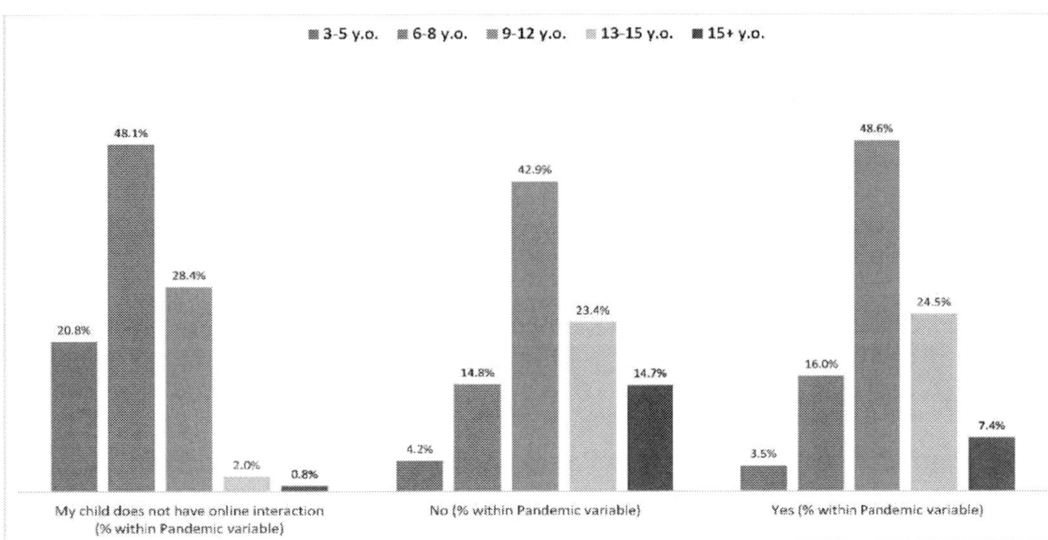

Figure 1. Comparison between the answers of the question if the children of the participants have changed their online behavior during the pandemic and the ages of the children (Cross-tabulation analysis between Pandemic variable and Children's age variable)

On top of that, the chi-square test between the pandemic variable and the knowledge variable $x^2(4, 1750) = 20.473$, $p < .001$, $V = .076$ indicates that parents who answer that they have enough knowledge to advise their child on how to stay safe online, report less that their child has been affected by the pandemic (28.6% vs. 37.1%).

These two last findings, about the discussion variable and the knowledge variable, reveal that digital literacy of parents may be the key to help overcome potential online risks of the children, especially during the pandemic.

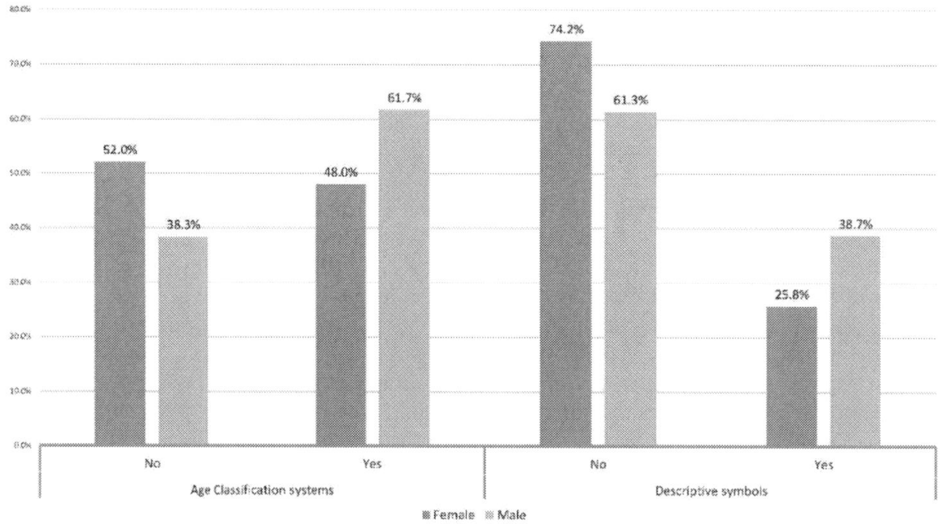

Figure 2. Comparison between the gender of the participants and if they are aware of the age classification systems and descriptive symbols

Furthermore, the chi-square test between the pandemic variable and the control variable $x^2(6, 1750) = 294.922$, $p < .001$, $V = .290$ revealed that there is a moderate association between the two variables. In this case, our Null Hypothesis is also rejected. According to cross-tabulation analysis between the two variables, parents who have answered that they have noticed change in their child's online habits after the outbreak of the pandemic are more likely to have answered that they are partially in control of the activity of their children (59.9% vs. 51.5%) or that they have no control of their child's online activity (16.1% vs. 14.6%).

By conducting chi-square test between the children's age variable and the control variable we reject the H_0, concluding that there is indeed association between these variables too x^2 $(12, 1750) = 280.099$, $p<.001$, $V = .233$. In specific, what we observe from Figure 3 is that parents of children aged 3-5 (57.5%) and 6-8 (49.2%), say that they are in control of what their children do online. Parents of children aged 9-12 mostly respond that they are partially in control (54.6%), but there is still a high percentage of parents (33.7%) who respond that they are in control. Parents of children aged 13-15 and 15+ mostly answer that they are partially in control (58.6% and 54.4%) but a high percentage of them also reports that they are not in control (20.7% and 31.3%) (Figure 3).

Finally, from the chi-square test between the pandemic variable and child's gen-der variable, we retain the null hypotheses that the two variables are independent $x^2(2, 1750) = .097$, $p = .953$, thus there is no association between the variables.

4.2 Results of the Evaluation of Parents Knowledge about Audiovisual Tools and Ratings for Parental Control

In the second part of our study, we examined to what extent parents know how to use age and descriptive content classification systems. The goal of a classification system is to provide parents advanced knowledge about media productions (on-demand-video, video games, etc.), that would allow them to make a good informed decision about whether their child should watch and/or engage with the media content without posing any harm (Gentile, 2008) (Gentile, et al., 2011) (Gentile, et al., 2005) (Bushman & Cantor, 2003).

From our analysis, we see that half of the parents (49.8%) do not know the existence of age classification systems such as the PEGI system (Konzack, 2012). What's more, the vast majority of them (72.1%) is not aware of what the descriptive content symbols of the PEGI system indicate (Table 3). At the same time, almost all parents wish to be informed about age ratings and potentially harmful content that is contained in the audiovisual content their children engage with (97.5% and 96.3%). The vast majority would prefer to have both kind of information provided, that is age ratings combined with content ratings (85.0%).

On the other hand, 22.6% of parents believe that classifications systems do not provide enough information for parents to keep their children safe from potentially harmful content (Table 3).

By conducting chi-square test between Participants' gender and the classification systems variable we reject the Ho, because we find that there is association between the gender of the parents and if they are familiar with the age classification systems x^2 (1, 1750) = 17.984, p < .001, V = .0.101. Specifically, what we observe is that the majority of male participants (Fathers) have responded that they are aware of age classification systems (like the PEGI scale) at 61.7%. On the other hand the majority of female participants (Mothers) have responded that the are not aware of the age classification systems at 52% (Figure 2). This observation might be based on the fact that males play more online games than females, so they are more familiar with age classification systems (Daskalaki, et al., 2020) (Chen, et al., 2018) (McKinnon-Crowley, 2020).

Moreover, we came to the conclusion that parents who have more than 10 years of experience online, are more familiar with age classification systems than parents who have less experience. This conclusion was drawn from the chi-square test between the online experience of the participants (Years of online activity form Table 1) and the age classification variable from Table 3. Specifically, we reject the Ho, as the x^2 (3, 1750) = 38.299, p < .001, V = .148, which indicates that there is association between these variables. From Figure 4 we see that the more online experience one has (in years) the more familiar she is with age classification systems. Only participants who have reported to have more than 10 years of experience, report in majority that they are aware of age classification system (55.2%).

The overall picture drawn, is that a big percentage of parents are not aware of important tools that could help them in the parental mediation task of their children, especially during the pandemic, although the majority of the them report to be savvy users and of higher education (65.9% over 10 years of online activity and 64.3% have college or bachelor degree) (Table 1).

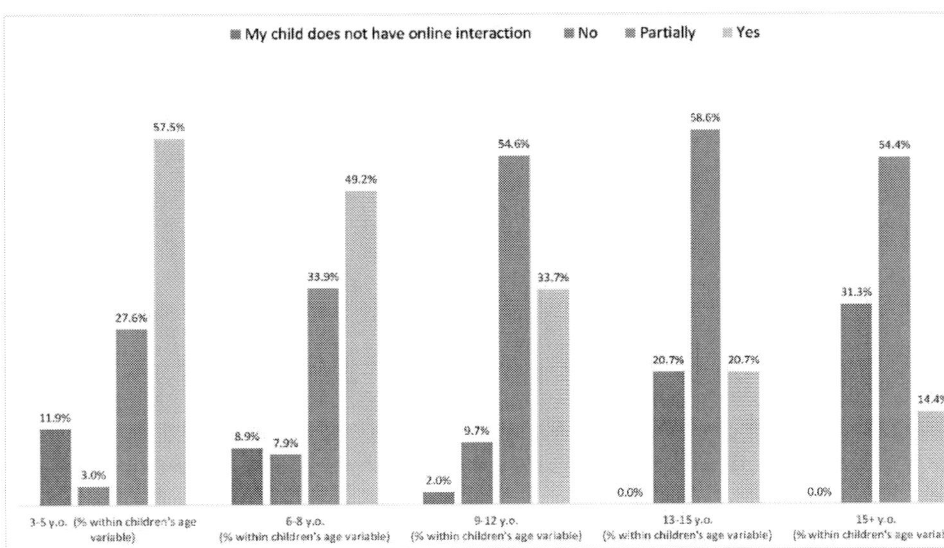

Figure 3. Comparison between children's age and if parents are in control of their online activity (Cross-tabulation analysis between children's age variable and control variable)

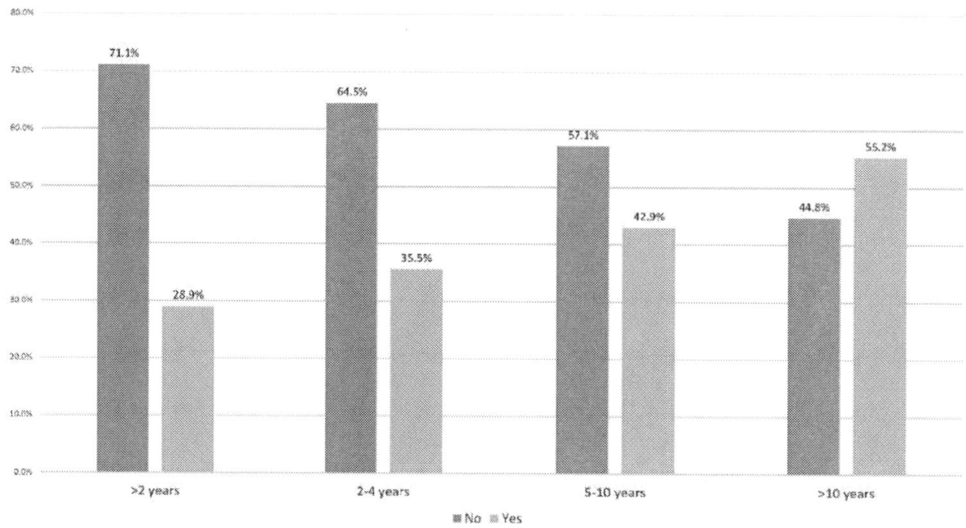

Figure 4. Comparison between the years of online experience of the participants (in years) and if they are aware of the age classification systems (Cross-tabulation analysis between years of online activity variable and the classification systems variable)

These finding reveal that there is a need for more effort on awareness raising and tools that could help parents choose what is best for their child, regarding online activities. Furthermore, it reveals that parent are not digitally literate when it comes to content classification systems.

5. LIMITATIONS

The underrepresentation of male participants might limit the generalization of the findings. On the other hand, the over-representation of female participants is a pattern that we come across regularly, as the audience demographics of the awareness platform of the Greek Safer Internet Center (SIC) comprises of approx. 65% Females and 35%Males. Furthermore, the followers of the social media accounts of the Greek SIC are 70% Females and 30% Males. As indicated from other researches (Connell, et al., 2015) mothers spend more time with their children than fathers on both weekdays and weekend days. Not surprisingly, the more time the parent reported spending with the child, the more likely they were to co-use media. Furthermore, other studies show that fathers tend to have less parental concerns compared to mothers (Yosi, 2020) (Pratt, et al., 2019). Lastly, the study is prone to certain biases, as data are self-reported from parents.

6. DISCUSSION AND CONCLUSION

Our survey showed that there is a high percentage of parents (29.8%) that report changes in the online habits of their children during the pandemic. Hence, the answer to our first research question is that a fair amount of parents, have noticed changes in the online behavior of their children. From a qualitative perspective, we indicated that some parents' responses reveal emotional distress, because of the complicated situation parents are positioned in, with their new roles during the pandemic, as educators and full-time entertainers.

Regarding our second research question, our research revealed that those parents who reported that they discuss more with their child about online safety have lower chances of reporting that their child has been affected by the pandemic. Moreover, we showed that parents who answer that report to have enough knowledge to advise their child on how to stay safe online, report less that their child has been affected by the pandemic. Overall, our research affirms that digital literacy of parents might be the key to overcome potential online risks of children, especially during the pandemic.

Another factor that has been proven crucial on how children coped with the pandemic was demographic factor and specifically the age of the child. Children aged 6-15 years old, seem to be more affected from the pandemic compared to children 3-5 and children 15+ years old. Notably, the age group 9-12, appears to be the age group, which shows the biggest percentage of parents noticing change in their child's online habits after the outbreak of the pandemic. What's more, the age group 9-12, is admittedly the crucial age where children make the first outbreak to the online world. For this specific age group, parents who report that they do not have the control or parents who report partially in control of the online activities of their children are more than parents who say that they are in control of the online activity of their children. The latter was not the case for the younger age groups.

For the older age groups 13-15 and 15+, parents who respond that they are not in control of their children online activities are more than parents who say that they are, regardless of the pandemic variable. Moreover, our research showed that the gender of the child and the residence (city or village) is independent of whether a child is more or less affected by the circumstances of the pandemic.

These findings reveal that the lockdown measures that have been taken from countries, due to the COVID-19 pandemic, accelerated the turning point where parents were in control of the online activities of their children and then began to lose it. This faster pace of changing of the online behavior of children, left parents unprepared and thus unable to react at the same pace.

Just as importantly, regarding our third research question, parents seem to be incompetent to make good informed decision about what is appropriate for their children online. This is obvious from the low percentages of parents reporting being aware of age and content classification systems online, but also from the fact that 51% of parents don't use parental control systems, either because they are not aware of how to use them or because they choose not to use them. Our statistical analysis showed that parents who have more than ten years of online experience but also male participants, are more familiar with age classification systems.

To conclude with, the COVID-19 pandemic initiated an extensive, sudden and dramatic digital transformation in the society. The pandemic forced children, to take an extraordinary digital leap. This required significant adjustments from the entire society. Parents had to take the lead in this sudden, unexpected digital transformation of children's basic education, without being prepared for it. In our survey, we showed that there is a need to put more effort on awareness raising on tools that could help parents choosing what is best for their child, regarding their online activities.

CONFLICT OF INTEREST

No potential competing interest was reported by the authors.

ACKNOWLEDGMENT

This research has been co-financed by the European Union and Greek national funds through the Operational Program Competitiveness, Entrepreneurship and Innovation, under the call RESEARCH - CREATE - INNOVATE (project code: T1EDK-02147).

REFERENCES

Attavar, S. P. K., 2021. Connected to devices, disconnected from children: struggles of urban, dual-earning parents in India during COVID-19. *Journal of Children and Media,* Volume 15, p. 138–141.

Bushman, B. & Cantor, J., 2003. Media Ratings for Violence and Sex: Implications for Policymakers and Parents. *American Psychologist,* pp. 130-141.

Chen, K. H., Oliffe, J. L. & Kelly, M. T., 2018. Internet Gaming Disorder: An Emergent Health Issue for Men. *American Journal of Men's Health,* Volume 12, pp. 1151-1159.

Christodoulaki, M. & Fragopoulou, P., 2010. SafeLine: reporting illegal internet content. *Information Management & Computer Security.*

Connell, S. L., Lauricella, A. R. & Wartella, E., 2015. Parental Co-Use of Media Technology with their Young Children in the USA. *Journal of Children and Media,* Volume 9, pp. 5-21.

Daskalaki, E., Psaroudaki, K. & Fragopoulou, P., 2018. EL-SIC: focus on better and Safer Online Experiences for Kids. *ERCIM NEWS,* p. 52–53.

Daskalaki, E., Psaroudaki, K., Karkanaki, M. & Fragopoulou, P., 2020. Understanding the online behavior and risks of children: results of a large-scale national survey on 10-18 year olds. *arXiv preprint arXiv:2008.10274.*

Dong, C., Cao, S. & Li, H., 2020. Young children's online learning during COVID-19 pandemic: Chinese parents' beliefs and attitudes. *Children and Youth Services Review,* Volume 118, p. 105440.

Dunton, G. F., Do, B. & Wang, S. D., 2020. Early effects of the COVID-19 pandemic on physical activity and sedentary behavior in children living in the US. *BMC Public Health,* Volume 20, p. 1–13.

Eyimaya, A. O. & Irmak, A. Y., 2021. Relationship between parenting practices and children's screen time during the COVID-19 Pandemic in Turkey. *Journal of pediatric nursing,* Volume 56, p. 24.

Gentile, D. A., 2008. The rating systems for media products. *Handbook of children, media, and development,* p. 527–551.

Gentile, D. A., Maier, J. A., Hasson, M. R. & de Bonetti, B. L., 2011. Parents' evaluation of media ratings a decade after the television ratings were introduced. *Pediatrics,* Volume 128, p. 36–44.

Gentile, D., Humphrey, J. & Walsh, D., 2005. Media ratings for movies, music, video games, and television: a review of the research and recommendations for improvements. *Adolesc Med Clin,* Volume 16, p. 427–46.

Hale, T. et al., 2021. A global panel database of pandemic policies (oxford covid-19 government response tracker). *Nature Human Behaviour,* p. 1–10.

Iivari, N., Sharma, S. & Ventä-Olkkonen, L., 2020. Digital transformation of everyday life–How COVID-19 pandemic transformed the basic education of the young generation and why information management research should care?. *International Journal of Information Management,* Volume 55, p. 102183.

Jiao, W. Y. et al., 2020. Behavioral and emotional disorders in children during the COVID-19 epidemic. *The journal of Pediatrics,* Volume 221, p. 264.

Kokolaki, E. et al., 2020. Investigating the dynamics of illegal online activity: The power of reporting, dark web, and related legislation. *Computer Law & Security Review,* Volume 38, p. 105440.

Konzack, L., 2012. Pan European game information (PEGI) system. *Encycl. Video Games: Cult. Technol. Art Gaming,* Volume 2, p. 474–476.

Lemay, D. J., Doleck, T. & Bazelais, P., 2021. Transition to online teaching during the COVID-19 pandemic. *Interactive Learning Environments,* Volume 0, pp. 1-12.

Livingstone, S. & Helsper, E. J., 2008. Parental Mediation of Children's Internet Use. *Journal of Broadcasting & Electronic Media,* Volume 52, pp. 581-599.

McKinnon-Crowley, S., 2020. Fighting Gendered Battles: On Being a Woman in a Contemporary Gaming Community. *Journal of Contemporary Ethnography,* Volume 49, pp. 118-142.

Montag, C. & Elhai, J. D., 2020. Discussing digital technology overuse in children and adolescents during the COVID-19 pandemic and beyond: On the importance of considering Affective Neuroscience Theory. *Addictive Behaviors Reports,* Volume 12, p. 100313.

Pavlenko, G. V. & Pavlenko, A. I., 2020. *Digital Literacy as a Condition for Positive Experience of the COVID-19 Lockdown for Families With Preschool Children.* s.l., Atlantis Press, pp. 507-512.

Pratt, M., Hoffmann, D., Taylor, M. & Musher-Eizenman, D., 2019. Structure, coercive control, and autonomy promotion: A comparison of fathers' and mothers' food parenting strategies. *Journal of health psychology,* Volume 24, p. 1863–1877.

Roe, A., Blikstad-Balas, M. & Dalland, C. P., 2021. The Impact of COVID-19 and Homeschooling on Students' Engagement With Physical Activity. *Frontiers in Sports and Active Living,* Volume 2, p. 205.

Spinelli, M., Lionetti, F., Pastore, M. & Fasolo, M., 2020. Parents' stress and children's psychological problems in families facing the COVID-19 outbreak in Italy. *Frontiers in Psychology,* Volume 11, p. 1713.

Vessey, J. A. & Betz, C. L., 2020. Everything old is new again: COVID-19 and public health. *Journal of pediatric nursing,* Volume 52, p. A7.

Vuorikari, R. et al., 2020. *How families handled emergency remote schooling during the Covid-19 lockdown in spring 2020-Summary of key findings from families with children in 11 European countries,* s.l.: s.n.

Wang, G. et al., 2020. Mitigate the effects of home confinement on children during the COVID-19 outbreak. *The Lancet,* Volume 395, p. 945–947.

Wong, R., 2020. When no one can go to school: does online learning meet students' basic learning needs?. *Interactive Learning Environments,* Volume 0, pp. 1-17.

Yates, D., Moore, D. & McCabe, G., 1999. *The Practice of Statistics. New York, NY: H.* s.l.:Freeman & Company.[Google Scholar].

Yosi, Y., 2020. Systematic review of the differences between mothers and fathers in parenting styles and practices. *Current Psychology,* Volume 9, pp. 1936-4733.

REFINEMENT OF THE QUANTITATIVE MODELS TO ESTIMATE USER'S FEAR IN EVACUATION ROUTE PLANNING: INTRODUCTION OF USER ATTRIBUTES AND NONLINEARIZATION OF THE MODEL

Hiroshi Furukawa[1] and Ryota Koshimizu[2]
[1]*Faculty of Engineering, Information and Systems, University of Tsukuba*
[2]*Department of Risk Engineering, University of Tsukuba*
1-1-1 Tenoudai, Tsukuba, Ibaraki, 305-8573, Japan

ABSTRACT

During disaster evacuation, fear or panic can force evacuees to make irrational decisions. The final goal of our project is the development of a navigation system that provide routes where evacuees go through reassured. The aim of this study is to improve the model created by our previous study. In the first stage of this study, we considered the user's attributes as additional factors in the fear estimation model, and also constructed the fear estimation model by nonlinearizing the model, i.e., Random Forest Regression and Support Vector Regression. By comparing the results with the previous model, we verified whether the improvement in model accuracy could be measured. The results showed that the model created by Random Forest Regression was the most versatile and the most accurate. In the second stage, in order to evaluate whether the proposed revised method improves the accuracy of the model, we conducted cognitive experiments using the route with the revised model and the shortest route. The results show that the mean value of the level of fear is lower for the revised method than for the shortest path. It is expected that the pedestrian navigation system based on the proposed method can provide routes where users can evacuate reassured, avoiding places where they may feel great fears.

KEYWORDS

Disaster Evacuation, Anxiety, Emotion Modeling, Reassured, Disaster Mitigation, Intelligent Transport Systems

1. INTRODUCTION

A problem that arises when disaster victims evacuate is that they do not know where to go. In the Kumamoto earthquake, some evacuees took refuge in places that were not designated by the local government. This made it difficult for the government to know the whereabouts of the evacuees (Funakoshi and Hatayama, 2017). In order to solve this problem and facilitate evacuation, evacuation support tools are needed that allow disaster evacuees to obtain appropriate information. Bernardini et al. (2019) analyzed behavioral data on earthquakes that occurred in New Zealand, Italy, and Japan. They noted that effective support for evacuees' decision-making should be provided to improve community resilience and personal safety, and identified individual device-based support tools as one of the main solutions.

Disaster navigation system has become popular as one of the tools to support disaster evacuation. In the disaster navigation systems available in the market, the route by the shortest distance is used to guide the route from the current location to the evacuation site. There are three problems with this method, considering the actual situation of evacuation. The first is that when a large-scale disaster occurs, building collapse and fire may occur together. In the Great Hanshin-Awaji Earthquake of 1995 as well as the Great East Japan Earthquake of 2011, many roads were blocked due to collapsed buildings (Yamamoto et al., 2017). During a disaster evacuation, road blockage is expected to make it difficult for navigation users to take the shortest route. No et al. (2020) present a method for assigning evacuation routes that considers both exposure to hazards and walking distance by estimating the danger zone of building collapse and incorporating it as a travel cost when crossing the road network.

The second problem is the occurrence of traffic jams and accidents that lead to increased evacuation time during disasters. There is no guarantee that the method of providing the shortest distance will be able to cope with the intense transportation demand during evacuation, nor is there any guarantee that there will not be intersections that become bottlenecks for accidents. Campos et al. (2012) proposed a method which applies a heuristic algorithm that iteratively defines two independent routes from the disaster area to each shelter, using the travel time and capacity of the transportation network as parameters, and assigns vehicle flows in the evacuation plan.

Third, even if a certain route is actually passable, the user may feel fear from the appearance of the road and avoid passing that road. In the 1964 Niigata earthquake, it was reported that evacuation was delayed due to fear of evacuation routes (Horiguti and Kosaka, 1984). A support tool that may be useful in solving this problem is a navigation application that guides evacuees to a route where they will not feel fear during evacuation activities. This study focused on this third problem.

As a tool to prevent panic among evacuees during disaster evacuation, the ultimate goal of this project is to develop a pedestrian navigation system that provides safe routes through which evacuees can avoid places where they feel great fear (Furukawa and Liu, 2018). Furukawa (2021) has created a model that quantitatively evaluates the fear that people feel during evacuation actions depending on the road conditions, with the goal of providing evacuees with a route that does not cause fear. The model they developed predicts the level of fear using multiple regression analysis, i.e., linear model, where the coefficient of determination is only 0.297 at the highest, which is a problem because it does not sufficiently predict the level of fear.

The purpose of this study is to improve the model proposed by Furukawa (2021) by addressing the significant individual differences in fear estimation and the limitations of the linear model. In the first stage of this study, we considered the user's attributes as additional factors in the fear estimation model, and also constructed the fear estimation model by nonlinearizing the model. In the second stage, in order to evaluate whether the proposed revised method improves the accuracy of the model, we conducted cognitive experiments using the route with the revised model and the shortest route.

2. BASIC IDEA OF EVACUATION ROUTE PLANNING

We proposed an evacuation route planning method that provides a safe route through which evacuees can avoid spots (man-made and natural structures and areas) that may cause them great fear (Furukawa and Liu, 2018). Figure 1 shows the situation assumed in the definition of the revised method.

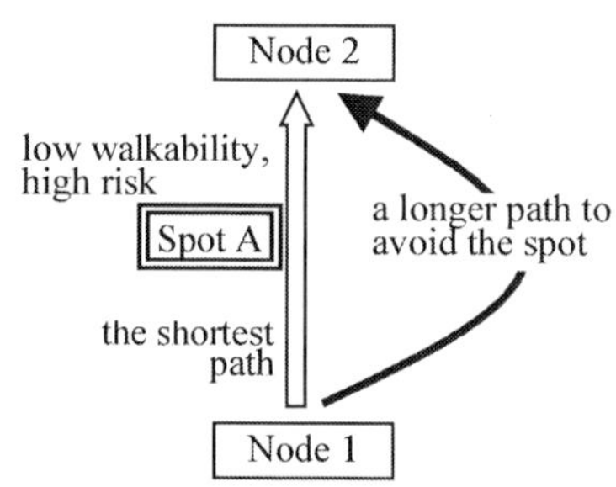

Figure 1. The situation assumed for the definition of the revised cost function

This method consists of three groups of models. The first group of models is a fear estimation model that estimates the user's fear level of physical factors (spots) on the route that may cause fear in evacuees. The second set of models estimates the allowable evacuation delay time based on the fear level estimated by the first set of models. In this method, the allowable delay time (Matsuda, et al., 2004) is used as the additional time that a user can tolerate to bypass a spot that causes great fear for the user. The third model is a cost function defined by equations (1) and (2).

$$\alpha = \frac{[time\ for\ the\ path\ with\ a\ fear\ spot]}{[time\ for\ the\ path\ with\ a\ fear\ spot] + [the\ acceptable\ time\ delay]} \tag{1}$$

$$[the\ revised\ cost\ of\ the\ detour\ path] = \alpha \times [original\ cost] \tag{2}$$

[*time for the path with a fear spot*] : Time required to walk the path with a fear spot.

[*original cost*] : Physical distance of the path with a fear spot. The distance is used for the conventional route planning method.

[*the revised cost of the detour path*] : The revised cost for the detour path, which is the path to avoid the fear spot.

As the value of the detour route increases for the user, i.e., as the acceptable delay time increases, the value of the revised cost becomes smaller. If the detour has a spot, the revised cost is used instead of the original cost. This cost function allows the fear of pedestrians to be considered in route planning.

3. PREVIOUS WORK AND OUR TARGETS

The aim of our previous work was identification of additional factors, along routes to improve the fear estimation model (Furukawa, 2021). A questionnaire survey was conducted to seek capable candidates of additional factors, and "size of the largest signboards" was selected as a new candidate. The second step was validation of the factors and the model through a cognitive experiment. 360-degree videos and a head-mounted display was used to display the images to the participants. The effectiveness of the new fear factor "size of the largest signboard" and creating a model group by segmentation were confirmed. The two modifications reduced the root mean square error of the fear estimation by 4.7% from the result without them. Also, the mean absolute error of the estimation decreased 8.6%.

The model developed in the previous study has a low coefficient of determination of 0.297, which is insufficient to be used for actual route guidance. Therefore, in this study, we took two approaches to improve the accuracy of the model.

The first is to add a new factor to the model that considers individual differences. From the data obtained in the previous study (Furukawa, 2021), it was assumed that individual differences were the cause of the low accuracy of the model. In order to improve the accuracy of the model, it is necessary to incorporate into the model factors related to individual differences that were not used in the previous study.

The second is the nonlinearity of the fear estimation model. In the previous study (Furukawa, 2021), the multiple regression analysis used to create the model is a linear model, and thus its representational capability is limited. Figure 2 shows the relationship between the average fear level of 20 participants in the experiment and the road width for 8 road locations without buildings among the data obtained in the previous study.

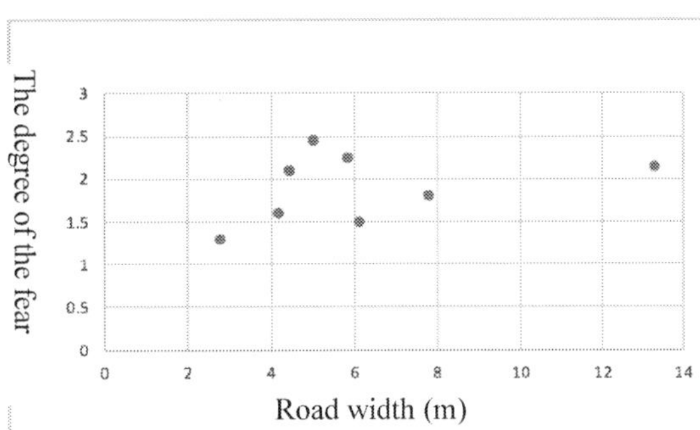

Figure 2. Relationship between road width and average fear level on roads without buildings

Figure 2 shows that the relationship between road width and average fear level is not linear. Therefore, if a multiple regression analysis is used to create the model, it is possible that the fear level cannot be expressed accurately. In order to solve this problem, this study aims to improve the accuracy of the model by applying a nonlinear model as the model creation method. Specifically, we will create models using the nonlinear regression models Random Forest Regression and Support Vector Regression, and select an appropriate model by comparing the results.

4. REFINEMENT OF THE FEAR ESTIMATION MODEL

4.1 Introduction of User Attributes to the Fear Estimation Model

In the fear evaluation model created by Furukawa (2021), the number of factors used to create the model was too small to create a sufficient fear evaluation model to be used as a navigation system. Therefore, in the model created in this study, individual differences are expressed by increasing the number of attributes used in the model. In the previous study, only road conditions were used to create the model. Preliminary research (Koshimizu, 2019) revealed that the fear of evacuation can be estimated by using the user attributes, so this study creates a fear evaluation model using "road conditions" and "user attributes."

In addition to "road width," "signboard," and "building," which have been used in previous studies, this study newly added "overhead wires," "train bridge," and "bridge" as factors. The three newly used factors were found to have an effect on the fear of disaster evacuation from the previous study. Therefore, these factors can be used to estimate the degree of fear, and were adopted as new road conditions in this study.

The following three user attributes were selected as factors for the new model. The reasons for the selection of each factor are explained below.

(1) Frequency of visiting the downtown area

This is used as a factor because preliminary research (Koshimizu, 2019) revealed that it has an impact on the fear of disaster evacuation. This is considered to be an attribute that indicates the user's physical strength and extroversion.

(2) Average value of user's fear of the "road with a train bridge" measured in the VR environment

In our preliminary study (Koshimizu, 2019), we found that the distribution of the participants' response fear of the six points of "roads with train bridges" was biased from the fear data obtained from the experiments in the VR environment and in the field. We used VR images and a head-mounted display, which is a display for VR viewing, as the environment to display the images to be evaluated to the participants. We believe that adding "the average value of the user's fear of 'road with a train bridge' measured in the VR environment" as a new user attribute will improve the representational ability of the model for roads with train bridges.

(3) Average value of user's fear of the "road with bridge" measured in the VR environment

From the preliminary study (Koshimizu, 2019) as well as (2), we found that there was a bias in the distribution of the participants' response fear of the four "roads with bridges" locations. In order to make it possible to express this bias of the fear level, we added "the average value of the user's fear level toward 'road with a bridge' measured in the VR environment" as a user attribute.

4.2 Nonlinearization of the Fear Estimation Model

In this study, we created and compared fear evaluation models using the three methods shown below. The three models selected were Multiple Linear Regression (MLR), which is a linear model used in previous studies, and Support Vector Regression (SVR) and Random Forest Regression (RFR), which are nonlinear models that are expected to improve model accuracy. We used scikit-learn, an open source machine learning library in Python, to implement the three evaluation models to be compared. MLR, SVR, and RFR were implemented using the scikit-learn modules model.LinearRegression, sklearn.svm.SVR, and sklearn.ensemble.RandomForestRegressor, respectively.

4.3 Results and Discussion

Fifteen participants in their twenties were subjected to the experiment. The average age was 22.53 years old, the highest age was 24 years old, and the lowest age was 20 years old. Ethical considerations were considered in the design of this experiment, which was approved by the ethics review board of our organization. The participants were paid for their participation in the experiment.

Participants in the experiment were asked to view 360-degree images of roads at 50 locations in Chiyoda Ward, Tokyo, using VR, and to respond to the degree of fear they felt when passing through the roads on a five-point scale. The participants were asked to rate their level of fear when passing through the roads on a five-point scale: 0: not fearful, 1: slightly fearful, 2: fearful but passable, 3: fearful and would like to avoid passing through, 4: very fearful and would not pass through.

We compared the results of MLR, SVR, and RFR using the response data of fear level obtained from the experiment. Using 5-fold cross validation, the coefficient of determination and root mean squared error (RMSE) values for each model were calculated. The results are shown in Table 1 and Table 2. From Tables 1 and 2, RFR took the highest value for the coefficient of determination, and also took the lowest value for RMSE. This result shows that RFR is the most suitable model for fear prediction. Therefore, the fear evaluation model using RFR is adopted in this study.

Table 1. Results of the coefficient of determination for test data

Type of the model	Average
MLR	0.304
SVR	0.281
RFR	0.490

Table 2. Results of the RMSE for test data

Type of the model	Average
MLR	0.913
SVR	0.934
RFR	0.783

5. A COGNITIVE EXPERIMENT FOR VALIDATION OF THE REVISED MODEL FOR FEAR ESTIMATION

A cognitive experiment was conducted to verify whether fear during evacuation behavior was reduced in the route created using the revised fear evaluation model and whether it was appropriate as an evacuation route. We asked the participants to walk from the same starting point to the destination point using both the "shortest route" and the "route created by the revised method." We compared the fear level data obtained in each trial.

5.1 Flow of the Cognitive Experiment

(1) In order to collect the user attributes "the average value of the user's fear of the road with a train bridge" and "the average value of the user's fear of the road with a bridge" measured in the VR environment in advance, the users were asked to answer the fear level at eight points using the VR environment.
(2) Move to the starting point of the walking experiment and ask the participants to walk from the starting point to the destination point in the "shortest path."
(3) Have the participants return to the starting point again, and walk from the starting point to the destination point using the "path created by the revised method."
(4) After arriving at the destination, the participants are interviewed to get their opinions about the route.

In order to take into account the effect of the order of the experiments, the order of (2) and (3) was switched depending on the participants.

5.2 Environmental Conditions of the Experiment

In this experiment, it is necessary to collect the data of fear of the road in the VR environment in advance. To collect the data in advance, we used HTC VIVE, a VR terminal.

We developed a navigation application using "ArcGIS Runtime SDK for Android" to show the route used in the walking experiment to the experiment participants. This application can create a route that passes through multiple specified points, and it can create a route that passes through all the nodes obtained by the Dijkstra method. In addition, the current location can be displayed on the map, so the application can be used in the same way as other navigation applications in the market.

The walking experiment was conducted around Chuo Ward, Tokyo. The starting point was the Kyobashi Trust Tower, and the destination point was the Seven-Eleven Kayabacho Station East Exit Store. The location was selected to cover the road conditions used in the model. According to the National Institute of Land and Infrastructure Management (NILIM), the critical walking distance for evacuation is reported to be 2.0 km (NILIM, 2006). Therefore, the starting point and the destination point were selected so that the route used in this experiment would be within 2.0 km.

The participants of the experiment were 10 in their 20' s. Ethical considerations have been considered in the design of this experiment, which has been approved by the ethics review board of our organization. We paid the participants for the experiment.

The routes were created using the user attribute data obtained from the participants in the experiment. The route created in this experiment was the same for all the participants in the experiment. The difference between the route and the shortest route is that the route is centered on the main street (wide street).

5.3 Data Acquired and Results of Analysis

We summarize the results of the evaluation of the degree of fear of all nodes for each path. Figure 3 is a box-and-whisker diagram showing the distribution of fear levels for the shortest route (29 nodes) and Figure 4 for the revised route (30 nodes). In the box-and-whisker diagrams, the x-axis shows the numbers of the points of the roads passed in the experiment and the y-axis shows the distribution of the fear of the 15 participants' responses to the corresponding roads.

The maximum value for both routes is compared. In the shortest route, there was a participant who answered "4", which is the maximum fear level, but in the revised route, the maximum fear level was "3." This is because the revised route avoided the road spot that recorded the fear level of 4 in the shortest route. This result indicates that the route using the revised method can avoid the route that is prone to extreme fear.

Table 3 shows the analysis of the data for each route. Table 3 shows that the mean value is lower for the revised method than for the shortest path. This result shows that the revised method is able to reduce the fear felt throughout the entire path.

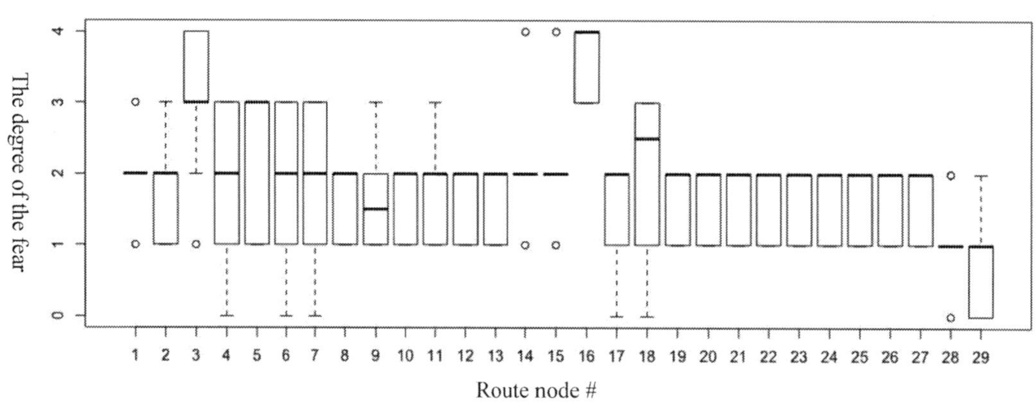

Figure 3. Distribution of the fear level answered by the experimental participants in the shortest route

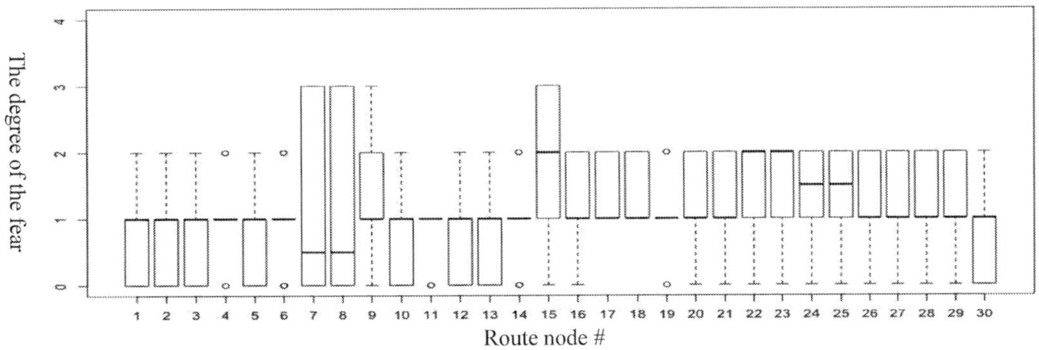

Figure 4. Distribution of the fear level answered by the participants of the experiment for the route created by the revised method

Table 3. Results of statistical analysis on the level of fear for each route

	The shortest route	The route created by the revised model
Average	1.802	1.137
Standard deviation	0.084	0.748
t-test	$p = 2.2e^{-16}$	

5.4 Discussion

Through comparison experiments for both the shortest path and the path using the revised model, we confirmed that the model created by the proposed method can be used to create a path that avoids fearful road spots. However, when compared to the shortest route, the road becomes longer instead of reducing the fear level. In a situation where aftershocks are possible, there would be users who would consider it risky to walk for a longer time. It is necessary to make some adjustments to the length of the path.

After walking both routes, the participants were asked which route they would prefer to take in the event of a disaster evacuation. 9 out of 10 participants chose the revised route. From this result, we can conclude that our method is able to create an evacuation route that is more appropriate than the shortest route for many users.

We tested the accuracy of the RF model using the responses of fear level for each road obtained in the evaluation experiment, and found that the coefficient of determination was 0.08. The reason for the low model accuracy may be due to the different districts. In the model validation experiment in Section 4, we used the same road data around Chiyoda Ward as the training data as the test data. However, in the evaluation experiment conducted in this section, the evaluation of roads in the office district around Chuo Ward was used, and it is thought that the value of the coefficient of determination became lower due to the different districts. It was confirmed that in order to make the method more versatile, it is necessary to build the model with various locations with different conditions.

Another limitation of this study is that the participants are limited to young university students. Since the basic usefulness of the proposed method has been confirmed, it is necessary to expand the target group of participants. Currently, we are planning to conduct a study with elderly people.

6. CONCLUSION

The final goal of our project is the development of a navigation system that provide routes where evacuees go through reassured. The aim of this study is to improve the model created by our previous study. In the first stage of this study, we considered the user's attributes as additional factors in the fear estimation model, and also constructed the fear estimation model by nonlinearizing the model, i.e., Random Forest Regression and Support Vector Regression. By comparing the results with the previous model, we verified whether the improvement in model accuracy could be measured. The results showed that the model created by Random Forest Regression was the most versatile and the most accurate. In the second stage, in order to evaluate whether the proposed revised method improves the accuracy of the model, we conducted cognitive experiments using the route with the revised model and the shortest route. The results show that the mean value of the level of fear is lower for the revised method than for the shortest path, and that the revised method is able to reduce the fear felt throughout the entire path.

From the results, it also was found that the versatility of the model needs to be improved. There is a possibility that the currently created regression model is only suitable for the roads in Chiyoda Ward. To solve this problem, we can expect to create a model with sufficient generality by using data from various different streets.

It is expected that the pedestrian navigation system based on the proposed method can provide routes where users can evacuate reassured, avoiding places where they may feel great fears.

ACKNOWLEDGEMENT

This work was supported in part by Grants-Aid for Science Research 20K12074 of the Japanese Ministry of Education, Science, Sports and Culture.

REFERENCES

Bernardini, G. et al., 2019. Proposing Behavior-oriented Strategies for Earthquake Emergency Evacuation: A Behavioral Data Analysis from New Zealand, Italy and Japan. *Safety Science*, Vol. 116, pp. 295-309.

Campos, V. et al., 2012. A method for Evacuation Route Planning in Disaster Situations. *Procedia - Social and Behavioral Sciences*, 54, pp. 503-512.

Funakoshi, K. and Hatayama, M., 2017, A study of Identification of Disaster Refugees in Kumamoto Earthquake 2016, Proceedings of DPRI Annual Meeting 2017, Kyoto, Japan, E02. (in Japanese)

Furukawa, H. (2021). Refinement of the quantitative models to estimate user's fear in evacuation route planning: A study on the effectiveness of physical factors for signboards. *In Intelligent and Reliable Engineering Systems*, CRC Press, pp. 55-62.

Furukawa, H. and Liu, Z., 2018. A qualitative model to estimate users' fear of environmental conditions for evacuation route guidance. *Intelligent Human Systems Integration: Proceedings of International Conference on Intelligent Human Systems Integration 2018*, Vol. 722, pp. 473–479.

Horiguti, T. and Kosaka, S., 1984, Study of Human Response on Earthquakes. *Comprehensive Urban Studies*, Vol. 23, pp. 77-92. (in Japanese)

Koshimizu, R., 2019, A Study of a Route Evaluation Model Considering User Attributes for Fear of Nighttime Evacuation. Graduation Thesis, Department of Information Science, University of Tsukuba.

Matsuda, M. et al., 2004. A Personalized Route Guidance System for Pedestrians. *IEICE Trans. on Fundamentals of Electronics, Communications and Computer Sciences*, Vol. 87, pp. 132–139.

NILIM, 2006. Manual of Supporting Vulnerable People in Flood. *Technical Note of NILIM*, No. 292.

No, W. et al., 2020. Balancing Hazard Exposure and Walking Distance in Evacuation Route Planning during Earthquake Disasters. *International Journal of Geo-Information*, Vol. 9, No. 432, pp. 1-14.

Yamamoto K, Li X., 2017. Safety Evaluation of Evacuation Routes in Central Tokyo Assuming a Large-Scale Evacuation in Case of Earthquake Disasters. *Journal of Risk and Financial Management*, Vol. 10, No. 3, 14.

METHOD FOR ISOLATING THE PATIENT AND IoT ABNORMALITY USING A BAYESIAN NETWORK

Ryoichi Sasaki[1], Akinori Ueno[1] and Jigang Liu[2]
[1]*Tokyo Denki University, 5 Senju-Asahi-Cho, Adachi-Ku, Tokyo 120-8551, Japan*
[2]*Metropolitan State University, 700 East Seventh Street, Saint Paul, MN 55106-5000, USA*

ABSTRACT

In recent years, Internet of Things (IoT) systems have become widespread. In the medical and health fields, the number of systems that use IoT to detect and diagnose patient abnormalities is increasing. Even if an abnormality in a patient is detected by such a system, it may actually be due to an abnormality in a component, such as the IoT. Therefore, when an abnormality in a patient is detected, we have developed a method to determine whether the abnormality is a patient abnormality or an abnormality in any part of the detection system using a Bayesian network. In addition, it was confirmed that by applying this method to a patient abnormality detection system using an under-sheet-type multi-vital IoT monitor in hospital, it is possible to isolate the cause of the abnormality appropriately and efficiently.

KEYWORDS

Bayesian Network, Medical IoT, Patient Abnormality, Cause Isolation

1. INTRODUCTION

In recent years, Internet of Things (IoT) systems have become increasingly widespread. In the medical and health fields as well, systems that use IoT to detect and diagnose patient abnormalities are increasing. Even if an abnormality in a patient is detected by such a system, the abnormality may actually be due to an abnormality in a component, such as the IoT. Therefore, when an abnormality in the patient is detected, it is necessary to have a method by which to determine whether the cause is an abnormality in the patient or any of the component abnormalities. The authors have developed a method for isolating the cause using a Bayesian network. At the same time, we have solidified the concept of a system referred to as the Integrated Abnormality Detection/Guide System, which is the target of the proposed method. This system consists of a patient abnormality diagnosis subsystem and an abnormality cause isolation subsystem. The patient abnormality diagnosis subsystem indicates to a nurse the patient to be treated first, and the abnormality cause isolation subsystem indicates to the remote maintenance (RM) personnel the component to be maintained next.

An experiment was conducted in which the proposed method was trial-applied to the abnormality cause isolation subsystem, targeting the under-sheet-type multi-vital IoT monitor as an IoT component for detecting patient abnormalities. As a result, it became clear that the proposed method can appropriately and efficiently isolate the cause of an abnormality.

Various methods have been proposed (for example, Lo, Flaus and Adrot (2019), Cai, Huang and Xie (2017), Chiremsel, Said and Chiremsel (2016), Tanwar (2020), Sasaki et al. (2018)) including methods using a Bayesian network, for isolating components that cause abnormalities when there is an abnormality in the system. However, there has been no proposal of a method for isolating the cause using a Bayesian network for medical IoT systems that monitor patient abnormalities.

In addition, in order to properly respond to the requirements of the system, the proposed method has the following characteristics.

(Characteristic 1) The proposed method has a mechanism that does not require an inappropriate flow of information, such as patient privacy information between the nurse, who is the manager of abnormal information, and RM personnel.

(Characteristic 2) If each patient or component is treated as one node of the Bayesian network, then the model becomes complicated, and the calculation takes time due to the large number of nodes. Therefore, the proposed Bayesian network treats them as one node or two nodes and identifies which patient or which component with which the node is associated before and after the calculation.

(Characteristic 3) In the proposed method, it is presumed that abnormal alerts may be issued for many patients at the same time due to component abnormalities. Therefore, we decided to treat the abnormal alarm of one patient and the simultaneous abnormal alarm of one or more other patients as separate nodes. By doing so, it can be expected that the cause of the failure can be appropriately and efficiently isolated.

The remainder of this paper is structured as follows. In Section 2, we introduce an overview of a Bayesian network and the Waikato Environment for Knowledge Analysis (Weka) program used for its modeling and simulation, whereas Section 3 outlines the under-the-sheet-type multi-vital IoT monitor used as an example medical IoT system in the present study. Section 4 describes the integrated monitoring/abnormality guide system concept, and Section 5 describes the Bayesian-based network abnormality cause isolation method and its trial application results. Finally, we conclude the present paper in Section 6.

2. OVERVIEW OF THE BAYESIAN NETWORK AND WEKA

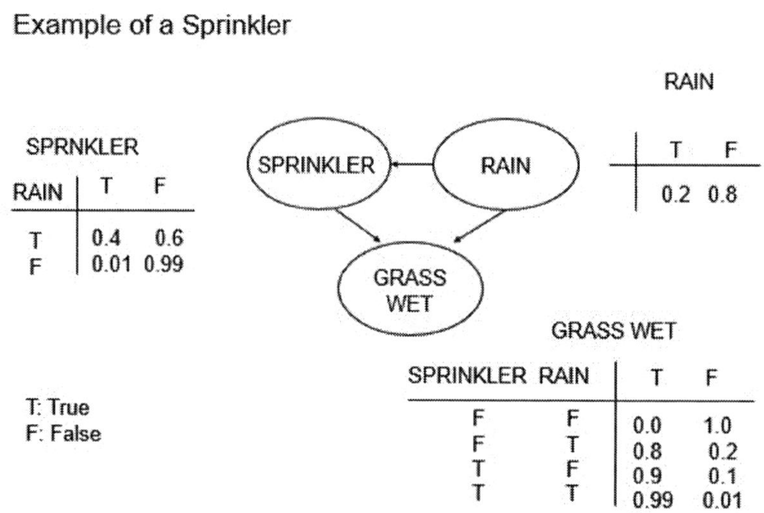

Figure 1. Example of a Bayesian network

A Bayesian network is defined in Nguyen and Do (2009) as "a probabilistic graphical model that represents a set of variables and their conditional dependencies via a directed acyclic graph (DAG)."

The example of a sprinkler is often used to explain a Bayesian network, as shown in Figure 1. The Bayesian network in this figure is composed of nodes and edges that represent causal relationships, and a conditional probability table (CPT) is provided for each node. These CPTs describe the probability for each condition composed of the values taken by the parent (upstream) node.

In the figure example, T represents true, and F represents false. Moreover, there are three nodes: RAIN (whether it has rained), SPRINKLER (whether the sprinkler has operated), and GRASS WET (whether the lawn is wet). In addition, edges (arrows) are drawn for each of these nodes. The edge from RAIN to SPRINKLER represents the cause and effect that "raining or not raining affects the probability that the sprinkler will operate". From the bottom line of the CPT in the upper-left corner of the figure, it can be seen that the "probability that the sprinkler will operate when it rains" is 0.01 (1%). Since it is useless to operate a sprinkler on a rainy day, the strongest assumption is that the sprinkler will not be operated under such conditions.

The structure modeling and probability of such a Bayesian network can be obtained by inputting data or can be determined by human subjective judgment. In the present study, the human subjective judgment method is adopted because this method targets a system that will be operated in the future.

If a Bayesian network can be modeled in this manner, then it is possible to obtain the probability value of the event "cause" when the "result" is known. For example, when the lawn is found to be wet, the probability of rain can be calculated. This probability value is sometimes called the posterior probability. In addition, when the result is known, both the knowledge and the event probability that causes the knowledge are obtained. This is sometimes called a simulation.

As defined in Holmes, Donkin and Witten (1994), Weka is machine learning software developed at the University of Waikato in New Zealand that is written in Java. Since one of the machine learning functions is a Bayesian network, Weka can be used to model and simulate a Bayesian network.

3. OVERVIEW OF THE UNDER-SHEET-TYPE MULTI-VITAL IOT MONITOR

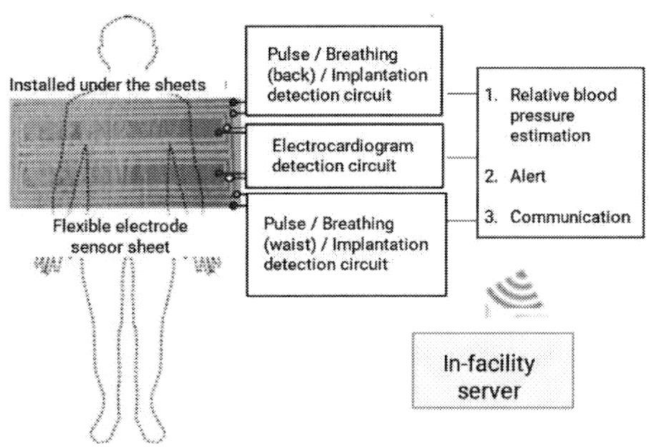

Figure 2. Under-sheet-type multi-vital IoT monitor

The IoT component targeted here is an under-sheet-type multi-vital IoT monitor (See Figure 2) shown in Takano and Ueno (2019). Monitoring is performed by installing the sensor under the bed sheet of the patient and using the sensor to measure his or her electrocardiogram, whether he or she is in or out of bed, his or her breathing condition, blood pressure, etc. The sensor also alerts the nursing staff if the sensor detects any abnormalities. This monitor can be used in hospitals and long-term care facilities.

In typical systems of this type, even if a patient abnormality alert has been issued, the alert is often traced to a component abnormality, such as a hardware failure, a program bug, a program change caused by a virus, or something similar. Therefore, a mechanism that can distinguish between patient and component abnormalities is needed, and if the cause of an abnormality is found to be component-related, then the same mechanism should be capable of estimating the cause and identifying the components that are most likely to be responsible for the alert.

4. CONCEPT OF INTEGRATED MONITORING/ABNORMALITY GUIDE SYSTEM

The integrated monitoring/abnormality guide system based on the proposed method for the under-sheet-type multi-vital IoT monitor proposed herein is designed for in-facility and RM servers and will be configured as shown in Figure 3. This system will be operated as follows:

(1) The patient monitoring function of each under-sheet-type multi-vital IoT monitor (hereinafter referred to as the IoT monitor) in the hospital is used to measure the electrocardiogram, blood pressure, respiratory status, bed leaving status, and so on, of the patient. The result is then sent to the in-facility server by LAN together with the component ID.

(2) The in-facility server uses the patient abnormality diagnosis function to determine whether a patient has an abnormality based on the measurement results of the vital data of the patient.

(3) If it is determined that there is an abnormality, then the component ID used by the patient with the abnormality is sent to the RM server.

(4) At the same time, an alert including the component ID, the corresponding room number, the patient ID, the type of abnormality, etc., is sent to the terminal of the corresponding nurse using wireless LAN.

(5) When a warning indicating the abnormality of the patient arrives, the nurse goes to the corresponding patient and checks whether there is any abnormality. If the patient is normal, then input the following information from the nurse terminal into the in-facility server:

(a) There was a patient abnormality alert, but there was no patient abnormality.

(b) The component ID corresponding to the target patient.

(6) The in-facility server sends the input result from the nurse to the RM server.

(7) The RM server has an abnormality cause isolation subsystem using Weka based on the Bayesian network. If a false alert about the abnormality of a patient is received, then the posterior probability of failure of each component in situations in which the results are known is calculated.

(8) The subsystem notifies the RM personnel of the component ID with a large posterior probability value that causes it as the component to be maintained next. The RM personnel checks whether the component is abnormal or normal and inputs the status to the system.

The methods described in (7) and (8) will be explained in more detail in the next section.

Here, the abnormality of the patient was not sent to the RM server, although (a) a patient abnormality alert was raised for the patient (despite the patient being normal), and (b) the component ID of the component used for the patient is input. This prevents patient privacy information that RM personnel should not know from being sent to the RM server. This corresponds to Characteristic 1 mentioned in Section 1.

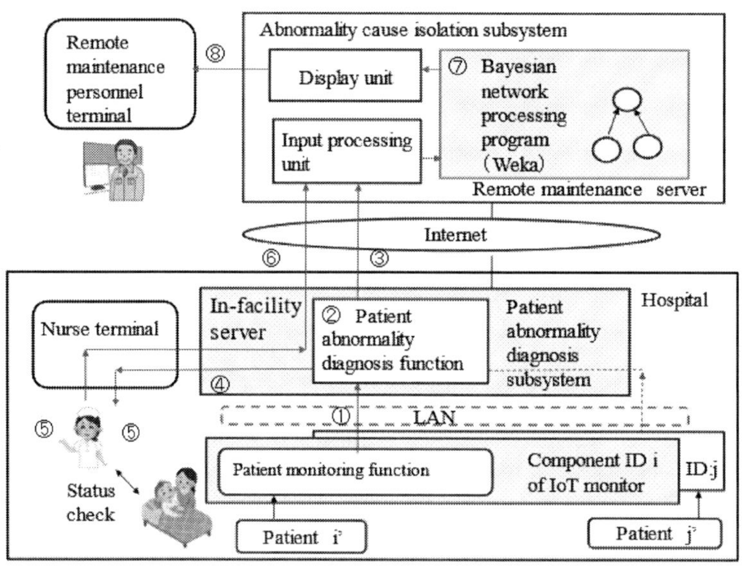

Figure 3. Configuration of the integrated monitoring abnormality guide system

5. BAYESIAN-NETWORK-BASED ABNORMALITY CAUSE ISOLATION METHOD AND ITS TRIAL APPLICATION RESULTS

5.1 Proposed Method

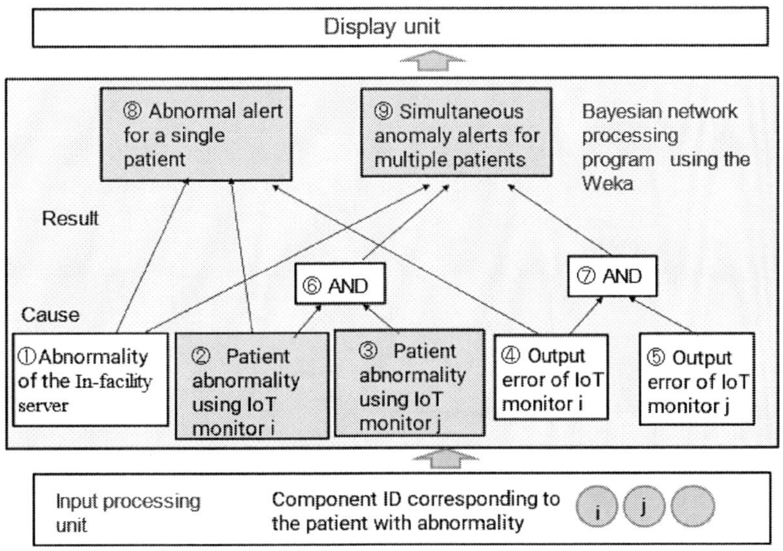

Figure 4. Abnormality cause isolation subsystem

In this section, we provide a more detailed explanation of the functions of the abnormality cause isolation subsystem implemented in the RM server of the proposed integrated monitoring/abnormality guide system (see Figure 3). This subsystem consists of (a) an input processing unit, (b) a Bayesian network processing program, and (c) a display unit. Here, Weka is used as the Bayesian network processing program.

As a result, we modeled the Bayesian network as shown in Figure 4. There are nine nodes in this model. The following five causes are the causes of abnormalities: ① Abnormality of the in-facility server, ② Patient abnormality using IoT monitor i, ③ Patient abnormality using IoT monitor j, ④ Output error of IoT monitor i, ⑤ Output error of IoT monitor j. The results are ⑧ Abnormal alert for a single patient and ⑨ Simultaneous abnormality alerts for multiple patients. The conditional probability tables of the nodes are described in Figures 5 and 6. These values are based on the following assumptions.

Patient Abnormality Occurrence Probability > IoT Monitor Abnormality Occurrence Probability > Server Abnormality Occurrence Probability

① Abnormality of the In-facility server

True	False
0.02	0.98

② Patient abnormality using IoT monitor i

True	False
0.1	0.9

③ Patient abnormality using IoT monitor j

True	False
0.1	0.9

④ Output error of IoT monitor i

True	False
0.05	0.95

⑤ Output error of IoT monitor j

True	False
0.05	0.95

⑥ ⑦ AND

Input		Output	
④	⑤	T	F
T	T	1	0
T	F	0	1
F	T	0	1
F	F	0	1

Figure 5. Conditional probability table (1)

⑧ Abnormal alert for a single patient

Input			Output	
①	②	④	T	F
T	T	T	0.99	0.01
T	T	F	0.9	0.1
T	F	T	0.9	0.1
F	T	T	0.9	0.1
T	F	F	0.8	0.2
F	T	F	0.8	0.2
F	F	T	0.8	0.2
F	F	F	0.0	1.0

⑨ Simultaneous anomaly alerts for multiple patients

Input			Output	
①	⑤	⑦	T	F
T	T	T	0.99	0.01
T	T	F	0.9	0.1
T	F	T	0.9	0.1
F	T	T	0.9	0.1
T	F	F	0.8	0.2
F	T	F	0.8	0.2
F	F	T	0.8	0.2
F	F	F	0.0	1.0

Figure 6. Conditional probability table (2)

In Bayesian networks, the conditions for entering one child node from multiple parent nodes are represented by OR conditions. However, considering simultaneous failures, it is necessary to use AND conditions, as in ⑥ and ⑦. Therefore, we decided to introduce the pseudo-conditional probabilities shown in the lower-right corner of Figure 5, referring to the method described in Reference [3]. This is to achieve Characteristic 3, as described in Section 1.

In addition, since one hospital has many patients and many monitors corresponding to each patient, treating them as a node complicates the model and takes time to calculate. Therefore, the Bayesian network model considered herein uses a method of treating them as one or two nodes and associating the node as an individual patient or component before and after calculation. This is to achieve Characteristic 2, as described in Section 1.

5.2 Application Results

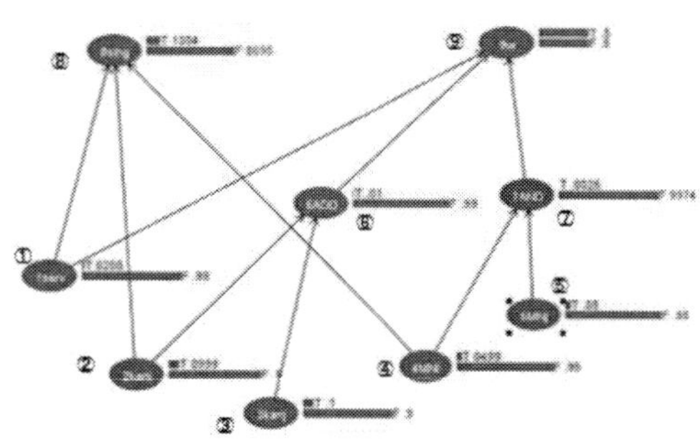

Figure 7. Prior probabilities for each node

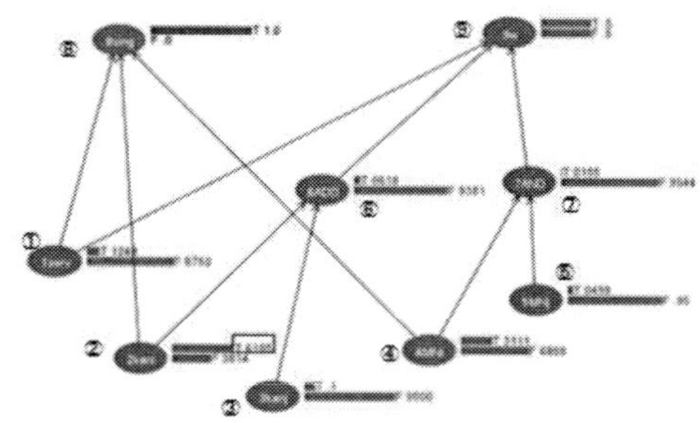

Figure 8. Posterior probabilities for each node when there is an anomaly alert for a single patient

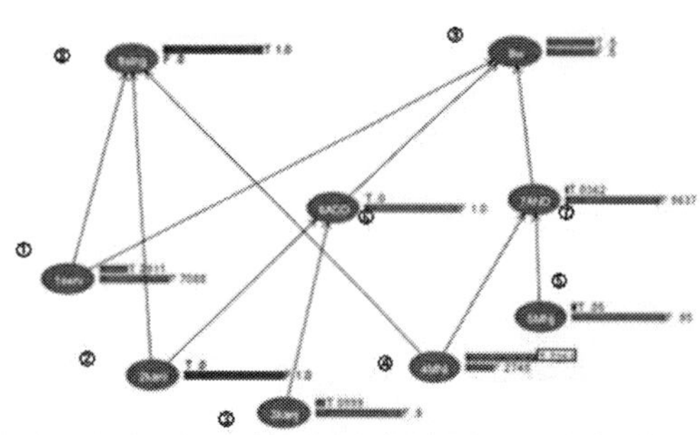

Figure 9. Posterior probabilities for each node when there is an anomaly alert for a single patient and this patient is not anomalous

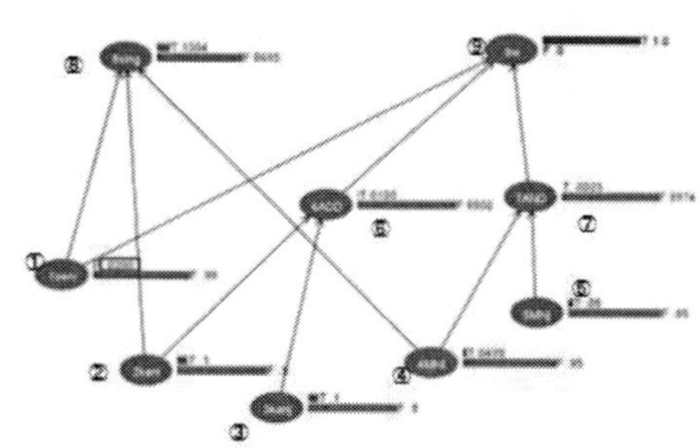

Figure 10. Posterior probabilities for each node when there are simultaneous anomaly alerts for multiple patients

The output results regarding the prior probabilities of each node are as shown in Figure 7 when the above Bayesian network structure and conditional probabilities are input to Weka. Here, T represents the probability of occurrence in the case of True, and F represents the probability of occurrence in the case of False. Node ① is described as T0200, which indicates that the probability of being True is 0.02, i.e., 2%, and indicates that the probability of being False is 0.98, i.e., 98%.

In addition, the posterior probabilities of each node calculated using Weka when there is an abnormality alert for a single patient, as shown in node ⑧, are as shown in Fig 8. Here, among nodes ①, ②, and ④, which are the inputs to node ⑧, the posterior probability is the largest for ② Patient abnormality using IoT monitor i, as shown in Figure 8, and the value of the probability is 61.85%.

In this situation, if the nurse confirms that there is no abnormality in the patient corresponding to IoT monitor i, the state of node ② can be fixed as False. Therefore, the probability of occurrence of other nodes is as shown in Figure 9. From this, it can be seen that, among the nodes ① and ④, the node with the highest posterior probability is the output error of IoT monitor i in ④. Let the RM personnel know this result and perform maintenance of IoT monitor i.

Furthermore, if simultaneous abnormality alerts for multiple patients of node ⑨ occur, then the post-occurrence probabilities of the other nodes are as shown in Figure 10. Among nodes ①, ⑥, and ⑦, which are directly connected to node ⑨, the largest abnormality is that of the in-facility server of node①, and the value of the probability is 2%. Notify the RM personnel of the result in this case and have the personnel perform maintenance.

5.3 Considerations

(1) The order of these patients and components to check next is consistent with the engineer's intuition. Therefore, this method can be considered to be appropriate. We also found that the calculations were completed instantly and were efficient.

(2) We attempted to determine what kind of components and patients should be checked next by changing the probability of patient abnormality and the probability of component abnormality in various ways. When multiple patient abnormality alerts are issued, the component to be checked next changes from the in-facility server to multiple corresponding patients when the in-facility server abnormality probability is less than half of the current estimated value. Similarly, the same result is obtained when the probability of abnormality of the patient is equal to or greater than 1.5 times the current estimated value. By carrying out such sensitivity analysis, the measures to be taken under various preconditions can be seen.

(3) The current method is to check the patient for abnormalities first, based on the concept of patient safety first. However, if reducing the burden on the nurse is desired in order to balance safety and efficiency, it is possible to make a decision in the abnormality cause isolation subsystem first and to determine whether the patient is likely to have an abnormality. Therefore, as shown in Figure 10, if an abnormality occurs in multiple patients at the same time, then there may be a method of first checking the in-facility server that is likely to be the cause

6. CONCLUSIONS AND FUTURE RESEARCH

(1) For an IoT system that detects patient abnormalities, we developed a method that uses a Bayesian network to isolate whether patient abnormality alerts are really due to patient abnormalities or component abnormalities.

(2) The proposed method also realizes the three characteristics described in Section 1 and is consistent with practical requirements.

(3) By applying the proposed method to a patient abnormality detection/guide system for under-sheet-type multi-vital IoT monitors, it was confirmed that the cause of the abnormality can be appropriately and efficiently isolated.

In the future, we would like to apply the proposed method to the actual field on a trial basis in order to make the probability of occurrence on the causal side more realistic. In addition, we would like to perform more precise modeling by classifying patient abnormalities as (a) electrocardiogram abnormalities, (b) blood pressure abnormalities, (c) respiratory abnormalities, or (d) bed-leaving abnormalities.

REFERENCES

Lo J. N., Flaus G, and Adrot O., (2019). Review of Machine Learning Approaches in Fault Diagnosis applied to IoT Systems, *International Conference on Control, Automation and Diagnosis (ICCAD)*, pp. 1-6.

Cai B., Huang L. and XieM., (2017). Bayesian Networks in Fault Diagnosis, in *IEEE Transactions on Industrial Informatics*, vol. 13, no. 5, pp. 2227-2240.

Chiremsel Z., R. Said N., and Chiremsel R, (2016). Probabilistic fault diagnosis of safety instrumented systems based on fault tree analysis and Bayesian network, *J. Failure Anal. Prev.*, vol. 16, pp. 747–760.

Tanwar S., (2020). Human Arthritis Analysis in Fog Computing Environment Using Bayesian Network 1. Classifier and Thread Protocol, *IEEE Consumer Electronics Magazine*, vol. 9, no. 1, pp. 88-94.

Sasaki R. et al., (2018). Development and Evaluation of Intelligent Network Forensic System LIFT Using Bayesian Network for Targeted Attack Detection and Prevention, *International Journal of Cyber-Security and Digital Forensics (IJCSDF)* vol.7, no4, pp344-353.

Nguyen L., Do P., (2009). Combination of Bayesian Network and Overlay Model in User Modeling, *ICCS 2009: Computational Science* – ICCS 2009 pp 5-14

Holmes G., Donkin A. and Witten I.H., (1994). WEKA: a machine learning workbench, *Proceedings of ANZIIS '94 - Australian New Zealnd Intelligent Information Systems Conference*, pp. 357-361.

Takano M. and Ueno A., (2019). Noncontact in-bed measurements of physiological and behavioral signals using an integrated fabric-sheet sensing scheme, *IEEE Journal of Biomedical and Health Informatics*, vol. 23, no. 2, pp. 618-630.

ARTIFICIAL INTELLIGENCE FOR NEXT GENERATION ENERGY SERVICES ACROSS EUROPE – THE I-NERGY PROJECT

Evangelos Karakolis, Sotiris Pelekis, Spiros Mouzakitis, Ourania Markaki, Katerina Papapostolou, Giorgos Korbakis and John Psarras
Institute of Communication and Computer Systems (ICCS) of National Technical University of Athens (NTUA), Greece

ABSTRACT

Artificial Intelligence (AI) holds the premise to transform the energy sector and the underlying value chain; scarcity of AI expertise in the energy community, fuzzy and unclear regulations on access to data, standards' immaturity and uncertain business cases are hampering though the full exploitation of its potential. In this context, the goal of this paper is to present the I-NERGY project, an Innovation Action that targets to promote AI in the energy sector by reinforcing the AI-on-demand (AI4EU) platform service offering and ecosystem. To this end, the paper introduces the I-NERGY project concept, the domain challenges it addresses and the target audience towards which it is addressed, exposes the project technical solution and pilot use cases that respectively incarnate, and exemplify and validate it and emphasizes its open call mechanism for providing financing support to third SMEs for energy use cases and AI services proliferation.

KEYWORDS

Artificial Intelligence, AI-on-Demand, Energy, AI4EU, Open Calls

1. INTRODUCTION

AI spreading in the energy sector is expected to dramatically reshape the energy value chain in the next years, by improving business processes performance, while increasing environmental sustainability, strengthening social relationships and propagating high social value among citizens. People's well-being, industrial competitiveness and the overall functioning of society are dependent on safe, secure, sustainable and affordable energy. AI is expected to radically transform the energy sector, redesign and shape the energy value chain and revolutionise the way through which Electric Power and Energy Systems (EPES) community is undertaking the business processes.

The use of AI is acknowledged to be of utmost importance for energy utilities to improve the performance of their business processes, and for power network operators to increase the stability of their operated network, within the renewable energy-based emerging decentralised paradigm. DeepMind AI managed to effectively achieve 40% energy savings for the Google Data Center operation (Yao, 2018). General Electric estimates that AI can enhance the production of a wind farm by 20% (GeneralElectric, 2019). AI transformation in the energy industry will directly influence international energy stability and economic prosperity (Nagy & Hajrizi, 2018).

At the same time, AI proliferation in the energy sector holds the premise for a larger environmental and social impact (Marinakis et al., 2020), by affecting environmental sustainability, strengthening social relationships among members of local communities and contributing to alleviate energy poverty. Energy fingerprinting might be leveraged to deliver different consumer-centred innovative AI-based services which bring high social value to individuals and/or local communities. Hence, AI can contribute to finding solutions to some of the most pressing societal challenges, such as the fight against climate change, environmental degradation and the challenges linked to sustainability. A large share of EPES stakeholders believe that AI will have a big impact on their business, since AI spreading will allow them to align their business processes to novel fine-grained near real time optimal energy system operation, within a context of rising share of deployed renewable energy. However, they are far to integrate AI in key business processes (Berger, 2018). Uncertain business cases, fragmented regulations, standards immaturity and low-technical SMEs workforce skills barriers are actually hampering the full exploitation of AI along the energy value chain.

In view of addressing these barriers in the European AI landscape and facilitate technology transfer from research to business, the first European Artificial Intelligence On-Demand Platform - AI4EU (EU, 2020) was launched in 2019 with the support of the European Commission under the H2020 program. The AI4EU platform[1] is a one-stop-shop for anyone looking for AI knowledge, technology, tools, services and experts. AI4EU aims at creating value, growth and jobs for Europe through a collaborative platform, which unites the AI community, promotes European values and supports research on human-centered and trustworthy AI. Nurtured within the AI4EU ecosystem, the I-NERGY project[2] specifically targets the promotion and support of AI in the energy sector with the following objectives:

- Reinforcing the AI-on-demand-platform for the energy sector with novel AI services and applications
- Reaching out to energy domain stakeholders to validate the developed applications and laying the foundation for a pan-European AI for energy ecosystem, boosting EU-scale data economy and use cases.

In this context, this paper introduces the I-NERGY project (started in January 2021 and ends in December 2023) that targets to promote AI in the energy sector by reinforcing the AI-on-demand (AI4EU) platform service offering and ecosystem. Specifically, I-NERGY's concept, technical approach and pilot use cases are presented and justified, alongside the project's open call mechanism that provides financial support to SMEs to develop energy use cases by leveraging AI.

2. RELATED WORK

AI can unlock significant value for energy utilities, in terms of improving their business processes, increasing power networks' stability and essentially achieving significant energy savings. However, energy companies often lack ICT skills to catchup with AI potential causing high demand for AI experts. Also, there are several consolidated silos not willing to share data and processes. Combined with the lack of semantic and business interoperability across different energy utilities, this hinders the high data potential in the energy domain. Contradictorily, there are various scientific publications that exploit AI to create value-adding services, dealing with electrical load forecasting, predictive maintenance for power networks or building facilities, citizen patterns' anomaly detection in smart buildings and smart grids, energy flexibility and demand response (DR).

Regarding load forecasting, (Guo et al., 2020) developed a short-term load forecasting model of multi-scale CNN-LSTM hybrid neural network that considers real-time electricity prices. The experimental results show that the proposed method has higher accuracy than other methods proposed in the literature. (Chen et al., 2018) focused also on short-term load forecasting. The authors developed a neural network forecasting method named NeuCast, enabling anomaly detection and forecasts under different temperature assumptions. Experiments in different datasets showcased considerable improvement over the state-of-the-art.

Concerning DR services, as the problem to be solved is more complex, there are different approaches. For instance, (Lu et al., 2018) and (Wen et al., 2015) formulate the problem of demand response as a reinforcement learning model. In the first case the proposed algorithm is price-based and adaptively decides the electricity price using an online learning process. In the second case, the proposed algorithm, named CAES, models both energy prices and residential devices usage as Markov decision processes and adapts to user preferences over time. On the other hand, (Baloglu & Demir, 2015) model the problem of demand response in a smart grid as a Bayesian game-theoretical model using a dynamic pricing scheme. Simulation results demonstrated that the proposed model evenly distributes the daily load in smart grid and therefore it is successful.

Furthermore, an example of predictive maintenance in building facilities is presented by (Bouabdallaoui et al., 2021), who propose ML and DL techniques, to identify failures in smart buildings. Their framework shows great potential to predict failures. Another example of ML-based predictive maintenance is presented in (Yeh et al., 2019). The goal is to predict the long-cycle maintenance time of wind turbines in a power company. The results of this approach reach high accuracy values and can be used for asset turbine maintenance.

Regarding anomaly detection, latest research has focused on detecting anomalies in citizen patterns in smart homes or smart grid installations. Different publications examine different types of anomalies. For instance,

[1] https://www.ai4europe.eu/
[2] https://i-nergy.eu/

(Novak et al., 2013) use self-organised maps to identify anomalies, mostly based on sensors' data, (Yamauchi et al., 2020) use home appliances connected to the internet, to detect cyber-attacks based on user behaviour. (De Benedetti et al., 2018) predict anomalies in photovoltaic systems operation, based on the comparison between the actual and predicted AC power production, while the latter is predicted via an ANN, using solar irradiance and PV panel temperature measurements. The experimental results seem satisfactory. Moreover, as this approach can identify system deviations' trends from the normal operation behaviour, it is suitable for predictive maintenance in photovoltaic systems.

From the presented approaches it is observable that, the proposed solutions are tailored to specific business requirements with specific data schemas. while they mostly focus on specific and narrow subtasks, instead of a system level approach. Hence, they cannot be easily applied by multiple similar stakeholders, as there are no commonly agreed interoperability procedures and usually measurements' metadata are not available. Therefore, the need for commonly accepted data interoperability standards among different systems should be priority, alongside a knowledge sharing culture across different stakeholders. I-NERGY aims at addressing this issue by providing reusable and interoperable data and AI models and setting standards for data and AI services interoperability in the energy domain and reinforcing AI4EU platform energy-related assets.

AI4EU project (Cortés et al., 2019) aims at reinforcing AI knowledge and resources sharing and bringing closer AI experts with different scientific domains. Other projects targeting to reinforce AI4EU assets are AI4Copernicus[3], aiming to bridge AI with earth observation and make AI4EU platform the digital environment of choice for users of Copernicus data; AIDIH Network[4], targeting to create a European Network of Digital Innovation Hubs with focus on AI; AIPlan4EU[5], aiming to bring AI planning to platform; BonsAPPs[6], focusing on SMEs digitalisation by facilitating access, implementation and make use of AI in an easy and affordable way; and StairwAI[7], aiming to ease low-tech users engagement to the AI-on-Demand platform.

Regarding the energy domain, there are also a few projects acknowledging the need for setting up interoperability standards as well as the fact that combining different types of data can unlock significant added value. For instance, BD4NRG[8] aims to enable improved operations for all stakeholders in the energy value chain by leveraging the potential of big data in the energy sector. Contrary to I-NERGY, BD4NRG focuses mostly on big data. On the other hand, MATRYCS[9]aims at reinforcing decision support operations in smart buildings through big data, AI and analytics technologies.

3. I-NERGY CONCEPT AND TECHNICAL APPROACH

Lack of EPES stakeholders' workforce ICT background is the reason they are far from integrating AI in key business processes. Moreover, lack of tools for capturing the real time dynamics, scarcity and competition for AI experts, the need for knowledge transfer to new contexts and accordingly for training new AI for each context, as well lack of optimal ways to explore and exploit cross-domain data, which are now being generated at an unprecedented rate, still incommode the complete introduction of AI in the energy sector.

In essence, I-NERGY's main objective is to capitalise on state-of-the-art AI, IoT, semantics and data analytics technologies and deliver an open modular framework for supporting AI-on-Demand in the energy sector. I-NERGY vision is to enable edge-level, AI-based, cross-sector, multi-stakeholder analytic tools for integrated and optimised smart energy management and to evolve, scale up and demonstrate an innovative energy-tailored AI-as-a-Service Toolbox, which will help towards achieving a techno-economic optimal management of the EPES value chain, especially when it comes to SMEs and non-tech industries, while leveraging on and complementing the AI resources and tools made available by the AI4EU platform. The project aims essentially at strengthening European-wise Research and Innovation on AI, through synchronizing, liaising, contributing, and extending the AI4EU Platform service and research across a variety

[3] https://ai4copernicus-project.eu/
[4] https://ai-dih-network.eu/
[5] https://www.aiplan4eu-project.eu/
[6] https://bonsapps.eu/
[7] https://cordis.europa.eu/project/id/101017142
[8] https://www.bd4nrg.eu/
[9] https://matrycs.eu/

of cross-fertilisation activities. Hence, the main focus is the development and sharing of state-of-the-art AI services that will be useful for both energy stakeholders and the European community.

I-NERGY main stakeholders cover the entire energy value chain, including Transmission System Operators (TSOs), Distribution System Operators (DSOs), Energy Services Companies (ESCOs), Policy makers (e.g., EC Directorates and Units), Facility Managers, Investors, governments, Citizens and Designers.

To address the aforementioned challenges, I-NERGY will develop an innovative technical solution. Figure 1 illustrates an initial version of the I-NERGY conceptual architecture. I-NERGY technical solution consists of several service layers, ranging from data management services (ingestion, storage, harmonisation etc.) to AI-enabled energy analytics applications and services. Specifically, it consists of the Data Services', the AI Trained Models', the Energy Analytics' Applications, and the I-NERGY – AI4EU Interconnection Layers.

The **Data Services Layer** will allow the ingestion, pre-processing and querying of heterogeneous data. Its most important components are the services for interoperability, data ingestion, data cleansing curation and preparation, as well as a common data model which secures that all data, being stored to I-NERGY platform adhere to predefined standards. With this approach the data can be used also by other stakeholders and services that use the same standards with little to no modifications.

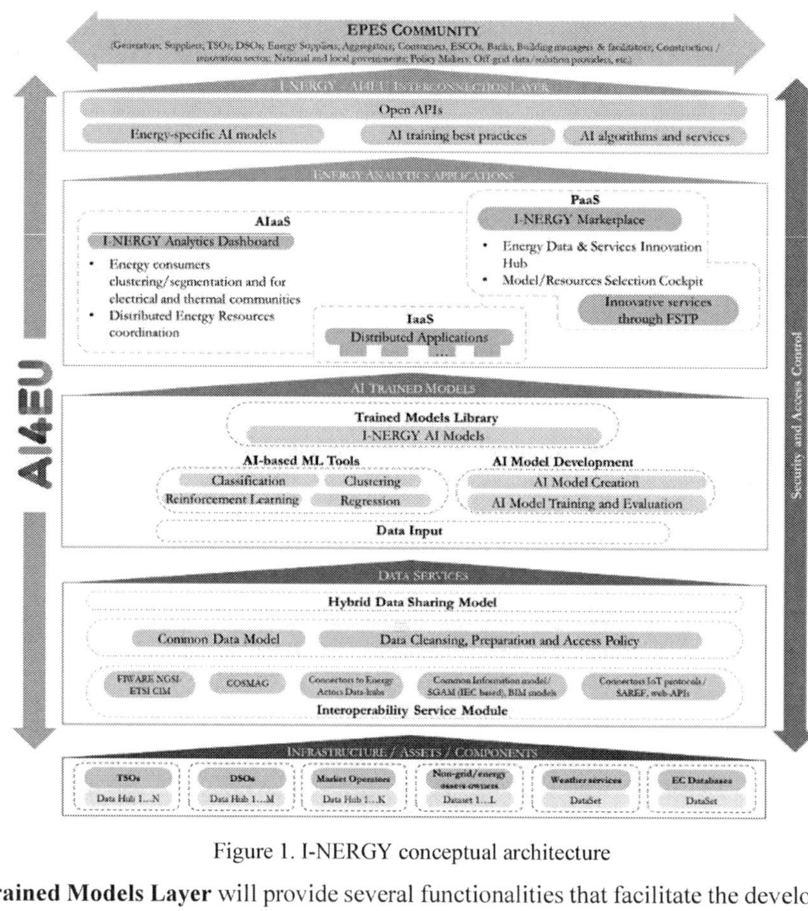

Figure 1. I-NERGY conceptual architecture

The **AI Trained Models Layer** will provide several functionalities that facilitate the development, creation and testing of new AI models. Moreover, it will be responsible for storing I-NERGY AI models. Some services to be provided in this layer are the ML models development toolbox, a trained models library and an AI model training and evaluation environment. The former will provide a library of state-of-the-art methods for AI model development, including several ML and DL technologies (e.g. scikit-learn, TensorFlow, Apache Spark MLib etc.), as well as transfer learning capabilities, whereas the latter will provide resources for efficient model training, and model evaluation utilities that monitor the accuracy of developed models over time and provide recommendations for improvements. The trained models library will be the marketplace of all I-NERGY trained models, to facilitate reusability and knowledge exchange among different stakeholders.

The **Energy Analytics Applications layer** is the closest layer to end users, providing them with energy analytics services (AI as a service) and applications that are stored in the AI trained models' layer. Moreover, visual analytics tools will be provided, to facilitate exploratory analyses on specific datasets. The analytics services will be served through APIs to end user applications and business intelligence systems, to provide them with accurate predictions, and facilitate enhanced decision making on critical issues, such as power network reliability and DR. Contradictorily, energy analytics applications will be mostly focused on digital twin applications creating physical systems' (e.g. networks, buildings and energy systems) digital representations, to perform simulations and tests for physical assets of I-NERGY pilots. Some energy analytics services and applications to be provided by this layer are electrical load forecasting, demand response, predictive maintenance for circuit breakers, anomaly detection in citizen patterns, digital twin for distributed energy resources (DER), prioritisation and risk assessment of energy efficiency investments, digital twin for electrical communities.

As reinforcing the AI4EU On-Demand platform, through utilisation, distribution and enrichment of the existing AI resources in the energy domain is a key I-NERGY objective, the **I-NERGY – AI4EU Interconnection Layer** is responsible for the bilateral communication between I-NERGY and AI4EU platforms. Additionally, it is responsible to make AI4EU trained models, data and other assets available to I-NERGY services, as well as to publish I-NERGY assets (services, datasets, documentation etc.) to AI4EU Catalog and onboard I-NERGY models and services to AI4EU Experiments for sharing AI knowledge and resources with a wider range of interested parties.

I-NERGY data, services and other assets will be available to users provided that they are authenticated and given authorisation to access the requested resources. Hence, I-NERGY platform has its own **Security and Access Control Module**, which is responsible for user authentication and authorisation. This module also provides mechanisms which ensure that security standards are holistically met during I-NERGY operation.

The developed assets (datasets, services, applications) will be available to EPES stakeholders as well as other researchers through AI4EU platform and I-NERGY Marketplace, according to the policies that have been defined by their owners, in order to reinforce AI knowledge in the energy domain across Europe.

4. PILOT USE CASES

The I-NERGY analytics framework will be applied, demonstrated and validated in real-life pilots involving 9 pilot hubs and 15 different use cases, distributed across three domains: (i) **AI for energy networks, aiming at the optimised operation of electricity and district heating networks.** Services relating to this domain will focus on grid asset management, predictive maintenance and enhanced reliability as well as electricity demand forecasting; (ii) **AI for Renewable Energy Sources (RES) generation in buildings, districts, communities.** These services will involve the forming and management of Virtual Power Plants (VPPs) functioning as flexibility providers, through the successful matchmaking of prosumers and green energy marketplaces; (iii) **AI for enabling synergies and implications on other energy and non-energy domains** such as heating, transport, water management, personal safety, finance and Ambient Assisted Living (AAL). Here, applications will focus on dynamic energy-efficient and end-user comfortable building-scale management, financial risk assessment and management of renewable investments, optimal energy management in buildings, and cross-sector energy-driven services including personal safety and care management services for the elderly.

Pilot sites will be accompanied by two testbed facilities and simulation-enabling digital twins (Boschert & Rosen, 2016), spanning across 8 European countries (Greece, Latvia, Italy, Portugal, Spain, Croatia, Slovenia and Germany). The large geographical coverage of the demo sites aims to support the EU-wide replicability and market take-up of AI-driven solutions in different socio-economical contexts, to maximise the I-NERGY services impact across Europe. The planned use cases are briefly described below.

AI for network assets' predictive maintenance, integrating off-grid data with condition-based monitoring. This pilot aims at assessing the condition of grid assets and specifically circuit breakers inside the Portuguese transmission network. DL techniques will be deployed to determine the failure probabilities of each asset based on historical oscillography data of circuit breaker tripping incidents and to provide answers to the challenges of predictive maintenance and effective maintenance plans implementation.

AI for network load forecasting towards efficient operational planning. This pilot's goal is to provide forecasts of aggregated and disaggregated electrical load timeseries for the Portuguese transmission system.

Applying state-of-the-art ML and DL-based short-term load-forecasting techniques on historical data, a load forecasting framework of various timesteps and forecasting horizons will derive, leading via self-monitoring and iterative learning to operational planning optimisation, and grid operations' reliability improvement.

AI for District Heating and Cooling Network (DHCN) load forecasting and optimisation of the production mix. This pilot consists of two use cases. The first regards the provision of accurate demand forecasts for a large DHCN managed by a Spanish facility manager by matching production with demand through energy demand predictions. Available data range from cooling and heating demand and production to RES production and weather forecasts. State-of-the-art ML will be applied to provide estimations of day-ahead future values of the energy demanded by the DHCN, aiming at decreasing its energy consumption and GHG emissions. The second one will leverage the produced demand forecasts, to investigate demand response schemes for matching demand with production. Given the RES stochasticity, this optimisation task will lead to a "greener" production mix.

AI for energy saving verification, increasing the trust on energy performance contracts (EPCs). This pilot will act as a decision support system for a Spanish ESCO by establishing a workflow to measure and verify energy and economic savings after energy efficiency related building renovations. Following, simulation and digital twins will be employed, leveraging the available historical data from smart meters and two natural gas boilers for heating and domestic hot water of a large building community, with the ultimate goal of improving the ESCO's business model through energy efficient refurbishments and reliable EPCs.

Cross-functional AI predictive analytics for integrated DSOs asset management and network operation. This use case's goal is to support a condition and risk-based maintenance of power components, owned by an Italian DSO. Data-driven predictive analytics will be applied on datasets relating to operational data, acquired from distribution network assets such as transformers and lines, as well as historical data on replaced assets. The expected result is the anticipated failure prediction at the low voltage side of secondary substations, leading to efficient infrastructure management, equipment's lifetime increase, and service interruption times' reduction.

AI-based consumption and flexibility prediction for local community optimal aggregation and flexibility trading. This pilot comprises two cases. The first aims to assist an Italian aggregator and DSO in forming and validating a decentralised VPP consisting of residential, commercial and industrial customers. Exploiting the availability of weather data and smart meter data, AI techniques will be used for load profiling, clustering and forecasting, seeking to form flexibility clusters amongst end-users. Based on such predictions, the aggregator will be accordingly selecting the appropriate flexible loads and consumers which better fit with the flexibility request, conveyed by the flexibility trading market. The second use case aims at coordinating with the local water network operator seeking to follow specific activation priority models for smart water pumps according to the electricity flexibility needs, hence realizing the synergy between electricity and water.

AI-based IoT-enabled PV module-level portfolio optimal predictive maintenance and PV-enhanced industrial plant optimal operation. This use case focuses on predictive maintenance of multiple utility and industrial scale PV plants in Italy, managed by an O&M and designer company of RES generation plants. Exploiting the abundance of near-real-time grid measurements, weather data, SCADA data and maintenance records from PVs, I-NERGY will employ ML and DL models for the prediction and detection of malfunctioning at decentralised module level. Major expected outcomes include improvement in operational efficiency of PV assets through the combined effect of optimised maintenance and increased assets efficiency and increased self-consumption from local RES leading to electricity cost reduction.

AI in EV charging infrastructure. This use case aims at optimizing the operation of EV charging stations owned by a Greek energy supplier. Given the data availability from publicly accessible charging stations relating to EV charging cost, duration and demand, ML-based predictive algorithms will enable load profile extraction and availability prediction of public charging stations based on timely distributions and average duration of charge transactions. Additionally, through AI-based variable pricing algorithms, the use case will allow for more efficient operation of charging stations and smooth load distribution amongst them.

AI for peer-to-peer renewable energy trading in virtual energy community. This use case will contribute to the establishment of a VPP, consisting of multiple households, distributed within multiple geographical areas of Croatia and managed by a local RES cooperative. In terms of datasets, PV generation measurements within each household and historical demand and generation are available alongside weather measurements collected across the grid. In this context, AI techniques will be employed, to enable community participation in the ancillary services market, and peer-to-peer energy trading within it, hence leading to innovative prosumer business models and their promotion across the citizens.

AI for the Ambient Assisted Living (AAL) and personal safety/security at home. This use case focuses on the development of services for personal safety, security and AAL in an elderly care house, managed by a Slovenian energy supplier in the context of a peer-to-peer energy trading platform. Available data include residential smart meters, ambient sensors, operational data from site assets (PV, heating, heat storage) and meteorological variables. Electricity fingerprinting methods will be applied for modelling the behaviour of specific devices, individuals and activities. Based on unsupervised ML techniques caregivers will be supported via alerts in case of anomalies, as well as living conditions, habits, and behaviour changes' monitoring.

AI for de-risking energy efficiency investments. This use case focuses on reducing the uncertainty linked to energy efficiency investments managed by a Latvian municipal energy agency. Historical heating and hot water consumptions along with meteorological variables and internal real-time ambient measurements will be collected for a small number of buildings, prior and following their renovation. Accordingly, AI will enable the extraction of knowledge regarding energy savings based on a few buildings and then its generalisation to other buildings with similar constructional characteristics leveraging knowledge from external databases. Hence, EPCs and other energy investments will be more reliable, cost-effective and of better quality.

AI for improved Energy Performance Certificates Reliability. This use case focuses on reinforcing the reliability of Energy Performance Certificates and is led by a Spanish municipal energy agency. Available data range from energy performance certificate and energy efficiency project databases to historical actual energy consumption data of buildings. AI algorithms will be tailored to detect patterns from real energy consumption data, distinguishing among the consumption derived from the energy fabric, energy systems and user behaviour. This will be contrasted to existing Energy Performance Certificates and raise alarms when AI-inferred energy values greatly differ from them.

AI for predicting the climate change impact in RES and energy demand at regional level. This use case is also led by a Spanish energy agency. AI methods will be applied on publicly available data such as Copernicus C3S (Buchwitz et al., 2018), aiming at producing an accurate climate change impact model for the region of Asturias. The model will enable predictions of future changing conditions derived from climate change related to the energy demand and RES, hence enabling the effective planning and deployment of RES.

5. I-NERGY OPEN CALLS

I-NERGY will significantly contribute to spreading and adoption of the AI along energy sector through the launch and management of two Open Calls, facilitating the access of energy vertical SMEs to finance while further validating I-NERGY use cases, promoting the development of new AI-driven technology components and energy services, and ultimately enriching the AI4EU resources and tools catalogue. The above will be achieved through the provisioning of Financial Support to Third Parties (FSTP). FSTP amounts to 2 M€, to be distributed to up to 25 bottom-up projects within a time period of 17 months for each call.

The selected projects will cover various application domains besides the energy sector (e.g. environment, society and economy), a wide range of experimentation areas, including AI applications in energy, Data governance and valorisation for energy services, Analytical applications in energy, Monitoring, energy usage optimisation, Predictive maintenance, and Demand forecast, and numerous challenges, enumerating network assets predictive maintenance, network loads and demand forecasting towards efficient operational planning, energy demand and supply prediction, energy storage management decisions, integrated TSOs / DSOs asset management, consumption and flexibility prediction, solar energy and photovoltaic applications, electric vehicles, trading in energy communities, energy efficiency investments and decision support systems, energy performance, energy savings and contracts, climate change and business environmental impact transformation, reinforcement learning in energy systems.

6. CONCLUSION AND NEXT STEPS

This paper presented I-NERGY, a project that aims to deliver an energy-specific open modular framework for supporting AI on demand in the energy sector and reinforce the AI4EU platform with new energy related assets (AI models, datasets and more), through state-of-the-art AI, IoT, semantics and data analytics technologies. The project motivation and the challenges to be addressed were presented in detail, alongside the project objectives and its relation to the AI4EU platform. A literature review on related approaches and projects on energy analytics services was also performed, to showcase the I-NERGY added value. The paper further presented the proposed technical architecture alongside the main services to be developed as well as the I-NERGY pilot use cases. The Open Calls, another important project aspect, were also described as they are expected to enrich the project know-how. As the project is in its first steps, there are no concrete results yet. However, several energy analytics services will be launched in the following months. The latter will be thoroughly evaluated, so as to refine technical developments and improve I-NERGY functionalities. Lastly, several assets will be published to AI4EU, enabling interested stakeholders to gain significant know-how and experiment with real data and state-of-the-art AI models.

ACKNOWLEDGEMENT

This work has been funded by the European Union's Horizon 2020 research and innovation programme under the I-NERGY project, Grant Agreement No 101016508.

REFERENCES

Baloglu U. B. et al, 2015. A bayesian game-theoretic demand response model for the smart grid. *International Journal of Smart Grid and Clean Energy*.

Berger R., 2018. *Artificial intelligence: A smart move for utilities*.

Boschert, S. et al, 2016. Digital Twin---The Simulation Aspect. In P. Hehenberger & D. Bradley (Eds.), *Mechatronic Futures: Challenges and Solutions for Mechatronic Systems and their Designers*, pp. 59–74

Bouabdallaoui Y. et al, 2021. Predictive maintenance in building facilities: A machine learning-based approach. In *Sensors*, Vol. *21*, No. 4.

Buchwitz M. et al, 2018. Copernicus Climate Change Service (C3S) global satellite observations of atmospheric carbon dioxide and methane. *Proceedings of the International Astronautical Congress, IAC*, *2018-October*(1), pp. 57–60.

Chen P. et al, 2018. *NeuCast: Seasonal Neural Forecast of Power Grid Time Series*.

Cortés U. et al, 2019. Trustworthy AI. The AI4EU approach. *Proceedings of Science*.

De Benedetti M. et al, 2018. Anomaly detection and predictive maintenance for photovoltaic systems. In *Neurocomputing*, Vol. *310*.

EU, 2020. White Paper On Artificial Intelligence - A European approach to excellence and trust. In *European Commission*.

GeneralElectric, 2019. *General Electric GE Launches the Next Evolution of Wind Energy Making Renewables More Efficient, Economic*.

Guo X. et al, 2020. A short-term load forecasting model of multi-scale CNN-LSTM hybrid neural network considering the real-time electricity price. *Energy Reports*, Vol. *6*, pp. 1046–1053.

Lu R., 2018. A Perspective on Reinforcement Learning in Price-Based Demand Response for Smart Grid. In *Proceedings - 2017 International Conference on Computational Science and Computational Intelligence, CSCI 2017*, pp. 1822–1823.

Marinakis V. et al, 2020. From big data to smart energy services: An application for intelligent energy management. In *Future Generation Computer Systems*, Vol. *110*.

Nagy K.et al, 2018. Beyond the Age of Oil and Gas – How artificial intelligence is transforming the energy portfolio of the societies. In *IFAC-PapersOnLine*, Vol. *51*, No. 30.

Novak M. et al, 2013. Anomaly detection in user daily patterns in smart-home environment. In *Journal of Selected Areas in Health Informatics*, Vol. *3*.

Wen Z. et al, 2015. Optimal demand response using device-based reinforcement learning. In *IEEE Transactions on Smart Grid*, Vol. *6*, No. 5, pp. 2312–2324.

Yamauchi M. et al, 2020. Anomaly Detection in Smart Home Operation from User Behaviors and Home Conditions. In *IEEE Transactions on Consumer Electronics*, Vol. *66*, No. 2.

Yao W., 2018. *Analysis on the Application of the Artificial Intelligence Neural Network on the New Energy Micro Grid*.

Yeh, C. et al, 2019. Machine learning for long cycle maintenance prediction of wind turbine. In *Sensors*, Vol. *19*, No 7.

CRITERIA FOR THE ANALYSIS OF SERIOUS GAMES INTERFACES IN VIRTUAL REALITY

André Salomão, Victor Nassar, Milton Vieira and Berenice Santos Gonçalves
Universidade Federal de Santa Catarina
Design Lab, R. Roberto Sampaio Gonzaga, 274, Florianópolis, Brazil

ABSTRACT

The article presents an analysis of two games considered serious games in the context of virtual reality platforms: Bus Simulator Drive and EarthQuake Simulator VR. The objective is to analyze how the interaction process occurs in these types of games, which elements make up the interfaces in serious games, how they are used, how they integrate into the context, which aspects are relevant to virtual reality, among other aspects. Both games interfaces were analyzed according to the criteria: Virtual world, Interactivity, Graphical interface, Metaphors, and Feedback. The analysis possible to establish a systematic decomposition of the serious game itself, discussing the elements that make up the interfaces, how they are used, how they integrate into the context, which aspects are relevant to virtual reality, among other contributions.

KEYWORDS

Serious Games, Interface, Virtual Reality

1. INTRODUCTION

The games industry has transformed since its emergence, acting as an entertainment activity for certain groups of individuals and presenting as a culture in society, including exploring different areas such as education, business, and medicine (Santanella, 2013). In the maturing process of games, this characteristic provided the development of the so-called "serious games", which are games that act to simulate ways of experiencing the real world, assisting in the acquisition of experience in activities and decision-making practices, in handling equipment, between others. Thus, it provides benefits for theoretical teaching and practical application of processes, aiding in knowledge and data production, allowing for professional improvement, and teaching in a controlled environment (Kapp, Blair & Mesch, 2014; Crookall, 2010; Michael & Chen, 2006).

LaValle (2017) argues that virtual reality is about the process to induce a specific behavior using artificial sensory stimulation, while the person has little or no notion of interference. Being inside the games means creating a mental immersion, putting the player inside a simulation, that is, a virtual world (Sherman & Craig, 2003). Due to technological advances and the ease with which information is propagated, the design process becomes more complex (Quintão & Triska, 2013).

Understanding this process, the purpose of serious games, the concepts of interfaces in the design area, and their application in the game universe are necessary to understand the complexity of building these games in virtual reality to work as knowledge for future research. Therefore, this article presents an analysis of two games considered serious games in the context of virtual reality platforms: Bus Simulator Drive and EarthQuake Simulator VR. The objective is to analyze how the interaction process occurs, which elements make up the interfaces in serious games, how they are used, how they integrate into the context, which aspects are relevant to virtual reality, among other aspects. Initially, there is a cut for the interface concepts used in the design environment and how they are applied in the games area. Afterward, the analysis criteria of how the interfaces are being worked in serious games and, consequently, in virtual reality are considered.

2. SERIOUS GAMES CHARACTERISTICS

The term serious games have its origin in the book by Clark Abt (1970). Although there are debates about the meaning, one of the considerations made is that they include games with the purpose of learning and training (Crookall, 2010). For Sherman & Craig (2003), serious games are games that use the medium to deliver a message, teach a lesson, or provide an experience. Zyda (2005) says that serious games aim to simulate practical situations of activities and can be used for training professionals and with an educational purpose, providing moments that encourage the precision of tasks and decision-making. In general, serious games have their goals aimed at learning certain situations, seeking to achieve specific results for tasks in the real world (Aldrich, 2009).

The design and creation process for serious games is not different from traditional games, however, while the later focuses on entertainment, the former focus on bringing these concepts and applying them in specialized content. Thus, they aim to train the user in an activity, through the simulation of a non-lethal environment, allowing the creation of a learning routine to improve the person's skills (Crokall, 2010). Among serious games applications, there is consolidated development in the medical area, the automotive industry, the agricultural sector, equipment handling, among others (Machado et al., 2011; Michael & Chen, 2006), including cases such as the process of a vaccination (Ogilvy Brasil, 2017) or the simulation of an earthquake (Lovreglio et al., 2018).

The development of games, in general, includes fundamental areas such as programming, art, audio, and production (Chandler, 2012), based on what is intended to be obtained for the game experience, that is, the entire process of player interactivity with the game and its details (Rouse, 2005). The sharp difference between games and serious games that affects the approach to the design process is precision (Michael & Chen, 2006). As serious games depend on creating a virtual environment that simulates a real-life activity, whatever the goal, the aesthetic part of the game is not prioritized, but how close the simulated activity and environment are to reality. In this sense, the interface is the point of contact between the user and the system, establishing an interaction process (Preece, Rogers & Sharp, 2013). Likewise, in games, the interface has the function of being the access point between the player and the virtual world established by the game (Sherman & Craig, 2003). But now, the interface will have the objective of making the player feel in control of the experience (Schell, 2008), in a way that does not exclude the concepts proposed by Santa Rosa & Moraes (2008) and Johnson (2001) in Human-Computer Interaction, that address how systems affect people, concerning the stimuli, information, responses, and actions that guide this process.

2.1 Interface in Serious Games

According to LaViola, et al. (2017) concept of the user interaction process (Figure 1), the User element represents the player who will interact with the system. The System is that will receive the information coming from the player, process it, and respond accordingly. Input Device represents any device for the player to send information to the system. Output Device is understood as the device that will receive this information coming from the system and will change it into content that the user can perceive whether visually, or any other type of perception.

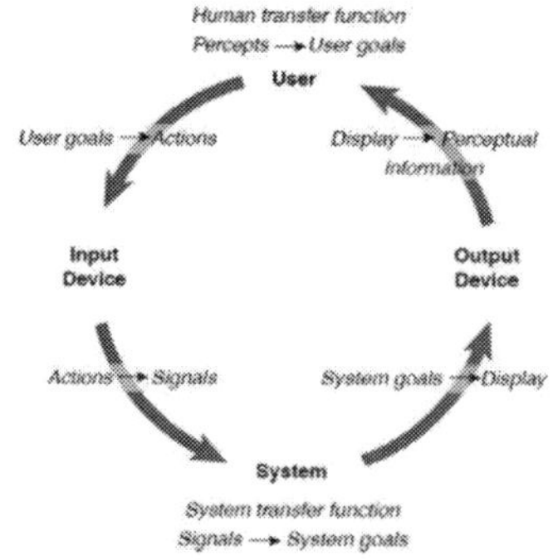

Figure 1. System transfer function cyclical process

While LaViola, et al. (2017) bring a more general approach to interfaces, Schell (2008) brings concepts to the scope of game design. According to Figure 2, it is noted that the concepts proposed by Schell (2008) about the interface in games are like those proposed by LaViola et al. (2017).

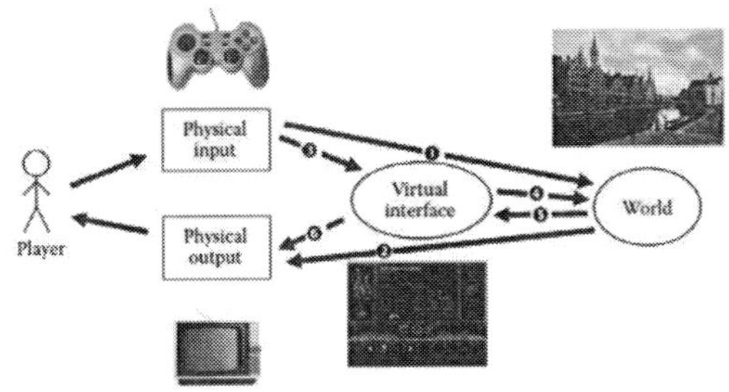

Figure 2. Schell's (2008) proposed concept to game interfaces

The term 'User' is the equivalent of the 'Player'. To simplify, Input and Output will be kept, but System, in this case, is divided into two new categories: Virtual Interface and World. Schell (2008) considers Virtual Interface, a "conceptual layer" between the World and the Player. This layer is composed of all the elements that are not necessarily part of the virtual world in which the player is interacting, but that support the player, containing the player Input and Output commands for the player. Inside what he calls this subtle layer are the elements that support the Player to interact with the game, such as the camera that is used to see the world, menus, buttons, icons, and more. The term 'World' will be simplified in the system proposed by LaViola, et al. (2017), as it contains only the elements that are parts of the virtual world, such as objects, game physics, scenarios, characters, and any other element that will make up the game universe. In Schell's (2008) scheme, despite the separation of each part of a game's interface, they work together, each step fulfilling a different role in the Player-World interaction.

This way the interface acts as an interaction tool between the systems, in this case, player, game, and the elements between them (Freitas, 2005), influencing how the player will fulfill the objective of serious games, as if the project if done poorly, noise is created between the player and the virtual world. In this sense, Moore's (2011) ideas about Graphical User Interface (GUI) are added, which focuses on the graphical part of the user interface, being all the imagery types that the player sees on the screen during the game.

Moore (2011) determines two categories of information: firstly in-game screens, which are used during the game, and secondly shell screens, which are used outside the game. Thus, an in-game screen is any screen that performs a function within the game, usually intending to inform the player about some functionality or event. For example, screens like the player's inventory, their combat screen, window, or menu with relevant types of information. This information can be static, meaning that the player does not directly interact with the information; or dynamic, meaning that it can interact with this interface.

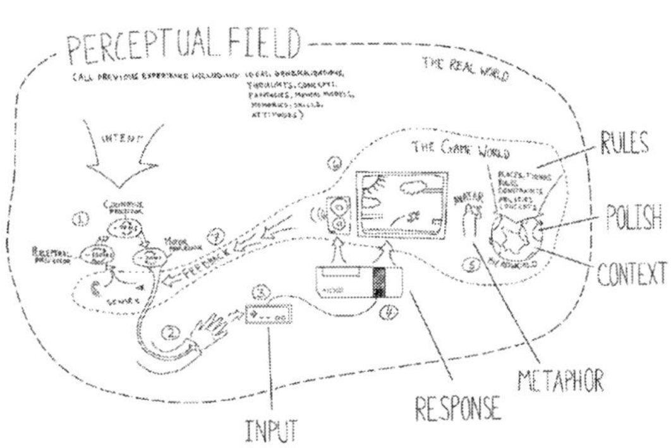

Figure 3. Field of perception adopted by Swink (2009)

In this context, it is relevant to understand how the player's perceptual field works in moments of interaction with the interface. Swink (2009) addresses the concept of "feeling" games, seeking to understand how the perception of human beings when interacting with virtual worlds works. This perception exists in different forms: visual, tactile, auditory, proprioceptive. Another point to be considered is that games allow the player to feel as if the virtual world were an extension of their body. Furthermore, these feelings are an ongoing process of skill-building and practice.

In figure 3, there is the field of perception that Swink (2009) adopted to explain how the player's perception process interacts with the virtual world. Note that the field has elements like the interface concepts proposed above. The player is divided into categories of brain processes. Input continues to play the same role. Output is included in the concept of feedback. Virtual Interface and World are contained in categories such as response, context, polish, metaphor, and rules. The 'Response' is how the system processes and modulates according to the player's input. Context is the space being simulated. Polish is the artificial effect that enhances the quality of the game. Metaphors are the representations that the game uses to generate an expected reaction from the player, with preconceptions that the player already has. Rules are arbitrary relationships between game variables that change the player's perception of game elements.

2.2 Criteria for Serious Games Analysis

To establish an analysis of interfaces in serious games, the criteria considered relevant for the proposal must be defined, to operationalize the comparison process. To conduct an analysis of interface elements in serious games, we sought to consider the main categories present in the literature by LaViola, et al. (2017), Schell (2008), Swink (2009), Moore (2011), Sherman & Craig (2003).

From this, the categories were separated into areas relevant to the Virtual Interface and World (Schell, 2008). The first will be deconstructed into two categories: Virtual World and Interactivity, while the second into three categories: Graphical Interface, Metaphors, and Feedback.

a) Virtual World: Sherman & Craig (2003) consider the virtual world to be any virtual space manifested through a medium and a description of the collection of objects in that space and its rules and governing relationships. In the gaming environment, the "context" of the game is the simulated space, that is, the physical space of the game's reality that includes the game rules (Swink, 2009).

b) Interactivity: In virtual reality, interactivity is any type of communication that takes place between the user and the virtual world mediated by input and output devices (Laviola et al., 2017). It is also considered how the player is placed in the scene, which avatar is used, that is, which character or object the player is incorporating and which tools he uses to interact with the virtual world (Sherman & Craig, 2003).

c) Graphical interface: It is divided into categories of the in-game screen and shell screen elements (Moore, 2011). The items on the player's screen environment that make up the interface are part of the information that guides the player, through images, texts, icons, and other options. In addition, some menus appear during or after the game, used to show information relevant to the player, such as their equipment list or score.

d) Metaphors: They relate to the player's perception of elements and interactions with objects within the game, in which experiences, ideas, and generalizations have a greater effect, as they are elements that come from the player's life experience (Swink, 2009). The function of metaphors in games is related to elements that are used in the interface to help the player's interaction in this world, these metaphors can be both visual and sound.

e) Feedback: It is the game's way of signaling information to the player on the interface if what he is doing is working or not (Moore, 2011; Swink, 2009). Feedback forms can be done in multiple ways, such as visual or audible. This element is fundamental in the context of Serious Games because it is how the game demonstrates the player's evolution in what is proposed as a goal.

3. METHODOLOGICAL PROCEDURES

This research aims to analyze how the interaction process occurs in serious games in virtual reality, seeking to operationalize the elements that make up the interfaces, understanding how they are used and how they integrate into the context. This research was carried out through an analytical study of serious games interfaces in virtual reality based on the criteria presented: Virtual World, Interactivity, Graphical Interface, Metaphors, and Feedback.

A survey was carried out on the Steam commercial game sales platform so that the selected games were commercially accessible to the public. It is important to consider that the goal of the game was within the concepts established by games that are considered serious games, simulating some type of real-world activity for training users in tasks that encourage decision-making in critical situations. In addition, we sought a serious game that also used the Virtual Reality system. Thus, the following games were selected: Bus Driver Simulator 2018 and Earthquake Simulator.

Figure 4. Bus Driver game

Bus Driver (Figure 4) is a game produced by the company KishMish Games, which aims to teach the user how to drive a bus. Thus, it is possible to interact with the bus from a touchscreen display, stopping at points for boarding and disembarking, in addition to finding different traffic depending on the time of day (Kishmish Games, 2018). EarthQuake (Figure 5) is a serious game launched in 2017 by the Lindero Edutainment company and applied to fire and earthquake survival training, teaching how to use the emergency kit and other actions to be taken (Lindero Edutainment, 2017).

Figure 5. EarthQuake game

4. ANALYSIS

After selection, both games interfaces were analyzed according to the criteria: Virtual world, Interactivity, Graphical interface, Metaphors, and Feedback.

4.1 Analysis – Bus Simulator Drive

a) Virtual world: The objective of the game is to include the player as a public transport bus driver. The player must follow the work route, stop at bus stops for passengers to board and disembark, as well as comply with traffic rules. As an example of world simulation, there is at the beginning of the game a simple trip from the train station to Lenin Square, at lunchtime on a working day and it is explained that that is why the bus is not crowded. Thus, it is observed that the game context has as basic rules: location context, time of day, number of passengers. It is also noted that although the game simulates elements of a real city such as buildings, signs, and traffic, the virtual world created is not a faithful representation of somewhere, in reality, it is just a fictional world called Virtual City. The elements that make up this world, such as scenery, buses, and people, are represented simply, with aesthetic fidelity only in form, but not in visual quality.

b) Interactivity: As the objective of the game is to create a simulation of how it is to drive a public transport bus, the player's avatar is the bus driver himself. Despite this, the game does not allow for character customization. Thus, the interaction takes place only with the elements present inside the bus, such as the steering wheel, buttons for opening and closing the door, and other elements that belong to the work of driving. As the game is played in first-person mode, with the player representing the driver, the camera replicates the player's neck movements with the virtual reality goggle. Thus, if the player looks to his right side in the direction where passengers board the bus, the game's camera simulates this movement as if it were the driver looking. It is also possible to consider the player's bus as an extension of the avatar, as the game does not separate the two during gameplay and interactions extend to elements found in traffic, such as other cars, signs, and the work route itself.

c) Graphical interface: At the beginning of the game, in virtual reality mode, there is the Menu with the basic options of Start, Options, and Exit the game (this screen is a shell-screen). When starting a game, there is a new interface, in which there is a list of scenario options for the player to select and where the context of the basic rules of the scenario is informed. During gameplay, the interface space is partially covered by the interior of the bus, including the steering wheel, bus buttons, and rearview mirror, with the rest of the space showing the simulated virtual environment around the bus. The dashboard for the driver to view data such as speed is considered an in-game screen. The bus has a screen on the right-hand side of the steering wheel with information about the route you should take, money earned from tickets, possible fines if you do something wrong. This monitor is inserted in the busy environment, working as if the driver had a tablet at his disposal while working. With this information, it is complex to classify it as a shell-screen or in-game screen, as this tablet plays the role of both, containing realistic information about a bus trip, such as passenger payment and the route you must take (in-game screen), but it is also used to inform the player of mistakes made (shell-screen). At the end of the journey, a new shell-screen menu appears to end the journey and take the player to the entry menu.

d) Metaphors: Several metaphors of the game Bus Driver are present in the context of the virtual world itself, such as traffic lights with red, yellow, and green, traffic signs with speed limits, bus stops, and pedestrian crossings. Others are inside the bus, such as the elements found on the driver's panel, such as speed markings and icons indicating functions such as opening a door, using a headlamp, among others. In addition to the visual part, the game tries to simulate the sounds of a traffic environment, such as horns and engine noise. All these elements are icons or symbols that players already live within everyday life. Two metaphors are not associative to the real world, such as the use of an imaginary line and arrows to indicate the path to be taken. However, this type of signaling is commonly used in GPS applications to guide the user on the route. In general, the game also uses green and red colors for positive and negative results.

e) Feedback: The first form of feedback found in the game is on the tablet, which contains information about whether the passenger boarded the bus and how much money he paid. During the course, lines and arrows are used to indicate if the path chosen by the player is correct. The game also uses a menu at the end of the route to inform the player's score, the amount earned in money with the tickets, in addition to approving or disapproving the activity performed.

4.2 Analysis – EarthQuake Simulator VR

a) Virtual World: The game teaches the user to survive disaster experiences such as fire and earthquake. These events are simulated with the player inside a house. In this scenario, the game explores areas of the house such as bedrooms, bathrooms, and kitchens. The context of the game is to simulate a dangerous event, such as a house fire, teaching the player how to react. For this, the player must fulfill a series of activities and instructions. The game has shortcomings in the aesthetic part, such as the unrealistic effect of fire and earthquake. However, it is noteworthy that the objective itself is to try to accurately simulate the necessary activities and movements that the player must do to survive such an extreme situation.

b) Interactivity: The EarthQuake game is performed in the first person, with the player in the avatar role. Therefore, the player's head movement works like the camera. During the game, objects scattered around the house such as fire extinguishers, books, and medicine chest are the interactive elements that the player has to use to survive. This interaction is done through the player's own hands. The game projects the player's movements from real life to the virtual world. Although the game simulates the movement of the head and hands, the locomotion movements are made through the so-called point-and-click, in which the player must use the controller to go by clicking where he wants to reach.

c) Graphical Interface: The game starts with a shell-screen with basic instructions on how to play. After that, the game uses television as an interface to contextualize the player with what is happening inside this virtual world and give tips for the player's survival. This is followed by a checklist inside the kitchen, which works as an in-game screen interface, containing information on how to prepare for an earthquake. Screen space is not blocked by any element, with the player's view unobstructed, and only elements of the scene itself are used to convey information to the player. When the game needs to demonstrate something that is not naturally part of the scenario, a graphical interface with the information appears. In addition, a narrator is informing the activities to be done. With that, the game uses a lot of audio instead of visual.

d) Metaphors: The EarthQuake game simulates a circle interface to indicate where you want to go. Within the checklist that the player must complete, each completed step is marked with a green correct sign. When the player needs to be in a specific position in the scenario, the game demarcates this area in green lines indicating that it is a safe place. In addition, there is an indication of green arrows along the path that the player must take to accomplish the objective. All these elements are pertinent to everyday elements of a player's life.

e) Feedback: When the player must assemble a survival kit with the necessary items, the game provides an interface on top of the backpack that works as a counter indicating the total number of items needed and how many have already been collected. In the checklist present in the scenario, every time the player puts an object inside the backpack, there is a green line and a correct sign marked above the item in the response. When the player fails to collect an item, the narrator warns that something is missing. Another element of feedback is a dog's bark, which is used to signal that the earthquake is about to start, and which gets louder when the earthquake is closer to happening. Lastly, if the player followed the instructions and survived the earthquake, you get a message that the activities were completed.

5. CONCLUSION

This article aimed to analyze the interaction process in serious virtual reality games. Therefore, it was necessary to establish criteria for analyzing computer systems and games in general that could be adapted to the analysis of serious games. The categories present in the literature by LaViola, et al. (2017), Schell (2008), Swink (2009), Moore (2011), Sherman & Craig (2003), defining as common criteria: Virtual World, Interactivity, Graphical Interface, Metaphors, and Feedback.

In this sense, an analysis of the serious games Bus Simulator Drive and EarthQuake Simulator VR was performed. Among the elements analyzed, it is considered that "interactivity" was noted to have the most influence on virtual reality, as this method brings devices that go beyond the common control, increasing not only the possibilities of interaction but also of replicating movements of the human being in the game. The other elements had highlights with less impact on the functioning of the interface. "Virtual world" benefited from the player's immersion in the universe. The "graphical interface" had its adaptation more from a technical point of view, because of virtual reality, its elements had to be modified for the output type that the virtual reality devices have. The same goes for the elements of "Metaphors" and "Feedback".

It is noteworthy that the analysis of serious games was not intended to determine whether a game is better than another or what problems the game presents. With this, the adoption of the criteria made it possible to establish a systematic decomposition of the serious game itself, discussing the elements that make up the interfaces, how they are used, how they integrate into the context, which aspects are relevant to virtual reality, among other contributions. To expand this research, it is proposed to analyze the user experience with games, addressing details of the player's interaction with the controls, how the player is being affected by changes, and how these actions are being reflected within the virtual world.

ACKNOWLEDGEMENT

We thank the Federal University of Santa Catarina. The financial support of CAPES. The Team in DesignLAB/UFSC and Tecmidia for the collaboration to this research.

REFERENCES

ABT C., Clark. 1970. *Serious games*. Viking Press. USA.

Aldrich, Clark. 2009. *The Complete Guide to Simulations and Serious Games: How the Most Valuable Content Will be Created in the Age Beyond Gutenberg to Google*. Pfeiffer; .

Chandler, Heather Maxwell. 2012. *Manual de Produção de Jogos Digitais*. 2nd ed. Bookman. Porto Alegre

Crookall, David. 2010 *Serious games, Debriefing, and Simulation/Gaming as a Discipline*. Sage Publications, New York.

Freitas, Julio C. 2005 O Design como Interface de Comunicação e uso em Linguagens Hipermidiáticas. *In O chip e o caleidoscópio: reflexões sobre as novas mídias*. SENAC. São Paulo

Johnson, S. 2001. *Cultura da interface: como o computador transforma nossa maneira de criar e comunicar*. Jorge Zahar. Rio de Janeiro, Brazil.

Kapp, Karl M. et al. 2014 *The Gamification of Learning and Instruction Fieldbook - Ideas into Practice.* Wiley: San Francisco, CA, USA.

Kishmish Games. 2018. *Bus Driver Simulator* 2018. web

Lavalle, Steven. 2017. *Virtual Reality*. Cambridge University Press, England.

Laviola, JR. Joseph J. et al. 2017. *3D User Interfaces Theory and Practices* Second Edition. Addison-Wesley, USA.

Lemos, A. (1997). Anjos interativos e retribalização do mundo. Sobre interatividade e interfaces digitais. *Revista Tendências* XXI, v.2. Lisboa: APDC, p. 19-29.

Lindero Edutainment. 2017. *EarthQuake Simulator VR*. Steam Store. Web

Lovreglio, R., et al. 2018. *Prototyping Virtual Reality Serious games for Building Earthquake Preparedness: The Auckland City Hospital Case Study*. ArXiv e-prints.

Machado, Liliane dos Santos. Et al. 2011. *Serious games* baseados em realidade virtual para educação médica. *Rev. bras. educ. med.*, Rio de Janeiro, v.35, n.2, p.254-262.

Michael, David. Chen. 2006. Sande. Serious games: Games That Educate, Train, And Inform. *Thomson Course Technology PTR.*

Moore, Michael E. 2011. *Basics of Game Design*. CRC Press Taylor & Francis Group, USA.

Ogilvy Brasil. 2017. *VR Vacine*. Ogilvy, Brazil.

Preece, Jennifer. Et al. 2013. *Design de interação: além da interação humano-computador.* 3 ed. Bookman, Brazil.

Quintão S., Fernanda, Triska, Ricardo. 2013. Design da informação em interfaces digitais: origens, definições e fundamentos. *Revista brasileira de Design da Informação*.

Rouse, Richard. 2005. *Game Design Theory & Practice*. Wordware Publishing, Inc.

Santaella, Lucia. 2013. *Comunicação ubiqua: Repercussões na cultura e na educação*. Paulus Editora, Brazil.

Santa Rosa, José Guilherme; Moraes, Anamaria de. 2008. *Avaliação e projeto de interfaces*. 2AB. Teresópolis, Brazil.

Schell, Jesse. 2008. *Second Edition The Art of Game Design A Book of Lenses*. CRC Press Taylor & Francis Group. USA,

Sherman, William; Craig, Alan. 2003. *Understanding Virtual Reality: Interface, Application, and Design*. Elsevier Science, USA.

Swink, Steve 2009. *Game Feel: A Game Designer's Guide to Virtual Sensation*. Elsevier, USA.

Zyda M. From visual simulation to virtual reality to games. *Computer.* 38 (9):25-32. 2005.

CLASSIFICATION OF METHODS AND ALGORITHMS FOR DETECTION OF FALLS IN OLDER ADULTS

Manuel Erazo-Valadez, Javier Ortiz-Hernandez, Angel Israel Daza-Castillo, Juan Antonio Miguel-Ruiz, Alicia Martínez-Rebollar and Yasmin Hernandez
The National Technological Institute of Mexico/CENIDET, Cuernavaca, México

ABSTRACT

Approximately 30% of older adults fall at least once a year and 50% of that number will fall twice. Likewise, the number of falls that an older adult may suffer rises with increasing age. Falls have a high morbidity and mortality rate and are considered a major public health problem. It is estimated that 7% of hospital visits by older adults are the result of a fall and 40% of these require hospitalization. This article presents some of the main detection methods and algorithms used for fall detection and discusses their advantages and disadvantages. Each of these methods and algorithms directly or indirectly requires varying processing, connectivity, storage, and portability capabilities and provides varying degrees of accuracy. Based on this analysis, an experimental development for fall arrest in older adults will be proposed that aims to achieve 95% accuracy using a minimally invasive wearable sensor.

KEYWORDS

Fall Detection, Methods and Algorithms, Wearable Sensors, Older Adults

1. INTRODUCTION

The World Health Organization (WHO) defines a fall as an unintentional event affecting a person that causes him or her to lose balance and impact the ground or other arresting surface (Durán et al., 2017). "The accelerated aging of the population has led to the emergence of a new public health problem: falls in the elderly" (da Silva-Gama & Gómez-Conesa, 2008).

It is estimated that during a year approximately 37.3 million falls occur in older adults, causing serious injuries in the people who suffered them (Silva-Fhon et al., 2019). Epidemiological studies have shown that one in three people over 65 years of age suffers a fall per year and half of these people suffer more than one fall (Varas-Fabra et al., 2006). Deaths of older adults aged 65 years and older as a result of falls account for three-quarters of fall deaths in the United States (Rubenstein & Josephson, 2002). The incidence and severity of injury from falls in older adults increases with age. With increasing age, the balance and response ability of the elderly is also affected (Kannus et al., 2014). The consequences of falls can be physical and psychological. The most common physical consequences are inflammations caused by the trauma and fractures occur in 6% of all falls. While the most common psychological consequences are loss of self-confidence, fear or anxiety to suffer a fall again (Varas-Fabra et al., 2006).

People aged 65 years and older are prone to suffer a greater number of falls. Due to their age, they may suffer from various chronic and/or degenerative diseases such as cardiovascular problems, nervous system disorders and osteoporosis, which can influence walking difficulties, loss of balance and movement (Rubenstein & Josephson, 2002), (Zorrilla & Dahily, 2011). Several studies have shown that people who take three or more medications are more likely to fall (Silva-Fhon et al., 2019), (Varas-Fabra et al., 2006). Some medications that increase the likelihood of a fall in the elderly are: psychotropic drugs, sedatives, hypnotics, antidepressants, benzodiazepines and neuroleptics (Rubenstein & Josephson, 2002), (Zorrilla & Dahily, 2011). A wide variety of extrinsic and intrinsic factors have been found to be associated with falls in this population group. The most common extrinsic factors are those related to the home environment and the intrinsic factors detected are: disabilities, exacerbated chronic diseases, previous falls, age-related body changes and multiple medication. The presence of two or more of these factors is associated with a higher probability of a fall occurring (De et al., 2002). Mexico is home to 15.4 million people aged 60 years or older, of whom 7.4 million live alone. Of these, 41.4% are economically active, while 69.4% suffer from some disability (Nacional & Unidas, 2020).

2. SYSTEMS, METHODS AND ALGORITHMS FOR FALL DETECTION

A systematic search related to fall detection systems was carried out in five databases, in which a total of 200 articles were obtained. Using various filters, 30 relevant articles using wearable sensors were obtained, of which 25 make use of threshold-based algorithms and 5 machine learning-based algorithms. 25 make use of threshold-based algorithms and 5 machine learning-based algorithms. Likewise, 10 articles were obtained based on environmental monitoring using infrared sensors, cameras or combined systems.

In the bibliographic review, the works obtained were classified into three groups: Systems, Methods or Algorithms.

-Systems are understood as the proposal of complete solutions related to fall detection. These solutions generally present complete prototypes that include all the necessary hardware and software to ensure the functionality of the solution. The proposed systems may be based on a single method or a combination of methods. Also, a given method can be implemented by an algorithm or by variants of a given algorithm. These systems may have associated with the fall detection various functionalities for example to notify the fall to a third person and describe in detail the devices and communication systems used.

-Methods are understood as the proposed use of a certain technique to detect and characterize the fall phenomenon.

-Algorithms refers to the programming required to computationally implement the detection method.

Two main types of fall detection methods are identified. Each of these methods may have some variants.

2.1 Fall Detection Methods based on Environmental Monitoring

This category includes detection systems that use sensors which are installed around the user's environment and are responsible for monitoring the activities performed by people on a daily basis. The most commonly used technologies in this type of detectors are infrared sensors and those that use cameras for monitoring (Pérolle & Etxeberria Arritxabal, 2006).

Advantages:

- The person does not wear any type of fall detection device, and may not even be aware that he or she is being monitored (Belshaw et al., 2010).
- The installed devices are continuously powered they do not rely on batteries (Yu et al., 2012).

Disadvantages

- Site furniture, people or other objects may affect the accuracy of fall detection (Mastorakis & Makris, 2014).
- Various technologies need to be installed to avoid blind spots within individual rooms
- High cost of implementation

2.2 Fall Detection Methods based on Wearable Devices

This category includes detection systems that use sensors that can be worn by a person without affecting activities of daily living. These systems generally use sensors embedded in mobile equipment such as smartphones, smart bracelets, wearable devices, etc. (Pérolle & Etxeberria Arritxabal, 2006). In this study, only works using 2-axis and 3-axis integrated accelerometers as sensing device were considered.

Advantages:

- Monitoring can be performed in multiple spaces, open or enclosed.
- Various types of sensors and constant monitoring in multiple spaces can be installed for monitoring.
- A single sensing device can provide an adequate degree of accuracy (Wang et al., 2014).
- Furniture, people or other objects are not an obstacle to its operation.
- By pre-installing the sensors in the installation, a constant power supply can be ensured.

Disadvantages:

- Device autonomy depends on battery backup.
- The user must remember to put on the wearable device correctly (Degen et al., 2003).
- The user can damage the device voluntarily or involuntarily impeding its functionality.

3. MAIN METHODS AND ALGORITHMS BASED ON WEARABLE DEVICES

3.1 Threshold-Based Fall Detection Methods

These algorithms use limits (thresholds) to detect different phases of the fall, usually upper limits, which when reached or exceeded trigger actions to analyze and verify that a fall has occurred.

Advantages:
- Low consumption of computational resources.
- Uses simple arithmetic calculations to perform drop detection (Tong et al., 2009).

Disadvantages:
- Difficult to determine the threshold that gives the best results.
- Poor choice of thresholds can lead to erroneous drop detections
- There is no standard for defining thresholds.
- Most of the research done has been tested only in controlled environments (Vallejo et al., 2013).

In the work "Development of an in-home fall monitoring platform for older adults", (Murray Toledo, 2020) they use a threshold-based fall detection algorithm. The implemented algorithm uses 3 different thresholds that are used to perform the detection of 3 phases of the fall: free fall, impact and rest. Figure 1 shows the flowchart of the algorithm operation (Murray Toledo, 2020).

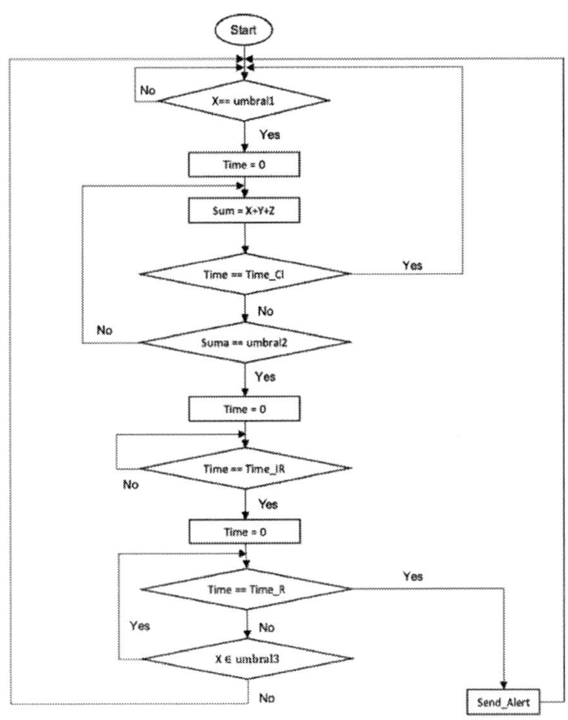

Figure 1. Flowchart of the work from figure in (Murray Toledo, 2020)

-Threshold 1 is used to detect the free fall phase, during this phase an acceleration in the x-axis similar to the acceleration of gravity is expected, so a threshold value 0.6 g was defined where g=9.82 m/s^2.

-Threshold value 2 was defined at 1.5 g and is used to detect the impact phase where the sum of the three accelerometer vectors (x-axis + y-axis + z-axis) is performed. The result of the sum must exceed the value of threshold 2 to detect that there was a deceleration of the body upon impact. Then, it will be determined if the threshold value is reached or exceeded in a time of 2 seconds, otherwise the value will be returned to the previous phase.

-Threshold 3 is the resting threshold, after the threshold is reached in the previous phase a time of 2 seconds is expected where the x-axis must remain with an acceleration within the range of threshold 3, the range is -0.5g to 0.5g, if in the established time it does not remain within the range the fall would not be detected, if it remains within the range the fall would be detected.

In the work "A smartphone-based fall detection system", they use a fall detection algorithm that is based on the occurrence of a 3g peak considered as the threshold that initiates the analysis of the following fall detection stages.

This remains in the sampling state in the first stage, until it detects a peak ≥3g and moves to the post-peak, at this point it waits for a lapse of 1000ms, in which there must not be any other peak and moves to the post-fall, otherwise it returns again to the post-peak. In the Post-fall it waits 1500ms, in which there is no activity and moves to the Activity-test, but if a new threshold peak is detected, it returns to the post-peak. In the Activity-test if it does not pass the test it returns to Sampling, but if it passes it is detected as a fall event (Valcourt et al., 2016).

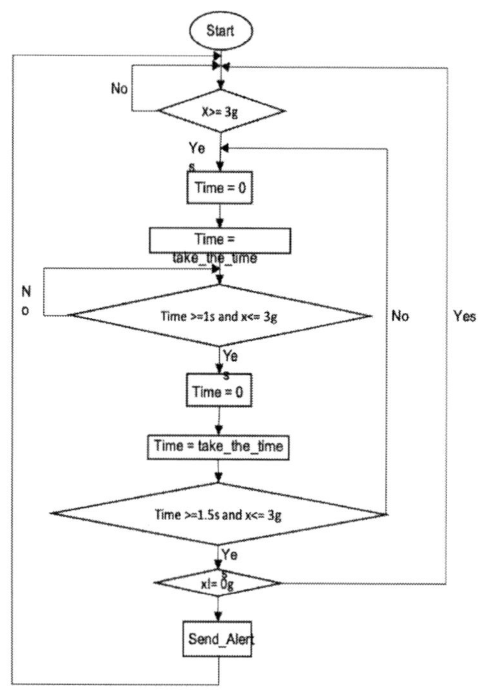

Figure 2. Threshold-based flowchart from figure in (Valcourt et al., 2016)

3.2 Machine Learning-Based Algorithms

3.2.1 Fall Detection Algorithms Based on Neural Networks

Neural network algorithms mimic the behavior of human thought, which passes information between neurons to obtain a result. They are composed of neurons that are themselves within a layer and communicate through links called weights. The weights can increase or inhibit the activation of the neurons with which it communicates.

Advantages:
- This type of algorithm can differentiate between activities of daily living and falls.
- By taking into account the nature of various activities it avoids errors.

Disadvantages:
- An extra device such as a computer is needed to perform the training of the network
- The application needs to be trained before use
- Consumes more computational resources
- Poor training of the neural network may influence the effectiveness of fall detection.

These types of algorithms implement a neural network that uses the collected data for classification in two ways: normal activity or fall. It is a feed forward network that consists of 3 layers and each layer has 5 neurons. The input of values to the network is the accelerometer data, this is connected to the first layer with the matrix W1kj which are the weights of the input layer connections and layer one. Layers one and two are connected by matrix W2kj, which contains the weights of the layer one and two connections. The matrix W3kj is the one containing the weights of the layer two and three connections. Between layer three and the output layer is the W4kj matrix, which contains the weights of the connections between these layers. Figure 3 shows the structure of the neural network used in this work (Vallejo et al., 2013).

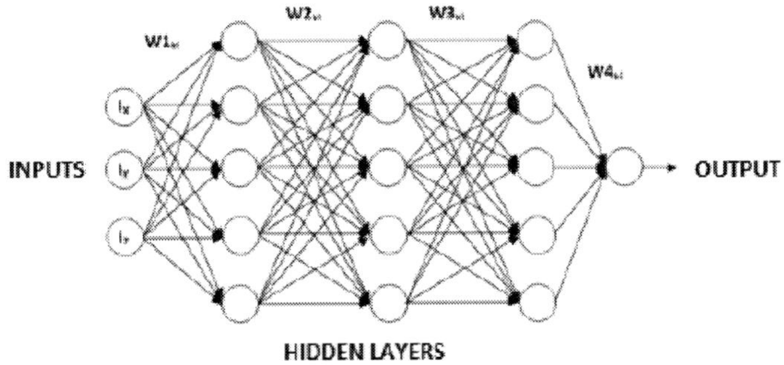

Figure 3. Structure of the neural network used for three-layer; five-neuron fall detection (Vallejo et al., 2013)

The stored data set was separated into two parts, the first subset of data includes data from 329 falls and 392 activities that the user performs in his daily life and was used to train the network. The second subset of data contains the data of 216 falls and 250 activities of daily life, this subset was used to test the performance of the neural network after being trained. The results of the tests carried out from the work of (Moran Garabito, 2017) are presented in Table 1.

Table 1. Results of tests performed

Training error rate	1.25%
Percentage of test error	1.07%
Percentage of undetected falls in training	1.52%
Percentage of falls undetected in testing	1.86%

3.2.2 Falling Detection Algorithms Based on Decision Trees

These types of algorithms use the comparisons that are present in the generated decision trees. The decision trees are generated using the minimum and maximum points in the acceleration taking into account daily life activities and different types of falls. Once having the trees, the algorithm is generated, using comparisons of the changes in acceleration to determine whether it is some activity of daily life or some type of fall.

Advantages:
- Simple implementation.
- Low consumption of computational resources.
- This type of algorithm can differentiate between activities of daily living and falls.

Disadvantages:
- Different experiments must be carried out to obtain the data that will be used to generate the decision trees.
- Poor experimentation in the measurement of falls can influence the effectiveness of fall detection.
- A large amount of data is needed to generate the decision tree and another to test the performance.

In (Moran Garabito, 2017), an algorithm is implemented that was developed using two types of decision trees. For the construction of the trees, the information obtained by a triaxial accelerometer was used, both from falls and from activities performed in daily life such as: walking, lying down, bending, descending stairs, jumping, sitting and climbing stairs. The decision trees use the maximum and minimum peaks and troughs that were detected in the acceleration when performing each of the activities and in the simulations of the falls. Figure 4 shows the decision tree generated for the minimum peaks of the accelerations

The decision trees generated are used to develop the algorithm. The algorithm works with 100 samples and with them the minimum and maximum acquired are determined, a filter is used to eliminate oscillations caused by breathing or low frequency activities, then the data enters the algorithm where by means of comparisons generated by the decision trees it is detected if the data is a fall of one of the activities of daily life that were taken into account.

The authors of the work indicate that the algorithm obtained 97% of true positives in the detection of falls and the remaining 3% as false positives (Moran Garabito, 2017).

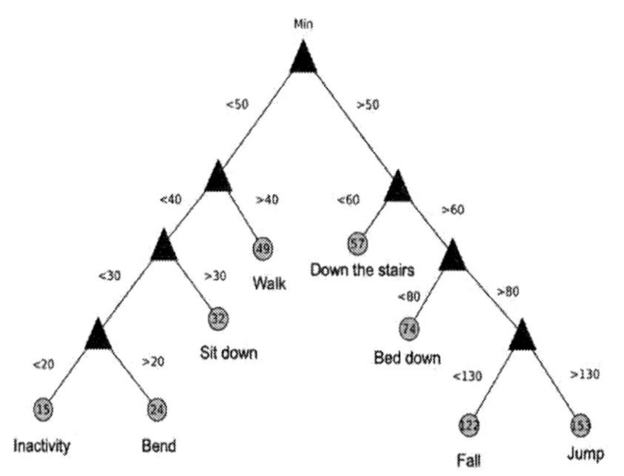

Figure 4. Decision tree of the minimum peaks obtained from the figure in (Moran Garabito, 2017)

4. CONCLUSIONS

Given the increase in the population of older adults worldwide, there is a growing need for solutions to problems presented by this segment of the population to help them lead a more autonomous life with greater well-being. Fall detection has become a very important issue due to the serious consequences of delaying timely assistance to the elderly. Current options for fall detection are very limited and difficult to access for most elderly people.

In this work we propose a classification of the types of algorithms for fall detection. Based on the algorithms it is intended to perform a coding of each of them and test them under the same conditions to identify the algorithm that delivers better results and comparing the number of errors in the detection of falls and activities of daily living.

An investigation of various works related to fall detection was conducted in order to observe and learn about them, with the aim of identifying the most appropriate methods for the development of a low-cost and reliable solution for fall detection. See table 2.

Table 2. Comparison of fall detection methods

Fall detection methods	**Accuracy**	**Processing requirements**	**Configuration requirements**
Thresholds	87.85%	Low	Low
Neural networks	98.4%	High	High
Decision trees	97%	Low	High

We identified three main methods, with some variants. They were compared considering their accuracy, as well as their processing requirements (processing time, complexity of the algorithms), as well as their configuration requirements (time and difficulty of the training and configuration of the method prior to its use). In the case of accuracy, the results obtained from the literature review were averaged. It was observed that the algorithms based on thresholds use different stages, constants and mathematical calculations to determine whether a fall has been detected.

We believe that the classification of these algorithms would facilitate the development of new fall detection systems and make it easier for the developers of these systems to choose the algorithm that suits their needs and the type of measurement device they will use.

ACKNOWLEDGEMENT

This work has been partially funded by the TecNM project 10489.21-P & PRODEP CENIDET-CA-18.

REFERENCES

Belshaw, M., Taati, B., Giesbrecht, D., & Mihailidis, A (2010). Intelligent Vision-Based Fall Detection System: Preliminary Results From a Real-World Deployment

da Silva-Gama, Z. A., & Gómez-Conesa, A. (2008). Factores de riesgo de caídas en ancianos : revisión sistemática Risk factors for falls in the elderly : *Rev Saúde Pública*, 42(5), 946–956.

De, S. P., Hernández, S., Moctezuma, A., Rodrigo, G., Ortega, G., & María, R. (2002). Caídas en el adulto mayor. Factores intrínsecos y extrínsecos. *Revista Medica del Instituto Mexicano Del Seguro Social,* 40(6), 489–493.

Degen, T., Jaeckel, H., Rufer, M., & Wyss, S. (2003). SPEEDY:a fall detector in a wrist watch. *Seventh IEEE International Symposium on Wearable Computers*, 2003. Proceedings., 184–187. https://doi.org/10.1109/ISWC.2003.1241410

Durán, E. R., Camarero, G. F. R., & Martínez-Esparza, E. H. (2017). Incidencia y características de las caídas en un hospital de cuidados intermedios de Barcelona. *Gerokomos*, 28(2), 78–82.

Kannus, P., Parkkari, J., Koskinen, S., Niemi, S., Palvanen, M., Järvinen, M., & Vuori, I. (2014). Fall-Induced Injuries and Deaths Among Older Adults. 281(20), 1895–1899.

Mastorakis, G., & Makris, D. (2014). Fall detection system using Kinect's infrared sensor. *Journal of Real-Time Image Processing*, 9(4), 635–646. https://doi.org/10.1007/s11554-012-0246-9

Moran Garabito, C. E. (2017). Algoritmo de detección de caídas en un sistema embebido. In Ciateq, A. C.

Murray Toledo, S. C. A. (2020). Desarrollo de una Plataforma de Monitoreo de Caídas dn Domicilio para Adultos Mayores.

Nacional, E., & Unidas, N. (2020). Comunicado De Prensa Núm . 337 / 19 10 De Julio De 2019 " Estadísticas a Propósito del Día Mundial de la Población (11 De Julio) ." INEGI, 337(19), 1–13. https://www.inegi.org.mx/contenidos/saladeprensa/aproposito/2020/Poblacion2020_Nal.pdf

Pérolle, G., & Etxeberria Arritxabal, I. (2006). Detector automático de caídas y monitorización de actividad para personas mayores. *Revista Española de Geriatría y Gerontología*, 41(Supl 2), 33–41. https://doi.org/10.1016/s0211-139x(06)73006-2

Rubenstein, L. Z., & Josephson, K. R. (2002). The epidemiology of falls and syncope. *Clinics in Geriatric Medicine*, 18(2), 141–158. https://doi.org/10.1016/S0749-0690(02)00002-2

Silva-Fhon, J. R., Partezani-Rodrigues, R., Miyamura, K., & Fuentes-Neira, W. (2019). Causas y factores asociados a las caídas del adulto mayor Causes and factors associated to falls among the Elder Causas e fatores associados aquedas no idoso. *Enfermeria Universitaria*, 16(1).

Tong, L., Chen, W., Song, Q., & Ge, Y. (2009). A research on automatic human fall detection method based on wearable inertial force information acquisition system. *International Conference on Robotics and Biomimetics*.

Valcourt, L., de La Hoz, Y., & Labrador, M. (2016). Smartphone-based Human Fall Detection System. *IEEE Latin America Transactions*, 14(2), 1011–1017. https://doi.org/10.1109/TLA.2016.7437252

Vallejo, M., Isaza, C. v., & Lopez, J. D. (2013). Artificial Neural Networks as an alternative to traditional fall detection methods. *Proceedings of the Annual International Conference of the IEEE Engineering in Medicine and Biology Society*, EMBS, 1, 1648–1651. https://doi.org/10.1109/EMBC.2013.6609833

Varas-Fabra, F., Castro Martín, E., Pérula de Torres, L. Á., Fernández Fernández, M. J., Ruiz Moral, R., & Enciso Berge, I. (2006). Caídas en ancianos de la comunidad: Prevalencia, consecuencias y factores asociados. *Atención Primaria*, 38(8), 450–455. https://doi.org/10.1157/13094802

Wang, J., Zhang, Z., Li, B., Lee, S., & Sherratt, R. S. (2014). An enhanced fall detection system for elderly person monitoring using consumer home networks. *IEEE Transactions on Consumer Electronics*, 60(1), 23–29. https://doi.org/10.1109/TCE.2014.6780921

Yu, M., Rhuma, A., Naqvi, S. M., Wang, L., & Chambers, J. (2012). A Posture Recognition-Based Fall Detection System for Monitoring an Elderly Person in a Smart Home Environment. *IEEE Transactions on Information Technology in Biomedicine*, 16(6), 1274–1286. https://doi.org/10.1109/TITB.2012.2214786

Zorrilla, A., & Dahily, G. (2011). Aspectos sociodemográficos de las caídas en ancianos atendidos por un Grupo Básico de Trabajo. *Journal of Physics A: Mathematical and Theoretical*, 44(8), 51. https://doi.org/10.1088/1751-8113/44/8/085201

5 YEARS OF EARLY MANAGEMENT OF SKIN CANCER BY TELE-DERMATOLOGY: WHAT HAVE WE LEARNED FROM REAL-WORLD DATA?

Myriam Le Goff-Pronost[1], Imad El Badisy[2], Quentin Dejonghe[3], Caroline De Pauw[3], Tanguy Lagorsse[3], Bastien Affeltranger[4] and Estelle Borne[5]

[1]*PhD, IMT Atlantique, LATIM, M@rsouin, Technopôle Brest Iroise – CS 83818 – 29238 Brest cedex 3 – France*

[2]*IMT Atlantique, France*

[3]*URPS Hauts-De-France, Lille, France*

[4]*PhD, Société française de santé publique (SFSP), France*

5Dr., Dermatologist, MD PhD, Clinique Vauban 10 avenue Vauban, 59300 Valenciennes, France

ABSTRACT

This paper presents a tele-expertise experiment in dermatology with the aim of early detection of skin cancers. This telemedicine system allows the general practitioner (GP) to send a request for an opinion to a distant dermatologist. Carried out in France (Hauts-De-France region) for 5 years, this experiment gathered real data exchanged between GPs and dermatologists, and accounting for a total of 1,812 tele-expertises. The results show that tele-expertise makes it possible to reduce the time taken to take charge of dermatology patients. It is also noted that the requests of GPs do not relate only to skin cancer, yet also to benign lesion. Based on a numerical model developed alongside with the experiment, the next challenge is to demonstrate the economic sustainability of tele-expertise in dermatology.

KEYWORDS

Tele-Dermatology, Skin Cancer, Expertise, Time Access, Real-World Data, Medico-Economic Sustainability

1. INTRODUCTION

Dermatology is a medical specialty that early recognized the usefulness of relying on new technologies to improve practice and, in some areas, to counterbalance declining medical demographics. Numerous studies have shown that tele-dermatology is a reliable and acceptable practice (Bashshur, 2015; Trettel, 2018). One of the first objective of tele-dermatology was to validate the images captured by communication tools and verify that image quality was sufficient and identical to that of physical examination (Coates, 2011; Chen, 2014). Telemedicine has proven to be a good communication tool between general practitioners (GP) and dermatologists (Van den Akker, 2001) as well as a vehicle for improving the skills of treating physicians (Pala, 2020).

Tele-dermatology has also shown strong utility in oncology for the detection of skin cancers via tele-expertise which allows the specialist remotely to make a diagnosis and organize treatment (Fabbrocini, 2011; Finnane, 2017), and to identify melanomas based on remote pictures (Chuchu, 2018). In fact, the detection of a skin cancer can come from the patient who himself notices a suspicious skin lesion or from the GP during a consultation for another reason, or during hospitalization. In addition, tele-expertise helps limit patient's travel burden from a medical practitioner to the next.

Tele-expertise offers three models of practice for the management of skin tumors:

- Advisory opinion and improving diagnosis accuracy;
- Triage of patients with benign vs. malignant lesions. Patients with skin cancer are given priority treatment;
- The appropriate medical direction and clinical follow-up, by validating the need to consult a specialist or not, or to be treated, biopsy or surgery.

In the case of skin cancer, the major issue it to establish diagnosis as early as possible, so as to prevent the further spread of malignant cells to other organs. But even if patients report changes in the pigmentation of their lesions, this may still lead to delayed care. Tele-expertise responds to a problem of medical demography. It facilitates access to expertise healthcare for various categories of the population, especially those located far from city centers where the medical demography is greater (Coutasses 2018). The shortage of medical doctors is indeed leading to creating long waiting time for first appointments. Tele-dermatology reduces waiting time and allows early assessment of the lesion and its treatment (Finnane, 2017).

The objective of this paper is to present an experiment carried out in France (Hauts-de-France region) for 5 years and to analyze the quantitative data obtained by the technological platform collecting and relaying tele-expertise in dermatology. The results in terms of time to treatment, addressed skin lesions, and patients' medical trajectory will be analyzed. The issue of remuneration for the medical act of providing tele-expertise will also be discussed, as a key factor in assessing medico-economical sustainability of this initiative.

2. METHODS

This is a retrospective, observational study based on data from real practice (RWD, Real World Data), i.e. data generated during routine clinical practice (Makady, 2017). The data come from a French experiment carried out from November 2015 to December 2020 in the Hauts-de-France region.

2.1 The French Experiment

Declining medical demographics of dermatologists is a reality in the Hauts-de-France region, with a 9.5% decrease over the 2007-2016 period and a density of 3.6 dermatologists per 100,000 inhabitants, vs. 5.1% in France (CNOM, 2016). Based on this observation and in order to promote faster treatment of patients with a suspicious skin lesion identified by their GP during a consultation, an organization making it possible to make the best use of the medical resources available in the region, has been developed.

This experiment began in November 2015 in the departments of Aisne, Oise and Somme, then extended in 2018 to the Hauts-de-France territory and is still in the experimentation phase. Using a dermatology tele-expertise software (online application), GPs can seek advice and/or action from a dermatologist.

Before being able to request an opinion on the dermatology tele-expertise application, GP must undergo training (first-hand, which has evolved into e-learning via a training platform, then into a webinar). The training aims at presenting the implementation of tele-expertise in dermatology, the use of the dedicated application, medical responsibility issues, and above all to deepen GPs clinical understanding of skin cancer screening, which actually was a strong request from these practitioners.

When a skin cancer is suspected, the procedure involves a sequence of activities. First, when the GP receives a patient with a suspicious dermatological lesion (identified by the doctor or by the patient himself), he offers the patient a tele-expertise, to which the patient may or may not consent.

Using a dermatology tele-expertise application available on a mobile phone, the GP completes a form containing patient information, takes photos and sends them to the dermatologist. The dermatologist has 7 days to respond, either by connecting to the platform available on a computer or to the application available on a mobile phone.

As soon as the expert opinion is generated by the dermatologist, the GP receives a notification on his application and can contact his patient to inform him of the expertise and the follow-up to be given (monitoring, appointment, etc.).

2.2 Available Data

The data available originate from two tele-expertise software platforms (Inovelan from 2015 to 2018 and Maincare from 2018 to 2020) used in the project. A total of 1,812 tele-expertise initiated by their GP with a remote expert opinion were implemented. The available data relate to the demographic and clinical profile of the patient, the dates of request for an opinion and the dates of expert return, the motive for the request, the type of skin lesion or tumor, the diagnosis proposed by the expert, the conduct to be taken following the diagnosis (e.g.: no treatment; meeting with dermatologist; clinical follow-up or surveillance by GP etc.). Also available are data of on online chat function allowing GPs and dermatologists to exchange more qualitative information.

3. RESULTS

3.1 Details on the Use of Tele-Expertise

1,812 tele-expertise requests were made between November 2015 and December 2020 by GP. Regarding gender of included patients, requests were made for 47% of men and 53% of women. The average age was 55.5 years old, the youngest was a baby and the oldest 99 years old. Patients with a history of skin cancer represented 14,5%.

There was a positive evolution in the number of tele-expertise from 2016 (n= 289) to 2020 (n=713). The number of doctors involved had evolved positively over the period. The number of GP increased from 36 in 2016 to 126 in 2020 and the number of dermatologists from 16 in 2016 to 25 in 2020. GPs have shown themselves to be more and more interested in tele-expertise. The number of dermatologists is limited in the Hauts-de-France region and due to the retirement of some of them, the number is decreasing a little over the project's time period.

3.2 A Request for Tele-Expertise not Limited to the Most Serious Cases

The objective of the tele-expertise was to enable a GP to contact a dermatologist for a suspected skin cancer. However, GPs requested a tele-expertise because they thought they were dealing with a skin cancer in only 6,6% of cases, a benign tumor in 13,47% of cases and expressed doubts in 66,50%. In the end, the dermatologists' responses did diagnose a malignant tumor in 14.84% of cases, a benign tumor in 42.39% of cases and they shared uncertainty in diagnosis based only on the medical file and photos for 35.9% of cases.

This is confirmed by the type of lesions detected by the dermatologist. The frequency of distribution of lesions with a malignant, benign or undefined character is presented in table 1. Only 28,44% of lesions are classified as skin cancers, while 5,9% are pre-cancerous lesions.

Table 1. Frequency of distribution of lesions

Cancerous lesions	Pre-cancerous lesions	Benign lesions	Not determined
Basal cell carcinoma (10,13%) Squamous cell carcinoma (3,97%) Bowen's disease (1,74%) Dubreuilh melanom (0,49%) Keratoacanthoma (0,8%) Unspecified skin cancer (11,31%)	Actinic keratosis (5,9%)	Naevus (21%) Seborrheic keratosis (18,95%) Angiome (1,49%) Histiocytofibrome (1,42%) Wart (0,93%) Cyst (0,93%) Fibroma (0,87%) Botriomycome (0,87%) Papillom (0,68%) Lentigo (0,31%)	Unspecified (17,38%) Others (1,67%)

The question then arises as to whether the use of tele-expertise may have been diverted from its initial objective and allows the GP easier access to the dermatologist for less urgent cases.

Tele-expertise improves medical regulation of patients depending on emergency level. In parallel with this analysis of system use in real-life, a qualitative study was carried out by social science researchers from EHESP School of Public Health. They demonstrated, based on a survey of GPs involved in the experiment, that "*tele-expertise is a well-accepted technological innovation in dermatology among GP, which enables the best use of the scarce medical resources [in dermatology] available in the region and to address the needs of patients*" (Marrauld, 2021). Moreover, the tele-expertise platform could reduce the time taken to access the dermatologist (Marrauld, 2021). This is one of the important consequences of tele-expertise development, which issue is addressed below.

3.3 Impact on patient care access time

Different access times are identified:

- The access times to the first dermatology consultation, that is, the waiting time for initial treatment;
- The average response time and diagnosis by the specialist which depends on whether the lesion is malignant or benign, the median waiting time for patients with melanoma was 14 days and 13.5 days for squamous cell carcinoma in the British study by May (2008);
- The time for implementing the action to be taken: biopsy, surgical intervention (excision). Excision make it possible to confirm the malignant character of a lesion. The tele-dermatology approach facilitates its access: the average time of biopsy of cancerous lesions was measured at 13.8 days for the traditional practice vs. 9.7 days for tele-dermatology (Kahn, 2013).

In the case of our study, we calculated the time between the date of request for a dermatologist's opinion by the GP, and the date of expertise transmitted by the dermatologist to the data exchange platform.

The average time between the tele-expertise request and the expert's return is 5.094 days on average (SD = 14,54). The median is 0,797. To compare this figure with the traditional time taken to take care of a dermatology patient in the region, we interviewed 13 general practitioners. They estimate at 171 days (5,7 months) the time to obtain an appointment with the dermatologist, despite the support in a coordinated care course started by the GP. The differential is 166 days and it is statistically significant.

Figure 1 shows the time between the result of the tele-expertise, and a new consultation with the dermatologist.

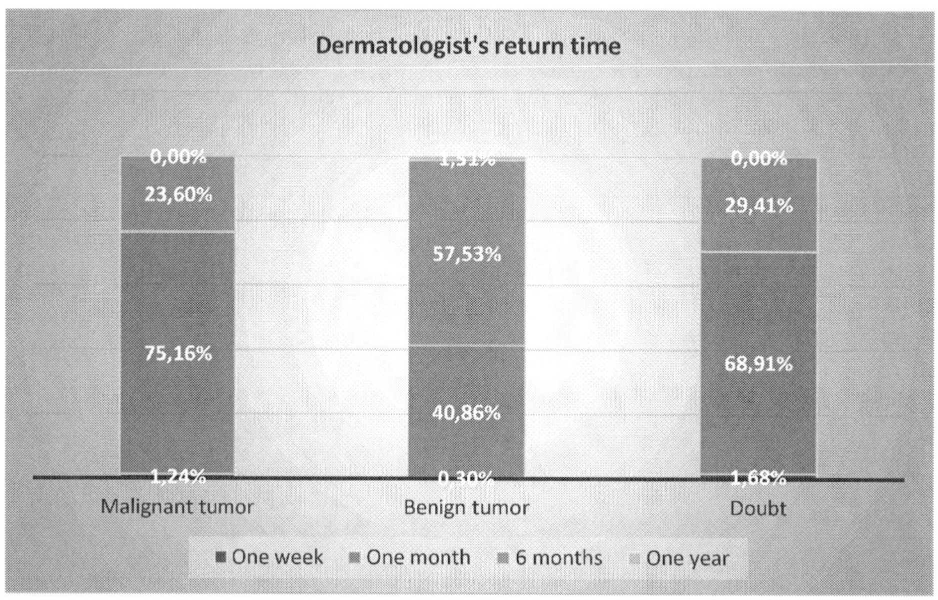

Figure 1. Delays between the result of the tele-expertise and a new consultation with the dermatologist

The dermatologist takes over the tele-expertise in less than a month when a skin cancer has been detected. Consultation times are longer for benign tumors because dermatologists will wait to follow the evolution of the lesion at 3 or 6 months in order to make the best medical decision. And when the diagnostic could not be clearly established by tele-expertise, the deadlines are also shortened. The use of a dermatoscope makes it possible to have a diagnosis with greater certainty, in particular for malignant lesions and then treat the patient as quickly as possible.

We can still conclude that tele-expertise makes it possible to reduce the time taken to obtain an appointment with the specialist medical doctor. This has been confirmed in other studies, without yet having a consensus on the duration gained. Börve (2013) shows a decrease in the time taken to obtain an appointment from 80 days to 2 days. He also noted a drop in the time taken for surgery (from 85 days to 36 days). In New Zealand, the average tele-dermatologist response time was 2.07 hours (McGoey, 2015). In the study by Coloma (2019) in Chile, the average time to be diagnosed with tele-dermatology was 12.6 days. This time was reduced by 6.4 days after the involvement of a new dermatologist in the team, which also shows that tele-dermatology certainly makes it possible to compensate for medical demographic problems, provided they are in sufficient number to provide a remote response. The differences in terms of number of days of patient care depends on the organization of the health system, medical demography and for tele-dermatology the size of the network of doctors involved, the number of requests, the ergonomics of the technological platform.

3.4 Impact on the Patient's Care Path

Tele-expertise, as it is organized in Hauts-de-France, does not change the course of the patient's care path, nor does it affect the role of the GP in the healthcare process or value chain. Only the access to the specialist is facilitated, in particular with access times being reduced. Following the tele-expertise, the dermatologists indicate whether a treatment is needed. The recommended course of action after the tele-expertise was as follows (Figure 2).

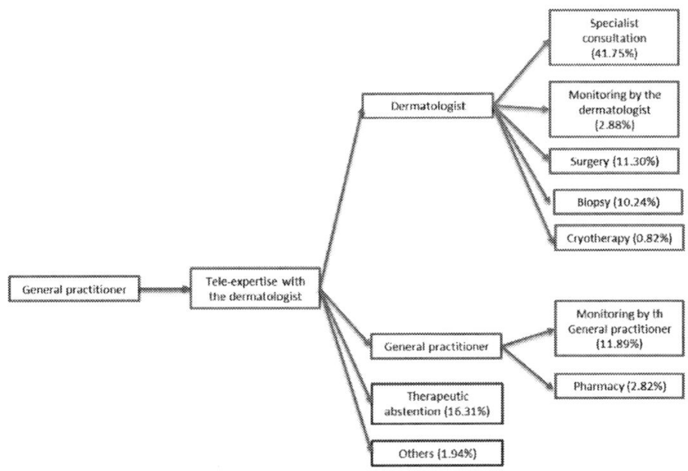

Figure 2. Actions to be taken recommended by the dermatologist following the tele-expertise

In 55.95% of cases, tele-expertise revealed a need for follow-up by the dermatologist. The GP is able to resume monitoring the patient for 11.90% of cases. But, in 16% of cases, the lesions observed did not require treatment and allows another patient to be cared for.

Even though there were only 25% of skin cancer detected, more than half of the cases required a visit to the dermatologist. Tele-expertise thus allows better care, even for mild cases.

This type of representation in the form of a decision tree will allow us to identify the savings achievable thanks to tele-expertise. Indeed, one of the current challenges is to determine the best business model for tele-expertise.

4. A CHALLENGE: THE REMUNERATION OF THE TELE-EXPERTISE ACT

At the economic level, Snoswell's systematic literature review (2016) shows that tele-dermatology is cost-effective, and the savings are greater, the more distant from the dermatologist's office patients are. This means less travel for patients (Ferrandiz, 2017), as well as an increase in their productivity because they lose fewer days of work. Patients also get treatments more quickly and some useless treatments are even avoided, such as for instance biopsies that are not required if the tumor is not benign.

From the dermatologist's point of view, tele-expertise helps save time because these medical specialists can treat each case more quickly (Whited, 2015; Ferrandiz, 2017), and because fewer cases are presented to them (due to the upstream triage of patients). In 2015, in their literature review, Gordon et al. confirm that economic analyzes of the early detection of skin cancer are still necessary and must be carried out (Gordon, 2015).

However, tele-dermatology implies that the GP completes the electronic files on the platform used, for some this can represent a double entry and a waste of time or they do not do it and the data is lacking. Therefore, the most impacting sustainability issue here is the lack of remuneration for this act in a number of countries, as well as the absence of an associated business model, that makes it worthwhile for the dermatologist to join.

Within the framework of the French experiment, avoided savings were observed in terms of kilometers avoided for patients, and less specialist consultations and examinations. These savings made, as well as the costs incurred (technology, coordination...), have yet to be measured. Two medico-economic research protocols are in progress.

The medico-economic results will also make it possible to adjust the level of remuneration for tele-dermatology acts for applicants and those required. In France, tele-expertise acts have been reimbursed by common law since February 2019. It is the first country to reimburse the tele-expertise act at a national level and for any doctor, whatever his specialty (Ohannessian, 2020). The question arises as to whether the amount invoiced is sufficient (from 12 to 20 € for the required doctor – medical expert – and from 5 to 10 € for the requesting – the GP). Compensation was then reviewed during the summer of 2021 (20 euros for the required doctor and 10 euros for the requesting doctor).

When this project was set up, a remuneration model was negotiated, namely 14 euros for a request for an opinion by a GP in addition to the classic consultation and 46 euros for the dermatologist during the diagnosis and / or the conduct to be taken issued. The remuneration was negotiated because the model based on article 36 of the law n°2013-1203 on the financing of Social Security for 2014 provided for the dermatologist 27 euros while the remuneration of the general practitioner was not determined. Note that the compensation model proposed in the context of the experiment, with regard to amendment 6 to the medical agreement, is superior to conventional negotiations.

The qualitative analysis carried out (Marrauld, 2021) showed that general practitioners were satisfied with the remuneration offered by the experiment, but this is not a priority. Their priority was really to be able to quickly access the dermatologist. On the other hand, for the dermatologist, carrying out an expertise takes time and they consider it necessary to be able to be remunerated at their fair value. They believe that the € 20 bill is insufficient, but that they are satisfied with the proposal made by the Hauts-De-France region. To maintain this level of remuneration, it is necessary to provide proof that the use of tele-expertise allows savings to the health system, which is why an economic evaluation will be carried out.

5. CONCLUSION

After 5 years of using tele-expertise in Hauts-De-France region, doctors and patients have shown an interest in treating suspicious skin lesions with the expert support from a remote dermatologist. Several advantages were highlighted: a feedback from dermatologists in reduced time, a slightly modified and more adapted treatment path, management of all types of lesions. Once these real word data have been submitted to an economic evaluation protocol, it could be justified to perpetuate this type of application of telemedicine, and to develop it further.

The major take-ways about these 5 years analysis are then:

- Tele-dermatology is a triage tool for the dermatologist, improving the chances of survival for patients and optimizing the consultation;
- for the GP, this allows easier access to the dermatologist and to benefit from companionship with the dermatologist, this would allow the GP to improve their skills;
- for the patient, this puts back into the care pathway people who have given up;
- finally, it is a real decision-making tool to monetize the financing of telemedicine.

The perspectives of this work are therefore to compare the real data on the use of tele-expertise with the real data on the consumption of care provided by patients, and to compare them to patients with traditional care. In addition, interviews with patients are planned to find out their perception of tele-expertise and their satisfaction with this new type of care.

ACKNOWLEDGEMENT

The authors wish to thank the Hauts-De-France Regional Health Agency (ARS) and the National Cancer Institute (INCa) for their funding of and support to the experiment.

REFERENCES

Bashshur, R. L. et al. 2015. The empirical foundations of teledermatology: a review of the research evidence, *Telemedicine and e-Health*, 21(12), pp. 953-979.

Börve, A. Et al. 2013. Mobile teledermoscopy-there's an app for that!, *Dermatol Pract Concept*, 3(2), pp. 41-48.

Chen, C.H. et al. 2014. Patient-centered wound teleconsultation for cutaneous wounds: a feasibility study, *Ann Plast Surg.*, 72(2), pp.220-4.

Chuchu, N. et al. 2018. Teledermatology for diagnosing skin cancer in adults, *Cochrane Database Syst Rev.*, *12*(12), CD013193.

Coates, D. F., Bowling, J., and Soyer, H. P. 2011. Telemedicine and Teledermatology. *Telemedicine in Dermatology*, 67.

Coustasse, A. et al. 2019. Use of teledermatology to improve dermatological access in rural areas, *Telemedicine and e-Health*, *25*(11), pp.1022-1032.

Fabbrocini, G. et al. 2011. Teledermatology: from prevention to diagnosis of nonmelanoma and melanoma skin cancer, *Int J Telemed Appl.*, 125762.

Ferrándiz, L. et al. 2017. Internet-based skin cancer screening using clinical images alone or in conjunction with dermoscopic images: A randomized teledermoscopy trial, *Journal of the American Academy of Dermatology*, *76*(4), pp.676-682.

Finnane, A. et al. 2017. Teledermatology for the diagnosis and management of skin cancer: a systematic review, *JAMA dermatology*, *153*(3), pp. 319-327.

Gordon, L. G., & Rowell, D. 2015. Health system costs of skin cancer and cost-effectiveness of skin cancer prevention and screening: a systematic review, *European Journal of Cancer Prevention*, *24*(2), pp.141-149.

Makady A. et al. 2017. What is real -world data? A review of definitions based on literature and stakeholder interviews. *Value Health*. *20*(7):858 - 865.

Marrauld L. et al. 2021

May, C., Giles, L., & Gupta, G. 2008. Prospective observational comparative study assessing the role of store and forward teledermatology triage in skin cancer, *Clinical and Experimental Dermatology: Clinical dermatology*, *33*(6), pp.736-739.

McGoey, S. T., Oakley, A., & Rademaker, M. 2015. Waikato teledermatology: a pilot project for improving access in New Zealand, *Journal of telemedicine and telecare*, *21*(7), pp. 414-419.

Ohannessian R. et al. 2020. France Is the First Country to Reimburse Tele-Expertise at a National Level to All Medical Doctors, *Telemed J E Health*.

Pala, P., Bergler-Czop, B. S., & Gwiżdż, J. M. 2020. Teledermatology: idea, benefits and risks of modern age–a systematic review based on melanoma, *Advances in Dermatology and Allergology/Postępy Dermatologii i Alergologii*, *37*(2), pp.159.

Snoswell, C. Et al. 2016. Cost-effectiveness of store-and-forward teledermatology: a systematic review, *JAMA dermatology*, *152*(6), pp. 702-708.

Trettel, A., Eissing, L., & Augustin, M. 2018. Telemedicine in dermatology: findings and experiences worldwide–a systematic literature review, *Journal of the European Academy of Dermatology and Venereology*, *32*(2), pp. 215-224.

van den Akker, T. et al. 2001. Teledermatology as a tool for communication between general practitioners and dermatologists, *Journal of Telemedicine and Telecare*, *7*(4), pp.193-198.

Whited, J.D. 2015. Teledermatology, *Med Clin North Am*. *99*, pp. 1365–1379.

PROPOSAL FOR A MODEL FOR DETECTING FAKE NEWS ON SOCIAL MEDIA IN MEXICO

Carlos Augusto Jiménez Zarate[1] and Leticia Amalia Neira Tovar[2]
Universidad Autónoma de Nuevo León, Mexico
[1]M. eng.
[2]Dra

ABSTRACT

The emission of false news on social networks has been increasing continuously, this work analyzes the different automatic detection techniques used for false news, proposes an integration of different machine learning algorithms in addition to the development of a new data set of news tweets in Mexico. To do this, an extraction of tweets from the Mexican media and from sites known as transmitters of false news in Mexico was carried out. The dataset classification test showed that it was the passive-aggressive algorithm that obtained the best accuracy with 79.6%.

KEYWORDS

Fake News, Machine Learning, Social Media

1. INTRODUCTION

The increase in the use of socio-digital platforms has brought with it an increase in harmful practices to social communication, such as the spread of fake news, the use of automated user accounts or profiles known as bots, but there are also the trolls that are users who regularly broadcast provocative and inflammatory content against other users in order to seek self-assertion (Fenoll., 2015).

In the spread of fake news, it is important to be able to analyze the users who are victims of fake news, and some users with certain personality characteristics are more likely to trust fake news (Shu et al., 2019).

Given the magnitude of the spread and spread of fake news, the application of various strategies to try to lessen the impact of fake news has been studied, such as putting warning messages on content categorized as fake news, ratings of the sources influenced the beliefs of the users and established that this rating is a viable measure for fake news (Kim et al., 2017).

But many of these messages have not been shown to have an impact on the detection of fake news by users of social networks (Ross et al., 2019)

There are dimensions such as: Age, gender, education and culture, as factors in the acceptance of fake news, but it is age that has the greatest influence on the acceptance of fake news (Rampersad et al, 2020).

Other users tend to share fake news due to behaviors such as fear of missing something, or fatigue in the use of social networks (Talwar et al., 2019).

The explosive growth of fake news and its impact on different areas such as democracy, justice and public trust has seen an increase in the demand for systems to detect fake news using new datasets, patterns and various latest generation (Zhou et al., 2019).

Perez-Rosas et al (2017) presented two data sets for the detection of fake news that cover seven different news domains, also described the extraction and validation process in great detail, identifying the linguistic differences between fake news and news real.

Kim et al (2018) determined that there is a bias in the information and that most users of social networks cannot distinguish a fake news from a real news, in such a way that, of 83 participants in their research, only one 17% were able to detect a fake news, and only one person was able to detect a fake news more than 60% of the time.

One of the current issues where fake news is having an important impact is in COVID-19, they carried out an investigation, in which they developed a Dateset that includes fake news data from public fact-checking sites such as PolitiFacts, Snopes7 and Boomlive, (Patwa et al., 2020).

Sharma et al (2021) implemented the detection of fake news, using machine learning algorithms, for which they used the "LIAR" dataset from the Politifact fact-checking site. For the preprocessing of the data, they started with data cleaning that consists of removing punctuations, eliminating empty words and the stemming function, which allows reducing a word to its root form, for example: Title, Title -> Title. They then implemented function generation to generate a number of characteristics, such as word count, frequency of large and single words, and n-grams. This in order for the algorithms to understand the text and perform the grouping and classification. Within this phase is the vectorization of the data, which is a process of encoding the text as whole numbers. Another vectorization method is the n-gram method quantifies all the combinations of adjacent words or letters of length "n" that can be found in the source text. For the detection of fake news, they used the algorithms of Naive-Bayes, Random Forest, Logistic Regression and finally the Passive-Aggressive Classifier. After testing the four algorithms, they determined in their research that the logistic regression algorithm was the one with the highest performance, reaching 75%.

The vast majority of research on fake news has focused on Twitter, but the Naive-Bayes classifier has obtained good results for Facebook, achieving an accuracy of 74% Granik et al (2017).

In addition, there are the artificial positioning strategies known as Astroturfing, which are campaigns that try to influence public opinion through the appearance of viralization of content in socio-digital networks, Astroturfing has two characteristics: The use of deception to hide the origins of the orchestrated campaigns and the lack of transparency of the sponsors of such campaigns (Leiser, 2016).

Khan et al (2019) carried out a benchmark between different pre-trained advanced linguistic models of Machine Learning for the detection of fake news, such as:

The BERT (Bidirectional Encoder Representations from Transformers), which is a model for learning contextual representations of unlabeled words. They focused on BERT-Base which has 12 layers with 12 attention heads and 110 million parameters.

RoBERTa (Optimized Focus). This model achieves better performance by using mini batches to train the model for a longer time through more data.

DistilBERT. It is a smaller, faster and cheaper and lighter version of the original BERT, they have 40% less parameters than the BERT-Base.

ELECTRA (Efficiently LEarning an Encoder that Classifs Token Replacements Accurately). This self-supervised learning model of language representation. This model takes an input text and randomly masks the text with an input token, ELECTRA is trained to distinguish real input tokens from fake input tokens.

ELMO (Language model embeddings). It is a contextualized word representation of a deep bidirectional model that is trained on a large text corpus. It has 2 layers and 93.6 million parameters.

Zervopoulos et al (2020) used various Machine Learning techniques, such as Naive Bayes, Suuport Vector Machine, C4.5 and Ramdon Forest, to be able to classify the linguistic characteristics of fake news, for this they took the tweets in English and Chinese from a Twitter database to classify fake news.

Gao et al. (2016) evaluated the performance of the convolutional neural network (RNN) algorithm and for the detection of rumors they determined a performance of 0.827.

Oshikawa et al (2018) implemented an investigation where they used various models of natural language processing (NLP) for the detection of fake news, others such as Cueva et al (2020) compared the natural language processing technique with various models of Artificial Intelligence , among them the Long Short Term Memory (LSTM), Gated Recurrent Unit (GRU) for this they built a Dataset that was based on a data set from the Kaggle platform, which offers various data repositories for different types of projects, including the detection of fake news.

Liu et al (2020) (2020) presented research for the early detection of fake news, through a neural network model which they named "Fake News Early Detection" or FNED, which is composed of three components. A multiple response function extractor that takes into account the text of responses and the user's profile, a mechanism that highlights important answers, and a grouping mechanism to perform feature aggregation.

Ksieniewicz et al (2019) exposed the different types of digital analysis that can be applied to a news item to detect whether or not it is fake news, among them, the reputation of the author of the news, an image analysis, to determine the context and the detection of manipulation, the analysis of text using natural language processing techniques, psycholinguistic or non-linguistic analysis, and finally the analysis of the news metadata. In addition, they emphasized the impact of fake news during the current COVID-19 pandemic, such is the case of fake news that claimed that "5G" cell phone antennas were causing the coronavirus.

Reis et al (2019), worked to determine new functions for the detection of fake news, also addressed the different analysis topics that can be performed on the text, such as:

Language characteristics (syntax) and they analyzed the characteristics with methods such as the bag of words, n-grams, labeling, number of words and syllables per sentence.

Monti et al (2019) developed a model for the detection of fake news focused on the study of its spread, taking into account data such as content, user profile and user activity. They determined that the structure and propagation of social networks are relevant characteristics that allow the adequate detection of fake news, and they also established that fake news can be detected efficiently in the first stages of propagation or diffusion.

2. DEVELOPMENT AND RESULTS

Figure 1 shows the proposed model to classify news as false or true, where the text of the tweet and the users who broadcast the content (news) are classified using machine learning algorithms. To find out if the content of a news item is false or real. To determine if a tweet is viral or not, social network analysis will be used, through which it will be determined by statistics of the number of likes by adding the number of retweets obtained for each tweet.

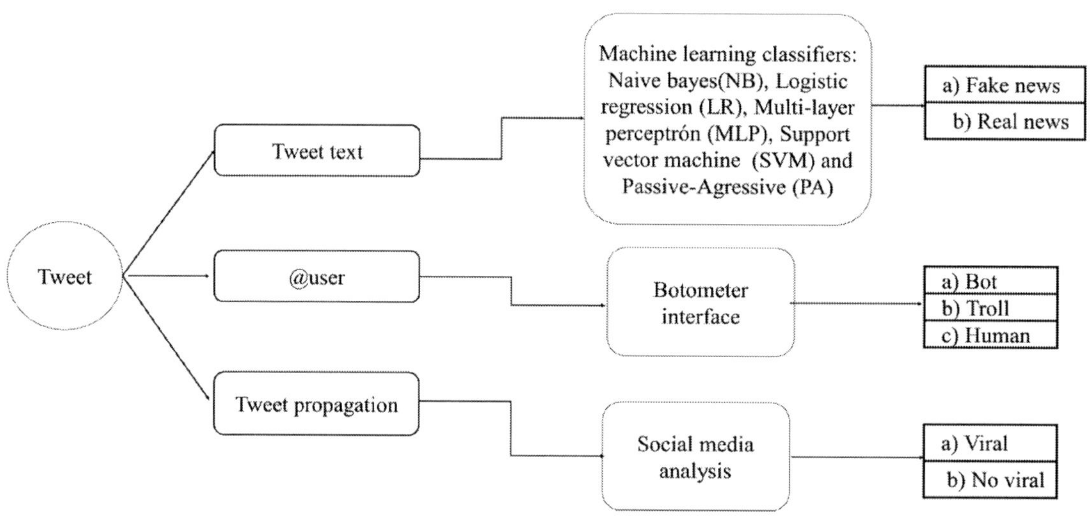

Figure 1. Fake news detection model in social media in Mexico

For this paper, only the first part will be addressed, which is the classification of the text of the tweet into fake news or real news. for which the construction of a dataset of news content broadcast on Twitter Mexico was carried out.

For the development of a dataset of Mexican media tweets, various Mexican news media accounts that have a Twitter account were taken into account; the Twitter API was used to extract the tweets.

To extract tweets, it is necessary to have the api keys provided by Twitter and establish the keywords or accounts from which the streaming will be carried out. Figure 2 shows the process for the development of the data set related to the news media in Mexico that have a Twitter account.

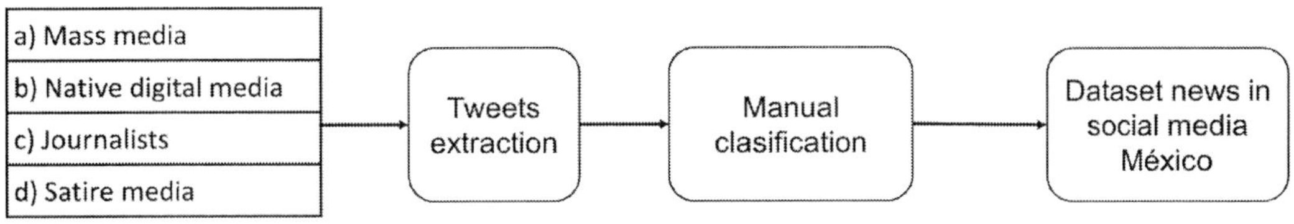

Figure 2. Dataset development process

Once the tweets were obtained, they were classified manually, for which a team of volunteers was formed, who were shown the definition of the Cambridge dictionary that says that fake new are: "False stories that seem to be news, spread on the internet or using other means, generally created to influence political opinions or as a joke". For the definition of news, the dictionary of the Royal Spanish Academy was used, which says the news is: Information about something that is considered interesting to disseminate; disclosed fact or new information regarding a matter or a person.

The total number of tweets extracted was 5,108 tweets, of which 1,126 tweets were manually classified in the two categories proposed for this work that are "fake news" or "real news"

This data set will be used to form the training data set. Table 1 shows us the classification percentages of the training data set, it can be seen that the percentage of tweets classified as false news represents 52.8% and the percentage of tweets classified as real news represents 47.1%, thus obtaining a balanced dataset.

Table 1.Types of tweets in the dataset (manual classification)

Tweets type	%
Fake news	52.8
Real news	47.1

Table 2 shows the structure of the dataset and the text of some of the tweets that were classified for the development of the new dataset of news tweets in social media in Mexico. It can be seen that it is composed of two columns, the first refers to the body of the tweet or plain text, and the second column is the label with which the content of the tweet or text was categorized.

Table 2. Sample of news tweets that were classified as false news (Fake) or real news (True)

Tweets text	Label
Peña Nieto sabía que Juan Gabriel estaba vivo pero le pidió ocultarse ha... https://t.co/bHK2IW9YRk vía @YouTube	FAKE
Captaron a Juan Gabriel en la marcha del orgullo gay 2019! https://t.co/drEe70MqdF vía @YouTube	FAKE
Solo llegaron tres mil dosis. El gobierno y Morena no paran de hacer el ridículo. https://t.co/hzLr0eUNUR	FAKE
AMLO autoriza nuevo partido de Elba Esther y le da $20 mil millones de ... https://t.co/zE9NOh6rso vía @YouTube	FAKE
El primer mandatario indicó que este "es el país con más #fraudes electorales en la historia... se tienen que termi… https://t.co/BAWcgXO5r7	TRUE
El sóftbol dará inicio a los Juegos Olímpicos de Tokio el miércoles, con el enfrentamiento entre Japón y Australi… https://t.co/YS4ENYzYov	TRUE
Funcionarios de la @Registraduria de #Colombia reconocieron el trabajo que realiza el @iecm en materia electoral… https://t.co/uP014m6OOX	TRUE
Guerrero retrocedió de semáforo verde a amarillo ante repunte de casos de #Covid19, informó el Gobernador Héctor As… https://t.co/0PoQRlqsxk	TRUE

There are various classification techniques such as:

The Naive-Bayes algorithm (NB). This algorithm is a posterior probability classifier. This algorithm assumes that for a sample X, its attributes X_1, X_ (2,) ..., X_ (n,) have a linear independence with respect to the value of the class, so that the conditional probability is presented as the product of the conditional probabilities of the attributes separately. This algorithm assumes that the occurrence or non-occurrence of any characteristic is not related to the occurrence or non-occurrence of any other characteristic (Frank et al., 2000).

Logistic regression (LR). This algorithm works in a similar way to linear regression, but they have a binomial response variable, and it is also capable of modeling probability based on individual characteristics. But since the probability is a ratio, what is modeled in this algorithm is the logarithm of the probability (Sperandei, 2014).

Multi-layer Perceptron (MLP). It is a supervised learning algorithm that learns from a function training on a dataset where "m" are the input dimensions and "o" are the output dimensions. Unlike logistic regression between the input and output layer there can be one or more non-linear layers called hidden layers. Although this algorithm is very common, it is also necessary to take into account some of the problems, such as the choice of parameters and network configuration, if there is a small learning rate it can lead to a slow convergence, but if there is a slow learning rate high this can cause jumps in the solution (Popescu, 2009).

Support Vector Machine (SVM). This algorithm can be described as a surface learning algorithm of two distinct classes of entry points. The SVM tries to draw a hyperplane to be able to classify vectors with a high degree of similarity (Evgeniou & Pontil, 2001).

Passive-aggressive (PA). This algorithm is also known as passive-aggressive online; it has a large margin for online ranking, they are called passive because if the prediction is correct, it maintains the representation and does not make any exchange and aggressive because if the prediction is incorrect, it makes changes in the representation, that is to say, some exchange in the representation can correct the prediction; its main parameters are: C. It is to formalize and denotes the penalty that the model will make in a prediction error; max_iter. It is the maximum number of duplications that the model performs on the training data (Suganthi, 2021).

Table 3 shows the precision results of the algorithms proposed for the fake news detection model, being the passive aggressive algorithm (PA) the one that obtained the best result for the test dataset of news tweets in Mexico, with a 79.6%, followed by the Naive Bayes (NB) algorithm who obtained an accuracy of 78.2%, the algorithm that obtained the lowest score was the multi-layer perceptron (MLP) with 71.6%. For this paper the user analysis and the analysis of the propagation of the tweets are left for a future delivery. However, it is proposed to perform the analysis of the user profile through the Botometer interface tool which uses a machine learning model, it also offers an API to integrate the analysis of several accounts through a simple open code and free access.

Table 3. Accuracy of algorithms for the classification of tweets of the proposed model for the detection of fake news on social media in Mexico

Algorithm	Accuracy
Naive-Bayes (NB)	78.2%
Logistic regresion (LR)	75.6%
Multi-layer Perceptron (MLP)	71.6%
Support vector machine (SVM)	76.0%
Passive-agressive (PA)	79.6%

3. CONCLUSION AND FUTURE WORK

The model presented proposes the integration of different algorithms of machine learning and integrating it with other analyzes such as the user profile and the level of spread or viralization of the news tweets. For this, a totally new data set was developed with tweets from the year 2021, made up of 1,126 tweets that were manually classified into real news (True) and false news (Fake). The test of the data set showed that it was the passive-aggressive algorithm that obtained the best classification result with 79.6% accuracy. Although the results are below 95%, it shows that the development of a new dataset of news tweets in Mexico is feasible. As future work, work will be done on the expansion of classified content, and the manual classification process will be reviewed to increase accuracy, the integration of the analysis of user profiles and the level of propagation or viralization; and thus, be able to implement the false news detection model in social networks in Mexico.

REFERENCES

Cueva, E. et al. (2020) "*Detecting Fake News on Twitter Using Machine Learning Models*," pp. 1–14.

Crammer, K. et al. (2006). Online Passive-Aggressive Algorithms. Journal of Machine Learning Research. 7. 551-585.

De, G.L., Sarracén, P. et al, (2019) "*Análisis y detección de odio en mensajes de Twitter.*"

Evgeniou, T. et al, (2001) "Support vector machines: Theory and applications," in *Lecture Notes in Computer Science (including subseries Lecture Notes in Artificial Intelligence and Lecture Notes in Bioinformatics)*. Springer Verlag, pp. 249–257. doi:10.1007/3-540-44673-7_12.

Fenoll, V. (2015) "*El trol de Internet. Estrategias de los usuarios para controlar el diálogo en los medios digitales durante el juicio de Francisco Camps,*" Dígitos. Revista de Comunicación Digital, 0(1), pp. 179–198. doi:10.7203/rd.v0i1.9.

Frank, E., et al, (2000) *Technical Note: Naive Bayes for Regression.*

Gao, W. et al. (2016) *Detecting rumors from microblogs with recurrent neural networks*. Available at: https://ink.library.smu.edu.sg/sis_research.

Khan, J.Y. et al. (2019) "*A Benchmark Study of Machine Learning Models for Online Fake News Detection.*" doi:10.1016/j.mlwa.2021.100032.

Kim, A., et al, (2018) *Combating Fake News on Social Media with Source Ratings: The Effects of User and Expert Reputation Ratings*. Available at: https://ssrn.com/abstract=3090355.

Kim, C. et al, (2017) "*Like, comment, and share on Facebook: How each behavior differs from the other,*" *Public Relations Review*, 43(2), pp. 441–449. doi:10.1016/j.pubrev.2017.02.006.

Ksieniewicz, et al, 2019). *Machine Learning Methods for Fake News Classification.* 10.1007/978-3-030-33617-2_34.

Leiser, M. (2016) "*AstroTurfing , ' CyberTurfing ' and other online persuasion campaigns,*" *European Journal of Law and Technology*, 7(1), pp. 1–27.

Liu, Y. et al, (2019) *Early Detection of Fake News on Social Media Through Propagation Path Classification with Recurrent and Convolutional Networks*. Available at: www.aaai.org.

Monti, F. et al. (2019) "*Fake News Detection on Social Media using Geometric Deep Learning.*" Available at: http://arxiv.org/abs/1902.06673.

Oshikawa, R., et al, (2018) "*A Survey on Natural Language Processing for Fake News Detection.*" Available at: http://arxiv.org/abs/1811.00770.

Patwa, P. et al. (2020) "*Fighting an Infodemic: COVID-19 Fake News Dataset.*" doi:10.1007/978-3.

Pérez-Rosas, V. et al. (2017) "*Automatic Detection of Fake News.*" Available at: http://arxiv.org/abs/1708.07104.

Popescu M. et al, (2009). Multilayer perceptron and neural networks. WSEAS Transactions on Circuits and Systems

Rampersad, G. et al, (2020) "*Fake news: Acceptance by demographics and culture on social media,*" *Journal of Information Technology and Politics*, 17(1), pp. 1–11. doi:10.1080/19331681.2019.1686676.

S. Garg et al, (2020) "Phony News Detection using Machine Learning and Deep-Learning Techniques," *2020 9th International Conference System Modeling and Advancement in Research Trends (SMART)*, 2020, pp. 27-32, doi: 10.1109/SMART50582.2020.9337120.

Shu, K., et al, (2019) "*Studying Fake News via Network Analysis: Detection and Mitigation,*" (January), pp. 43–65. doi:10.1007/978-3-319-94105-9_3.

Sperandei, Sandro. (2014). Understanding logistic regression analysis. Biochemia medica. 24. 12-8. 10.11613/BM.2014.003.

Suganthi, B. (2021). *"FAKEDETECTOR:Effective fake news deteccion with Passive Aggressive Algorithm".* Science, technology and development. ISSN: 0950-0707. Volume X Issue IX SEPTEMBER 2021. Page 193.

Talwar, et al, (2019). Why do people share fake news? Associations between the dark side of social media use and fake news sharing behavior. Journal of Retailing and Consumer Services. 51. 72-82. 10.1016/j.jretconser.2019.05.026.

Zervopoulos, A. et al. (2020) "*Hong Kong Protests: Using Natural Language Processing for Fake News Detection on Twitter,*" *IFIP Advances in Information and Communication Technology*, 584 IFIP, pp. 408–419. doi:10.1007/978-3-030-49186-4_34.

Zhou, X. et al. (2019) "*Fake News: Fundamental theories, detection strategies and challenges,*" in *WSDM 2019 - Proceedings of the 12th ACM International Conference on Web Search and Data Mining*. Association for Computing Machinery, Inc, pp. 836–837. doi:10.1145/3289600.3291382.

TRUST AND CYBERSICKNESS IN VR-MARKETING – INVESTIGATING IPD AND CYBERSICKNESS, AND THEIR EFFECTS ON TRUST, CUSTOMER VALUE, NPS, CROSS- AND UP-SELLING

Roger Seiler, Thierry Brodmann and Thomas Keller
Zurich University of Applied Sciences, St.-Georgen-Platz 2, P.O. Box, CH-8401 Winterthur, Switzerland

ABSTRACT

VR (virtual reality) is rapidly gaining attention from academia and the business world. The cost for hardware is diminishing, and consumer HMDs (head-mounted displays) are becoming increasingly affordable, thereby driving the popularity of this technology. Because immersive experiences can foster positive emotions, VR has also gained the attention of marketing departments. However, the virtual world comes with a risk of systems akin to motion sickness, and in VR, this is known as "cybersickness". In this study, cybersickness and its effects on customer-related constructs such as trust, customer value, cross- and up-selling, and NPS (net promoter Score) are experimentally tested. The IPD (interpupillary distance) is manipulated, and an SSQ (simulator sickness questionnaire) is used to test for sickness. Since cybersickness negatively affects customer value, NPS, and consumer trust in the vendor, we conclude that it is necessary to prevent this to ensure monetary and non-monetary customer values remain high.

KEYWORDS

VR,Cybersickness, IPD, Trust, Customer Value, NPS

1. INTRODUCTION

VR is becoming increasingly popular in production, product design of physical products (Farsi et al., 2020), and entire factories (Grieves, 2014) have digital twins. VR and AR (augmented reality) are fuelling the future of business (Wen, 2019), and even IoT and smart city concepts are considering extended reality (XR) (Andrade & Bastos, 2019) and investigating this emerging technology. When exploring virtual worlds, users immerse themselves in a digital space and respond emotionally to this experience. Therefore, it is no surprise that this has caught the attention of academia and business alike. Hard- and software, as well as knowledge and skills for implementing these experiences, come at a cost, and the latter in particular are rare. However, the price of HMDs is diminishing (Economist, 2020), and with the growing use of this technology, it is becoming increasingly accessible. Furthermore, drivers of the adoption of HMDs are composed of utilitarian as well as hedonic benefits, while health and privacy issues exist as barriers (Herz & Rauschnabel, 2019).

A link between enjoyment in VR and purchase intention has also been found (Manis & Choi, 2019). Indeed, VR can positively influence spatial presence, which in turn affects enjoyment (Shafer et al., 2018), and enjoyment diminishes the tendency towards cybersickness (Israel et al., 2019). Despite these positive effects, VR does not come without its problems, and understandably, cybersickness negatively affects (Shafer et al., 2018) the attractions of a virtual world.

This study investigates customer-related constructs such as trust, customer value, cross- and up-selling, and NPS as these are relevant specifically to both marketing and commercial success in general.

The paper is structured as follows: A literature review is initially conducted before the research questions and hypotheses are derived. We then describe the methodology and data collection before moving on to the analysis, discussion, concluding results, and implications.

2. LITERATURE

Empirical evidence suggests that positive effects of VR and AR can be seen in education (Garzón et al., 2019; Radu, 2014; Reisoğlu et al., 2017), smart cities (Lv et al., 2016), health care and medicine (Barsom et al., 2016), teamwork (Salvetti et al., 2018), premium and luxury retailing (Harren et al., 2019), and in VR-supported e-commerce (Papadopoulou, 2007). Nevertheless, the latest research on AR (Rese et al., 2017) and VR (Tussyadiah et al., 2018) suggests that hedonic and affective aspects should be taken into account, and trust will also be considered in this study. In a travel planning situation, immersion promotes positive behavioural intentions (Disztinger et al., 2017), so purchasing intentions and concepts related to products or services are included in this study.

Trust is generally called for when websites are visited, and this plays a role when interacting with artefacts (Beatty et al., 2011; Kim et al., 2008; Kim & Peterson, 2017). Furthermore, trust can positively affect our online purchasing actions (Chang & Chen, 2008; Kim & Peterson, 2017; Tang et al., 2012) and also has a role in virtual environments. VR has the potential to build (Kugler et al., 2019; Salantri, 2018) and even rebuild trust (Shahrdar et al., 2019). Similarly, AR can also build trust (Bilgili et al., 2019), which in turn has a positive impact on consumer purchase intentions (Lu et al., 2016) and satisfaction (Das, 2016; Papadopoulou, 2007). This tends to affect business success in general and, specifically, customer value (e.g. purchase intention).

The concept of customer value can be categorised into market and resource potentials (Tomczak & Rudolf-Sipötz, 2006). The former contains monetary aspects (e.g. purchases and cross- and up-selling), whereas the latter includes non-monetary elements (e.g. information- and referral potential such as word of mouth) (Tomczak & Rudolf-Sipötz, 2006). Hippner and Wilde differentiate between transaction and relation potentials of customers (Hippner et al., 2011; Hippner and Wilde, 2006), while the former are monetary and the latter aspects of a non-monetary nature (e.g. referral, information, and cooperation potential). Word-of-mouth (WOM) recommendation is an example of a non-monetary customer value.

Empirical evidence suggests that cross-selling is enhanced by face-to-face interaction and not by mediated communication (Värlander & Yakhlef, 2008). Nevertheless, the effects of trust on cross-selling behaviour are pointed out by Värlander and Yakhlef (2008). Consequently, as VR has the potential to build (Kugler et al., 2019; Salantri, 2018) and even rebuild trust (Shahrdar et al., 2019), it is unclear which effect holds in a cross-selling VR situation. Customer monetary value is also affected by trust (Kim & Peterson, 2017), and WOM or referrals can be positively influenced too (Ladeira et al., 2016). Similarly, emotions can affect the perception of service quality, be a significant predictor of satisfaction, and lead to WOM recommendations (White, 2010). Hence, if an immersive VR experience positively affects emotions, both satisfaction and WOM can be enhanced – and both are relevant for NPS.

The NPS, developed by Reichheld (2003), is based on a single question asking whether you would recommend a product/service to a friend on a scale from 1–10. Responses between 1 and 6 are called detractors, and responses 9 and 10 are called promotors. Answers 7 and 8 are categorised as passive. The NPS is calculated by subtracting the number of detractors in percentages terms from the number of promoters. Industry has widely adopted this score for measuring customer satisfaction as it is easy to apply in a business context and allows for benchmarking and comparisons within and between sectors.

The effect VR has on purchase intentions is device-dependant (Martínez-Navarro et al., 2019), and as mentioned above, cybersickness can also be an issue (Bruck & Watters, 2011; Davis et al., 2014; Israel et al., 2019; Shafer et al., 2018). No one feeling nauseous is likely to be in the best condition to make an important purchase. Adjusting the IPD of your HMD when exploring virtual worlds is crucial to clear vision, and failing to do so can lead to cybersickness, as empirical evidence shows (Kim & Park, 2019). Interestingly a larger-than-ideal IPD seems to prompt cybersickness more often than a lower-than-ideal IPD (Kim & Park, 2019). Since the evidence is unclear about how cybersickness affects customer value in VR-supported marketing and whether the wrong IPD can induce cybersickness, our research questions are as follows: *How does cybersickness affect customer-related constructs in VR? (RQ1)* and *How does IPD affect cybersickness in VR marketing? (RQ2).*

3. METHODOLOGY

Although this is a preliminary study, it tested for reactions using a questionnaire after exposing participants to a VR application. The test group has an IPD in their HMD that did not correspond to their actual IPD, which empirical evidence suggests might trigger cybersickness (Kim & Park, 2019). In our experiment, an offset of +6 mm was used.

Figure 1. Motorboat rental – VR island

Figure 2. Foot (red) and boat (yellow) routes

Mayer and Davis trust scales were used (Mayer et al., 1995; Mayer & Davis, 1999) to ensure easy comparison with earlier research. In addition, the three dimensions of "integrity", "competence", and "benevolence" from Mayer and Davis were shortened by Dreiskämper et al. (2016) to account for the motorboat scenario.

Customer value measurement was in line with Tewes (2003), building on the theory presented earlier in this paper. In addition, purchasing behaviour (intention to rent a motorboat), cross-selling (diving equipment rental for the boat trip), up-selling (a higher price for a more powerful motorboat), and referential potential in form of the NPS were all measured. Apart from the NPS, all ratings were measured on a five-point Likert scale.

This study used a common scale to measure cybersickness and compare these results to earlier research. Although it has its critics (Stone Iii, 2017), one of the most popular (Balk et al., 2013; Rebenitsch, 2015; Rebenitsch & Owen, 2016) scales for measuring cybersickness is the simulator sickness questionnaire (SSQ) – subdivided into nausea (SSQ-N), disorientation (SSQ-D), and oculomotor (SSQ-O). In line with Kennedy et al. (1993), the questionnaire was only filled out by participants who had already experienced VR to prevent the possibility of symptoms being triggered by suggestion alone. An exception to this approach was made for customer value; before being immersed in VR, participants were asked to answer the customer value questions as a baseline and provide their socio-demographic data. After the VR experience, customer value questions were repeated, and the difference between the baseline (pre-VR) and customer value (post-VR) was calculated.

In line with existing theory and empirical evidence, we derived the hypotheses in Table 1 below.

Table 1. Overview of the hypotheses

#	Text	Result
1	The intensity of cybersickness affects customer value in VR marketing.	Accept
2	Cybersickness affects purchase intention.	Accept
3	Cybersickness negatively affects trust.	Accept
4	Cybersickness negatively affects cross-selling.	Reject
5	Cybersickness negatively affects-up-selling.	Reject
6	Cybersickness negatively affects NPS.	Accept
7	A poorly set HMD IPD adjustment increases cybersickness.	Reject
8	A poorly set HMD IPD adjustment increases cybersickness nausea (SSQ-N).	Reject
9	A poorly set HMD IPD adjustment increases cybersickness oculomotor (SSQ-O).	Reject
10	A poorly set HMD IPD adjustment increases cybersickness disorientation (SSQ-D).	Reject

The authors could not identify clear empirical evidence for the effects of cybersickness and its impact on customer value. Nevertheless, cybersickness shows numerous adverse effects on the VR experience in general. Therefore, Hypothesis 1 states that cybersickness negatively affects customer value (H1) as if one feels nauseous, this is also likely to affect the ability or desire to shop (H2). For this reason, we hypothesise that cybersickness negatively affects trust (H3), cross- (H4), up-selling (H5), and NPS (H6). Furthermore, based on the research by Kim and Park (2019), we hypothesise that a poorly set HMD IPD intensifies the symptoms of cybersickness (H7). Hypotheses 8–10 are derived from H7 but in a more detailed manner to better understand the effects of cybersickness in our chosen scenario and context. Therefore, we hypothesise that a poorly set HMD IPD will support SSQ-N (H8), SSQ-O (H9), and SSQ-D (H10). The experiment used the same virtual boat simulator as in our earlier project. Here, the application had a boat jetty (see Figure 1.), and to get there, participants followed blue markers (see Figure 2.). The walking element in VR to reach the boat was intentionally added to help participants familiarise themselves with the environment and ensure everyone had the same amount of time in VR. This was important for the poorly adjusted IPDs to take effect (The treatment group had 6 mm added to their correct and physically measured IPDs.). After reaching the boat jetty, participants were asked to board the boat and navigate along yellow buoys in the water, leading to a destination flag. The buoys marking the way also ensured that participants did not stay from the route either intentionally or otherwise. Figure 2 depicts the virtual world's red (walking) and yellow (boat) paths.

A pilot study was conducted to identify problems with the questionnaire (including the setup of the experiment and the comprehension of the instructions) and the general scenario. As a result, minor revisions to the instructions and the section of the questionnaire asking about prior knowledge were made. R was used to analyse the data and the following packages (readxl, car, robustbase, ggplot2, psych, apaTables, and plot.lmSim). Twenty participants took part in the main study, although two had to drop out at the preliminary walking stage as they were already experiencing symptoms associated with cybersickness before they had got into the boat. This reduced our final sample to 18.

4. RESULTS, DISCUSSION, IMPLICATIONS, AND LIMITATIONS

Data collection was conducted in the spring term of 2020 with nine people in the treatment group and nine in the control group. The average participant age was 32 (SD = 13.79), and six were female and twelve were male. Fourteen participants had no prior experience of VR applications, and of the remaining four, three had experienced cybersickness in the past.

Correlations were calculated, and SSQ-T (see above) scores correlated with the customer value delta. A strong correlation between the customer value and SSQ-N, SSQ-O, and SSQ-D was observed. Therefore, H1 stating that cybersickness affects customer value is accepted. A negative correlation between trust and SSQ-O: ($r(15) = -.49$, $p = .043$); SSQ-D: ($r(15) = -.59$, $p = .012$); and SSQ-T: ($r(15) = -.49$, $p = .048$) was also observed. Furthermore, a negative correlation was observed between SSQ-T, SSQ-N, SSQ-O, SSQ-D, and purchase intention. Therefore, not only does cybersickness affect customer value (H1) and purchase intention (H2), but trust is also negatively affected by cybersickness, and thus, H1, H2, and H3 are accepted.

Cross- (H4) and up-selling (H5) do not correlate with SSQ-T or the significant subscales, so H4 and H5 are rejected. NPS, however, strongly and significantly correlates with SSQ-T and its subscales leading to the acceptance of H6. Regarding the IPD and its influence, non-significant effects were reported since neither Welch-test for group comparison showed significant effects although all mean values of the SSQ scales were higher in the treatment than in the control group (SSQ-T: Mt = 53.61, SD = 56.94; SSQ-T: Mc = 26.18, SD = 14.84; SSQ-N: Mt = 39.22, S.D = 54.06; SSQ-N: Mc = 13.78, SD = 18.54; SSQ-O: Mt = 37.06, SD 39.65; SSQ-O: Mc = 23.58, SD = 13.90; SSQ-D Mt = 74.24, SD 68.19; SSQ-D: Mc = 34.03, SD = 17.21). Furthermore, we calculated a dummy variable where SSQ-T >20 was coded as 1 and smaller as 0, resulting in a binary variable. Here too, no significant group comparison differences were reported. Accordingly, hypotheses 7–10 are rejected.

The preliminary results of this study were discussed and analysed using correlation analysis, suggesting that cybersickness negatively correlates with purchasing intentions and NPS – thus lowering the intention to recommend a product or service to others. However, the same cannot be said for cross- and up-selling. Interestingly, trust seems to correlate positively with cross- but not up-selling, just as up-selling correlates with purchasing intention. Such an observation may be due to more complex correlations between the present constructs than bivariate correlations. Indeed, cybersickness seems to correlate with customer value, making it a relevant construct for businesses seeking to implement VR applications. Furthermore, trust correlates negatively with cybersickness, suggesting that cybersickness influences trust. Earlier research and literature both indicate that this can be detrimental to business success. Consequently, trust is a relevant construct regarding immersive VR experiences in a business context.

VR has been shown to be a promising technology for businesses seeking to enhance emotions in customer interaction and immersive experiences. Furthermore, this study suggests that it is crucial to avoid cybersickness as a general rule and, more specifically, in a business setting. Failing to do so may negatively affect trust, NPS, customer value, and ultimately, purchase intention.

This study was conducted in the shadow of a worldwide pandemic, so there may have been self-selection bias in the sample. In addition, this initial study must be labelled as early-stage research, and the results may be different for a representative sample. Similarly, the results may differ in other scenarios or products.

Finally, as this study does not measure actual purchasing behaviour, the laboratory findings might vary if participants were in an alternative purchasing decision and context in the field. As participants were given a fixed route (blue markers and yellow buoys), they may have exhibited behaviour (e.g. walking more slowly or looking around) that would not have been observed in the absence of such guidance. Furthermore, this study analysed the data through correlation. However, the authors want to emphasise that although correlations may point towards causation, they cannot imply causation as this can only be achieved in an experiment where manipulation checks and confounding variables are rigorously controlled. Adding to the results of this preliminary study could be done by increasing the convenience sample size used here due to the worldwide pandemic situation.

In this study, referral and positive word of mouth were measured using the NPS and it is acknowledged that in the most recent publications, a further concept called "net emotional value" (Müller et al., 2021) was introduced. Instead of counting on a single question to measure satisfaction, emotions are presented and measured to create net emotional value as augmented (Batdi & Talan, 2019; Javornik, 2016) and virtual worlds (Reisoğlu et al., 2017; Schutte & Stilinović, 2017) can foster emotional responses. Since both AR and VR (Hamari & Keronen, 2017; Huang & Liao, 2015; Tussyadiah et al., 2018) can generate a feeling of presence, the authors suggest that net emotional value could be used to enrich to the findings of this study.

Our correlation analysis in the discussion section suggests that indirect effects may be present (e.g. trust) rather than bivariate correlations. Therefore, a further opportunity for research seeking to extend these preliminary results would be to employ more advanced statistical methods such as structural equation modelling (SEM), which can handle direct and indirect effects.

This study focuses on renting a motorboat, so it would be interesting to see if product type (e.g. search, experience, or trust goods) plays a role since the perceived risk (and the need for trust) may be different depending on the situation.

5. CONCLUDING REMARKS

The results in this study are promising, and companies seeking to optimise purchase intention, NPS, customer value, and trust will find that VR applications generate emotions showing positive effects on these business-relevant constructs. However, it is crucial to mitigate cybersickness as this can undo the very benefits which VR is trying to promote.

REFERENCES

Andrade, T., Bastos, D., 2019. Extended Reality in IoT scenarios: Concepts, Applications and Future Trends, in: 2019 5th Experiment International Conference (Exp.at'19). Presented at the 2019 5th Experiment Conference (exp.at'19), IEEE, Funchal (Madeira Island), Portugal, pp. 107–112. https://doi.org/10.1109/EXPAT.2019.8876559

Balk, S.A., Bertola, D.B., Inman, V.W., 2013. Simulator Sickness Questionnaire: Twenty Years Later. Driving Assessment Conference 7, 257–263.

Barsom, E.Z., Graafland, M., Schijven, M.P., 2016. Systematic review on the effectiveness of augmented reality applications in medical training. Surgical Endoscopy 30, 4174–4183. https://doi.org/10.1007/s00464-016-4800-6

Batdi, V., Talan, T., 2019. Augmented reality applications: A Meta-analysis and thematic analysis. Turkish Journal of Education 8, 276–297. https://doi.org/10.19128/turje.581424

Beatty, P., Reay, I., Dick, S., Miller, J., 2011. Consumer Trust in e-Commerce Web Sites: A Meta-study. ACM Comput. Surv. 43, 14:1-14:46. https://doi.org/10.1145/1922649.1922651

Bilgili, B., Özkul, E., Koç, E., Ademoğlu, M.O., 2019. An Investigation of Augmented Reality Applications from the Perspectives of Brand Trust and Purchase Intentions of Customers, in: Grima, S., Özen, E., Boz, H., Spiteri, J., Thalassinos, E. (Eds.), Contemporary Issues in Behavioral Finance, Contemporary Studies in Economic and Financial Analysis. Emerald Publishing Limited, pp. 53–64. https://doi.org/10.1108/S1569-375920190000101005

Bruck, S., Watters, P.A., 2011. The factor structure of cybersickness. Displays 32, 153–158. https://doi.org/10.1016/j.displa.2011.07.002

Chang, H.H., Chen, S.W., 2008. The impact of online store environment cues on purchase intention: Trust and perceived risk as a mediator. Online Information Review 32, 818–841. https://doi.org/10.1108/14684520810923953

Das, G., 2016. Antecedents and consequences of trust: an e-tail branding perspective. Intl J of Retail & Distrib Mgt 44, 713–730. https://doi.org/10.1108/IJRDM-06-2015-0089

Davis, S., Nesbitt, K., Nalivaiko, E., 2014. A Systematic Review of Cybersickness, in: Proceedings of the 2014 Conference on Interactive Entertainment - IE2014. Presented at the the 2014 Conference, ACM Press, Newcastle, NSW, Australia, pp. 1–9. https://doi.org/10.1145/2677758.2677780

Demeure, V., Niewiadomski, R., Pelachaud, C., 2011. How is believability of a virtual agent related to warmth, competence, personification, and embodiment? Presence: teleoperators and virtual environments 20, 431–448.

Disztinger, P., Schlögl, S., Groth, A., 2017. Technology Acceptance of Virtual Reality for Travel Planning, in: Schegg, R., Stangl, B. (Eds.), Information and Communication Technologies in Tourism 2017. Springer International Publishing, Cham, pp. 255–268. https://doi.org/10.1007/978-3-319-51168-9_19

Dreiskämper, D., Pöppel, K., Strauß, B., 2016. Vertrauen ist gut …. Zeitschrift für Sportpsychologie 23, 1–12. https://doi.org/10.1026/1612-5010/a000156

Economist, 2020. Headset technology is cheaper and better than ever. The Economist Technology QUARTERLY.

Farsi, M., Daneshkhah, A., Hosseinian-Far, A., Jahankhani, H. (Eds.), 2020. Digital Twin Technologies and Smart Cities, Internet of Things. Springer International Publishing, Cham. https://doi.org/10.1007/978-3-030-18732-3

Garzón, J., Pavón, J., Baldiris, S., 2019. Systematic review and meta-analysis of augmented reality in educational settings. Virtual Reality 23, 447–459. https://doi.org/10.1007/s10055-019-00379-9

Grieves, M., 2014. Digital twin: manufacturing excellence through virtual factory replication. White paper 1, 1–7.

Hamari, J., Keronen, L., 2017. Why do people buy virtual goods: A meta-analysis. Computers in Human Behavior 71, 59–69. https://doi.org/10.1016/j.chb.2017.01.042

Harren, B., Seiler, R., Müller, S., 2019. Augmented Reality und Virtual Reality im Premium- und Luxus-Retail, in: Uhl, A., Loretan, S. (Eds.), Digitalisierung in der Praxis. Springer Fachmedien Wiesbaden, Wiesbaden, pp. 183–195. https://doi.org/10.1007/978-3-658-26137-5_12

Herz, M., Rauschnabel, P.A., 2019. Understanding the diffusion of virtual reality glasses: The role of media, fashion and technology. Technological Forecasting and Social Change 138, 228–242. https://doi.org/10.1016/j.techfore.2018.09.008

Hippner, H., Hubrich, B., Wilde, K.D., 2011. Grundlagen des CRM, 3rd ed. Gabler, Wiesbaden. https://doi.org/10.1007/978-3-8349-6618-6

Hippner, H., Wilde, K.D., 2006. Grundlagen des CRM: Konzepte und Gestaltung. Gabler Verlag, Wiesbaden.

Huang, T.-L., Liao, S., 2015. A model of acceptance of augmented-reality interactive technology: the moderating role of cognitive innovativeness. Electron Commer Res 15, 269–295. https://doi.org/10.1007/s10660-014-9163-2

Israel, K., Zerres, C., Tscheulin, D.K., Buchweitz, L., Korn, O., 2019. Presenting Your Products in Virtual Reality: Do not Underestimate cybersickness, in: Nah, F.F.-H., Siau, K. (Eds.), HCI in Business, Government and Organisations. ECommerce and Consumer Behavior, Lecture Notes in Computer Science. Springer International Publishing, Cham, pp. 206–224. https://doi.org/10.1007/978-3-030-22335-9_14

Javornik, A., 2016. 'It's an illusion, but it looks real!' Consumer affective, cognitive and behavioural responses to augmented reality applications. Journal of Marketing Management 32, 987–1011. https://doi.org/10.1080/0267257X.2016.1174726

Kennedy, R.S., Lane, N.E., Berbaum, K.S., Lilienthal, M.G., 1993. Simulator Sickness Questionnaire: An Enhanced Method for Quantifying Simulator Sickness. The International Journal of Aviation Psychology 3, 203–220. https://doi.org/10.1207/s15327108ijap0303_3

Kim, D.J., Ferrin, D.L., Rao, H.R., 2008. A trust-based consumer decision-making model in electronic commerce: The role of trust, perceived risk, and their antecedents. Decision Support Systems 44, 544–564. https://doi.org/10.1016/j.dss.2007.07.001

Kim, H., Park, J.H., 2019. Effects of Simulator Sickness and Emotional Responses When Inter-pupillary Distance Misalignment Occurs, in: Karwowski, W., Ahram, T. (Eds.), Intelligent Human Systems Integration 2019, Advances in Intelligent Systems and Computing. Springer International Publishing, Cham, pp. 442–447. https://doi.org/10.1007/978-3-030-11051-2_67

Kim, Y., Peterson, R.A., 2017. A Meta-analysis of Online Trust Relationships in E-commerce. Journal of Interactive Marketing 38, 44–54. https://doi.org/10.1016/j.intmar.2017.01.001

Kugler, T., Ye, B., Motro, D., Noussair, C.N., 2019. On Trust and Disgust: Evidence from Face Reading and Virtual Reality. Social Psychological and Personality Science 194855061985630. https://doi.org/10.1177/1948550619856302

Ladeira, W.J., Santini, F. de O., Araujo, C.F., Sampaio, C.H., 2016. A Meta-Analysis of the Antecedents and Consequences of Satisfaction in Tourism and Hospitality. Journal of Hospitality Marketing & Management 25, 975–1009. https://doi.org/10.1080/19368623.2016.1136253

Lu, B., Fan, W., Zhou, M., 2016. Social presence, trust, and social commerce purchase intention: An empirical research. Computers in Human Behavior 56, 225–237. https://doi.org/10.1016/j.chb.2015.11.057

Lv, Z., Yin, T., Zhang, X., Song, H., Chen, G., 2016. Virtual Reality Smart City Based on WebVRGIS. IEEE Internet of Things Journal 3, 1015–1024. https://doi.org/10.1109/JIOT.2016.2546307

Manis, K.T., Choi, D., 2019. The virtual reality hardware acceptance model (VR-HAM): Extending and individuating the technology acceptance model (TAM) for virtual reality hardware. Journal of Business Research 100, 503–513. https://doi.org/10.1016/j.jbusres.2018.10.021

Martínez-Navarro, J., Bigné, E., Guixeres, J., Alcañiz, M., Torrecilla, C., 2019. The influence of virtual reality in e-commerce. Journal of Business Research 100, 475–482. https://doi.org/10.1016/j.jbusres.2018.10.054

Mayer, R.C., Davis, J.H., 1999. The effect of the performance appraisal system on trust for management: A field quasi-experiment. Journal of Applied Psychology 84, 123–136. https://doi.org/10.1037/0021-9010.84.1.123

Mayer, R.C., Davis, J.H., Schoorman, F.D., 1995. An integrative model of organisational trust. Academy of management review 20, 709–734.

Müller, S., Seiler, R., Völkle, M., 2021. Measuring emotions in customer relationships: Can NEV replace NPS? Presented at the EMAC Conference, Madrid, Spain.

Papadopoulou, P., 2007. Applying virtual reality for trust-building e-commerce environments. Virtual Reality 11, 107–127. https://doi.org/10.1007/s10055-006-0059-x

Radu, I., 2014. Augmented reality in education: a meta-review and cross-media analysis. Personal and Ubiquitous Computing 18, 1533–1543. https://doi.org/10.1007/s00779-013-0747-y

Rebenitsch, L., 2015. Managing cybersickness in virtual reality. XRDS 22, 46–51. https://doi.org/10.1145/2810054

Rebenitsch, L., Owen, C., 2016. Review on cybersickness in applications and visual displays. Virtual Reality 20, 101–125. https://doi.org/10.1007/s10055-016-0285-9

Reichheld, F., 2003. The one Number You Need to Grow. Havard Business Review, 81 (12) 46–54.

Reisoğlu, I., Topu, B., Yılmaz, R., Karakuş Yılmaz, T., Göktaş, Y., 2017. 3D virtual learning environments in education: a meta-review. Asia Pacific Educ. Rev. 18, 81–100. https://doi.org/10.1007/s12564-016-9467-0

Rese, A., Baier, D., Geyer-Schulz, A., Schreiber, S., 2017. How augmented reality apps are accepted by consumers: A comparative analysis using scales and opinions. Technological Forecasting and Social Change 124, 306–319. https://doi.org/10.1016/j.techfore.2016.10.010

Salantri, D., 2018. Trust in Virtual Reality. University of Nottingham, Nottingham UK.

Salvetti, F., Bertagni, B., Ingrassia, P., Prattico, G., 2018. HoloLens, Augmented Reality and Teamwork: Merging Virtual and Real Workplaces. International Journal of Advanced Corporate Learning 11, 44–47. https://doi.org/10.3991/ijac.v11i1.9228

Schutte, N.S., Stilinović, E.J., 2017. Facilitating empathy through virtual reality. Motivation and Emotion 41, 708–712. https://doi.org/10.1007/s11031-017-9641-7

Shafer, D.M., Carbonara, C.P., Korpi, M.F., 2018. Factors Affecting Enjoyment of Virtual Reality Games: A Comparison Involving Consumer-Grade Virtual Reality Technology. Games for Health Journal 8, 15–23. https://doi.org/10.1089/g4h.2017.0190

Shahrdar, S., Park, C., Nojoumian, M., 2019. Human Trust Measurement Using an Immersive Virtual Reality Autonomous Vehicle Simulator, in: Proceedings of the 2019 AAAI/ACM Conference on AI, Ethics, and Society - AIES '19. Presented at the the 2019 AAAI/ACM Conference, ACM Press, Honolulu, HI, USA, pp. 515–520. https://doi.org/10.1145/3306618.3314264

Stone Iii, W., 2017. Psychometric evaluation of the Simulator Sickness Questionnaire as a measure of cybersickness. Graduate Theses and Dissertations. https://doi.org/10.31274/etd-180810-5050

Tang, J., Gao, H., Liu, H., Das Sarma, A., 2012. eTrust: Understanding Trust Evolution in an Online World, in: Proceedings of the 18th ACM SIGKDD International Conference on Knowledge Discovery and Data Mining, KDD '12. ACM, New York, NY, USA, pp. 253–261.

Tewes, M., 2003. Der Kundenwert im Marketing. Deutscher Universitätsverlag, Wiesbaden. https://doi.org/10.1007/978-3-663-09615-3

Tomczak, T., Rudolf-Sipötz, E., 2006. Bestimmungsfaktoren des Kundenwertes: Ergebnisse einer branchenübergreifenden Studie, in: Günter, B., Helm, S. (Eds.), Kundenwert: Grundlagen – Innovative Konzepte – Praktische Umsetzungen. Gabler Verlag, Wiesbaden, pp. 127–155. https://doi.org/10.1007/978-3-8349-9288-8_6

Tussyadiah, I.P., Wang, D., Jung, T.H., tom Dieck, M.C., 2018. Virtual reality, presence, and attitude change: Empirical evidence from tourism. Tourism Management 66, 140–154. https://doi.org/10.1016/j.tourman.2017.12.003

Värlander, S., Yakhlef, A., 2008. Cross-selling: The power of embodied interactions. Journal of Retailing and Consumer Services 15, 480–490. https://doi.org/10.1016/j.jretconser.2008.01.003

Wen, C., 2019. Gartner: Fueling the Future of Business [WWW Document]. Gartner. URL https://www.gartner.com/en (accessed 5.5.20).

White, C.J., 2010. The impact of emotions on service quality, satisfaction, and positive word-of-mouth intentions over time. Journal of Marketing Management 26, 381–394. https://doi.org/10.1080/02672571003633610

ENHANCEMENT OF AI-BASED IMPLEMENTATION USING A ONE-STAGE DETECTOR ALGORITHM FOR THE DETECTION OF COUNTERFEIT PRODUCTS

Eduard Daoud, Nabil Khalil and Martin Gaedke
Technische Universität Chemnitz, Germany

ABSTRACT

Counterfeit products are a major problem that the market has been facing for a long time. According to the Global Brand Counterfeiting Report 2018 "Amount of Total Counterfeiting, globally has reached to 1.2 Trillion USD in 2017 and is Bound to Reach 1.82 Trillion USD by the Year 2020", a solution to this concern has already been researched and published by the authors in previous research papers published in e-society 2020 and IADIS journal, but the issue with the previously mentioned solution was that the object detection performance and accuracy needed to be improved. In this paper, a comparison between the current YOLO (You Only Look Once) algorithm used in the new implementation and the SSD (Single Shot Detector) algorithm, the faster R-CNN (Region-Based Convolutional Neural Networks) used in the old implementation, is made in the context of the present task to discuss and prove why YOLO is a more suitable option for the counterfeit product detection task.

KEYWORDS

Anti-Counterfeiting, Machine Learning, Deep Learning, Image Recognition, Object Detection

1. INTRODUCTION AND CURRENT PROBLEM

Counterfeited products have been a huge problem to the whole world market for a long time, there have been many types of research focused on solving this specific problem and only one solution was found proposing the use of machine learning and object detection to allow end-user to be able to verify and authorize products using only an image that contains the product quality certificate logos and marks. This solution was published by Eduard, et al. (2020) and it uses SSD by Liu, et al. (2016) and Faster R-CNN by Ren, et al. (2016) machine learning algorithms for detecting logos and marks in images. Logos and marks in product images are likely to be small, and these images will not always be in a high resolution, and that is one of the difficulties that make it hard for the SSD algorithm to detect small objects efficiently. Before we start, we will explain the reason why YOLOv4 by Alexey & Chien-Yao (2020) is a suitable option. Two different architectures are used in object detection tasks; the first one is the two-stage detectors which include the famous regional-based detectors like R-CNN by Girshick, et al. (2013), Fast R-CNN by Girshick (2015), and Faster R-CNN which are used for different tasks. The other object detection architecture is the one-stage detector, which includes SSD and YOLOv4, even though SSD and YOLO are using the same architecture, the way the network in each algorithm is constructed and the way they work is different. The differences between the one-stage detector and the two-stage detectors as well as the difference between SSD and YOLOv4 will be explained in the next sections.

2. STATE OF THE ART ANALYSIS

According to Alexey & Chien-Yao (2020), there are two popular types of object detectors, two-stage detectors, and one-stage detectors.

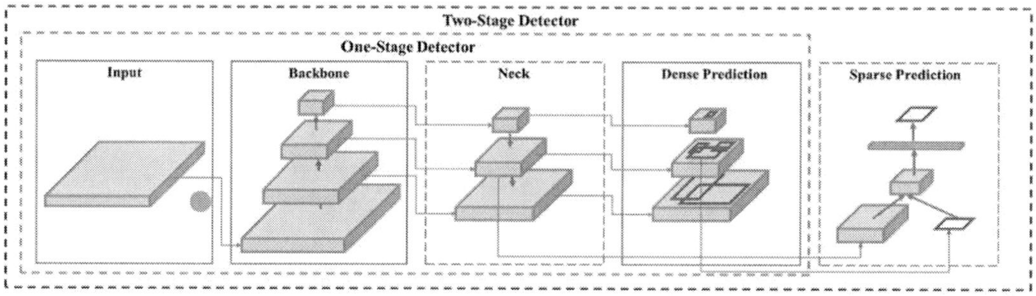

Figure 1. The difference between the two-stage and one-stage detectors according to Alexey & Chien-Yao (2020)

The image above illustrates the difference between the two-stage and the one-stage detector. The two-stage detector focuses on Faster R-CNN implementation by Girshick (2015) and the single-stage detector focuses on SSD and YOLOv4 implementation by Alexey & Chien-Yao (2020). The CertificateOk platform resulting from the research of Eduard, et al. (2020) uses the Faster R-CNN implementation and the proposed new implementation uses the YOLOv4 implementation as a framework. As in Manuel, et al. (2020) & Shilpa, et al. (2021), the Faster R-CNN contains two main elements: The region proposal network (RPN), and the Fast R-CNN header network. At the beginning of the detection, a CNN is used to extract the features on the image as a whole; in previous versions of R-CNN, feature extraction was applied for each region of interest (ROI) separately, which increases the inference time. Then the RPN utilizes the sliding windows' technique on the output of the feature map to generate proposals on each location with anchors (reference boxes) that were on the feature map and predict whether this location contains an object or not. The anchors that the RPN uses come in different shapes and sizes to be able to correctly predict whether there is an object in the given region of interest or not. After that, all the detected regions will be passed through a network to calculate the score of having an actual object in that region. The final step of the first stage is having the top regions of interest cropped using the ROI pooling layers. In the second stage, the results of the ROI pooling will be sent to the fully connected Fast R-CNN network for classification and localization, which is referred to in Figure 1 as Sparse Prediction.

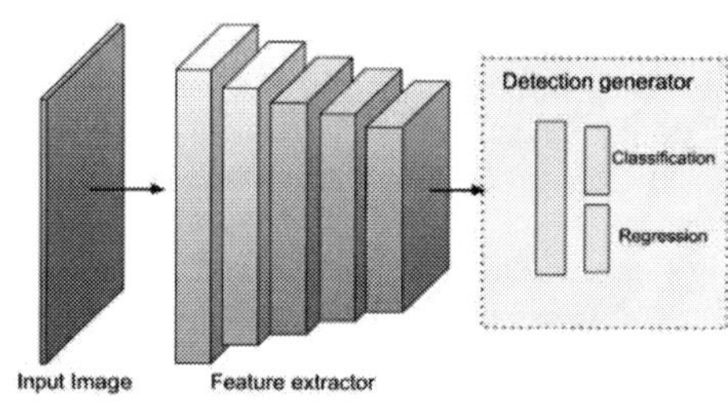

Figure 2. One-stage detector according to Manuel, et al. (2020)

On the other hand, there is the one-stage detector which includes SSD and YOLO algorithms. As shown in Figure 1 and Figure 2 the one-stage detectors detect the bounding boxes as well as the predicted class in one step. The one-stage detector, single-shot detector, or SSD by Liu, et al. (2016) uses VGG-16 as a feature extractor, which is the same feature extractor used by Faster R-CNN by Girshick (2015), VGG-16 is a convolutional neural network model first proposed by K. Simonyan and A. Zisserman of the University of Oxford in their work "Very Deep Convolutional Networks for Large-Scale Image Recognition". SSD inference starts by dividing the image into multiple grids and then for each grid it makes prediction boxes, with the anchor of these boxes being in the middle of the grid. And predicts the existence of all the object classes that we have. As shown in Figure 3 SSD predicts with different convolutional sizes and sends the predicted classes to the final overall prediction to be able to improve accuracy.

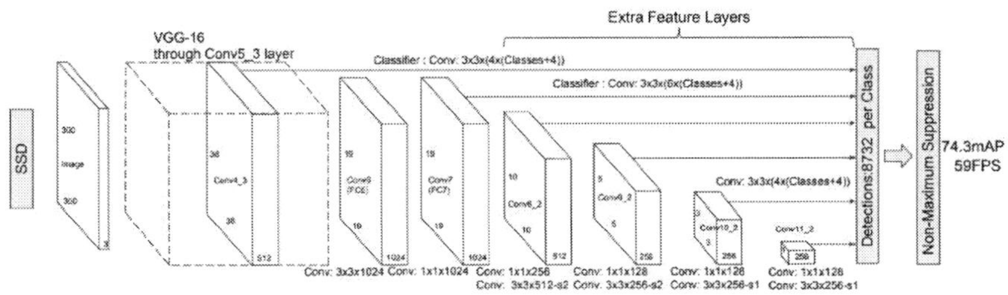

Figure 3. Single-shot detector as in Liu, et al. (2016)

One of the challenges and problems with SDD, as described in Liu, et al. (2016), is that the detection step leads to numerous prediction boxes. This problem is solved by non-maximum suppression, which is a technique for combining multiple boxes belonging to the same object Jan, et al. (2017).

The second one-stage detector and the one that will be the focus of this research is 'you only look once' or YOLOv4 by Alexey & Chien-Yao (2020). YOLO by Joseph, et al. (2016) was introduced in 2016 as a state-of-the-art real-time detection algorithm, and since then the development and improvement of YOLO have never stopped. The way YOLO works is a little different from the way SSD by Liu, et al. (2016) works, YOLO starts by dividing the image into an $S \times S$ grid, for each grid a B number of bounding boxes are created along with the confidence in these boxes, if the object center was detected in one of the grids, that grid will be in charge of detecting the whole object, each bounding box inside the grid will contain 5 predictions (x, y, h, w, and c) while X and Y represent the center of this box, H and W are the height and the width and C is the confidence, in the end for the whole YOLO predictions can be put as $(S\times S\times(B\times 5 + C))$, and for each grid, only one prediction will be constructed with each class probability, this can be expressed like $(B\times 5+C)$ Joseph, et al. (You Only Look Once:Unified, Real-Time Object Detection, 2016).

As an example, from our case - detection fake product -, shown in Figure 4 we detect the TUV SUD logo so the grid that contains the logo will result in Pc =1 which means that there is an object in this grid and the (x, y, h, w) for this logo and the classes probabilities which will be zero for the first and last class and 1 for the second class which indicates that the detected object belongs to the second class.

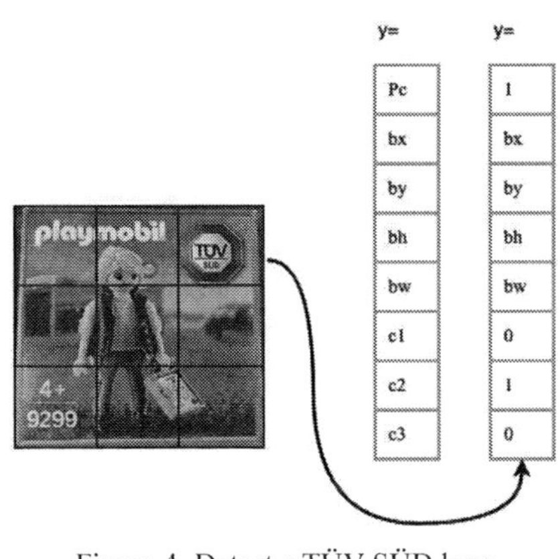

Figure 4. Detect a TÜV SÜD logo

YOLOv2 by Joseph & Ali (2016) included some improvements like 'Higher Resolution Classifier', 'Multi-Scale Training', 'Fine-Grained Features' and Darknet-19 architecture that include 19 convolutional layers as a feature extractor, alongside other improvements that increased the accuracy and the performance of YOLOv2 over YOLOv1 and made the detection of smaller objects much better.

YOLOv3 by Redmon & Farhadi (2019) featured huge improvements in the feature extractor as it uses Darknet-53 has 53 convolutional layers which is much deeper than Darknet-19 which was used in YOLOv2. YOLOv3 makes predictions like Feature Pyramid Networks or FPN Tsung-Yi, et al. (2017), FPN constructs two pathways, bottom-up which increases the semantic value but with lower resolution, and top-down which offers higher resolution but low semantic value. Figure 5 shows the way FPN works, the top level is a low-resolution high-semantic representation that helps detect larger objects, and the lower level is a high-resolution layer that helps detect smaller objects, and in the middle layers connections between the reconstructed layers and feature maps is made for better location accuracy Tsung-Yi, et al. (2017).

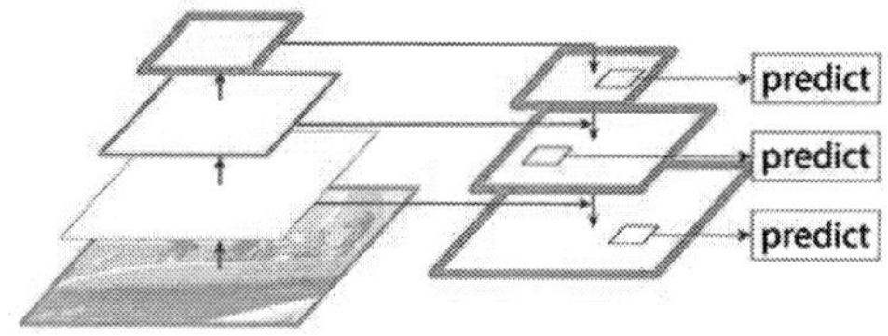

Figure 5. Feature pyramid networks as in Tsung-Yi, et al. (2017)

While YOLOv3 uses multiple layers like FPN and also uses the high-resolution layer, SSD by Liu, et al. (2016) only uses the upper layers for inference and does not reuse the higher-resolution feature maps as shown in Figure 6 and that makes SSD a bad choice for detecting small objects like a logo or quality marks Tsung-Yi, et al. (2017).

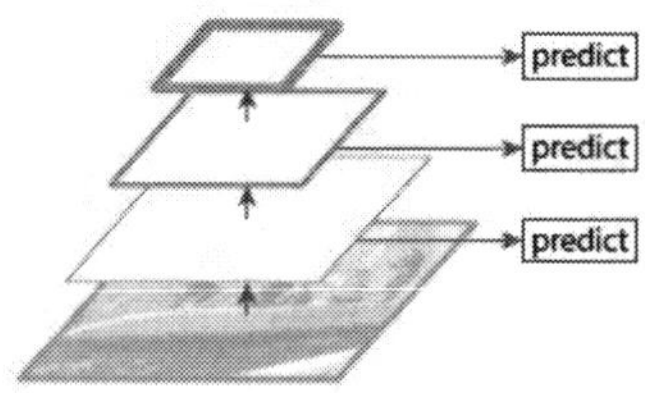

Figure 6. Pyramidal feature hierarchy as in Tsung-Yi, et al. (2017)

YOLOv4 by Alexey & Chien-Yao (2020) improves the mean average precision (mAP) by 10% over YOLOv3, and it includes changes in different aspects of the algorithm, first YOLOv4 uses CSPDarknet53 as a feature extractor which is a feature extractor that can learn, it takes the input and divides that input into two parts, one part will go through the dense layer and the other will be concatenated at the end to get the final dense layer result Chien-Yao, et al. (2020), YOLOv4 also added a spatial pyramid pooling (SPP) Kaiming, et al. (2015) after the CSPDarknet53 to be able to generate fixed-length features regardless of the size of the feature maps. A key change in YOLOv4 is that it uses a modified Path Aggregation Network (PANet) Shu, et al. (2018) instead of the FPN that was used in YOLOv3, PANet tries to enhance the way FPN works and increase its accuracy and performance. PANet uses "FPN backbone, bottom-up augmentation, adaptive feature pooling, Box branch, and a fully connected fusion" Shu, et al. (2018).

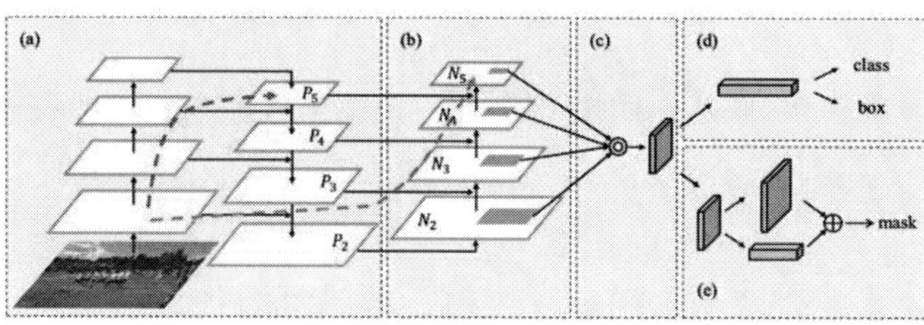

Figure 7. Path aggregation network architecture as in Shu, et al. (2018)

As shown in Figure 7 part (a) and (b) shows the "FPN backbone" and the "bottom-up path augmentation" this helps preserve the spatial information while keeping the length of the layers short. Part (c) is the "adaptive feature pooling" it uses features from all layers and lets the network choose the useful features; it also performs "ROI Align operation" on feature maps. (d) and (e) represent the "Fully-connect Fusion" which is used to make accurate mask prediction with a high location sensitivity. YOLOv4 uses PANet with a small modification, instead of adding layers and forming a new layer YOLOv4 preform concatenation between the input layer and the previous one.

Based on this evidence and insights, this paper implements a new performant and user-friendly solution. In the next section, we present the concept behind the new solution and the technical architecture of the application and then go into more detail about the implementation phase.

3. CONCEPT AND TECHNICAL ARCHITECTURE

The approached application is developed in a way that allows the end-user to easily verify products using smartphones, cameras, or a picture from the internet. This allows a high majority of end-consumers to detect fake products.

The application will receive the image that contains the logo and possible marks in an HTTP request; after that, the image will be sent to OpenCV YOLOv4 trained model for detection. After detection is completed, the results will be sent to the user in a JSON Response so that the user can easily view the results on any device.

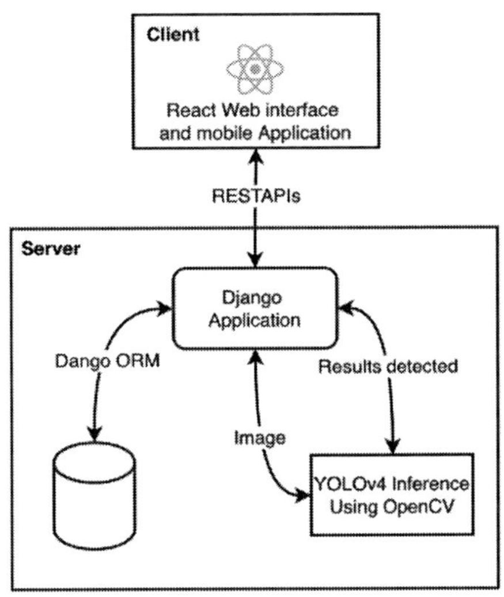

Figure 8. The concept of the proposed application

As shown in Figure 8, the client-side can be a ReactJS application on the web or React Native application on smartphones. The user will send an image from the client-side to the web servers via Rest APIs along with other information (metadata, request user info). The server-side has two main parts, the Django application, which will receive the request and extract the necessary data from it, and the OpenCV deep learning inference using YOLOv4. To verify the concept as a whole and the proposed application, which focuses in particular on the detection of counterfeit products, we implement the solution in the next section and train the model with the logo of the certification body and the quality mark of TÜV SÜD AG as one of the largest European certification bodies and VDE e.V. as one of the largest technical-scientific associations in Europe in the field of safety and quality in electrical, information and medical technology.

4. IMPLEMENTATION

Certain steps are necessary to build a high-efficiency machine learning solution that can identify labeled logos/marks correctly from product images. The first step is to decide which computer vision algorithm to use, in our case YOLOv4 seems the most reasonable algorithm because of its high ability to detect a small object and its very high performance compared to other algorithms. After that, the dataset should be created including both correct and wrong logos/marks to use this dataset later in the training process.

We are going to use the dataset that was used in the previous implementation by Eduard, et al. (2020) of CertificateOk 1 and improve it a bit by adding more samples, the dataset that was used contained around 600 images of different shapes and different logo/marks dimensions. After creating the dataset, a suitable labeling tool was used like YOLO_Label2, which is an open-source labeling tool that creates label files easily and efficiently. After labeling the whole dataset it is recommended to split the dataset by 80% for training and 20% for testing and validation. We used the transfer learning technique which is using pre-trained weights file in our case YOLOv4 pre-trained weights to speed up the training process and enhance the accuracy and performance.

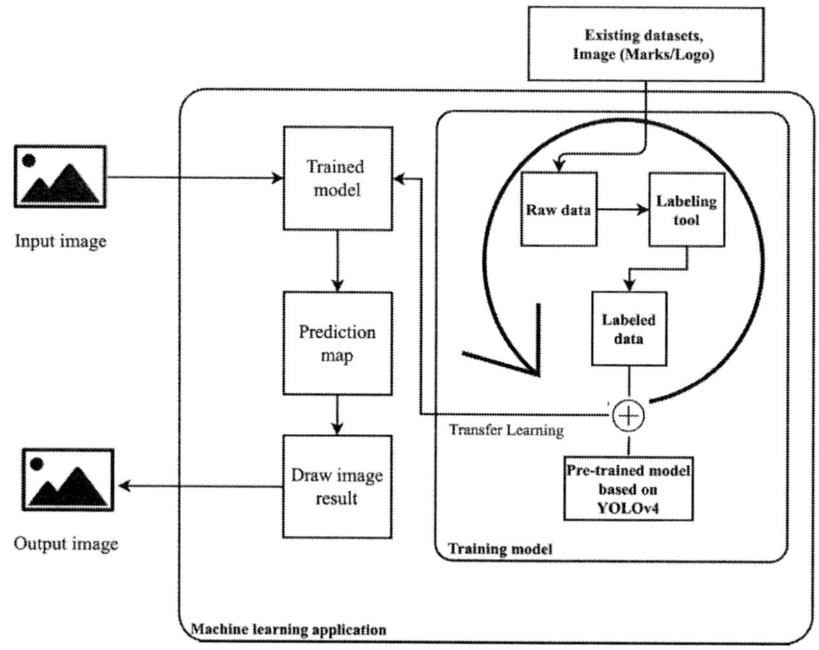

Figure 9. Implementation to YOLOv4 model adapted from Eduard, et al. (2020)

The training step is a continuous step, which means it can be repeated using saved weights to increase accuracy until the model achieves its highest mean Average Precision (mAP).

The trained model weights will be used by OpenCV3 deep learning inference since OpenCV has a good integration with darknet4 which is an open-source neural network that is used in building YOLOv4. The backend will be implemented using Django5 which is an open-source python web framework and integrating OpenCV with Django OpenCV-python library will be used. On the client-side ReactJS will be used for creating a customizable application with high stability. In the following section, we evaluate our approach before we headline the summary and an outlook on our work.

5. EVALUATION AND CHALLENGES

The proposed solution to fight counterfeit products has several advantages over normal counterfeit counters, it empowers the end-user to be able to verify and report products without the need for any special tools, only an image of the product that contains the logo/marks of the manufacturer is considered enough for our machine learning application to decide if the product is counterfeit or original.

[1] https://app.certificateok.de/Consumer accessed at 9th of January 2022
[2] https://github.com/developer0hye/Yolo_Label accessed at 9th of January 2022
[3] https://opencv.org/ accessed at 9th of January 2022
[4] https://pjreddie.com/darknet/ accessed at 9th of January 2022
[5] https://www.djangoproject.com/ accessed at 9th of January 2022

One of the biggest challenges during the implementation of any AI application is collecting and creating a good dataset to use in training. Our focus was improving the implementation of the CertificateOk application by switching from Faster R-CNN and SSD to YOLOv4, and as discussed in section 2 (State-of-the-art analysis) YOLOv4 showed much better results with smaller objects.

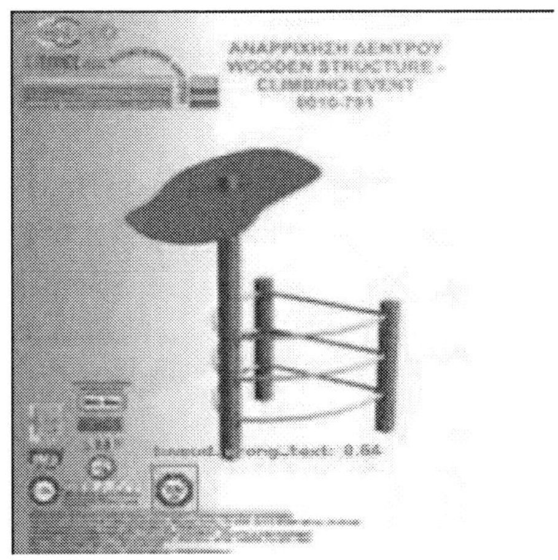

Figure 10. Detection example using old implementation

The image in Figure 10 shows a product image with TUV SUD fake logo with a low resolution and small logo size; the old implementation was SSD and Faster R-CNN could not detect the logo/marks of that size on multiple images with the same sizes. To compare the performance between the old implementation and the new one, both were deployed on the same Ubuntu server,

Figure 11 demonstrates the query with the same file and under the same conditions (Hardware environment and internet connection) completely different response experience.

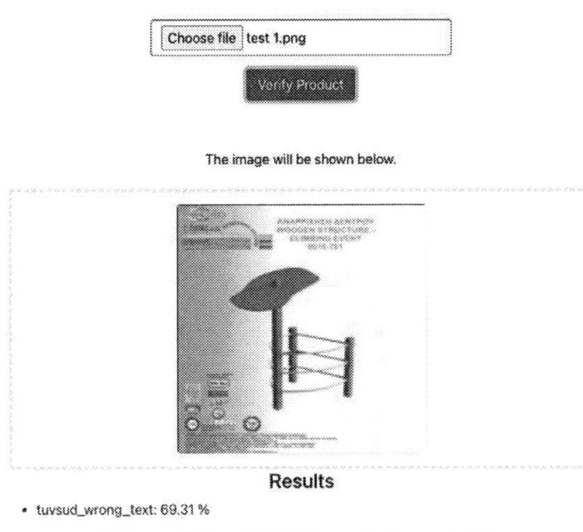

Figure 11. Detection example using the new implementation

The old implementation receives the response after 15 seconds, while the new implementation 6 receives the final response of 600~900 MS, which is a huge improvement over the old implementation.

[6] http://aiapp.certificateok.de:8008/ accessed at 9th of January 2022

6. CONCLUSION AND OUTLOOK

In conclusion, this paper highlighted the difference between one-stage detectors with a focus on SSD Liu, et al. (2016) and YOLO with its different versions and two-stage detectors with a focus on Faster R-CNN Ren, et al. (2016). The highlight of that research is that YOLOv4 Alexey & Chien-Yao (2020) perform better on **lower resolution and small objects** than SSD or Faster R-CNN specifically because of the following the way FPN make a prediction which was first adopted in YOLOv3 Redmon & Farhadi (2019) and later in YOLOv4 PANet was used which make YOLOv4 even better in detecting smaller objects Alexey & Chien-Yao (2020).

In future work, the focus could be on collecting more data samples and working closely with big certificate issuers to cover a variety of options. There is also the possibility to improve the existing application by giving the certificate issuer the ability to upload their logos/marks, and it gets added to the model training process, that way in the future certificate issuer can change or update their logos and have that directly reflected on CertificateOk system.

In the end, the possibilities of using AI and machine learning in preventing counterfeit products are huge and there is always room for improvement, and empowering end-users that will make the marked a safer and a more transparent place for customers.

REFERENCES

Alexey, B. & Chien-Yao, W. a. H.-Y. M. L., 2020. YOLOv4: Optimal Speed and Accuracy of Object Detection, s.l.: s.n.

Chien-Yao, W. et al., 2020. CSPNet: A new backbone that can enhance learning capability of cnn, s.l.: IEEE.

Eduard, D., Martin, G., Dang, V. & Hung, N., 2020. IMPROVING FAKE PRODUCT DETECTION USING AI- BASED TECHNOLOGY, s.l.: 18th International Conference e-Society.

Girshick, R., 2015. Fast R-CNN, s.l.: s.n.

Girshick, R., Donahue, J., Trevor, D. & Jitendra, M., 2013. Rich feature hierarchies for accurate object detection and semantic segmentation, s.l.: s.n.

Jan, H., Rodrigo, B. & Bernt, S., 2017. Learning non-maximum suppression, Saarbrücken, Germany: Max Planck Institut für Informatik.

Joseph, R. & Ali, F., 2016. YOLO9000: Better, Faster, Stronger, s.l.: s.n.

Joseph, R., Santosh, D., Ross, G. & Ali, F., 2016. You Only Look Once: Unified, Real-Time Object Detection, s.l.: University of Washington.

Kaiming, H., Xiangyu, Z., Shaoqing, R. & Jian, S., 2015. Spatial Pyramid Pooling in Deep Convolutional Networks for Visual Recognition, s.l.: s.n.

Liu, W. et al., 2016. SSD: Single Shot MultiBox Detector. s.l., arXiv preprint, arXiv:1512.02325.Manuel, C.-G., Jesús, T.-M. & Pedro, L.-B. a. J. G.-G., 2020. On the Performance of One-Stage and Two-Stage Object.

Redmon, J. & Farhadi, A., 2019. Yolov3: An incremental improvement. s.l., arXiv preprint arXiv:1804.02767.

Ren, S., He, K., Girshick, R. & Sun, J., 2016. Faster R-CNN: Towards Real-Time Object Detection with Region Proposal Networks. s.l., In Advances in neural information processing systems (pp. 91-99)..

Shilpa, S., Mamta, K. & Trilok, K., 2021. A Real-Time Integrated Face Mask Detector to Curtail Spread of Coronavirus, s.l.: s.n.

Shu, L. et al., 2018. Path aggregation network for instance segmentation, s.l.: IEEE.

Tsung-Yi, L. et al., 2017. Feature Pyramid Networks for Object Detection. s.l., IEEE Conference on Computer Vision and Pattern Recognition (CVPR).

DEVELOPMENT OF E-COMMERCE IN TIMES OF THE CORONA CRISIS

Darius Zumstein[1], Carmen Oswald[1] and Claudia Brauer[2]
[1] *Zurich University of Applied Sciences, Institute of Marketing Management*
Theaterstrasse 17, 8400 Winterthur, Switzerland
[2] *Management Center Innsbruck, Universitätsstrasse 15, 6020 Innsbruck*

ABSTRACT

In 2020 and 2021, the coronavirus crises lead to an extraordinary e-commerce growth. Based on an empirical study among 365 online retailers in Switzerland and Austria, the e-commerce developments during the corona crises were investigated. Nine out of ten online retailers demonstrate a sustainable e-commerce growth, and more than half have gained many new customers. In addition, many existing customers buy more frequently from online retailers, and/or buy larger quantities. In 2020, most online shops had a strong order increase in product groups like garden, do-it-yourself, toys, furniture, sports equipment, and food (more than 20% per year). Due to the e-commerce growth, online retailers are faced with different challenges in procurement, management, customer service, distribution, and IT. Moreover, new sales channels like messenger and social commerce arise and classical formats are adapted. Therefore, omni-channel retailers test showrooms, click and collect, experiential, self-service, or pop-up stores. Finally, this contribution provides strategic and operational implications for online shop operators.

KEYWORDS

E-commerce, Digital Commerce, e-Commerce Trends, Onlines Sales, Coronavirus Crisis, Digital Sales, Digital Services

1. INTRODUCTION: THE GROWTH OF E-COMMERCE

The coronavirus crisis has raised many questions for online traders in relation to e-commerce. In recent years, online sales have grown steadily, as evidenced by the multitude of scientific articles and practical contributions, Therefore, the economic importance of e-commerce for many companies is empirically proved in different studies (Wölfle & Leimstoll 2021, Zumstein & Steigerwald 2018, 2019; Zumstein, Oswald & Brauer 2021). According to a survey by the Swiss Retail Association in cooperation with Swiss Post and GfK, sales of Swiss online shops grew to over 13.1 billion Swiss francs in 2020, which is 27% more than in 2019 (Swiss Post 2021). In 2020, in Austria 15 billion euros were spent on online purchases of physical goods. This corresponds to a share of 68% of the total e-commerce expenditure of Austrians (Austrian Retail Association 2021). In 2021, the B2C (business-to-consumer) e-commerce growth rate in Switzerland was 37% and in Austria 7%. However, the e-commerce growth rate in European countries varied from 1% in Estonia up to 77% in Greece (Lone, Harboul, Weltevreden 2021). In eastern European countries, the e-commerce growth rate was often higher-than-average (Moldova 49%, North Macedonia 37%, Hungary 35%, Poland 34%, Albania 33% and Croatia 32%). While Spain (29%) and Portugal (23%) had high growth rates too, in large economies they were lower (France 9%, United Kingdom and Germany 2%).

Due to the coronavirus crisis, many retailers have had to close stationary shops temporarily and to adopt sales strategies because of the lockdowns and changed purchase behaviour. However, to continue the business purpose, many retailers either expanded the product range and stock of their online shops, or they introduced a new one. With this development, however, far-reaching operational changes were necessary. Research from previous years shows that markets, marketing, data, information technology (IT) and logistics were the main challenges for online shop operators (Zumstein & Steigerwald 2019, Zumstein & Oswald 2020). However, the operational changes and challenges of online retailers due to the coronavirus crisis have not been much investigated scientifically so far. This paper therefore aims to answer the following research question: *How did e-commerce develop among Swiss and Austrian online retailers during the coronavirus crisis?*

This contribution is structured among a market research literature and based on the results of the conducted study from online retailers operating in the Swiss and Austrian market. It shows the predicted sustainable growth of e-commerce in those markets and the growth in orders among different product categories during the Corona crisis. Furthermore, the growth on turnovers of new and existing online customers is discussed. Additionally, the relevance of sales channels in e-commerce and their development are focused. A special focus lies on changes regarding retail stores, personal sales and trade fairs as well the development of stationary stores and new sales formats. In the last part, the development and intensity of challenges in e-commerce are presented. The paper closes with the conclusion and recommendations for online retailers.

2. LITERATURE

Even though Switzerland and Austria are geographically close, the Swiss and Austrian e-commerce markets are not identical and show different market conditions.

Regarding to a conducted study in 2020, the Swiss e-commerce revenue was in 2020 with 27 billion Euro higher than the Austrian online revenue with 23,2 billion Euro. The biggest percentage (58%) of bought goods in Switzerland were physical goods whereby in Austria it was 10% more revenue by physical goods (68%). Swiss consumers are spending more on services (23%) than Austrian consumers (16%). In total, physical goods worth 18.2 billion Euro were purchased online in Switzerland in 2020 and 15.7 Billion Euro in Austria (nets DACH, 2020). On the consumer side, data privacy and security concerns decreased significantly, and the Swiss population has become more impatient regarding waiting times for deliveries and value the faster shopping in stationary shops more strongly (Rudolph, Klink & Hoang, 2021). In Austria the transformation from traditional catalog to online retailing thus appears to be almost complete. Three quarters of all Austrians have already made purchases from online retail whereby especially among consumers over 40 and among women, distant selling become strongly more important during the pandemic (Austrian Retail Association, 2021).

3. RESEARCH DESIGN

The growth in e-commerce in recent years and the online boom since the beginning of the coronavirus crisis were important reasons for conducting this study for the fourth time after 2018, 2019 (Zumstein & Steigerwald, 2018, 2019), and 2020 (Zumstein & Oswald, 2020). Its aim was to find out more about current developments in online retailing in Switzerland and Austria. The subjects of this research project were all online retailers in Switzerland and Austria with a .com, .ch, or .at domain that are registered and operate in Swiss and Austrian markets. As in most recent projects, the focus is not only on large online shops but on smaller and medium-sized enterprises (SMEs). The data for the study was collected from 8 June to 4 September 2021 as part of a quantitative online survey using Qualtrics software. Of the online retailers contacted, 365 participants completed the majority of the questionnaire. The sample size (n) is 365 unless otherwise stated. The survey was able to reach the target group via LinkedIn, newsletters, emails, specialist groups in the social media, and the contact forms of online shops. The questionnaire contained in total 55 questions including follow up questions. 284 Swiss (78%) and 63 Austrian online shops (17%) took part in the 2021 online retailer survey.

4. RESEARCH RESULTS

4.1 Growth in E-Commerce

The extent of the Swiss and Austrian e-commerce growth in sales is surprising: 88% of the 316 online shops surveyed grew overall in 2020 compared to the previous year. Of these, 23% of online stores saw growth increase slightly, between six and 15%. 29% grew strongly, between 16 and 29%, and for 36% of online stores, sales growth increased very strongly (over 30%). These, coronavirus-related, sales growth figures are unusual and reminiscent of the boom times of the 1950s and 80s. Only eight percent of retailers report that online sales remained the same in 2020, with between minus five and plus five percent growth. Only four percent of the respondents saw their online shop sales declining last year.

Moreover, one of four online retailers expect a strong sustainable sales growth. Other 69% of the online shop operators believe that the current e-commerce boom will grow moderately. Therefore, nine out of ten online retailers in e-commerce expect an overall sustainable sales growth. A small number, four percent each, forecast only temporary growth or no growth at all. In the actual e-commerce boom, online shops benefited in four ways: Firstly, purchases shifted from offline to online; secondly, demand for many products increased (see Chapter 4.2); thirdly, new customers were acquired online; and fourthly, existing customers made more and/or more frequent purchases online (see Chapter 4.3).

4.2 E-Commerce Growth per Product Category

The study focused on the number of online orders for the product ranges or groups in the e-shops has developed since the pandemic started in March 2020 (Zumstein et al. 2021). Figure 1 clearly shows that online orders over all product groups increased slightly or strongly in 2020 compared to the previous years' sales period. Since the coronavirus crisis, the number of orders in the *garden and do-it-yourself* (DIY) segment have increased the most overall: They increased sharply (more than 20%) or slightly (minus five to minus 19%). For 22% of respondents, orders increased slightly, and for 68% of them, orders for garden and DIY products increased strongly by more than 20% compared with the previous year. This increase in orders can be explained by changes in consumers' leisure and work behavior (home office). In spring 2020 and 2021, many home and garden products were ordered when people had to stay at home and spent a lot of time looking after their homes, balconies, terraces, and gardens. The second strongest growth in e-commerce was in the *sporting goods* sector: For two-thirds of the online shops, online sales of sporting goods grew by more than 20% year-on-year, while a further 21% recorded slightly growing sales. For example, more bicycles and e-bikes were sold online than ever before. *Online grocers* have been among the big winners since the pandemic, with more than half of them selling more than 20% more food online compared to 2019, and another quarter selling at least five to 19% more. Temporarily, the share of grocery online sales quintupled at times from three to as much as 15%.

Cosmetics also grew strongly online for more than half of the retailers surveyed, and slightly for a quarter of them, with sales only declining in rare individual cases. Very similar figures can be observed in the *toys and furniture sectors*: Online order growth was strong for half and slight for a third of retailers. While *multimedia and electrical devices* were still in very high demand online in the spring of 2020, demand flattened out later in the year, with 47% reporting strong sales growth and another 29% at least slight growth. It was a similar story for non-prescription *drugs*, which have seen increased demand online since the coronavirus crisis. Three out of four online pharmacies or drugstores grew slightly or strongly. *Watches and jewellery* are also increasingly sold online. This sector grew strongly for 42% of watch and jewellery retailers, and slightly for another third. Sales in *online fashion* were surprisingly positive: Most online clothing and online shoe retailers reported strong growth (45%) or slight growth (31%).

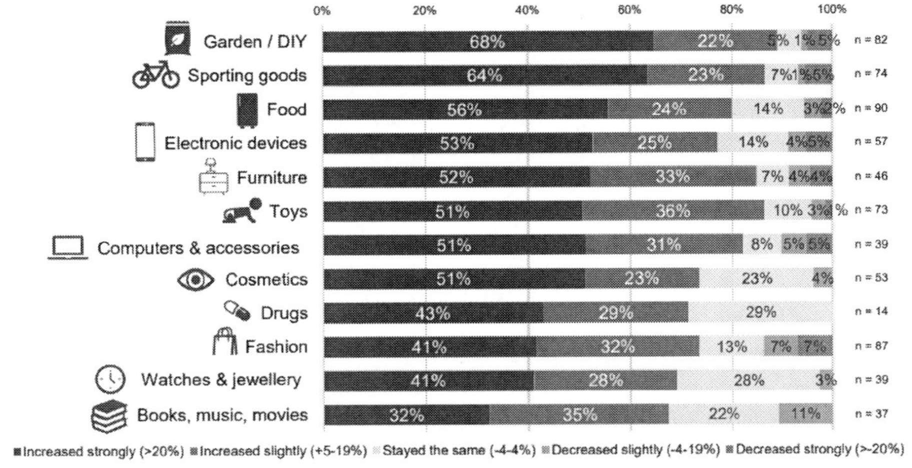

Figure 1. Online order growth per product category in the Corona year 2020 compared to 2019

For *computers and accessories*, strong (41%) or slight (37%) sales growth can be observed; only a few online retailers (seven percent) saw a slight or strong decline in orders. Now that everyone has finished equipping their home offices, the strong sales growth from the first half of 2020 has declined in relative terms.

Online orders for products such as *books, music, and films* (including downloads) rose by 56% year-on year overall, far outstripping the 16% decline.

4.3 E-Commerce Growth on Turnover of New and Existing Customers

The e-commerce growth also led to *new customers*. When asked whether a relatively large number of new customers had been acquired in their online shops since the start of the coronavirus crisis, the results were astonishing: 89% of the online retailers had acquired new customers, and more than half had even acquired a very large number of new customers. Only eight percent stated that they had acquired few or no new customers.

This strong growth in new customers is remarkable and, in many cases, comes at the expense of the stationary retail trade. In response to the follow-up question about revenues involving new customers, the following distribution emerged, as can be seen in Figure 2 on the right: 16% achieved *above-average turnover* and for two-thirds, this was average. For 11% of the respondents, new customer turnover was below average (Zumstein et al. 2021). It can be concluded that the new customers acquired during the coronavirus crisis do not generate significantly more revenue for most online retailers than existing customers.

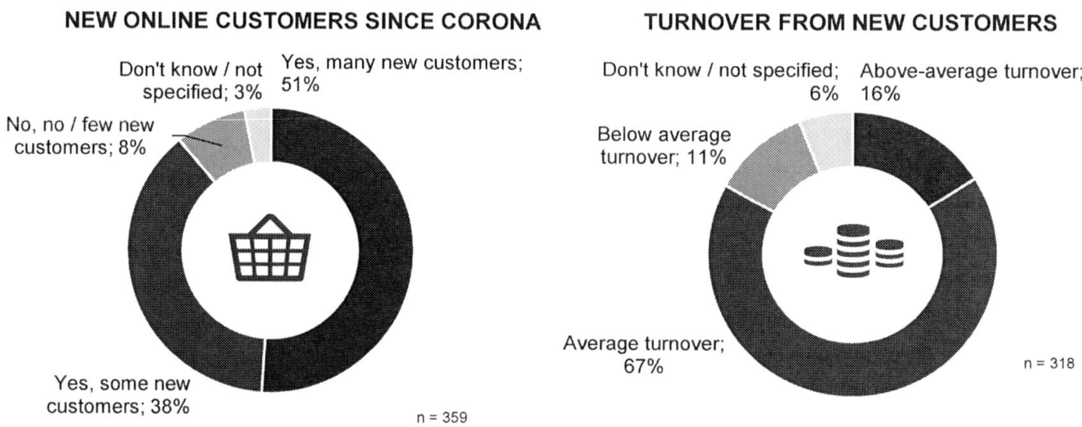

Figure 2. New online customers since corona and turnover from new customers

The question about the development of online sales and purchase frequency of existing customers of online shops revealed surprising results. One in five online retailers reported that customers not only bought more frequently online since the coronavirus crisis, but that they also *bought more*, i.e., at a higher volume or with a higher basket value. For 18% of the online retailers, existing customers did not buy more, but they *bought more frequently*. One in ten reported a higher volume, even if the purchase frequency of existing customers remained the same. For a good third of retailers, existing customers purchased the same amount and with the same frequency in the online shop as before the coronavirus crisis.

Retailers operating their online shop have been able to profit from the e-commerce boom in different ways: Firstly, almost all have gained new customers, and secondly, half have sold more frequently and/or more to existing customers online than before coronavirus crisis. However, this extraordinary sales growth with new and existing customers depends on an effective e-commerce strategy, a suitable product and pricing policy, professional marketing, and the ability to master the various operational challenges.

4.4 Relevance of Sales Channels in E-Commerce

It is shown that the majority of sales are broadly based and that customers can place their orders via several distribution channels. In 91% of cases, the retailers operate their *online shop(s)* themselves; only nine percent have outsourced them. 90% of the online retailers consider the online shop to be relevant to sales, which was to be expected (compare Figure 3 an Zumstein et al. 2021).

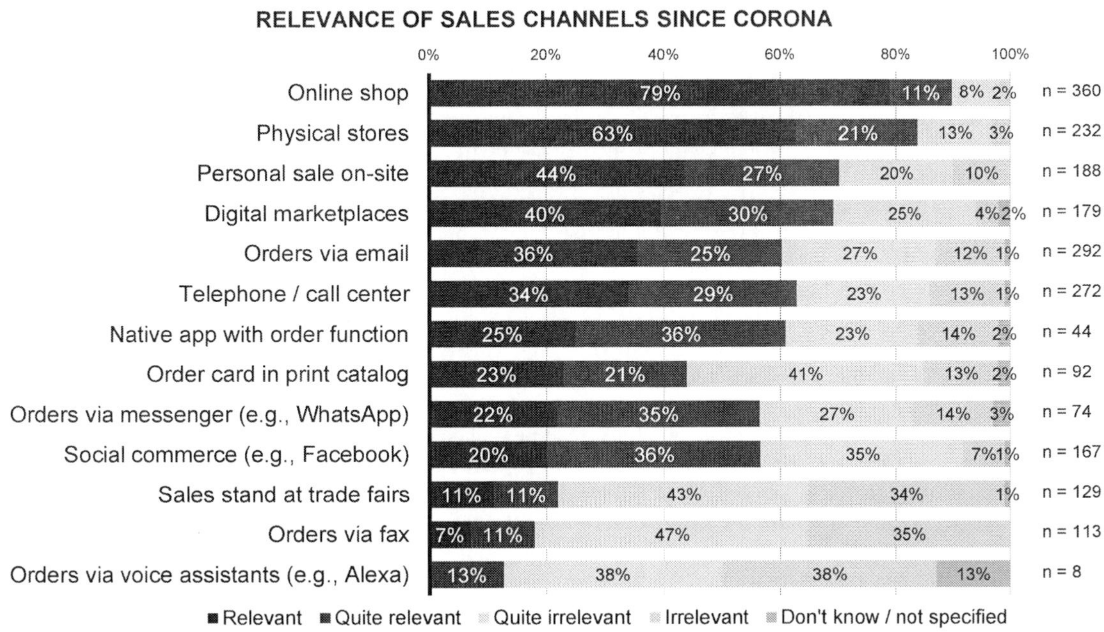

Figure 3. Relevance of sales channels since the coronavirus crises

Two-thirds of online retailers also sell their goods and services in *physical stores* with sales areas they operate themselves. As can be seen in Figure 3, brick and mortar stores rank second and are (somewhat) relevant to sales for 84% of respondents. Around 57%, mainly B2B online retailers, generally trade physically and in person – for example, through sales representatives or sales assistants. This sales channel is also (somewhat) relevant to sales for two-thirds of retailers

Orders per e-mail is relevant to sales for 36% (mostly in B2B businesses), and somewhat sales relevant for a further 25%. Four out of five online shops accept orders placed by *phone*, either through their customer service or a call center. Interestingly, 34% consider the telephone or smartphone to be a channel relevant to sales, and a further 29% see it as somewhat sales relevant. Remarkably, *Digital marketplaces* like Amazon gain in importance: It became an additional relevant online sales channel for 70% of all online retailers.

Half of online retailers already use *social commerce* via social networks to sell their goods and services, above all Facebook (Marketplace or Shops), Instagram Shops, TikTok and LinkedIn. The large reach of social platforms makes social commerce an attractive, additional form of marketing and sales and is therefore relevant to sales for one in five retailers, and somewhat relevant for one in three.

4.5 Changes Regarding Retail Stores, Personal Sales, and Trade Fairs

Retailers were asked whether they expect more customers to return to their brick-and-mortar stores once the coronavirus crisis has passed. Only ten percent believe that many customers will return to *brick-and-mortar stores* because they prefer the personal shopping experience. Over half of the omni-channel retailers expect slightly more consumers to shop in physical retail stores again after the coronavirus crisis. Reasons are that customers appreciate being able to shop *online and offline*. Almost a quarter of the retailers expect shopping behavior to remain as it is now. Only six percent assume that fewer customers will visit stores in the future because they mainly want to shop online.

Regarding the situation of *personal on-site sales*, only one in eight respondents expects to sell much more in person again once the coronavirus crisis has been defused. The named reasons are that customers value personal contact with sales personnel or, in the case of B2B, field sales staff. Every second online retailer assumes that there will be more customer visits as customers are advised both on- and offline. Similarly, one-third of the online retailers will return to *physical trade fairs* after the coronavirus crisis. Physical selling at trade fairs is considered by one third, but not at as many as before. Eight percent of previous exhibitors will no longer exhibit at trade fairs because of the high costs involved or other reasons.

4.6 Development of Stationary Stores and New Sales Formats

The rise of e-commerce is often blamed for the fact that customers are shopping less in stationary stores. As a matter of fact, many physical stores, especially small shops in cities and villages, had to close, in recent years. The coronavirus crisis and the conducted lockdowns das intensified this process. Operators of brick-and-mortar stores were asked whether they thought that this trend will continue. Only three precent think that the death of physical shops will continue as before. Half of the retailers believe that there will be a trend towards *fewer physical retail stores*. One in eight brick-and-mortar retailers believes that brick-and-mortar stores will remain. One-third reject the notion of the death of physical stores because they believe in *new sales formats*.

In the follow-up question as to what new sales formats there will be in stationary retail in the future, there were various answers: 55% of the store operators are relying on *showrooms*. This means that only a selected part of the product range is exhibited or shown in physical stores, while the entire range is available in the online shop. Most omnichannel providers have also introduced a *click-and-collect* or click-and-reserve option. Products are ordered or reserved online and then picked up in the stationary retail store. The same principle applies to *pick-up stores*, where online purchases can be picked up at the company's or a third party's pick-up station. Many retailers rely on *customer experiences* to make stationary retail stores attractive. Experiential stores should offer customers experiences and inspiration that they would not get online. *Events* also seem to be more popular again among some of the omni-channel retailers surveyed, at least after some of the Corona measures have been relaxed. *Pop-up stores* (temporary shops, or markets in vacant buildings) were also a frequently mentioned new sales format. Another omni-channel strategy, for 27% of the respondents, is *advisory shops and service centers* that provide customers added value by personal advice and services. Other 11 retailers are attempting to attract customers back to stationary stores by *partnering* with other businesses. For example, they combine retail and gastronomy by opening shops in bars, takeaways, or restaurants.

Another retail trend confirmed by 10 of the respondents are *self-service stores* (autonomous stores), in which customers pay for goods without the help of a cashier but by using an app, scanning device, or another mobile solution. Self-checkout replaces sales staff, digitizes and automates the stationary point of sale (POS). Unmanned forms of distribution enable sales 24 hours a day, seven days a week. Similarly, *vending machines* were mentioned by five respondents. Some omni-channel retailers rely on *flagship stores and branding stores*.

Shop-to-store or shop-in-shop formats are also being tested by online retailers. In addition, due to growing e-commerce, individual providers are expanding their brick-and-mortar stores into logistics hubs in order to ship goods quickly to their online customers. Finally, some retailers are experimenting with *virtual reality* (VR) or *augmented reality* (AR) and trying to integrate these technologies into their brick-and-mortar store concepts.

4.7 Challenges in E-Commerce

With the development of e-commerce in times of Corona crises, the annual survey on the challenges in e-commerce has been conducted since 2018. This allows a comparison of *different challenges* before and after the crisis. The study results show that the challenges faced by online retailers are constantly shifting.

In 2020, the focus was primarily on management, as decisions regarding personnel, the implementation of protection measures, the introduction of home working, and strategy or product range alignment had to be made. Currently, the main problem lies in *procurement*: Seven out of four online retailers report that their suppliers cannot deliver or that they can only deliver with delays (see Figure 4 and Zumstein et al. 2021). Importers are faced with many problems because international supply chains have become interrupted, are slower, or more expensive. The *market* ranks second in the current barometer of e-commerce problems: 70% of retailers agreed that, for example, increasing competition and price competition in the market represent a major or medium challenge. In 2020, the market was even less of an issue, ranking only ninth, with 25% of retailers agreeing. *Marketing* is also seen as a major challenge by 21% of respondents and as a medium challenge by 35% of them. Specific marketing challenges include rising costs or prices, especially for Google and Facebook, growing complexity, reduced effectiveness, and efficiency, or budget cuts.

Customer service currently remains a major (21%) or medium challenge (38%) for online retailers when it comes to the increasing number of customer inquiries or complaints. The situation has also worsened considerably with regard to *information technology* (IT): while just 25% agreed with this problem in 2020, more than twice as many agreed with it in 2021, at 58%. *Sales* also became more difficult in 2020 and 2021: 18% see major challenges, and another 36% see medium challenges when it comes to click-and-collect or omni-channel sales.

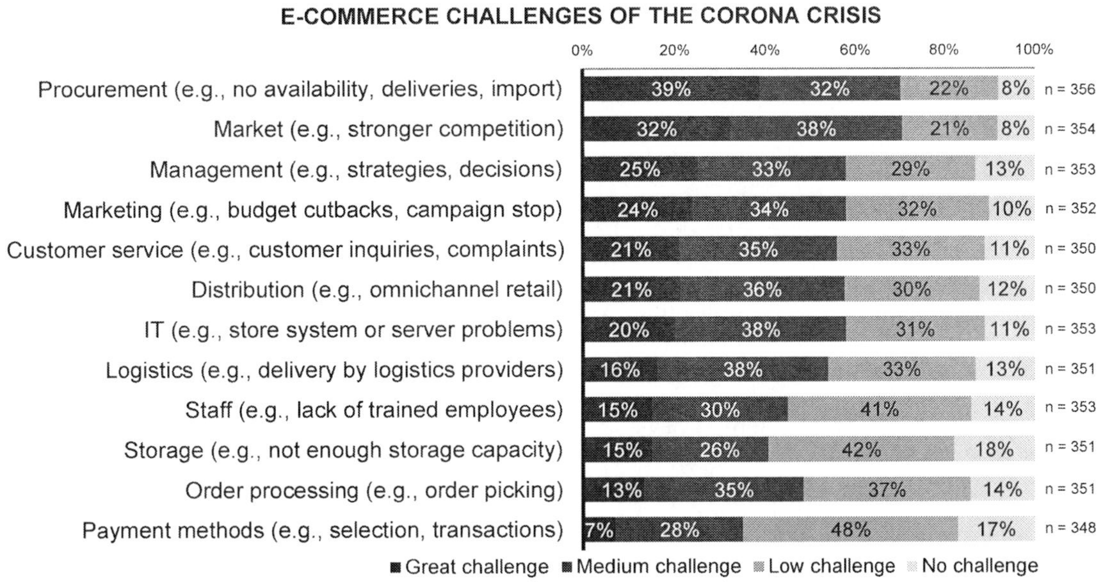

Figure 4. Biggest challenges of online shop operators

Order processing, i.e., the timely handling of the high number of orders during the Corona crisis demand shock, posed a key challenge for online retailers in the first half of 2020. In the meantime, most retailers have effective ways to handle their order processing, such as picking and commissioning, as they have taken appropriate measures and increased resources. In Figure 4, only 48% still consider *picking* to be a challenge .

Many retailers have introduced a new online shop, since the start of the Corona crisis. In addition to staff and web shops, there was also frequent investment in warehousing. *Warehouse capacities* were systematically expanded by most retailers. Numerous online retailers had learned their lesson from the supply bottlenecks in spring 2020 and increased their stock in 2021.

Regardless of the industry, many retailers have been strengthening their *online presence* since the coronavirus crisis and investing in presenting themselves in their best light. Many small niche online shops are experiencing strong growth, which is challenging many managers in terms of personnel and organization.

5. CONCLUSION

The study pointed out the development of e-commerce in Switzerland and Austria in times of the corona crises. The boom and growth in this sector due to lockdowns and a shift from stationary to online shopping led to the focus on the growth itself and the impacts that come with it. Such as the acquisition of new customers and a constant turnover by existing customers. The impacts and developments of sales channels due to the growth led to new channel and sales formats. In addition, the annual survey made it possible to monitor the special challenges in times of crisis and shows that measures in *budgets, warehousing, personnel or distribution* have been implemented.

The results of the study are limited to the Swiss and Austrian online retailer market whereby more Swiss online retailer participated than Austrian online retailers. This due to the primary inclusion of the Austrian partners and market leading into a minor notoriety and initiative building of a network of Austrian online retailers. Furthermore, the study is a quantitative study and it is a descriptive market research to gain insights and capture developments in the online retailing sector. The study gives an overview of some important aspects of the *development in online retailing* in times of the corona crisis but does not claim to be complete.

As a result of the online study nine areas of recommendations for online retailer could be identified. As there are management, sales, online shop, services, IT, marketing, organization, warehouse and logistics.

1. **Management**: The result of the shift from offline to online in all business areas have been budget adjustments and investments. Therefore, it is important to consider digitalization as part of the overall

business strategy, across all processes and employees involved. To adapt to changes in the market as an online retailer it is recommended to optimize work, warehouse and logistics processes constantly.

2. **Sales:** Those retailers and manufacturers who support their business broadly via various offline and online sales channels reduce the risks and dependence on individual channels. Among the digital sales channels, particular focus should be placed on an online shop, digital marketplaces, social media platforms, and apps
3. **Online shop**: With an own online shop, one can reduce dependencies and react more quickly and flexibly to changes in demand. Product range expansions and marketing activities can thus be implemented quickly when the market, customer needs, or user behavior change
4. **Services**: Online retailers should provide their users with various functions and services. These are product filters and finders, recommendations of alternative and additional products, watch lists and wish lists, product ratings, discount codes, and free shipping. Omnichannel retailers should offer services such as click and collect, in-store product availability, and store finders. Since the start of the crisis, some innovative retailers have introduced new digital services such as virtual store tours, video advice, live chat, or a chatbot.
5. **IT**: Due to the constantly changing usage patterns and needs, flexible, expandable online shop and payment systems should be in use and seamlessly integrated with the relevant information systems such as ERP, CRM (customer relationship management), CMS (content management systems), PIM (product information management), cash register, controlling, analytics, and warehouse systems.
6. **Marketing**: The shift of the offline marketing budget to digital marketing should ensure that a suitable marketing mix, especially in terms of digital marketing tools, is managed for each online shop.
7. **Organization**: Functioning processes and IT are not enough to be successful in e-commerce. Flexible and agile teams in the various areas, including purchasing, sales, marketing, IT, logistics, and distribution are essential for a well-positioned digital business. Enabling work from home, offering webinars and digital consultations, as well as conducting digital training and further education motivate employees.
8. **Warehouse**: This research confirms that the design of scalable warehouse capacities and storage areas are important criteria in the success of e-commerce business. The majority of online retailers have invested heavily in warehousing. Some have also added warehouses and redistributed their human resources.
9. **Logistics**: Logistics capacities are constantly being optimized and expanded, as this study shows. There continues to be a shift from stationary shopping to pure online shopping, which can be anticipated through adapted logistics processes and flexibly deployable personnel.

Finally, online retailers should continue to analyze the developments in this challenging environment and anticipate and face any discernible changes. *Flexibility in management and organization* as well as budget shifts are important factors to face the instable times of crises.

REFERENCES

Austrian Retail Association (2021). eCommerce Studie Österreich - Konsumentenverhalten im Distanzhandel. KMU Forschung Austria.

Lone, S., Harboul, N., & Weltevreden, J. W. J. (2021). *2021 European E-commerce Report*. Hogeschool van Amsterdam. Retrieved from https://www.cmihva.nl/wp-content/uploads/2021/09/EuropeanEcommerce-Report-2021.pdf

Nets DACH (2020). E-Com Report Dach 2020. Retrieved from https://www.concardis.com/ecom-report-2020.

Rudolph, T., Klink, B. & Hoang, M. (2021). Der Schweizer Online-Handel – Internetnutzung Schweiz 2021. A study by the University of St. Gallen.

Trade Association. swiss (2021). Online retail market Switzerland. HANDELSVERBAND.swiss. Retrieved from https://handelsverband.swiss/facts/facts-zur-schweiz

Wölfle, R., Leimstoll, U. (2021). E-Commerce-Report Schweiz 2021 - Standortbestimmung im Schweizer Handel, Basel: FHNW. Retrieved from https://www.e-commerce-report.ch.

Zumstein, D., Steigerwald, A. (2018). Swiss Online Retailer Survey 2018 – Digital Commerce. A study by the Lucerne University of Applied Sciences and Arts. Lucerne: HSLU.

Zumstein, D., Steigerwald, A. (2019). Online Retailer Survey 2019 – Opportunities and challenges in sales and marketing of Swiss online shops. A study by the Institute of Marketing Management. Winterthur: ZHAW. Retrieved from https://digitalcollection.zhaw.ch/bitstream/11475/18746/5/Onlinehaendlerbefragung_2019.pdf.

Zumstein, D., Oswald, C., (2020). Online Retailer Survey 2020 – Sustainable growth of e-commerce and challenges in times of crisis. A study by the Institute of Marketing Management. Winterthur: ZHAW. Retrieved from https://digitalcollection.zhaw.ch/bitstream/11475/20912/3/2020_Zumstein-Oswald_Swiss-Online-Retailer-Survey.pdf

Zumstein, D., Oswald, C., (2021). Online Retailer Survey 2021 – Empirical Findings on the E-Commerce Boom in Switzerland and Austria. Winterthur: ZHAW. Retrieved from www.zhaw.ch/storage/hochschule/medien/news/2021/210908-zhaw-studie-onlinehaendlerbefragung-2021-EN.pdf

STUDYING GAMIFICATION AS A TOOL FOR COLLECTING DATA

André Salomão, Bruno Dal Ponte Pavei da Silva, Júlio Monteiro Teixeira, Nicolas Canale Romeiro and Milton Luiz Horn Vieira
Universidade Federal de Santa Catarina
Design Lab, R. Roberto Sampaio Gonzaga, 274, Florianópolis, Brazil

ABSTRACT

It is already knowledge that games themselves are good at motivating their players, usually by focusing on three main cores, time, rewards, and pleasure. The core of gamification is the user, in the case of gamification, being treated like a player, therefore any system that the player interacts with, how to motivate they are consequently driving the result of said system. This research aimed to analyze the application of the concept of avatar gamification in a digital platform. For this, analyzes of the profile of different users of this platform were carried out to find out if it was possible to identify the psychological profile of everyone according to the concepts of Bartles (1996). The result found indicates that, although the platform allows customization and priority level of what the user can demonstrate on their profile page, the available elements made it possible to identify trends for only three player profiles on the platform.

KEYWORDS

Design, Avatar, Game, Gamification.

1. INTRODUCTION

It is already knowledge that games themselves are good at motivating their players, usually by focusing on three main cores, time, rewards, and pleasure. The core of gamification is the user, in the case of gamification, being treated like a player, therefore any system that the player interacts with, how to motivate they are consequently driving the result of said system. Therefore, the more the designer understands its audience, who are playing their product, both at the current time and prospective, the easier will be to design features that will drive their behavior towards the game's goal (Zichermann & Cunningham, 2011).

Nannan Xi and Juho Hamari (2019) wrote an article about the relationship between gamification, brand engagement, and brand equity, where they asked 824 users from the Xiaomi and Huawei communities about different gamification tools, they interacted within each of them. One of the issues concluded by the researchers was the fact that they could not generalize their results to another community or on a broader scale due to their methodology, their gamification elements were first grouped and then analyzed, instead of being identified and analyzed individually so they could generalize the results afterward.

This article proposes to take a few steps back regarding Nannan Xi and Juho Hamari's (2019) article to have results that can be generalized to a different culture or community of people. The article takes the element of gamification, groups them, separates them into different categories, and then collects information about how the users interact with these elements. Our goal is to use one single gamification element, in this case, we chose the 'avatar' element, to collect data and information about the platform's users to create personas and then base those personas in game's psychology profiles to figure out which gamification-type of tool the developers should focus on according to their target audience. The idea is that studying first a gamification element 'avatar' that can collect real data about the target audience can lead to proper categorization of the remaining gamification elements based on gamer's psychology, which therefore allows better generalization of results.

2. PROCEDURES

The procedure adopted for this research is the case study aims, according to Gil (2002), to carry out an in-depth study of one or a few objects in a way that allows broad and detailed knowledge of the object of study. Complementing Gil, Dresch, et al. (2015) state that it is a research method used to investigate a problem within a context in which they occur, through comparison of data collected by the research, which seek to identify theoretical categories that can serve to generate new theories, therefore, the case study aims to describe a phenomenon, test theory, and create theory.

According to Gil (2002), of the purposes mentioned for the use of this research method, the ones that best fit the present investigation are (i) to describe the situation of the context in which a particular investigation is being carried out and (ii) to explain the causal variables of a given phenomenon in very complex situations that do not allow the use of surveys and experiments.

Complementary to Gil (2002), to reach the objectives of research on a case study, according to Dresch, et al (2015), the research must go through some steps: (i) define the conceptual structure, where it seeks to consult the existing literature related to the research topic and describe propositions & demarcate research boundaries, (ii) plan the cases, in this step it will be selected which objects of study will be used as an example to carry out the in-depth study, defining itself which and how they will be analyzed, (iii) collect data from the defined object of study, record what was found when in contact with the object of study, (iv) data analysis, prepare an analysis from the collected data, seeking to group them according to their similarities and identify causal relationships, (v) generate a report, demonstrate the theoretical implications of the study.

Following this methodology, this research, therefore, proposes to analyze the 'avatar' gamification element in different profiles of a platform to understand this phenomenon for the future exploration of this concept as a tool for collecting data from platform users. First, then (i) a theoretical survey will be carried out on the concepts of game design, gamification, and avatars (ii) followed by the selection of the object of study, in this case, the use of the gamification concept on avatars within the Steam sales platform by through the search for user profiles that fit within the concepts established in the first step. Define (iii) the different public profiles of platform users to analyze the content and later (iv) cross-reference information present in the profiles with the concepts raised in the theoretical foundation. Finally (v), generate a discussion about the implications of the research according to the results found.

3. GAME DESIGN & GAMIFICATION

Throughout history, games have gained different functions and practices, according to McGonigal (2011), games can be defined according to common characteristics present in the structure of their experiences, being composed of goals, rules, feedback system, and voluntary participation. The goal is related to the player's purpose when participating in the game, according to the expected result of the developed activities (McGonigal, 2011). Being able to portray, at the end of the game, according to the completeness of these activities or one of its sections, contemplating the completion of a task that guides the player (Vianna et.al., 2013). Subsequently, the rules ground the space of possibilities to complete the goals, stimulating creative and strategic perception (McGonigal, 2011). Its function is to balance the possibilities of the game, to predict behavior according to the players' actions (Vianna et.al., 2013).

The feedback system helps in the motivation process corresponding to the player's progression, as a metric of the established goal (McGonigal, 2011). In addition to providing a performance return to user interactions with activities, related to their actions (Vianna et.al., 2013). Voluntary participation is consistent with the player's consent to the structure of the game, its optional and intentional presence per the characteristics of the challenge (McGonigal, 2012). It complements the consensus between the system and the user, and its disposition to the proposed conditions (Vianna et.al., 2013).

Due to the digital industry, gamification was spread in the second half of 2010 (Deterding, 2011), from a TED conference by Jane McGonigal, an American designer on the subject (Vianna et. al., 2013). For McGonigal (2011) the motivational retribution found in games results in positive emotions, showing its applicability in experience planning, considering the perspective of game developers in solving problems. Burke (2015) explains that, although gamification shares characteristics with video games and reward programs, according to the user's voluntary involvement in systems that feature interactive mechanics, it differs in its primary motivator. According to the author, the purpose of games is exclusively for entertainment, in which the experience planning is consistent with the player's immersion. Reward programs have the purpose of creating value for the consumer in transactions and rewarding them with tangible gratifications on an already established performance. Otherwise, the purpose of gamification is aimed at engaging at an emotional level, with the perception of value over actions through the user's process, according to solutions that re-signify the meaning present in their behavior. This motivation is the result of intrinsic and extrinsic rewards, in which the participation and autonomous actions of the user, added to constant feedback, result in the achievement of significant goals (Burke, 2015). Its definition can be analyzed in contrast to other concepts, according to Deterding et. al. (2013) in Figure 1, differing from toys and playful design on the horizontal axis. Considering play as a playful and spontaneous activity (Vianna, et. al., 2013).

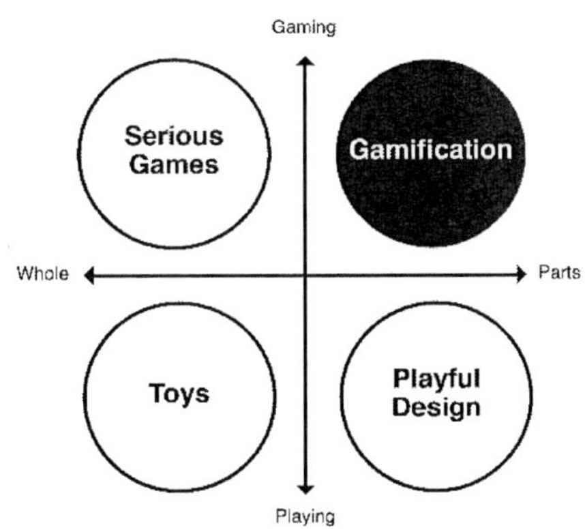

Figure 1. Concepts quadrant chart

In this context, games are distinguished from forms of entertainment by the consistency of their characteristics, limiting the game space with rules and objectives (Gray; Brown; Macanufo, 2010). In the same way, gamification uses game elements but differs in the totality of elements used (Alves, 2015). Considering the resources found in games to build gamified experiences, Werbach and Hunter (2012) present the components in the way the game is played, according to dynamics, mechanics, and components. The existing modules in the user experience reside in their dynamics, corresponding to patterns based on actions responsible for the direction and structure of the system. Activity states, on the other hand, are classified by their mechanics, in-game practices, and behaviors, composing the use and foundation of their components. As a foundation, we have its components according to analogies that give function to the game system (Alves, 2015).

Dynamics are abstract concepts present in the experience system, which help in the development of activities. According to the authors, the main dynamics are (i) Constraints: Stimulate strategic thinking by limiting the possibilities of completing an objective; (ii) Emotions: Motivate the player by completing the proposed objectives according to an information feedback system; (iii) Storytelling: Explain the circumstances of the game in its context to engage the player; (iv) Progression: Rewarding the player's advancements in proportion to the recognition of their activities and; (v) Relationship: Interacting socially within the game environment.

To give action to the dynamics, mechanics are explored, defining the possibilities of interactions, according to procedures that govern a game. (Vianna et.al., 2013). Unlike the rules found in the structure of a game with access to players, the mechanics of a game are interconnected to their experience, according to the descriptive mechanisms that influence the game's outcome. (Adams; Dormans, 2012). Considering that the players are the protagonists of the game (Vianna et.al., 2013) and that the design of experiences is focused on the user, Alves (2015) highlights the existence of different variations of players, having types of learning and temperaments distinct.

Bartle (1996) describes that these distinct behaviors can be classified according to the way people interact with the game. Composed of four abstract terms evidenced in the player's motivation process, referenced as socializers, explorers, achievers, and killers (Figure 2).

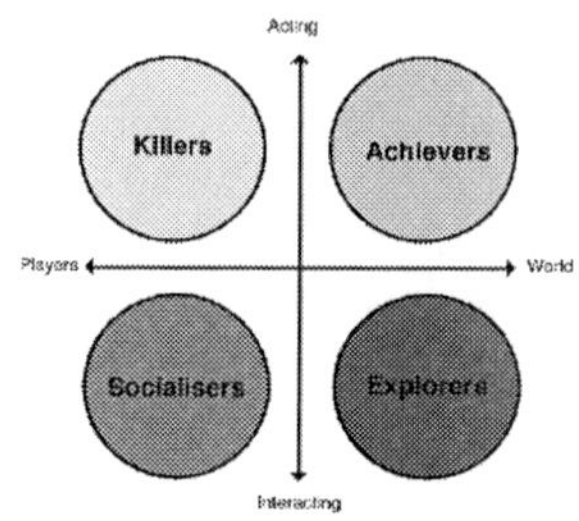

Figure 2. The four archetypes of player's motivation process

Each quadrant categorizes the extreme of interest in the players' motivations, the horizontal axis divides the player's preference between interacting with other players or exploring the game universe, while the vertical axis defines the player's choice to interact with the game system or act about him (Bartle, 1996). Achievers are the type of players interested in acting in the game world, are driven by the game's objectives, like to accumulate points, levels, and rewards that make you stand out from other players. On the other hand, explorers are motivated by interaction with the game, they seek to know all the information about the game system and for them, this discovery is the reward. When the interest is turned to interaction with other players, we have socializers, emphasizing collaboration between users and seeking the social aspect of a game. Finally, assassins categorize players with a competitive spirit, have a desire to become skilled among their peers, and crave a reputation for their abilities.

4. PERSONAS & AVATARS

It is possible to interpret the typologies proposed by Bartle (1996) as positioning strategies and exploration of optional niches. Considering that its polarization is objective the characteristics of each quadrant, we can relate each of these as extremes of personalities and consequent opportunities for investigation, aimed at developing research that has part of their user process in a gamified system or games. Present in another field of knowledge, aimed at representing ideal users, according to explicit assumptions about their actions. Personas assist in the empathetic decision-making process by creating a user-oriented focus of engagement (Adlin, Pruitt, 2010).

Personas are simulated representations of characters to represent a user or group of peers comprehensively, are used in research and development of projects aimed at people, aiming at the comprehensive interpretation of data, and are related to the study of similar social behaviors. It is a tool that makes use of qualitative and quantitative data to better understand the customer of a brand, product, or service, and predict their actions in controlled environments. (Herskovitz, Crystal, 2010; Cooper, et.al., 2007). Its use is not limited only to user creation and development processes for specific products, but also to any system that can include the user as part of its process, visible in its participation as a creative tool in different development methods. To create a persona, a process of documenting common characteristics, conceived through information, is necessary.

According to Nielsen et.al (2015), based on a market analysis regarding the persona development processes of different organizations, the characteristics necessary to compose a persona involve demographic factors, personality types, lifestyles, day-to-day life. day of the individual, performance scenarios, simulated situations, and especially the relationship between the user and the brand, in the connection of the experience with its products and services, among more information, with the general objective of empathically understanding the needs of the consumer. On the other hand, in the literal representation of the user in digital systems, we find avatars, as to dimensions of data that, combined with the identification of typologies of players, offer relevant data for the construction of a persona of a gamified system, presented in the next section.

Avatars are manifestations of a user of the digital environment, applied as a graphic or pictorial representation of two-dimensional and three-dimensional universes. They act as a mechanical extension representing a personal profile and aim to simulate an identity providing a customized experience. (Alves, 2015). This involvement and immersion in the digital environment are based on the principle of new forms of entertainment along with sensory exposure and the user's procedural authority, which enable significant opportunities for narrative entertainment (Murray, 2003). According to Castranova (2003), avatars come from the expansion of digital environments and the need to present their users through interfaces, due to their natural evolution, have expanded to video games and other systems and interfaces we use. They can be represented by choices that simulate characteristics of a profile in the system, carrying meanings associated with the symbols. As a form of simple visual identification shown in the example in Figure 3, when registering a new user in the Windows XP operating system, the user is suggested to associate a pictorial image and a set of characters to represent their environment in the system.

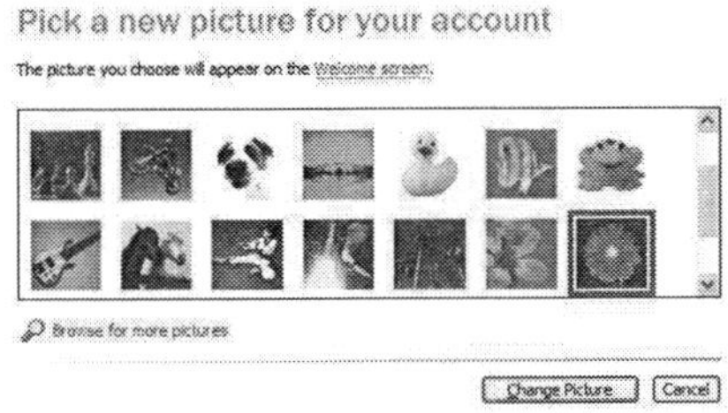

Figure 3. Avatar

In addition, Teichrieb (1999) presents two representation possibilities for avatars: (I) a graphical user representative, as in the previous example, and (ii) a representative capable of developing additional functions, acting as intelligent agents governed by rules of interactions. According to the author, when used as information agents, the premises of the development of (a) actions based on simple rules, with the capture of sensors, (b) reactive to external actions, concerned with the state of the environment, are governed by (a) c) cognitive systems, storing the state of the environment and assimilating its characteristics with the environment and (d) optimizers performing activities combined with the current situation of the environment. According to Muray (2003), the proportionality of digital immersion is associated with a good resolution of the environment in which the user is inserted. In this way, avatars represent a positive alternative to the degree of involvement of virtual systems (Teichrieb, 1999) Therefore, it is essential to understand how the interaction with avatars can impact the user experience and the beginning of this ideation how can we understand the impact that personalization.

5. DISCUSSION

Following the established procedures, after a theoretical survey on the topics of game design, gamification, avatars & personas, we sought to establish how to identify in each Steam platform user profile, possible indicators following the hypothetical-deductive logic for profile identification of each user within the quadrant proposed by Bartles (1996). For this, the profile of different users was analyzed to identify whether it was possible to establish a psychological profile to the profile, if so, where the user fits within the concept of Bartles (1996), and if not, what information was lacking to reach a conclusion regarding this user. The first profile analyzed will be used to find out which elements are present on the profile page and which of these elements are fixed or changeable according to the user's desire.

These identifiers will help in the analysis of each of the profiles, consequently, the choice of identifiers that are adjustable can better reflect its psychological profile. About the user himself, he has the option to modify his name, profile picture, and a brief description of himself. In addition, the user can customize their profile page, being able to change the background image, theme, which insignia are highlighted, which are their favorite groups, they can also change privacy options, such as public profile or not. The part of personal highlights is more flexible for the user to highlight what is of most interest to him, where depending on the item he chooses to highlight, it may be a better indicator on establishing what kind of psychological profile he fits within the concept of Bartles (1996).

For privacy reasons, all information that could expose the identity of a user of any of the profiles analyzed here will be suppressed, and only public Steam profiles will be used. For this article, 50 different profiles were analyzed to seek information that allows the identification of their archetype of player. Within these profiles, 20% presented insufficient information for a complete analysis, among the remaining 80% we picked three users to be discussed below which had highlighted indicators that enable their identification in one of Bartles' archetypes (1996), the rest present information that indicates characteristics of different archetypes, but not the possibility to highlight one.

User 01, represented by figure 4, chose as a brief description of himself to redirect the viewer to two different websites, the first called SteamLadder, used to identify the rank of the Steam user profile within the ecosystem, and the second called SteamRep, which evaluates the user's reputation within the same ecosystem, both sites indicate that the player has characteristics of an achiever, as he wants to show his achievements through his reputation & ranking.

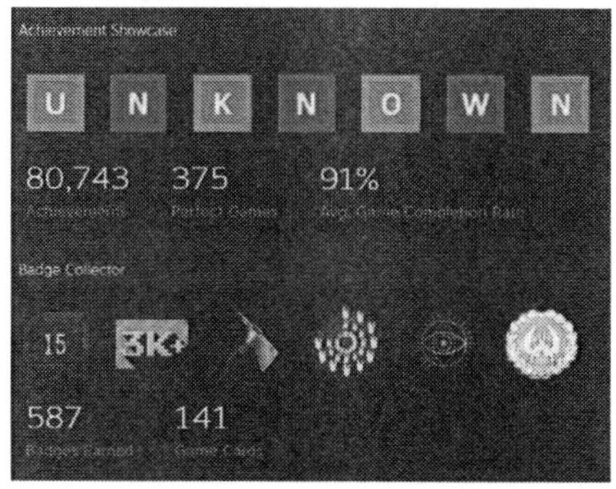

Figure 4. Achiever profile

On their profile page, the user chose to demonstrate as the main highlight elements such as the number of achievements and the percentage of avg game completion rate of 91%, suggesting that on average the player completes 91% of the available achievements, not only does he seek to be a completionist, as he also likes to expose his achievement collection to other users, the rest of his profile is aimed at demonstrating his achievements in different ways. As the player chooses mostly to expose highlighted elements of their achievements, such as rank level or percentage of achievement of goals, the player fits the profile of Achiever proposed by Bartle (1996) without presenting other elements that could indicate another psychological profile.

User 02, represented by figure 5, did not describe in his profile information any element that would indicate his psychological type, however, in his profile, he chose as an image, one that symbolizes action, in addition, the player mostly presents games of player-versus-player profiles, in addition, the profile has a much lower rate of goal achievement within games. Therefore, the lack of exposure of specific elements demonstrates that he does not have an achiever tendency, but the high preference and recorded time in games like Counter-Strike: Global Offensive (almost two thousand hours of game), a popular shooting game First-person video that pits the player against another player, and other similar games like PUBG: Battlegrounds (837 hours of gameplay), demonstrate an inclination to be a killer type player, who is more interested in games where he can enter in conflict with others.

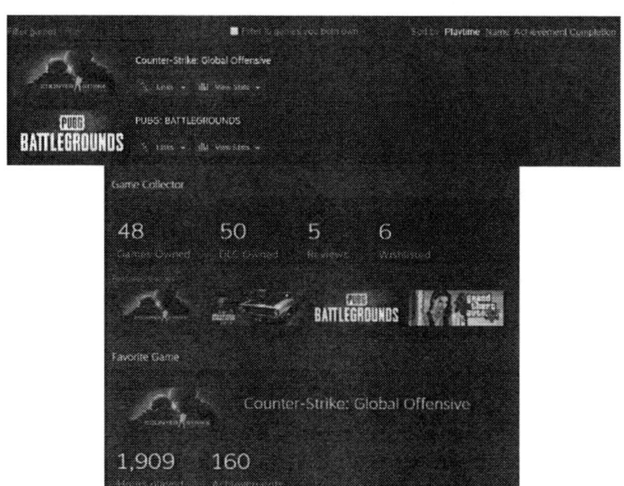

Figure 5. Killer profile

User 03, represented by figure 6, placed personal information such as his or her tastes as a description in his profile, the idea of being open to new interactions with other users, such as exchanging items. The user follows this information by highlighting in their profile a long list describing their tastes such as major games, television shows, movies, music, artists, food, and drink, as well as prerequisites for accepting new friend requests. In addition to the focus on providing personal information for new relationships with other platform users, the player is present, at the time of this research, in 57 different user groups on the Steam platform, more than the 15 groups that user 02 is in, but less than the 210 that user 01 is, in addition, the player currently has around 295 friends added to the platform, compared to user 01 keeps this information private and user 02 has 147 added. The player also demonstrates an aptitude for the player versus player games, having as a favorite game, Counter-Strike: Global Offensive, which gives him the connotation of being a killer type of player.

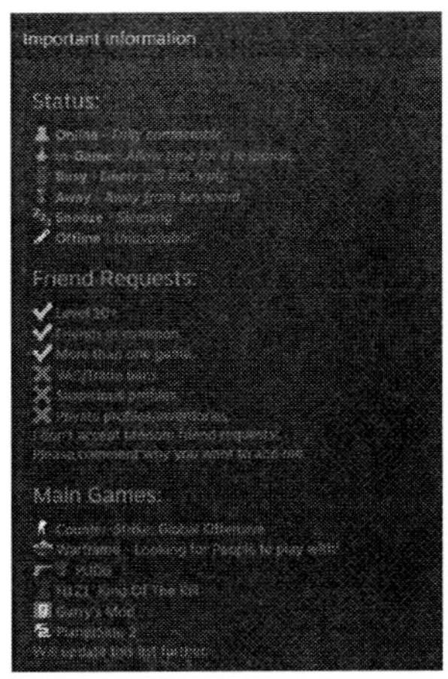

Figure 6. Socializer profile

Overall, although the profile has elements of a killer-type player, because it places a strong emphasis on social issues, as a prerequisite for adding user 03 to your friend's list, it indicates that the user is more concerned about socializing with users who have the same or similar profile, so he is likely to be categorized as a socializer's profile user. In these three users chosen for analysis, it was possible to see that there are clear indicators and preferences of each one of the users that enable the inclination of their psychological profile within the concepts established by Bartles (1996). User 01, despite having some elements that can be categorized as socializers, such as the high number of group participation, his number of friends was private, and the rest of the information in his profile showed a tendency to prioritize his achievements inside the steam platform. User 02 also follows the same logic, he has some characteristics of an achiever's profile, but he prioritizes information about games in preference to the player against player, which indicates a killer-type player profile. On the other hand, user 03, like user 02, in the sense that he has a taste for player versus player games, but in his profile, he is more concerned with demonstrating his personality, and citing prerequisites for other players who want to interact with him on the platform.

What these three mentioned users have in common, along with the availability of the information available on the Steam platform for player customization, is the fact that it is difficult to define how prone the user is to the explorer profile, as few indicators allow the player exposes his preference for exploration over the other three profiles, possibly the best indicator is hours played in games that allow the player to explore in an open universe, but this type of example is not easily replicated on any gamified platform that wants to identify if your user profile is of the explorer type.

6. CONCLUSION

This research goal was to analyze the application of the concept of avatar gamification in a digital platform. For this, analyzes of the profile of different users of this platform were carried out to find out if it was possible to identify the psychological profile of everyone according to the concepts of Bartles (1996). The result found indicates that, although the platform allows customization and priority level of what the user can demonstrate on their profile page, the available elements made it possible to identify trends for only three player profiles on the platform.

For a future gamified system that uses the concept of the avatar to collect data on the psychological profile of each user, to identify how to proceed with the development of the platform according to the target audience, it is necessary to establish options for the user who identify him clearly and less subjectively what his preferences are. Because with only information found in the Steam user profile, it is possible to find an inclination to a type of archetype, but it is not possible to say with 100% certainty. In the ideal situation, the gamified system should allow the designer or project manager to draw conclusions with a higher level of confidence.

ACKNOWLEDGEMENT

We thank the Federal University of Santa Catarina. The financial support of CAPES. The Team in DesignLAB/UFSC and Tecmidia for the collaboration to this research.

REFERENCES

Adams, Sean; Morioka, Noreen; StonE, Terry Lee 2006. Logo design workbook: A hands-on guide to creating logos. Rockport Publishers.

Adlin, Tamara; Pruitt, John. 2010 The essential persona lifecycle: Your guide to building and using personas. Morgan Kaufmann,.

Aline, Dresch et al. 2015 Design Science Research: Método de pesquisa para avanço da ciência e tecnologia. Bookman. Brazil

Alves, Flora. 2015. Gamification: como criar experiências de aprendizagem engajadoras. DVS editora.

Bartle, Richard. 1996. Hearts, clubs, diamonds, spades: Players who suit MUDs. Journal of MUD research, v. 1, n. 1, p. 19.

Burke, Brian. Gamificar: como a gamificação motiva as pessoas a fazerem coisas extraordinárias. DVS Editora, 2015.

Castronova, Edward. 2003. Theory of the Avatar. Available at SSRN 385103.

Cooper, Alan; Reimann, Robert; Cronin, David. 2013. About face 3: the essentials of interaction design. John Wiley & Sons.

Deterding, Sebastian et al. 2011. From game design elements to gamefulness: defining" gamification". In: Proceedings of the 15th international academic MindTrek conference: Envisioning future media environments. p. 9-15.

Gil, A. C. 2002. Como elaborar projetos de pesquisa. Editora Atlas, São Paulo, Brazil.

Gray, Dave; Brown, Sunni; Macanufo, James. 2010 Gamestorming: A playbook for innovators, rulebreakers, and changemakers. " O'Reilly Media, Inc.".

Herskovitz, Stephen; Crystal, Malcolm. 2010. The essential brand persona: storytelling and branding. Journal of business strategy.

Mcgonigal, Jane. 2011. Reality is broken: Why games make us better and how they can change the world. Penguin.

Murray, Janet. 2003 Hamlet no holodeck. São Paulo: Unesp.

Nielsen, Lene et al. 2015. A template for design personas: analysis of 47 persona descriptions from danish industries and organizations. International Journal of Sociotechnology and Knowledge Development (IJSKD), v. 7, n. 1, p. 45-61.

Teichrieb, Verônica. 1999. Avatares como guias interativos para auxílio na navegação em ambientes virtuais tridimensionais. Universidade Federal de Pernambuco, Recife (Dissertação de mestrado).

Vianna, Ysmar et al. Gamification, Inc: como reinventar empresas a partir de jogos. Rio de Janeiro: MJV, 2013.

Zichermann, Gabe; Cunningham, Christopher. 2011. Gamification by design: Implementing game mechanics in web and mobile apps. " O'Reilly Media, Inc.".

Werbach, Kevin; Hunter, Dan. 2012. For the Win: How game thinking can revolutionize your business. Wharton Digital Press.

AN ONLINE EXPERIMENT ON THE STEREOTYPE CONTENT MODEL (SCM) AND CHATBOTS – DOES SWAPPING THE PICTURE MAKE A DIFFERENCE?

Roger Seiler and Sonja Wüest
Zurich University of Applied Sciences
St.-Georgen-Platz 2, CH-8400 Winterthur, Switzerland

ABSTRACT

Chatbots have become quite popular in recent years, and research on the topic has gained momentum. In this study, we address whether the stereotype content model applies in the context of chatbots. Furthermore, we consider whether swapping the image of a person in the chatbot interface makes a difference in terms of the SCM. An online experiment was conducted to A/B-test different chatbot versions, and the results suggest that the SCM applies. Furthermore, a chatbot can be perceived as warm and competent, with friendliness, in particular, fostering online trust. This, in turn, is a business-success-relevant construct in an online setting. Therefore, if a trustworthy chatbot is to be implemented, the SCM is considered relevant and necessary for implementing such a bot.

KEYWORDS

Chatbots, Stereo Content Model, Trust, Online Experiment, A/B-Testing

1. INTRODUCTION

Since ELIZA (Weizenbaum, 1966) and A.L.I.C.E. (Wallace, 2009), chatbots have further evolved and become integrated as voice assistants in operating systems. Market size and growth estimates are high, and the field of application ranges from healthcare and banking to retail (Intelligence, n.d.). Furthermore, an extensive analysis of patents highlights their importance and how this technology is moving towards supporting and assisting customers (Pantano & Pizzi, 2020). This results in a shift from personal support to an automated and more technical touch (Pantano & Pizzi, 2020). A more virtual and digital customer service approach is emerging, so the question of how social aspects should be addressed arises. Personalisation and social presence are constructs related to this (Verhagen et al., 2014). The more human the bot appears, the more people can relate to it (Wilson et al., 2017). Because relational aspects (e.g. trust) can play a role in business success and e-commerce (Beatty et al., 2011; Kim et al., 2008; Kim & Peterson, 2017; Köksal & Penez, 2015) and prior research has an emphasis on technical aspects (Pantano & Pizzi, 2020), this research contributes to the chatbot literature by testing whether the SCM applies in the given context. Furthermore, the question can be answered by swapping the chatbot picture to create a chatbot personality that users and potential customers perceive as positive.

This research builds on the work of Fiske et al. (2007, 2002) and Cuddy et al. (2008), which stated that universal dimensions of warmth and competence exist and when these meet robots, it is a double-edged sword (Tay et al., 2014). Furthermore, the SCM was introduced by Casciaro and Lobo (2005) based on the research previously mentioned.

This paper contributes to the current literature by applying the SCM in a chatbot context and conducting an online experiment (A/B-test) to ascertain whether the model also holds. This is especially relevant to e-commerce as purchase behaviours have changed due to the pandemic (Gao et al., 2020). Valaskova et al. (2021) commented that shopping patterns have changed, and 65% of consumers intend to maintain these new purchasing habits in the future. Furthermore, online service and support are applications where chatbots have replaced humans by drawing on deep learning, natural language processing (NLP), natural language understanding (NLU), and natural language generation (NLG) to interact with customers (Mohamad Suhaili et al., 2021). Building online trust is essential, as is clarifying the relevance of the model, since it can be used to guide companies seeking to work with chatbots. The following section provides an overview of the relevant concepts through a literature review.

2. LITERATURE

Empirical research suggests that trust is a key success factor in online commerce (Beatty et al., 2011; Kim et al., 2008; Kim & Peterson, 2017; Köksal & Penez, 2015). This is especially relevant since the question of trusting the faceless and intangible takes place online (Beldad et al., 2010). Linked to this is the aspect of social presence that can arise when artefacts with social cues are perceived by users or customers (Verhagen et al., 2014). Social presence and social cues are both relevant when considered in the context of purchase intentions (Botha & Reyneke, 2015; Lu et al., 2016).

The SCM (Casciaro & Lobo, 2005) extends the work of Fiske and Cuddy by creating a model based on the two dimensions of sympathy and competence to categorize stereotypes (see Figure 1). Casciaro and Lobo proposed (according to the two dimensions in their model) a stereotypical "incompetent jerk" (low competence and low sympathy), a "competent jerk" (high competence but low sympathy), a "lovable fool" (high sympathy but low competence) and a "lovable star" (high sympathy and high competence) (Casciaro & Lobo, 2005). When picking who to work with, people tend to opt for the lovable star (Casciaro & Lobo, 2005). Furthermore, Casciaro and Lobo (2005) point out that the sympathy dimension affects the building up of trust. Indeed, this is in line with van der Holst who stated that this holds for e-commerce, but in health care, it is competence that fosters trust (Holst, 2021). This model has found its application in education (Niemiec & Ryan, 2009), brand management (Aaker et al., 2012), health care (Drevs, 2013), information technology (Franklin et al., 2013), nonprofit organisations (Aaker et al., 2010), and sales (Zawisza & Pittard, 2015). Furthermore, these dimensions also seem to hold in the context of human-robot interaction (HRI) (Christoforakos et al., 2021; Tay et al., 2014).

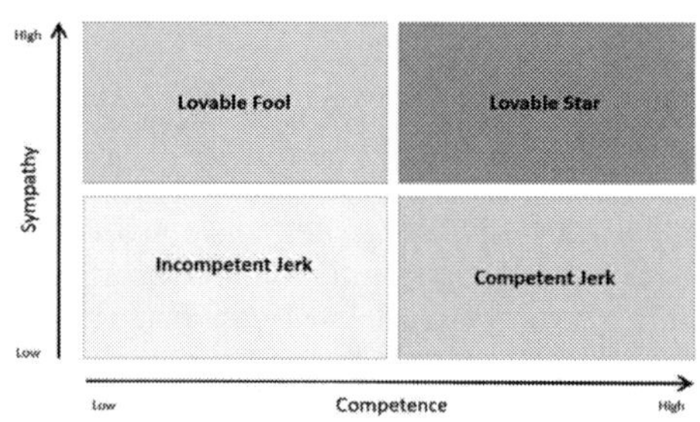

Figure 1. SCM by Casciaro & Lobo (2005)

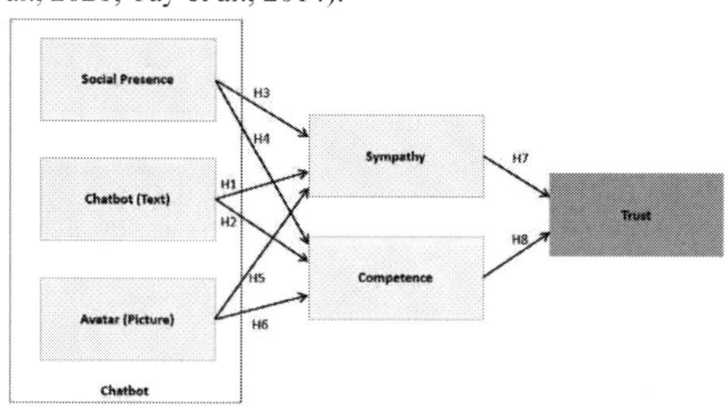

Figure 2. Conceptual Model

Trust can develop when visiting websites (Ba & Pavlou, 2002; Lee et al., 2015; McAllister, 1995; D. H. McKnight et al., 2002; H. D. McKnight et al., 2002) and hence, can play a role when interacting with artefacts (Beatty et al., 2011; Kim et al., 2008; Kim & Peterson, 2017) or a specific technology (Mcknight et al., 2011). Furthermore, past research has shown that trust not only builds in human relationships but also when interacting with robots (Christoforakos et al., 2021). Even in mediated communication in general, trust can be formed (Pan & Steed, 2016). Trust builds upon first perceptions (Hampton-Sosa & Koufaris, 2005), and past empirical research suggests that images can help build trust (Steinbrück et al., n.d.). This is in line with Wood et al. (2008), who found evidence that verbal and non-verbal cues can foster trust in car sales based on a perception of the sympathy and competence of the salesperson.

Social presence plays a role in electronic mediated communication because an avatar displayed in a chat box has positive effects on perceived interactivity, social support, and trust (Chattaraman et al., 2014). Mediated communication can lead to the perception of social cues as well as the feeling of being close to the other party (Biocca et al., 2003).

Based on the work of Wood et al. (2008), Fiske et al. (2007, 2002), Cuddy et al. (2011, 2008, 2007) and Casciaro and Lobo (2005), we constructed the conceptual model (see Figure 2) for this research. Additionally, the hypotheses were derived from earlier research (see Table 1 for an overview).

Table 1. Overview of the hypotheses

#	Text	Result
1	Text communication influences perceived sympathy.	Accept
2	Text communication influences perceived competence.	Accept
3	Social presence influences perceived sympathy.	Accept
4	Social presence influences perceived competence.	Reject
5	Avatar (picture) influences perceived sympathy.	Reject
6	Avatar (picture) influences perceived competence.	Reject
7	Sympathy influences trust.	Accept
8	Competence influences trust.	Accept

3. METHODOLOGY

The chatbot was implemented as a mock-up using Botsociety software. The pictures were tested in a previous study where students were asked to assign images to the corresponding stereotypes of the SCM. The "lovable fool" and the "incompetent jerk" pictures drawn from the earlier study were used here as stimulus material. Furthermore, text from a previous study by Rozumowski et al. (2017) was used. User responses were identical. The layout of the chatbot is designed to resemble a messaging app communication (e.g. Facebook Messenger). Both chatbots have the same name to avoid potential bias, and both chatbots introduce themselves as financial advisors.

Table 2. Overview of the chatbots and the online experiment procedure

		1. E-mail with an invitation to the experiment. 2. Starting page with welcome and scenario. 3. Ice-breaker questions to test knowledge about chatbots. 4. Randomization (Chatbot 1 [Lovable Star] / Chatbot 2 [Incompetent Jerk]). 5. Sympathy 6. Competence 7. Trust 8. Social presence 9. Affinity to technology 10. Socio-demographic questions
Chatbot "lovable star"	Chatbot "incompetent jerk"	The process overview

The scales in the conceptual model are drawn from existing literature for reasons of rigour as well as comparability to prior research. Sympathy, competence, and trust are based on the scales used in McCroskey and Teven (1999) and the scale for social presence as in Bailenson et al. (2001).

In addition, control questions were used (e.g. hair colour and if the chatbot image was wearing glasses or not). Additionally, affinity to technology was measured as a control variable using the scales from Grabner et al. (2016). A manipulation check was implemented using the SCM, and participants had to categorise their Avatar according to this. If they matched, the manipulation check was rated as successful.

A pre-test was conducted before the final invitation e-mail was sent to participants. Before the experiment started, they were given a short text about their scenario. Here, they were asked to watch the interaction with a chatbot as they would like to know more about a particular pension plan. Randomisation was used to determine which chatbot the participant saw (an overview of the procedure is listed in Table 2).

Data analysis was conducted with SPSS 25 and before data analysis, cleansing and recoding of reverse-coded items took place. Missing values were labelled as such to exclude them from further analysis, and the answer given was compared to the scales and values below or above the scale (seven-point scales were used). One case was identified and deleted from the data set.

4. RESULTS AND DISCUSSION

The survey was online for 18 days and 936 student participants were contacted, of which 156 opened the invitation link contained in the e-mail. On the welcome page, 25 participants aborted, and a further 19 did not continue the survey after being asked the knowledge questions about chatbots. A further 32 people chose not to continue after being randomly assigned to a chatbot. This left 76 participants that completed the questionnaire (N=76).

Of the 76 participants, 47 are females and 29 are males. 53.9% of the participants are students (of which 65.8% were employed part-time). 75% of the participants have a Bachelor's degree or higher, and 57.9% live in an urban region. 47.4 % already have a pension plan. 68.4% of the participants consider themselves technology-competent, while 80.1% understand what "chatbot" means (both answers were self-reported); however, only 21.5% use chatbots (this low figure is not necessarily out of anxiety since 73.7% reported no security concerns regarding the technology).

The "lovable star" group had an average age of 27.4 years (SD = 4.2), and 57.9% were female. On the other hand, the average age of the "incompetent jerk" group was 28.9 years (SD = 5.3), and 65.8% were female. A Chi-square test did not show any significant group differences regarding age, gender, type of employment, education, place of residence (rural/urban), or having a pension plan. Therefore, the randomised assignment to the groups (Chatbots 1 and 2) was successful, and further analysis could be conducted.

The reliability analysis was conducted by calculating Cronbach's Alpha values. All the Cronbach's Alpha values of the constructs used in this study were above the recommended cut-off value of .7 stated in Nunally (1978). Hence, a group comparison was conducted using the Mann-Whitney U-Test. Significant group difference can be reported for sympathy: $U = 516$, $r = .25$, and $p = .032$; competence: $U = 242$, $r = .57$ and $p < .001$; and trust: $U = 425$, $r = .36$, and $p = .002$. Therefore, the "lovable star" was perceived as more sympathetic, competent, and trustworthy than the "incompetent jerk". However, the social presence construct shows a non-significant group difference: $U = 671$, $r = .06$, and $p = .592$.

Table 3. Overview of construct reliability

Construct (# items)	**Cronbach's Alpha**
Sympathy (6)	.872
Competence (6)	.863
Trust (5)	.823
Social presence (5)	.735
Affinity to technology (5)	.725

An overview of the hypotheses is given in Table 1. Regarding sympathy a cross-table analysis (>= 5 = high sympathy, <5 = low sympathy) and Chi-square test were conducted χ^2 (1, N = 76) = 13.625, $p = .000$. Cramer's V was calculated, and the value of .423 $p = .000$ is in the middle range, and in terms of the Odds Ratio the "lovable star" was 6.2 times more sympathetic than the "incompetent jerk". Hence, H1 is accepted.

Competence was analysed in the same way. χ^2 (1, N = 76) = 21.111, p = .000. Cramer's V was calculated, the value of .527 p = .000 was in a strong range, and in terms of the Odds Ratio the "lovable star" was 10.5 times more competent than the "incompetent jerk". Hence, H2 is also accepted.

Spearman's correlation coefficients were calculated to test for the effects of social presence on perceived sympathy. The Spearman's correlation coefficient (two-tailed) was r(74) = .240, p = .036, which is a weak but significant correlation. Consequently, H3 is accepted.

Spearman's correlation coefficients were also calculated to test for the effects of social presence on perceived competence. The Spearman's correlation coefficient (two-tailed) was r(74) = -.044, p = .708, which is very weak and there was no significant correlation. Hence, H4 is rejected.

The question regarding the Avatar and his appearance was used to test H5. Participants who did not know or were unable to state the Avatar's hair colour or if he was wearing glasses were put into the group that did not perceive the Avatar. All participants answering the questions correctly were put into the group that consciously perceived the Avatar. The Chi-square test was not significant for either the "lovable star": χ^2 (1, N = 76) = .016, p = .584 or the "incompetent jerk": χ^2 (1, N = 76) = 3.031, p = .298 . Hence, no effect of the appearance of the Avatar on sympathy was reported, and H5 is accordingly rejected.

The same test was then conducted for H6 to determine whether the Avatar's appearance influenced perceived competence. The Chi-square test was calculated for the "lovable star": χ^2 (1, N = 76) = 0.215, p = .643 and for the "incompetent jerk": χ^2 (1, N = 76) = 1.406, p = .236. Because no significant effect was reported, H6 must also be rejected.

Regression analysis was used in a further analysis of the data. Sympathy as an independent variable and trust as a dependent variable were included in the model (R^2 = .53, β = .675, p < .001). Hence, H7 is accepted. Competence as an independent variable and trust as a dependent variable were included in the model (R^2 = .41, β = .493, p < .001). Hence, H8 is accepted.

The null hypothesis that communication does not influence the perception of chatbots can be rejected. However, this study suggests an effect on sympathy and competence and, in turn, trust. The text used seems to influence perceived sympathy as well as competence, while social presence has a significant effect on sympathy but not on competence.

The rejection of H5 and H6 is not in line with empirical evidence from earlier research and Avatar appearance was deemed not to influence perceived sympathy or competence. Since sympathy and competence positively affect trust, the SCM applies in the context of chatbots.

5. IMPLICATIONS, LIMITATIONS, AND FURTHER RESEARCH

The results of this research suggest that social presence and the chatbot text have a positive effect on the perceived sympathy of a chatbot. Therefore, companies seeking to implement a chatbot perceived as competent and likeable should consider the SCM when implementing and testing their chatbots. Furthermore, they are advised to pay attention to details such as text, which affects sympathy and competence. In times of artificial intelligence and platforms to implement conversational agents (e.g. Azure, Amazon Web Services, Google Cloud, IBM Bluemix, and others), it could make a difference to customer perception of chatbots if the text is adapted or trained in line with the SCM. This aspect affects both sympathy and competence – and ultimately trust. Therefore, according to empirical evidence (Beatty et al., 2011; Kim & Peterson, 2017), this is business-success-relevant because it influences online customer decisions (Kim et al., 2008).

The data analysed in this study suggest that swapping a picture is insufficient since the Avatar's image influenced neither sympathy nor competence. However, further analysis is needed to explain why this was the case here as past research suggests that changing a picture may be all that is required. One possible reason is that social presence has a more significant effect than the image itself.

It must be noted that the sample in our study comprising students is not representative of the entire population. However, one advantage for us was that this younger age group was generally familiar with the concept of chatbots. Indeed, earlier research does not categorically reject the use of student sampling such as MTurk or convenience adult samples (Krupnikov & Levine, 2014). Students samples are considered legitimate provided they are adequate (e.g. in early-stage research) as conducted in this paper (Ferber, 1977). Students samples can also be used for initial marketing research (Ashraf & Merunka, 2017).

This study presented chatbot interaction to participants in an online experiment, and the results may have been different in a field study (in the context of an actual business transaction and interaction). Furthermore, the results may differ depending on the products used in the exchange. In this study, a financial setting and scenario were used for prior research, and these were not changed for reasons of comparability. Despite this, later findings may differ since the importance of sympathy and competence (and their effects on trust) depend on the context (see van der Holst (2021) for differences in e-commerce and heath care).

As this study did not rely on real-life customer interaction, further research could conduct a field study where user-interaction is actively implemented into the study design (or by using a live chatbot). Since past literature suggests that pictures are quite powerful when evaluating sympathy and competence in the context of the SCM, a possible further experiment could extend the research by adding an additional group of chatbots without images. This could shed light on this subject and may lead to insights into why some studies show effects and others do not.

Furthermore, this research used statistical methods that do not account for direct and indirect effects. Consequently, a possible further research opportunity would be to replicate this study and use structural equation modelling (SEM) and other suitable statistical analysis methods to account for direct and indirect effects that might be present when researching in the context of the SCM.

6. CONCLUSION

The results of this study suggest that the SCM holds in the context of chatbots. Furthermore, perceived competence and sympathy are antecedents to building trust. This is important when humans interact with artefacts, such as visiting an online store or seeking assistance from a company's chatbot. As we have already stressed, trust is generally relevant to business success, so it makes sense to have artefacts fostering trust in line with the SCM.

This study suggests that swapping a picture is insufficient. Indeed, constructs such as social presence have to be considered as well when implementing a customer experience (CX) in line with the SCM. This study also suggests social cues and text play a role; therefore, it is advisable to introduce these aspects into a chatbot in addition to an image. Because cloud platforms provide a fast and easy way to do this, it is essential to pay attention to the whole interaction and, for example, to customise the text in terms of the SCM.

As subjective and complex customer perception involves testing whether the chatbot and its cues are perceived, these can make the difference between an artefact being perceived as a "lovable star" or an "incompetent jerk". The latter would have a negative impact on business, whereas the former would contribute to business success.

REFERENCES

Aaker, J., Vohs, K.D., Mogilner, C., 2010. Nonprofits Are Seen as Warm and For-Profits as Competent: Firm Stereotypes Matter. Journal of Consumer Research 37, 224–237. https://doi.org/10.1086/651566

Aaker, J.L., Garbinsky, E.N., Vohs, K.D., 2012. Cultivating admiration in brands: Warmth, competence, and landing in the "golden quadrant." Journal of Consumer Psychology 22, 191–194. https://doi.org/10.1016/j.jcps.2011.11.012

Ashraf, R., Merunka, D., 2017. The use and misuse of student samples: An empirical investigation of European marketing research. Journal of Consumer Behaviour 16, 295–308. https://doi.org/10.1002/cb.1590

Ba, S., Pavlou, P.A., 2002. Evidence of the Effect of Trust Building Technology in Electronic Markets: Price Premiums and Buyer Behavior. MIS Quarterly 26, 243–268. https://doi.org/10.2307/4132332

Bailenson, J.N., Blascovich, J., Beall, A.C., Loomis, J.M., 2001. Equilibrium Theory Revisited: Mutual Gaze and Personal Space in Virtual Environments. Presence: Teleoperators and Virtual Environments 10, 583–598. https://doi.org/10.1162/105474601753272844

Beatty, P., Reay, I., Dick, S., Miller, J., 2011. Consumer Trust in e-Commerce Web Sites: A Meta-study. ACM Comput. Surv. 43, 14:1-14:46. https://doi.org/10.1145/1922649.1922651

Beldad, A., de Jong, M., Steehouder, M., 2010. How shall I trust the faceless and the intangible? A literature review on the antecedents of online trust. Computers in Human Behavior, Advancing Educational Research on Computer-supported Collaborative Learning (CSCL) through the use of gStudy CSCL Tools 26, 857–869. https://doi.org/10.1016/j.chb.2010.03.013

Biocca, F., Harms, C., Burgoon, J.K., 2003. Toward a more robust theory and measure of social presence: review and suggested criteria. Presence: Teleoper. Virtual Environ. 12, 456–480. https://doi.org/10.1162/105474603322761270

Botha, E., Reyneke, M., 2015. The Influence of Social Presence on Online Purchase Intention: An Experiment with Different Product Types. Looking Forward, Looking Back: Drawing on the Past to Shape the Future of Marketing. Proceedings of the 2013 World Marketing Congress 180–183.

Casciaro, T., Lobo, M.S., 2005. Competent jerks, lovable fools, and the formation of social networks. Harvard business review 83, 92–9, 149. https://doi.org/10.1037

Chattaraman, V., Kwon, W.-S., E. Gilbert, J., Li, Y., 2014. Virtual shopping agents: Persona effects for older users. Journal of Research in Interactive Marketing 8, 144–162. https://doi.org/10.1108/JRIM-08-2013-0054

Christoforakos, L., Gallucci, A., Surmava-Große, T., Ullrich, D., Diefenbach, S., 2021. Can Robots Earn Our Trust the Same Way Humans Do? A Systematic Exploration of Competence, Warmth, and Anthropomorphism as Determinants of Trust Development in HRI. Front. Robot. AI 8. https://doi.org/10.3389/frobt.2021.640444

Cuddy, A.J.C., Fiske, S.T., Glick, P., 2008. Warmth and Competence as Universal Dimensions of Social Perception: The Stereotype Content Model and the BIAS Map. https://doi.org/10.1016/S0065-2601(07)00002-0

Cuddy, A.J.C., Fiske, S.T., Glick, P., 2007. The BIAS map: Behaviors from intergroup affect and stereotypes. Journal of Personality and Social Psychology 92, 631–648. https://doi.org/10.1037/0022-3514.92.4.631

Cuddy, A.J.C., Glick, P., Beninger, A., 2011. The dynamics of warmth and competence judgments, and their outcomes in organisations. https://doi.org/10.1016/j.riob.2011.10.004

Drevs, F., 2013. How patients choose hospitals: Using the stereotypic content model to model trustworthiness, warmth and competence. Health Serv Manage Res 26, 95–101. https://doi.org/10.1177/0951484813513246

Ferber, R., 1977. Research By Convenience. Journal of Consumer Research 4, 57–58. https://doi.org/10.1086/208679

Fiske, S.T., Cuddy, A.J.C., Glick, P., 2007. Universal dimensions of social cognition: warmth and competence. Trends in Cognitive Sciences 11, 77–83. https://doi.org/10.1016/j.tics.2006.11.005

Fiske, S.T., Cuddy, A.J.C., Glick, P., Xu, J., 2002. A model of (often mixed) stereotype content: Competence and warmth respectively follow from perceived status and competition. Journal of Personality and Social Psychology 82, 878–902. https://doi.org/10.1037/0022-3514.82.6.878

Franklin, D., Kiefer, B., Laird, C., Lopez, F., Pham, C., Suarez, J., Waite, R., Conrad, P., Boe, B., Nilsen, K., Hill, C., Len, M., Dreschler, G., Aldana, G., Almeida-Tanaka, P., 2013. Assessment of computer science learning in a scratch-based outreach program, in: Proceeding of the 44th ACM Technical Symposium on Computer Science Education - SIGCSE '13. Presented at the Proceeding of the 44th ACM technical symposium, ACM Press, Denver, Colorado, USA, p. 371. https://doi.org/10.1145/2445196.2445304

Gao, X., Shi, X., Guo, H., Liu, Y., 2020. To buy or not buy food online: The impact of the COVID-19 epidemic on the adoption of e-commerce in China. PLOS ONE 15, e0237900. https://doi.org/10.1371/journal.pone.0237900

Grabner, C., Tiwari, R., Buse, S., 2016. Mobile Banking aus der Perspektive der Nutzer, in: Grabner, C., Tiwari, R., Buse, S. (Eds.), Perspektiven des Mobile Banking in Deutschland: Implikationen auf Basis einer Untersuchung von Angebot, Nutzern und Umfeld. Springer Fachmedien, Wiesbaden, pp. 59–108. https://doi.org/10.1007/978-3-658-12788-6_6

Hampton-Sosa, W., Koufaris, M., 2005. The Effect of Web Site Perceptions on Initial Trust in the Owner Company. International Journal of Electronic Commerce 10, 55–81. https://doi.org/10.1080/10864415.2005.11043965

Holst, E.M. van der, 2021. Designing for Trust: A neuroscientific and design perspective on trust within a professional context. https://doi.org/10.3990/1.9789036551762

Intelligence, I., n.d. Chatbot market in 2021: Stats, trends, and companies in the growing AI chatbot industry [WWW Document]. Business Insider. URL https://www.businessinsider.com/chatbot-market-stats-trends (accessed 6.14.21).

Kim, D.J., Ferrin, D.L., Rao, H.R., 2008. A trust-based consumer decision-making model in electronic commerce: The role of trust, perceived risk, and their antecedents. Decision Support Systems 44, 544–564. https://doi.org/10.1016/j.dss.2007.07.001

Kim, Y., Peterson, R.A., 2017. A Meta-analysis of Online Trust Relationships in E-commerce. Journal of Interactive Marketing 38, 44–54. https://doi.org/10.1016/j.intmar.2017.01.001

Köksal, Y., Penez, S., 2015. An Investigation of the Important Factors Influence Web Trust in Online Shopping. Journal of Marketing and Management; Beverly Hills 6, 28–40.

Krupnikov, Y., Levine, A.S., 2014. Cross-Sample Comparisons and External Validity. J Exp Polit Sci 1, 59–80. https://doi.org/10.1017/xps.2014.7

Lee, J., Lee, J.-N., Tan, B.C.Y., 2015. Antecedents of cognitive trust and affective distrust and their mediating roles in building customer loyalty. Information Systems Frontiers 17, 159–175. https://doi.org/10.1007/s10796-012-9392-7

Lu, B., Fan, W., Zhou, M., 2016. Social presence, trust, and social commerce purchase intention: An empirical research. Computers in Human Behavior 56, 225–237. https://doi.org/10.1016/j.chb.2015.11.057

McAllister, D.J., 1995. Affect- and Cognition-Based Trust as Foundations for Interpersonal Cooperation in Organisations. Academy of Management Journal 38, 24–59. https://doi.org/10.5465/256727

McCroskey, J.C., Teven, J.J., 1999. Goodwill: A reexamination of the construct and its measurement. Communication Monographs 66, 90–103. https://doi.org/10.1080/03637759909376464

Mcknight, D., Carter, M., Thatcher, J., Clay, P., 2011. Trust in a specific technology: An Investigation of its Components and Measures. ACM Transactions on Management Information Systems 2, 12–32. https://doi.org/10.1145/1985347.1985353

McKnight, D.H., Choudhury, V., Kacmar, C., 2002. Developing and Validating Trust Measures for e-Commerce: An Integrative Typology. Information Systems Research 13, 334–359. https://doi.org/10.1287/isre.13.3.334.81

McKnight, H.D., Choudhury, V., Kacmar, C., 2002. The impact of initial consumer trust on intentions to transact with a web site: a trust building model. The Journal of Strategic Information Systems 11, 297–323. https://doi.org/10.1016/S0963-8687(02)00020-3

Mohamad Suhaili, S., Salim, N., Jambli, M.N., 2021. Service chatbots: A systematic review. Expert Systems with Applications 184, 115461. https://doi.org/10.1016/j.eswa.2021.115461

Niemiec, C.P., Ryan, R.M., 2009. Autonomy, competence, and relatedness in the classroom: Applying self-determination theory to educational practice. Theory and Research in Education 7, 133–144. https://doi.org/10.1177/1477878509104318

Nunally, J., 1978. Psychometric theory. McGraw-Hill, New York.

Pan, Y., Steed, A., 2016. A Comparison of Avatar-, Video-, and Robot-Mediated Interaction on Users' Trust in Expertise. Front. Robot. AI 3. https://doi.org/10.3389/frobt.2016.00012

Pantano, E., Pizzi, G., 2020. Forecasting artificial intelligence on online customer assistance: Evidence from chatbot patents analysis. Journal of Retailing and Consumer Services 55, 102096. https://doi.org/10.1016/j.jretconser.2020.102096

Rozumowski, A., Hari, J.J., Dermody, J., 2017. Warmth and competence: how to become a trustworthy "Lovable Star" in business, in: The 50th Academy of Marketing Conference, Hull, 3.-6. Juli 2017. Academy of Marketing.

Steinbrück, U., Schaumburg, H., Duda, S., Krüger, T., n.d. A Picture Says More Than A Thousand Words - Photographs As Trust Builders in E-Commerce Websites 2.

Tay, B., Jung, Y., Park, T., 2014. When stereotypes meet robots: The double-edge sword of robot gender and personality in human–robot interaction. Computers in Human Behavior 38, 75–84. https://doi.org/10.1016/j.chb.2014.05.014

Valaskova, K., Durana, P., Adamko, P., 2021. Changes in Consumers' Purchase Patterns as a Consequence of the COVID-19 Pandemic. Mathematics 9, 1788. https://doi.org/10.3390/math9151788

Verhagen, T., van Nes, J., Feldberg, F., van Dolen, W., 2014. Virtual customer service agents: Using social presence and personalisation to shape online service encounters. Journal of Computer-Mediated Communication 19, 529–545. https://doi.org/10.1111/jcc4.12066

Wallace, R.S., 2009. The Anatomy of A.L.I.C.E., in: Epstein, R., Roberts, G., Beber, G. (Eds.), Parsing the Turing Test: Philosophical and Methodological Issues in the Quest for the Thinking Computer. Springer Netherlands, Dordrecht, pp. 181–210. https://doi.org/10.1007/978-1-4020-6710-5_13

Weizenbaum, J., 1966. ELIZA—a Computer Program for the Study of Natural Language Communication Between Man and Machine. Commun. ACM 9, 36–45. https://doi.org/10.1145/365153.365168

Wilson, J.R., Lee, N.Y., Saechao, A., Hershenson, S., Scheutz, M., Tickle-Degnen, L., 2017. Hand Gestures and Verbal Acknowledgments Improve Human-Robot Rapport, in: Kheddar, A., Yoshida, E., Ge, S.S., Suzuki, K., Cabibihan, J.-J., Eyssel, F., He, H. (Eds.), Social Robotics, Lecture Notes in Computer Science. Springer International Publishing, Cham, pp. 334–344. https://doi.org/10.1007/978-3-319-70022-9_33

Wood, J.A., Boles, J.S., Babin, B.J., 2008. The Formation of Buyer's Trust of the Seller in an Initial Sales Encounter. Journal of Marketing Theory and Practice VO - 16 27. https://doi.org/10.2753/MTP1069-6679160102

Zawisza, M., Pittard, C., 2015. When Do Warmth and Competence Sell Best? The "Golden Quadrant" Shifts as a Function of Congruity With the Product Type, Targets' Individual Differences, and Advertising Appeal Type. Basic and Applied Social Psychology 37, 131–141. https://doi.org/10.1080/01973533.2015.1015130

UNDERSTANDINGS AND PERSPECTIVES ON BLENDED LEARNING IN A BRAZILIAN PRIVATE UNIVERSITY IN THE CONTEXT OF TRANSFORMATIONS

Katiúscia Akemi Nasu Nogueira and Maria Cristina Lima Paniago
Universidade Católica Dom Bosco - UCDB
Campo Grande, MS, Brazil

ABSTRACT

The definitions and denominations of blended learning vary considerably. The Covid-19 pandemic has favored a lack of differentiation by indistinctly naming models of emergency remote education through the term blended learning. Hence, the several ways of understanding blended learning are echoed in the diversity of practices that can be adopted. This paper is a snapshot of a masters' study that aimed at analyzing the understandings and teachers' practices related to blended learning in a private university in Brazil. During the time of this study, the institution was going through intense internal transformations and an uncertain external context full of unpredictability due to the pandemic situation. This is a case study, and it has a qualitative and exploratory approach. Data was collected from the analysis of institutional documents and semi- structured interviews with instructors from the university. The theoretical framework and literature review uses Bacich, Tanzi Neto and Trevisani (2015); Horn and Staker, (2015); Kanuka and Rourke (2013); Moran (2013); Moreira and Monteiro (2013); Morin (2015); Paniago (2016); and Tori (2009; 2017). The findings were analyzed through a content analysis lens, and showed multiple understandings of the concept of blended learning, relative incomprehension of how to support active learning in various spaces in an integrated manner. In these instructors' practices and beliefs, the ICT are primarily used to provide a more personalized pace of study with some element of students' organization concerning time and space. The pandemic was contextualized as a driving factor for the expansion of blended courses, but it does not follow in the same proportion an approach to valorization and development of the faculty.

KEYWORDS

Blended Learning, Distance Education, Digital Technologies

1. INTRODUCTION

Literature on blended learning highlights the diversity of concepts that involve the theme of polysemy and ambiguities (Friesen, 2012; Kanuka & Rourke, 2013). The Covid-19 pandemic complicates these understandings by suddenly expanding the use of information and communication technologies (ICT) in educational practices (Moreira and Schlemmer, 2020; Hodges et al., 2020). In the face of new routines, blended learning takes on a polysemic meaning. Appenzeller et al. (2020) emphasize the need to understand that there is a difference between the emergency strategy adopted for the continuity of classes, called emergency remote learning and blended learning. Moreira and Schlemmer (2020, p. 9) define emergency remote learning as a temporary teaching model that "involves the use of totally remote teaching solutions identical to the practices of physical environments". For these authors, in this emergency, a classroom as an ecosystem is not constituted or robust. The goal of emergency online education is to provide temporary and quick access during the emergency period.

In Brazilian Higher Education, this context is still experiencing the exponential expansion of Distance Education programs, which in the last ten years (2009-2019) had an increase of 378.9% in the number of students starting their undergraduate courses in such modality (INEP, 2020). Also, a 145.24% growth in the number of blended courses offered between 2017-2018 (Censo EAD.BR, 2018).

Recently, through law No. 2,117 of December 6, 2019, the Ministry of Education (MEC) expanded the authorization for Higher Education Institutions to introduce more distance learning modality credits in the pedagogical and curricular organization of their on-site undergraduate courses. That alone could increase the total course load of each course by 20% to 40% (MEC, 2019). This flexibility of the workload though, allows for different combinations between online and classroom teaching, enabling new configurations of Brazilian Higher Education. It also provides opportunities for institutions to offer undergraduate programs through blended learning education.

That said, this study aims at analyzing the understandings and teaching practices related to blended teaching in an in-person Biological Sciences undergraduate teaching program. This program is offered at a private university in the State of Mato Grosso do Sul, Brazil. The study investigates the difficulties in understanding blended learning given the diversity of concepts, nomenclatures, and ambiguities that became more complex due to the current pandemic scenario. Based on these findings, the research investigates how this will affect the use of ICT in blended pedagogical practices. In addition, this article intends to contribute to the theoretical foundation that informs the understandings of the features of blended learning and to reflect on pedagogical practices.

2. BLENDED LEARNING

2.1 History and Literature Review

The term blended learning – used throughout this paper - emerged in the US around the 2000s. Initially, it focused on corporate education (Friesen, 2012; Moreira & Schlemmer, 2020). While English-speaking countries use the nomenclature b-learning, blended learning is still predominant. In Brazil, the term was translated as hybrid teaching (Moran, 2021; Martins, 2016). Some of the terminologies adopted are bimodal system (Moran, 2013), blended learning (Moran, 2013), blended learning (Tori, 2009); b-learning (Moreira & Monteiro, 2013); blended (e)learning (Moreira & Monteiro, 2013); multimodality (Schlemmer & Moreira, 2020).

Between 2006 and 2007, after the publications by Curtis Bonk and Charles Graham in the US and Randy Garrison and Norman Vaughan in Canada, there has been a change in the use of the term, sparking interest in blended learning in Higher Education, rather than in the corporate training sector (Friesen, 2012).

More recently, in the period 2011-2013, understandings about blended learning were added in the research studies by Clayton Christensen, Michel Horn and Heather Staker. The publications discuss innovation theories, propose a concept and a taxonomy for blended learning.

In Brazil, blended learning starts as mixed presence and expands into Higher Education, based on the possibility of offering up to 40% of the credit hours in the distance learning modality in some of the different undergraduate programs (Moran, 2021).

Valente (2014) argues that the plurality of nomenclatures characterizes a transitional phase in which several activities and distance education models coexist. The author highlights that blended learning enables pedagogical practices in which the student develops an active role to signify and understand the information. The conceptual discussion is also addressed by Moreira and Monteiro (2013, p. 86) who argue that blended learning "can be understood as a highly complex communication process", pointing out that the result of the implementation of blended education programs can have effects varying accordingly to the configuration adopted.

Machado (2018) understands blended learning as a methodological approach that integrates ICT to personalize teaching and promote active learning; the author separates and distinguishes the concepts "mixed presence" and "blended learning" by stating that, while in the mixed presence there is a separation between online and face-to-face activities, in blended learning there is integration and connection between the different spaces. Martins (2018) states that the different meanings attributed to blended learning vary according to the use that the institution/author/course intends to demonstrate. The author also states that there is no conceptual consensus shared by authors who research this topic.

The main result of the literature review indicates that, even though blended learning in Higher Education is associated with the combination of the in-person and distance education modalities, the concept is evolving towards the understanding of a more sophisticated, broad, and complex concept. The studies come closer to the understanding that blended learning, from the perspective of the mere combination of modalities, is reductionist and does not contemplate the possibilities of an approach that presupposes personalized teaching, student-centered learning and the use of digital technologies as a means and not an end in itself (Valente, 2014; Moreira & Monteiro, 2013; Sousa & Schlünzen Junior, 2018; Silva, 2016; Martins, 2016; Andrade, 2018; Machado, 2018).

2.2 Theoretical Framework

Based on Kenski (2012), Moreira and Schlemmer (2020), we can see that ICT use can happen through different methodological approaches. These approaches vary from more instructional ones which focus on the unidirectional transmission of information to more interactive approaches in which the teaching and learning processes occur amidst a multidirectional communication. Following this lens, the goal is not centered on the content, nor on the instruction/instructor, but it is on the dialogical relationship among all individuals. Vaughan (2016) stresses that blended learning is a teaching methodology in which students and instructors share responsibilities and move from passive to more active learning. Following this methodology, individuals learn how to learn and take on more responsibility for their learning in an active learning environment both in in-person and online settings.

Research conducted by Horn and Staker (2015) define blended learning as an education program linked to an educational institution. In this approach, part of the teaching and learning process takes place through an integrated experience with online learning and personalized teaching is articulated with competence-based learning to provide student-centered learning.

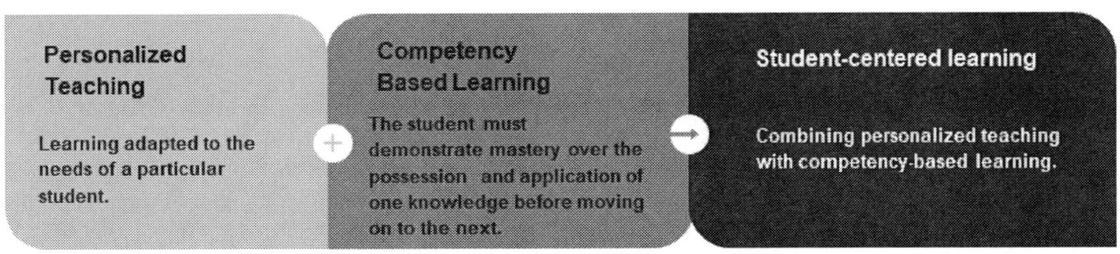

Source: This figure was designed by the authors based on Horn and Staker (2015)

Figure 1. Student-centered learning

Following this perspective, blended learning has some key elements: *Autonomy:* students' autonomy is related to learning how to manage their own learning, a learn how to learn process (Pires, 2015; Vaughan, 2016). *Personalization:* the development of autonomy happens gradually, and it requires cooperation and monitoring from the instructor. Moreover, it suggests either personal support or more personalized study plans (Bacich, Tanzi Neto & Trevisani, 2015; Schneider, 2015). *Flexibility:* blended programs entail more flexibility in their course projects in terms of thinking of goals, strategies, and methods (Tori, 2017). *The ICT:* the technologies contribute to the personalization of learning and offer a variety of resources to the students (text, videos, animations, audios, etc). Technologies also provide a more personalized rhythm of study. The systems and platforms used can also afford data that shows the students' development; through continuing evaluation processes, the instructor can plan and replan classes based on the identified data in addition to the individual and collective needs of their students (Horn & Staker, 2015; Lima & Moura, 2015; Rodrigues, 2015).

3. METHODOLOGY

A case study is, according to Yin (2015, p. 17), an empirical investigation that "deeply examines a contemporary phenomenon ('the case') in its context of the real world [...]". The contemporary educational phenomenon that justifies this case is blended learning in a private higher education institution. This institution expands the percentage of distance education workload of distance education programs, reconfigure different courses pedagogical projects, and implement new platforms such as LMS (Learning Management System), mostly during the Covid-19 pandemic. This research, therefore, aims at understanding contemporary events rather than controlling them. We investigate such phenomenon of blended learning in its context of real-world

(Yin, 2015); are interested in the perspectives of the participants (Minayo, 1994); and intend to contribute to the understanding of educational phenomena from a qualitative lens (Creswell, 2010; André, 2013).

The higher education institution used in this research is private, and it has high-quality evaluation done by the Brazilian Ministry of Education. The university offers 53 undergraduate courses (32 in-person courses, and 21 in distance education) in the different areas of education, health, social sciences, agriculture, engineering, and humanities. The campus infrastructure includes a veterinarian hospital, clinic, gymnasium, a farm-house school, and labs (e.g., communication, technology, and health). The institution has other 27 branches across the Brazilian country that physically support distance education. It also has post-undergraduate programs both in-person (32 different courses) and distance education (46 other courses), in addition to 6 graduate programs (master's and doctorate), including an international master's program.

The course explored here – Biological Sciences – is one that prepares future students to teach. It is an in-person course that has a total of 4,080 credit hours. Around 29.71% of these credit hours are offered through an online approach. This course has its core curriculum in 22 other disciplines, and they are all offered in-person, too. Besides, the other 18 disciplines of the course are offered in the distance education model, and 13 are offered in a blended format. The students in this course take disciplines in the field of the Biological Sciences and also in Education (e.g., sociology of education). The latter usually serves other teaching areas as well. The participants in this study were intentionally selected, after all the list of faculty members was carefully considered. Our goal was to recruit participants who were "well informed" (Yin, 2015, p. 117) and able to provide relevant insights about the research goals. In total, there were 5 instructors, and one of them also exercises the role of coordinator in the program. They all have experiences with courses and disciplines that combine both in-person and online teaching. They have worked at the university for over 3 years, are between 33 and 61 years old, and have extensive experience teaching in Higher Education – 5-26 years. Three participants have got their master's (n=60%), and 2 are PhDs (n=40%).

The intentional recruitment of participants tried to contemplate the multiple experiences in a transdisciplinary exercise (Morin, 2015), which means bringing instructors from different areas of knowledge (pedagogy, letters, biology, biomedicine, immunology).

Data collection happened from March to April of 2021. The collected data comes from institutional documents such as the Institutional Development Plan, the Institutional Pedagogical Project, and the Course Pedagogical Project, and from information gathered in semi-structured interviews which happened via Google Meet. According to Minayo (2008), the methods used in a qualitative inquiry allow mediation between the theoretical and methodological aspects and its empirical reality. Yin (2015) stresses that interviews are sources of the most important information for this type of study.

Data analysis happened from May to June of 2021. The meaning-making processes (Creswell, 2020; André, 2013) included the elaboration of two facets of analysis that emerged in the study. The limitations of this study relate mostly to the health crisis as the study took place during the rapid advancement of Covid-19 outbreaks in Brazil (FIOCRUZ, 2021) and in the state of Mato Grosso do Sul (SES MS, 2021). Indeed, these factors impacted the participation and availability of more participants.

4. FINDINGS AND DISCUSSION

The ethics committee of research with human beings approved this research. This paper kept all personal information anonymous and did not provide the name of the participating university nor the participants' names. The letter "P" followed by non-sequential numbers identifies the participants.

4.1 The Instructors' Concepts

Understandings. The results showed multiple understandings when the instructors were asked about their concepts of blended learning. Predominantly, participants understood blended learning as a combination of the in-person and distance education modalities. Some responders mentioned they had just heard about or had contact with the terminology, and that makes it harder for them to adopt and work with blended learning in classroom. Sometimes, more than one participant indistinctly associated blended learning to emergency online learning.

P86: "For me, blended learning is considered as a teaching methodology, which will combine both in-person and distance learning, but blended learning will also offer you a flexibility in both these environments, virtual and in-person [...] So, blended learning for me, it enables us to overcome this view that the whole class is doing the same thing at the same time".

P39: "From what I understand, it is that in some courses, some determined field studies will be applied in-person, including those with practicum, or a more theory-practice approach [...]. And those disciplines or courses that are more basic and general for everyone, and that could be used by more than one course, those will move onto the virtual, onto distance education. These last ones will be developed online".

P12: "Because today, we have a lot of difficulties in understanding what blended learning is, and how it should be worked with. If you see the information we have, you will see that it exists... we will have bigger... we will have the most diverse number of definitions of blended learning".

P70: "For me, blended learning is that one that goes... that has an in-person meeting with students, then partially it is in-person and partially remote, which happens with the help of different platforms [...]".

Discussion: As it could be observed in the blended learning literature, the flexibility of having multiple possibilities and models associated to the selection of different conceptions about blended learning can result in contradictory implications. On one hand, the different conceptions promote the popularity and expansion of blended learning. On the other hand, however, these views make it complex to understand what blended learning actually is and its implications after implementing and performing it (Graham, 2006; Friesen, 2012; Kanuka & Rourke, 2013). Along with Horn and Staker's (2015) stance, there is a need for "broader" (p. 37) parameters which will not limit the possibilities that blended learning fosters. However, Graham (2006), Hanuka and Rourke (2013), and Horn and Staker (2015) also recognize that broad definitions can generate more misunderstandings around blended learning, making it more complex even to use it in practice. Graham (2006) then proposes the need for a more restricted definition that reflects the core characteristics of blended teaching. Minayo (1994), for instance, say that concepts have a communicative feature and that itself should allow interlocutors to understand them.

Andrade (2018) contributes to the empirical results that were highlighted by some instructors who mentioned about pedagogical practices. Paniago (2016) says that instructors have been challenged to teach beyond the context of a classroom, and have been asked to use different media, audiovisual, and technological resources within the reconfiguration of spaces and practices of blended learning.

Perspectives. For the participants, the pandemic will favor the introduction of some of the distance education credits in in-person courses. This means that part of the adopted methodologies of teaching in a blended format should be more permanent in a post-pandemic moment. Teachers mention that the expansion is more related to financial and cost pressures than efforts to improve educational practices. They also mention that this expansion causes impacts related to remuneration and teaching work.

P52: "It is because I have been doing an analysis, I have noticed that several employers, after this period of time, can also do an analysis and notice that institutions will profit more from keeping the employee at home. That can start adopting that, not only in education, but other areas too [...] So I think a lot of it will remain". In reference to the choice of blended learning the teacher states: "It seems to me to be a decision based... on the economic part of the university prevailing over the pedagogical part".

P12: "So, I believe that at this moment, we could be going through a transition [...]. But I believe that a 100% in-person teaching will not happen again".

Discussion: Moran (2012, p. 129) states that the option of expanding blended learning is related to the digital culture that our society is in today, along with strategies of institutions to decrease their costs.

4.2 Digital Technologies

Technology. The virtual learning environment (VLE) was the type of technology mentioned by all participants in the study. The VLE has been the main resource used to combine both in-person and online learning. Its use has been reflected under two aspects: to provide access to content and to allow students to personalize their own time and space.

P39: "[...] the material and the content are there and the student will work on them whenever they think it is better. They will schedule their own time".

P12: "Part of the course is offered through distance learning anyways. Students access a virtual environment, do the readings and the activities, do an assignment according to the orientation of the learning unit, and at the same time, they contact the professor of the course who attends the student and supervise them in an in-person approach".

Integration. For basically all instructors who responded the questions for this study, it is challenging to integrate educational practices in both in-person and online settings at the same time.

P52: "We have to make the discipline move as integrated as possible. They [students] enter the platform, they do the activities. And I look there, in addition to having to set up the activities, I bring some of the discussions to my room, just to make it look more unison".

P70: "Because I bring content from the platform to discuss it during the class: 'ah in that exercise, in that problem with the platform that you solved, you said that, why did you say that?'. So, I try to bring this to the class [in person]".

P12: "And we need to, we would need to make this link so that the student understands that distance education content is not separate, or that it is loose, free, and with no one taking care of it there. [...]. But there has to be a connection so that the student doesn't get lost. Because otherwise they will reach the end of the course and will say: I took two courses, one in-person and another in distance education".

Discussion: For Moran (2003, p. 59), the pedagogical project of a given course should integrate the in-person and the digital as "curricular components that are inseparable". That is, to sustain that both virtual and physical spaces should be equally important to maximize the possibilities of more flexible, collaborative, and personalized teaching and learning processes.

Autonomy. Methodologies such as blended learning, where the learning strategies are centered on the effective participation of students, contribute to a better engagement, autonomy, and participation of the students in the teaching and learning processes (Horn & Staker, 2015; Bacich, Tanzi Neto & Trevizani, 2015). However, most participants did not mention the use of ICT and blended learning as an opportunity to develop an autonomous and active learning. Some participants did understand that an autonomous and active learning is conditional to a successful blended syllabus, but not one that should be developed and improved during the whole course.

P39: "You can clearly notice that those who are not committed cannot sustain themselves. They do not thrive. They end up staying and soon enough dropping off".

P52: "I think that the distance education system generally requires the students to be mature, so they can be autonomous. And most of the younger students do not have that".

5. CONCLUSION

This study aims at analyzing the understandings and teaching practices related to blended learning during pandemic outbreaks. Our discussions highlighted challenges towards the complexity and diversity of conceptualizing blended learning, observed in the different teaching practices of participants. Furthermore, the study showed the relative misunderstandings around integrated practices in both in-person and online settings. The relevance of this discussion has acquired such a dimension that currently the National Council of Education has announced the proposal for an Ordinance that will bring concepts to broaden the understanding of blended learning in Brazil. Most of our participants affirmed that the pandemic would contribute to the expansion of blended courses with impacts on teacher development and work. However, only a few participants suggested that such expansion will increase the possibilities of students' autonomy development through blended learning. And the ICT have been used for content access and offered students flexibility in their re-signification of time and space.

ACKNOWLEDGEMENT

This research study has had the support of CAPES (https://www.gov.br/capes/pt-br), a foundation linked to the Ministry of Education, which funds master's programs in Brazil.

REFERENCES

Andrade, J. Z. de. (2018). *Aprendizagem híbrida e adaptativa: caminhos na relação educação e tecnologias*. Tese de Doutorado em Educação. Pontifícia Universidade Católica do Rio de Janeiro, Departamento de Educação.

André, M. (2013) O que é um estudo de caso qualitativo em educação? *Revista da FAEEBA - Educação e Contemporaneidade*, Salvador, Vol. 22, No. 40, pp. 95-103, jul./dez.

Appenzeller S. et al (2020). Novos tempos, novos desafios: estratégias para equidade de acesso ao ensino remoto emergencial. *Revista Brasileira de Educação Médica*, Brasília, Vol. 44, Supl. 1, pp. 01-06.

Bacich, L., Tanzi Neto, A., Trevisani, F. de M. (2015). *Ensino híbrido: personalização e tecnologia na educação*. Porto Alegre: Penso.

Ministério da Educação (MEC). (2019). *Portaria nº 2.117, de 6 de dezembro de 2019*. Brasília, available at: <https://www.in.gov.br/en/web/dou/-/portaria-n-2.117-de-6-de-dezembro-de-2019-232670913> (accessed 6 July 2020).

Censo EAD.BR. (2019). *Relatório analítico da aprendizagem a distância no Brasil 2018*. Organização ABED - Associação Brasileira de Educação a Distância. Curitiba: InterSaberes.

Creswell, J. W. (2010). *Projeto de pesquisa: métodos qualitativo, quantitativo e misto*. 3. ed. Porto Alegre: Artmed.

Fundação Oswaldo Cruz (FIOCRUZ). (2021). *Brazil faces the worst scenario since the beginning of the pandemic*, available at: <https://portal.fiocruz.br/en/news/brazil-faces-worst-scenario-beginning-pandemic> (accessed 01 June 2021).

Friesen, N. (2012). *Report: defining blended learning*, available at: <http://learningspaces.org/papers/Defining_Blended_Learning_NF.pdf> (accessed 05 January 2019).

Graham, C. R. (2006). Blended learning systems: definition, current trends, and future directions. In: Bonk, C. J. et al. (Ed.). *The handbook of blended learning: global perspectives, local designs*. São Francisco, CA: Pfeiffer Publishing.

Hodges, C. et al. (2020). The Difference Between Emergency Remote Teaching and Online Learning. *Educause Review*, available at: <https://er.educause.edu/articles/2020/3/the-difference-between-emergency-remote-teaching-and-online-learning> (accessed 02 October 2020).

Horn, M. B., Staker, H. (2015). *Blended: usando a inovação disruptiva para aprimorar a educação*. Porto Alegre: Penso.

Instituto Nacional de Estudos e Pesquisas Educacionais Anísio Teixeira (INEP). (2020). *Censo da Educação Superior 2019: notas estatísticas*, available at: < https://www.gov.br/inep/pt-br/areas-de-atuacao/pesquisas-estatisticas-e-indicadores/censo-da-educacao-superior/resultados> (accessed 10 February 2021).

Kanuka, H., Rourke, L. (2013). Using blended learning strategies to address teaching development needs: How does Canada compare? *Canadian Journal of Higher Education. La Revue canadienne d'enseignement supérieur*, Vol. 43, No. 3, pp. 19-35.

Kenski, V. M. (2012). *Educação e tecnologias: O novo ritmo da informação*. 8. ed. Campinas: Papirus.

Lima, L. H. F., Moura, F. R. (2015). O professor no ensino híbrido. In: Bacich, L., Tanzi Neto, A., Trevisani, F. de M. (Orgs.). *Ensino híbrido: personalização e tecnologia na educação*. Porto Alegre: Penso.

Machado, N. S. (2018). *Fazendo o semipresencial e sonhando com o ensino híbrido na graduação, a voz dos estudantes: uma análise comparativa de modelos pedagógicos nos cenários público e privado*. Dissertação de Mestrado Profissional em Educação e Novas Tecnologias. Centro Universitário Internacional Uninter.

Martins, L. C. B. (2016). *Implicações da organização da atividade didática com uso de tecnologias digitais na formação de conceitos em uma proposta de ensino híbrido*. 2016. Tese de Doutorado em Psicologia. Universidade de São Paulo, Instituto de psicologia da Universidade de São Paulo.

Minayo, M. C. S. (1994). Ciência, técnica e arte: o desafio da pesquisa social. In: Deslandes, S. F. et al. (Orgs.). *Pesquisa social: teoria, método e criatividade*. 21. ed. Petrópolis, RJ: Vozes.

Moran, J. M. (2013). Ensino e aprendizagem inovadores com apoio de tecnologias. In: Moran, J. M., Masetto, M. T., Behrens, M. A. *Novas tecnologias e mediação pedagógica*. 21. ed. rev. atual. Campinas: Papirus.

Moran, J. (2021). O Ensino Híbrido: emergência ou tendência? Gazeta do Povo. *Educação & Mídia*, available at: <https://www.gazetadopovo.com.br/vozes/educacao-e-midia/o-ensino-hibrido-emergencia-ou-tendencia/> (accessed 16 March 2021).

Moreira, J. A., Schlemmer, E. (2020). Por um novo conceito e paradigma de educação digital onlife. *Revista UFG*, Vol. 20, pp. 01-35.

Moreira, J. A., Monteiro, A. (2013). Blended learning: uma estratégia dinâmica ao serviço da educação. In: Henriques, H. M. G. (Org.). *Educação e formação de professores: história(s) e memória(s)*. Portalegre: Instituto Politécnico de Portalegre. Escola Superior de Educação.

Morin, E. (2015). *Introdução ao pensamento complexo*. 5. ed. Porto Alegre: Sulina.

Paniago, M. C. L. (2016). Narrativas eclipsadas e ressignificadas de docentes e discentes sobre/na cibercultura. *Revista Educ. Públ.*, Vol. 25, No. 59/1, p. 355-365.

Pires, C. F. F. (2015). O estudante e o ensino híbrido. In: Bacich, L., Tanzi Neto, A., Trevisani, F. M. (Orgs.). *Ensino híbrido: personalização e tecnologia na educação*. Porto Alegre: Penso.

Rodrigues, E. F. (2015). A avaliação e a tecnologia: a questão da verificação de aprendizagem no modelo de ensino híbrido. In: Bacich, L., Tanzi Neto, A., Trevisani, F. M. (Orgs.). *Ensino híbrido: personalização e tecnologia na educação*. Porto Alegre: Penso.

Secretaria de Estado de Saúde de Mato Grosso do Sul (SES MS). (2021). *MS quebra mais um recorde na pandemia: 60 mortos em 24h*, available at: <https://www.saude.ms.gov.br/ms-quebra-mais-um-recorde-na-pandemia-60-mortos-em-24h/> (accessed 27 March 2021).

Schlemmer, E., Moreira, J. A. (2020). Ampliando conceitos para o paradigma de educação digital OnLIFE. *Revista Interacções*, Vol. 16, No. 55, pp. 103-122.

Schneider, F. (2015). Otimização do espaço escolar por meio do modelo de ensino híbrido. In: Bacich, L., Tanzi Neto, A., Trevisani, F. M. (Orgs.). *Ensino híbrido: personalização e tecnologia na educação*. Porto Alegre: Penso.

Silva, M. R. C. (2016). *Ensino híbrido em cursos de graduação presenciais das universidades federais: uma análise da regulamentação*. Dissertação de Mestrado em Educação. Universidade Federal de Mato Grosso, Instituto de Educação.

Sousa, S. O., Schlünzen Junior, K. (2018). Blended Learning: reflexões sobre os atributos de uma aprendizagem mista. *Interações*, Vol. 14, No. 47, pp. 98-121.

Tori, R. (2009). Cursos híbridos ou blended learning. In: Litto, F. M., Formiga, M. M. M. (Orgs.). *Educação a Distância: o estado da arte*. São Paulo: Pearson Education.

Tori, R. (2017). *Educação sem distância: as tecnologias interativas na redução de distâncias em ensino e aprendizagem*. 2. ed. São Paulo: Artesanato Educacional.

Valente, J. A. (2014). Blended learning e as mudanças no ensino superior: a proposta da sala de aula invertida. *Educar em Revista*, Curitiba: Editora UFPR, Edição Especial, No. 4, pp. 79-97.

Vaughan, N. (2016). Princípios da boa prática em Ensino Híbrido. *Programa Questão de Pesquisa*, Secretaria Geral de Educação a Distância (SEaD) da Universidade Federal de São Carlos (UFSCar), available at: <https://www.youtube.com/watch?v=d4lCxR6bOZU> (accessed 27 March 2021).

Yin, R. K. (2015). *Estudo de caso: planejamento e métodos*. 5. ed. Porto Alegre: Bookman.

DEPICTING U.S.-CHINA DISPUTES ON TECH GIANTS THROUGH SOCIAL MEDIA: AN ATTEMPT OF COMPUTATIONAL POLITICAL COMMUNICATION

Yekai Xu* and Mingqi Xie**,[1]
*Graduate School of Interdisciplinary Information Studies, University of Tokyo
Hongo, Bunkyo-ku, Tokyo, 113-0033, Japan
**Schwarzman College, Tsinghua University, Haidian District, Beijing, China

ABSTRACT

Computational political communication based on big data analytics of social media texts brings a prospecting framework to understand the public's perception of and interaction with political issues globally. This study collects a large scale of user-generated Twitter data to delineate online political communication dynamics upon U.S.-China disputes. Tech giants Huawei, Tencent, and ByteDance are chosen as epitomes of the U.S.-China power game to grasp more detailed opinions. Seven English-speaking countries: the U.S., the U.K., Canada, Australia, New Zealand, India, and Pakistan, are selected as keywords for filtering among tweets collected from March 2020 to March 2021 across the globe. Automated text-based sentiment analysis is conducted. This study shows that the popularity of discussions about given countries and companies is inconsistent and might be event-induced. Also, the discourse of all these companies is interrelated rather than separated. This research facilitates future studies on fine-grained, categorized, and automated sentiment & discourse analysis to depict a broader panorama of online public opinion.

KEYWORDS

Big Data, Social Media, Computational Political Communication, U.S.-China Disputes, Tech Giants, Twitter

1. INTRODUCTION

Big data analytics and social media are shedding new light on the interdisciplinary study of both political science and communication studies. For the first time in history, researchers are faced with profuse politics-related information and comments generated by ordinary citizens on social media, empowering them to explore the dynamics of public opinion on critical issues.

U.S.-China bilateral relation has become one of the most influential agendas in contemporary global politics. Over the past few years, starting from increasing mutual tariffs to the escalating conflicts embodied in almost every aspect of the two countries' interaction including international governance and national security, U.S.-China disputes have drastically altered the ecosystem for global trade, investment, and supply chains. Most specifically, within Trump Administration, from the blacklisting of semi-conductor suppliers for Huawei to the ban of TikTok and WeChat, tech giants with a Chinese background are to a great extent posed as epitomes of the competitive power game scenario (Lu et al. 2019; Rosset 2019).

Despite its friendly and goodwill showbiz in the first two years, the Trump administration has then embedded a pivot of America's policy towards China. Published in December 2017, "National Security Strategy of the United States of America" initiates Washington's novel definition of China as a "competitor", "rival", "adversary", and "revisionist power", which served as a curtain-raiser for the upheaval until this day (The White House 2017). With rising nationalism domestically and intensifying pressure externally, Chinese decision-makers, on the other hand, have also been adopting a more "assertive" and "uncompromising" approach in both Aussenpolitik and Innenpolitik which inevitably accounts for de facto "lex talionis" deadlock (Clarke 2020).

---

[1]The two authors have made equal contributions to this paper. * xu-yekai@g.ecc.u-tokyo.ac.jp, ** mingqi.xie@sc.tsinghua.edu.cn

The post-COVID-19 pandemic era has witnessed an exacerbated "decoupling" between the two major powers (Bernes et al. 2020). A vis-à-vis confrontation and retaliation has been projected to not only the sphere of trade but more structurally impacting the network of "global tech" constructed via cooperative efforts within the last two decades. As a milestone of the ongoing industrial revolution, a new phase of globalization, and the forefront of free trade, international tech giants have their roots in crossing-border information exchange, and simultaneously contribute to deepening the connection of the "global village" (Barevičiūte 2010; Fatma & Bharti 2019; Wyne 2020).

Huawei, with its headquarter located in Shenzhen, is a leading telecommunication hardware manufacturer and flagship smart device company in China. In 2020, this 5G titan has ultimately met with the suppression from the U.S. featuring the forced outage of its semi-conductor suppliers including TSMC, Samsung, and SK Hynix (Guo et al. 2019). China-based software companies have also been dramatically impacted in 2020 by the "Clean Network" action plan of the U.S. government. TikTok, a ByteDance-made social media app for short videos, and WeChat, another app for instant messaging, audio, and video calls owned by Tencent, are subsequently included in the blacklist by Washington. Not until these latecomer high-tech innovators enjoyed their unprecedented international boom, they are confronted with the strike that may end their game in the U.S. or even all U.S. allies (Setretary of State 2020).

This study looks into Huawei, ByteDance, and Tencent for their representativeness of hardware and software providers impacted by U.S.-China disputes, and for their huge user scale and global influence. Moreover, WeChat has its major income from the Chinese Mainland while TikTok is an international market-oriented app. This can also serve as a comparison. Internet tech giants are considered to be the watershed of China's rise as a global competitor in technology, innovation, and tertiary industry whereas at the same time an epicenter of China's "challenge" and "threat" to the U.S.

In this digital era, while state behaviors, state-company relations, and geopolitical power plays can be more precisely and directly depicted from the macroscopical policy-making level, the public's perception and interaction also constitute a fundamental sector to the decision-making process, possibly more profoundly than ever. Twitter, among all major global social media platforms, has its characteristics as an internationally connected, weak ties-based "public sphere", facilitating this research to depict a more comprehensive view of U.S.-China disputes (Castells 2008; Habermas et al. 1974; Williams 2017). Therefore, this study chooses Twitter data for delineating online political communication dynamics.

In this work, names of seven major English-speaking countries, namely, the United States, the United Kingdom, Canada, Australia, New Zealand, India, and Pakistan, are selected as keywords for filtering among all the Twitter data collected over twelve months across the globe. The U.S., U.K., Canada, Australia, and New Zealand are also known as the "Five Eyes Alliance", which is an intelligence-based strategic ally group with its origin as "UKUSA" from the Second World War (Albers et al. 2016). This study also notices the strong geopolitical proximity between India, Pakistan, and China. These two South Asian countries, acknowledged as the biggest English-speaking countries adjacent to China and together populated over 1.5 billion, cast a huge impact on China's overseas market and foreign strategies (Sun 2020). Names of the three Chinese tech giants, Huawei, Tencent, and ByteDance, are also used to target relevant tweets.

How does online public opinion perceive and respond to the disputes between America and China? What is the picture of social media discourse on specific tech giants? To our knowledge, this is the first study dedicated to answering these questions. In the second section, we will provide a concise review of the transition of political communication studies, and point out its promising future for both social and data scientists. Then, we go on to introduce preliminary findings of our Twitter data analysis. Discussions and conclusions are offered at the end. This study hopes that the publication of the dataset, and the insights the dataset provides after applying certain computational methods, can inspire and facilitate more social and data science researchers to create meaningful scholarly works.

2. EXISTING WORKS: ACHIEVEMENTS, DEFICIENCIES, AND EXPECTATIONS

This section summarizes existing works in understanding the dynamics of public opinion, pointing out its shift from traditional media to social media and the impetus behind it. We show that large-scale social media data ensures a promising future for the interdisciplinary study of political communication as well as social simulating and modeling.

2.1 Traditional Media and Surveys in the Beginning: Efforts by Social Scientists

Media framing of certain countries, issues, or important figures has long been one of the most popular topics among political communication researchers. The manually-coded methods, e.g., text analysis, discourse analysis, and content analysis, are widely adopted in the studies of images and agendas constructed by different media sources, while a majority of the research by social scientists still focus on traditional media, namely newspapers, magazines, TVs, etc.

In recent years, China has won more and more attention to its international image presentation. Golan & Lukito (2015) describes the rise of China via looking into American newspapers' "opinion articles" on China. Golan and Lukito reckon that opinion journalism, including "editorials" and "co-eds" of major newspapers, embodies the most clearly how a country's elite community thinks about specific issues. This research mainly utilizes the inductive qualitative analysis framework, looking into the Wall Street Journal (WSJ) editorials and the op-eds on China's rise. The text analysis focuses on key statements, positive or negative attitudes, and the use of quotes. It presents that "economic partnership," "internal dispute," "geopolitical threat," and "economic threat" are the main categories of WSJ's narrative framework. Golan and Lukito carried out the analysis based on a belief that the elites of society are responsible and influential to foreign policymaking. Similar frameworks are universally adapted in social scientists' research on media framing and international image-related topics.

While public opinion's response to certain countries and issues is becoming more well-attended in academia these days, classic methodologies including surveys are applied in numerous social science research. Yang (2020) carried out a study on how China's image affects China's product selling in the United States. Focusing on public opinion as a critical factor in this research, participants were recruited in a medium city of Ohio in both ways: printed and online questionnaires (on Facebook). However, this approach to depicting public opinion about China's country-of-origin image still faces questions that whether it is comprehensive enough and if there exist more efficient ways to do the research.

The Verb In Context System (VICS) is also an early attempt to understand the mentality of people, especially political leaders (Schafer & Walker 2006). Based on the 1969 study of the "operational code" (George 1969), the VICS analyzes people's political opinion and beliefs on power, predictability, the role of chance, etc., through their use of verbs found in public accessible speeches and policy text. An exhaustive dictionary was established to provide reference to the orientation of each verb, e.g., friendly or hostile, optimistic or pessimistic. The VICS is widely used for studying political figures (Cuhadar et al. 2017; Dyson 2007; Renshon 2008; Renshon 2009; Walker 2011), where methods including "Leadership Traits Analysis (LTA)" are adopted to depict the process of political decision making of leaders—for example, analyzing leaders' personality influences during disputes and even armed conflicts (Dyson 2006). However, the methods' generalization to the public remains somehow stagnant, at least partly due to a lack of available texts written by the general public.

2.2 The Advent of Social Media: Promises for Data Scientists

Entering the era of social media, the openness and user-generating nature of cyberspace empower the general public to express and construct online discourse. According to a Pew Research Center report, more than 40% of American adults accessed information for the 2016 presidential election via social media, which provides a simple example of this ubiquitous phenomenon nowadays. The rapid development of computer science enables data scientists to directly study the public's opinion for the first time. Opposite to traditional researchers' focus on limited information sources and small target population, data scientists have been working to discover more latent and complex information from broader social media data.

Sentiment analysis is a frequently employed technique for studying social media data in text modality. The basic goals of sentiment analysis are emotion recognition and polarity detection (Cambria 2016; Poria et al. 2017). Many researchers used this method to explore country images, evaluate international relations, and predict electoral results. Chen et al. (2020) and Xu et al. (2020) are both event-based country image studies with Twitter data, observing online public opinion during the 70th anniversary of the People's Republic of China and the COVID-19 pandemic, respectively. Their data was retrieved through Twitter Streaming API, and sentiments towards China (positive, negative, neutral) were analyzed with machine learning algorithms trained on manually labeled data. Their features include: 1) Xu et al. collected and compared English and

Chinese data, while Chen et al. focused on English discourse. It was found that a significant opposition existed between the online public opinions towards China of the two languages. 2) Chen et al. provided fine-grained sentiment analysis by dividing online public opinion towards China into seven categories: Politics, Economy, Foreign affairs, Culture, Epidemic situation, Anti-epidemic measures, and Racism. They revealed that the gradual increase in negative politics-, foreign affairs-, and racism-related tweets and the decrease in non-negative epidemic situation-, anti-epidemic measures-related tweets resulted in the overall sentiments' transition from non-negative to negative towards China. 3) Chen et al. displayed the different patterns in the attitudes of Congress members, media, and social bots, showing that social bots were more likely to spread negative sentiments towards China, while media were usually non-negative. For U.S. congress members, the Republicans were more negative than the Democrats. 4) Xu et al. explored how positive and negative tweets were distributed among different countries and found that states enjoying better diplomatic relations with China generally had a positive view towards China. 5) Xu et al. obtained word vectors for the top 100 frequently and uniquely used words for both English and Chinese, positive and negative tweets through the word2vec technique. Preferred topics of distinct languages and sentiments were analyzed, e.g., positive Chinese tweets primarily focused on celebration activities while negative Chinese tweets tended to talk about broader issues like Hong Kong.

Chambers et al. (2015) modeled relations between states using sentiments revealed in tweets with country names. Seventeen months of Twitter data were collected, and the aggregated sentiments for nation pairs were calculated with a support vector machine. The results indicated an alignment between human polls and social media sentiments, verifying the validity of applying social media data to infer international relations.

Predicting election results with social media data is also a focus for researchers. Related works include (D'Andrea et al. 2019; Jungherr et al. 2017; Lopez et al. 2017; Tsirakis et al. 2017). Other papers addressing online public opinion towards political events include Adams-Cohen (2020), Leong & Ho (2021), McGregor (2019), etc.

2.3 The Era of Interdisciplinary Collaboration: Computational Political Communication

Despite the considerable endeavor and contributions the above-mentioned works made to the emerging field of computational political communication, their shortcomings are also prominent. Their implications for social challenges are vague. With their vision limited to describing general pictures, the advanced computational techniques are not fully utilized to answer more meaningful questions and bring about possible solutions. Meanwhile, a lack of real-time, or 'nowcast,' analysis, which has the potential to detect major events at an early stage and provide governments and the society with necessary notifications, also stands out as a significant deficiency for existing studies.

From the global communication perspective, it can be anticipated that a more comprehensive and real-time computational research on social media will become increasingly significant for academia and policy-makers. Computational political communication is undoubtedly a rising field for interdisciplinary collaboration, with social scientists' intrinsic dedication to find questions and create meanings and data scientists' capability to initiate more sophisticated quantitative research. Data scientists should be encouraged to engage in more of this interdisciplinary area, honing and experimenting with their methodologies and theories (Margolin 2019; van Atteveldt & Peng 2018). So, below presents a demo analysis with Twitter data.

3. A DEMO FOR DATA COLLECTION AND ANALYSIS

3.1 Data Collection

The data analyzed in this study is collected through Twitter Streaming API, which allows users to retrieve tweets with designated hashtags. Since the dataset is expected to support research in a broader context and is not specific to this work, the hashtags for retrieving data are designed to include all major countries in the world (5 permanent members in the UN security council, G20 countries, OECD countries) and countries enjoying close contact with China (member states of Shanghai Cooperation Organization and the Association of Southeast Asian Nations, North Korea). The collection started on March 4, 2020, and will continue for several years. This dataset is open to all researchers. This study uses the data from March 4, 2020, to March 14, 2021, including a total of 148,725,018 tweets.

Then, we filter the collected data with the following criteria: a tweet should simultaneously include names or synonyms of at least one of the seven English-speaking countries and the names or synonyms of at least one of the three Chinese tech giants. The names and synonyms are shown in Table 1. Please note that the names and synonyms are case-insensitive since all the tweets and names would be changed into the lower case before filtering. At last, a total of 149,339 tweets were selected for this study.

Table 1. Names and synonyms of countries and companies

Type	Names and synonyms
Countries	'the us', 'UnitedStates', 'United States', 'the states', 'America', ' uk ', 'UnitedKingdom', 'United Kingdom', 'Britain', 'Canada', 'Australia', 'aussie', 'NewZealand', 'New Zealand', 'India', 'Pakistan'
Companies	'huawei', 'hua wei', 'bytedance', 'byte dance', 'zijietiaodong', 'zi jie tiao dong', 'tiktok', 'tik tok', 'douyin', 'dou yin', 'tencent', 'tengxun', 'teng xun', 'wechat', 'weixin', 'wei xin'

3.2 Data Analysis – Quantitative Characteristics and Linguistic Preferences

This part reveals the quantitative characteristics and linguistic preferences of tweets linked to different countries and companies.

Figure 1 displays the number of tweets about the seven chosen countries and the three selected companies from March 4, 2020, to March 14, 2021. It can be found that the ups and downs in popularity of country-company topics are significant: rarely mentioned on most days and intensively discussed in certain periods, possibly after an important event. Some events may induce massive discussions related to the same company in multiple countries, e.g., following India's ban on TikTok on June 29, 2020, a peak of related tweets appear in Australia, India, the U.K., and the U.S. Also, public attention towards the three companies is uneven. Huawei receives the most mentions when people are simultaneously talking about Australia, Canada, New Zealand, and the U.K., while ByteDance enjoys an overwhelming popularity in India, Pakistan, and the U.S.

Figure 2 reveals the word vectors of frequently mentioned words (appeared more than 500 times in our collected corpus) by tweets related to different countries and companies. Limited by space, this paper only shows the word vectors of Australia, Pakistan, U.K., and U.S.-related tweets. The word vectors were calculated through word2vec. It can be observed that, for any given country, words from tweets related to different companies generally form only one cluster, entangling with each other rather than distributing separately. It indicates that the discourse of all these companies is inter-related. The colors also provide an intuitive image of which company is more widely discussed, e.g., the prominent green in the U.K. picture tells that Huawei was more frequently talked about.

3.3 Data Analysis – Sentiment of the Tweets

This section uses an unsupervised sentiment analysis method to show the attitudes of Twitter users when they mention the countries and companies of interest.

The algorithm in this study is an adapted version of the fuzzy rule-based unsupervised sentiment analysis technique developed by Vashishtha and Susan for analyzing social media posts (Vashishtha & Susan 2019). Every tweet was classified as positive, negative, or neutral with the Mamdani system and nine fuzzy rules.

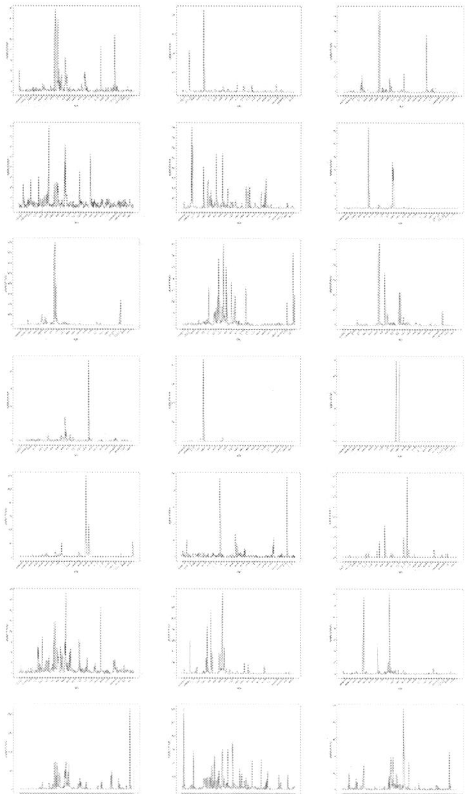

Figure 1. Number of tweets discussing the seven countries and the three companies, from March 4, 2020 to March 14, 2021 (*From top to down: Australia, Canada, India, New Zealand, Pakistan, the United Kingdom, the United States; from left to right: ByteDance, Huawei, Tencent*)

Please download all the original figures at https://drive.google.com/file/d/1T_fHpKVz1Z79Fo2I-4QPqva3DIVzaZU2/view?usp=sharing.

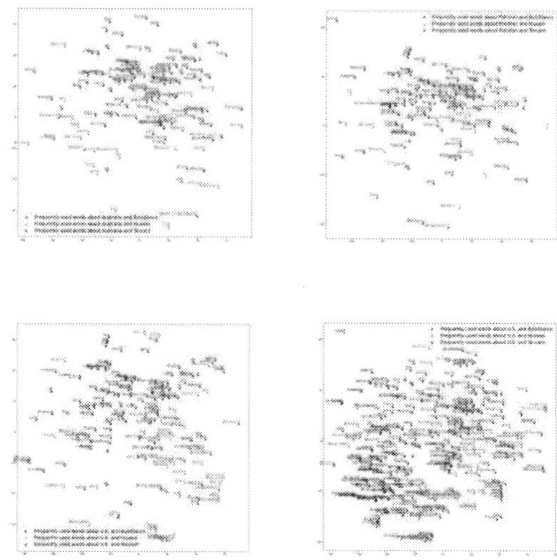

Figure 2. Word vectors of frequently mentioned words (*top-left: Australia; top-right: Pakistan; down-left: the U.K.; down-right: the U.S.*)

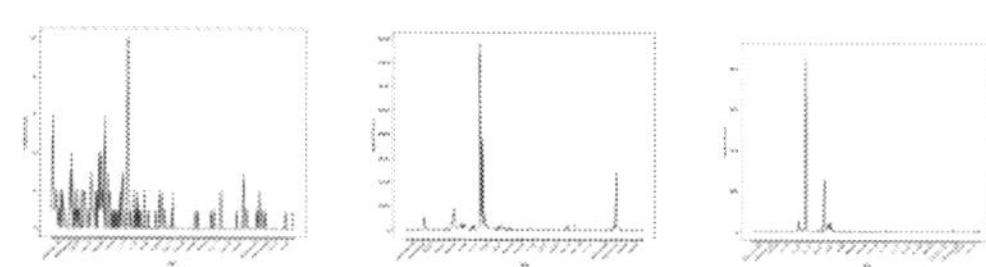

Figure 3. Number of positive (*left*), neutral (*middle*) and negative (*right*) tweets mentioning India and Bytedance

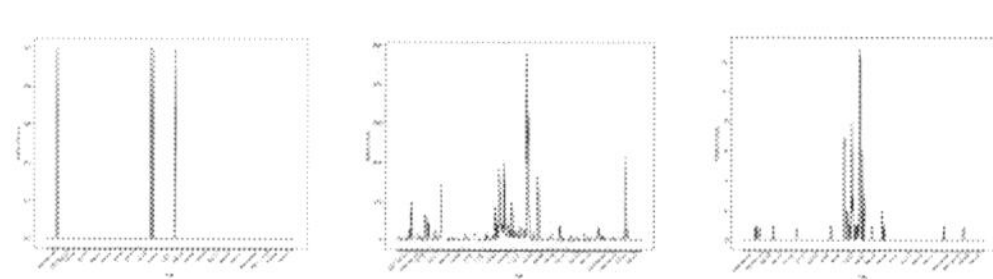

Figure 4. Number of positive (*left*), neutral (*middle*) and negative (*right*) tweets mentioning the U.S. and Tencent

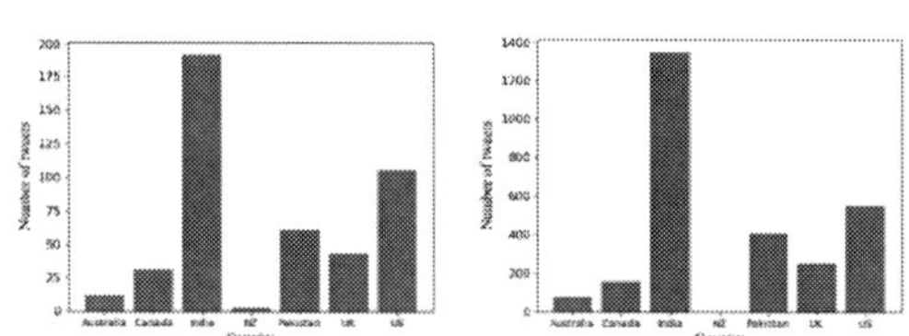

Figure 5. Number of positive (*left*) and negative (*right*) tweets about Chinese tech giants when mentioning the seven English-speaking countries

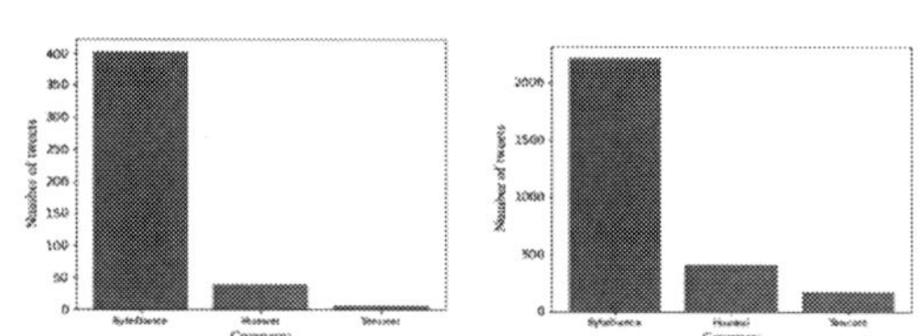

Figure 6. Number of positive (*left*) and negative (*right*) tweets about the seven English-speaking countries when mentioning Chinese tech giants

Figures 3 and 4 are the fluctuations of the number of positive and negative tweets mentioning selected country-company pairs. It can be observed that most tweets are neutral, but negative tweets also significantly outnumber positive ones.

Figures 5 and 6 show the number of positive and negative tweets in our data set about every country and company. India and ByteDance are the ones that attract the most attention on Twitter when discussing issues about countries and Chinese tech giants. And the rankings of the number of positive and negative tweets containing country names and company names are generally the same.

4. CONCLUSIONS AND DISCUSSIONS

In the past few years, the bilateral relation between U.S.-China has been witnessing a "freefall," posing concern to global governance and international order. With its crossing-border and user-generated nature, social media provides a promising field for computational political communication research, enabling us to understand the mechanism of online public opinion's perception of and interaction with global politics.

This study highlights the prospect computational political communication has for people's understanding of political events in the digital era. After summarizing researchers' efforts spanning traditional media and survey to large-scale social media data, we introduce a new Twitter dataset and provide an example for the use of such data by revealing its quantitative features and sentiment characteristics.

Future research will include 1) From social scientists' perspective: generating more political communication questions that can a) be solved with large-scale social media data and computational methods, and b) facilitate high-quality social governance that optimizes the living experience of all; 2) From data scientists' perspective: under the principle of respecting privacy, developing more fine-grained sentiment analysis algorithms for digital media contents to discover the political leanings of Internet users and the mechanisms for online political communication. Realizing real-time analysis is another promising task.

REFERENCES

Adams-Cohen N. J., 2020. Policy Change and Public Opinion: Measuring Shifting Political Sentiment with Social Media Data. *In American Politics Research*, Vol. 48, No. 5, pp. 612-621.

Albers S. et al, 2016. Strategic Alliance Structures: An Organization Design Perspective. *In Journal of Management*, Vol. 42, No. 3, pp. 582-614.

Barevičiūte J., 2010. The Locality of the "Global Village" in the Aspect of Communication: Pro et contra m. McLuhan. *In Limes: Cultural Regionalistics*, Vol. 3, No. 2, pp. 184-194.

Bernes T. et al, 2020. Challenges of Global Governance Amid the COVID-19 Pandemic. Council on Foreign Relations (CFR).

Cambria E., 2016. Affective Computing and Sentiment Analysis. *In IEEE Intelligent Systems*, Vol. 31, No. 2, pp. 102-107.

Castells M., 2008. The New Public Sphere: Global Civil Society, Communication Networks, and Global Governance. *In the Annals of the American Academy of Political and Social Science*, Vol. 616, No.1, pp. 78–93.

Chambers N. et al, 2015. Identifying Political Sentiment between Nation States with Social Media. *Proceedings of the 2015 Conference on Empirical Methods in Natural Language Processing*. Lisbon, Portugal, pp. 65-75.

Chen H. et al, 2020. Country Image in COVID-19 Pandemic: A Case Study of China. *In IEEE Transactions on Big Data*, Vol. 7, No. 1, pp. 81-92.

Clarke M., 2020. Beijing's Pivot West: The Convergence of Innenpolitik and Aussenpolitik on China's 'Belt and Road'? *In Journal of Contemporary China*, Vol. 29, No. 123, pp. 336-353.

Cuhadar E. et al, 2017. Personality or Role? Comparisons of Turkish Leaders across Different Institutional Positions. *In Political Psychology*, Vol. 38, No. 1, pp. 39-54.

D'Andrea E. et al, 2019. Monitoring the Public Opinion about the Vaccination Topic from Tweets Analysis. *In Expert Systems with Applications*, Vol. 116, pp. 209-226.

Dyson S. B., 2006. Personality and Foreign Policy: Tony Blair's Iraq Decisions. *In Foreign Policy Analysis*, Vol. 2, No. 3, pp. 289-306.

Dyson S. B., 2007. Alliances, Domestic Politics, and Leader Psychology: Why Did Britain Stay out of Vietnam and Go into Iraq? *In Political Psychology*, Vol. 28, No. 6, pp. 647-666.

Fatma A. and Bharti N., 2019. Perception vs. Reality: Understanding the US–China Trade War. *In Transnational Corporations Review*, Vol. 11, No. 4, pp. 270-278.

George A. L., 1969. The 'Operational Code': A Neglected Approach to the Study of Political Leaders and Decision-making. *In International Studies Quarterly*, Vol. 13, No. 2, pp. 190-222.

Golan G. J. and Lukito J., 2015. The Rise of the Dragon? Framing China's Global Leadership in Elite American Newspapers. *In International Communication Gazette*, Vol. 77, No. 8, pp. 754-772.

Guo L. et al, 2019. Huawei's Catch-up in the Global Telecommunication Industry: Innovation Capability and Transition to Leadership. *In Technology Analysis & Strategic Management*, Vol. 31, No. 12, pp. 1395-1411.

Habermas J. et al, 1974. The Public Sphere: An Encyclopedia Article (1964). *In New German Critique*, No. 3: pp. 49-55.

Jungherr A. et al, 2017. Digital Trace Data in the Study of Public Opinion: An Indicator of Attention toward Politics Rather Than Political Support. *In Social Science Computer Review*, Vol. 35, No. 3, pp. 336-356.

Leong A. D. and Ho S. S., 2021. Perceiving Online Public Opinion: The Impact of Facebook Opinion Cues, Opinion Climate Congruency, and Source Credibility on Speaking Out. *In New Media & Society*, Vol. 23, No. 9, pp 2495-2515.

Lopez J. C. A. D. et al, 2017. Predicting the Brexit Vote by Tracking and Classifying Public Opinion Using Twitter Data. *In Statistics, Politics and Policy*, Vol. 8, No. 1, pp. 85-104.

Lu C. et al, 2019. Perspectives on the Global Economic Order in 2019: A U.S.-China Essay Collection. Center for Strategic and International Studies (CSIS).

Margolin D. B., 2019. Computational Contributions: a Symbiotic Approach to Integrating Big, Observational Data Studies into the Communication Field. *In Communication Methods and Measures*, Vol. 13, No. 4, pp. 229-247.

McGregor S. C., 2019. Social Media as Public Opinion: How Journalists Use Social Media to Represent Public Opinion. *In Journalism*, Vol. 20, No. 8, pp. 1070-1086.

Poria S. et al, 2017. A Review of Affective Computing: from Unimodal Analysis to Multimodal Fusion. *In Information Fusion*, Vol. 37, pp. 98-125.

Renshon J., 2008. Stability and Change in Belief Systems: The Operational Code of George W. Bush. *In Journal of Conflict Resolution*, Vol. 52, No. 6, pp. 820-849.

Renshon J., 2009. When Public Statements Reveal Private Beliefs: Assessing Operational Codes at a Distance. *In Political Psychology*, Vol. 30, No. 4, pp. 649-661.

Rosset C., 2019. Huawei Ban Means the End of Global Tech, 17 May 2019. Foreign Policy. Available from: https://foreignpolicy.com/2019/05/17/huawei-ban-means-the-end-of-global-tech/. [18 November 2021].

Schafer M. and Walker S. G., 2006. Operational Code Analysis at a Distance: The Verbs in Context System of Content Analysis. *Beliefs and Leadership in World Politics*: Palgrave Macmillan, New York. pp. 25-51.

Secretary of State, 2020. The Clean Network. U.S. Department of State. Available from: https://www.state.gov/the-clean-network/. [21 September 2020].

Sun Y., 2020. China and South Asia Crisis Management in the Era of Great Power Competition. Norwegian Institute for International Affairs (NUPI).

The White House, 2017. National Security Strategy of the United States of America. Available from: https://trumpwhitehouse.archives.gov/wp-content/uploads/2017/12/NSS-Final-12-18-2017-0905.pdf. [18 November 2021].

Tsirakis N. et al, 2017. Large Scale Opinion Mining for Social, News and Blog Data. *In Journal of Systems and Software*, Vol. 127, pp. 237-248.

van Atteveldt W. and Peng T.-Q., 2018. When Communication Meets Computation: Opportunities, Challenges, and Pitfalls in Computational Communication Science. *In Communication Methods and Measures*, Vol. 12, No. 2-3, pp. 81-92.

Vashishtha S. and Susan S., 2019. Fuzzy Rule based Unsupervised Sentiment Analysis from Social Media Posts. *In Expert Systems with Applications*, Vol. 138, pp. 112834.

Walker S. G., 2011. Anticipating Attacks from the Operational Codes of Terrorist Groups. *In Dynamics of Asymmetric Conflict*, Vol. 4, No. 2, pp. 135-143.

Williams C. B., 2017. Introduction: Social Media, Political Marketing and the 2016 US Election. *In Journal of Political Marketing*, Vol. 16, No. 3-4, pp. 207-211.

Wyne A., 2020. How to Think about Potentially Decoupling from China. *In The Washington Quarterly*, Vol. 43, No. 1, pp. 41-64.

Xu Y. et al, 2020. Understanding Online Public Sentiments: A Machine Learning-Based Analysis of English and Chinese Twitter Discourse during the 2019 Chinese National Day. *Proceedings of the 2nd International Multidisciplinary Information Technology and Engineering Conference (IMITEC 2020)*. Kimberley, South Africa, pp. 1-9.

Yang C., 2020. How China's Image Affects Chinese Products in a Partisan-motivated US Market. *In Global Media and China*, Vol. 5, No. 2, pp. 169-187.

TEEN SOCIAL MEDIA USE DURING COVID-19: PARENT PERCEPTIONS AND OVERSIGHT

Vanessa P. Dennen, Hui Shi, Stacey A. Rutledge, Lauren M. Bagdy, Daeun Jung, Stephen Bunn, Casey Cargill, Catherine Cosgrove and Amber Hedquist
Florida State University, Tallahassee, FL USA

ABSTRACT

The paper investigates how parents of American teenagers navigated teen social media use during the early months of the COVID-19 pandemic, amid school closures and stay-at-home orders. Through an online survey, parents of teenagers reported on teen engagement, happiness, and social media use along with their own levels and types of oversight related to that social media use. Findings showed that parents perceived their teens to be similarly or less engaged in school and social activities than usual, and generally happy with social media use contributing somewhat to that happiness. Parental monitoring of social media use was the same or lower than during pre-pandemic times overall, with some significant differences related to parent gender, teen age, and teen gender.

KEYWORDS

Social Media, Parent, Teenagers, Pandemic, COVID-19

1. INTRODUCTION

In spring 2020, much of the world swiftly shut down in response to the COVID-19 pandemic. Specific responses to the pandemic varied by country and region, but stay at home orders were common, leaving people to increasingly rely on their phones and computers to connect with the outside world. Social media specifically provided a platform through which phones and computers could unite people, and thus has played a prominent role in pandemic life. Among its many functions have been maintaining existing social connections, developing and supporting community networks, entertainment, and crowdsourcing information at the local, national and global levels. For many people, social media was a primary way of learning how others were experiencing the pandemic and having social interactions with people outside of one's household during the first months of the pandemic.

Teenagers may have been forced into household isolation in spring 2020, but this did not mean that they lacked social interaction. For American teenagers, who were already heavy users of both mobile phones and social media pre-pandemic (Anderson & Jiang, 2018), social media networks and established patterns of use were already in place. For many teens, their social media networks and experiences are intertwined with their school networks and experiences (Dennen, Rutledge, et al., 2020; Rutledge et al., 2019). In other words, teens use social media to connect outside of school to support peer relationships and identity development (Dennen, Choi, et al., 2020). When physically in schools, where social media and mobile phone use are complex and multifaceted (Greenhow et al., 2019) and may be restricted or eschewed in favor of face-to-face interactions (Garcia, 2017), teens are likely to discuss things they have seen on social media (Dennen, Rutledge, et al., 2020; Rutledge et al., 2019). Thus, during Spring 2020, when schools at all levels shifted to emergency remote learning (Hodges et al., 2020) for the remainder of the school year as a safety precaution, high school students experienced not only an educational disruption (Colvin et al., 2022), but also a social one. School closures and isolation have been blamed for a range of ill effects on teens (Tan, 2021), and in particular teen mental health issues (Meherali et al., 2021). Other effects experienced by teens during this time include increased screen time (Ceylan et al., 2021) and sedentariness (Rossi et al., 2021).

Both teens and their parents struggled during the lockdown when they were largely limited to each other for in person social interaction. For teens, this period was marked by an increase in mental health issues and negative behaviors (Breaux et al., 2021), with established family relationships moderating how these issues were internalized and externalized (Skinner et al., 2021). Social media offered a way to maintain friendships outside the household and communicate with friends during the early months of the pandemic (Dennen, Rutledge, et al., 2021a, 2021b), but its use was more situated or visible in the household than usual, where parents could directly monitor things like time spent online.

The triadic relationship between teens, social media, and their parents is complex. Social media can be a source of positive outcomes, but also a source of peril for teens. Parents themselves often look to social media to support their parenting (Dennen, Jung, et al., 2021). Parental monitoring of social media use, starting in the pre-teen years, can lead to more positive outcomes for teens (Fardouly et al., 2018). However, at some point parent oversight must be relaxed, with control over online decisions ceded to the teen. Not only is it developmentally appropriate for teenagers to have privacy and make their own social decisions, but it also connects to the important development of digital literacy skills. This situation can prove challenging, with parents as a primary source of both guidance and discipline over an activity that occurs in a virtual space where parents are not welcome.

2. PURPOSE AND RESEARCH QUESTIONS

The purpose of this study is to investigate parent perspectives on and oversight of teen social media use during the early months of the COVID-19 pandemic. The parent perspective is an important one for three reasons. First, parents are usually the responsible party providing teenagers with access to mobile phones and Internet service for social purposes. In this position, parents serve as potential technology gatekeepers. Second, contemporary parenting involves monitoring teenagers' mobile phone and social media use, along with teaching them to be responsible users (Dennen et al., 2019). Third, parents typically live and interact with teenagers daily and can offer perspectives on their teenager's activities and moods. Although a parent's report on teen attitudes and behavior is secondary data, parents are nonetheless keen observers of teen behavior. Parents are often used as a source of data about teen social media use (e.g., Wallace, 2021). Additionally, this study focuses on how parents monitor and respond to their teenager's social media use, in which case they directly self-report information.

The study focuses specifically on teen engagement and happiness along with parent social media restrictions and monitoring in the immediate wake of the pandemic. Of interest here is whether parents perceived that their teen's everyday life was affected by the pandemic and whether they became less restrictive about online activities as a result. The research questions that guided this study are:

1. Did parents perceive a difference in their teen's engagement regular activities during the early months of the pandemic?
2. Did parents perceive social media as an important component of teens happiness during the early months of the pandemic? Did perceptions of happiness differ by age and gender?
3. Did parents adjust their social media monitoring behaviors in the early months of the pandemic? Did parent oversight differ by gender and age?
4. What was the relationship between parent oversight and perceived level of teen social media use during the early months of the pandemic?

3. METHOD

To address the research questions, a survey study was conducted during the summer of 2020. The study was approved by the researchers' Institutional Review Board.

3.1 Participants

Participants in this study were 641 parents or guardians of teenage children in the United States. The sample included parents representing 44 of the 50 states. Each participant reported data on up to three teenagers, with a total of 921 teenagers represented in the data set (see Table 1 for an overview of demographics). Although most respondents indicated they were female and in a mother role, the gender balance of teenagers was more even. The 4.5% of participants in the other role were stepparents, grandparents, and legal guardians. For brevity, the term parent is used throughout this study to indicate individuals in a parent or parent-like role. Most of the teens were white, and they were evenly split between younger teenagers, defined as between ages 13-15, and older teenagers, defined as between ages 16-19.

Table 1. Family Demographics ($N_{(parents)}$ = 641, $N_{(teens)}$=921)

Demographic Variables	N	Percentage
Parent Gender		
Female	560	87.4%
Male	78	12.2%
Non-binary	3	0.5%
Parent Role in Family		
Mother	560	87.4%
Father	52	8.1%
Other roles	48	4.5%
Teen Gender		
Female	430	46.7%
Male	480	52.1%
Non-binary/unknown	11	1.2%
Teen Race		
White	691	75.0%
Black	78	8.5%
Hispanic or Latinx	56	6.1%
Asian	21	2.3%
Other races	75	8.1%
	N	M(SD)
Age of teens	921	15.5(1.83)
Younger Group (13-15)	482	52.3%
Older Group (16-19)	439	47.7%

3.2 Data Collection

Data collection occurred via an online survey using the Qualtrics survey platform. All participants opted into the survey after first being presented with a study information sheet. The survey itself consisted of parent demographics, followed by a question about how many teenagers were in the parent's household. For each teenager in the household, up to a maximum of 3 teenagers, parents were asked a block of questions about the teen's demographics, the parent's oversight of the teen's social media use, and the parent's observations and perceptions of the teen's social media use. The survey was advertised to parents using paid advertisements on Facebook and Instagram during July 2020. Parents could follow a link embedded in the ad to access the survey. At the conclusion of the survey they could enter a drawing to win one of four $25 gift cards.

3.3 Data Analysis

Data analysis focused on descriptive analysis of responses to answer the first three research questions, and a chi-square tests of independence to explore demographic differences for research questions two and three. For the chi-square analyses we explored differences across three demographic variables, parent gender, teen gender, and teen age. Teen age was grouped into younger (13-15) and older (16-19) teens (see Table 1) based on the typical legal driving age in the United States, which is 16 years old. This division was meaningful because for many teens independence is associated with driving (Scott-Parker, 2018). In another study conducted during the early period of the pandemic, teens who were able to drive reported more interactions with friends and the outside world than younger teens (Dennen, Rutledge, et al., 2021b). Finally, logistic regression was used to answer the fourth research question.

4. FINDINGS

4.1 Parent Observation of Teen Engagement and Happiness

Around half of the parents reported that their teens were less engaged in school and social activities during the early months of the pandemic when compared to pre-pandemic times (see Table 2). Notably, some parents perceived that their teen's engagement in school or social activities increased during this period. Despite the perceived decrease in engagement for many teens, most parents reported that their teen's happiness was at a medium or high level. Similarly, social media was reported to be important to teen happiness during this time at either a medium or high level. A chi-square test of independence showed no differences in happiness related to teen gender or age.

Table 2. Teen engagement and happiness

	Less	Same	More
School Engagement	459 (49.8%)	231 (25.1%)	209 (22.7%)
Social Engagement	507 (55.0%)	268 (29.1%)	135 (14.7%)
	Low	Medium	High
Happiness	74 (8.0%)	366 (39.7%)	481 (52.2%)
SM Importance	83 (9.0%)	317 (34.4%)	521 (56.6%)

4.2 Parent Social Media Oversight

Parents were asked to indicate whether their social media restrictiveness and monitoring activities had changed during the early months of the pandemic. As reported in Table 3, most parents reported that their monitoring was about the same, but a sizable minority reported that they had become less restrictive during this time. When asked about specific forms of oversight, the greatest changes were reported about monitoring and restricting the amount of time teens spend online. Specifically, parents loosened their oversight with regards to time.

Chi-square tests of independence were used to examine differences based on parent gender, teen gender, and teen age (see Table 4). There was a significant relationship between parent gender and level of oversight, $\chi2$ (2) = 6.403, p = .038. The post-hoc tests showed that mothers were more likely than fathers to reduce restrictions during this time, whereas fathers were more likely than mothers to increase restrictions. For example, 24.5% of fathers increased their monitoring of with whom their teens interacted online compared to only 14.8% of mothers.

There were also significant differences in oversight based on the age of the teens, $\chi2$ (2) = 15.08, p = .001. For every item, parents were more restrictive with younger teens (age 13-15) than they were with older teens (age 16-19). Additionally, parents reported being more likely to have increased conflicts about social media use with younger teens.

Teen gender did not show significant differences when parents reported about oversight in general, $\chi2$ (2) = 4.232, p = 0.12. However, there were significant differences when focused specifically on monitoring who teens interact with. A post-hoc test showed that parents were more restrictive with daughters than they were with sons.

Table 3. Changes in parental monitoring activities

	Less restrictive	About the same	More restrictive
Parental monitoring of teen's social media use	187 (20.3%)	656 (71.2%)	78 (8.5%)
Monitoring Activities	Less	About the same	More
I monitor what they post online.	101 (11%)	683 (74.2%)	137 (14.9%)
I monitor who they interact with online.	117 (12.7%)	659 (71.6%)	145 (15.7%)
I monitor how much time they spend online.	227 (24.6%)	527 (57.2%)	167 (18.1%)
I restrict the amount of time they spend online.	291 (31.6%)	509 (55.3%)	121 (13.1%)
I have conflict with my teen about their online activities.	153 (16.6%)	616 (66.9%)	152 (16.5%)

Table 4. Chi-square results of the impact of family factors on teens' social media use

	Parent gender χ^2 (df)	Teen gender χ^2 (df)	Teen age χ^2 (df)
Level of monitoring	6.403 (2)**	4.232 (2)	15.08 (2)***
Monitoring activities			
I monitor what they post online.	2.939 (2)	0.972 (2)	17.263 (2)***
I monitor who they interact with online.	6.729 (2)**	7.727 (2)**	26.942 (2)***
I monitor how much time they spend online.	9.524 (2)**	5.812 (2)	22.801 (2)***
I restrict the amount of time they spend online.	8.882 (2)**	3.706 (2)	6.569 (2)**
I have conflict with my teen about their online activities.	1.569 (2)	1.435 (2)	7.504 (2)**

Note. **$p<0.05$, ***$p<0.01$

4.3 Oversight and Level of Use

To explore the relationship between changes in parent monitoring and level of teen social media use, we did an ordered logistic regression. The results showed that heavy teen use of social media was significantly associated with decreased parents' oversight (β=-.239, Wald's χ^2=14.243, p<0.001). The logistic regression model indicated that parents whose teens are heavy social media users less restrictively monitored those teens (OR = 0.787, 95% CI = 0.696, 0.892).

5. DISCUSSION AND CONCLUSION

These findings suggest that parents recognized that their teens were less engaged in typical school and social media activities (research question 1). Although most parents did not feel that their teens experienced a dip in happiness, they nonetheless recognized the importance of social media to their teens for maintaining social connections during a stressful time (research question 2). These findings were corroborated by teens in a parallel survey study (Dennen, Rutledge, et al., 2021a) and are consistent with another study that found both parents and teens experienced increased reliance on social media during the early pandemic (Drouin et al.,

2020). Addressing research questions 3, parents responded accordingly by either relaxing their oversight, including time restrictions, or by maintaining the status quo. Finally, lower rates of restriction and monitoring were associated with heavier teen social media use, at least in terms of parental perceptions (research question 4). The many parents who reported no change in their oversight behaviors combined with the association between less restrictive parents and higher teen social media use implies that prior to the pandemic they had already established effective ways of parenting their teens related to social media use. In this sense, the term *effective* is relative and assumes that whatever arrangement was in place pre-pandemic balanced factors like safety, maturity level, and parent-child conflict in a manner that led to satisfactory outcomes.

In the roughly 30% of cases in which parent monitoring changed, we did not collect data that explains the change. However, various explanations can be considered. In cases where parents and teens experienced greater togetherness at home, parent exposure to teen behaviors may have increased. In particular, this phenomenon may explain the significant difference based on parent gender, which somewhat challenges findings from a pre-pandemic study which suggest that mothers are more engaged in social media monitoring (Wallace, 2021). During the pandemic, an increase in parents working at home may have given fathers greater exposure than usual to their teen's online behaviors. This awareness may have led them to try to enact new limits.

Conversely, parents who previously enforced restrictions and monitored teen use closely may have been too tired to continue this practice or may have swiftly concluded that the benefits outweighed the risks of allowing their teens to use social media and to have privacy while they use it. Without social media during this time, important peer interactions may have been lost, delaying the continuous development of interpersonal skills and social competencies (Hussong et al., 2021). Given the frequent perception that social media was contributing to teen happiness, this is a logical conclusion. It is also supported by findings from another study in which parents reported that they think monitoring teen social media use is a good idea, but they are uncertain of their efficacy (Douglas et al., 2020). Alternately, after spending more time together than usual some parents may have concluded that restrictions were not necessary, mimicking Bulow et al.'s (2021) finding that behavioral controls were ceded to autonomy in some instances during this time.

This study confirms prior studies that suggest parents are more heavily involved in monitoring the social media use of younger teens in comparison to older teens (Douglas et al., 2020; Wallace, 2021). A reduction in monitoring as teens get older is developmentally appropriate. Parents can provide greater guidance and set firmer limits when their children are first learning to use the medium, ideally helping to establish healthy online behaviors and awareness of perils to avoid. As teen knowledge and parent trust both increase, parent oversight can recede.

Differences based on gender appear to be more complex. This study found differences on a single issue, specifically *who* their teen interacted with. The greater concern about daughters' interaction partners may reflect fear of sexual predators along with the stereotyped double standard that suggests girls are more likely to be prey in this context. Such stereotypes have played out in other studies of teen online behaviors. For example, Douglas et al. (2020) found that parents of sons were more concerned than parents of daughters about teens watching sexually explicit material online.

This study provides a glimpse at parent perceptions and oversight of teen social media use during a time of high stress and uncertainty. The sample represents individuals who are social media users already and who opted in to participate, which is a limitation of the study. A survey of parents who are not social media users may have led to different findings. Such parents would not have experienced parallel increased reliance on social media alongside their teens as the pandemic began, nor would they understand as effectively how social media functions. Continued research into this area would be valuable, examining how the triadic teen, parent, and social media relationship evolves more generally as teens age and within specific circumstances.

ACKNOWLEDGEMENT

This research was funded by a Collaborative Collision: COVID-19 Seed Grant at Florida State University.

REFERENCES

Anderson, M., & Jiang, J. (2018). *Teens, social media & technology 2018*. Pew Research. http://www.pewinternet.org/2018/05/31/teens-social-media-technology-2018/

Breaux, R., Dvorsky, M. R., Marsh, N. P., Green, C. D., Cash, A. R., Shroff, D. M., Buchen, N., Langberg, J. M., & Becker, S. P. (2021). Prospective impact of COVID-19 on mental health functioning in adolescents with and without ADHD: protective role of emotion regulation abilities. *J Child Psychol Psychiatry, 62*(9), 1132-1139. https://doi.org/10.1111/jcpp.13382

Bulow, A., Keijsers, L., Boele, S., van Roekel, E., & Denissen, J. J. A. (2021). Parenting adolescents in times of a pandemic: Changes in relationship quality, autonomy support, and parental control? *Dev Psychol, 57*(10), 1582-1596. https://doi.org/10.1037/dev0001208

Ceylan, S. S., Erdoğan, Ç., & Turan, T. (2021). Investigation of the effects of restrictions applied on children during COVID-19 pandemic. *Journal of pediatric nursing, 61*, 340-345. https://doi.org/10.1016/j.pedn.2021.09.013

Colvin, M. K., Reesman, J., & Glen, T. (2022). The impact of COVID-19 related educational disruption on children and adolescents: An interim data summary and commentary on ten considerations for neuropsychological practice. *The Clinical Neuropsychologist, 36*(1), 45-71. https://doi.org/10.1080/13854046.2021.1970230

Dennen, V. P., Choi, H., & Word, K. (2020). Social media, teenagers, and the school context: A scoping review of research in education and related fields. *Educational Technology Research and Development, 68*, 1635-1658. https://doi.org/10.1007/s11423-020-09796-z

Dennen, V. P., Jung, D., Cargill, C., & Hedquist, A. (2021). Social media and parenting support: A systematic scoping review (2010-2019). *International Journal on WWW/Internet, 19*(2), 1-18.

Dennen, V. P., Rutledge, S. A., & Bagdy, L. M. (2019). Social media use in high school settings: Rules, outcomes, and educational opportunities. In *Proceedings of the 10th International Conference on Social Media and Society* (pp. 205-213). ACM. https://doi.org/10.1145/3328529.3328561

Dennen, V. P., Rutledge, S. A., & Bagdy, L. M. (2020). (Dis)connected: The role of social networking sites in the high school setting. *American Journal of Education, 127*(1), 107-136.

Dennen, V. P., Rutledge, S. A., Bagdy, L. M., Bunn, S., Jung, D., Cargill, C., Cosgrove, C., Hedquist, A., & McWaters, S. (2021a, April 8-12). *Teenage social media use in the time of COVID-19: Resilience, connection, entertainment, and learning* [Conference Poster]. American Educational Research Association, http://aera21-aera.ipostersessions.com/Default.aspx?s=6C-5D-EC-AD-C6-F2-B8-14-3B-70-E6-3C-62-67-53-69

Dennen, V. P., Rutledge, S. A., Bagdy, L. M., Bunn, S., Jung, D., Cargill, C., Cosgrove, C., Hedquist, A., & McWaters, S. (2021b). Virtual independence: Teen social media use during the summer of quarantine. In P. Kommers & M. Macedo (Eds.), *International Conference on Web Based Communities and Social Media 2021* (pp. 211-215). IADIS.

Douglas, K. D., Smith, K. K., Stewart, M. W., Walker, J., Mena, L., & Zhang, L. (2020). Exploring parents' intentions to monitor and mediate adolescent social media use and implications for school nurses. *J Sch Nurs*, 1059840520983286. https://doi.org/10.1177/1059840520983286

Drouin, M., McDaniel, B. T., Pater, J., & Toscos, T. (2020). How parents and their children used social media and technology at the beginning of the COVID-19 pandemic and associations with anxiety. *Cyberpsychology, Behavior and Social Netwworking, 23*(11), 727-736. https://doi.org/10.1089/cyber.2020.0284

Fardouly, J., Magson, N. R., Johnco, C. J., Oar, E. L., & Rapee, R. M. (2018). Parental control of the time preadolescents spend on social media: Links with preadolescents' social media appearance comparisons and mental health. *J Youth Adolesc, 47*(7), 1456-1468. https://doi.org/10.1007/s10964-018-0870-1

Garcia, A. D. (2017). *Good reception: Utilizing mobile media and games to develop critical inner-city agents of social change*. MIT Press.

Greenhow, C., Galvin, S. M., & Staudt Willet, K. B. (2019). What Should Be the Role of Social Media in Education? *Policy Insights from the Behavioral and Brain Sciences, 6*(2), 178-185. https://doi.org/10.1177/2372732219865290

Hodges, C., Moore, S., Lockee, B., Trust, T., & Bond, A. (2020). The difference between emergency remote teaching and online learning. *EDUCAUSE review, 27*.

Hussong, A. M., Benner, A. D., Erdem, G., Lansford, J. E., Makila, L. M., Petrie, R. C., & Team, S. C.-R. (2021). Adolescence amid a pandemic: Short- and long-term implications. *J Res Adolesc, 31*(3), 820-835. https://doi.org/10.1111/jora.12671

Meherali, S., Punjani, N., Louie-Poon, S., Abdul Rahim, K., Das, J. K., Salam, R. A., & Lassi, Z. S. (2021). Mental health of children and adolescents amidst COVID-19 and past pandemics: A rapid systematic review. *Int J Environ Res Public Health, 18*(7). https://doi.org/10.3390/ijerph18073432

Rossi, L., Behme, N., & Breuer, C. (2021). Physical activity of children and adolescents during the COVID-19 pandemic: A scoping review. *Int J Environ Res Public Health, 18*(21). https://doi.org/10.3390/ijerph182111440

Rutledge, S. A., Dennen, V. P., Bagdy, L. M., Rowlett, J. T., & Burnick, S. (2019). Exploring adolescent social media use in a high school: Tweeting teens in a bell schedule world. *Teachers College Record Yearbook, 121*(14).

Scott-Parker, B. (2018). "You're so used to having someone tell you what to do": Experiences of young drivers during the provisional licence phase. *Transportation Research Part F: Traffic Psychology and Behaviour, 56*, 508-521. https://doi.org/https://doi.org/10.1016/j.trf.2018.03.027

Skinner, A. T., Godwin, J., Alampay, L. P., Lansford, J. E., Bacchini, D., Bornstein, M. H., Deater-Deckard, K., Di Giunta, L., Dodge, K. A., Gurdal, S., Pastorelli, C., Sorbring, E., Steinberg, L., Tapanya, S., & Yotanyamaneewong, S. (2021). Parent-adolescent relationship quality as a moderator of links between COVID-19 disruption and reported changes in mothers' and young adults' adjustment in five countries. *Dev Psychol, 57*(10), 1648-1666. https://doi.org/10.1037/dev0001236

Tan, W. (2021). School closures were over-weighted against the mitigation of COVID-19 transmission: A literature review on the impact of school closures in the United States. *Medicine, 100*(30), e26709-e26709. https://doi.org/10.1097/MD.0000000000026709

Wallace, L. N. (2021). Differences in social media monitoring practices based on child and parent gender. *Family Relations, 70*(5), 1412-1426. https://doi.org/10.1111/fare.12568

A QUINQUENNIUM MAPPING LITERATURE REVIEW ON BIG DATA ANALYTICS IN TOURISM AND HOSPITALITY

Nikolaos Misirlis and Dirk van der Steenhoven
HAN University of Applied Sciences, 6826CC, R31, Arnhem, The Netherlands

ABSTRACT

Big data analysis can change the global tourism and hospitality industry, providing deeper knowledge and greater insights and increased relationships regarding e-travelers. The purpose of this study is to present a mapping literature review and a research articles' classification regarding big data and social media data exploitation representing a fuel of innovation in tourism and hospitality. The review covers 24 articles from peer review journals, over the last decade, presenting the Boolean technique followed for the data-extraction method. The articles are classified in several distinct modules and research thematic areas and sub-areas. The findings of this study reveal, among others, the most studied areas, trends and tendencies for big data analysis in tourism and hospitality. Our literature review revealed several emerging research approaches, focused on, but not limited to: social media platforms and other data sources, type of analysis (data analytics, model analytics and geospatial analytics), tools and methodologies and outcomes, to wit market research and decision-making in tourism. This study is the first using mapping literature review techniques on focused articles related to BD analysis regarding tourism and hospitality, presenting a complete, increasing and continuously editable framework for future research. Thus, tourism BD analysis provides significant challenges in the relationship between businesses and their customers, offering superior buying and support experiences with a view to enhancing customer choice and expectations.

KEYWORDS

Big Data, Tourism, Hospitality, Social Media, Literature Review

1. INTRODUCTION

Big Data (BD) represents a disruptive technology that is already modifying the business intelligence. The main idea behind the BD remains always the need of data analytics in order to increase business insights and take better decisions (Daniel et al., 2010). Big Data is by all means an innovative and powerful tool for enhancing the capabilities and the decisions of the travel and hospitality industry, in specific: predicting tourism demand and individual preferences, understanding the tourists from their online behavior, influencing, monitoring and evaluating their satisfaction and designing personalized services and tailored experiences (Rammstedt and John, 2007).

There are many misunderstandings regarding BD and its definition. The basic definition is "datasets which could not be captured, managed, and processed by general computers within an acceptable scope" (Chen et al., 2014). For many researchers the BD's definition remains debatable, with current literature containing 43 different definitions(Mayeh et al., 2012), but none universally accepted (Grubmüller et al., 2013). BD defers from the traditional data analysis, since bigger variety (range of data types and sources), volume (amount of data) and velocity (speed of data in and out) are being involved, also known as the 3V's of the big data analytics. Some authors add another V on the equation, the Veracity (Beyer and Laney, 2012), creating this way the 4V definition and others the Validity and Volatility, ending up to talk about the 6Vdefinition, which is the most complete today (Chatzipavlou et al., 2015, Gandomi and Haider, 2015, Karanatsiou et al., 2017, Boyd, 2006, Hatzithomas et al., 2017, Misirlis et al., 2017). According to a recently consensual definition (Karanatsiou et al., 2017) "Big data represents the information assets characterized by such a high volume, velocity and variety to require specific technology and analytical methods for its transformation into value". Differences on definitions have to do most with the different opinions of researchers on what part of data is more important. Some believe that variety and velocity are the most important aspects of BD and others that volume is everything. On the other side, all researchers agree that data science differs from Big Data and that the final interpretation step remains perhaps the most crucial throughout the process (Yang et al., 2011).

A problem that arises from the study of BD is the complexity of data. Yet, there is no deep understanding upon the complexity and furthermore how to address, rather than understand complex data. In literature there is a lack of knowledge regarding distribution, complexity understanding and association relationships (Grubmüller et al., 2013).

For this purpose, we propose a framework of Input, Process and Outcomes modules with specific research thematic areas of BD analytics in tourism and hospitality incorporating a complete literature review table, in order to overcome the aforementioned issues. The present chapter is structured as follows: the next session presents the literature review methodology used. Consequently, we propose a conceptual framework categorizing the recent literature in specific thematic areas regarding BD analysis in tourism and hospitality. Last, we conclude with the research implications and future studies.

2. LITERATURE REVIEW - METHODOLOGY

In literature there are several frameworks for diverse fields related to road or accident data (Bullinger et al., 2010, Nanos et al., 2017, Misirlis and Vlachopoulou, 2018a), health data (Podobnik, 2013, Asur and Huberman, 2010, Xie et al., 2012, Rohm et al., 2012, Chen et al., 2014, Beyer and Laney, 2012, Jani et al., 2014, Song and Liu, 2017), decision making processes (Kontopoulos et al., 2013, Bartolini et al., 2015, Misirlis and Vlachopoulou, 2018b, Siemens and Long, 2011, Briggs, 1976, Kao and Craigie, 2014), behavioral analysis (Hatzithomas et al., 2017), education (Lieberman, 2014) or eGovernment (Gosling et al., 2003), with the list for the applied fields to seem endless. In this study we focus on tourism and hospitality investigating Input, Process, and Outcome modules, related to BD analysis. Using Boolean phrases we collected 24 articles that match entirely our research. We searched articles from ScienceDirect, Scopus and Google scholar, removing conference articles, book chapters and white papers.

Useful conclusions can be drawn from the year's distribution Figure 1. In 2014 only 3 articles fitted our Boolean research, 4 in 2015 and 4 in 2016. A large increase in publications is noticed in 2017 with 12 (50% of the considered articles) research papers. Our research stops in 2017 so the one article with 2018 as a date is not representative of the tendency for that year. Future similar research can contribute on that data. The fact that there is an increase of publication equal to 300% (2017 respect to 2016) shows that there is a continuous increasing interest of academics and practitioners regarding big data in tourism.

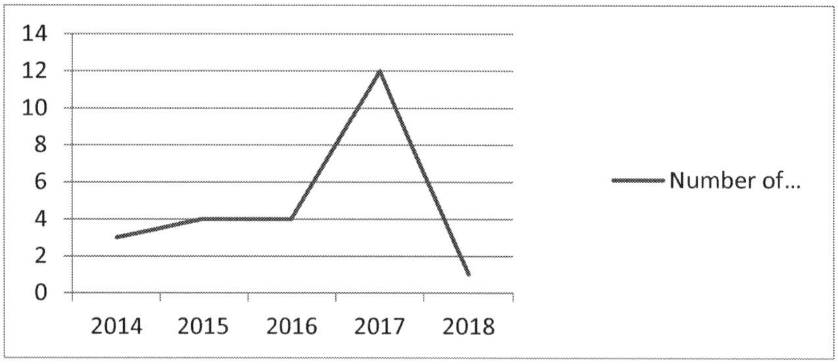

Figure 1. Year distribution of articles

The 24 articles were then studied in order to continue with the mapping literature review. The articles were initially divided in 10 categories. Consequently the keywords were unified in distinct categories so as to end up to the 4 categories of research thematic areas that form the final 3 modules on our review. Table 1 presents the articles collected and divided on the 3 modules, 4 research thematic areas including sub-areas, namely: Data Sources & Social media platforms (where the data come from), BD Analytics: types of analysis, tools & methodologies (how the data will interpret the information/ knowledge) and Value (market research & decision-making in tourism and hospitality). On Table 1 we provide the definitions for each module and research thematic area before presenting the articles for each category and the relevant statistics, research and results.

Data source represents the first approach on Big Data Analysis procedure. Data originated from online actions of users form the Input module. These data include information on segments such as social media (social networking sites, microblogs, vlogs or blogs etc), websites, mobile devices, customer relationship management apps, e-transactions and search engines queries. This User Generated Data (UGD) benefits the BD analysis by creating a large amount of data in order to uncover patterns, correlations and other insights. The relevant tools, after the UGD collection, use multiple techniques and methods, to gain value from the aforementioned data (Misirlis and Vlachopoulou, 2018a).

The 3 basic types of analysis are: data, model and geospatial with the first category to be related mostly with statistical analysis, the second with the use of specific scientific models, both theoretical and practical and the third category with data analysis related to geographical or spatial aspects.

Analytic tools and methodologies can be especially useful in helping companies in tourism and hospitality sector mine and refine data to determine valuable information for optimizing business outcomes. In specific, predictive analytics gives marketing professionals more insight into customer preferences depending on timely and reliable tourism big data analysis, based on both the quality of the big data and the customer feedback mechanisms.

Value is frequently seen as another important characteristic of big data due to its novel application in various areas related to the tourism industry. First, collecting, correlating, and analyzing tourism big data from customer interactions across channels enhances tourism demand predictions. Secondly, measuring tourists' satisfaction leads to customers' pleasure and loyalty. The customer should be at the center of all big data efforts. Third, personalized marketing activities and targeted tourism experiences design are extremely powerful opportunities that can be obtained from big data (Jani et al., 2014).

Table 1. Modules, research thematic areas and sub-areas definitions

Modules	**Research thematic areas**	**Research thematic sub-areas**	**Definitions**
Input: where the data come from	Data sources	Social media platforms Websites, mobile devices, CRM, e-transactions, search data, etc.	Articles that analyze issues related to the inputs required for exploiting big data, such as data inputs, data sources, technological and organizational resources and capabilities. Specifically this category incorporates articles that focus on data originated from social media platforms
Process: how the data will interpret the information/ knowledge	Analytics: Type of analysis	Data	Articles focused on methods or tools strictly related to the statistical analysis of BD
		Model	Articles focused on specific scientific models (theoretical and practical) that are used on BD analysis
		Geospatial	Articles that analyze data with specific geographical or spatial aspects
	Analytics: Tools & Methodologies	Articles that use specific tools and methodologies in order to conduct text, sentiment or predictive analysis. Methodologies from machine learning algorithms are used as well as statistical analysis for BD	

Modules	Research thematic areas	Research thematic sub-areas	Definitions
Outcomes: market research & decision-making in tourism and hospitality	Value	Tourism demand predictions Measuring tourists' satisfaction & preferences Personalized marketing activities and targeted tourism experiences design	Articles that analyze the BD impact on marketing research and the decision-making process on tourism: predicting tourism demand, measuring tourists' satisfaction, designing personalized marketing activities and targeted tourism experiences

We noticed that the majority of the articles fit in more than one category. Hence on Table 2, we categorize the articles to the most dominant and representative module, except from few cases.

Table 2. Articles distribution on: Modules, research thematic areas and sub-areas

Modules	Research thematic areas	Research thematic sub-areas	Articles
Input: where the data come from	Data sources	Social media platforms	Kim et al. (2017), Su et al. (2016), Önder (2017), García-Palomares et al. (2015), Salas-Olmedo et al. (2018), Liu and Mattila (2017), Mariani et al. (2016)
		Websites, mobile devices, CRM, e-transactions, search data, etc.	Guo et al. (2017), Raun et al. (2016)
Process: how the data will interpret the information/ knowledge	Analytics: Type of analysis	Data	Dolnicar and Ring (2014); Gunter and Önder (2016); K. Kim et al. (2017); Xiang, Schwartz, Gerdes Jr, and Uysal (2015)
		Model	Gao, Zhang, Lu, Wu, and Du (2017); Guo, Barnes, and Jia (2017); He, Liu, and Xiong (2016); X. Li, Pan, Law, and Huang (2017); Marine-Roig and Anton Clavé (2015); Zhang, Lan, Qi, and Wu (2017)
		Geospatial	Huang et al. (2017), (2016), Önder (2017), Supak et al. (2015), García-Palomares et al. (2015), Raun et al. (2016), Salas-Olmedo et al. (2018)
	Analytics: Tools & Methodologies	Xiang et al. (2015), Kim et al. (2017), Li et al. (2017), Guo et al. (2017)	
Outcomes: market research & decision-making in	Value	Tourism demand predictions	Dolnicar and Ring (2014); Li, Pan, Law, and Huang (2017); Gunter and Önder (2016); Supak et al. (2015); Raun, Ahas, and Tiru (2016);

Modules	Research thematic areas	Research thematic sub-areas	Articles
tourism and hospitality			Salas-Olmedo et al. (2018); Fuchs, Höpken, and Lexhagen (2014); Song and Liu (2017)
		Measuring tourists' satisfaction & preferences	Xiang, Schwartz, Gerdes Jr, and Uysal (2015); K. Kim et al. (2017); Zhang, Lan, Qi, and Wu (2017); Li, Pan, Law, and Huang (2017); Guo et al. (2017); Marine-Roig and Anton Clavé (2015); Su, Wan, Hu, and Cai (2016); Miah, Vu, Gammack, and McGrath (2017); Fuchs, Höpken, and Lexhagen (2014); Jani et al. (2014)
		Personalized marketing activities and targeted tourism experiences design	He, Liu, and Xiong (2016); (Huang et al., 2017); García-Palomares, Gutiérrez, and Mínguez (2015); Liu and Mattila (2017); Mariani, Di Felice, and Mura (2016); Y. Li, Hu, Huang, and Duan (2017)

The Input module contributes with 7 and 2 articles for each one of the two thematic areas. The Analytics thematic area contributes with 17, in total, articles, almost evenly divided to the second and third sub-module. The analytics module uses methodologies from data analysis, such as text analysis (Xiang et al., 2015), sentiment analysis (Kim et al., 2017), Latent Dirichlet Allocation (Guo et al., 2017) and fuzzy algorithms (Gao et al.) with emphasis mostly on user-generated data, a field that gathers the interest of practitioners, since it can benefit both contributor and host.

3. DISCUSSION – FUTURE IMPLICATIONS

It is clear that Big Data became one of the most emerging fields of science that will lead the years to follow research. As it is occurs from the literature review, a wide variety of technologies is applied in the implementation of the big data. Today's advanced analytics tools and methodologies enable tourist organizations to extract insights from data with previously unachievable levels of sophistication, speed and accuracy. Scientists and practitioners hope to mine the insights from BD information/ knowledge, gaining full advantage of the BD value. Managers believe that since even small data is useful, the size of the utility level at the big data will be even greater, since the data is even more sophisticated. This study is the first using mapping literature review techniques on focused articles related to BD analysis regarding tourism and hospitality, presenting a complete, increasing and continuously editable framework for future research. Hence, the timely use of big data for forecasting and decision-making using proper approaches and methods is the best way to capitalize the benefits of big data. Thus, tourism BD analysis provides significant challenges in the relationship between businesses and their customers, offering superior buying and support experiences with a view to enhancing customer choice and expectations. The danger is in assuming that insights and ingenuity naturally lie inside Big Data rather than inside of the creative management of the data. Therefore, Big Data can support decision-making, but cannot replace the strategic management (Song and Liu, 2017, Misirlis and Vlachopoulou, 2018b). Additionally, legal restraints and data protection rules are developing worldwide, preventing their uncontrolled use. There is an increased interest of the restrictions of data use of customers regarding the security and the General Data Protection Regulation, the GDPR (Bartolini et al., 2015, Tankard, 2016).

Our research has concluded that articles are almost equally distributed across all framework modules and thematic areas and sub-areas. Nearly the same number of articles belongs to each module. Considering areas and sub-areas also, we notice that the articles are distributed almost equally also here. From this fact we conclude that researchers and practitioners of the field show the same interest in all three main modules in terms of Big Data Analysis Management in Tourism and Hospitality.

We believe that the mapping of the literature is crucial since a researcher or a practitioner should take into consideration the existing research regarding Input, Process and Outcomes, regarding specific thematic areas, in order to achieve better insights. This last conclusion is further strengthened by the fact that the majority of the articles fit in more than one module or sub-module. Methodologies and tools are in most cases mixed. Researchers need to study in depth the entire process so as to have a complete understanding of Big Data. There is a need to further study in depth in geographical specific areas choosing data sources, analysis tools & methodologies for specific marketing objectives.

Big data analysis in tourism and hospitality suggest that the future may belong to those tourist organizations and firms best able to collect analyze and use data responsibly, creating unified data views and tourists' insights, aligning company offerings and customer needs, in order to shape and deliver enhanced services and experiences.

REFERENCES

Asur, S. & Huberman, B. A. 2010. Predicting the Future with Social Media. *Proceedings of the 2010 IEEE/WIC/ACM International Conference on Web Intelligence and Intelligent Agent Technology - Volume 01*. IEEE Computer Society.

Bartolini, C., Gheorghe, G., Giurgiu, A., Sabetzadeh, M. & Sannier, N. 2015. Assessing IT security standards against the upcoming GDPR for cloud systems.

Beyer, M. A. & Laney, D. 2012. The importance of 'big data': a definition. *Stamford, CT: Gartner*, 2014-2018.

Boyd, D. 2006. A blogger\'s blog: Exploring the definition of a medium. *Reconstruction,* 6.

Briggs, K. C. 1976. *Myers-Briggs type indicator*, Consulting Psychologists Press Palo Alto, CA.

Bullinger, A. C., Hallerstede, S. H., Renken, U., Soeldnet, J.-H. & Moeslein, K. M. Towards Research Collaboration – a Taxonomy of Social Research Network Sites. AMCIS 2010 Proceedings, 2010.

Chatzipavlou, I., Misirlis, N. & Vlachopoulou, M. Smartphone Medical App use: A Survey Among Medical Students at Aristotle University of Thessaloniki. MCIS, Mediterranean Conference on Information Systems, 2015.

Chen, M., Mao, S. & Liu, Y. 2014. Big data: A survey. *Mobile Networks and Applications,* 19, 171-209.

Daniel, Z., Hsinchun, C., LUSCH, R. & SHU-HSING, L. 2010. Social Media Analytics and Intelligence. *Intelligent Systems, IEEE,* 25, 13-16.

Dolnicar, S. & Ring, A. 2014. Tourism marketing research: Past, present and future. *Annals of Tourism Research,* 47, 31-47.

Gandomi, A. & Haider, M. 2015. Beyond the hype: Big data concepts, methods, and analytics. *International Journal of Information Management,* 35, 137-144.

Gao, W., Zhang, Q., Lu, Z., Wu, D. & Du, X. Modelling and application of fuzzy adaptive minimum spanning tree in tourism agglomeration area division. *Knowledge-Based Systems*.

García-Palomares, J. C., Gutiérrez, J. & Mínguez, C. 2015. Identification of tourist hot spots based on social networks: A comparative analysis of European metropolises using photo-sharing services and GIS. *Applied Geography,* 63, 408-417.

Gosling, S. D., Rentfrow, P. J. & Swann Jr, W. B. 2003. A very brief measure of the Big-Five personality domains. *Journal of Research in Personality,* 37, 504-528.

Grubmüller, V., Götsch, K. & Krieger, B. 2013. Social media analytics for future oriented policy making. *European Journal of Futures Research,* 1, 1-9.

Guo, Y., Barnes, S. J. & Jia, Q. 2017. Mining meaning from online ratings and reviews: Tourist satisfaction analysis using latent dirichlet allocation. *Tourism Management,* 59, 467-483.

Hatzithomas, L., Misirlis, N., Boutsouki, C. & Vlachopoulou, M. Effects of Personality Traits on Facebook Use. 5th International Conference on Contemporary Marketing Issues, 2017.

Huang, Z., Cao, F., Jin, C., Yu, Z. & Huang, R. 2017. Carbon emission flow from self-driving tours and its spatial relationship with scenic spots – A traffic-related big data method. *Journal of Cleaner Production,* 142, Part 2, 946-955.

Jani, D., Jang, J.-H. & Hwang, Y.-H. 2014. Big Five Factors of Personality and Tourists' Internet Search Behavior. *Asia Pacific Journal of Tourism Research,* 19, 600-615.

Kao, P.-C. & Craigie, P. 2014. Effects of English usage on Facebook and personality traits on achievement of students learning English as a foreign language. *Social Behavior and Personality: an international journal,* 42, 17-24.

Karanatsiou, D., Misirlis, N. & Vlachopoulou, M. 2017. Bibliometrics and altmetrics literature review: Performance indicators and comparison analysis. *Performance Measurement and Metrics,* 18, 16-27.

Kim, K., Park, O.-J., Yun, S. & Yun, H. 2017. What makes tourists feel negatively about tourism destinations? Application of hybrid text mining methodology to smart destination management. *Technological Forecasting and Social Change,* 123, 362-369.

Kontopoulos, E., Berberidis, C., Dergiades, T. & Bassiliades, N. 2013. Ontology-based sentiment analysis of twitter posts. *Expert Systems with Applications,* 40, 4065-4074.

Li, X., Pan, B., Law, R. & Huang, X. 2017. Forecasting tourism demand with composite search index. *Tourism Management,* 59, 57-66.

Lieberman, M. Visualizing Big Data: Social Network Analysis. Digital Research Conference, 2014.

Liu, S. Q. & Mattila, A. S. 2017. Airbnb: Online targeted advertising, sense of power, and consumer decisions. *International Journal of Hospitality Management,* 60, 33-41.

Mariani, M. M., Di Felice, M. & Mura, M. 2016. Facebook as a destination marketing tool: Evidence from Italian regional Destination Management Organizations. *Tourism Management,* 54, 321-343.

Mayeh, M., Scheepers, R. & Valos, M. Understanding the role of social media monitoring in generating external intelligence. *In:* LAMP, J., ed. Australasian Conference on Information Systems (23rd : 2012 : Geelong, Victoria), 2012 2012 Geelong, Victoria. ACIS, 10.

Misirlis, N., Nanos, I. & Vlachopoulou, M. A Roadmap to Social Media Analytics. 6th International Symposium & 28th National Conference on Operational Research, 2017.

Misirlis, N. & Vlachopoulou, M. 2018a. Social media metrics and analytics in marketing – S3M: A mapping literature review. *International Journal of Information Management,* 38, 270-276.

Misirlis, N. & Vlachopoulou, M. 2018b. A unified framework for decision-making process on social media analytics. *Springer Proceeding in Business and Economics,* In Press.

Nanos, I., Misirlis, N. & Manthou, V. Cloud Computing Adoption and E-government. 6th International Symposium and 28th National Conference on Operational Research, At Thessaloniki, Greece, 2017.

Önder, I. 2017. Classifying multi-destination trips in Austria with big data. *Tourism Management Perspectives,* 21, 54-58.

Podobnik, V. An analysis of facebook social media marketing key performance indicators: The case of premier league brands. Telecommunications (ConTEL), 2013 12th International Conference on, 26-28 June 2013 2013. 131-138.

Rammstedt, B. & John, O. P. 2007. Measuring personality in one minute or less: A 10-item short version of the Big Five Inventory in English and German. *Journal of Research in Personality,* 41, 203-212.

Raun, J., Ahas, R. & Tiru, M. 2016. Measuring tourism destinations using mobile tracking data. *Tourism Management,* 57, 202-212.

Rohm, A., Milne, G. R. & Kaltcheva, V. The role of online social media in brand-consumer engagement. Direct/Interactive Marketing Research Summit Proceedings, 2012.

Salas-Olmedo, M. H., Moya-Gómez, B., García-Palomares, J. C. & Gutiérrez, J. 2018. Tourists' digital footprint in cities: Comparing Big Data sources. *Tourism Management,* 66, 13-25.

Siemens, G. & Long, P. 2011. Penetrating the Fog: Analytics in Learning and Education. *EDUCAUSEreview online.*

Song, H. & LIU, H. 2017. Predicting tourist demand using big data. *Analytics in smart tourism design.* Springer.

Su, S., Wan, C., Hu, Y. & Cai, Z. 2016. Characterizing geographical preferences of international tourists and the local influential factors in China using geo-tagged photos on social media. *Applied Geography,* 73, 26-37.

Supak, S., Brothers, G., Bohnenstiehl, D. & Devine, H. 2015. Geospatial analytics for federally managed tourism destinations and their demand markets. *Journal of Destination Marketing & Management,* 4, 173-186.

Tankard, C. 2016. What the GDPR means for businesses. *Network Security,* 2016, 5-8.

Xiang, Z., Schwartz, Z., Gerdes Jr, J. H. & UysaL, M. 2015. What can big data and text analytics tell us about hotel guest experience and satisfaction? *International Journal of Hospitality Management,* 44, 120-130.

Xie, Y., Cheng, Y., Honbo, D., Zhang, K., Agrawal, A., Choudhary, A., Gao, Y. & Gou, J. 2012. Probabilistic macro behavioral targeting. *Proceedings of the 2012 workshop on Data-driven user behavioral modelling and mining from social media.* Maui, Hawaii, USA: ACM.

Yang, M., Kiang, M., Ku, Y., Chiu, C. & LI, Y. 2011. Social Media Analytics for Radical Opinion Mining in Hate Group Web Forums. *Journal of Homeland Security and Emergency Management.*

INSTRUCTOR TEACHING EXPERIENCE WITH ONLINE DISTANCE LEARNING FOR PRACTICAL DESIGN COURSES AFTER COVID-19

Miha Kim and Dong-Yeong Lee
University of Hanyang, The South Korea

ABSTRACT

Due to COVID-19, all classes in schools have been converted to distance learning using online platforms. However, various problems were raised when converting face-to-face classes to online distance learning. In particular, the difficulties were more pronounced for practical design courses because they include practical experience.
In this context, this study focused on actual online distance learning classroom cases in design education. Based on the qualitative case study methodology, four instructors were interviewed about their experience with distance learning courses that actively utilized online platforms for college design courses as research cases.
In design education, which aims at interdisciplinary and convergence thinking, online distance learning is meaningful in that it can expand experience and opportunities for the overall formative design through the development of technology. On the other hand, there are clear limitations in terms of practical production activities for existing online distance learning methods. Therefore, it is necessary to explore whether to develop classes based on the recently used effective activities or whether to find new strategies in the case that these limitations are fundamental to online distance learning.

KEYWORDS

Distance Learning, Design Education, Education after COVID-19, Practical Online Teaching

1. INTRODUCTION

Education around the world began to actively utilize information and communication technology as the COVID-19 pandemic began. In this era of transformation, the Ministry of Education of Korea judged that it would be impossible to execute the school's normal academic schedule, and they issued a recommendation that included avoiding face-to-face courses and conducting distance learning (Ministry of Education, 2020).

However, various problems were raised while switching most courses to distance learning. In particular, since design universities primarily involve practical applications, the tuition is usually higher than other majors. Not only is the use of facilities restricted due to COVID-19 but there are many cases in which lectures and assignments were replaced with videos or teaching materials, and this change inevitably led to a growing number of complaints from learners. Some universities partially allowed face-to-face practical courses to facilitate smooth progress; however, COVID-19 has continued to be an obstacle, and limited face-to-face courses are expected to continue until the situation stabilizes.

In this context, this article attempts to discuss the implications for design education by focusing on actual distance learning cases at college. Using a qualitative case study approach, we examine the teaching experience of instructors who have experienced distance learning, the types of challenges they have faced, and future possibilities and reflections.

1.1 Online Distance Learning after COVID-19

Distance learning is essentially a form of education in which instructors and learners do not meet face-to-face. Simonson et al. (2006) defined the basic components of distance learning in four ways: institutionally-based, separation of instructors and learners, interactive telecommunication, and sharing of learning experiences through the media. The purest form of distance learning requires that participants are separated by both time and space (Keegan, 1996). However, currently, with the development of technology, instructors and learners can communicate simultaneously even if they are spatially separated. Currently, in distance education discussions, various cases such as blended learning or flip learning have been explored.

The results of analyzing more than 240 studies show that there is no significant difference between traditional classroom education and distance learning, and that distance learning can be as effective as face-to-face education (Russell, 1999, as cited in Simonson, 2006). The types of online distance learning held at Korean universities after COVID-19 are shown in Table 1 (J.H. Oh, 2020).

Table 1. Types of online distance learning

Real-time video lecture	**Pre-recorded video lecture**	**Lecture recording and teaching materials**	**Utilization of existing media**
Instructor and learner meet at a specific time and interact in real time.	Video materials are produced and posted in a classroom or studio using camcorder equipment.	A file is created and posted by adding the instructor's voice to the teaching materials such as PPT or images.	Instructors select and provide existing videos addressing class-related content.
		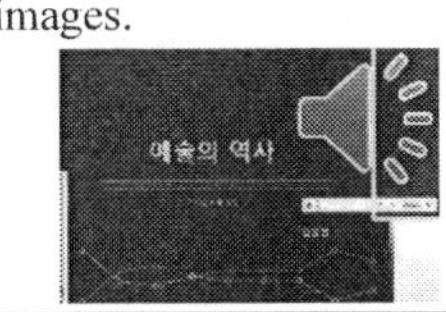	

Different from traditional classroom instruction, where learners rely heavily on instructors, distance learning allows learners to learn autonomously; additionally, remote communication is not just a means of education but a system that communicates through media (Moore & Kearsley, 1996). In other words, distance learning pursues learning with high learner autonomy and independence, but it is planned learning and requires strategies that require active activities and experience from learners within the remote system.

1.2 Practical Design Courses

In education, practice refers to a form of learning accompanied by physical activity. In this article, the practical design course involves a process of observation, discovery, and application based on a specific theory, and these courses focus on practice that facilitates educational goals.

Design addresses both aesthetic and functional aspects based on mass production and a functionalist philosophy with the development of machinery and technology since the 19th century. The design process is quite complex and diverse. Designers work individually or jointly, begin spontaneously due to creative inspiration, and proceed precisely according to close market analysis, prospects, and technical background (Heskett, 1980). Therefore, in practice, design courses not only involves the creation of aesthetic works but also includes various activities such as field surveys, group activities, and technology utilization.

1.3 Proposal

Currently, few studies conducted in Korea have focused on the process of converting existing face-to-face courses to distance learning using online platforms (J.U. Do, 2020). In Korea, the importance of distance learning has not emerged as dramatically as it has in other countries because physical access to educational institutions is more accessible compared to other countries with large national areas. The majority of studies were primarily conducted to discover the availability of media.

This case study explores the difficulties and strategies used to overcome the limitations of remote design courses by interviewing instructors who designed and operated actual design practical courses. This exploration could provide insight into the problems experienced by instructors and an exploration of the implications that should be considered in instructional system design for distance learning courses related to design in the educational field.

2. METHOD

This case study focused on specific situations and collected in-depth data using various sources of information such as observation, interviews, and documents (Creswell & Poth, 2018). Case studies have a naturalistic approach and are sensitive to complexity and interaction in a specific context (Stake, 1995), so it is necessary to define cases that can be categorized using certain characteristics, such as the specific time or place, during this process. The important consideration when conducting these types of studies is not to provide generalized statistics based on a quantitative collection of events but to expand and define theories by considering cases, and accordingly, this study was conducted by collecting multiple cases and finding interrelationships and deriving meanings within a context.

2.1 Research Process

Researchers can use the maximum deviation method to present various perspectives on specific cases (Creswell & Poth, 2018). In this article, it was judged that various variables such as the guidelines, situations, course contents, and teaching characteristics of the instructor could not be generalized, so multiple cases were selected. However, the characteristics of the instructors who participated in the interviews were different.

A few extensive and non-judgmental questions can facilitate the emergence of the participants' narratives (Charmaz, 2006). The interview was guided deliberately to five open topics: The guidelines and responses from the school, issues regarding the usability of online platforms, things that have been replaced or changed, the experience of running the courses, and the participant's opinion on the role of each subject in terms of country, school, instructor, and learners. Recorded videos of actual courses, teaching materials, evaluation, learner assignments, and guidelines from the Ministry of Education and each school during the classes' periods of operation were collected and analyzed. Since all the instructors who participated in the interview agreed to provide the data on the condition of anonymity, some data containing information or images that could reveal the subject's identities were deleted or reconstructed.

Table 2. Participant information

Type	Age group	Course	Teaching experience	Most used platform
Instructor A	30s	Project of design	6-year	Blackboard
Instructor B	30s	Project of design	2-year	Zoom
Instructor C	50s	Industrial design	11-year	Zoom
Instructor D	60s	Visual design	23-year	YouTube, Web log

Table 3. Interview proceedings

Type	Date	Additional interview
Instructor A	August 27, 2020, 6:20-7:10PM.	· Telephone (30 minutes) · Letters exchanged twice
Instructor B	September 7th, 2020, 4:00-5:00 PM.	· Zoom meeting (40 minutes) · Letters exchanged once
Instructor C	September 17, 2020, 2:00-3:40PM.	· Letters exchanged twice
Instructor D	September 10th, 2020, 12:00-1:40PM.	· Letters exchanged twice

2.2 Analysis

The notion of story is central to research on teaching and learning (Frelin, 2013). An average of 95 minutes of conversation was collected for each interviewee, including phone questions and answers, and transcription of the oral data collected through this process was conducted.

General data analysis of qualitative research involves a coding process in which sub-themes are classified, named, and then woven into a larger category or topic for later comparison (Creswell & Poth, 2018).

Accordingly, all of the experiences of the instructors who participated in the interview were derived, and then the experiences that were unrelated to overlapping experiences or research topics were filtered out. The concepts of attributes were then collected and categorized using case analysis and continuous comparison of the subject (Charmaz, 2006). In quantitative analysis, the category names may be applied when they are from other researchers, or the vocabulary used by the research participants can be determined by the researcher (Merriam, 2009), and in this article, the researcher applied the vocabulary of the higher concept.

3. RESULTS

According to the Ministry of Education's guidelines, which proposed the detailed method for class management involves collecting opinions from teachers and learners and entrusting the implementation to their discretion (Ministry of Education, 2020), the specific experiences of each instructor's case were different. In each case, the statements were examined by dividing them into "Impasse", which was experienced while operating distance learning courses in design subjects, "Attempt" for smooth teaching in courses, "Potential" found in this process, and "Reflection". Twenty-five subcategories and 12 core topics were derived using meaningful statements.

Table 4. Instructor teaching experiences with online distance learning for practical design courses

Categories	Core topics	Subcategories
Impasse	Carry a burden alone.	(A)(B)(C)(D) Not enough time to prepare for online distance learning. (A)(B)(C)(D) The environment and support are insufficient. (A)(C)(D) The instructor feels the difficulties and limitations of using the online platform. (A)(C) Instructors are tired of things that they do not have to do in face-to-face courses.
	Never get over things.	(A)(B)(C)(D) The instructor feels the limitations of making activities and effects. (C)(D) It is difficult to communicate online rather than face-to-face.
	Meaningless evaluation standard.	(A)(B)(C)(D) It is hard to reflect the learners' participation and attitudes in the evaluation.
	Students who can't concentrate.	(D) A skeptic about real-time online distance learning. (D) Learners who are not voluntary.
Attempt	Variety of uses for online platforms.	(B)(D) Try to activate the use of online platforms for interaction. (A)(D) Adjusted class contents for learners to be able to adapt to the new teaching method. (C) Different online platforms are used according to class contents and activities.
	Specific instructions for learning.	(B) Various activities are presented so that learners can focus. (B)(C) Class rules are set and reflected in grades.
Potential	Students who adapt well to online distance learning.	(A)(B)(C)(D) Learners' good use of online platforms. (A)(B) Learner's approach instructors more easily.
	Discover the advantages of online distance learning.	(A)(B)(D) The advantages of distance learning when using online platforms. (A)(B)(D) It is useful if distance and face-to-face methods are mixed.
	The learning effect is valid depending on the situation.	(C)(D) Distance learning is not a big problem for senior students. (B) Face-to-face learning is not necessary. (B) There is no significant difference between distance learning and face-to-face classes in terms of results.
Reflection	The direction of future online distance learning for design education.	(A)(B)(C) In future distance learning, changes in educational content and goals are needed. (C) Distance learning is positive but limited.

Training is needed to improve delivery skills.	((B)(D) Online remote classes require lecture skills that are different from face-to-face classes.
Control and rules that ignore each course are poison.	(D) Instructors require autonomy when using the platform. (D) Time standards cannot be applied to design course subjects.

Instructor A = (A), Instructor B = (B), Instructor C = (C), Instructor D = (D)

All instructors had no experience with distance learning, and they had difficulties because the environment or support for the courses was not suitable. To induce the full participation of learners in distance learning using online platforms, it is essential to establish an environment in which both learners and instructors can smoothly access the online system before classes begin (Salmon, 2013).

> "Basically, the Wi-Fi provided by the school does not connect well with the Blackboard for security reasons. I had to change some settings to connect, but it wasn't working, so I used the Tethering function. The same goes for students." (Instructor A)

Instructor C's school used its own learning management system(LMS) before starting distance learning. However, it was inconvenient to use in practical classes, and there was no function in terms of real-time classes. Since then, the school has provided data and educational programs regarding the use of Zoom so that real-time distance learning can be conducted, but they are not useful. Rather, Instructor C had to work much harder because of the guidelines for posting records of the course on the school's LMS.

> "In the school guidelines, there should be evidence to see if the class was actually held or not. So I uploaded a class video. Also, submit assignments, give feedback, check attendance by LMS, but the actual class is operated at Zoom. I had to work twice and three times." (Instructor C)

Prensky (2001) referred to the generation born between 1980 and 2000 as Digital Natives. Compared to learners, instructors were not familiar with the digital environment, so they felt difficulty and became tired of communicating online.

> "The biggest problem with online is that I'm not good at it. I can't use it, not used to online. Instructors are in a hurry. Why isn't this turning on? That's how I lose all the trust in the class by students." (Instructor D)

The problem regarding the instructor's ability to use the online platform was also revealed in the experiences of Instructors A and C. Instructor D easily adjusted the difficulty of the last task among the three project tasks in the class, but learners did not reach the level expected by the instructor. In fact, in Korea, concerns have been raised that the ability to discriminate has decreased as most universities have changed the evaluation method for their grades to absolute evaluation (M.H. Cho, 2020). In distance learning, it is difficult to control learners who do not focus on classes, and there are limitations in forming rapport. Therefore, curricula and evaluation criteria that are distinctly different from face-to-face classes must be applied.

> "I split it into small unit groups. If there are about 20 students over, they don't talk to each other. They didn't concentrate. Feel awkward and shy. So divide into small groups, communication takes place within them, and projects are carried out. And while I feedback to other students' groups, they solve the task in my directions. I think that kind of interaction was good." (Instructor B)

The most representative limitations appeared when providing solid visuals that are not implemented on digital screens.

> "The quality of the mock-up is important. These course contents were to made mock-up. But now the focus is on how well they show the work online rather than actual things."(Instructor A)

> "They could select a target user, and do various platforms, products, services, environments, and exhibitions that fit the needs of the target. But, most of the students showed in service design. Limitations seem to have come naturally from the environmental aspect." (Instructor B)

> "They don't know how it can improve the completeness of the mock-up. No matter how much I talk, I can't explain it well. Also, they all look similar through the camera. I can't see the details." (Instructor C)

On the contrary, distance learning was more efficient in senior classes centered on personal production activities, and the results of tasks such as data collection and field research were superior to a face-to-face class. Due to the nature of distance learning, where guidance and learning processes are recorded, it can be seen that it has a positive effect on post-class review and reflection.

In the case of learners, when engaging in distance learning, they asked instructors questions more frequently, and they quickly accepted the new ways of the class and teaching methods online and showed more preference.

> "Because the records are left, students remind them of every comment. It is much more realistic than words that flow. So I said every word more carefully." (Instructor A)

> "Except for some practical courses, it's the same as a face-to-face anyway. Rather, if they come in person, you have to wait for the instructor's criticism for a long time. There was no problem with the 4th-grade graduation exhibition course. They're good on their own." (Instructor C)

> "Regardless of the quality of the task, it can be seen that they tried to reflect my feedback by watching the video very meticulously. Even if it's not a COVID-19, I think that kind of online learning is very beneficial."(Instructor D)

Table 5. Learner assignments in distance learning of instructor B

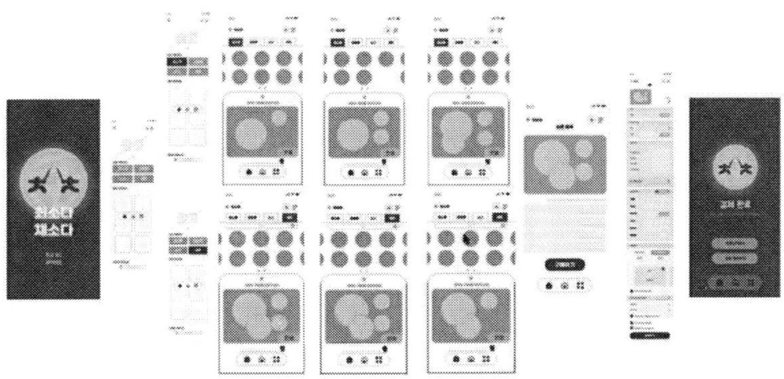

Table 6. Learner assignments in face-to-face classes(above) and distance learning(below) of instructor C

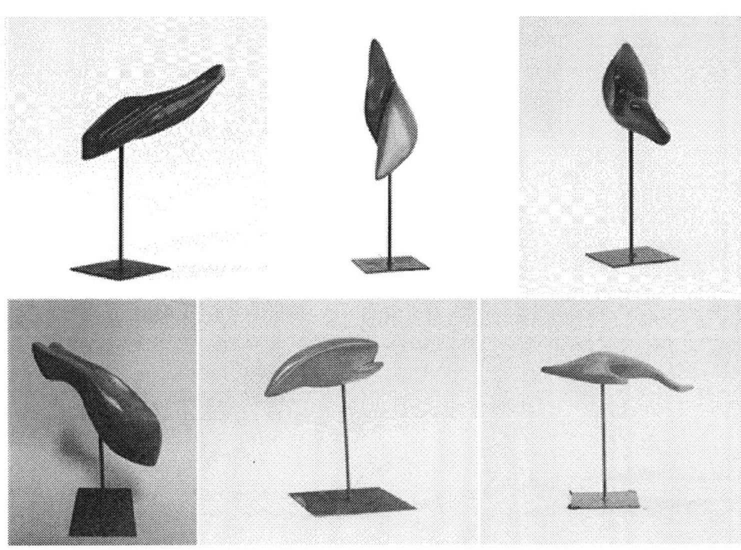

After the course, the instructors felt that the educational goals, contents, outcomes of distance learning and face-to-face classes were different, and the teaching method should also be different. Therefore, blended learning-type classes mixed with distance and face-to-face methods were considered the best.

"Theoretical classes or presentations can be heard (online) well and clearly seen. It was much better." (Instructor A)

"I think the curriculum of Korean design is very biased toward teaching the skills. For example, students who study the humanities also use it in other fields or their own positions, not only in writing or writing books. The design likewise can use in a wide variety of fields" (Instructor B)

In addition, the improvement of lecture delivery skills through video media, the use of the platform according to the subject, and the guarantee of autonomy by the teaching method should be supported.

4. DISCUSSION

Distance learning is positive in that it can expand experiences and opportunities for overall design centering on technological development. However, there are clearly practical activities that cannot be realized through distance learning. Therefore, it is necessary to discuss whether to develop classes that focus on currently used effective activities to find new strategies in the case that these limitations are fundamental to distance learning.

4.1 Practical Activities for Online Distance Learning

There are many restrictions on communication through video media, but in some activities, it is possible to find components that were similar to or more effective than a face-to-face class. Learner satisfaction according to the type of distance learning is much higher for classes using video media than those that provided only teaching materials and assignments (D.J. Lee, & & M. S. Kim, 2020). Therefore, in distance learning, video media should be considered.

First, in the case of all instructors, a validation of whether practical classes for visual design could be implemented on the screen was derived. The validity of implementation depends on whether the visual component can be completely checked in the video media, and if the final task performed by the learner is a practical task delivered in the form of digital graphics or video, the limitations of distance learning can be negated.

In particular, it was found that there was no difficulty in remote guidance through video media in courses for senior students. According to the statements from instructors C and D, they were already familiar with the university's courses and formative practical activities and were 'on their own'. Since the role of the instructor is simply to provide appropriate feedback according to the activity stage, it was possible to flexibly and efficiently manage the course and learning schedule. When a tutorial or demonstration for practical activities is needed, the learner's understanding is higher when they are provided videos than when they are experienced in real time.

4.2 Blended Learning

Blended learning provides a variety of learning methods that are suitable for learners' needs by properly mixing distance learning and face-to-face class, providing efficient access to knowledge through various delivery media, mitigating Spatio-temporal constraints, and reducing the cost of teaching and learning (Graham, 2003). Instructor D predicted that the best teaching method could be facilitated if approximately one-third of all courses were guaranteed face-to-face class time. Learners can watch video classes at any time without requiring time, physical presence, and cost of attending the classroom, and the rest of the class can then focus on theoretical learning and research activities.

Opinions were divided among the instructor regarding group activities and tasks, but it was found that overall, research activities by students proceeded smoothly. Blended learning is a strategy that can overcome the limitations of both distance learning and face-to-face classes and also make use of their strengths.

4.3 Mechanisms that Facilitate Class Activity

For enjoyable learning and knowledge creation to occur based on a certain sense of purpose within the learning group, a support device that promotes activities is needed (Y.M. Yu, 2018). In the case of Instructor B, it can be seen that the degree of participation improved when the learning group was divided into small units and group activities were conducted. Instructors B and C required small task units to be performed and communicated about them frequently. Instructor C set rules so that the activities were completed during class time. The results were all effective. In distance learning, providing units of knowledge repeatedly and presenting specific methods for learners and instructors are consistent with previous studies (J.K. Lee, J. K., Jeon, 2018; Y.K. Lim, Kim, 2019), which show that acting as thinking facilitators can activate learner participation. For all of the instructors' courses, learners were competent at using the online platform and were also active in communication with instructors. Given the research results (Y. Noh, 2019) that interest in the platform itself can lead to an interest in learning, efforts are needed to find the most suitable online platforms for classes and apply them in combination.

4.4 Social Network for Sharing Instruction Strategies

It was noted that designing blended learning-oriented classes that mix distance learning and face-to-face class methods is not only much more difficult than traditional classrooms but also costs three times as much (Bersin, 2003). However, even regular meetings by instructors were reduced or omitted due to COVID-19, and they had difficulty finding communities with which to share information.

The Ministry of Education and schools left a significant portion of the class management at the instructor's discretion, and the instructors used an unfamiliar online platform and remotely operated the class. During this process, it was found that the instructor felt considerable fatigue due to collective guidelines that did not account for the characteristics of the class, an unstable online access environment, digital infrastructure, and an increased workload. If each case is shared and in-depth research and class development are conducted to account for these problems, the burden for individual instructors can be relieved and continuous growth for remote classes can be expected.

4.5 Provision of Standardized Guides and Systems for Design Practical Courses

The design process for distance learning requires a supportive teaching guide and systems at the national or institutional level should be based on these guidelines. Practical support for the use of online platforms and digital devices by instructors is needed. All of the instructors stated that although they majored in design and had relatively frequently used online platforms or digital devices, some had difficulty using them in class.

Instructors and learners should be provided with an environment for smooth online access. The first step in ensuring that learners have the motivation and willingness to participate in distance learning classes is to construct an environment in which online systems can be accessed smoothly (Salmon, 2013).

In addition, evaluation criteria suitable for distance learning should be prepared. In all of the instructors' cases, in terms of learner evaluation, it was difficult to apply the existing face-to-face class standards. In the post-COVID-19 era, distance learning is no longer a substitute but a regular teaching model. A standardized instructional design model for distance learning that considers the characteristics of the design field should be developed.

5. CONCLUSION

Distance learning courses are based on information and communication technology. Online, distance has disappeared, and there is only an infinite virtual space. Therefore, how can educators and administrators make this virtual space an effective place for teaching and learning? Even though the 'Place' is not necessarily visible, to make the 'Space' into the 'Place' is to give value (Tuan, 1977). While the virtual world is not necessarily visible, to make the virtual space into an educational place provides value. When classes use online spaces and learners' positive experiences accumulate, the online space will become a meaningful place for learning and provide a new classroom that transcends physical limitations due to distance.

The development of information and communication technology, which is also the core of the 4th Industrial Revolution, removes distance and connects the world (Cairncross, 1998). The rapid development and dissemination of technology have completely changed the way learners obtain and process information, but education is still following the traditional implementations without understanding the needs of learners (Prensky, 2001). In particular, distance learning in design education, which involves many practical activities, is only an alternative to face-to-face classes, and attempts to reconstruct or develop existing classes into online remote classes have not yet emerged. The gap between online virtual space and real space will gradually narrow. Now is the time to find specific ways to change for the future of education.

REFERENCES

Bersin, J. (2003). *The blended learning book: best practices, proven methodologies, and lessons learned*. San Francisco: Pfeiffer.

Cairncross, F. (1998). *The Death of Distance: How the Communications Revolution will Change our Lives*. London: Orion Business.

Charmaz, K. (2006). *Constructing grounded theory. A practical guide through qualitative analysis*. London: Sage.

Creswell, J. W., & Poth, C. N. (2018). *Qualitative Inquiry and research design: choosing among five approaches*. Thousand Oaks, CA: Sage.

Do, J. U. (2020). An Investigation of Design Constraints in the Process of Converting Face-to-face course into Online Course. *Journal of Education & Culture*, *26*(2), 153-173.

Graham, C. R. (2006). *Blended learning systems: definition, current trends, and future directions*. San Francisco: Pfeiffer.

Heskett, J. (1980). *Industrial Design*. Oxford: Oxford University Press

Keegan, D. (1996) *Foundations of distance education (3rd ed)*. London, UK: Routledge.

Lee, D. J. & Kim, M. S. (2020). University students' perceptions on the practices of online learning in the COVID-19 situation and future directions. *Multimedia-Assisted Language Learning*, *23*(3), 359-377.

Lee, J. K. & Jeon, M. G. (2018). The Effect of Flipped Learning applied at Problem-solving Math class in University. *Korean Association for Learner-Centered Curriculum And Instruction*, *18*(4), 571-599.

Merriam, S. B. (2009). *Qualitative research: A guide to design and implementation*. San Francisco, CA: Jossey-Bass.

Ministry of Education. (2020, April 10). *Recommendations for the operation of bachelor's degrees in 2020*. https://www.moe.go.kr/boardCnts/view.do?boardID=294&boardSeq=79917&lev=0&searchType=null&statusYN=W&page=2&s=moe&m=020402&opType=N

Moore, M. G., & Kearsley, G. (1996). *Distance education*. Belmont: Wadsworth

Noh, Y. (2019). A Study on Factors affecting Learner's Satisfaction with Google Classroom. *The Academy of Customer Satisfaction Management*, *21*(4), 71-89.

Oh, J. H. (2020). The future after COVID-19, the era of learning from the era of education (Issue &Analysis No. 421). Gyeonggi: GRI

Prensky, M., (2001). Digital natives, digital immigrants part 1. *On the Horizon*, *4*(5), 1-6.

Salmon, G. (2013). *E-tivities: The key to active online learning*. ProQuest Ebook Central: https://ebookcentral.proquest.com

Simonson, M., Smaldinon, S., Albright, M., & Zvacek, S. (2006). *Teaching and learning at a distance: foundations of distance education (3ed)*. London: Pearson Education

Stake, R. E. (1995). *The art of case study research*. Thousand Oaks, CA: Sage.

Tuan, Y. F. (1977). *Space and Place: The Perspective of Experience*. Minnesota: University of Minnesota Press.

Yu, Y. M. (2018). Knowledge ecology. Seoul: Parkyoung Book

REDUCING FOOD WASTE WITH VIRTUAL REALITY (VR) TRAINING – A PROTOTYPE AND A/B-TEST IN AN ONLINE EXPERIMENT

Roger Seiler[1], Daniel Fankhauser[1] and Thomas Keller[2]
[1]*Zurich University of Applied Sciences, St.-Georgen-Platz 2, P.O. Box, CH-8401 Winterthur, Switzerland*
[2]*Zurich University of Applied Sciences, Theaterstrasse 17, P.O. Box, CH-8401 Winterthur, Switzerland*

ABSTRACT

Food waste is an important issue in the global warming debate. In this study, a virtual reality (VR) application was built from the insights and requirements of a focus group. The VR prototype was then validated using A/B-testing in an online experiment due to COVID-19 restrictions. VR is considered suitable for transferring information and building awareness regarding the topic of food waste. However, it is necessary to maintain the right balance between an informative and a serious gaming application. VR scenarios that people enjoy using have positive learning effects. Furthermore, scenarios that feature gamification elements are rated more highly regarding intention to use, which, in turn, benefits learning.

KEYWORDS

VR, Food Waste, A/B-Test, Online, Experiment

1. INTRODUCTION

Food waste is an important topic (Jeswani et al., 2021), a real problem (Praktischer Umweltschutz, 2020), and an entire generation has been labelled with the term (Priefer et al., 2014). In households every year, 1.3 billion tons of food are wasted globally, and household-associated food waste accounts for up to a trillion dollars of economic loss (Principato et al., 2021). Furthermore, the topic is relevant because in 2019 worldwide (2600 cities in 160 countries), 7 million people protested openly about climate change (Aaron, 2019). However, empirical evidence suggests that habits can change if food waste is documented (Arnd I. Urban, 2015). Fighting food waste by handing out flyers is not an option as this is neither environmentally friendly nor necessary in a world of smartphones. Until now and as far as the authors are aware, approaches utilising VR remain a research gap. This conclusion is backed by work on the pervasive fridge (a smart fridge concept) by Rouillard, who hypotheses that it may worth investigating augmented reality (AR) to measure the purchased quantities of food and thereby avoid waste. (Rouillard, 2012).

This study aims to reduce food waste through the application of VR in answering the following research question: *How can a VR application contribute to reducing food waste?*

This paper is structured as follows: Following a literature review, there is an overview of the state of the art, a description of the research method, data analysis, discussion, and presentation of findings. To conclude, we address research limitations, further research opportunities, and any implications.

2. LITERATURE

The term "waste" refers to a loss and, in our case, relates to the deliberate or unintentional waste of food. Some authors further distinguish between avoidable and unavoidable waste (Beretta & Hellweg, 2019). Inedible food waste is categorised as "unavoidable", whereas food waste resulting from a change in preference or distribution problems is labelled "avoidable" (Beretta & Hellweg, 2019). Reasons for avoidable food waste include inadequate storage facilities, expiry dates on products, and personal preferences.

Reasons for food waste are manifold, but Schneider (2008) emphasises socio-cultural aspects and information deficits (Schneider, 2008). Furthermore, portion sizes, sales discounts, and overestimation of the shelf life (Kapp et al., 2017) are reasons why avoidable food waste occurs. Countermeasures such as shopping planning and reducing information deficit (Priefer et al., 2014) are also suggested. Kapp et al. also recommend education and training for individuals as a possible countermeasure (Kapp et al., 2017).

Numerous meta-analyses conclude that VR and AR can positively affect motivation and learning success (Garzón et al., 2019; Radu, 2014; Tekedere & Göke, 2016). For example, gamification specifically can be used for educational purposes and play a role in intrinsic motivation in traffic education (Vogelsberg, 2008). This concept is also used in further education (Fritz, 1997). Serious gaming is a game-based learning approach and extends the pure recreational effect of traditional gaming by providing an added value (Stieglitz, 2015). In pedagogical research, serious games are used to study human behaviour and decision-making (Lang et al., 2012). Furthermore, in certain situations where physical risk exists, simulations and serious games may be a valid training option (e.g. firefighting or flight simulation) (Stieglitz, 2015) since errors could be fatal in real life but not in the world of VR. Hence, using VR simulation for training purposes is much safer.

Although food waste is not usually associated with an immediate risk to life, information transfer via VR seems a good approach to close the food-waste knowledge deficit because positive effects on motivation, learning success, and long-term memory have been reported in empirical studies.

3. METHODOLOGY

This study is composed of two stages or phases. In the first (qualitative) specification phase, a focus group was used to gather specifications for developing the VR prototype before transitioning into the second phase. In the (quantitative) validation phase, A/B-testing in an online experiment with a questionnaire was used to gain insights into which approaches are best to help reduce avoidable food waste.

The first phase can be divided into three steps: (i) preparation, (ii) the focus group round, and (iii) qualitative content analyses. A stimulus was presented at the beginning of the focus group, and guiding questions were used to aid the group discussion. The third step was conducted following the qualitative content analysis, according to Mayring (2015).

Derived from the qualitative phase, the quantitative phase was implemented using LimeSurvey as an online survey tool. As COVID-19 prevented the initially planned lab experiment, a video guiding viewer through the two versions of the prototype (one prototype has gamification elements while the other one does not) was shown to participants in the online survey. The distribution of executable files was considered but dismissed as participants typically do not have the necessary VR hardware or suitable systems. In addition, this could have introduced biases resulting from different hardware configurations. Therefore, randomisation was used to determine which of the two videos was shown to participants.

The gamification prototype (see Figure 1) has high scores, instant graphical feedback, and sound effects, while the non-gamified version does not have these elements.

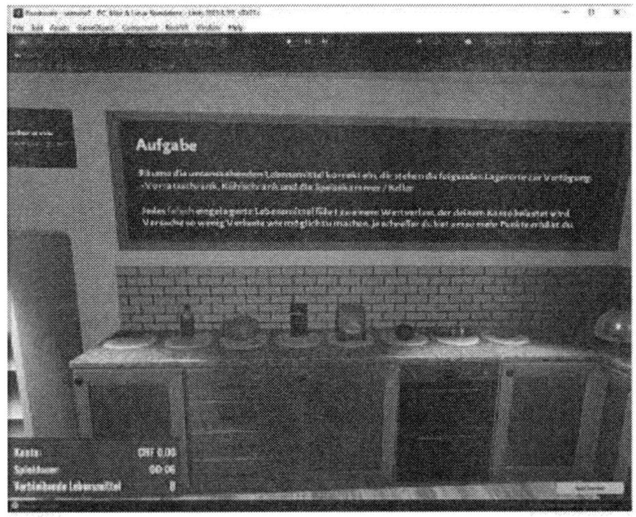

Figure 1. VR prototype

Building on the work of Sagnier et al. (2020), a conceptual model (see Figure 2) was derived and used to derive the hypothesis of this study.

Based on the technology acceptance model (TAM) (Davis, 1986), H1, H2, and H3 were derived (see Table 1 for an overview of all hypotheses), stating the perceived ease of use (PEOU, H1) and perceived usefulness (PU, H2) affecting intention to use (ITU) as well as PEOU affecting PU (H3). Pragmatic quality (PQ) positively affects PEOU (H4a) and PU (H4b); hedonic quality stimulation (HQS) positively affects PEOU (H5a) and PU (H5b); personal innovativeness (PI) positively affects PU (H6a) and ITU (H6b). Venkatesh and Bala (2008) propose that perceived enjoyment (PE) has a positive effect on PEOU (H7a) and ITU (H7b). Furthermore, the authors of this paper hypothesise that the perceived learning outcome (PLO) has a positive effect on the ITU (H8). A note regarding the hypotheses H9–H11 must be made as they were derived after analysing the data and finding significant correlations (see Section 5 and Table 2).

The questionnaire relied on the Likert five-point scale except for the socio-demographic variables, hedonic constructs, and pragmatic quality. The last two were measured on a five-point semantic differential. The PEOU is a 3 item, and PU is a 4 item construct, both based on Kolitz (2008). ITU is a four-item construct drawn from Kolitz (2008), and PE is a six-item construct, based on Balog and Pribeanu (2010). The second items were removed in PE and ITU as they did not apply to the VR scenario. PI has four items based on Lu et al. (2005), whereas PQ and HQS are both seven-item constructs measured by a semantic differential based on Pivec (2006). Finally, PLO is a three-item construct based on Hirdes (2016).

Table 1. Overview of the Hypotheses

#	Text	Result
1	Perceived ease of use positively affects intention to use.	Reject
2	Perceived usefulness positively affects intention to use.	Accept
3	Perceived ease of use positively affects perceived usefulness.	Accept
4a	Pragmatic quality positively affects perceived ease of use.	Reject
4b	Pragmatic quality positively affects perceived usefulness.	Accept
5a	Hedonic quality stimulation has a positive effect on perceived ease of use.	Reject
5b	Hedonic quality stimulation has a positive effect on perceived usefulness.	Accept
6a	Personal innovativeness positively affects perceived usefulness.	Reject
6b	Personal innovativeness positively affects intention to use.	Reject
7a	Perceived enjoyment positively affects perceived ease of use.	Reject
7b	Perceived enjoyment positively affects perceived usefulness.	Accept

#	Text	Result
8	Perceived learning outcome positively affects intention to use.	Accept
9	Perceived enjoyment has a positive effect on perceived learning outcome.	Accept
10	Hedonic quality stimulation has a positive effect on perceived learning outcome.	Accept
11	Perceived usefulness has a positive effect on perceived learning outcome.	Accept

4. DATA ANALYSIS

This section of the paper covers the qualitative and quantitative phases of the research. The qualitative phase was coded with the MAXQDA Analytics Pro 2020 software, and three main categories were identified: (i) development, (ii) design, and (iii) information transfer. In the following paragraphs, aspects mentioned by the focus group participants are described by addressing the categories and subcategories identified in the content analysis.

In the first main category (development), four subcategories were identified: scenario, concept, task, and goals. In the "scenario" subcategory, storage when shopping, minimum shelf-life date, and fridge are reported. Storage covers storage aspects when shopping as well as questions of how to store food once it has been brought home. In "minimum shelf life date", opening cupboards and deciding if the food is edible based on the shelf-life date is established, while in "fridge", one must determine whether food must be put in the fridge or not.

In the "concept" subcategory, the product's life cycle is prolonged or shortened depending on the choice of where to store the food. Players get immediate feedback and responses on the effects their choices have. The game informs players what influences their choices have on the shelf life of the products. For example, a growing or diminishing pile of food waste symbolises whether that decision was right or wrong depending on the storage choice. Furthermore, the game ensures players understand the consequences of their actions.

In the "task" subcategory, a player has a list showing the current and upcoming task. The game does not offer written instructions since the task (storing food purchases at home correctly after returning from shopping) is intuitive. An avatar could provide step-by-step guidance if necessary but not offer hints or explicit instructions.

In the "goals" subcategory, players learn where best to store groceries, decide whether food is still safe or not (even if the shelf-life date has expired), and make informed decisions for themselves. Furthermore, awareness of the consequences of food waste should be heightened.

In the second main category (design), four subcategories were identified: location, interaction, objects, and grocery (objects). In the "location" subcategory, the game should be played where the fridge normally stands. Furthermore, the game should provide a standard use case, common when storing groceries at home, and a familiar environment.

In the "interaction" subcategory, players interact with products and store them. It should be possible to interact and turn the product to see if queues exist regarding the proper storage of the food. Objects that should be present are a fridge, a shelf, and a shopping basket. Familiar and popular foods such as yoghurt or salt should be used in the scenario.

In the third main category (information transfer), two subcategories were identified: feedback and the type of information transfer. In the "feedback" subcategory, textbox information with links to possible storage options is suggested. Feedback is displayed as a textbox, and if a product is not stored correctly, the text turns red. If players make a mistake, they receive a notification about why that action or choice is wrong and why. Standard gamification concepts such as winnable points or coins are also an option.

In the "type of information transfer" subcategory, a combination of visual and textual feedback is proposed, and a focus on visual elements is recommended. Information transfer can also be enhanced with an avatar or mascot.

Based on this qualitative information, the VR prototype requirements are derived and classified as functional (F) or non-functional (NF). The functional requirements are providing a shopping basket, visualisation of task, consequences of storage choices, game progression, and money wasted. Non-functional requirements implemented in the prototype are interaction and intuitive gameplay.

To highlight the consequences of poor storage choices, a price for each food item was set. For example, coffee beans should be stored in the cupboard, meat, fish, cheese, and milk in the fridge, pasta on the shelf, and banana and tomatoes in the pantry. If a wrong storage choice is made, the value of the food is reduced. This system should provide an incentive to avoid food waste within the game scenario. Furthermore, a scoring system with points was introduced to augment the scenario with gamification and provide a further incentive to avoid food waste.

5. RESULTS, DISCUSSION, IMPLICATIONS, AND LIMITATIONS

Data collection was conducted in the spring of 2020 with 95 participants, although some questionnaires were incomplete, leaving 78 for further processing. A control question was used to check if people had actually seen the VR application as they were asked to name the storage option not available in the application. Socio-demographic variables come first, with education being measured by degree because interest in technology, as well as food waste, may be different among these categories.

The sample consists of 29 female (37.2 %) and 49 male (62.8 %) participants. When looking more closely at scenarios one and two, there are 15 and 14 females and 24 and 25 male participants, respectively. The participants are relatively young (M=36.12, SD=9.20). Regarding education, 39 participants (50%) hold a degree from a university of applied sciences, 13 participants (16.7 %) hold a university degree, ten participants (12.8 %) have a professional diploma, six participants (7.7%) hold an apprentice degree, eight participants (10.3%) hold a college degree, and two participants (2.6%) stated "other educational degree".

First, the constructs were tested for reliability. Cronbach's Alpha values of the construct are as follows: PU (α=.84), PEOU (α=.91), ITU (α=.91), PE (α=.84), PI (α=.88), PQ (α=.82), HQS (α=.91), and PLO (α=.92). The values are all well above the cut off value of .7 generally used in empirical research (Nunally, 1978). Further data analysis could now be conducted.

By comparing the mean values of the two scenarios (with and without gamification), all variables showed significant differences except PEOU and PI (see Table 3). Therefore, the analysis was continued, and correlations were interpreted.

Table 2 shows an overview of correlations. Hypotheses were accepted if correlations between the constructs addressed in the hypothesis correlate significantly. The correlations suggest that H1 must be rejected because the correlation analysis is not significant. However, the constructs in H2 show positive correlations, so H2 is accepted. Similarly, the constructs of H3 shows significant correlations, so H3 is accepted. The constructs in H4a do not correlate significantly, whereas those in H4b do. Consequently, H4a is rejected and H4b accepted. The constructs in H5a do not show significant correlation, so H5a is rejected. However, the constructs of H5b correlate significantly, and H5b is accepted. Both H6a and H6b show no significant correlations and are rejected. The correlation of constructs in H7a is not significant, but those of H7b are, so H7a is rejected and H7b accepted. The constructs in H8 correlate significantly, and H8 is accepted.

During correlation analysis, further hypotheses (H9, H10, and H11) can be derived from the data analysis, not in the TAM referenced in the theory section of this paper. PE correlates with PLO (H9), HQS correlates with PLO (H10), and PU correlates with PLO (H11). Therefore, these hypotheses are added to the overview (see Table 1).

Table 2. Overview of Correlation for Scenario 2 (with gamification)

Hypothesis	Construct 1	Construct 2	Scenario 2	Result
H1	PEoU	ITU	.065	✗
H2	PU	ITU	**.717****	✓
H3	PEoU	PU	**.373***	✓
H4a	PQ	PEoU	.187	✗
H4b	PQ	PU	**.473****	✓
H5a	HQS	EoU	.302	✗

H5b	HQS	PU	**.709****	✓
H6a	PI	PU	-.080	✗
H6b	PI	ITU	-.028	✗
H7a	PE	PEoU	.267	✗
H7b	PE	ITU	**.613****	✓
H8	PLO	ITU	**.628****	✓
#H9	PE	PLO	**.599****	✓
#H10	HQS	PLO	**.539****	✓
#H11	PU	PLO	**.597****	✓

* $p < .05$, ** $p < .01$ (both two tailed)

Table 3. Overview of group comparison

Variable	t	df	Sig. (2-tailed)	Mean Difference	Std. Error Difference	CI 95% Lower	CI 95% Higher
PU	-6.301	76	.000	-1.10897	.17600	-1.45951	-.75844
PEOU	-1.245	76	.217	-.27350	.21965	-.71097	.16396
PI	.419	76	.676	.05128	.12225	-.19219	.29476
PLO	-5.096	76	.000	-1.19658	.23480	-1.66422	-.72894
PQ	-3.983	71.204	.000	-.52747	.13242	-.79149	-.26345
HQS	-5.051	76	.000	-.83150	.16463	-1.15938	-.50362
ITU	-6.188	76	.000	-1.39316	.22514	-1.84156	-.94477
PE	-4.602	76	.000	-.75385	.16382	-1.08011	-.42758

6. DISCUSSION

In line with prior research on TAM, PEOU does not show significant effects on ITU, but PU does. Pragmatic quality has effects on PU but not on PEOU. Accordingly, HQS shows positive effects on PU but not on PEOU. PI did not affect PU or ITU, which is somewhat surprising as one could argue that PI may also lead to ITU. PE has positive effects on ITU but not on PEOU. PLO has positive effects on PLO. Therefore, the TAM seems to hold in the context of VR and reducing food waste by immersive experiences.

The dependant variable PLO is noteworthy as correlations were found but were not initially in the derived hypotheses. Nevertheless, data suggests that PE, HQS, PU, and PLO correlate. This is in line with prior research findings; therefore, the conclusions of this study are reported, and the correlations added to the overview as new hypotheses.

7. IMPLICATIONS

Research on VR suggests that this has a positive effect on education (Ai-Lim Lee et al., 2010; Garzón et al., 2019; Radu, 2014). The results of this study confirm that this holds in the contest of food waste too because PE, HQS, and PU positively correlate with PLO. Furthermore, PE positively correlates with ITU the VR application. These preliminary results are promising for organisations seeking to raise awareness regarding the topic and to combat food waste by letting individuals immerse themselves in virtual worlds and discover ways to avoid food waste in real life. Furthermore, the results of this study suggest that this does not have to be an arduous learning path since perceived enjoyment was significantly higher in the gamification enriched VR application than in the non-gamified one. Hedonic quality stimulation was also significantly higher. This supports the suggestion that learning can be a hedonic and enjoyable task, especially when interaction and immersion into virtual worlds are involved. Consequently, creating such worlds is highly recommended because the perceived learning outcome was also significantly higher with the treatment than in the control group.

8. LIMITATIONS

The authors want to highlight that these results are based on correlation analysis. The results should, therefore, be taken as preliminary initial results to inspire further research activities. Furthermore, this study was conducted under the shadow of a worldwide pandemic and the initially planned lab experiment was adapted to enable the quantitative phase to take place online. Consequently, results may differ because the tests were not carried out in laboratory conditions. Empirical research and the meta-analysis mentioned in the literature section of this study suggest that the effects would probably be even stronger if real immersion in the VR application had been experienced. This is because the VR application would leave a greater impression on the user than the online video we were obliged to resort to.

9. FURTHER RESEARCH

This study has a specific scenario, namely, deciding where to store food purchases in the home. Therefore, earlier stages such as the actual shopping or writing of a shopping list may be opportunities for further research towards avoiding food waste. Furthermore, the scenario used in this study is located at home in a familiar environment, so effects resulting from social influences (such as desirability) do not play are role. However, stronger social influences on food-wasting behaviour may well be present in a shared setting such as an office kitchen. Such influences could be further evaluated. A further research opportunity could also arise by varying the price and the products involved. Further research might choose more advanced research methods such as regression and structural equation modelling (SEM) as the correlations reported in this research suggest that direct and indirect effects may be present.

10. CONCLUDING REMARKS

The results of this study are promising and perceived learning outcomes are higher with gamification than without. Furthermore, awareness regarding food waste can be raised with the VR prototype presented in this paper as well as tangible results in terms of food not wasted. The results of this study suggest that this does not have to be a tough learning path but can be pleasurable because learning is based on interaction and takes place in a realistic, albeit virtual context. Therefore, we hope this application will be helpful since its perceived usefulness was significantly higher with the treatment than in the control group. In conclusion, we believe that avoidable food waste can be reduced using the VR application presented in this study, and we invite researchers to contribute and build on these preliminary findings.

REFERENCES

Aaron, 2019. 7.6 million people demand action after week of climate strikes [WWW Document]. Global Climate Strike. URL https://globalclimatestrike.net/7-million-people-demand-action-after-week-of-climate-strikes/ (accessed 6.10.21).

Ai-Lim Lee, E., Wong, K.W., Fung, C.C., 2010. How does desktop virtual reality enhance learning outcomes? A structural equation modeling approach. Computers & Education 55, 1424–1442. https://doi.org/10.1016/j.compedu.2010.06.006

Arnd I. Urban, G.H., 2015. Wertstoffhof - Chancen, Entwicklungen, ..., Schriftenreihe des Fachgebietes Abfalltechnik UNIKAT. Kassel University Press, Kassel.

Balog, A., Pribeanu, C., 2010. The Role of Perceived Enjoyment in the Students' Acceptance of an Augmented Reality Teaching Platform: a Structural Equation Modelling Approach. SIC 19. https://doi.org/10.24846/v19i3y201011

Beretta, C., Hellweg, S., 2019. Lebensmittelverluste in der Schweiz: Mengen und Umweltbelatung. Wissenschaftlicher Schlussbericht. ETH Zürich, Zürich.

Davis, F.D., 1986. A technology acceptance model for empirically testing new end-user information systems: Theory and results (PhD Thesis). MIT.

Fritz, J., 1997. Edutainment - Neue Formen des Spielens und Lernens?

Garzón, J., Pavón, J., Baldiris, S., 2019. Systematic review and meta-analysis of augmented reality in educational settings. Virtual Reality 23, 447–459. https://doi.org/10.1007/s10055-019-00379-9

Hirdes, E., 2016. Beschreibung von wiederverwendbaren Prozessen zur Erreichung von Lernzielen in Serious Games, Research on IT / Service / Innovation / Collaboration. Kassel University Press, Kassel.

Jeswani, H.K., Figueroa-Torres, G., Azapagic, A., 2021. The extent of food waste generation in the UK and its environmental impacts. Sustainable Production and Consumption 26, 532–547. https://doi.org/10.1016/j.spc.2020.12.021

Kapp, B., Sajovitz, P.L., Strobel, C., Pöchtrager, S., 2017. Die Einstellung von Wiener KonsumentInnen zum Thema Lebensmittelverschwendung.

Kolitz, K., 2008. Systemdesign im Market-Engineering - Experimente zu Teilnehmerverhalten und Technologieakzeptanz, Studies on eOrganisation and Market Engineering. Universitätsverl., Karlsruhe.

Lang, F., Püschel, T., Neumann, D., 2012. Serious Gaming. Spiele als experimentgestützte Evaluationsmethode.

Lu, J., Yao, J.E., Yu, C.-S., 2005. Personal innovativeness, social influences and adoption of wireless Internet services via mobile technology. The Journal of Strategic Information Systems 14, 245–268. https://doi.org/10.1016/j.jsis.2005.07.003

Mayring, P., 2015. Qualitative Inhaltsanalyse, 12., überarb. Aufl. ed, Beltz Pädagogik. Beltz, Weinheim.

Nunally, J., 1978. Psychometric theory. McGraw-Hill, New York.

Pivec, M., 2006. Affective and emotional aspects of human-computer interaction, The future of learning, 1572-4794. IOS Press, Amsterdam; Washington, DC.

Praktischer Umweltschutz, 2020. Das Problem Food Waste.

Priefer, C., Jörissen, J., Bräutigam, K.-R., 2014. Food Waste Generation in Europe.

Principato, L., Mattia, G., Di Leo, A., Pratesi, C.A., 2021. The household wasteful behaviour framework: A systematic review of consumer food waste. Industrial Marketing Management 93, 641–649. https://doi.org/10.1016/j.indmarman.2020.07.010

Radu, I., 2014. Augmented reality in education: a meta-review and cross-media analysis. Personal and Ubiquitous Computing 18, 1533–1543. https://doi.org/10.1007/s00779-013-0747-y

Rouillard, J., 2012. The Pervasive Fridge. A smart computer system against uneaten food loss, in: Seventh International Conference on Systems (ICONS2012). Saint-Gilles, Réunion, pp. 135–140.

Sagnier, C., Loup-Escande, E., Lourdeaux, D., Thouvenin, I., Valléry, G., 2020. User Acceptance of Virtual Reality: An Extended Technology Acceptance Model. International Journal of Human–Computer Interaction 1, 1–15. https://doi.org/10.1080/10447318.2019.1708612

Schneider, F., 2008. Online-Fachzeitschrift des Bundesministeriums für Land- und Forstwirtschaft, Umwelt und Wasserwirtschaft.

Stieglitz, S., 2015. Gamification – Vorgehen und Anwendung. HMD 52, 816–825. https://doi.org/10.1365/s40702-015-0185-6

Tekedere, H., Göke, H., 2016. Examining the Effectiveness of Augmented Reality Applications in Education: A Meta-Analysis. International Journal of Environmental and Science Education 11, 9469–9481.

Venkatesh, V., Bala, H., 2008. Technology Acceptance Model 3 and a Research Agenda on Interventions. Decision Sciences 39, 273–315. https://doi.org/10.1111/j.1540-5915.2008.00192.x

Vogelsberg, S., 2008. Verkehrserziehung durch Edutainment, Lebenslang lernen. Logos-Verl., Berlin.

MOBILE LEARNING GAMES WITH AUGMENTED REALITY IN A PARK - SYSTEM FOR CLASSIFICATION OF QUESTIONS FOR QUIZ GAME CREATION

Lúcia Pombo and Margarida M. Marques
Research Centre on Didactics and Technology in the Education of Trainers (CIDTFF)
Department of Education and Psychology, University of Aveiro, 3810-193 Aveiro, Portugal

ABSTRACT

This study used Bloom's Revised Taxonomy to examine 30 questions produced for a mobile quiz game with augmented reality contents to be explored in a formal learning context, in an urban green park, in Portugal. The game was co-created by 14 in-service teachers involved in a 50h training that aimed to promote the collaborative development of open digital educational resources that foster Science, Technology, Engineering and Mathematics (STEM) learning based on game approach and supported by mobile devices in outdoor settings. This is a qualitative study, based on the questions planning documents produced by the teacher trainees, which was treated using a hybrid process of inductive and deductive content analysis. The results indicate that teachers developed questions that, in the learner point of view, fall in the lower taxonomy levels, namely Remember, Understand, Apply and Analyze. Moreover, the most frequent type of question required "Direct application" of contents already known to real situations and mobilization of information expected to have been already covered at school, in a "Consolidation" approach. The empirical results suggest that the highest levels of Bloom's Revised Taxonomy (Evaluate and Create) are only achievable, during the process of game creation, and not while playing the game. Suggestions were made regarding future research, such as to analyze the process of game co-creation by teachers familiar with this classification system, to triangulate with the current study. This work is relevant for teacher trainees and teachers to promote higher quality game-based learning in teaching practices, as well as its associated resources.

KEYWORDS

Classification of Questions, Mobile Learning, Game-Based Learning, Teacher Training, Qualitative Study

1. INTRODUCTION

The concept of Mobile Learning Games has become popular in teaching and learning contexts as they can mobilize various types of skills. The main idea is to use game mechanics, such as competition, rewards, or simply curiosity in order to captivate the learners' attention and impulse them to learn (Dondlinger, 2007). There are a lot of different types of mobile learning games. Location-based mobile learning games bring together four of the most popular and current eLearning trends: mobile learning, digital storytelling, gamification, and location-based learning (Johnson et al., 2015), to unlock educational content through storytelling, rich digital media, location-awareness, maps, augmented reality (AR), and gamification strategies (Edmonds & Smith, 2017).

Location-based is one of the most interesting kinds of mobile learning games even when explored in formal contexts, as it implies to go out of four classroom walls and go to nature spaces where users can explore. Mobility also opens the possibility of situated learning in various physical settings. It turns learning into a personal and engaging experience where surroundings are linked to educational contents. Location-based mobile learning games can shift the focus from mere identification of content to interactive discovery that enhances and extends the way students experience learning from the environment and with each other (Edmonds & Smith, 2016).

When used correctly, game features enhance the learners' experience with emotion, which has positive effects on engagement and memory (Marfisi-Schottman & George, 2014), and therefore they promote situated cognition and authentic learning in educational environments. Although the benefits of mobile learning games have been recently studied, there are few reports of teachers being involved in the creation of learning apps as well as embedded resources. Therefore, it is crucial to investigate further to identify characteristics of situated learning environments, which led to specifying characteristics of authentic activities that teachers and instructional designers can use when designing learning experiences. For that purpose, Reeves and colleagues (2002) propose ten characteristics that provide students the opportunity to: (i) engage in problems/projects with real-world relevance; (ii) address ill-defined problems and (iii) complex tasks through sustained investigation; (iv) examine tasks from differing perspectives with the support of diverse resources, and (v) collaborate with other learners and (vi) reflect on their learning experiences. Additionally, for instructors who wish to provide authentic learning experiences, the work that students undertake should (vii) be applicable to a variety of subject areas; (viii) integrate with assessments; (ix) result in meaningful products; and (x) reflect a variety of solutions and possible competing outcomes. The authors also sought to emphasize that authentic learning in mobile education is feasible with intentional instructional strategies and appropriate educational technologies.

Considering the above-mentioned it is vital to provide teacher training to support teachers to use educational applications, to design proper activities and games, and adapt them to their course material and specific learning situations. It is also important to involve teachers in the creation of tools that enable the development of educational games, and moreover to provide them investigation evidences that mobile learning games, compared to other types of learning materials, can allow the construction of new concepts by players in a much funnier, interactive and dynamic way (Sampaio et al., 2012), and that their use in education can contribute to an increase of students' motivation and skills development (Sindre, 2009). For example, mobility offers new possibilities for enriching games and enhancing the users' experience by taking advantage of real objects (e.g. plants, buildings, tiles) in real contexts (e.g. natural parks, archeological or geological sites) (Daniel et al., 2009). Several studies have also shown that physical excitement caused by walking, running or jumping during the game increases player engagement (Bianchi-Berthouze, 2013). When combined with quiz games, a treasure hunt game can have additional benefits. A treasure hunt is a game in which players attempt to find hidden items with a series of clues. Because this type of game pushes players to explore the environment and get familiar with it, it is very well appropriate to teach about the characteristics of real items, locations and environments.

User friendly quiz games with immediate feedback, whether the student answers correctly or incorrectly, can provide valuable information in order to improve engagement in the game, and most of all, it can provide pedagogical benefits if the feedback is constructive and motivational. Game rewards such as extra points or unlocking the next part of the story, can also help motivate the learners to physically move to the next location (Marfisi-Schottman & George, 2014) to successfully conclude the game, and with learning gains. As the process of constructing educational mobile games can be as beneficial as the act of playing, and as there is a scarcity of educational resources for educational mobile games with AR, which integrate curriculum contents, the authors developed a teacher training workshop focusing on designing learning materials and questions to integrate in a mobile app. Therefore, this paper emerges from the need to create a classification system suitable for questions integrated in AR mobile games, in an outdoor context, to provide a greater diversity and a better quality of educational resources and questioning, towards constructivist pedagogy and situated and authentic learning. For that purpose, a process articulating inductive and deductive coding was applied. The theory-driven categories were the categories of cognitive processes from the revised Bloom's Taxonomy: Remember, Understand, Apply, Analyze, Evaluate, and Create (Anderson et al., 2001). These were articulated with data-driven categories, regarding the classification of quiz questions. The idea is to develop a system for classification of questions that can be used by teachers to diversify the type of questions they create, prompting different cognitive levels and also producing challenging questions. This classification system is also useful to support the evaluation of educational resources.

The implications for practice of this study is that teachers should be encouraged to use mobile apps integrating quiz games to increase new learning or provide consolidation activities in a different environment. Teachers also should facilitate mobile learning quiz game opportunities to encourage learning outside of the classroom. The system for classification of questions should be helpful to support teachers to design and use mobile app-based quiz games, and integrate them in their classes.

2. METHODOLOGICAL OPTIONS

This work presents a qualitative study (Merriam & Tisdell, 2015) based on documents produced by teacher trainees, which were treated using a hybrid process of inductive and deductive content analysis (Bardin, 2016; Xu & Zammit, 2020). The study's main aim is to develop a system for classification of questions integrated in mobile quiz games for outdoor contexts, based on the work developed by 14 in-service teachers under a 50h teacher training workshop. Qualitative studies are one of the most common forms of research in Education and require a flexible and data-driven research design (Hammersley, 2013). Hence, the focus is on developing rich descriptions of the phenomena under study, as contextual data are required for other researchers and practitioners to be able to relate the study findings to their own work contexts (Kivunja & Kuyini, 2017).

The research question is: How can a system for classification of questions support teachers in creating mobile learning games, adapted to their own contexts, and integrating diverse cognitive levels? Hence, to answer this question, two research objectives were defined:

1. To develop a system for classification of questions for mobile learning games;
2. To observe teachers using the system for classification of questions during the process of quiz questions creation.

The focus of this contribution is the first objective, as the revision of literature did not provide a classification system ready to be used by teachers. The second research objective will be pursued in future research efforts, in order to fully answer the formulated research question.

Follows the description of the context and participants in this study, as well as the data collection and analysis procedures (Section 2.2).

2.1 Teacher Training Workshop

The context of this study is a teacher training workshop, which has been described in previous studies (Marques & Pombo, 2021a; Marques & Pombo, 2021b). The training aimed to promote the collaborative development of open digital educational resources that foster Science, Technology, Engineering and Mathematics (STEM) learning based on game approach and supported by mobile and AR technologies in outdoor settings.

The educational resources were developed for the EduPARK app (http://edupark.web.ua.pt/mobile_app, accessed on 12 October 2021). It was created under the EduPARK project, funded by FEDER and FCT (2016-19) and that is still running. The EduPARK app supports exploration of AR contents developed for the Aveiro green park (Portugal) in a free mode, and in a play-the-game mode. The game supported by the app is an interdisciplinary quiz treasure hunt that integrates educational AR contents, images, audios and videos. Hence, most games available through the app foster interdisciplinary learning, one of the features of authentic activities according to Reeves (2002). The game structure is organized in the following loop (Figure 1): (i) give instructions to find a different AR marker in each location of interest (Figure 1B); each marker unlocks the access to information relevant to answering a series of questions related to that specific location; (ii) explore the AR contents, e.g., a specific botanical species with information about its origin, its flowers and leaves, and other curiosities (Figure 1C); (iii) present a multiple-choice question, with associated content - text, audio or image (Figure 1D); and (iv) give feedback to answers and award points, if the answer is correct (Figure 1E). The exploration of AR contents (B and C) is not mandatory, nor the inclusion of media files (image, audio and video) in all the questions. The game mascot is a female monkey, who lived in the park some time ago, and who guides the players and gives them formative feedback after answering; for example, when an incorrect answer is given, the mascot explains the right answer. Hence, the game structure implements several game features commended in the literature, such as prompting to physically move to different locations to find treasures or AR contents from hints, providing immediate feedback to game performance and gathering points (Marfisi-Schottman & George, 2014).

The app was developed to support social constructivism approaches to learning (Burr, 2015), where the users' construction of meaning is influenced by the interaction of the learners' prior knowledge with the new experiences, as well as by interactions with others. Thus, the project team recommends the exploration of the app in groups, to facilitate collaboration and discussion towards authentic learning experiences (Reeves et al., 2002), although it can be used individually as well.

Previous studies revealed the app has a high usability and educational value from basic to high education contexts (Pombo & Marques, 2019; Pombo & Marques, 2020; Pombo et al., 2019), which may facilitate teachers' adoption of the involved emergent technologies (mobile AR) and educational approaches (game-based learning). To promote teacher adoption of these innovative and effective approaches, a workshop accredited with 50 h (25 h in face-to-face sessions and 25 h of autonomous work) of continuous training for teachers was conducted between October 2020 and January 2021.

A B C D E

Figure 1. Selected screens of the EduPARK app and game (in Pombo & Marques, 2021)

Teacher trainees were characterized through data collected in a questionnaire. The analysis of its results was presented previously (Marques & Pombo, 2021a), so follows only the information needed to understand this study's results.

From the 16 teachers attending the workshop, 14 gave informed consent to participate in this study. The workshop's teacher cohort profile matches closely the Portuguese teacher profile according to PORDATA (https://www.pordata.pt/, accessed on 26 September 2021) in terms of: (a) gender, as 12 females and 2 males participated in the study; and (b) experience, as 12 teachers had more than 21 years of experience. Most teachers had a high degree (10 teachers), which is mandatory by Portuguese Law. The subjects taught were: (a) mathematics in the 3rd cycle of basic education (CBE) or in secondary teaching (3 teachers); (b) physics and chemistry in the 3rd CBE or in secondary teaching (6 teachers); (c) nature sciences in the 3rd CBE (1 teacher); and (d) mathematics and nature sciences in the 2nd CBE (6 teachers) (Marques & Pombo, 2021a).

The workshop trainers were the authors of this study and have several years of experience as science education researchers. The workshop created opportunities for teacher trainees and researchers to collaborate in the development of high-quality open educational resources for STEM learning, accessed through the EduPARK app. The quality and relevance of the resources were supported by the integration of recommendations from the literature on effective teaching and learning methodologies, particularly when seeking to take advantage of mobile and AR potential. The produced resources (questions and associated images, audios and videos) are articulated with the National Science Curriculum and grounded in real educational contexts.

The workshop involved several activities, including group discussion and reflection on mobile learning, AR in education, and game-based learning; exploring games with the EduPARK app, as if teachers were students, in the Aveiro green park; and collaborative design and development of quiz questions and resources for a new EduPARK game, in two cycles of refinement. The created game is directed at 2nd and 3rd CBE students and it is available through the EduPARK app, in Portuguese.

The process of questions development was conducted in work groups (four groups of three teacher trainees and two groups of two). In the first cycle of game co-creation, trainees planned a first version of quiz questions, and associated resources, using a digital word document template. They were supported by the workshop trainers for ideas generation and suitability checks. A minimum of five quiz questions was asked for each group. For each question, the groups:

a) identified the curricular framing - subject(s), schoolyear, topics and aimed learning;
b) selected one point of interest in the park that offers learning opportunities under the identified curricular framing;
c) formulated one introduction to the question (optional), the question itself, up to four short answer options (indicating the correct one(s)), and differentiated feedback to the answer, whether is it correct or incorrect;
d) identified the resources to be explored under the question - previously developed AR contents, videos, audios and/or images;
e) predicted the level of difficulty for the target school level; and
f) attributed points, in case of correct answer.

Followed a presentation of the developed work (quiz questions and respective educational resources) by each work group. The presentation was followed by a big group discussion, for formative evaluation and suggestion of improvements, from other teacher trainees and trainers. The best three questions of each group were selected through a voting system where each participant anonymously selected the best question in each group and justified his/her opinion.

In the second cycle of co-creation, the evaluation and comments collected from the big group discussion were taken into consideration to improve the three most voted questions. Each group delivered an improved version of their work, to be compiled by teacher trainees into a functional and coherent game accessed through the EduPARK app. A test of the co-created game was conducted. For that, teachers explored their game in the park, using mobile devices and took notes in order to propose new improvement suggestions. A new big group discussion allowed conducting the final refinement of the game.

Finally, each group presented a final version of their planning document, with the group quiz questions and educational resources, for assessment, as part of the requirements for obtaining a continuous teacher training certificate.

2.2 Data Collection and Analysis

In this qualitative study a hybrid process of inductive and deductive content analysis (Bardin, 2016; Xu & Zammit, 2020) was used to interpret raw data: quiz questions (introduction, question formulation, answer options, associated resources and feedback) planned by six groups of teacher trainees. Four groups produced five questions, as required; one group produced six questions; and another group produced twelve questions. A document compiling the first five questions of each group was created, to keep balanced input from each group. It includes a total of 30 questions. Each question received a code similar to the following, G1.1, meaning that this was the first question of G1.

The analysis approach integrated data-driven codes with theory-driven ones based on the revised Bloom's Taxonomy (Anderson et al., 2001). In a first step, an inductive analysis was conducted, which originated a first version of question categories and their description. In this initial analysis, each question was read and the associated educational resources were analyzed, to produce tentative categories, drawing on the data and bearing in mind the aim of the study. In a second phase, the categories were revised and organized according to the revised Bloom's Taxonomy, with the different cognitive levels. The coding process for each category was manually conducted simultaneously by two researchers, who are also the authors of this paper, through a peer debriefing process.

3. RESULTS AND DISCUSSION

This section presents and discusses the system for classification of questions (Table 1) that resulted from the analysis of the 30 questions produced by 14 in-service teachers, in groups, which were integrated in a mobile quiz game with AR contents in the EduPARK app to be played in an urban green park, in the context of a 50h training course. Overall, the results indicate that teachers developed questions that, in the learner point of view, fall in the lower levels of Bloom's Revised Taxonomy, namely Remember, Understand, Apply and Analyze.

Results reveal that the most frequent type of question produced by the teachers required "Direct application" of contents already known to real situations (10 questions) and was produced by all but one group, revealing that most teachers acknowledge the importance of this type of question. An example question is about a structure delimited by marble walls near by a statue in the park, representing a geometric figure formed by a rectangle and a semi-circle. The students are asked to select the correct option that allows them to calculate the figure's area. In the feedback a figure is presented. It explains the figure is composed of two geometric figures and how the area is calculated for each one. The result is the sum of the two figure's areas. Hence, this type of question is framed in engaging in problems/projects with real-world relevance, contributing to authentic experiences, promoting engagement and motivation to learn and better equipping learners to succeed in college, careers, and adulthood (Reeves et al., 2002). Moreover, as school content is related with real world places, objects and situations, games with this type of questions may engage students emotionally, which, according to Marfisi-Schottman and George (2014), has positive effects on engagement and memory, promoting situated cognition and authentic learning.

Table 1. System for classification of questions for mobile learning games with AR and frequency of questions in each questions category

Bloom's Taxonomy	Questions category	Description of questions category	Frequency	Id Questions
Remember - recall facts and basic concepts	Consolidation	The question mobilizes information already covered at school.	8	G1.3, G2.4, G3.1, G3.2, G4.1, G4.4, G5.2, G6.4
Understand - explain ideas and concepts	Observation	The question requires the user to observe the surroundings.	4	G1.5, G4.3, G4.5, G5.3
Apply - use information in new situations	Direct application	The question requires mobilizing information already covered at school to use in a real and specific situation.	10	G2.2, G2.5, G3.3, G4.2, G5.1, G5.4, G6.1, G6.2, G6.3, G6.5
	Selection of information	The question requires the exploration of AR contents, videos, audios or images and selection of the information needed.	4	G1.1, G1.4, G2.1, G.5.5
Analyze - draw connections among ideas	Relation of new information	The question requires relating new information from different origins (e.g. from the question introduction and from the AR content).	4	G1.2, G2.3, G3.4, G3.5

The second most frequent type of question prompted the mobilization of information expected to have been already covered at school, in a "Consolidation" approach (8 questions) and was produced by all groups. Once more this type of question was considered relevant by in-service teachers. An example of a "Consolidation" question starts with the fact: "The mallard is a constant presence in the Park's lake. The male and female have different colors. Click on the video icon". The video shows both male and female mallard individuals and describes their main physical differences. The question is: "Physical differences (feather color, size…) between male and female are related to…" Four options are given and students are supposed to already know from previous experiences that physical differences are related to reproduction. In the feedback it is explained that these differences (e.g., the male's attractive colors) increase the chance of mating. The relevance of constructive and motivational feedback is also pointed out by Marfisi-Schottman and George (2014), who acknowledged it can provide engagement in the game, and most of all, it can boost pedagogical benefits.

In three of the other types of questions were included four questions each: i) "Observation", which requires the user to observe specific features of the surroundings to understand phenomena, and it is associated to the Understand category of the Bloom's Revised Taxonomy; ii) "Selection of information", requiring the exploration of AR contents, videos, audios or images that help to answer correctly the question, and is related to Apply in Bloom's revised Taxonomy, where it is important to select and use information in new situations; and iii) "Relation of new information", when it requires relating new information from different origins (e.g. from the question introduction and the AR content), linked to Analyze in Bloom's Revised Taxonomy, where it is needed to make connections among different ideas.

An example of "Observation" question is one where it is mandatory to observe the birds in the lake to answer the number of such populations in that habitat, linking students' surroundings with curricular contents. It is worth noting that one of the features claimed in the literature as interesting in location-based mobile games, the mobility to go out of the classroom to explore nature (Edmonds & Smith, 2016), necessarily involves observation. And, notably, half of the teacher groups took advantage of the mobility allowed by mobile devices to promote situated learning, by creating observation questions, turning learning into a personal and engaging experience (idem).

Finally, "Information selection" and "Relation of new information" questions were created by half of the teacher groups. These types of questions require students to go through multimedia resources (including AR contents), as advised by Edmonds and Smith (2017). The latter type of question requires a higher cognitive level, as students not only need to select information from different media supports (Apply level in Bloom's Revised Taxonomy), but also have to relate different information from distinct origins (Analyze level in Bloom's Revised Taxonomy). Moreover, AR contents also scaffolds learning through the exploration of real objects in real contexts, a feature relevant in authentic learning environments (Reeves et al., 2002). This is only possible as the EduPARK game is not just a quiz game, but it has other complementary resources supporting students' learning (Pombo & Marques, 2020).

When observing the type of questions produced by each group of teachers, we found that G6 produced questions in 2 categories, G3 and G4 produced in 3 categories, and G1, G2 and G5 produced in 4 categories. Hence, although some teachers already produced questions classified in several categories, there are teachers that still produced questions in only 2 or 3 categories. This result seems to indicate that, maybe unconsciously, some teachers intended to diversify the type of questions, which is also a concern when they create other resources, such as instruments of assessment (e.g., written tests). However, this is not true for all. The authors' expectation is that all teachers will be able to create more diversified questions at the cognitive level, through the use of this classification system.

In a final reflection, the highest levels of Bloom's Revised Taxonomy, Evaluate and Create, seem achievable only in the process of creation of questions, and not while playing the game. For example, the Evaluate level was observable only during the process of game creation, when teachers selected the best question produced by each group and justified their opinion, through a voting system. Also, the Create level was identified during the process of question creation, which implies not just formulating a question, but also creating a feedback system and a set of other media resources that complement the question. It also implies considering the question suitability to a determined point of interest in the park, offering learning opportunities under a certain curricular framing.

4. CONCLUSION

Mobile learning games with AR in the outdoors should be spread among all learning levels, as it can mobilize various types of skills and consolidate learning in different environments. These games also contribute with positive effects on engagement and memory (Marfisi-Schottman & George, 2014), as they may promote situated cognition and authentic learning in formal and non-formal education, and also extend the way students experience learning from the environment and with each other (Edmonds & Smith, 2016). In addition, quiz games combined with treasure hunting allows the construction of new concepts by players in a much funnier, interactive and dynamic way (Sampaio et al., 2012).

This work highlights the importance of providing specialized training in supporting teachers to use mobile apps integrating quiz games, motivating them to include mobile outdoor learning in their teaching practices. More importantly, these initiatives empower teachers with the proper skills to collaboratively design and create mobile learning games. The system for classification of questions, developed in this work, is intended to increase teachers' consciousness regarding the creation of a higher variety of questions, as well as its associated feedback and resources. This way, they can prompt different cognitive levels, according to Bloom's Revised Taxonomy (Anderson et al, 2001), and promote higher quality game-based learning in teaching practices. For example, this system supports teachers becoming aware that questions from the categories "Direct application" and "Consolidation" are particularly suitable for integration with formal assessments in the classroom, to provide evidence of the learning gains from playing mobile quiz games with AR contents in real outdoor situations.

This study has a small number of participants, which allows a deeper analysis to uncover key aspects of the study more clearly (Merriam & Tisdell, 2015). Hence, no statistical generalization is intended. The aim was to develop a first version of a classification system to be used in future research. This should analyze the process of game co-creation by teachers in new training initiatives, where they are familiar with this system for classification of questions in the task of game creation, to triangulate with the current study.

ACKNOWLEDGEMENT

This work is financially supported by National Funds through FCT – Fundação para a Ciência e a Tecnologia, I.P., under the project UIDB/00194/2020. The EduPARK project was funded by FEDER funds through the COMPETE 2020-Operational Programme for Competitiveness and Internationalisation (POCI), and by Portuguese funds through FCT, Grant N. POCI-01-0145-FEDER-016542. The work of the second author is funded by national funds (OE), through University of Aveiro, in the scope of the framework contract foreseen in numbers 4, 5 & 6 of article 23 of Decree-Law 57/2016 of August 29 changed by Law 57/2017 of July 19.

REFERENCES

Anderson, L.W., Krathwohl, D.R., Airasian, P.W., Cruikshank, K.A., Mayer, R.E., Pintrich, P.R., Raths, J. and Wittrock, M.C., 2001. *A Taxonomy for Learning, Teaching, and Assessing: A Revision of Bloom's Taxonomy of Educational Objectives.*

Bianchi-Berthouze, N., 2013. Understanding the Role of Body Movement in Player Engagement. *Human Computer Interactions*, Vol. 28, No. 1, pp. 40–75.

Burr, V., 2015. *Social Constructionism.* (3rd ed.). Routledge/Taylor & Francis Group.

Daniel, S., Harrap, R. and Power, M., 2009. Getting into Position: Serious Gaming in Geomatics, In T. Bastiaens, J. Dron & C. Xin (Eds.), Proceedings of E-Learn 2009, Government, Healthcare, and Higher Education (pp. 213-219). Vancouver, Canada: AACE. https://www.learntechlib.org/primary/p/32463/

Dondlinger, M.J., 2007. Educational video game design: A review of the literature. *Journal of Applied Educational Technology*, Vol. 4, No. 1, pp. 21–31.

Edmonds, R. and Smith, S., 2017. From playing to designing: Enhancing educational experiences with location-based mobile learning games. *Australasian Journal of Educational Technology*, 33(6). 41.

Hammersley, M., 2013. *What is Qualitative Research?* London and New York: Bloomsburry

Johnson, L., Adams Becker, S., Estrada, V. and Freeman, A., 2015. *NMC Horizon Report: 2015 Higher Education Edition.* Austin, TX: The New Media Consortium.

Kivunja, C. and Kuyini, A.B., 2017. Understanding and Applying Research Paradigms in Educational Contexts. *International Journal of Higher Education*, 6(5), 26–41. https://doi.org/10.5430/ijhe.v6n5p26

Marfisi-Schottman, I. and George, S., 2014. Supporting Teachers to Design and Use Mobile Collaborative Learning Games. *International Association for Development of the Information Society*, ICML, Madrid, Spain.

Marques, M.M. and Pombo, L., 2021a. Teachers' experiences and perceptions regarding mobile augmented reality games: A case study of a teacher training. Proceedings of INTED2021 Conference (pp. 8938–8947). IATED. https://blogs.ua.pt/cidtff/wp-content/uploads/2021/03/87544.pdf

Marques, M.M. and Pombo, L., 2021b. The Impact of Teacher Training Using Mobile Augmented Reality Games on Their Professional Development. *Education Sciences*, 11(8), 404. https://doi.org/10.3390/educsci11080404

Merriam, S.B. and Tisdell, E.J., 2015. *Qualitative Research: A Guide to Design and Implementation* (4th ed.). Wiley.

Pombo, L. and Marques, M.M., 2019. Learning with the Augmented Reality EduPARK Game-Like App: Its Usability and Educational Value for Primary Education. *Intelligent Computing.* CompCom 2019. Advances in Intelligent Systems and Computing (Vol. 997, pp. 113–125). Springer. https://doi.org/10.1007/978-3-030-22871-2_9

Pombo, L. and Marques, M.M., 2021. Guidelines for Teacher Training in Mobile Augmented Reality Games: Hearing the Teachers' Voices. *Education Sciences*, 11(10), 597. https://doi.org/10.3390/EDUCSCI11100597

Pombo, L. and Marques, M.M., 2020. The potential educational value of mobile augmented reality games: The case of EduPARK app. *Education Sciences*, 10(10), 287. https://doi.org/10.3390/educsci10100287

Pombo, L., Marques, M.M., Afonso, L., Dias, P. and Madeira, J., 2019. Evaluation of a mobile augmented reality game application as an outdoor learning tool. *IJMBL*, 11(4), 59–79. https://doi.org/10.4018/IJMBL.2019100105

Reeves, T.C., Herrington, J. and Oliver, R., 2002. Authentic activities and online learning. In T. Herrington (Ed.) *Research and Development in higher education: Quality conversations.* Vol. 25 (pp. 562–567). Hammondville: HERDSA.

Sampaio, B., Morgado, C. and Barbosa, F., 2012. Collaborative quiz game developed with Epik. IADIS *International Conference on Cognition and Exploratory Learning in Digital Age*, pp. 308–301.

Sindre, G., Natvig, L. and Jahre, M., 2009. Experimental Validation of the Learning Effect for a Pedagogical Game on Computer Fundamentals. *IEEE Transactions on Education*, Vol. 52, No. 1, pp 10–18. doi: 10.1109/TE.2007.914944

Xu, W. and Zammit, K., 2020. Applying Thematic Analysis to Education: A Hybrid Approach to Interpreting Data in Practitioner Research. *International Journal of Qualitative Methods*, Vol 19.

LEARNING COMMUNICATION WITH AUTISTIC PEOPLE WITH A MOBILE SERIOUS ROLE-PLAYING GAME

Dixit Bharatkumar Patel[1], Xavian Ogletree[1] and Yong Pei
Department of Computer Science and Engineering, Wright State University, Dayton, Ohio 45435, USA

ABSTRACT

While serious role-play games have been developed for individuals with autism spectrum disorders to learn social interactions and emotions, there is a lack of role-playing games that teach people without autism the necessary communication skills to engage and interact effectively with autistic people. In this research, we present a mobile serious role-playing game as a comprehensive expert-guided experiential and cognitive learning tool, consisting of instruction, play, review, and discussion, that helps achieve enhanced learning outcomes while enabling an independent-learning workflow. By making it available for both iOS and Android devices, it has the potential to help spread the awareness of autism and help create a more inclusive environment for autistic people at schools, universities, and communities.

KEYWORDS

Mobile Learning, Experiential Learning, Role Play, Serious Games, Autism Spectrum Disorder, Virtual Reality

1. INTRODUCTION

More than 200,000 students with autism spectrum disorders (ASD) will arrive on campuses around the United States over the next decade (Borrell, 2018; Pinder-Amaker, 2014)). However, periods of transition are particularly difficult for high school students with ASD entering a postsecondary setting (Wei, et al, 2013). Providing appropriate support to these students is essential to assisting students to achieve a higher quality of life, increased productivity, positive social interactions inside and outside of the classroom, and decreased reliance on subsequent or perpetual disability services post-graduation (Geller, et al, 2009; Goldstein, et al, 2008). Programs such as The RASE initiative (Rando, et al, 2016) provide transition coaching services that team a coach with a student with an autism diagnosis to assist the adjustment period from high school to college. The transition coaches are experienced juniors, seniors, or graduate students without an autism diagnosis; and, if being properly trained and sufficiently prepared, they can effectively help students with ASD in key competency areas: time management and organization, resiliency, advocacy, social skill development and study skills/technology use (Rando, et al, 2016).

However, training student coaches and other care providers to engage with clients with ASD is challenging. For example, the coaches have been socialized throughout their lives to be especially polite and verbose when dealing with a topic that is difficult to discuss (for example – hygiene concerns or feedback on a problem). On the other hand, students with ASD prefer direct, action-based statements that are clear indicators of the expected behavior on their part (Milestones, 2021), such as "I need you to take a shower every day. You can choose the time, but it must be once a day". Another example is the need for a coach to engage in open-ended questions than a yes or no answer with the client, but the open question also has to be clear and not too broad. For example, it is better to say, "Tell me about one thing you are particularly proud of from high school." versus "Do you like Sci-Fi shows?" or "What do you do for fun?". The first is a yes or no answer and the second is too general. As is the case in many social, behavioral, and health science education, it requires much role-play or real-play practice along with expert guidance for transition coaches to make improvements in their proficiency. Unfortunately, due to the limited availability of the professional standardized client and instructional experts, transition coaches currently have very limited opportunities to practice in an

[1] (Equal Contribution)

expert-guided role-play training session. As a result, because of inadequate training and a limited number of prepared candidates, these proven interventions, such as transition coaching services, are under-utilized in practices.

2. APPROACH

The primary aim and contribution of this research are to harness the latest advances in mobile computing, serious games, augmented/virtual reality (AR/VR), and human-computer teaming technologies to address the current challenge of coaching the transition coach to effectively interacting, engage, and build rapport with their student clients with ASD. By uniquely harnessing the built-in multi-modal capabilities of widely available and cost-effective iOS and Android smart devices, we have created and demonstrated a fully immersive first-person view experiential learning-based mobile serious role-play game through which the transition coach candidates can interact with the virtual standardized client with ASD under the guidance of a virtual expert instructor. Furthermore, our mobile serious game approach provides a more objective, accurate, and continuous assessment of trainees' performance in real-time, without having to demand a potentially prohibitive amount of time and effort from the human expert trainers. The improved assessment of individual performance has the potential to provide evidence for the expert instructors to quickly modify specific exercises to maximize training outcome and scalability by identifying each individual's progress and needs, thus supporting the more efficient evidence-based training curriculum.

2.1 Related Serious Role-Playing Games for Autism

Serious role-playing games provide a user experiential learning of the targeted skills and allow practices of a wide range and flexible combination of skill sets and scenarios without incurring potentially prohibitive costs and risks of real plays (Othlinghaus-Wulhorst, et al, 2020). It has been of particular interest and benefits for the training of social skills (Michael, et al, 2006; Daniau, 2016; Zheng, et al, 2021).

Serious role-playing games have also been created and used to support the social skill development of individuals with autism spectrum disorders (ASD) (Tang, et al, 2019; Kokol, et al, 2020; Grossard, et al, 2017; Wouters, et al, 2013). These serious games aim to teach social interactions and emotions to autistic people. However, there is a lack of such role-playing games in the market to help teach people without autism the necessary communication skills to interact effectively with autistic people.

3. DESIGNS

In this research, we aim to design and create a mobile serious role-playing game that encourages and enables everyone to (i.) learn and understand the behaviors of autistic people; (ii.) improve their communication skills to interact with them; and (iii.) be able to easily access the training using mobile devices, such as smartphones, tablets, iPads, etc.

3.1 Skill Acquisition Goals

In the current version of the game, we focus on helping the learner to acquire two important skills when interacting with autistic people:

- using direct, action-based communications.
- dealing with the nonverbal behaviors that could potentially interfere with the ongoing conversation.

3.2 Enabling Technologies

In this section, we will discuss the related technologies that help enable effective and efficient virtual role-playing.

3.2.1 High-Fidelity Virtual Character

Particularly, we investigate the level of hologram fidelity required to facilitate a smooth integration of Alice, the virtual character with ASD as shown in Figure 1, in a real-world setup to simulate a realistic encounter between the learner and Alice. The High-fidelity hologram may lead to a better perception of the virtual character in a static mode but at the cost of high computation that may produce potentially prohibitively long delays and result in degraded perception in a dynamic mode where contents need to be constantly updated on a mobile device. A particular adaptation effort is made to find the right balance to maximize the usability of these devices.

3.2.2 Embedded Virtual Expert to Guide and Review the Role-Plays

As pointed out by Zheng et al. (2021), serious games may improve social skills when used alongside in-person discussion. Serious role-playing games create a complex learning situation that warrants instructional support to facilitate experiential learning. Thus, serious games need to be used in tandem with instruction, play, review, discussion, and debriefing to help learners achieve the learning outcomes (Eng, 2021).

In this research, we have designed, created, and embedded Dr. Erika Parker, a virtual expert instructor, into the game flow. Figure 2 illustrates a review and discussion session led by the expert instructor to help the learner understand the difference between indirect speech and direct speech; moreover, how to convert an indirect speech statement to its corresponding direct speech statement. Such review, discussion, and guidance are made available through the entire training to help enhance the cognitive learning process on top of the experiential learning provided by the role-plays. The learner has the option to request more examples and discussion if needed. Therefore, it provides a comprehensive tool that enables the users with totally independent learning.

Figure 1. Alice with ASD

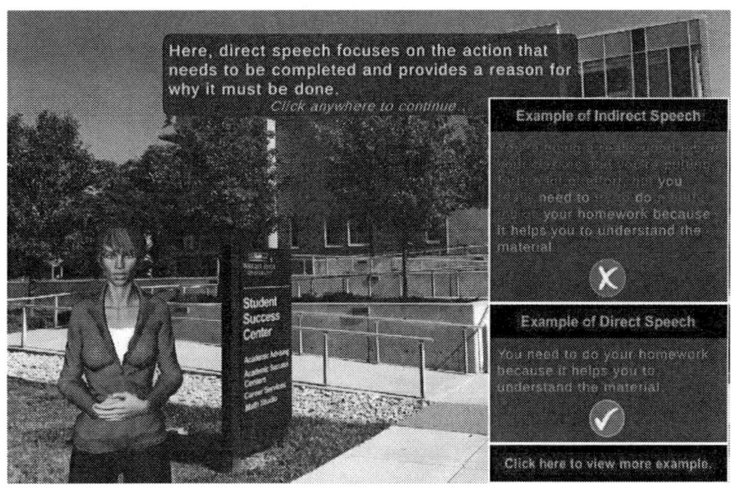

Figure 2. Prof. Erika Parker, the Embedded Virtual Expert, Provides Case Reviews via a Virtual Whiteboard

3.2.3 Mobile Game available for both iOS and Android Devices

A learner can download this serious role-playing app from the App Store (iOS) or Google Play (Android). The simulation can be completed at any time or place on a tablet or smartphone. These mobile devices, when coupled with the cloud provided services, provide multi-modal capabilities in addition to hologram visuals, such as voice, video, text, speech recognition, eye/gaze/attention tracking, or gestures to support multi-modal learning contents and interactions and multimodal assessments to maximize the learning outcomes. Therefore, it makes it significantly easier to access when compared to other delivery methods, such as VR goggles, laptop/desktop computers, etc. Thus, we believe it will make it easier for people without Autism to access resources and help that is required to learn how to communicate with autistic people.

4. DEMO AND RESULTS

We have designed, created, and released a serious role-playing game that demonstrates the feasibility and robustness of such a mobile computing enabled independent learning/training solution. The following demo results in present samples and offers validations for our design.

4.1 Preview of the Game

When starting the application, the user will be welcomed by Prof. Erika Parker, the virtual expert instructor as shown in Figure 3, who will guide and facilitate the entire training as the instructor of the contents, the reviewer of the plays, and the facilitator of the discussions. It is followed by the introduction of the learning objectives of this serious role-playing game. Then Alice, the standardized client with ASD and an 18 years old new college freshman, is introduced as shown in Figure 4.

Figure 3. The expert instructor - Prof. Erika Parker

Figure 4. Introduction of Alice

4.2 Direct, Action-based Communication

In this part of the game, the learner is taking the role of a college resident assistant who will meet with Alice in the office as shown in Figure 5. Scripted role-plays, as shown in Figure 6, are particularly designed and adopted to create a rich learning experience on how to communicate effectively in direct and action-based communication when interacting with autistic people. The learner can try different communication styles/options and then observe the corresponding response of Alice, thus supporting the cognitive learning process of the learner. To further enahance the learning, Prof. Erika Parker will provide an immediate review of the plays and facilitate the focused discussion on the communication strategy. Further roleplays may follow if needed based on the learner's performance and progress as shown in Figure 7 and 8.

Figure 5. Direct Communication Training Module

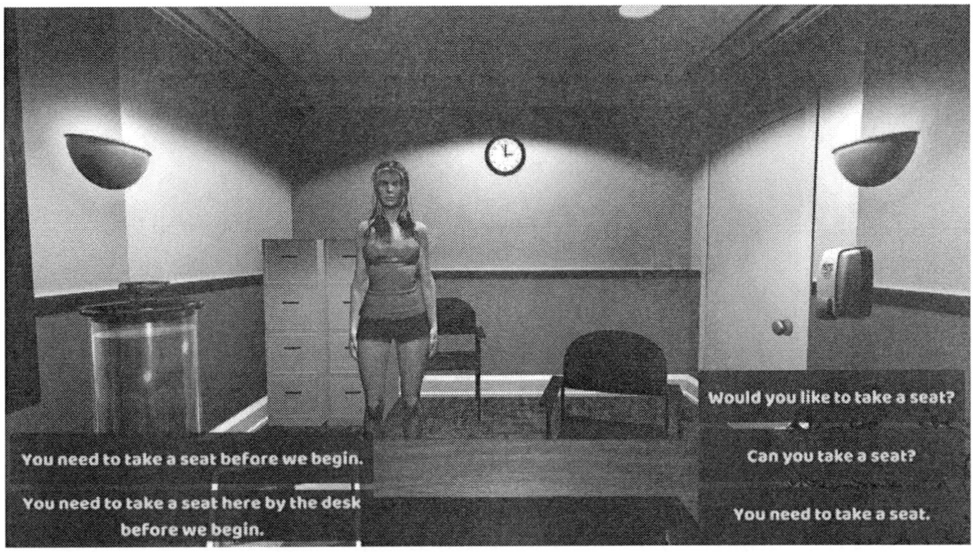

Figure 6. Scripted Direct Communication Role-Plays

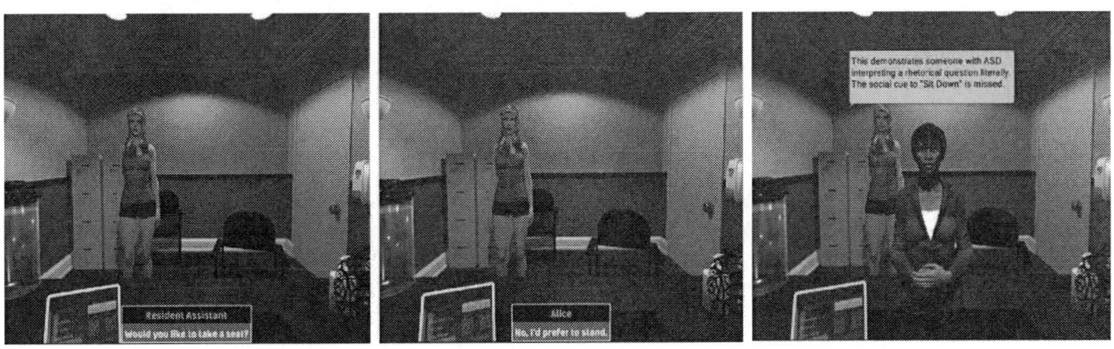

Figure 7. Sample Role-Plays and Reviews in the Direct Communication Module

Figure 8. Sample Role-Plays and Reviews in the Direct Communication Module

4.3 Dealing with Nonverbal Interfering Behaviors during Conversation

In this part of the game, the learner is again taking the role of a college resident assistant who will meet with Alice in the office as shown in Figure. 9. The game takes full advantage of the graphical capabilities of a mobile device to provide the high-fidelity presentation of a range of subtle Nonverbal Interfering Behaviors for the role-plays. Scripted role-plays, as shown in Figure 10, are designed to practice how to deal effectively with such Nonverbal Interfering Behaviors in order to ensure a smooth and engaging conversation. The learner can try different intervention options and then observe the corresponding response of Alice. Prof. Erika Parker will provide an immediate review of the plays and a focused discussion on the intervention strategy. Further roleplays may follow if needed based on the learner's performance and progress as shown in Figure 11 and 12.

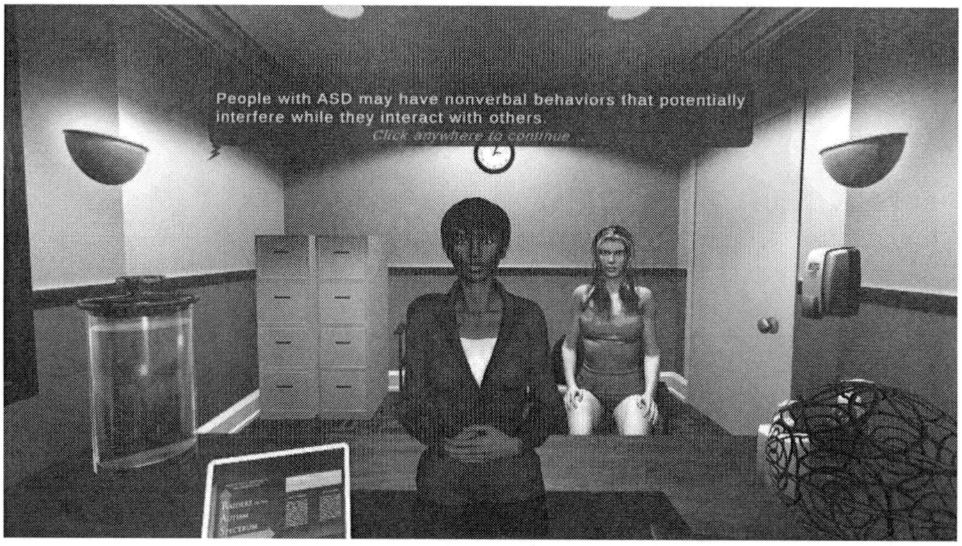

Figure 9. Nonverbal Interfering Behaviors Training Module

Figure 10. Scripted Nonverbal Interfering Behaviors Role-Plays

Figure 11. Sample Role-Plays and Reviews in the Nonverbal Interfering Behaviors Module

Figure 12. Sample Role-Plays and Reviews in the Nonverbal Interfering Behaviors Module

5. CONCLUSION

An effective and practical solution that helps people to independently learn and practice with ease on how to communicate effectively with autistic people will significantly improve learning efficiency and outcome, and more importantly, help spread the awareness of autism and encourage more people to understand, engage and interact effectively with them. In this research, we have successfully designed and developed a mobile serious role-playing game as a learning tool that harnesses the latest advances in mobile computing, serious game, virtual reality, and human-computer teaming. It resembles a comprehensive expert-guided experiential and cognitive learning process consisting of instruction, play, review, and discussion that help achieve enhanced learning outcomes via an independent-learning workflow. The release of the game for both iOS and Android devices further expands the potential reach of this learning tool and helps spread the awareness of autism and help create an inclusive environment at schools, universities, and communities.

Future works may consider the use of AR and AI capabilities to provide richer multimodal content and assessment. A trial study may also be warranted to establish a comprehensive understating of how such serious role-play games can help people improve communication with autistic people.

ACKNOWLEDGEMENT

We appreciate the contributions to this project by Heather M. Rando of the Raiders on the Autism Spectrum Excelling (RASE) program at Wright State University.

REFERENCES

Brendan Borrell, (2018), How colleges can prepare for students with autism, 23 MAY 2018, https://www.spectrumnews.org/features/deep-dive/colleges-can-prepare-students-autism/

Daniau S. The Transformative Potential of Role-Playing Games—: From Play Skills to Human Skills. Simulation & Gaming. 2016;47(4):423-444. doi:10.1177/1046878116650765

Eng, D. (2021, September 28). Playing serious games. Retrieved December 31, 2021, from https://www.universityxp.com/blog/2021/9/28/playing-serious-games

Geller, L. L., & Greenberg, M. (2009). Managing the transition process from high school to college and beyond: challenges for individuals, families, and society. Social Work Mental Health, 8, 92-116.

Goldstein, G., Allen, D. N., Minshew, N. J., Williams, D. L., Volkmar, D. L., & Klin, A. (2008). The structure of intelligence in children and adults with high functioning autism. Neuropsychology, 22, 301-312.

Grossard, Charline & Grynspan, Ouriel & Serret, Sylvie & Jouen, Anne-Lise & Bailly, Kevin & Cohen, David. (2017). Serious games to teach social interactions and emotions to individuals with autism spectrum disorders (ASD). Computers & Education. 113. 10.1016/j.compedu.2017.05.002.

Kokol P, Vošner HB, Završnik J, Vermeulen J, Shohieb S, Peinemann F. Serious Game-based Intervention for Children with Developmental Disabilities. Curr Pediatr Rev. 2020;16(1):26-32. doi: 10.2174/1573396315666190808115238. PMID: 31393252.

Michael, D., and Chen, S. (2006). Serious Games: Games that Educate, Train, and Inform. Boston, MA: Thomson Course Technology.

Milestones Autism Resources, Best Communication Practices for Interacting with Autistic People, https://www.milestones.org/get-started/for-community-at-large/interacting-with-autistic-people. Accessed on December 31, 2021.

Othlinghaus-Wulhorst, Julia & Hoppe, H.. (2020). A Technical and Conceptual Framework for Serious Role-Playing Games in the Area of Social Skill Training. Frontiers in Computer Science. https://doi.org/10.3389/fcomp.2020.00028.

P. Wouters and H. van Oostendorp, "A meta-analytic review of the role of instructional support in game-based learning," Computers & Education, vol. 60, no. 1, pp. 412–425, 2013.

Pinder-Amaker, S. (2014). Identifying the unmet needs of college students on the autism spectrum. Harvard Review of Psychiatry, 22, 125-137.

Rando, H., Huber, M. and Oswald, G. (2016). An academic coaching model intervention for college students on the autism spectrum. Journal of Postsecondary Education and Disability, 29(3), 257-262.

Tang JSY, Falkmer M, Chen NTM, Bölte S, Girdler S. Designing a Serious Game for Youth with ASD: Perspectives from End-Users and Professionals. J Autism Dev Disord. 2019 Mar;49(3):978-995. doi: 10.1007/s10803-018-3801-9. PMID: 30377883.

Wei, X., Yu, J., Shattuck, P., McCracken, M., & Blackorby, J. (2013). Science, technology, engineering, and mathematics (STEM) participation among college students with an autism spectrum disorder. Journal of Autism and Developmental Disorders, 43, 1,539-1,546.

Zheng LR, Oberle CM, Hawkes-Robinson WA, Daniau S. Serious Games as a Complementary Tool for Social Skill Development in Young People: A Systematic Review of the Literature. Simulation & Gaming. 2021;52(6):686-714. doi:10.1177/10468781211031283

LEVERAGING SMARTPHONE AFFORDANCES FOR EFL EMERGENCY REMOTE TEACHING

Peter Ilic
University of Aizu, Aizu-Wakamatsu, Fukushima, Japan

ABSTRACT

This study will benefit educators, curriculum developers, and researchers interested in the affordance of mobile ICT for education and especially how smartphones can be leveraged to provide better online learning outcomes for emergency remote teaching. The current global health concerns have forced many educators to rapidly adapt learning materials intended for in-class use to online activities. This research developed from this sudden need to understand how ICT could be efficiently leveraged to create an emergency remote teaching off-site learning environment for EFL learners in Japan. A questionnaire was employed to better understand the learners' degree of smartphone adoption in relation to their EFL collaborative educational activities. The goal was to use an exploratory data analysis technique (biplots) to gain a better insight into the current affordances that the students feel the smartphone offers. This information could then inform the migration of educational materials. The results indicate that during collaborative learning activities, for this sample population, communicating through email/texting was by far the most widespread use of the smartphone. This is followed by the less popular voice communications and internet use. In addition, the results support the idea that students perceive the smartphone as an anytime and anywhere device in the sense that it is carried by them throughout the day. Finally, in the context of the study, students used the smartphone as an electronic dictionary regularly and as an internet information gathering tool.

KEYWORDS

Mobile Learning, Emergency Remote Teaching, Curriculum Design, Biplot Analysis, Collaborative Learning, ICT, EFL

1. INTRODUCTION

The COVID-19 crisis forced a rapid shift away from traditional face-to-face, blended, and hybrid learning experiences to fully off-site learning, so necessitating a forgoing of the usual planning and design (Schultz and Demers, 2020). This emergency remote teaching (ERT) is a temporary shift of instructional delivery to an alternate delivery mode due to crisis circumstances (Hodges et al., 2020). Education that would otherwise be delivered face-to-face or as blended or hybrid courses is migrated to remote teaching during a crisis or emergency. The primary objective is to provide interim access to instruction and instructional supports so it is quick to set up and is reliably available during an emergency or crisis (Hodges et al., 2020). This study developed from this need to understand how Information and Communications Technologies (ICT) could be efficiently leveraged to create an ERT off-site learning environment for English as a Foreign Language (EFL) learners in Japan.

In this study, a questionnaire was employed to better understand the learners' degree of smartphone adoption in relation to their collaborative educational activities. The target technology in this study is the smartphone because it was the one device that the participants all owned and is ubiquitous in Japan (Ilic, 2021). Also, the place of smartphones in education has attracted considerable attention as the technology has matured (Kukulska-Hulme and Viberg, 2018). When asking students to rapidly switch from in-class to off-campus classes, it is essential for educators and administrators to understand the availability of devices that students already have access to or can be provided by the educational institution (Ilic, 2020). With this information on device availability educators may minimize the stress of this migration by utilizing devices to which students are already familiar. While it is beyond the scope of this study to provide a complete answer to the selection of ICTs that can best be incorporated, it does take a small step in that direction by focusing on one of the most common, the smartphone.

The goal was to use an exploratory data analysis technique (biplots) to gain a better insight into the current affordances that the students feel the smartphone offers them in order to aid in the design and migration of the collaborative activities, which will be an essential part of a planned course curriculum for EFL learners. The well-known importance of collaborative activities for language learning (Laurillard, 2009, Stahl et al., 2006) means that ICT affordances, in this case, those of the smartphone, are likely to aid in expanding the learning space beyond the traditional classroom by acting as a bridging tool (Ilic, 2014) that can operate across ever-changing contexts and learning spaces (Pachler, 2010).

A secondary goal was to gain an understanding of the students' relationships to the smartphone technology; this again is to direct the curriculum design as well to give the researcher a clearer image of what the students' everyday relationship is to this technology. With a clearer picture of the students existing digital ecosystem (Ilic, 2020), curriculum designers can better leverage the affordances that students have become accustomed to in their daily lives, so minimizing the impact of classes changing from on-campus to off-campus.

2. METHODOLOGY

2.1 Study Design

The research design is a case study to rapidly investigate the impact of mobile phones on collaborative learning activities in a university setting. The methodology utilized can best be described as a mixed methodology (qualitative and quantitative data), exploratory approach. Qualitative data was collected in the form of open-ended questions through an online questionnaire. The data was coded and converted into quantitative data to be analysed.

The participant sample in this study was drawn from a larger population of undergraduate students studying EFL at a four-year private university in Tokyo, Japan. The students were all between the ages of 18 and 20 years and living in Japan during the study period. There was a total of 94 students (n=94) who volunteered to complete the questionnaire.

2.2 Questionnaire

Since this was an exploratory study, open-ended questions were used to allow a wide range of possible answers from participants (Buckingham and Saunders, 2004). These 12 open-ended questions were used:

1. I always use my mobile phone to ...
2. Most of the time, I use my mobile phone to...
3. I sometimes use my mobile phone to...
4. I rarely use my mobile phone to...
5. I never use my mobile phone to...
6. I use my mobile phone when I...
7. I carry my mobile phone...
8. I use my mobile phone to study by...
9. A good mobile phone is...
10. A good mobile phone can...
11. Unfortunately, mobile phones are...
12. I wish my mobile phone could...
13.

Questions 1 to 6 were intended to gather affordances of smartphones as perceived by the participants, with question 8 directed specifically at study affordances. Question 7 collects evidence of the availability of smartphones. Finally, questions 9 to 12 gather participant impressions of the technology itself.

The answers were collected in English through an online system and classified thematically into codes. In line with the exploratory nature of this study, thematic coding (Ezzy, 2002) was used to allow the coding to emerge from the data as opposed to forcing a predetermined coding. All coding was performed by the researcher. The coding categories and the number of responses for each are included in Table 1. This resulted in 44 coded themes that emerged from these open-ended questions. These themes represent the factors that the students' perceived as related to their smartphone use.

2.3 Biplot Analysis

The data was analyzed using a biplot analysis (Gower and Hand, 1996). A biplot is a dimensional reduction technique that aims to represent both the observations and variables of a matrix of multivariate data on the same plot. There are many variations of biplots, and perhaps the most widely used one is implemented based upon principal component analysis (PCA). The data used is two-mode two-way data. Two-mode data is represented by the questions and the coded answers, each of which represents one mode. Two-way data is two-dimensional matrix data which is the numerical values of how many times each code was given as an answer for each question. For example, in the data in Table 1, *voice* was given as an answer to question 1 eleven times.

The biplot results for questions 1 through 5 are shown in Figure 1, and those for questions 6 through 12 are in Figure 2. The lines radiating out from a center point represent the variables which in this case are the open-ended questions 1 through 12. The numbers represent the coded answers to these questions. Each code and corresponding number can be seen in Table 1. The biplot results in Figure 1 and Figure 2 can tell us three important pieces of information about the data.

The first piece of information the biplot displays is the relationship between the questions as represented by the difference in angle between the lines. The smaller the angle between two lines then the more intimate the relationship or similarity of those variables, which in this case are the questions. For example, in Figure 1, question 1 (variable 1) and question 2 (variable 2) have a closer relationship than do question 1 and question 3. This might be due to the similarity in the term "always" used in question 1 and the term "most of the time" used in question 2.

The second relationship expressed in the biplot is between the questions, again as represented by the lines, and the coded answers represented by the numbers. This relationship is represented by the distance from the coded number on the plot to the center point of the lines. The farther away from the center point of a line that a number appears then the closer the relationship. In Figure 1, the point labeled number 2 is farther away from the center point of line 1 than is number 18. This indicates that code number 2 (email/texting) has a closer relationship to line 1 (question 1) than number 18 (general communications). One way to clearly see the distance is to draw a line from each number down through each line so it crosses at a 90-degree angle. These lines have been added in Figure 1 for numbers 2 and 18 as an example. Now it is clear that number 3 (internet) has a closer relationship to line 3 (question 3) than number 2 (email/texting).

The third piece of information provided by the biplot is the relationship among the coding numbers themselves. This is similar to the traditional principal component plot, where the distance between the numbers represents the relationship. The closer the numbers are, the stronger the relationship they have, or in other words, the more similar they are. Again, looking at Figure 1, it is clear that code 1 (voice) has a much stronger relationship to code 3 (internet) than it does to code 2 (email/texting).

3. RESULTS AND DISCUSSION

The biplot in Figure 1 includes questions 1 to 5, and all 44 coded data items and had a cumulative proportion of 0.57 for component 1, 0.78 for component 2, 0.94 for component 3, 0.97 for component 4, and 1.00 for component 5. Since the biplot process produces a two-dimensional image, we can only see component 1 and component 2. This means that Figure 1 can visually represent 78% of the total data structure. The biplot in Figure 2 includes questions 6 to 12 and all 44 coded data items and has a cumulative proportion of 0.68 for component 2, which means it represents 68% of the total data structure in two dimensions.

In Figure 1, question 1 ("I always use my mobile phone to …") is closely associated with "email/texting" (code 2) and has a much weaker association with "general communication" (code 18) "Email/texting" is also associated with question 2 ("Most of the time, I use my mobile phone to…") but to a slightly smaller degree because the added line crosses the variable line at a closer point to the center point of the lines. Question 3 ("I sometimes use my mobile phone to…") is strongly related to "voice" (code 1) and, to a slightly weaker extent, "internet" (code 3). Question 5 ("I never use my mobile phone to…") is strongly related to "television" (code 8) and "e-money" (code 11).

Considering Figure 2, question 7 ("I carry my mobile phone…") is strongly related to "anytime/anywhere" (code 29), which supports the idea that a smartphone is a ubiquitous tool for these participants. Question 8 ("I use my mobile phone to study by…") is strongly related to "dictionary" (code 14) and "internet" (code 3). "Unknown" (code 44) is also weakly related to this question of the study.

The questionnaire data were analyzed using a biplot which gave three different insights into the data. These included the relationship between the questions themselves, between the coded items and questions, and between the coded items themselves. The results indicate that the affordance of email/texting is by far the most common use of the smartphone, followed distantly by voice communications and internet searches. In addition, the affordance of anytime and anywhere use is indicated by the students carrying it throughout the day. In terms of education, it is used as an electronic dictionary and as an internet search portal which suggests that they are familiar with viewing websites on their smartphones so would transfer to a typical Content Management Systems (CMS) with ease.

The majority of coded terms can be seen in bunches close to the center point of the lines in the biplots. This indicates that they are very similar in that they had little relation to the questionnaire items. In future research, an alternative analysis technique other than biplots will need to be employed to better understand these relationships. But questions 1, 3, 5, 7, and 8 had a significant relationship to item voice, email/texting, internet, TV, e-money, games, audio, dictionary, or anytime/anywhere. This indicates that out of the 12 original questions, only the following five (1, 3, 5, 7, 8) reveal useful information:

1. I always use my mobile phone to …
3. I sometimes use my mobile phone to…
5. I never use my mobile phone to…
7. I carry my mobile phone…
8. I use my mobile phone to study by…

This suggests that a far shorter questionnaire could be used in a future study to gain the same amount of information. Of the five remaining questions, all but question 5 could be seen as asking for the popular affordances of the mobile phone. As mentioned above, these affordances include mobility, communication, and access to information through the internet. Alternatively, question 5 asks for affordances the participants do not associate with smartphones. These affordances include TV, e-money, games, and audio.

Table 1. Student survey results

Bi Plot Codes and Relationship Values													
Code #	*Code Value*	*Q1*	*Q2*	*Q3*	*Q4*	*Q5*	*Q6*	*Q7*	*Q8*	*Q9*	*Q10*	*Q11*	*Q12*
1	Voice	11	10	38	6	0	2	0	0	0	1	0	0
2	Email/Texting	55	39	3	2	2	7	0	1	0	1	1	1
3	Internet	6	26	21	9	5	2	0	34	0	5	0	3
4	Pictures	0	1	15	5	1	1	0	0	1	1	0	1
5	Video	0	0	0	1	1	0	0	0	0	0	0	2
6	Audio	1	4	2	14	8	1	0	4	0	0	0	4
7	Video Call	0	0	0	1	3	0	0	0	0	0	0	0
8	TV	0	1	1	21	17	0	0	0	0	9	0	4
9	Clock	3	4	2	0	0	0	0	0	0	0	0	0
10	E-Ticket	0	0	0	0	0	0	0	0	0	0	1	0
11	E-Money	0	0	2	5	29	0	0	0	0	0	0	0

Code #	*Code Value*	*Q1*	*Q2*	*Q3*	*Q4*	*Q5*	*Q6*	*Q7*	*Q8*	*Q9*	*Q10*	*Q11*	*Q12*
12	Games	0	1	1	11	13	0	0	1	0	0	0	0
13	Navigation	0	0	1	4	2	3	0	1	0	1	0	1
14	Dictionary	0	0	1	2	1	0	0	40	0	0	0	0
15	Schedule	0	0	0	3	2	0	0	0	0	0	0	0
16	Reading	0	0	1	1	0	0	0	0	0	0	0	0
17	Take Notes	1	0	1	1	0	0	0	0	0	0	0	0
18	General Comm.	15	1	1	0	0	20	0	3	0	0	0	0
19	Functions/Apps	0	1	1	4	1	0	0	0	7	15	1	11
20	Expense	0	0	0	0	0	0	0	0	3	0	19	7
21	Photo Size	0	0	0	0	0	0	0	0	7	0	5	4
22	Screen	0	0	0	0	0	0	0	0	0	0	3	0
23	Interface	0	0	0	0	0	0	0	0	0	2	0	2
24	Battery	0	0	0	0	0	3	0	0	3	5	6	9
25	Memory	0	0	0	0	0	0	0	0	0	2	0	2
26	Signal	0	0	0	0	0	0	0	0	0	5	2	5
27	Camara Quality	0	0	0	0	0	0	0	0	1	18	1	4
28	Memory	0	0	0	0	0	0	0	0	0	0	0	1
29	Anytime/Anywhere	0	0	0	0	0	4	87	0	0	1	0	0
30	Home	0	0	0	0	0	0	0	1	0	0	0	0
31	Travel	0	1	0	0	0	11	0	0	0	0	0	0
32	School	0	0	0	0	0	2	5	0	0	0	0	0
33	Free time	0	0	0	0	0	27	0	0	0	0	0	0
34	Emotion	0	0	0	0	0	5	0	0	0	3	0	0
35	Ease of use	0	0	0	0	0	0	0	0	9	3	10	3
36	Useful	0	0	0	0	0	0	0	0	8	4	0	1
37	Personal	0	0	0	0	0	0	0	0	11	0	0	4
38	Physical Quality	0	0	0	0	0	0	0	0	9	9	17	15
39	Speed	0	0	0	0	0	0	0	0	1	6	1	5
40	International	0	0	0	0	0	0	0	0	0	1	0	2
41	Health Danger	0	0	0	0	0	0	0	0	0	0	8	0
42	Overuse	0	0	0	0	0	0	0	0	0	0	11	0
43	Lost	0	0	0	0	0	0	0	0	0	0	2	0
44	Unknown	2	5	3	4	9	6	2	9	34	2	6	3

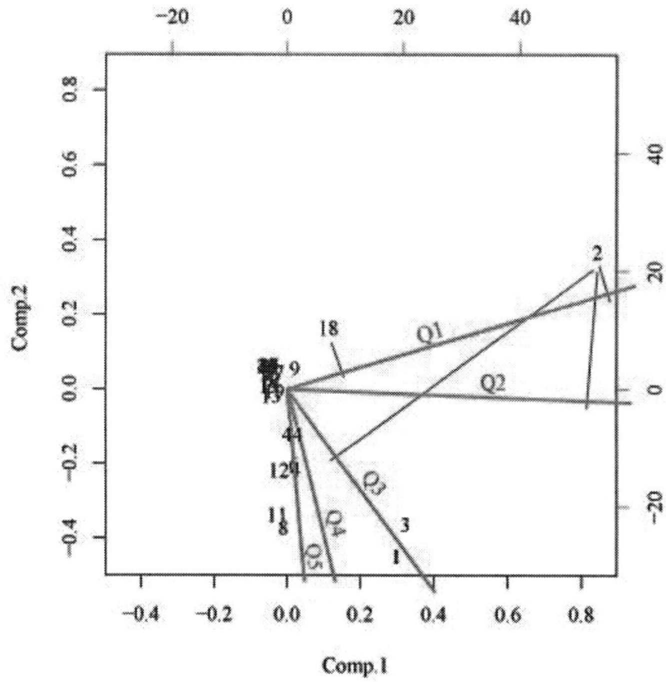

Figure 1. Biplot Questions 1 to 5

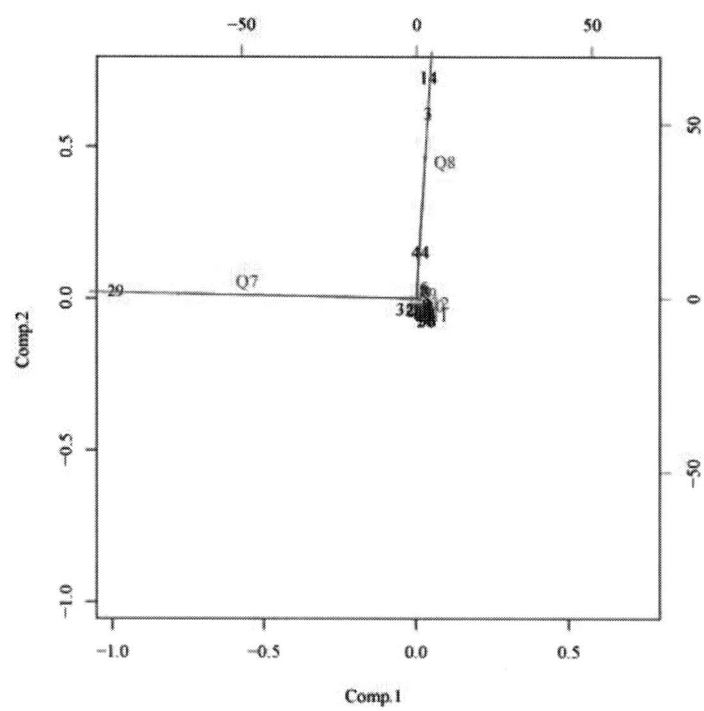

Figure 2. Pilot Study – Biplot Questions 6 to 12

4. CONCLUSION

These results indicate that among this sample population communicating through email/texting is by far the most widespread use of smartphones. This is followed by voice communications and internet use, which are less popular. In addition, the results provide evidence for the common idea that the smartphone is an anytime and anywhere device for the participants in the sense that it is carried throughout the day. Finally, in the context of this study, the smartphone is used as an electronic dictionary regularly and as an internet information gathering tool.

These results can be used by educators faced with ERT deadlines to adapt how the collaborative activities are designed and presented to the students. Designing collaborative activities that utilize the students' already established familiarity with asynchronous email/text communication modes over other modes are supported by these results. Also supported is the idea of providing mobile access to the activities through an internet-based CMS. The near-continuous connection the students have with the mobile phones may make the completion of the activities more likely as the students will not be constrained by time as in a traditional classroom.

The limitations of this study restrict how broadly the results can be applied. The participants are all of similar in age, cultural background, socioeconomic level, and living in Tokyo, Japan, where the communication infrastructure is well established (Ilic, 2021). Future research could expand the sample size and level of diversification to determine whether these findings are broadly geographically applicable. Also, an alternative analysis technique could be employed to investigate the relationship between the codes that were tightly packed into the center of the biplot diagrams in figures 1 and 2. In addition, the ever-changing digital ecosystem of students means this data could quickly become outdated as new affordances become available to students through the next generation of smartphone technologies. With this in mind, a multi-year study of student perceptions of their digital ecosystems and how they change would be another possible direction for further research.

ACKNOWLEDGEMENT

This research was funded by a grant from the Japanese Ministry of Education, Culture, Sports, Science and Technology (MEXT).

REFERENCES

buckingham, A. & Saunders, P. 2004. *The survey methods workbook : from design to analysis,* Cambridge, UK; Malden, MA, Polity.

Ezzy, D. 2002. *Qualitative analysis: Practice and innovation,* London, Routledge.

Gower, J. C. & Hand, D. J. 1996. *Biplots,* London, Chapman & Hall.

Hodges, C. B., Moore, S., Lockee, B. B., Trust, T. & Bond, M. A. 2020. The difference between emergency remote teaching and online learning.

Ilic, P. 2014. The Relationship between Students, Mobile Phones and Their Homework. *In:* Kalz, M., Bayyurt, Y. & Specht, M. (eds.) *Mobile as a Mainstream – Towards Future Challenges in Mobile Learning.* Springer International Publishing.

Ilic, P. Mapping the Digital Ecosystem for Education. 2020 Sixth International Conference on e-Learning (econf), 6-7 Dec. 2020 2020. 275-278.

Ilic, P. 2021. The Challenge of Information and Communications Technology in Education. *SHS Web of Conferences,* 102, 01009.

Kukulska-Hulme, A. & Viberg, O. 2018. Mobile collaborative language learning: State of the art. *British Journal of Educational Technology,* 49, 207-218.

Laurillard, D. 2009. The pedagogical challenges to collaborative technologies1. *International Journal of Computer-Supported Collaborative Learning,* 4, 5-20.

Pachler, N. 2010. *Mobile learning : structures, agency, practices,* New York, Springer.

Schultz, R. B. & Demers, M. N. 2020. Transitioning from Emergency Remote Learning to Deep Online Learning Experiences in Geography Education. *Journal of Geography,* 119, 142-146.

Stahl, G., Koschmann, T. & Suthers, D. 2006. Computer-supported collaborative learning: An historical perspective. *In:* Sawyer, R. K. (ed.) *Cambridge Handbook of the Learning Sciences.* Cambridge,: Cambridge University Press.

GRADUATE EMPLOYABILITY SKILLS DEVELOPMENT THROUGH REFLECTION AND SELF-ASSESSMENT USING A MOBILE APP

Maria Iqbal[1], Lars Jørgen Fredheim[1], Hege Annette Olstad[1], Aisha Abbas[2] and Sobah Abbas Petersen[1]
[1]*Dept. of Computer Science, Norwegian University of Science & Technology, Trondheim, Norway*
[2]*University of the West of Scotland, UK*

ABSTRACT

As university students' journey through their studies, their minds are fixed on a common end goal, that of graduating with flying colours and landing their dream job. They aim for achieving the top grades and focus on their studies, assignments, and exams. In this journey, the students often overlook or underestimate the importance of developing some skills that employers may consider important for their jobs. In this paper, we present a prototype of a mobile application that stimulates university students to reflect upon their experiences and assess the skills they may develop that would help them towards their dream job. The mobile application is designed to support students to recognize employability skills, conduct a self-assessment of their skills, document their skills in terms of the experiences that contributed to the development of the skills and to provide learning resources for improving skills. This work is conducted within the EU ERASMUS+ program.

KEYWORDS

Global Employability Skills, Mobile App, Reflection, Experience, Documentation, Self-Assessment

1. INTRODUCTION

University students are ambitious and envision their future in the light of their dream job once they receive their university degree. Their academic journey comprises of courses, assignments, projects, exams, and performance in the study modules, which is the priority of every student (Bass & Eynon, 2009). During this period, students are usually not able to appreciate the significance of employability skills needed to achieve their dream job and are essential to suffice the requirements of employers. With a focus on the fulfilment of academic requirements, students are usually not aware of employability skills that they acquire during their university (Bass & Eynon, 2009) . Formal education mostly organizes learning content in a way that mirrors the structures of academic disciplines, such as biology, mathematics, and history. Real-life problems and challenges, however, rarely fall neatly into the field of a single discipline. Similarly, assessments are based on what a student has learned rather than the non-directly observable constructs and how a student may apply what has been learned. Consequently, the students have gaps in their cognitive structures, which could affect the way they apply their competences (Cowley, Bedek, Ribeiro, Heikura, & Petersen, 2012). Universities are expected to develop graduates' employability to prepare them for the world of work (Cassidy, 2006; Cedefop, 2017; Suleman, 2017) and employability skills have recently increased in their significance.

Skills are often discussed along with the concepts of competence and knowledge. The meaning of the concept of competence is broader than the concept of skill as competencies incorporates a set of skills together with abilities and knowledge (Kennedy, Hyland , & Ryan, 2009). Employability skills can thus be defined as the transferable skills needed by an individual to perform a task and would make them employable. Along with a good technical understanding and subject knowledge, employers often outline a set of skills they want from an employee. A review of the literature has shown the significance of reflections to bring unknown learning to light especially when supported with evidence (Rolfe et al, 2001). Reflection has been used as a catalyst to invoke skill awareness and the need for skill acquisition in students. The questions identified for the critical reflection in the model by Rolf et al (2001) provides reference to determine components of the skill that focus on reflection and can be saved as evidence. For example, experience is identified as the component of a skill that enables a student to reflect on what part of the experience and include "What did I do?" Or what was the assigned task that has helped me acquire some skills beyond what I study?

The work presented in this paper has been conducted as a part of the European ERASMUS+ project GES App (Global Employability Skills). The main aim of the project is to develop a mobile application to allow students to plan, record and evidence the acquisition and development of Global Employability Skills (GES) throughout their university journey (GES, 2020). Thus, the project includes background studies and requirements elicitation for designing a mobile application that would help to achieve the aim of the project. In this paper, we present the prototype of the mobile application, the GES App, that encourages graduates and university students to identify their employability skills by reflecting upon the process. The design of the GES App aims to facilitate students in their skill identification and assessment processes by providing relevant information about employability skills. The skill assessment process includes documentation of evidence of acquired skill in terms of experiences, artifacts, and references.

The affordances of mobile technologies have long been identified as an effective means of supporting learners in many learning related activities, e.g., context-based and situated learning (Parsons, Thomas, & Wishart, 2016). It also supports students to learn or identify learning related content and activities with prompt accessibility. No doubt, one of the most significant properties of mobile technologies is its ubiquitousness, that it is handy and could be used for bite-sized learning, when the learner has some spare time or is stimulated by their surroundings. Similarly, reflecting upon their global employability skills and documenting them could be done at such a moment, either when a student realizes that they have acquired a new skill or enhanced their level of the skill, or if they simply have some minutes to spare and would like to document their skills. The main goals of the GES App are to support skill identification through reflection, self-assessment in terms of evidence and supporting students to acquire good habits in reflecting upon their employability skills and documenting them regularly. This research aims to address the current gap in research and technologies that support university students in acquiring and documenting employability skills. The main contribution of this work is to underline the significance of employability skills awareness among students and graduates while identifying the process to facilitate them through mobile technology.

The rest of this paper is organized as follows: Section 2 provides an overview of related work; Section 3 describes the method; Section 4 provides the conceptual framework for the GES App and the design of the prototype, and Section 5 discusses and concludes the paper.

2. RELATED WORK

Many students do not consider their GESs until after graduation and focus on their final exam results. In the layers of learning that lead to the results, there are several invisible skills that are relevant for employability, both for the students and employers (Bass & Eynon, 2009). An under-regulated aspect of employability research, according to St Jorre and Oliver (2018), is precisely to get the students involved in their employability skills during education (St Jorre & Oliver, 2018).

Technologies such as the GES App have the potential to make the invisible visible as it includes both reflections and evidence of learning so called artifact, which aligns with previous findings related to electronic portfolios (ePortfolios) (Eynon, Laura, & Török, 2014; Kuh, O'Donnell, & Schneider, 2017; Ring, Waugaman, & Brackett, 2017). Reflections are central to raising awareness around what is learned, but to identify skills, students will have to move into, through, and out of learning experiences (Coulson & Harvey, 2013). Moving into, through, and out of learning experiences is very similar to Rolfe et al.'s (Rolfe et al, 2001) reflective model, an established approach to reflection. The model is based upon three main questions: What? So what? Now what? and for each main question a set of guiding questions. Rolfe et al.'s (2001) reflective model was initially developed for critical self-evaluation for nursing. Since then, the model has been used in several areas, where the guidance questions are adapted to the goal and the purpose of the reflection. Ring, Waugaman and Brackett (2017) adapted Rolfe et al.'s (2001) model in a study where the participants were from the Health Sciences and Biosystems Engineering (Ring, Waugaman, & Brackett, 2017). The study aimed to examine how creating an ePortfolio impacted a student's ability to perform in a job interview. The guidance questions were designed to help the students connect past experiences with present understanding and future use or action.

There is a close link between the reflection model used by Ring, Waugaman and Brackett (2017), and self-assessment, as this type of reflection facilitates self-assessment (Yan & Brown, 2017) which involves learners making judgements about their achievements and the outcomes of their learning (Boud & Falchikov, 1989). Achievements and outcomes of the learning can be identified through the guiding questions. The judgements are based on evidence about performance collected from others, such as teachers and peers, and/or themselves, including their internal intuitions, emotions, and physical sensations (Sargeant et al, 2010). ePortfolios have been shown to make students aware of what they have learned because they need to reflect and evaluate upon their work to select suitable artifacts (Johnsen, 2012; Ring, Waugaman, & Brackett, 2017). Self-grading, rubrics, guidance questions or prompts are also used in digital tools such as ePortfolio, apps or other platforms to support students' self-assessment and enable them to select suitable artifacts that evidence and demonstrate students' skills, competencies, or learning acquired from education, training, or work (Johnsen, 2012; Xiaojun, 2016; Ramsey, Khann, & Weston, 2017).

3. METHODOLOGY

For the development of the GES App, the "Design Thinking" methodology is used. For the problem-solving the Design Thinking methodology offers a solution-based approach that is not only iterative but also a non-linear process. The five stages as defined by Hasso-Plattner Institute of Design at Stanford (the "d. school") are: Empathise, Define, Ideate, Prototype and Test, as shown in Figure 1 (Plattner, Leifer, & Meinel, 2009).

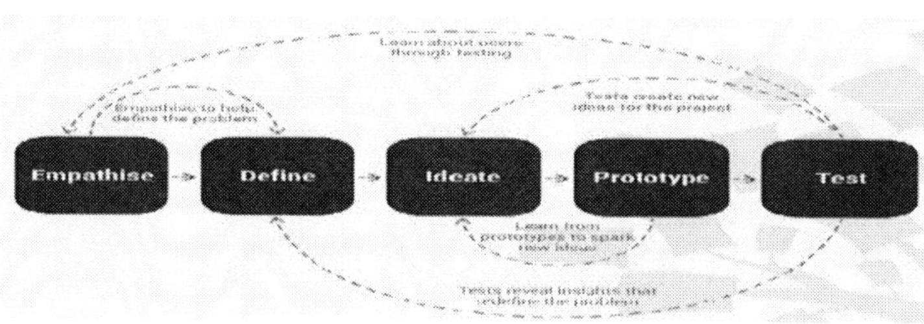

Figure 1. Stages in Design Thinking Process by Hasso-Plattner Institute of Design at Stanford

Being non-linear and iterative, the methodology is flexible and allows revaluation of the output of one phase based on the evaluation of the output of a successive phase. A brief overview of outputs of five phases of the process are as follows:

Empathise: The empathetic study of the problem has offered knowledge of what "Employability Skills" are? For this purpose, focus group interviews were used with stratified sampling of participants based on three characteristics of interest, that is if participants are students/job seekers, employers, or academic teachers. The process resulted in an understanding of employability skills among different focus groups.

Define: Through requirement elicitation of information gathered from the focus groups, the need of awareness for GES was identified and high-level requirements were defined.

Ideate: The conceptual framework for skills and activity design are the main outputs of this phase. The conceptual framework was defined for users to understand employability skills and activities were identified to motivate users for the need of skill recognition, acquisition, and development.

Prototype: The Figma prototype is the high-fidelity key output of this phase in which interactive mock-ups were designed for the GES mobile app depicting different activities of the application.

Test: GES App mobile app, developed in Unity, is the output of this phase.

In this paper, the agile development approach is adopted to Ideate and develop the conceptual framework for skills and the prototype of the mobile app. The rapid prototyping approach has been followed and the Figma user interface prototyping application has been used for designing the core functionalities and the interactive user interface. The Figma prototype has been used to conduct usability studies and to obtain feedback from users.

4. CONCEPTUAL FRAMEWORK AND DESIGN

The conceptual framework for skills is formulated over the notion of a crowd-sourced skills repository and is referred to as the Skills framework. The framework deliberates on all aspects that are identified as important to document skills and assist the reflection process of the user. This includes skill evidence in form of experiences, artifacts or references, skill level and skill goals to achieve the dream job.

4.1 Skills Conceptual Framework

Based on the requirement analysis and existing employability models (Saunders & Zuzel, 2010), the devised conceptual model for the GES App can be described as shown in Figure 2.

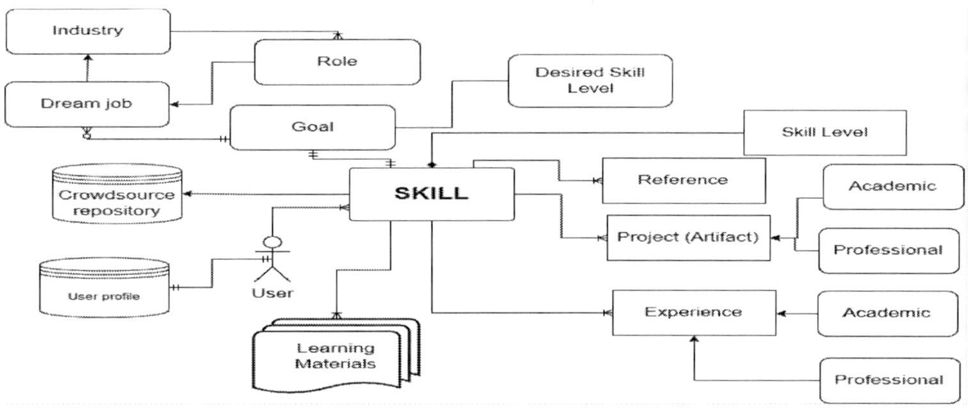

Figure 2. Conceptual Framework for graduate Employability Skills

Important components of the conceptual model are described in the following sub-sections.

4.1.1 Skills for Reflection

"Skill" is the central component of the skill framework. This component supports the goals of the application to recognize the skills acquired, while determining the skill level through reflection and evaluating the identified skill with the support of evidence that leads to the other important components of the framework that are "Experience", "Artifacts" and "References". A "Skill" is stored in a crowdsourced repository, and it is assessed in terms of skill level.

Crowdsourced repository of skills: not only enables the storing of the list of employability skills from literature, but also allows users to contribute and share with other users.

Skill Level: is used to allow the user to define the proficiency of their skill, based on the Dreyfus model (Dreyfus, 2004). Skill level is included so that the user can do a self-assessment of their skill through reflection and define one's level as a novice, advanced beginner, competent, proficient, or expert.

4.1.2 Evidence of Skill

The evidence of possessing a skill is documented in the form of "Experience", "Artifact" and "Reference".

Experience: indicates the process through which the user either has gained the skill or practiced it. Assessment of the experience reflects upon the skill acquired during the tenure. One skill can be acquired through one or multiple experiences and one experience can support many skills.

Artifact: represents the output achieved as the result of the application of one or more skills. An artifact can be associated with academic or professional experience.

Reference: This is a common practice to use references in a resume or CV. The same concept has been used as part of the skill framework that allows validation of the skill through a human source. One skill can have multiple references to support the evaluation of the skill.

4.1.3 Components of Skill Development

Skill Development is also an integral part of the objectives defined in the introduction of this paper. Self-assessment and reflection of the skill in light of the user's desired job can stimulate the skill development behaviour in the user. To support the process, 'dream job' and 'goal' are included in the Skill framework.

Dream Job: facilitate users to identify the need for skill development by defining the job or role, they want to attain in the future. Every dream job requires a skill set as defined by the industry. This enables users to compare their present skill set with the required skill set for the dream job and leads to the identification of the "Skill gap" (McKenney & Handley, 2019).

Goal: Acknowledging a skills gap through dream job can motivate users to learn or improve skills and encourage them to define a goal. The goal can be identified as the need of improving skill level by the user or learn new skills through different learning resources.

4.2 App Design Integrating Skill Framework

Integrating the components of the skill framework, activities for the mobile application are identified and incorporated in the GES App design (Fredheim, 2021). The complete design of the app is beyond the scope of this paper. Hence, we have focused on the activities that are designed to support students to reflect upon their employability skills through identifying and documenting them.

Add a New Skill: This activity is based on the main component of the framework that is "Skill". The main goal of the activity is to enable the user to add acquired skills to their profile. The crowdsourced repository supports the activity by offering a list of employability skills to browse from or to add the skill to the repository allowing other users to access it. This activity aims to facilitate the evaluation process of skill through reflection. The add option depicted by the (+) sign provides an option to add a new skill as shown in Figure 3 part (a). Users can assess their skill level as per the level of expertise as shown in Figure 3 part (b) below. Figure 3 part (c) shows an overview of the skill profile saved by the user. In the skill profile, a skill card shows information regarding skill level in terms of stars, number of experiences associated with skill and number of artifacts that support as evidence of the skill.

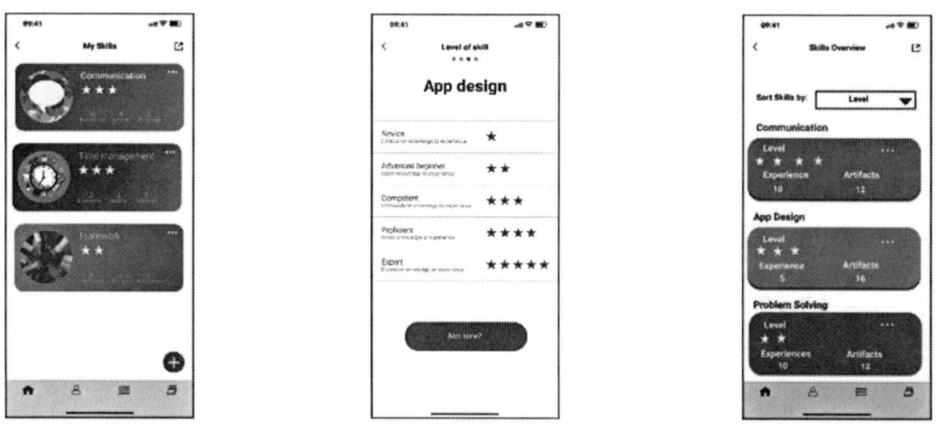

(a) (b) (c)

Figure 3. Add skill activity where (a) shows the option to add skill to user profile, (b) shows the evaluation of skill into skill level and © shows an overview of skills added to profile

The crowdsourced repository not only supports users to browse from the list of skills available through the GES App, but also enables users to identify the learned skills by acquiring more information about the skill through definitions and examples. The screenshot from the crowdsourced repository in Figure 4 part (a) shows the list of skills stored in the repository from which users can search for skills. If the skills are not in the skills repository, the user can add a new skill to their profile and the crowdsourced repository which can be accessed by other users as well. Descriptions of skills are also stored in the repository as shown in Figure 4 part (b) defining skills with examples for learning.

(a) (b)

Figure 4. Cropped screenshots of crowdsource repository in design where (a) shows the list of skills available in repository and (b) shows definition and examples of the selected skill

Document evidence of skill: Documentation of the evidence of skills allows the user to assess what has helped them to acquire the skill and how they can showcase the skill. This activity along with the skill assessment in the light of reflection encourages the sense of skill development process in user. The skill evidence documentation is integrated in application design by allowing the user to record experiences, artifacts they may have developed and a referee that could voucher for the experience.

Documentation of Experience: As defined in the conceptual framework, the experience is recorded as evidence that shows the implementation or acquisition of skill through any process. The app design enables the user to record the experience regarding the skill as shown in Figure 5 part (a). The process of acquiring skills can be academic like projects, seminars, courses, etc., or practical in terms of internships, projects or job as shown in Figure 5 part (b). For experience evaluation App design enables the user to assess skills from a role perspective. Assessment of experience in terms of these skills enables the app to substantiate the execution in 5 level metrics that correspond to "Very good", "Good", "Moderate", "Poor" and "Very poor" and can be summarized in terms of points as shown in Figure 5 part (c).

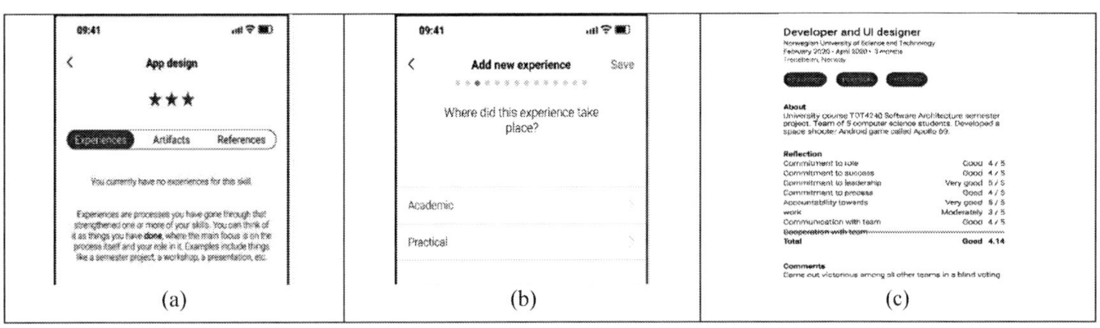

Figure 5. A cropped screenshot of adding experience as evidence in the app where part (a) shows the option to add experience (b) shows the option to select if the experience is academic or practical (c) shows the experience evaluated in terms of quantity

Documentation of artifact: The following activity provides evidence for skill as a potential output of experience. The GES app design enables the user to document the artifact in terms of different types of elements such as a tangible object, online or multimedia content, image, link, repository, video, or a note, etc. The recorded artifact can be used as evidence to support multiple skills in the user's profile. The recorded evidence along with the skill level assessment can be viewed in the skill card as shown in Figure 3 part (c).

References record: The component of reference is used in the framework to support skill through validation by human resources. The design allows the user to record the details of the reference for verification of skill however, consent of reference is required for this purpose. One reference can validate one to many skills of the user and added references are visible in the skill card as shown in Figure 3 part (c).

5. DISCUSSIONS AND CONCLUSION

Students are usually assessed based on what they have learned during their academic life that often lacks the depiction of real-life challenges which not only influence the way they practice their competencies but also obstruct the process of employability skill development because of lack of awareness (Bass & Eynon, 2009). It has become evident from the literature review that reflection supports the process of self-assessment (Boud & Falchikov, 1989; Yan & Brown, 2017). Using this concept in the GES App development project along, with requirement analysis of gathered data, enabled us to explore the probability of enhancing the element of awareness for employability skills, supporting it with the relation between reflection and self-assessment while utilizing the affordances of mobile technologies in learning related activities.

The two activities defined in this paper (add skill and add evidence) are designed to promote the self-assessment process in the user while reflecting on an employability skill they have acquired. The activity of adding skills is not only designed for users to add known skills to their profile but also prompt them to think if they have any skills that they are not aware of due to ignorance or lack of knowledge, as previous studies have proven to be effective when students develop ePortfolios (Johnsen, 2012; Ring, Waugaman, & Brackett, 2017). For this purpose, a crowdsourced repository has been used that provides a user with the list of common employability skills, with descriptions of the skills. In addition, if a desired skill is not available in the skills repository, the user is also able to add and share the skill through the skills repository. The self-assessment process is initiated while adding a new skill to the user's profile, where the user needs to determine their skill level. This process also stimulates reflection upon their skills and experiences that led to the skill. The reflection process is further enhanced while documenting the evidence of the skill in the form of experiences, artifacts, and references. The self-assessment of experience allows users to reflect upon what they have done in the light of defined skills and enables users to recognize the need for learning or improving. Both activities play a strong role in the initiation of skill development by allowing users to understand the skills gap for their dream job.

Based on the components of the skill framework, more activities are designed to encourage the process of skill development that enhance the overall compatibility with competency frameworks of different organizations while focusing on enabling users to determine their dream job and to realize the skills gap while facilitating them with learning resources to improve skills and employment readiness. The main limitation of this work is the lack of a full-scale user evaluation. We have conducted formative evaluations of some of the concepts and improved the design. The next step in our research is the evaluation of the design by university students in Norway, the UK, Poland and Greece, the partners in the project.

ACKNOWLEDGEMENT

This work has been conducted as a part of the Graduate employability skills App (GES-App) project, supported by a KA203 - Erasmus + Strategic Partnerships for higher education, grant; KA2, Cooperation for Innovation and the Exchange of Good Practices; Grant Agreement no: 2019-1-UK01-KA203-062146 and partly by the Norwegian Centre for Excellent IT Education ExcitED, funded by the Norwegian Research Council. The authors would like to thank the participants of the project and the evaluations.

REFERENCES

Bass, R., & Eynon, B. (2009). The Difference that Inquiry Makes: A Collaborative Case Study of Technology and Learning, from the Visible Knowledge Project. Retrieved 10 21, 2021, from https://blogs.commons.georgetown.edu/vkp/files/2009/03/bass-revised-2.pdf

Boud, D., & Falchikov, N. (1989). Quantitative Studies of Student Self-assessment in Higher Education: A Critical Analysis of Findings.". *Higher Education, 18 (5), 529–549.* Retrieved from https://link.springer.com/article/10.1007/BF00138746

Cassidy, S. (2006). Developing employability skills: Peer assessment in higher education. *Education and Training*, 508 - 517. doi:10.1108/00400910610705890

Cedefop. (2017). Defining, writing and applying learning outcomes: a European handbook. Luxembourg: Publications Office.

Coulson, D., & Harvey, M. (2013). Scaffolding student reflection for experiencebased learning: a framework. *Teaching in Higher Education, 18(4): 401-413.* doi:10.1080/13562517.2012.752726

Cowley, B. U., Bedek, M., Ribeiro, C., Heikura, T., & Petersen, S. A. (2012). The Quartic Process Model to Support Serious Games Development for Contextualized Competence-Based Learning and Assessment. In *Handbook of Research on Serious Games as Educational, Business and Research Tools.* IGI Global Publishers. doi:10.4018/978-1-4666-0149-9.ch025

Dreyfus, S. (2004). The five-stage model of adult skill acquisition. *Bulletin of science, technology & society, 24*(3), 177-181. doi:https://doi.org/10.1177/0270467604264992

Eynon, B., Laura, G. M., & Török, J. (2014). What Difference Can ePortfolio Make? A Field Report from the Connect to Learning Project. *International Journal of ePortfolio, 4(1), 95-114.* Retrieved from https://eric.ed.gov/?id=EJ1107844

Fredheim, L. J. (2021). *Mobile Application for Graduate Employability Skills - A proof-of-concept.* Norwegian University of Science and Technology Masters.

GES. (2020). *Project.* Retrieved from Graduate Employment Skills: https://ges-app.com/index.php/project/

Janosik, S. M., & Frank, T. E. (2013). Using ePortfolios to Measure Student Learning in a Graduate Preparation Program in Higher Education. *International Journal of ePortfolio 3(1), 13-20.* Retrieved 02 05, 2020, from https://eric.ed.gov/?id=EJ1107813

Johnsen, H. (2012). Making Learning Visible with ePortfolios: Coupling the Right Pedagogy with the Right Technology. *International Journal of ePortfolio 2(2), 139-148.* Retrieved from https://files.eric.ed.gov/fulltext/EJ1107610.pdf

Kennedy, D., Hyland , Á., & Ryan, N. (2009). Learning Outcomes and. In *In Best of the Bologna Handbook* (pp. 59 -76). Berlin, Germany: DUZ International .

Kuh, G., O'Donnell, K., & Schneider, C. G. (2017). HIPs at Ten. *The Magazine of Higher Learning, 49(5), 8-16.* doi:https://doi.org/10.1080/00091383.2017.1366805

McKenney, M., & Handley, H. (2019). Identifying and Quantifying Personnel Skill Gaps. *Proceedings of the Human Factors and Ergonomics Society Annual Meeting,* (pp. 332 - 336). doi:https://doi.org/10.1177/1071181319631078

Parsons, D., Thomas, H., & Wishart, J. (2016). Exploring Mobile Affordances in the Digital Classroom. *International Conference Mobile Learning.*

Plattner, H., Leifer, L., & Meinel, C. (2009). *Design-thinking.* Landsberg am Lech: Mi-Fachverlag.

Ramsey, P. L., Khann, S., & Weston, J. (2017). Designed for Learning: use of Skill Tracker in Veterinary education. *sia Pacific Management and Business Application 5(1), 53-63.* doi:10.21776/ub.apmba.2016.005.01.4

Ring, G., Waugaman, C., & Brackett, B. (2017). The Value of Career ePortfolios on Job Applicant Performance: Using Data to. *International Journal of ePortfolio 2(1), 225-236.* Retrieved 02 05, 2020, from https://files.eric.ed.gov/fulltext/EJ1159904.pdf

Rolfe et al. (2001). *Critical reflection for nursing and the helping professions: A user's guide.* Basingstoke: Palgrave Macmillan.

Sargeant et al, J. H. (2010). The Processes and Dimensions of Informed Self-assessment: A Conceptual Model. *Academic Medicine 85 (7):,1212–1220.* doi:doi: 10.1097/ACM.0b013e3181d85a4e

Saunders, V., & Zuzel, K. (2010). Evaluating Employability Skills: Employer and Student Perceptions. *Bioscience Education,* 1 - 15. doi:https://doi.org/10.3108/beej.15.2

Schneckenberg, D., Ehlers, U., & Adelsberger, H. (2011). Web 2.0 and competence-oriented design oflearning—Potentials and implications for higher education. *British Journal of Educational Technology, 42(5), 747-762.* doi: https://doi.org/10.1111/j.1467-8535.2010.01092.x

St Jorre, T., & Oliver, B. (2018). Want students to engage? Contextualise graduate learning outcomes and assess for employability,. *Higher Education Research & Development, 37(1), 44-57.* doi:https://doi.org/10.1080/07294360.2017.1339183

Suleman, F. (2017). The employability skills of higher education graduates: insights into conceptual frameworks and methodological options. *Higher Education, 76*, 263 - 278.

Washer, P. (2007). Revisiting Key Skills: A Practical Framework for Higher Education. *Quality in Higher Education, 13 (1), 57 - 67.* doi:10.1080/13538320701272755

Xiaojun, C. (2016). Evaluating Language-learning Mobile Apps for Second-language Learners. *Journal of Educational Technology Development and Exchange (JETDE), 9 (2), 39-51.* doi:10.18785/jetde.0902.03

Yan, Z., & Brown, G. T. (2017). A cyclical self-assessment process: towards a model of how students engage in self-assessment. *Assessment & Evaluation in Higher Education,.* Retrieved from https://doi.org/10.1080/02602938.2016.1260091

SHORT PAPERS

HEALTHY JOB. WORK AND HEALTH JUST A CLICK AWAY

Dalia Gallico
Università San Raffaele Roma, Italy

ABSTRACT

From a survey by the "European Agency for Safety and Health at Work" about 45% of the interviewees believe they accuse work-related stress, about 20% accuse of endure long and irregular working hours and over 59% complain of difficult interactions with their counterparts such as: customers, patients, students, etc.
Healty Job, is the name of the new app to improve the experience of thousands of users struggling with the stress and inconvenience caused by their work and internal phenomena.
The genesis of this app stems from the need to respond to the great change in the post-pandemic world of work, guaranteeing top quality services and support to accompany users to face all critical situations relating to psychophysical well-being within the habitual workplace.
According to the creators themselves, thanks to a series of researches, they managed to extrapolate a great sense of dissatisfaction among workers. Workers who, every day, have to face all those situations in the workplace, typical of "work-related stress, stress related to work activity that occurs when the demands of the workplace exceed the ability of the worker to deal with them, or check them "(source INAIL 2021).
This situation is due to the increasing pressures of work rhythms and incorrect attitudes, which in large and small companies, lead to inequality in the treatments that managers apply towards their subordinates. Last but not least, the recent pandemic emergency has brought about a major change in our working habitat which, transforming itself from corporate to domestic, has generated a great sense of inadequacy, due to often unsuitable and uncomfortable environments.

KEYWORDS

M.learning, Work, Health, Community, Co-working, Metaverse, Smartworking

1. INTRODUCTION

The pandemic and the consequent lockdown that we have suffered has transformed our habits, undermined our securities and undermined our certainties. In addition to hitting us from a human point of view, COVID forced us to change our approach to work. The long period of housewife constraint has accelerated a process of digitization of the world of work that has led to the use of more and more tools such as teleworking and smart working. Personally I spent 3 months in smartworking, alone at home. In this period I have reflected a lot on the world of work and above all on how this event had influenced and was perceived in a different way by each of us. I noticed this talking with colleagues, friends and acquaintances, each of them had different opinions on the issue and therefore also different inconveniences and benefits. Among the main changes in lifestyle we can talk about what has been an awareness on the part of workers, in fact, agile work has brought us back to discover the importance of affections and their private interests. In an Italian study, over 48% of respondents said, just 3 months after starting work from home, that they have an extra hour a day off that they use for their loved ones and for their passions. Abroad, this phenomenon has led to the creation of the so-called "Quitting economy" or "Great resignation", that is, more and more workers are resigning en masse in order to devote more time to their loved ones and interests.

2. VISION

HEALTHY JOB's vision is to help and assist the worker in dealing with all those situations that generate severe difficulties and the formation of pathologies deriving from the stress of work on a daily basis. The goal of HEALTHY JOB is to help respond to the targets required by Agenda 2030, and precisely to goal n ° 8 point 5: *"By 2030, ensure full and productive employment and decent work for women and men, including young people and people with disabilities, and fair remuneration for jobs of fair value".*

We dream of a change, an inner and personal revolution that starts from enhancing self-awareness and what is happening around us, from self-learning of how to react and manage stress in the workplace. HEALTHY JOB wants to represent an easy to use and above all discreet tool, which helps those in difficulty to face difficult situations in the workplace, increasing their awareness through listening desks, mindfulness tools to manage anxiety and maintain work focus and a series of podcasts in detail designed to inspire and motivate a change in approach to the problem. A friendly service in which to take refuge, a sort of multimedia pampering that increases one's strength of spirit and connects the user with a community that understands him and shares the same difficulties until he feels welcomed in a SAFE area. An app that adds VALUE to people's lives and that increases the meaning of all that audience of applications engaged in social issues.

3. THE CONTEST

A survey carried out by the European Agency for Safety and Health at Work already shows worrying data from a research of 2019. The survey collects responses made to ordinary workers and therefore is an effective mirror of the feelings of the European working class. From the survey about 45% of the interviewees believe they accuse work-related stress, about 20% accuse of endure long and irregular working hours and over 59% complain of difficult interactions with their counterparts such as: customers, patients, students, etc.

1. COWORKING.

Shared workspaces are a reality that has become increasingly popular in recent years and allows to share a workspace with others.This work experience, as well as the obvious economic advantages given by the savings on renting an office, gives those who are part of it the opportunity to be contaminated and to collaborate with people with different professional skills that they would normally never have been so close to. It is an environment that facilitates the creation of new collaborations and the mutual influence of different subjects in a meltingpot of creativity and innovation.

Shared work spaces are a reality that in recent years is gaining ground and allows to better reflect these characteristics in fact the coworking spaces correspond more and more to highly unconventional environments, the total absence of division between the various workstations, the presence of relaxation areas, informal rooms, gyms and rooftops for sharing represent the backbone of the philosophy of these places, where it is not difficult to find workstations where you can lie down to work and meeting tables where you can be side by side with complete strangers. We are not talking about the workplace but about Community.

2. SMARTWORKING

Smart working dictated by the recent health emergency has induced a strong change in our working habits and the rapid digitization process then imposed a change in our homes which very often our spaces were not ready to bear. Smart working brings both benefits and disadvantages.

On the one hand, the lack of social interaction and the absence of separation between living and working spaces has often led to a feeling of discomfort in workers, while the greater availability of free time and greater working flexibility led many to prefer this system. Smart working is not a passing event, in fact large companies are moving towards a hybrid system that allows them to assimilate most of the advantages both from the company side and from the worker side.

Surely this trend is changing in our spaces, our furnishings and also the way we choose the properties to buy by providing spaces that can be adequately dedicated to work.

3. METAVERSE AND DIGITAL SPACES

At the end of October Mark Zuckerberg (CEO of Facebook) on the occasion of the name change of his company launched an idea of the internet, the metaverse. Meta (new name of the Zuckerberg Group) has made it known that it is developing a digital and three-dimensional world that will be usable by all through augmented reality.

In this digital world, the US company promises to offer previously unthinkable possibilities, especially from the point of view of interaction.

In fact, it will be possible to experience this world through avatars and interact with others thanks to digital tools in immersive spaces such as those of a video game, and work as if we were in close contact with our colleagues and not simply through a screen as in smart working.

This will significantly change what the work experience is and will allow you to collaborate with people who are also very distant but without the coldness of a call or an email.

Just think of what representation of normality would be to walk with a colleague to the meeting room of a completely digital space, show him graphics and digital prototypes, being able to "handle" them as if he were present. A new perspective where the biggest tech companies are heading and that will surely upset our work experience in the future.

4. THE PROJECT HEALTHY JOB

The functionalities of the new application are divided into three specific aspects of the psychology of work. The first function is that of the listening desk, where users can get in touch with professionals specialized in occupational psychology. Professionals, who will have the role of guiding users in a rehabilitation process; of acceptance and action towards one's work situation, dealing with issues such as bullying and the burnout syndrome.

1. ASK

Section dedicated to psychological support. In this area, users have the opportunity to get in touch with a team of professionals to help them cope with their moment of difficulty in the workplace.

This activity can be carried out in two different ways:

- video call - live chat

2. LISTEN

Section dedicated to the app's podcast services. This is the section where the user can find hundreds of podcasts focused on the world of work, the psychological approach to the world of work and self-help and personal motivation. A series of stories, interviews and insights that aim to better understand the environment around us, the roles and one's attitude towards it. In this section it is also possible to find good practices for physical workers and activate notifications for the visual cooling of those who work at the video terminal.

Instead, we find a more didactic-cultural purpose in the second function; in fact, the app will allow you to access a mini podcast platform totally focused on content relating to the topic or preparatory to it. The collaboration of developers with the "leading" realities of the sector such as Spotify and Ted Talk is fundamental.

3. MEDITATE

Section to the world of mindfulness. In this part of the app we offer guides for performing easy mindfulness exercises with the aim of relaxing and maintaining concentration based on self-awareness and what you are doing. Last but not least, the third function which is the most interactive, as there is a section dedicated to mindfulness, a series of exercises to be performed in the headphones where a voice will guide the user to control his own breathing and to carry out micro-exercises that allow you to find immediate serenity, focus and inner peace.

4. FORUM Another section of the app will be dedicated to creating a community where users with the same problems can get in touch through a dedicated forum.

Moving on to a more objective analysis, some considerations must be taken into account: even if this service, as composed by the Italian company, does not yet have a full expression in the digital sector and therefore could be considered a pioneer in the field, there will be an answer in terms of subscriptions to this product? Are users ready to bring their personal problems into a digital context and thus give up that human interface they are used to? On the other hand, the creators argue that precisely the apparent detachment of the digital tool is the key to bringing people closer to this kind of issues, very often in fact the fear of opening up, and the idea of confiding in someone about their problems. it slows down those who are subject to it since in the first case shyness plays a fundamental role and can be overcome thanks to the detachment of the digital medium, while in the second case sometimes the acceptance of the problem itself is the main obstacle to be faced and the "light dress" "Of this app would help in solving the problem. We live in an era of constant and sometimes radical changes. Digital technology has an important impact in our daily life by completely changing the way we face new challenges from work to relationships, in short, our way of experiencing the world. The urgency is to acquire new understanding and new skills, as most jobs will undergo radical changes related to technologies. Work becomes sharing, of spaces of ideas also of lifestyles; a concept now known thanks to "Coworking", the professional completely overcomes the phase of isolation; since culturally speaking he does not necessarily come into contact with professionals in the same sector, this brings a great mental openness.

The creators of this app ask nothing more than to reveal features such as flexibility, and more importantly the absence of hierarchies, and ultimately, a clear sense of innovation, which in this case is understood as the concrete application of a idea. The purpose of this app to be a first approach to self-help, an assessment tool that helps to take those micro actions that allow us to better relate to others and help us improve our self-esteem and start to divert from that road that leads to work-related stress disorders. On the other hand, the direction that the world of work is taking is that represented by the increasingly intense process of dematerialisation and the creation of virtual realities in which we would experience moments of leisure but above all moments of work, collaborations and cultural exchanges. The environments we will get used to will be a negative version of the phygital, where we ourselves will be the analog elements immersed in the digital world.

5. THE MODALITY

1. Compatibility: All videos are optimized for mobile devices. The fact that they are played correctly with computer's browser does not guarantee that they work correctly on mobile devices.
2. Ease of use: mobile content scrollable, so you don't have to leave a page to interact with as many. contents and as many options as possible.
3. Impact: high-quality images and carefully edit them to maximize detail, with particular attention to size specifications (even when shrinking to fit smaller screens).
4. User Experience: All buttons on the screen are easy to use for mobile users. For this reason, reduced number of clicks required to complete an action. Focus on one action at a time, removing unnecessary screen changes or clicks.
5. Attention to the device: not all the actions you normally perform on a PC are equally simple on a smartphone.
6. Responsibility: a responsive template for everything, even for emails.
7. Content Length: Short paragraphs with often intersperse text and images.
8. Engagement: analyze how long users are likely to use their smartphone. According to one study, the average length of a mobile session is 10 minutes.
9. Content Indexing: Simplify content formatting to make it easier to find the most useful information. Clear titles, bulleted lists, images and icons to attract attention.

6. CONCLUSION

The main tech companies are developing these new technologies with huge investments, and this puts us in the position of absolutely not being able to ignore this trend, a few months ago Facebook became the protagonist of a futuristic showoff presenting its vision of the world digital

From this point of view, it is not surprising that Healthy Job represents a step forward in this direction, and expresses it in many aspects, interesting was the exposure of what will be the promotion and distribution channels, because, if it is logical to expect a promotion digital and social, it must be taken into account that the company's marketing offices have entered into agreements with the main trade union associations in order to use their channels to be proposed as a support and help tool to enhance workers' rights.

This move was carefully designed to fill that portion of the public, which covers an age group that currently works but is not accustomed to social media and the internet, so the dissemination of the tool through the trade unions seeks that target audience. people who are attentive to their identity as a worker, as a member of the aforementioned lists, but who, due to lack of familiarity with IT means, would not have been able to access them. From a more traditional point of view, the app will benefit from sponsorship on the spotify podcast platform and, in collaboration with Ted Talk, will present a live youtube on the occasion of Labor Day next

May 1st. The event will be punctuated by the alternation of the airing of the most famous speeches presented over the years in the various TedXs around the world and targeted interviews with experts and professionals in the sector with a large representation of psychologists and developers of the Italian app.

There will be publications in magazines and newspapers nationwide and TV shows at strategic times for the chosen target. In terms of business, the social soul of the initiative is immediately evident. In fact, the app already in its free version will guarantee a minimum usability useful for users who, in exchange for the usual advertising, will have access to all sections of the app and will be able to request psychological consultations online at a price in line with the market. Surely, by subscribing to the subscription plan, you can get the most out of the app by having unlimited access to the podcast and the mindfulness section as well as being able to get a very interesting discount for the consultations mentioned above. The hope is that the impetus towards such a delicate issue, on the part of the creators, represents a starting point and is taken as an example by more and more start-ups like this one that try to combine innovation with social utility every time. The creative ferment, which our startuppers demonstrate every day, really has a lot to offer to society, so let's hope that these initiatives also develop in the world of health, in policies in favor of social inclusion, in tools for the elderly and how repellent against bullying in our schools. If this necessarily implies the introduction of marketing systems and social logic that we are used to understanding as "questionable", then that's welcome! There is no innovation without compromise and we have a duty, as modern citizens, to interpret such systems as an indispensable form of patronage. We accept these innovations that the digital age, in which we are now immersed, offers us and we try to make the best of them for us and for future generations.

REFERENCES

Chet Hosmer, Carlton Jeffcoat, Matthew Davis, Thomas McGibbon (2011), "Use of Mobile Technology for Information Collection and Dissemination", Data & Analysis Center for Software, March 2011.

Crescente, Mary Louise; Lee, Doris (2011). "Critical issues of M-Learning: design models, adoption processes, and future trends". Journal of the Chinese Institute of Industrial Engineers 28 (2): 111–123.

Douch R., Savill-Smith C., Parker G. and Attewell J. 2010. Work-based and vocational mobile learning: Making IT work. London, LSN. http://issuu.com/steveb123/docs/100186

Elias, Tanya (February 2011). "Universal Instructional Design Principles for Mobile Learning". International Review of Research in Open and Distance Learning 12 (2): 143–156.

Georgiev, T., Georgieva, E. and Smrikarov, A. (2004). ME-Learning: A new stage of E-Learning. Proceedings International conference on Computer Systems and Technologies, CompSysTech' 2004, IV.28, 1-5.

Kahle-Piasecki, Lisa; Miao, Chao; Ariss, Sonny (2012). "Managers and the Mobile Device: M-Learning and m-business - Implications for the United States and China". Journal of Marketing Development and Competitiveness 6 (1): 56–68.

Keegan, D. (2005) The Incorporation of Mobile Learning into Mainstream Education and Training. Proceedings of mLearn2005- 4th World Conference on mLearning, Cape Town, South Africa, 25-28 October 2005. http://www.mlearn.org.za/CD/papers/keegan1.pdf

Masters, K.; Ng'ambi D. (2007). "After the broadcast: disrupting health sciences' students' lives with SMS". Proceedings of IADIS International Conference Mobile Learning. Lisbon, Portugal. pp. 171–175. ISBN 978-972-8924-36-2.

Mobile Learning Community. Mobile Learning History. 2010.

Moore, J. (2009). "A portable document search engine to support off-line mobile learning". Proceedings of IADIS International Conference Mobile Learning. Barcelona, Spain.

Mostakhdemin-Hosseini, A. and Tuimala, J. (2005). Mobile Learning Framework. Proceedings IADIS International Conference Mobile Learning 2005, Malta, pp 203-207.

Nyiri, K. (2006) Time and Communication in F. Stadler and M. Stöltzner (eds) Time and History: Proceeding of the 28 International Ludwig Wittgenstein Symposium, Kirchberg am Wechsel, Austria 2005.

Plant, S. (2000): On the Mobile. The Effects of Mobile Telephones on Social and Individual Life. http://www.motorola.com/mot/documents/0,1028,333,00.pdf

Saylor, Michael (2012). The Mobile Wave: How Mobile Intelligence Will Change Everything. Perseus Books/Vanguard Press. p. 176. ISBN 978-1593157203.

Singh, Mandeep (2010). "M-Learning: A New Approach to Learn Better". International Journal of Education and Allied Sciences 2 (2): 65–72.

Sørensen, C., L. Mathiassen, & M. Kakihara (2002): Mobile Services: Functional Diversity and Overload, presented at New Perspectives On 21st-Century Communications, May 24-25, 2002, Budapest, Hungary.

RECOGNITION OF ARM POSITIONS OF DEMENTIA PATIENTS VIA SMARTWATCHES USING SUPERVISED LEARNING

Sergio Staab and Ludger Martin
RheinMain University of Applied Sciences, Wiesbaden, Germany

ABSTRACT

Currently, about 46.8 million people worldwide have dementia. More than 7.7 million new cases occur every year. Causes and triggers of the disease are currently unknown, and a cure is not available. This makes dementia, along with cancer, one of the most dangerous diseases in the world. In the field of dementia care, this work attempts to use machine learning to classify the activities of individuals with dementia in order to track and analyze disease progression and detect disease-related changes as early as possible. In collaboration with two care communities, exercise data is measured using the Apple Watch Series 6. Consultation with several care teams that work with dementia patients on a daily basis revealed that many dementia patients wear watches. In this project data from the aforementioned sensors is sent to the database at 20 data packets per second via a socket. DecisionTreeClassifier, KNeighborsClassifier, Logistic Regression, Fast Forest, Support Vector Machine, and Multilayer Perceptron classification algorithms are used to gain knowledge about locating, providing, and documenting motor skills during the course of dementia. As a first step, arm position sequences are to be identified, from which different fine-granular activities are to be classified later.

KEYWORDS

Human Motion Analysis, Machine Learning, Dementia

1. INTRODUCTION

As a result of demographic changes, there are far more new cases of illness than deaths among those already ill. If there is no breakthrough in prevention and therapy, the number of dementia patients will increase to 74.7 million by 2030 and to around 131.5 million by 2050 according to population projections. In Germany alone, this corresponds to an average increase of around 40.000 dementia patients per year or around more than 100 per day, according to the German Federal Ministry for Health (Bundesministerium für Gesundheit 2020).

The shortage of junior staff due to the lower birth rate is leading to a decrease in population figures and a massive increase in people in need of care. This work deals with the machine tracking of activities during the course of dementia by means of sensor technology. Main part of this work is a system that is able to collect data from smartwatches in real time and send it to a server for further processing via a Web-Socket.

In cooperation with several nursing communities, with this work the measurement of training data using Smartwatch starts. A consultation with various nursing teams that work with people suffering from dementia on a daily basis has shown that many patients wear watches. Smartwatches allow for an unobtrusive way of measuring data. These devices usually integrate the following: global positioning system (GPS), accelerometer, light sensor, gyroscope, magnetometer, ambient temperature sensor, heart rate monitor, oxymetry sensor, skin conductance sensor, and skin temperature sensor.

This work answers the following question: Which Apple Watch sensor technology and which machine classification algorithms can be used to detect arm positions in dementia treatment?

2. RELATED WORK

Health information technologies have been revolutionizing healthcare for years. The variety and range of software and hardware technologies as well as the number of applications has increased considerably. There is an increasing global demand for the implementation of health information technologies in hospitals, clinics, and homes according to Lau et al. (Lau et al. 2019). In their work, they investigate the current status of mobile devices and software in relation to health information. In contrast to traditional health interventions originating from clinical researchers, mobile health applications are often developed commercially with little input from clinical researchers or consumers. Portable devices such as smartwatches and fitness tapes are becoming increasingly popular in all demographic groups, from children to older adults. Reasons for this increase are fitness tracking and health monitoring. According to Malu and Findlater, detecting mental and physical disorders and supporting people with difficulties can significantly improve the health of users (Malu and Findlater 2016). Several of these applications are based on data collected by sensors on smartwatches, including heart rate monitor, GPS, accelerometer, and gyroscope. Various interaction techniques make smartwatches unique and ubiquitous as a data tracking device. The literature supports this statement in various works of the past years.

Ravi et al. (Ravi et al. 2007) have successfully measured various human activities using an accelerometer. Shoaib et al. (Shoaib et al 2015) have used both smartphones and smartwatches together to identify various daily human activities.

Dong et al. (Dong et al. 2013) as well as Ramos-Garcia and Hoover (Ramos-Garcia and Hoover 2013) have measured eating cycles of smartphones users. In these studies, accelerometers and gyroscope sensor data from smartphones were used. Da Silva and Galeazzo (Da Silva and Galeazzo 2013) obtained various data on eight daily actions using accelerometer data, using an EZ-430 Chronos smartwatch. It should be noted that the detection of general activities is possible using accelerometers and gyroscope sensors. However, it is necessary to realize these activities for the health-related data in a much more fine-grained way. A crucial point is the arm movement detection. In their project in which only inertial sensors of the smartwatch were used, Jose Manjarres et al. (Jose Manjarres et al. 2019) present the challenge of recognizing human behavior by means of arm motion detection and its possibilities. They were able to calculate the workload according to the Frimat method using trained random forest with an accuracy of 97.5% in validation and 92% accuracy in real-time tests with 20 subjects.

Xu et al. (Xu et al. 2015) classified hand and finger gestures as well as characters from smartwatch motion sensor data. Similarly, Riaz et al. (Riaz et al. 2015) and Tautges et al. (Tautges et al. 2011) attempted to reconstruct body movements using several portable devices by comparing accelerometry data with the data generated from motion detection.

The present work is most similar to the project of Serkan Balli et al. (Serkan Balli et al. 2018). In their work, using an accelerometer and gyroscope in a smartwatch, the authors extracted 14 features from the obtained sensor data, condensed them through a dimensionality reduction algorithm filter and tested several methods (C4.5, SVM, random forest and kNN methods) for classifying human actions on five subjects to identify the following activities: brushing teeth, walking, writing on paper, writing with the keyboard, and vacuuming. The study shows how well machine activity classifications can be realized using the sensor technology of smartwatches. For example, writing using the kNN method was rated with a success rate of over 98%. Random forest and C4.5 methods classifies the action walking with 100% accuracy. The present project extends the applied motion sensors (accelerometer and gyroscope) by the pedometer and heart rate sensors. The authors expect that this will represent an improvement beyond the state of the art.

This work demonstrates the potential that smartwatches offer for the healthcare sector. In the following, the prototype is described.

3. CONSTRUCTION – MACHINE LEARNING

For this work, a standalone watchOS application for the Apple Watch Series 6 was implemented using state-of-the-art technology. The application communicates with a WebSocket that both outputs the watch data packets to a user interface and stores them in a MySQL database. The backup of the data is used for further machine processing.

The application provides methods for querying motion and health data, temporarily saving data in the smartwatch memory, labeling data, and an interface for exchanging sensor data with a web server via WebSocket. In case of complications, backup methods can trigger a resend of sensor data generated in a session. Instead of caching sensor data in a CSV file on an iPhone, this work enables direct reuse of sensor data on the server side in real time.

The sensor technology in the focus of this work controls through the application in detail accelerometer, gyroscope, gravity, and heart rate sensor as well as the electrical heart sensor (ECG). Figure 1 provides an overview of the work. Accelerometer, gyroscope, and magnetometer contribute to the mathematical calculation of the device orientation. The gravitational acceleration can be used to determine where south is, and the magnetic field vectors can be used to determine where north is from the device's point of view.

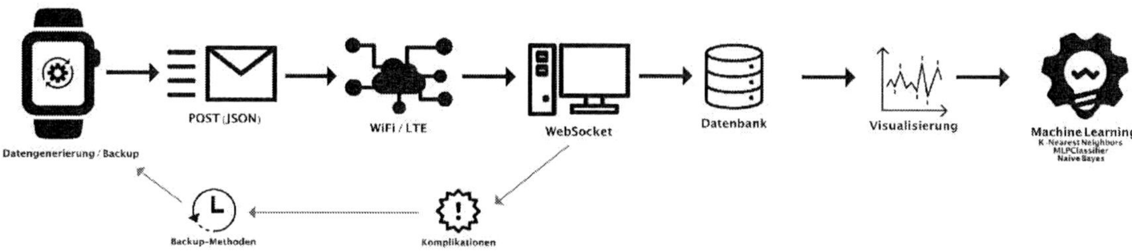

Figure 1. Overview

Rotation values of the gyroscope are integrated to estimate the deviation from the previous position. Thus, the combination of several sensors is used to calculate the attitude and to use the strengths of each sensor to compensate or minimize the weaknesses of each sensor. Since an acceleration sensor picks up any forces such as vibrations, this can cause unwanted noise. All movement and health data tracked by the realized application is first stored as arrays in a respective predefined structure and then encoded as JSON and then prepared for data exchange.

The data per second does not represent a temporal progression, but only a snapshot of the sensors. The data we tracked is at the temporal frequency of 20 hertz (Hz). Each of the data packets tracked at intervals of 50 milliseconds contains the following parameters: accelUserX, accelUserY, accelUserZ, attitudePitch, attitudeRoll, attitudeYaw, gravityX, gravityY, gravityZ, gyroX, gyroY, gyroZ, and heartrate.

When creating the test and training data, it was agreed that the movement would be approximately six seconds long. With one data record every 50 milliseconds, this corresponds to 20 data records per second and thus 200 data records in total (20 data records/second * 10 seconds). It has been found that the prediction accuracy improves significantly if instead of averaging 200 data per label at 20 Hz for the 12 features (4 sensors * x, y, z), the amount of data per half second is averaged and a new feature is formed from each averaging. This results in 240 features with 20 data sets per second and 12 original features. The data was divided into blocks of 0.5 seconds, with the mean value over the values being calculated for each block. Thus, twelve values must be determined for each feature (20 * 0.5 seconds = 10 seconds). In the example of 200 lines (= 10 seconds), the average of a block is thus formed over 10 lines. With a label duration of 220 lines (= 11 seconds), this results in 12 lines (rounded down to 20). In order to include these in the calculation of the average, they are distributed to the individual data sets (in this case to the first eight data sets). This ensures that there are always exactly twelve features for a value (e.g., AttitudePitch1, AttitudePitch2, ..., AttitudePitch20). The actual duration of the labels is thus variable, while the number of features remains constant. In summary, the length of the label determines the number of features, and the amount of data per feature is determined by the frequence (Hz) of the sensor.

4. RESULTS

The previously described methodology was applied to different classification algorithms in a series of experiments. Five subjects were included, generating 60 labels per arm position sequence. Figure 2 shows the different arm position sequences of the subjects.

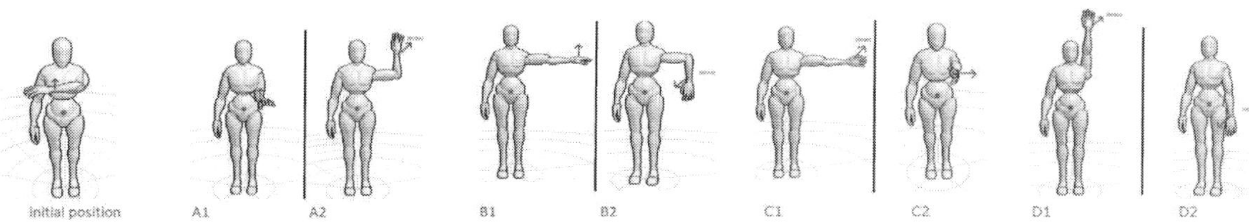

Figure 2. Arm position sequences

Each sequence (A to D) consists of two arm positions, each held for 3 seconds. The measurement rate of 20 Hz results in 4 * 5 * 60 * 20 = 24,000 data sets per test series. The subjects wore the watch on their dominant hand at all times. The test and training data were created separately, i.e. the data of one subject were compared with the data of the other four subject. The test series shows how the best classification algorithms perform with different sensors (cf. Table 1).

Table 1. Predictive power of two classification algorithms with different sensors

Algorithms	Sensors / Prediction	Sensors / Prediction	Sensors / Prediction	Sensors / Prediction
Logistic R.	Acceleration 65.56%	Attitude 96.67% Acceleration, Attitude 96.94%	Gyro 85.24% Gyro, Acceleration 89.44% Gyro, Attitude 96.94%	Gravity 99.44% Gravity, Acceleration 100% Gravity, Attitude 99.46% Gravity, Gyro 100%
Fast Forest	Acceleration 97.5%	Attitude 96.67% Acceleration, Attitude 99.72%	Gyro 98.33% Gyro, Acceleration 98.33% Gyro, Attitude 99.44%	Gravity 100% Gravity,Acceleration 99.72% Gravity, Attitude 100% Gravity, Gyro 100%

An important finding are the clear results of the Gravity Sensor alone and in combination with any other sensor. It seems that by changing the gravity, the hand position can be clearly defined.

The good results of the hand rotation detections represent another important finding. We initially assumed that heart rate and arm movements would provide clear data on respective activities; however, this assumption was wrong. Over 80 % of the performance are a result of hand movement and rotation detection. A visual comparison also confirms the high performance of the hand motion sensor technology. Figure 3 shows the direct comparison of the data between the acceleration sensor on the right and the gravity sensor on the left.

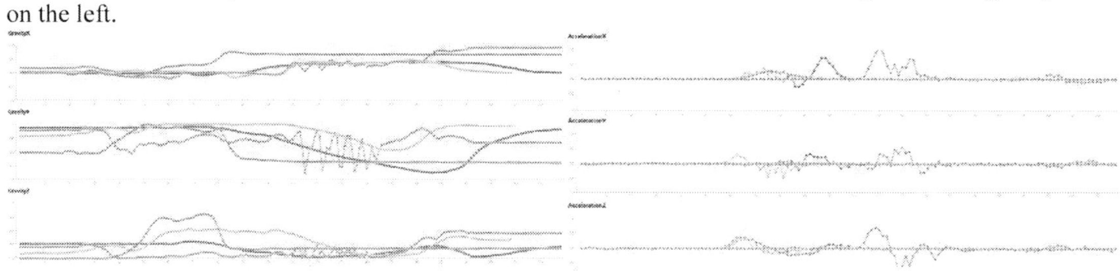

Figure 3. Comparison Acceleration Sensor (right) and Gravity Sensor (left) – A: Turquoise, B: Orange, C: Blue, D: Red

The differences in the movements are clearly visible with the Gravity Sensor, which also makes it easier for the classifier to classify them. This is a crucial piece of knowledge, hence the sensor technology must be given much more weight. It is the decisive factor that enables the recognition of very similar movements.

5. CONCLUSION

Based on our research, the interaction of the accelerometer, attitude sensor, gyroscope and G-sensor in combination with Logistic Regression and Fast Forest algorithms turns out to be the strongest combination for classifying arm position sequences. It should be noted that as a sole sensor, the G-sensor axes (Gravity - X, Y and Z) perform best. The magnetometer worsens the classification, and the heart rate plays a minor role in arm position sequences so far.

This work answers the question about the classifier and the required sensor technology for the detection of arm positions using smartwatches:

- Logistic R: G-sensor and Acceleration, G-sensor and Gyroscope
- Fast Forest: G-sensor, G-sensor and Attitude, G-sensor and Gyroscope

In the next step, based on this work, we will test the classification reliability of the favored algorithms with the four sensor systems on different frequency und on different activities, which in turn can only be recognized via the hand position. As one possibility, we will now try to classify very similar activities. For example, with the state of the art, movements such as drinking (bringing a glass to the mouth), eating (bringing a fork or spoon to the mouth) cannot be distinguished, since the sensory system hardly shows any differences due to the almost identical movement. It is these movements that we can now attempt to investigate using our work and the classifiers and sensors previously evaluated.

REFERENCES

Balli, S., Arif Sağbaş, E., Peker, M., 2018. Human activity recognition from smart watch sensor data using a hybrid of principal component analysis and random forest algorithm, *SAGE journals*, Vol.52, pp 37-45.

Bundesministerium für Gesundheit, 2020. Online-Ratgeber Demenz, https://www.bundesgesundheitsministerium.de /presse/pressemitteilungen/2020/3-quartal/nationale-demenzstrategie.html

Da Silva, FG., Galeazzo, E., 2013, Accelerometer based intelligent system for human movement recognition, *IEEE*, Bari, Italy. DOI:10.1109/IWASI.2013.6576063

Dong, Y., Scisco, J., Wilson, M., 2014, Detecting Periods of Eating During Free-Living by Tracking Wrist Motion, *IEEE*, Volume: 18, pp. 1253 – 1260. DOI:10.1109/JBHI.2013.2282471

Lau, F., Bartle-Clar, J., Bliss, G., Borycki, E., Courtney, K., Mu-Hsing Kuo, A., Kushniruk, A., Monkman, H., Vahabpour Roudsari, A., 2019, *Improving Usability, Safety and Patient Outcomes with Health Information Technology*, IOS Press.

Malu, M., Findlater, L., 2016, Toward Accessible Health and Fitness Tracking for People with Mobility Impairments, Proc. 10th EAI Int. Conf. Pervasive Comput. Technol., pp. 170–177.

Manjarres, J., Narvaez, P., Gasser, K., Percybrooks, W., Pardo, M., 2019, Physical Workload Tracking Using Human Activity Recognition with Wearable Devices, MDPI, DOI: https://doi.org/10.3390/s20010039

Ramos-Garcia, RI., Hoover, AW., 2013, A Study of Temporal Action Sequencing During Consumption of a Meal, *ACM*.

Ravi, N., Dandekar, N., Mysore, P., 2007, Activity Recognition from Accelerometer Data on a Mobile Phone, Springer, Berlin, Heidelberg, DOI: https://doi.org/10.1007/978-3-642-02481-8_120

Riaz, Q., Tao, G., Krüger, B., Weber, A., 2015, Motion reconstruction using very few accelerometers and ground contacts, AMC, DOI: https://doi.org/10.1016/j.gmod.2015.04.001

Shoaib, M., Bosch, S., Scholten, H., 2015, Towards detection of bad habits by fusing smartphone and smartwatch sensors, *IEEE*, DOI:10.1109/PERCOMW.2015.7134104

Tautges, J., Zinke, A., Krüger, B., Baumann, J., Weber, A., Helten, T., Müller, M., Seidel, H., Eberhardt, B., 2011, Motion reconstruction using sparse accelerometer data, *ACM*, DOI: https://doi.org/10.1145/1966394.1966397

Xu, C., Pathak, P.H., Mohapatra, P., Finger-writing with Smartwatch, 2015, A Case for Finger and Hand Gesture Recognition using Smartwatch, *ACM*, DOI: https://doi.org/10.1145/2699343.2699350

INTEGRATION OF QUICK RESPONSE (QR) CODE FOR AGRICULTURAL PRODUCT TARIFF COLLECTION AND VIRTUAL PAYMENT TRANSACTIONS

Richard Myrick T. Arellaga[1], Jermine V. Dacanay[1], Rhealyn B. Valenzuela[1], Melvin F. Ellorin[2] and Jose Alberto D. Pataweg[2]
[1]*Department of Engineering and Architecture, Urdaneta City University, Urdaneta City, Pangasinan, Philippines 2428*
[2]*Local Government Unit, Urdaneta City, Urdaneta City, Pangasinan, Philippines 2428*

ABSTRACT

Covid-19 pandemic that affects the whole world today. Local governments support all possible solutions to limit the exposure of its people to the disease. It promotes cashless and contactless transactions even in purchasing necessary goods. And since the government's strength comes from the revenues, refining the existing process is essential to survive this pandemic.
The government imposes market tariffs to raise revenue, and many developing nations like the Philippines use taxes. In establishing trading hubs all over the country, the government also ensures income from market activities. Urdaneta City Bagsakan market is one of the biggest trading hubs of agricultural products in Northern Luzon.
This study is about developing an automated tariff payment collection system for agricultural products like fruits and vegetables and livestock. It primarily aims to provide cashless and contactless transactions in collecting tariffs at Urdaneta City, Pangasinan. Currently, the collection of tariffs is still in manual collection and process. Reporting is done afterward by encoding the daily reports on a spreadsheet and is not always on time. It also includes a large amount of workforce to facilitate collection. Some anomalies always come up with the manual tariff payment, leading to the inaccuracy of reports affecting revenue. The system automates cash collection and produces reporting in real-time. It can also keep track of the list of traders that can facilitate the elimination of illegal trading. The system has two parts – (1) a mobile application to be used by traders, and (2) a cashiering system intended for market staff and administrators in the Bagsakan market. The mobile application for traders provides a contactless procedure of product valuation and tariff computation. It also has an electronic wallet to deliver a cashless transaction in tariff payment. The cashiering system for the market administrators for the following objectives: (1) provide support in loading the trader's app electronic wallet, (2) offer assistance to new trader's transactions, and (3) ensure valid transactions of tariff payment in trading hubs.

KEYWORDS

Agricultural Product Tariff System, Quick-Response (QR) Code, Cashless and Contactless Transactions, Electronic Wallet, Mobile Application Technology

1. INTRODUCTION

The existence of trading hubs in different provinces in the Philippines is beneficial to both traders and buyers, aiding farmers to sell their crops and other products. The government imposed market tariffs primarily to raise revenue. Many developing nations like the Philippines use tariffs as a way of raising revenue. In establishing trading hubs all over the country, the government also ensures gain from market activities.

Currently, the collection of tariffs is in manual collection and process. Reporting is done afterward by encoding the daily reports on a spreadsheet and is not always on time. It also includes a large amount of staffing to facilitate collection. With the manual method of tariff collection, some anomalies always come up, leading to the inaccuracy of reports affecting revenue. At present, there is intense competition between bank wallets and third-party e-wallets for payment transactions (Teng, S., & Khong, K. W. (2021).

This study focuses on developing an electronic wallet-based tariff collection system using Quick-Response (QR) Code for a cashless and contactless system for agricultural products in Urdaneta City 'Bagsakan' Market. Its specific objectives are: (1) Offer a cashless and contactless transaction in product tariff assessment and payment; (2) Use Quick Response (QR) code in agricultural product tariff assessment; (3) Develop electronic wallet for tariff payment transactions; and (4) Deliver a solution in providing reliable government transactions through a mobile cashiering application.

2. BODY OF PAPER

Many of our daily transactions move to cashless systems. However, most of the implementations are seen only for essential goods and transportation. Other local government units also offer cashless systems but only for permits. The mobile tariff collection system, to be called marketIS is customized for the Urdaneta City Bagsakan Market.

2.1 Project Problem Definition and Objectives

This study focuses in finding solution to the following problems:

1. What is the present process in Urdaneta City Bagsakan Market in terms of: (a) product tariff assessment; and (b) tariff payment?
2. What technology-based solution can offer a cashless and contactless transaction of product tariff assessment and payment?
3. How is Quick Response (QR) code technology be applied in the present market process of Urdaneta City Bagsakan Market in terms of: (a) of product tariff assessment; and (b) tariff payment?
4. How mobile cashiering application can provide option to reliable government transactions?

This project is also open and prepared for future system expansion to cover central business district transactions to the Local Government Unit. As a mobile application, the marketIS will serve as a wallet-based tariff collection system. It has the following advantages and features: offer a cashless and contactless transaction in product tariff assessment and payment; use Quick-Response (QR) code in agricultural product tariff assessment; use Quick-Response (QR) code for transaction records; an electronic wallet for tariff payment transactions; provide real-time tariff assessment and payment transactions; and deliver a solution in providing reliable government transactions through a mobile cashiering application.

2.2 Market Tariff Payment Solution

This project is an offered solution for a cashless and contactless fulfillment of transactions. Due to the Covid-19 pandemic, traders in Urdaneta City Market are at risk. But to fulfill the needs of the government through revenues, market transactions must continue. The proposed solution in collecting market tariffs in Bagsakan Market of Urdaneta City is an information system through a mobile application that automates market transactions. Market transactions that for automation are as follows: (a) product valuation and assessment; (b) traders' registration; (c) issuance of product tariff amount based from product valuation and assessment transaction; (d) tariff payment using the electronic wallet, and (e) mobile cashier application for market officials.

2.2.1 Trader's Identification Information using Quick-Response (QR) Code

To be able to use the full feature of the system, the trader must download and install the mobile application of the system. It requires the trader to provide a valid identification cards, e.g Government issued ID to confirm the details inputted. If no valid ID is available, the trader can opt for certificates proving residency, e.g. Barangay Clearance, NBI Clearance and the like.

Once, account has been created, the system will provide a Trader Identification ID card with assigned QR code. This code contains the information about the trader. Also, this Trader Identification card shall be used in all transactions related to the system. Figure 1 presents the Trader's Identification Card with assigned QR code generated by the system.

Figure 1. Trader's Identification Card as scanned by the system

2.2.2 Automated Product Valuation

The mobile application automates the valuation and assessment of agricultural products delivered in Urdaneta City Bagsakan Market. This mobile application shall be made available to every trader who wants to sell Urdaneta City Bagsakan Market. Using this application, any seller must register their names and contact information first. When the system confirms the trader's information, registration of kinds of products to sell follows. This registration will continue to product assessment by determining the type of agricultural product.

2.2.3 Automatic Tariff Computation

The mobile application automatically performs the tariff computation, and the application will then compute the total tariff to pay. Tariff payment has two (2) options: (1) payment using electronic wallet load, and (2) by using an account card for first-time users without prior registration as a market trader.

This option shall result in the generation of QR codes for successful transactions as a receipt. The second option is by using a physical account card by paying directly to the City Market Office, and (2) mobile payment using the mobile application as an electronic wallet.

2.2.4 Tariff Payment Using the Electronic Wallet

Another essential feature of the mobile application is the electronic wallet function. The traders' account with an electronic wallet holds a digital amount for paying product tariffs. Payment transactions are only possible if the electronic wallet has enough amount equivalent to the computed tax. Figure 2 presents the mobile application features for the trader.

Figure 2. Mobile application features for the trader

2.2.5 Mobile Cashier Application

Market administrators will use the mobile cashier application. Market administrators are previously issuing stubs with the equivalent amount for product tariff. It is also the task of the market administrator to accept the payment and record every transaction.

Market officials shall use a separate mobile application that caters to the following tasks: (1) Loading station of electronic wallet for mobile tariff payment system, (2) Trader registration of arriving traders without mobile application, and (3) accepting payments of sellers without access to trader's mobile application.

2.3 System Design and Discussions

The tariff mobile collection system integrates Quick Response (QR) Code for Tariff Collection and Virtual Payment Transactions of agricultural products delivered by traders in Urdaneta City Bagsakan Market. Automated transactions are as follows: (a) traders' registration, (b) product valuation and assessment, (c) issuance of product tariff, (d) the electronic wallet, and (e) the Cashiering system.

2.3.1 Trader's Registration

A registration intent will be made for initial users to collect information about the trader's profile such as name, address, place of origin of products, products, and vehicle information used to deliver goods. Upon registration, each trader will have an assigned unique identifier to be used in transactions inside the Bagsakan Market. When a user is already registered, the app will default to a login intent.

Since its application for a government transaction, the researchers included the issuance of a trader's card. The trader must present the card in every transaction in the Urdaneta City Bagsakan market, and this is to ensure security. Figure 3 presents the use-case diagram of the system for the two main actors, the trader and the market cashier.

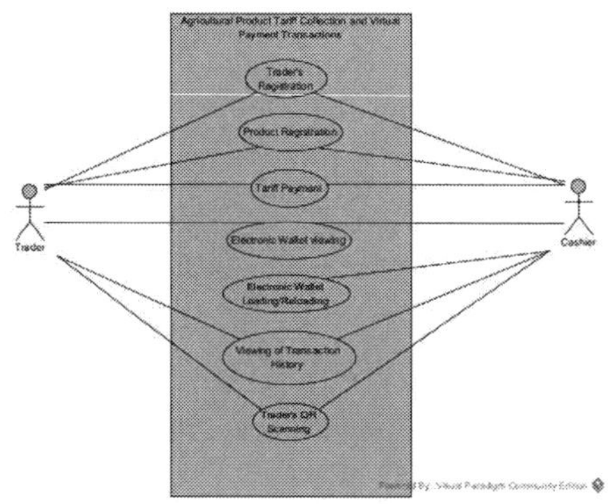

Figure 3. Use Case Diagram of the System

2.3.2 Product Valuation and Assessment

The mobile application will include a preset assessment of goods based on the usual procedure done. Product assessment determines the type of agricultural product. The trader can also view the current prices of goods in the application.

2.3.3 Issuance of Product Tariff

The system shall generate a Quick Response (QR) code reader for payment transactions. Each transaction will also be having corresponding timestamps, and these transaction details are reflected in QR code for verification later upon the trader's arrival in Bagsakan market.

2.3.4 Using the Electronic Wallet

The electronic wallet is one of the notable features of the project. Its primary purpose is to provide an automatic cashless and contactless payment after tariff assignment. Digital cash is used for tariff payment for cashless and contactless transactions. The mobile application also reflects all the transactions in real-time.

Loading an amount to the electronic wallet was done through the cashiering system. This cashiering system accompanied the mobile tariff transaction system intended for market administrators assigned in tariff collection.

2.3.5 The Cashiering System

The researchers included an accompanying automated system to support the project goal of providing a cashless and contactless transaction in Urdaneta City Bagsakan Market. This cashiering system is intended only for market administrators assigned to tariff collection. Mobile Cashiering system has the following features: (1)Loading for trader's electronic wallet ; (2) Generation of transaction details in QR code; (3) Registration of new traders; (4) Product valuation ; (5) Auto-Tariff generation for valuated products; (6) Checking of transactions history through QR; and (7) Transaction history viewing page.

The cashiering system can also keep track of the list of traders. This feature aids in the elimination of illegal trading. Then, a more secure collection of tariffs is assured, resulting in high revenue for the local government. Figure 4 presents the process flow of the system.

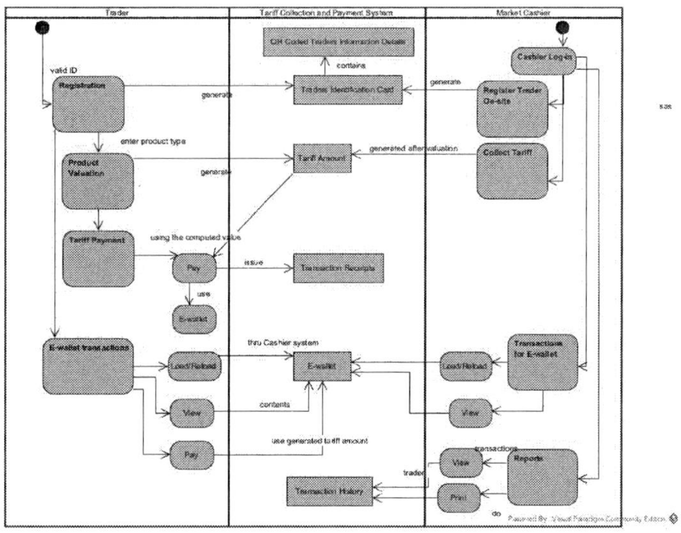

Figure 4. System Process Flow

2.4 Implementation

This system is a product tariff collection system and virtual payment transaction from registered traders with QR coded Identification Card. The use of QR code helps in proper documentation of transactions. It also promotes transparency by providing real-time reports from the acquired transactions of the system. Figure 5 presents the system architecture.

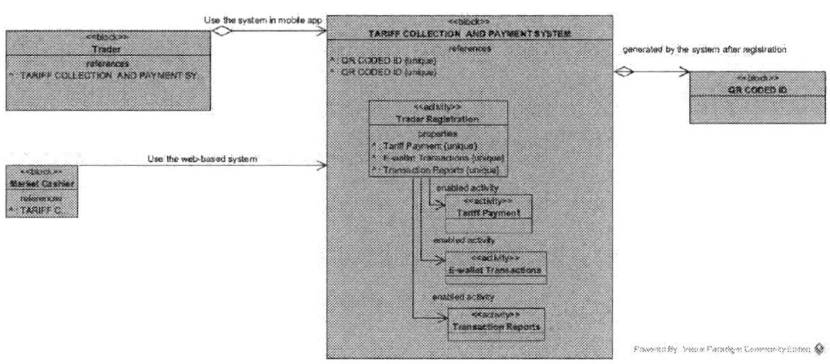

Figure 5. Project System Architecture

3. CONCLUSION

The researchers recommends the implementation of the automated tariff collection system for agricultural products. The system can benefit different agricultural trading hubs in the Philippines, where manual apportionment of tariffs is still in practice. Subsequently, this system also promotes cashless and contactless transactions and new standard practices amid Covid-19 pandemic.

With the manual collection, anomalies always come up, leading to the inaccuracy of tariff collection, significantly affecting revenue. The system also offers a secure system collection of tariffs for assured government gain. Transactions log aids in providing reliable transactions. Also, collecting payment is directed towards the Governments's Treasury electronically for a more secure revenue collection.

The electronic wallet can also expand applications in paying other transactions in local government. It can be extended to cover the whole central business district transactions to the Local Government Unit.

ACKNOWLEDGEMENT

The researchers would like to acknowledge the following: *The Department of Science and Technology* in believing in the contribution of this project study for the benefit of Filipino people; *The City Government of Urdaneta* for providing the means of making this study successful; *Urdaneta City University* for the platform of doing this project; and above all, *To God Almighty* for the blessing of life to be part of this endeavor. Thank you from our hearts.

REFERENCES

Caya, M. V. C., et. Al., *"Cashless transaction for resort club amenities using RFID technology,"* 2017IEEE 9th International Conference on Humanoid, Nanotechnology, Information Technology, Communication and Control, Environment and Management (HNICEM), Manila, 2017, pp. 1-5, doi: 10.1109/HNICEM.2017.8269488.

Conrad, E., Misenar, S., & Feldman, J. (2016). *Chapter 9 - Domain 8: Software Development Security (Understanding, Applying, and Enforcing Software Security).* In E. Conrad, S. Misenar, & J. Feldman (Eds.), *CISSP Study Guide (Third Edition)* (Third Edition, pp. 429–477). Syngress. https://doi.org/https://doi.org/10.1016/B978-0-12-802437-9.00009-6

Dewan, S. G., & Chen, L. (2005*). Mobile Payment Adoption in the US: A Cross-industry,* Crossplatform Solution. *Journal of Information Privacy and Security, 1*(2), 4–28. https://doi.org/10.1080/15536548.2005.10855765

Geambasu ,Cristina Venera et.al., "*Influence Factors for the Choice of a Software Development Methodology*" https://core.ac.uk/display/6261795?source=3

Hansson J., Xiong M. (2009) Real-Time Transaction Processing. In: LIU L., ÖZSU M.T. (eds) *Encyclopedia of Database Systems*. Springer, Boston, MA. https://doi.org/10.1007/978-0-387-39940-9_721

Majumder, A., et. Al., Pay-Cloak: A Biometric Back Cover for Smartphone with Tokenization Principle for Cashless Payment.

Mallat, N. (2007). *Exploring consumer adoption of mobile payments – A qualitative study. The Journal of Strategic Information Systems, 16*(4), 413–432. https://doi.org/https://doi.org/10.1016/j.jsis.2007.08.001

Nam G. (2021), Bringing the QR Code to Canada: The Rise of AliPay and WeChatPay in Canadian e-Commerce Markets. In: Arai K., Kapoor S., Bhatia R. (eds) *Proceedings of the Future Technologies Conference (FTC) 2020*, Volume 3. FTC 2020. Advances in Intelligent Systems and Computing, vol 1290. Springer, Cham. https://doi.org/10.1007/978-3-030-63092-8_42

Stefanou, C. J. (2003). System Development Life Cycle. In H. Bidgoli (Ed.), *Encyclopedia of Information Systems* (pp. 329–344). Elsevier. https://doi.org/https://doi.org/10.1016/B0-12-227240-4/00176-3

Tee, H., & Ong, H. (2016). Cashless payment and economic growth. *Financial Innovation, 2*, 1-9.

Teng, S., & Khong, K. W. (2021). Examining actual consumer usage of E-wallet: A case study of big data analytics. *Computers in Human Behavior, 121*, 106778. https://doi.org/https://doi.org/10.1016/j.chb.2021.106778

Tiwari, S. "An Introduction to QR Code Technology," 2016 International Conference on Information Technology (ICIT), Bhubaneswar, 2016, pp. 39-44, doi: 10.1109/ICIT.2016.021.

Wang, Y., & Shah, C. (2016). Exploring support for the unconquerable barriers in information seeking. *Proceedings of the Association for Information Science and Technology, 53*(1), 1–5. https://doi.org/https://doi.org/10.1002/pra2.2016.14505301106

CITIZEN IDENTIFICATION: CONCEPTS, PRINCIPLES AND OPINIONS – THE CASE OF MOZAMBIQUE

Paulo Maculuve and Luis Amaral
School of Engineering, Centro Algoritmi, University of Minho, Braga, Portugal

ABSTRACT

Citizen identification system in a digital economy context is fundamental for the citizen but also for the State in its role as a public service provider. Even for the legal system, since justice cannot be enforced in the absence of accurate identification of the players, under the risk of punishing the innocent and glorifying the criminals. Therefore, indubitable identity is also a social justice element (Hoover, 1972).

A variety of identification methods have been developed, throughout the years, to ensure indubitable identity. The use of biometrics has been effective and, with technological development, many innovative technologies have been used, such as smart cards that allow the portability of biometric information as part of Citizen Identification.

The Mozambican citizen identification system (ID System) is evolving. In the context of several strategic reforms of the public sector in Mozambique, particularly e-governance, many initiatives were carried out to enhance the identification system. However, there are still challenges concerning interoperability, process alignment and the boosting of Information and Communication Technologies (ICT) potential.

At the end of this paper, conclusions and recommendations focused on the rationalization, process alignment and enhancement of the ID System are presented, through the development of an Institutional and Logic Model of the Mozambican citizen Identification system, to ensure that the Information System concept (processes, people, and technology) is rationalized, according to the work systems theory (Alter, 2013).

KEYWORDS

Citizen Identification, Interoperability, E-Governance

1. INTRODUCTION

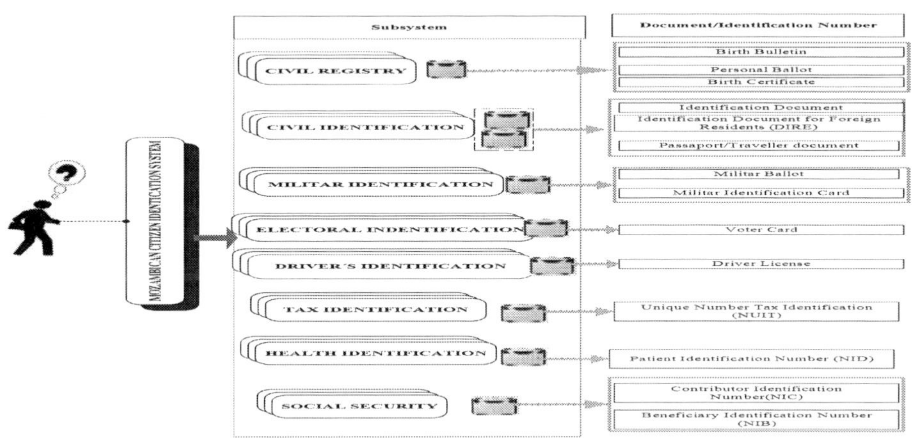

Figure 1. Macro vision of the Mozambican citizen identification system

Identification is the action and effect of identifying or being identified, and it is related to identity, which is a set of unique features of a person compared to others. Identity is the knowledge that a human being has regarding itself (dos Santos, 2013).

The human concern to identify people in a unique and distinguished way (indubitable, individual or distinct identity) dates back to years before Christ (BC). For instance, several methods to identify people have been developed (de Araújo & Pasquali, 2004).

Figure 1 illustrates the Mozambican citizen Identification system, which comprises various subsystems, in which each has its process and database, to produce its respective documents in an isolated way, in a sort of "Island" systems or Information Systems silos (Amaral, 2021).

It is worth highlighting that the objective of this article is focused on the citizen identification system, which is a responsibility of the state to create and/or maintain as part of its obligations towards the Citizen and vice-versa.

In the context of an Electronic Governance (e-governance) strategy, the Mozambican government has been taking actions towards the implementation of a citizen identification model rooted in ICTs potentialities, among which, the following are distinguished: (1) creation of a multi-sectorial team, that developed the concept of Unique Citizen Number Identification Card (NUIC, in Portuguese acronyms); (2) introduction of new documents formats (ID, DIRE and passport/travel document), based on biometric elements (Decretos 11,12 e 13/2008, de 4 de Abril); (3) revision of the Civil Registry Code (Lei 12/2018, de 4 de Dezembro), adopting the NUIC principle in the Civil Registry process, among others.

Taking into account the current Mozambican ID system and considering ICTs potential, it is worth performing a study about the Mozambican citizen identification model that will respond to challenges like security, privacy and availability of citizen identification data in all its life cycle. As portrayed in Figure 2, this life cycle starts at birth (materialized in legal affairs, through Birth Registration).

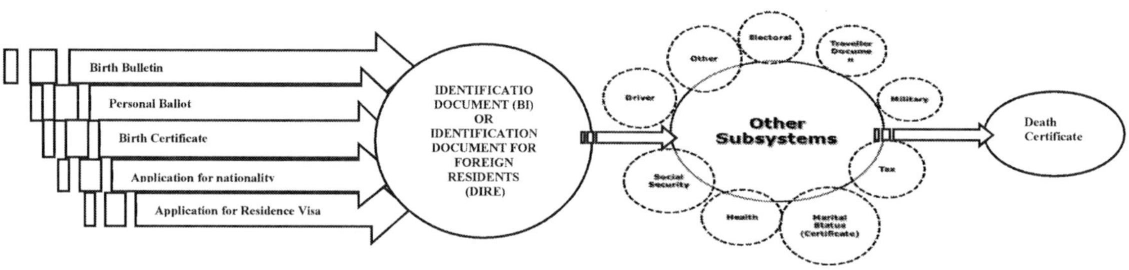

Figure 2. Simplified vision of the citizen life cycle under the identification point of view

2. THE CONCEPT OF CITIZEN AND ITS IDENTIFICATION

For a better framework of the subject of study, Mozambican citizen identification system, and to understand the philosophical foundations of the topic, it is essential to perform a bibliographic review of the concepts.

2.1 Citizen Concept

A key feature of a rule or law is its subjection to legal norms, since that is where the boundaries that determine the actions of its players - the government and the governed (the citizen) - are established through a set of rights and obligations, agreed as citizenship.

The citizenship concept dates back to Classical Antiquity. The French Revolution, in 1789, rose the awareness of citizenship with the proclamation of the "Droit de L'Homme et du Citoyen" (The Declaration of the Human Rights and of the Citizen), which, in general, advocated the effective participation of an individual in each community, according to the duties and obligations established and to be observed by all members of that community (Palazzo, 2021).

From that assumption, many states incorporated in their constitution and/or ordinary laws a variety of definitions alongside, for example: (a) In terms of the Portuguese Constitution (Constituição Da República, 1976) all citizens are entitled to the rights and subject to duties assigned in the Constitution; (b) According to Melo (1998; p.78)[1], it was verified that there was an evolutionary expansion of the citizenship concept, which

[1] In Dos Santos (2013)

was extended to civil, political and social rights, and more recently, duties regarding collective interests; (c) According to the Constitution of the Federal Republic of Brazil, (Constituição Federal, 2016) men and women have equal rights and duties in constitutional terms; (d) In terms of the Constitution of the Republic of Mozambique (Constituição da Republica, 2004), men and women are equal under the law in all scopes of political, economic, social, and cultural life.

Therefore, according to the constitution, a citizen can be defined by a set of rights and duties that enable them to participate in political and economic activities (Furtado, 2010).

For the identification system, according to our proposal, the citizen can be defined under two perspectives, namely, (1) citizen as a natural simple and pure person, and (2) citizen as a natural complex person, whereby:

(a) A Citizen as a natural simple and pure person, reflects the individual as a simple person of legal relations. In this perspective, the citizen engages in social legal relations from its birth registration, where he or she is assigned citizenship and visibility before the legal system of a given country, reflecting its initial stage of life, gifted by rights, but exempted from exercising them directly and personally.

(b) A Citizen as a natural complex person reflects his/her interaction with the complex legal environment. In this perspective, the citizen is empowered to exercise directly and personally, its rights and duties, contemplating several qualities acquired from its participation in multiple processes of life, namely: (1) health care user; (2) taxpayer; (3) voter; (4) driver; (5) social security system contributor or beneficiary; among others.

2.2 Citizen Identification

Establishing the identity of an indisputable person was a matter of concern of various generations in humanity. Identification is the action and effect of identifying or identify better. It is the action of recognizing someone as their own.

For Federico Olóriz Aguilera (1855-1912)[2], "identification is the most frequent and elementary act of a social life". It makes use of all senses, vision, smell, hearing, tact, and taste to identify people and things. However, when there is a need for accurate identification, to "praise" or "accuse" someone, it is important to have an indisputable identification, which characterizes the difference from another similar person. A variety of methods were developed and adopted by different countries to promote indisputable identification along the development of humanity (de Araújo & Pasquali, 2004), namely:

(a) Name is the oldest method used by human beings to recognize their peers and things that surround them.

(b) Ferret, a method based on the use of an iron tool, warmed out to tag criminals, slaves and animals.

(c) Mutilation is a method that consists in amputating parts of the body.

(d) Tattoos are a method that consists of tattooing the internal part of the right forearm with letters or number.

(e) Photography, the photographic method is used to complement other methods, such as the name.

(f) Part of the body, identification system based on measures of the exterior part of the ear canal, using an instrument called "otometer".

(g) Dental Arch is a method used to identify people that committed civil and criminal activities

(h) Anthropometry, based on the principle that the human skeleton does not change after 21 years, collected various processes and created a data basis with measures of different parts of the human body to compare with those from criminal cases reported at the time.

(i) Papilloscopy, commonly designated "fingerprints" or currently treated by biometry, consists of differentiating people, based on biophysical characteristics that do not change with time and that do not replicate in other human beings.

The use of some of these methods was limited due to their fragility or unhuman character, but also because they are difficult to file and search. Initially, identification aimed to determine ownership of animals, slaves, and personal objects. Over time, the priority was to prove the identification of harmful people in society, and, with the evolution and modernization of humanity, each person must carry responsive identification (timely, security and availability) and Current challenges demand identification systems with specific characteristics, namely, security and privacy of citizen's data to face cyber-crimes.

---

[2] In Dos Santos, (2013)

Considering the need to exchange information there is also a requirement for a key (the Unique Citizen Identification Number) associated with biometric elements, as well as the use of data storage technology, commonly known as "chip", standardized by the International Standard Organization (ISOxxxx).

3. THE CURRENT MOZAMBICAN IDENTIFICATION SYSTEM - STATE OF ART

After this brief contextualization, in the current section, we describe the current Mozambican Citizen Identification System, obeying the two perspectives of the definition of Citizen (according to our proposal):

3.1 The Citizen Identification: Citizen as a Natural Simple and Pure Person

The citizen identification in this perspective is expressed by birth registration and civil identification.

(a) Civil Registry, s subsystems that keeps birth registration information. The documents of this subsystem are (1) Birth bulletin; (2) Personal Ballot; (3) birth certificate.

(b) Civil Identification, a subsystem that keeps the database about the identification of nationals or naturalized citizens (that acquire Mozambican nationality) or those who required residence visas. The resulting documents from this subsystem are: (1) Identification Document (ID); (2) Identification Document for Foreign Residents (DIRE); (3) Passport/Traveler Document.

3.2 The Citizen Identification: Citizen as a Natural Complex Person

Table 1. Macro vision of the attributes of several Mozambican identification subsystems

#	Document (Subsystem)	Attributes																						
		Name[3]	Father	Mother	Residential Address	Professional Address	Document Number[4]	Birth Day	Marital status	Place of Birth	Tel	Fax	Email	Biometry	Nationality	Sex	Height	Expiry Date	Issuing Entity	Issuing Date	Place of Issue	Profession	Signature	photography
1.	Birth bulletin	•	•	•	•	•	•	•	X	•	X	X	X	X	•	•	X	X	•	•	•	X	X	X
2.	Personal Ballot	•	•	•	•	•	•	•	X	•	X	X	X	X	•	•	X	X	•	•	•	X	X	X
3.	Birth certificate	•	•	•	•	•	•	•	•	•	•	•	•	X	•	•	X	X	•	•	•	•	X	X
4.	Identification Document	•	•	•	•	•	•	•	•	•	•	•	•	•	•	•	•	•	•	•	•	•	•	•
5.	Identification Document for Foreign Residents (DIRE)	•	•	•	•	•	•	•	•	•	•	•	•	•	•	•	X	•	•	•	•	•	•	•
6.	Passport/Traveller Document	•	•	•	•	•	•	•	•	•	•	•	•	•	•	•	X	•	•	•	•	•	•	•
7.	Military Identification	•	•	•	•	•	•	•	•	•	•	•	•	X	•	•	•	•	•	•	•	•	•	•
8.	Electoral Identification	•	•	•	•	•	•	•	•	•	•	•	•	•	•	•	X	•	•	•	•	•	•	•
9.	Drivers' Identification	•	•	•	•	•	•	•	•	•	•	•	•	•	•	•	X	•	•	•	•	•	•	•
10.	Tax Identification	•	•	•	•	•	•	•	•	•	•	•	•	X	•	•	X	•	•	•	•	•	X	X
11.	Health Identification	•	•	•	•	•	•	•	•	•	•	•	•	X	•	•	X	•	•	•	•	•	X	X
12.	Social Security Identification	•	•	•	•	•	•	•	•	•	•	•	•	X	•	•	X	•	•	•	•	•	•	•

[3] The name structure and other elements are not standardized (for example, in some cases names and surnames are an unique name, in other cases the given names and surnames are different attributes).

[4] The structure of the document number is not uniform in deferments subsystems

The citizen identification in this perspective is expressed in the diverse subsystems, namely: (a) Health Identification maintains the citizen database that goes through the public hospital, assigning them the Patient Identification Number (NID) to access the clinical file; (b) Tax identification keeps citizens' databases and entities in compliance with tax obligations. The essence of the subsystem is the assignment of the Unique Number Tax Identification (NUIT); (c) Military Identification keeps database from national citizens above 18 years of age, eligible for military service. The documents required are (1) Military Ballot and (2) Military Identification Card; (d) Electoral Identification keeps a database from citizens with electoral capacity and the document used is the voter card; (e) Drivers′ Identification keeps a database from citizens enabled to drive motor vehicles and the document used is the driver′s license; and (f)Social Security Identification, database from (contributors and beneficiaries) of the social security, resulting in the creation of two identifiers, namely: (1) Contributor Identification Number and (2) Beneficiary Identification Number.

Each of the identification subsystems holds its own attribute set. In Table 1, there is a macro vision of the attributes of the different subsystems of the Mozambican citizen identification.

4. ANALYSIS OF THE MOZAMBICAN CITIZEN IDENTIFICATION SYSTEM

ICT in an age of the knowledge economy, where the differentiating factor is digitalization, accurate identification of the citizen is crucial.

The trend of the citizen identification systems is based on the smart card technology, which allows the portability of relevant information of an indubitable identity, which carries, at least: (1) Unique Citizen Identification Number; (2) Database about the citizen registry; (3) Identification document based on a smart card; (4) Essential data visible in the identification document (photography, name (s), birth date and others; (5) Biometric data, digital signature and other information usually stored in the database and/or in chips, visible only with an appropriate reader; among others.

For Mozambican citizens, the birth registry is mandatory and free of charge in the first 180 days of the citizens' life (Lei 12/2018, de 4 de Dezembro, 2018). However, many children, in rural areas, are not registered at birth for several reasons, emphasis on the following: (1) parents′ unawareness about the importance of the registry, they do so, when there is a demand, for instance, when a child is about to enroll in the first year of school; (2) in some cases, naming a child is preceded by traditional rituals, that in most cases delay the child registration.

As shown in Figure 1, each institution manages its processes, from the collection, storage, and citizens′ database, spends vast resources (human, material and financial) maintaining common citizen's data, disregarding standard principles and/or interoperability procedures, resulting in the duplication of records in several subsystems, therefore, identification of the citizen becomes complex and generates huge waste.

In general, exchange of information between ID subsystems is done manually, making it difficult and complex to develop new public and private services.

Currently, the citizen acts as the interoperability enabler between different subsystems, by providing information about changes in its registry along its life cycle and lack of interoperability demands that the citizens go to countless Government Institutions to request several identification documents, contributing to high levels of bureaucracy and higher costs for both the citizen and the state.

Most of the documents within the identification systems do not have a unique and common citizen identifier. Most recently, the inclusion of the ID number in passports and driver license was ordered. Thus, it is necessary to extend this procedure to all subsystems; the challenge is that the majority of the subsystems do not have biometric data, putting at stake the principle of indubitable identity.

Given the situation, the development of studies about the Mozambican citizen identification system is crucial.

5. CONCLUSIONS, RECOMMENDATIONS AND PROPOSALS FOR FUTURE DEVELOPMENTS

According to Figure 2, from the citizen's identification perspective, the life cycle begins in the Civil Registry (materialized by Birth Registry) subsystem, and ends in the same subsystem, through the issue of a death certificate. Therefore, the Civil Registry subsystem is the foundation of all identity systems that is why all efforts toward modernization must ensure an accurate interconnection between this and other systems.

The Mozambican citizen identification system portrays problems in two dimensions: (1) remarkably high and avoidable costs to the citizen; (2) it does not allow for responsive (safe, timely and available) information regarding citizen identification to help the state in its diverse administrative actions, including those that are harmful to government sustainability, namely, corruption, organized crime, and counter-terrorism.

Recalling Table 1 and making an attribute analysis, we verify that some subsystem documents like, for example, the Civil Registry contains redundant information. Therefore, we recommend binding it in one, the Birth Certificate, with updated information, and automatically eliminate the rest (Birth Bulletin and Personal Ballot, as illustrated in Figure 3.) An enhanced study may determine the rationalization of other subsystems.

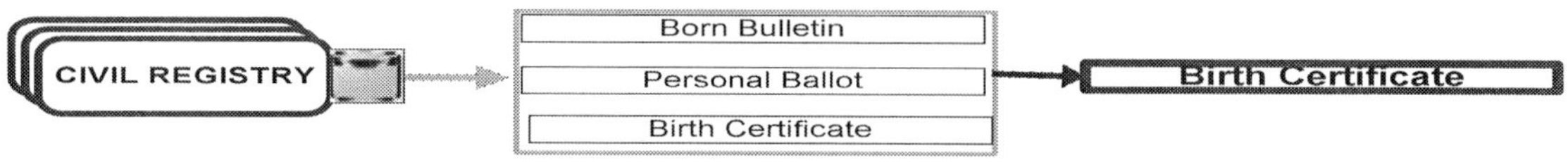

Figure 3. Rationalization of the Civil Registry subsystem

The Work System Theory (WST) demands interoperable information systems, which is absent from the Mozambican citizen identification system, making it dysfunctional, in a sense that it will not produce the results for which it was conceived efficiently (Alter, 2013).

Taking into account the above description, a study about the citizen identification systems, developed in these two views, is recommended, namely:

(a) The development of an interoperable Citizen Identification Conceptual Model to guarantee efficiency in the delivery of services in the public sector.

(b) The creation of an institutional base for the management, maintenance and techno-legal control of the citizen identification system in a holistic vision and with a sustainable architecture (planned; developed; implemented and maintained).

A concept study in the proposed view becomes important because a citizen identification system, founded in a modern and contemporary architecture that responds to current and next generations' challenges, will contribute to an efficient function of the public administration, as well as the democratization of the country and justice (Hoover, 1972).

REFERENCES

Alter, S. (2013). Work System Theory: Overview of Core Concepts, Extensions, and Challenges for the Future. *Business Analytics and Information Systems - Http://Repository.Usfca.Edu/at/35.*

Amaral, L. (2021). Sistemas de Informação na Administração Pública. In *Livro Branco* (1st ed., Vol. 1). APSI.

AMICCI, P. A. (2015). Identificação Criminal. *Https://Www.Eduvaleavare.Com.Br/Wp-Content/Uploads/2015/05/Artigo2.Pdf, 5*, 1–22.

de Araújo, M. E. C., & Pasquali, L. (2004). Histórico dos Processos de Identificação. *Http://Www.Institutodeidentificacao.Pr.Gov.Br/Arquivos/File/Forum/Historico_processos.Pdf.*

dos Santos, C. M. (2013, March 21). *Hermenêutica e o conceito jurídico de cidadão na ação popular no paradigma do Estado Democrático de Direito.* Revista Jus Navigandi.

Furtado, M. G. (2010). *A formação do Cidadão conforme a Constituição da República Federativa do Brasil de 1998.* https://www.teses.usp.br/teses/disponiveis/2/2140/tde-13122010-160747/publico/MARCELO_FURTADO_Dissertacao.pdf - 27-09-2021

Constituição da República, (1976) (testimony of Governo da Republica de Portugal).

Decreto de actualização de BI, DIRE e Passaporte, (2008) (testimony of Governo de Moçambique).

Decreto 67/2017, de 01 de Dezembro – Quadro de Interoperabilidade para o Governo Electrónico, (2017) (testimony of Governo de Moçambique).

Lei 12/2018, de 4 de Dezembro, Código de Registo Civil, (2018) (testimony of GOVERNO DE MOÇAMBIQUE).

Constituição Federal, (2016) (testimony of Governo Federal).

Hoover, J. E. (1972). The Role of Identification in Law Enforcement: An Historical The Role of Identification in Law Enforcement: An Historical Adventure. *St. John's Law Review*, *46*(4), 1–20.

Palazzo, F. P. (2021). A cidadania e as três leis de Newton. *Revista Consultor Jurídico.*

A CONCEPTUAL MODEL FOR REPRESENTATION (TRANSFER) PROCESSES

Tobias Huhmann and Chantal Müller
University of Education Weingarten, Germany

ABSTRACT

In mathematics education the learner's own transfer of representations within the same as well as between different levels of representations is an essential indicator to develop understanding. Digital media have expanded the possibilities of representing, learning with representations, and transfer processes of representations. This opens up a new spectrum of representation (transfer) processes in which these possibilities must be identified, analyzed, researched, and evaluated from a mathematical educational point of view. For this characterization process we developed the model Representation-Transfer-Spectrum. As an example, the use of the model is illustrated with an arithmetic learning object. Based on the characterization of *possibilities* that are implemented in the application, an important question to be researched is, which *realities* can be identified during individual task processes with the application? The goal for research and teaching is a "specific sensitivity for media (use) in mathematics education", so that analogue and digital media can be analyzed in a potential-oriented way in order to orchestrate them for better teaching and learning.

KEYWORDS

Mathematical Concepts, Learning with Analogue and Digital Representations, Transfer of Representations, Cognitive Demands

1. THEORETICAL FRAMEWORK

With digital media, the possibilities of representation have developed fast with regard to temporal and local availability. They can be manipulable, dynamizable, connected and synchronous. In mathematics education, learning with representations and especially the learner's own transfer processes of representations within the same and between different levels of representations, are seen as essential to develop understanding in the process of learning mathematics (Wittmann, 1981). For this purpose, new forms of representations, levels of representations, possibilities of combinations and representation transfer processes in teaching and learning contexts have to be 1. identified, 2. analyzed and 3. evaluated from a mathematical educational point of view. Thereby, the question arises, which cognitive demands are supported or replaced by digital media or are still placed on learners by learning mathematics (Huhmann & Müller, 2020, 2022a in press, 2022b in press)?

Representing and representations pursue two basic intentions. In *representing* the focus is *on doing*, on *externalizing one's own thinking* for communication with oneself and with others. Representing for oneself takes place in order to relieve and support one's own thinking processes through what is (visually) represented, in order to orient oneself in one's own thinking and to shape the further thinking process. Representing for others is done to communicate one's own thoughts through what is (visually) represented. It also helps to explain where words are missing for oneself and for others. The (visual) information can support to get into exchange with others, to communicate about one's own thoughts and to justify findings about relationships and regularities with the help of what is represented (Duval, 2006). *Representations* serve for the process of representing *as a tool to present one's own perceptions and ideas externally*. So, the intention of representations is to document information which is volatile (Huhmann, 2013; Wollring, 2006). Representation transfer processes are always required when at least two representations are given. They have to be compared on one or between different levels of representation – the levels acting, iconic, symbolic (see Bruner, 1971). A representation transfer is also required when a new representation has to be constructed based on a given one. In both cases, given elements of one representation have to be related to given or to be constructed elements of another representation. A purposeful use of different representations can create learning opportunities to explore relationships between representations and to recognize basic structures (Kuhnke, 2013).

Based on the models of acquisition and representation of knowledge (Piaget, 1972; Bruner, 1971), further models can be found for identifying and analyzing representation possibilities and representation transfer processes. Lesh et al. (1987) focus in their model on different analogue representation forms and associated representation transfers. The model is extended by a technological form of representation by Johnson (2018), with which digital media (e.g. manipulable and moveable pictures as further forms of representation) are basically covered. Further distinctions and specific features of representations with digital media as well as learning with these digital representations remain out of consideration. The model of multiple external representations according to Ladel (2009) is based on Bruners (1971) model and levels of representation - enactive, iconic, symbolic. It focuses on elaborated representation possibilities with digital and analogue media. However, it does not focus on the identification and analysis of representation transfer processes.

In summary, we see a research desideratum in the model-theoretical identification and analysis of representing, representation possibilities, and representation transfer processes in learning with analogue and digital media.

2. REPRESENTATION-TRANSFER-SPECTRUM

Based on the models of Piaget (1972) and Bruner (1971) as well as on the extended new representation possibilities offered by digital media, we have developed an extended model as a representation transfer spectrum (cf. Figure 1). With this model we want to identify, analyze, and evaluate from a mathematics educational point of view learning in terms of perceiving and acting with analogue and digital media:

1. *Identify*: In which levels are representing, the representations and the representation transfer processes located?
2. *Analyze*: Which cognitive demands are associated with representing, the representations and the representation transfer processes? Which cognitive demands are placed on learners and which are replaced or supported by media?
3. *Evaluate*: Which representing, representations and representation transfer processes are suited from a mathematic educational perspective?

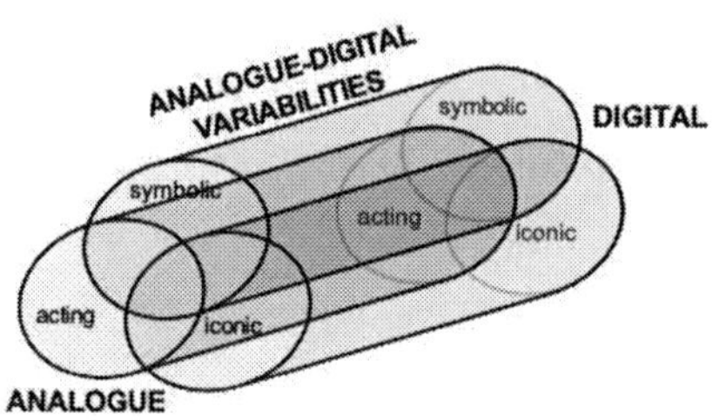

Figure 1. Representation-Transfer-Spectrum (Huhmann & Müller, 2020, 2022a in press, 2022b in press)

Learning objects and activities can be located in the individual areas analogue, digital or analogue-digital. Within these areas, a further assignment to the different levels of representations takes place. We also include the intersections in the model under the term "levels of representations" because representations cannot always be assigned to just one level of representation. If representations contain elements from different levels of representations e.g. depictions and at the same time descriptions (Schnotz & Bannert 2003), they are to be placed in the corresponding intersection.

With regard to the digital and analogue-digital area, there is an urgent need to research (Krauthausen, 2012, 2020) possible representations of the learning objects, and the suitability of the representation-transfer-spectrum to identify, analyze, and to evaluate representation (transfer) processes from a mathematics education point of view. For the digital area, central questions arise: What are the characteristics of the different levels of representations, and what are the characteristics of the different representations? Which learning objects can be located in their digital representation on which level? The analogue-digital area forms a spectrum between the analogue and the digital area. This area is to be investigated with regard to the representations of learning objects and activities in terms of possibilities and their characteristics. This involves the identification and analysis of analogue-digital variabilities - in the sense of variable parts closer to the analogue or digital level as well as with variable foci in or between the three diameters of the respective area. In this area, augmented reality and virtual reality applications, among others, are to be considered in a future-oriented manner. Representation transfer processes become visible in this model by connecting the activities located on the representation levels with arrows, so that the transfer from an initial representation, which is given to learners, to a final representation, which learners are supposed to construct by themselves or relate the both given ones, is recognizable. Representations become visible by dots in the levels.

In order to answer the introducing question, we will visualize representation transfer processes for a selected activity from arithmetic lessons in elementary school. Therefore, we use the representation-transfer-spectrum and analyze the representation transfer processes with regard to the cognitive requirements placed on learners or taken over by the digital medium.

Activity: Find all decompositions in two parts of the number 12 and document them. To find different decompositions, learners place chips in an analogue or virtual twenty frame (Urff, 2009). Discovered decompositions are documented.

Implementation analogue:

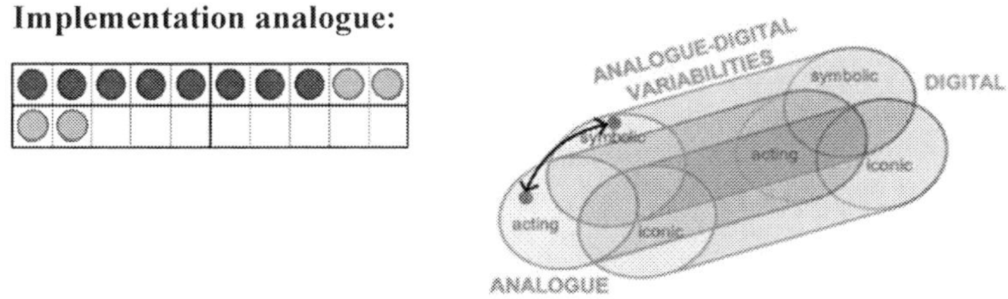

Figure 2. Representation-Transfer-Spectrum - implementation analogue

Cognitive requirements: Learners have to structure the number of chips of a color as an independent subset, recognize it and assign a symbolic number sign to the respective subset. With the assigned number signs, an addition term matching the iconic representation must be developed and represented by the learners. The assigned number signs will be defined as first summand and second summand and documented in writing.

Learners must perform the cognitive requirements of structuring and of the representation transfer processes between the acting-iconic level and the symbolic level.

Implementation digital:

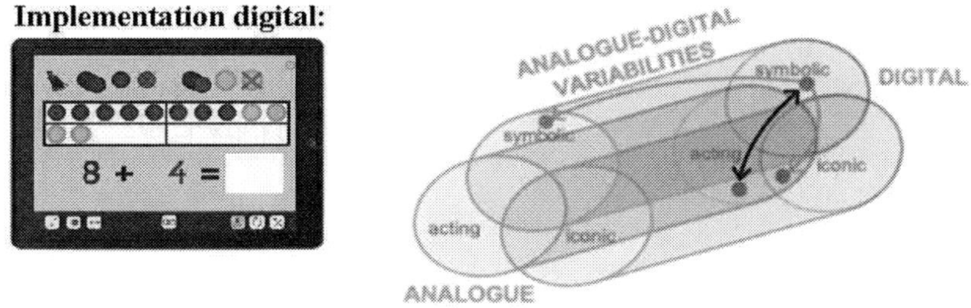

Figure 3. Representation-Transfer-Spectrum - implementation digital

Cognitive requirements: Learners place virtual chips in the virtual twenty frame. For each virtual action of placement, a symbolic addition term corresponding to the iconic representation is displayed, which is synchronously and automatically generated by the system. If red chips are added or removed, the symbolic 1st summand changes automatically. Accordingly, the 2nd summand changes automatically when virtual blue chips are placed. By tapping a placed chip, the color of this chip can be changed. For example, if there are 8 red and 4 blue chips in the virtual twenty frame and the 3rd red chip is colored blue by tapping on it, the newly colored blue chip is automatically shifted in the entire arrangement so that the set is displayed structured as 7 red and 5 blue chips. This means that the system automatically structures the set according to the color characteristic. Learners do not have to identify the quantity of chips of the same color in order to assign them to the symbolic numeral. A relation can be identified by a visual comparison of colors of chips and numerals. Likewise, this can take place via the comparison of impacts on the action-iconic-virtual or on the symbolic-virtual level and of effects on the automatically synchronously generated representation level. By the color configurations given by the digital medium and by the connection of the representation levels also the definition and order of 1st and 2nd summands is fixed.

The representation transfer processes described and the cognitive requirements are taken over here by the digital medium and do not have to be performed independently by the learner.

With the digital implementation of the activity, new documentation possibilities and representation transfer processes arise. These possibilities are visible in the representation-transfer-spectrum by grey arrows and the corresponding points. On one hand, the decompositions found of the number 12 can be documented in an analogue written form. On the other hand, the digital media offers the possibility to create screenshots of the found decompositions, so that they are digitally documented in an active-iconic way.

3. FINDINGS AND PERSPECTIVES

The activity Find all decompositions served here as an example to demonstrate the use of the Representation-Transfer-Spectrum. First, we identified and made visible, which forms of representation exist at which levels of representation and which representation transfer processes are demanded.

By comparing the implementation analogue and the implementation digital the different representation transfer processes became visible. Based on this the cognitive demands which are placed on learners and which are supported or replaced by digital media could be analyzed. We consider the suitability of the model from two perspectives: Can it serve as a model of thinking and analysis to make lesson planning and design decisions regarding a purposeful use and orchestration of different media? Can the representation-transfer-spectrum serve as a model of thinking and analysis for characterizing applications, for researching the applications with regard to the ways in which learners proceed with them, and for identifying, analyzing, and further developing analogue and digital representation possibilities with the help of applications?

From the perspective of research possibilities of action and affordances (Gibson, 1977), that means possibilities of action implicit in the medium, where made visible with the help of the model. With this first step we can answer our research question: Which possibilities are implemented in the application? Now the second step is to find out which realities can be identified during individual task processes with the application? Therefore further research is needed.

To summarize, with the help of the model, possibilities and realities of use are to be identified and made visible. The goal of this model is to characterize learning objects and their use in the context of (digital) media with regard to (new) forms of representation, (new) levels of representation and (new) representation transfer processes as well as (new) combination possibilities of representation.

The future-oriented question is which significance the representation-transfer-spectrum may have as a model of thinking and analysis for learning with analogue and digital media, also in other educational disciplines. The associated goal for research and teaching is a "specific sensitivity for media (use) in (mathematics) education", so that analogue and digital media are analyzed in a potential-oriented manner in order to orchestrate them for better teaching and learning.

REFERENCES

Bruner, J. S. (1971). Über kognitive Entwicklung. [About cognitive development]. In J. S. Bruner, R. R. Olver & P. M. Greenfield (Eds.), *Studien zur kognitiven Entwicklung.* Ernst Klett Verlag.

Gibson, J. J. (1977) The theory of affordances. In R. Shaw & J. Bransford (Eds.), Perceiving, Acting and Knowing (1st ed, pp. 67–82). Routledge. https://doi.org/10.4324/9781315467931

Huhmann, T. (2013). *Einfluss von Computeranimationen auf die Raumvorstellungsentwicklung.* [Influence of computer animation on the development of spatial imagination]. Springer Spektrum. https://doi.org/10.1007/ 978-3-658-03805-1

Huhmann, T., & Müller, C. (2022 in press a). Learning mathematics with media - representing, representations and representation transfer processes. CERME12.

Huhmann, T., & Müller, C. (2022 in press b). Darstellen, Darstellungen und Darstellungstransferprozesse - im Spektrum analoger und digitaler Medien. [Representing, Representation and Representation Transfer Processes - in the Spectrum of Analogue and Digital Media]. In B. Brandt, L. Bröll & H. Dausend (Eds.), *Digitales Lernen in der Grundschule III.* Waxmann.

Huhmann, T., & Müller, C. (2020). Zur Synchronität und Vernetzung von Darstellungsebenen für den Darstellungstransfer. [On the synchronicity and the connectivity of representation levels for the representation transfer]. In H.-S. Siller, W. Weigel, & J. F. Wörler (Eds.), *Beiträge zum Mathematikunterricht 2020* (p. 1473). WTM-Verlag. https://doi.org/10.37626/GA9783959871402.0

Duval, R. (2006). A cognitive analysis of problems of comprehension in a learning of mathematics. Educational Studies in Mathematics, 61(1–2), 103–131. https://doi.org/10.1007/s10649-006-0400-z

Johnson, E. L. (2018). A New Look at the Representations for Mathematical Concepts: Expanding on Lesh's Model of Representations of Mathematical Concepts. Forum on Public Policy Online. https://eric.ed.gov/?q=source%3A%22Forum+on+Public+Policy+Online%22&ff1=dtySince_2017&id=EJ1191692

Krauthausen, G. (2020). Vier Ebenen der Digitalisierungsdebatte. [Four levels of the digitization debate]. In G. Krauthausen et al. (Eds.), *Tablets im Grundschulunterricht – Fachliches Lernen, Medienpädagogik und informatische Bildung* (pp. 140–145). Schneider.

Krauthausen, G. (2012). *Digitale Medien im Mathematikunterricht der Grundschule.* [Digital media in mathematics lessons at elementary school]. Spektrum Akademischer Verlag. https://doi.org/10.1007/978-3-8274-2277-4

Kuhnke, K. (2013). Vorgehensweisen von Grundschulkindern beim Darstellungswechsel. Eine Untersuchung am Beispiel der Multiplikation im 2. Schuljahr. [Procedures of elementary school children in changing representations. A study using the example of multiplication in the 2nd grade]. Springer Spektrum.

Ladel, S. (2009). *Multiple externe Repräsentationen (MERs) und deren Verknüpfung durch Computereinsatz. Zur Bedeutung für das Mathematiklernen im Anfangsunterricht. [Multiple external representations (MERs) and their linkage through computer use. On the importance for learning mathematics in early education].* Verlag Dr. Kovač.

Lesh, R., Post, T. R., & Behr, M. (1987). Representations and Translations among Representations in Mathematics Learning and Problem Solving. In C. Janiver (Eds.), *Problems of Representation in the Teaching and Learning of Mathematics* (pp. 33–40). Lawrence Erlbaum.

Piaget, J. (1972). *Theorien und Methoden der Erziehung.* [Theories and methods of education]. Fischer Taschenbuch.

Schnotz, W., & Bannert, M. (2003). Construction and interference in learning from multiple representation. *Learning and Instruction, 13*, 141–156.

Urff, C. (2009). Virtuelles Zwanzigerfeld. [Virtual twenty frame]. http://www.lernsoftware-mathematik.de/cms/?p=503

Wittmann, E. C. (1981). *Grundfragen des Mathematikunterrichts.* [Fundamental questions of mathematics teaching]. Vieweg.

Wollring, B. (2006). Kindermuster und Pläne dazu - Lernumgebungen zur frühen geometrischen Förderung. [Children's patterns and plans for them - learning environments for early geometric fostering]. In M. Grüßing & A. Peter-Koop (Eds.), *Die Entwicklung mathematischen Denkens in Kindergarten und Grundschule: Beobachten - Fördern - Dokumentieren* (1st ed., pp. 80–102). Mildenberger.

PUBLIC E-ADMINISTRATION: UNDERSTANDING THE PERCEPTION OF TAXES BY GENERATION Y AND GENERATION Z

Tereza Zichová
Faculty of Informatics and Statistics, Prague University of Economics and Business, Czech Republic

ABSTRACT

Electronic participation has become more important than ever in the last two years. The pandemic in Europe since 2020 has accelerated the transition of governments to e-governments. However, countries still face many challenges in developing e-government. One of the problems is a lack of understanding of e-participation civic actors. Since, Generation Y and Generation Z are important internet users, their attitude towards public e-services is a crucial influential factor. The purpose of this study is to identify areas of potential challenges of public e-administration that result from tax perception of Millennials and Z Generation. Cochran's Q test examines the effectiveness equality of different proposals to change the perception of tax payment. Data were collected from 158 respondents through two questionnaire surveys. By understanding the main factors influencing citizens when paying taxes and premiums, e-government systems can offer suitable solutions when designing individual interfaces for citizens. A primary finding of this research highlights three critical influencing factors; firstly, knowing how and for what the levies will be used, secondary the option of choosing which public areas part of the levies will go to, and tertiary the importance of public finance transparency. The research identifies opportunities for considering citizens' tax perception when designing an e-tax administration interface. By understanding the taxpayers, the government can improve the development of e-government systems.

KEYWORDS

E-participation, E-Administration, E-Government, Taxes, Taxpayers' Attitude, Citizens' Perception

1. INTRODUCTION

Despite the high level of investments, long-term development of e-government systems and hight digital literacy, in some countries, it is still not possible to achieve the required level of its use by citizens. According to the Supreme Audit Office research published in 2020, only 0.5% of the total number of 8.7 million Czech citizens over the age of 18 used the citizen portal when communicating with the authorities (Supreme Audit Office, 2020). In the study about media coverage of e-tax portal, Zichová (2021) emphasizes the issue of tax administrative burden, notoriously problematic government public projects, and political distrust and influence. When developing an e-government project, it is essential to understand the ideologies and interrelated relationships of all the people involved (Kassen, 2020).

The research focuses on the importance of user-centric transformation and user-friendly principles, which define citizens not only as taxpayers, but also as users, clients, and consumers (Wimmer and Holler, 2003; Yu, 2008). States have a responsibility to develop high-quality e-services (Barnes and Vidgen, 2004) with a potential to increase e-participation (Kumar et al., 2007). A positive perception by citizens helps with the implementation and willingness to use the e-government projects (Abu-Shanab & Harb, 2019). Suki and Ramayah (2010) identified the main factors influencing the intention of using e-Government services to be: compatibility, perceived usefulness, approach, simplicity of use, interpersonal influence, external influence, self-efficacy, easing conditions, subjective standards and rules, and behavioural control. Fang (2002) describes successful features for a concept, practice, and development of the electronic government. He emphasizes a need for transparency, ease of use, and digital structure with an interface that simplifies transactions individually and the whole process of administration (Fang, 2002). Navigation facilities and accessibility of the tax e-administration were identified as important quality criteria of the e-government websites (Saha et al., 2012). Additionally, Chen (2010) assesses the quality of a system and information according to its ease of use, interactivity and accuracy focus, timeliness, and sufficiency of the information provided to citizens. Thanks to the simple design, appropriately selected functionalities, and website layout, users complete their tax-related tasks with minimal effort (Saha et al., 2012). Yeh and Lin (2008) examine the relationship between design elements and users' feelings.

Following the important role of citizens' tax perception, the paper focuses on a subsequent research question related to the surveyed sample of respondents. What are the most common perceived factors influencing the relationship to the payment of taxes by Generation Z and Generation Y? In connection with this research question, the author lists some possible e-government responses in the discussion section. To assign the effectiveness of individual factors, a Cochran's Q test is applied with a null hypothesis H0, that there are no significant differences in effectiveness, and an alternative hypothesis H1, that there are significant differences in effectiveness.

2. RESEARCH METHODS

The research method consists of a questionnaire survey. Respondents took place voluntarily by self-collection using mailing and a snowball sampling on social networks. They chose any number of options within the multiple-choice question: *What would change your perception of taxes?* Eight predefined answers were selected based on a literature search (Grimmelikhuijsen & Meijer, 2012; Langella, C. et al., 2021; Kim and Lee, 2012; Brown, 1979; Dahlby 2002): (1) *If the Czech Republic had a different current political situation.* (2) *If the Czech Republic had a different political past.* (3) *If the public finances were more transparent.* (4) *If I knew how and for what my levies would be used.* (5) *If I could choose which public areas part of my levy would go to.* (6) *If the Financial Administration offered more user-friendly support.* (7) *If the Financial Administration communicated more friendly.* (8) *If the employees of the Financial Administration communicated more friendly.* Respondents could also check the option I don't know / I can't judge or write their further opinion in an open answer.

Cochran's Q non-parametric statistical test on the significance level of 0.05 is used to determine whether the proportion of successes of facilitating the perception of taxes is equal across eight groups mentioned above (1)-(8). H0: The proportion of successes is equal for all the groups. H1: The proportion is different for at least one group. Dichotomous variables are categorical variables with two categories or levels: *Yes* (It will change my perception of tax payments.), *No* (It will not change my perception of tax payments.). The continuity correction has been applied. Cochran's Q test is chosen to use, because it determines whether there are differences in effectiveness between related categories. Calculations were performed in Statistical Software XLSTAT. The 158 responses were adjusted in order to exclude illogical, unrelated responses and respondents from other age groups. The representative dataset of the questionnaire survey consists of 146 answers, nationally 81% Czechs, 15% Slovaks, and 4% others, demographically, 82% women and 18% men. In terms of a long-term residence, a relatively even distribution was achieved: 31% respondents of the capital city of Prague, 44% of the city (with a population of over 3,001) and 25% of the municipality (with a population of up to 3,000). For the interpretation of the results, it is also important to note the predominant answers of respondents aged 18–25 years (69%, older from Generation Z) and 26–41 (31%, Generation Y/Millennials) with completed secondary education by graduation (45%) and university education (43%). Age classification into generations corresponds to the analysis of the Pew Research Center (Dimock, 2019). 86% of respondents are not entrepreneurs. Of the remaining 14% of self-employed persons, 19% of respondents perform their activities for more than 5 years.

3. RESULTS

The following Figure 1 shows the different percentage of groups: (1) *If the Czech Republic had a different current political situation.* (2) *If the Czech Republic had a different political past.* (3) *If the public finances were more transparent.* (4) *If I knew how and for what my levies would be used.* (5) *If I could choose which public areas part of my levy would go to.* (6) *If the Financial Administration offered more user-friendly support.* (7) *If the Financial Administration communicated more friendly.* (8) *If the employees of the Financial Administration communicated more friendly.*

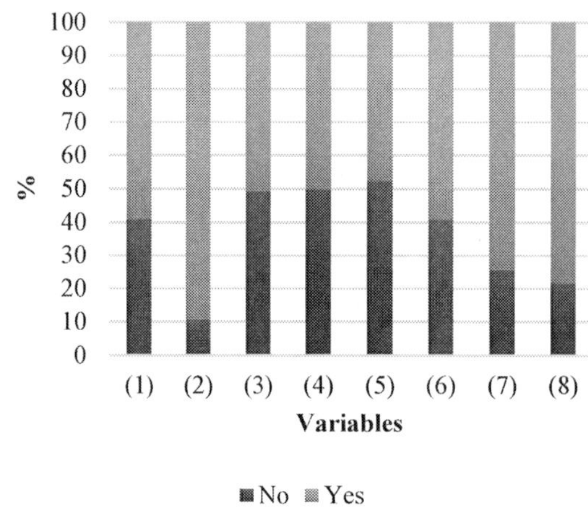

Figure 1. Percentage of the variables. Source author

Table 1 describes frequencies of categories *Yes* and *No*. The results show the highest proportion of factor 5. Respondents from Generation Y and Generation Z consider their free choice regarding the allocation of their taxes as a significant factor influencing their relationship to the payment of taxes. Transparency of public finances and knowing exactly what their fees are used for are also important to them.

Table 1. Summary statistics. Source author

Variable	Categories	Counts	Frequencies	%
(1)	No	77	77	59.231
	Yes	53	53	40.769
(2)	No	116	116	89.231
	Yes	14	14	10.769
(3)	No	66	66	50.769
	Yes	64	64	49.231
(4)	No	65	65	50.000
	Yes	65	65	50.000
(5)	No	62	62	47.692
	Yes	68	68	52.308
(6)	No	77	77	59.231
	Yes	53	53	40.769
(7)	No	97	97	74.615
	Yes	33	33	25.385
(8)	No	102	102	78.462
	Yes	28	28	21.538

Cochran's Q test (Table 2) outcomes underline a different equality of effectiveness of the groups. As the computed p-value is significantly lower than the significance level alpha = 0.05, the null hypothesis H0 is rejected, while the hypothesis H1: The proportion is different for at least one group, is not rejected. This means there is sufficient evidence to assume that factors influencing the perception of paying taxes lead to different proportions of success to change the perception.

Table 2. Cochran's Q test results. Source Author

Q (Observed value)	104.024
Q (Critical value)	14.067
df	7
p-value (one-tailed)	<0.0001
alpha	0.050

4. DISCUSSION

The results of the research resonate with the public choice theory which emphasizes the equal status of state and taxpayer. According to taxpayer sovereignty, taxpayers react positively when they are allowed to allocate part of their taxes to a specific purpose (Brown, 1979). Other essential factors for e-government adoption are trust (Park, 2008) and transparency (O'Neill, 2006). Even though researchers have different opinions about the direction of the effect of transparency on trust, positive effects of transparency are mentioned more often. The attention to government transparency is inspired by the highlighting of the new management movement on making government more responsible (Pollitt & Bouckaert, 2004).

The important question is how the government can learn from citizens' tax perceptions. It is not just a technical solution, but it is necessary to examine the feasibility and impacts of the changes on other variables. To adapt the interface to different types of users, the interface must be simple and effective for all the different groups of users. The interface should be built on interaction models based on the results of testing user interaction. Developers should think about the extent of users' knowledge and try to adjust the systems to the standards of participatory design, user-centred design, and user innovation. Users of the system should actively take part in its co-creation to reflect their preferences (Simonofski et al., 2019).

The public sector, unlike the private sector, usually has a lower motivation to develop customer-driven, resp. user-driven strategy. While private companies compete with several other competitors to gain customer loyalty, the public sector can remain more or less assured because it has its source of revenue secured by the state. The question remains whether private companies should replace the role of the Financial Administration and related tax departments. Why should not state organizations themselves design a system that is optimal for users and they do not have to search for it in different places on the internet for several life situations? An associated matter also remains the psychological effect on the motivation for the payment of taxes and the fulfilment of obligations to the state based on higher attractiveness and a certain degree of possible higher popularity of the user-oriented e-government interface. It would be possible to examine the influence of such a proposed interface on the psychological perception of legal obligations of citizens. Whether, for example, filing tax forms in a simple and clear form in conjunction with gamification and instructive explanation of obligations will have a positive effect on the tax perception.

5. CONCLUSION

The paper highlights the need to understand users to design e-government services that citizens will be willing to actively use. The purpose is to examine the factors influencing the perception of taxes by Generation Z and Generation Y and the level of importance of these factors. As the most commonly perceived factor was found the possibility of deciding where to allocate their taxes. Secondarily, the research points out the importance of education and providing information on what levies are used for. The government should also pay attention to assure public finance transparency. People pay more attention to the current political situation than the political past when they perceive taxes. User-friendliness of the system support is considered to be more influential than the friendliness of the Financial Administration communication. Cochran's Q test confirms significant differences in the effectiveness of eight influencing factors.

Due to multiple responses and the nature of the variables, it was necessary to omit some statistical tests which would show other interesting findings. The question should be reworded in further research so that further facts about the investigated area can be ascertained. The dataset could be extended with more responses and analysed with a Delphi qualitative tool. A Cochran's Q test can have some theoretical and procedural limitations when blocks are not randomly selected from the population. The paper's contribution lies not only in the results regarding the influencing factors when perceiving taxes but also in the discussion of the concept of the taxpayer as a respectable client of the state e-government system. E-government system users should be constantly engaged in improving it. Results can be beneficial for the future development and improvement of e-government projects and can bring new incentives to representatives, commissioners, officials, and other stakeholders. The study can be followed by assessing the applicability of changes in the e-government user interface based on citizens' preferences. It would be appropriate to go along with an additional quantitative survey focused on age-diverse respondents in order to ensure greater representativeness and applicability of the results.

REFERENCES

Abu-Shanab, E., & Harb, H. (2019). E-Government Research Insights: Text Mining Analysis. *Electronic Commerce Research and Applications*, 38. https://doi.org/10.1016/j.elerap.2019.100892

Barnes, S. J., & Vidgen, R. (2004). Interactive e-government services: modelling user perceptions with eQual. *Electronic Government*, 1(2), 213–228. https://doi.org/10.1504/EG.2004.005179

Brown, D. J. (1979). The Case For Tax-Target *Plans Journal of Education Finance*, 5(2), 215–224. http://www.jstor.org/stable/40703229

Chen, C. (2010). Impact of quality antecedents on taxpayer satisfaction with online tax-filing systems – an empirical study. *Information & Management*, 47, 308–15. https://doi.org/10.1016/j.im.2010.06.005

Dahlby, B. (2002). Taxing choices: issues in the assignment of taxes in federations. *International Social Science Journal*, 53(167), 93-101.

Dimock, M. (2019). Defining generations: *Where Millennials and Generation Z begins*. Pew Research Center. https://www.pewresearch.org/fact-tank/2019/01/17/where-millennials-end-and-generation-z-begins/

Fang, Z. (2002). E-government in digital era: concept, practice, and development. International journal of the Computer, the Internet and management, 10(2), 1–22.

Grimmelikhuijsen, S.G. and Meijer, A.J., 2012. Effects of Transparency on the Perceived Trustworthiness of a Government Organization: Evidence from an Online Experiment. *Journal of Public Administration Research and Theory*, 24(1), 137–157.

Kassen, M. (2020). E-participation actors: understanding roles, connections, partnerships, *Knowledge Management Research & Practice*, 18(1), 16–37. https://doi.org/10.1080/14778238.2018.1547252

Kumar, S., Baishya, K., Sreen, N., Sadarangani, P. H. & Samalia, H. V. (2021). Impact of National Culture on E-Government Development. Journal of Global Information Management, 29 (2), 1–22. https:// doi.org/10.4018/jgim.2021030101

Langella, C. et al. (2021). Financial reporting transparency, citizens' understanding, and public participation: A survey experiment study. *Public Administration*. https://doi.org/10.1111/padm.12804

O'Neill, O. (2006). Transparency and the Ethics of Communication. In *Transparency: The Key to Better Governance?*, edited by C. Hood and D. Heald, 75-90. Oxford: Oxford University Press.

Park, R. (2008). Measuring Factors That Influence the Success of E-government. In *Proceedings of the 41st Hawaii International Conference on System Sciences*, January 7-10, Waikoloa, Big Island, Hawaii.

Pollitt, C., & G. Bouckaert. (2004). Public Management Reform. A Comparative Analysis. Oxford: Oxford University Press, second edition.

Saha, P., Nath, A. K., & Salehi-Sangari, E. (2012). Evaluation of government e-tax websites: An information quality and system quality approach. *Transforming Government: People, Process and Policy*, 6(3), 300–321. http://doi.org/10.1108/17506161211251281

Simonofski A., Snoeck M., & Vanderose B. (2019). Co-creating e-Government Services: An Empirical Analysis of Participation Methods in Belgium. In R. Bolivar, & M. Pedro (Eds.), *Setting Foundations for the Creation of Public Value in Smart Cities. Public Administration and Information Technology* (Vol. 35, pp. 225–245). Springer. https://doi.org/10.1007/978-3-319-98953-2_9

Suki, N., M. & T. Ramayah (2010) User Acceptance of the E- Government Services in Malaysia: Structural Equation Modelling Approach. *Interdisciplinary Journal of Information, Knowledge, and Management*, 5, 15.

Supreme Audit Office (2020, July 13). *The state has spent about 300 million crowns on access to electronic public administration services, but few citizens use it* [Press Release]. https://www.nku.cz/cz/pro-media/tiskove-zpravy/stat-vynalozil-na-pristup-k-elektronickym-sluzbam-verejne-spravy-zhruba-300-milionu-korun--vyuziva-jej-ale-malo-obcanu-id11361/

Wimmer M. A. & Holler U. (2003). Applying a Holistic Approach to Develop User-Friendly, Customer-Oriented E-Government Portal Interfaces. In N. Carbonell, & C. Stephanidis (Eds.), Universal Access Theoretical Perspectives, Practice, and Experience. UI4ALL 2002 (pp. 167–178). *Lecture Notes in Computer Science* (Vol. 2615). Springer. https://doi.org/10.1007/3-540-36572-9_13

Yeh, C.-H., Lin, Y.-C. (2008). User-centered design of web pages. In Gervasi, O. et al. (Eds.), Computational Science and Its Applications. ICCSA 2008 (pp. 129–142). *Lecture Notes in Computer Science* (Vol. 5073). Springer. https://doi.org/10.1007/978-3-540-69848-7_12

Yu, C.-C. (2008). Building a Value-Centric e-Government Service Framework Based on a Business Model Perspective. *Lecture Notes in Computer Science*, 5184/2008, 160–171. https://doi.org/10.1007/978-3-540-85204-9_14

Zichová, T. (2021). E-Government Digital Czechia: E-Tax Portal Discourse. In *IDIMT-2021* Pandemics: Impacts, Strategies and Responses [online]. Kutná Hora, 01.09.2021–03.09.2021. Linz: Trauner Verlag, 2021, 133–140.

OBS SHARE AND MULTIVIEW: TWO METHODS FOR SHARING STUDENT WORK IN DISTANT TEACHING

Jun Iio
Faculty of Global-Informatics, Chuo University
1-18 Ichigaya-Tamachi, Shinjuku-ku, Tokyo, 162-8478, Japan

ABSTRACT

The COVID-19 pandemic has forced us to conduct online lectures at universities. Regarding ordinal courses in which teachers give their lectures and students simply listen, migrating online took place easily in a relatively straightforward way with the help of online meeting tools, such as Zoom, Webex, Google Meet, and Microsoft Teams. However, we faced some difficulties in the online migration of practical training courses. Particularly, in software development courses, a teacher must be able to monitor student learning progress to help them correct errors, check student code, provide advice, etc. This paper presents two proposals for sharing student progress in distant teaching for software development courses.

KEYWORDS

Real-Time Sharing, Student Desktop, OBS Studio, Google Colaboratory

1. INTRODUCTION

Many university teachers worldwide have been forced to provide lectures through the Internet in 2020 because of the COVID-19 pandemic. There is no exception for teaching computer science classes (Brooks et al., 2021). Fortunately, online meeting tools, such as Zoom, Webex, Google Meet, and Microsoft Teams, have become widespread (Singh and Awasthi, 2020), and students have become accustomed to using them. Additionally, various tips shared among teachers (Sandars et al., 2020) have helped them conduct distant teaching. Overall, it is relatively easy to migrate lectures online for regular classes, where teachers give lectures and students simply listen to them.

However, classes in universities are not limited to lectures. There are several difficulties in providing practical training courses online (Liu, W. et al., 2020). Particularly, for computer science classes, teaching programming is accompanied by practical training, such as writing appropriate code and testing software (Liu, A., 2020). In many cases, writing codes is necessary. Therefore, transitioning classes from offline to online for these types of courses is relatively complicated.

To conduct online practical training for writing adequate code or testing software, a teacher must monitor students' progress in their learning. This paper proposes two typical and straightforward methods that can aid in distant teaching, namely, sharing student desktops or notebooks, which are representative of student progress, among teachers and students.

2. PROPOSED METHODS

This section proposes two methods for real-time sharing of student working conditions. One method uses OBS Studio[1] and Zoom[2], and the other uses Google Colaboratory (hereinafter referred to as Colab)[3].

[1] https://obsproject.com/
[2] https://zoom.us/
[3] https://colab.research.google.com/

2.1 OBS Share: Sharing Student Desktops

It would be helpful to use multiple monitors for student desktops when teaching for software development education is conducted. Various systems for sharing desktops have been proposed (Ohshima et al., 2017), and there is a simple method to realize desktop sharing using OBS Studio. OBS Studio is an open-source broadcasting software package, and many teachers utilize it to conduct online classes (Rosenthal and Walker, 2020, Kristandl, 2020).

The combination of OBS Studio with online meeting tools allows classroom participants to share their desktops in real time (see Figure 1).

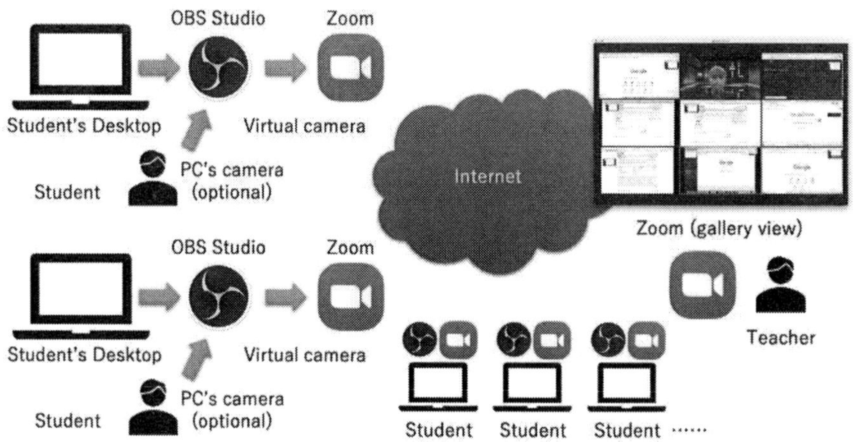

Figure 1. Overview of using OBS Studio to share student desktops

On November 22, 2021, eight students and the author attempted to set up a distant teaching environment using OBS Studio and Zoom[4]. Installing OBS Studio seemed to be easy for the students and they did not encounter any significant troubles. Figure 2 shows the teacher's desktop screen where the teacher monitors students desktop using Zoom's gallery view mode.

Figure 2. The teacher can monitor student desktops using Zoom's gallery view mode in real time

[4] Zoom can be replaced with other online meeting software.

The preparation steps can be summarized as follows:

1. Let every student install OBS Studio and start the program.
2. Let OBS capture each student's desktop by selecting capture screen as the source and begin sending it using a virtual camera by selecting start virtual camera from the control section.
3. Start Zoom and connect to the meeting.
4. Change Zoom's camera source setting to the virtual camera provided by OBS.

These steps allow students to share their desktop screen to Zoom, enabling the teacher to monitor what the students are doing in real time. During preparation, some students using Mac encountered minor issues, such as being unable to capture desktops or being unable to find OBS's virtual camera in Zoom's camera section.

Several significant issues encountered in configuring the described environment and critical points for troubleshooting are outlined below:

- Selecting the option of "use as a virtual camera" in the configuration of OBS on its first use.
- Providing permission to access screen capture and other devices in the security configuration of the control panel.
- Starting Zoom after completing OBS configuration. Zoom will not find the camera provided by OBS if Zoom is started before OBS configuration is completed.
- Turning off Zoom's virtual background.
- After all configuration steps are completed, the windows of OBS and Zoom should be minimized.

2.2 MultiView: Sharing Student Notebooks

The second option is to share student notebooks using software such as Jupyter Notebook[5] and Colab. However, this option has limitations in terms of language restrictions. Specifically, the notebook environment can host only Python and several other programming languages.

For example, the case using Colab is illustrated here. Colab is a cloud service, and it runs on the cloud computing environment. Therefore, it should be suitable if the client machine does not have significant computational power. Although the setup of Colab also requires several steps, it is easier than that of OBS and Zoom.

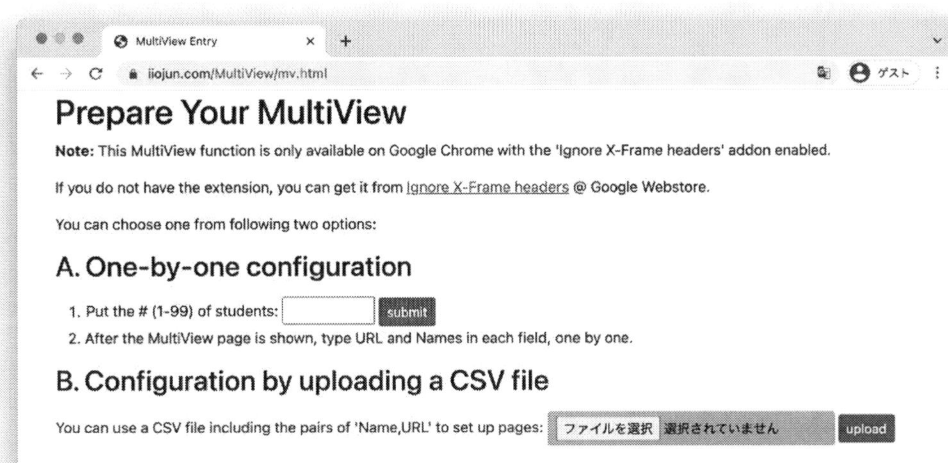

Figure 3. Configuration page of MultiView, which provides two methods for configuration

[5] https://jupyter.org/

The essential component of this option is to share student Colab notebooks with the teacher. This allows the teacher to check student progress at any time. Additionally, the teacher can communicate with students by commenting on or modifying their code.

MultiView was developed to capture a complete view of all student progress, rather than using the gallery view in Zoom with OBS. This is a simple program implemented using PHP and JavaScript. The source code for MultiView is available at https://github.com/iiojun/MultiView.

Figure 3 presents a screenshot of the MultiView setup page. The MultiView system provides two setup options: one-by-one configuration and semi-automatic setup by uploading a configuration file.

2.2.1 One-by-one Configuration

The first option is the one-by-one configuration method. Initially, the teacher enters the student number and clicks the submit button on MultiView's configuration page (see Section A. in Figure 3). Then, a page that contains a small section with the entered student number appears (see Figure 4 (A)). Each page is embedded as an inline frame, which is shrunk to half size.

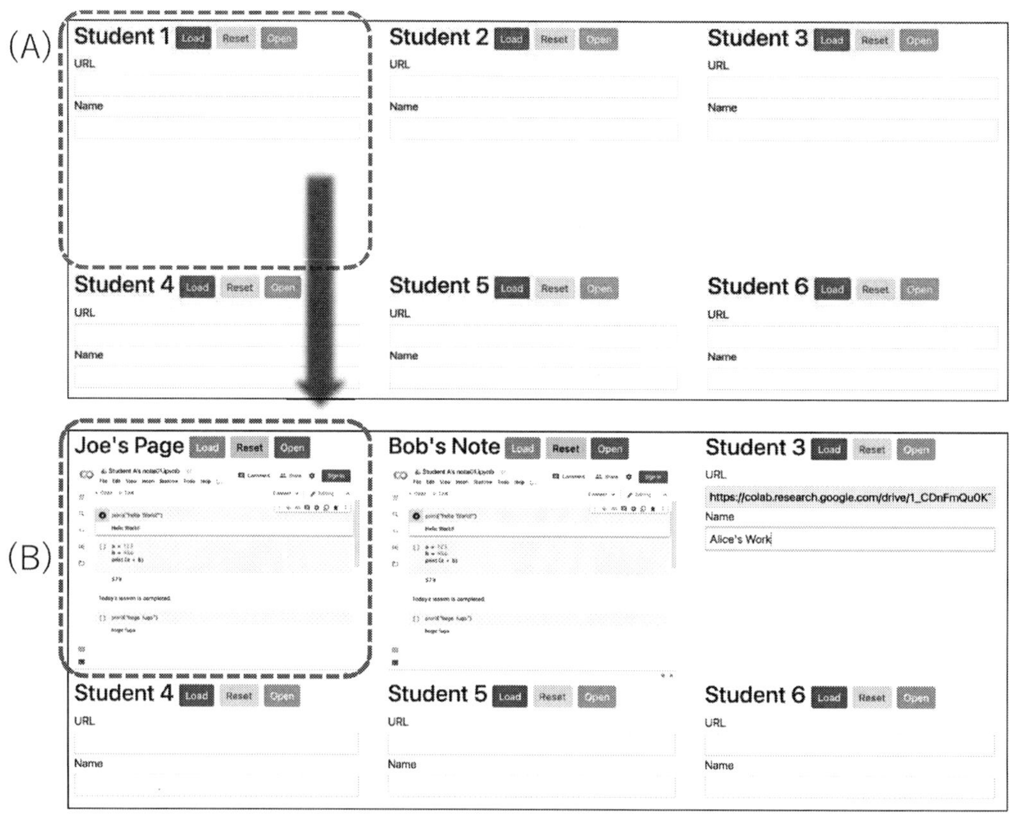

Figure 4. MultiView's main page, which has a configured number of small sections

Each block contains three buttons: *load*, *reset*, and *open*. In the initial stage, only the *load* button is enabled. Each page also has text fields to fill in the URL and name. After specifying the URL and name, a half-size webpage appears on the page section by clicking the *load* button.

Figure 4 (B) shows that the teacher has configured two pages: Joe's page as Student 1 and Bob's page as Student 2. These pages are embedded in the main page. These pages are synchronous with student pages. Although there is a subtle time lag, the teacher can confirm the actual status of student progress.

Specifying a student's name is not mandatory. If the name field is empty, only the placeholder "Student #" is used. When the page is embedded, the *load* button is disabled, while the *reset* and *open* buttons are enabled. Pressing the *reset* button removes the embedded page and reverts it to the initial state. The *open* button opens the page in a new window in the browser. If a shrunken page is not suitable for teaching, the teacher can access a regular independent page by clicking this button.

2.2.2 Bulk Configuration

To configure pages semi-automatically, MultiView has another option for embedding student Colab pages. If you select this option, you only need to prepare a CSV file that includes student names and the URLs of their notebooks in pairs on one line for each student, which are separated by commas, and upload it to the server.

By specifying a CSV file using the file chooser on MultiView's configuration page and uploading it (see Section B. in Figure 3), all web pages corresponding to the listed names will appear embedded on the main page.

Note that a standard web browser cannot accommodate MultiView functions for security reasons (Huang et al., 2012). The user must implement the "Ignore X-Frame headers" addon[6] for Google Chrome to enable MultiView's functionality.

3. CONCLUSIONS AND FUTURE WORK

In this paper, two methods were proposed to share multiple student desktops or notebooks simultaneously. OBS sharing, which is realized using OBS Studio and Zoom, is independent of the choice of programming language. Therefore, it would be helpful not only for computer science courses but also for other fields. MultiView, which shares student notebooks from Colab on a web page, is suitable for programming education. It is highly dependent on the synchronization ability of the Colab page sharing function.

This paper discussed how to implement the two methods mentioned above. These methods should be evaluated and compared in actual distant teaching scenarios. Experiments and evaluations for this purpose remain for future work. In addition, there are some other services to share the remote desktop. Comparison to such services should be considered.

REFERENCES

Brooks, A., Hardin, C., Scianna, J., Berland, M. and Legault, L.H, 2021. Approachesto Transitioning Computer Science Classes from Offline to Online. *Proceedings of the 26th ACM Conference on Innovation and Technology in Computer Science Education V. 1*, pp. 81–87.

Huang, L.S., Moshchuk, A., Wang, H.J., Schecter, S. and Jackson, C., 2012. Clickjacking: Attacks and defenses. In *21st {USENIX} Security Symposium ({USENIX} Security 12),* pp. 413–428.

Kristandl, G., 2020. "All the world's a stage"–the Open Broadcaster Software (OBS) asenabling technology to overcome restrictions in online teaching. *Compass: The Journal of Learning and Teaching at the University of Greenwich,* Vol. 14, No. 2, pp.1–16.

Liu, A., 2020. August. Design of Blending Teaching Mode for Software Testing Course. In *15th International Conference on Computer Science & Education (ICCSE)*, pp. 816–821. IEEE.

Liu, W., Zhang, H., Li, J., Bian, X., Luan, C. and Gao, J., 2020. August. Researchand Practice of Online Teaching in Construction Training Courses Against the Background of COVID-19 Epidemic. In *2020 International Conference on Social Science, Economics and Education Research (SSEER 2020)*, pp. 59–62. Atlantis Press.

Ohshima, Y., Freudenberg, B. and Amelang, D., 2017. Kanto: a multiparticipant screen-sharing system for Etoys, Snap! and GP. In *Proceedings of the 3rd ACM SIGPLAN International Workshop on Programming Experience*, pp. 7–10.

Rosenthal, S. and Walker, Z., 2020. Experiencing Live Composite Video Lectures: Comparisons with Traditional Lectures and Common Video Lecture Methods. *International Journal for the Scholarship of Teaching and Learning*, Vol. 14, No. 1, Article. 8.

Sandars, J., Correia, R., Dankbaar, M., de Jong, P., Goh, P.S., Hege, I., Masters,K., Oh, S.Y., Patel, R., Premkumar, K. and Webb, A., 2020. Twelve tips for rapidly migrating to online learning during the COVID-19 pandemic. *MedEdPublish*, Vol. 9, No. 1, p.3068.

Singh, R. and Awasthi, S., 2020. Updated Comparative Analysis on Video ConferencingPlatforms-Zoom, Google Meet, Microsoft Teams, WebEx Teams and GoToMeetings. *EasyChair: The World for Scientists*, pp.1–9.

[6] https://chrome.google.com/webstore/detail/ignore-x-frame-headers/gleekbfjekiniecknbkamfmkohkpodhe

E-LEARNING COURSE OF SOFTWARE FOR TEXTILE DESIGN

Ion Razvan Radulescu[1], Antonio Dinis[2], Benny Malengier[3], Andrej Cupar[4], Mirela Blaga[5] and Radek Polansky[6]
[1]*INCDTP – Bucharest, Str. L. Patrascanu 16, 030508 Bucharest 3, Romania*
[2]*University of Minho, Department of Textile Engineering, Campus de Azurem, Guimaraes, Portugal*
[3]*Ghent University, MATCH, Technologiepark-Zwijnaarde 70A, Gent, Belgium*
[4]*University of Maribor, Institute of Engineering Materials and Design, Smetanova 17, Maribor, Slovenia*
[5]*Technical University "Gh. Asachi" – Iași, Faculty DIMA,Str. D. Mangeron 29, Iași, Romania*
[6]*University of West Bohemia, Faculty of Electrical Engineering, Univerzitni 2795/26, 301 00 Pilsen, Czech Republic*

ABSTRACT

Industry 4.0 and digitization are nowadays important trends in the textile industry. The need for well-prepared professionals in software for the design and modelling of textile products requires the creation of up-to-date educational resources. Virtual learning supported by e-learning offers the instruments to continue education during pandemic restrictions. As such, six research and education providers on the European level have joined forces to create educational resources in e-learning format for students and professionals in textiles: the content is related to software for design and modelling of weaving, knitting, virtual prototyping of clothing, embroidery of e-textiles and experimental design, as well as technology transfer. The educational resources were implemented on the Moodle e-learning platform of the Erasmus+ project (www.advan2tex.eu/portal/) and will be further used to support classroom / virtual courses with students and professionals in textiles. The paper introduces the course and its foreseen impact within the current context.

KEYWORDS

E-textiles, Software, Design, Modelling, Higher Education Students, Professionals

1. INTRODUCTION

Our paper presents Open Educational Resources (OERs) in the field of software for the design and modelling of e-textile materials. The resources are structured on six modules in relation to the leading textile technological fields: weaving, knitting, clothing, embroidery, and experimental design, plus a module on technology transfer. The resources are available in six European languages: Czech, Dutch, English, Portuguese, Romanian and Slovenian. The state-of-the-art of our OERs is based on three main pillars:

1. The significance of e-learning for safety during a pandemic;
2. The e-textiles as a future trend and niche of modern textile products;
3. The software solutions for textile design.

Aim of the paper is to present the prepared OERs as response to a current need from the world-of-work.

1. E-learning is a well-established technique and has gained a new significance during the pandemic (Grosseck et al., 2020). A close link is related to the Emergency Remote Teaching Environment (ERTE), enabling online learning in critical situations, like the current COVID-19 pandemic. The main idea is to shift classroom learning towards virtual learning in emergency situations with a well-established conceptual framework (Whittle et al., 2020). Many Vocational Education and Training (VET) schools and Higher Education (HE) universities have organized virtual teaching courses for the last two years in Europe and worldwide. The main challenge of online teaching was to keep the trainees connected to the course, bridge activities needing direct interaction with the tutor (such as support with direct questions), and evaluate assignments. E-learning courses could support part of these challenges, for they enable flexible learning hours with the possibility to study within the most convenient timeslots, it allows synchronous and asynchronous communication methods between tutor and trainee, such as Chat and Forum for Q&A, and

they permit precise evaluation of assignments via multiple-choice tests and questionnaires. Some other challenges where virtual learning and e-learning have drawbacks are a lack of interaction control. However, the e-learning resources with open access are of substantial support for improving the learning process in various disciplines and for different target groups. Such resources are called Open Educational Resources (OER) (Grosseck & Craciun, 2020). OERs have a content-centred approach focusing on creating and reusing resources (Ehlers, 2011). In recent years, the quality improvement of OERs has been a challenge for reaching a more practice-centred approach and a better interaction between tutors and trainees. The so-called Open Educational Practices (OEP) are the future trend and include the online teaching experiences and best practices within the educational resources as well (Grosseck et al., 2020). Looking at the field, we can conclude that e-learning brings valuable support to classroom and virtual learning and that it has reached more significance during the pandemic.

2. E-textiles have emerged with the progress of spinning techniques by producing metallic yarns and with the progress of electronics by miniaturization of electronic components. Various descriptions and classifications of e-textiles have been proposed, depending on their subsystems (Carames & Lamas, 2018) or their integration techniques (Simegnaw, 2021). The subsystems of an e-textile are: sensing, actuation, control, communication, location, power, storage, and display subsystem. The possible integration techniques are: mechanical connectors, soldering, sewing and embroidering, hybrid solder and sewing, electrical conductive adhesive, inkjet, and 2D screen-printing, three-dimensional (3D) printing, stretchable electronics, and finally, the latest trend of electronic connections on threads (e-threads). Some of the main applications of e-textiles are: baby vest connected to a laptop (not wirelessly) for monitoring of vital signs, smart suit for elderly people for collection of physiological data – transmitted by Wi-Fi to a remote server, smart suits for athletes for collection of ECG and accelerometer data via Bluetooth and smartphone, etc. As such, e-textiles represent a future trend in the textile industry, in correlation with the European strategy in the textile field, which is focused on high value-added products.

3. Software for textile design emerged with the evolution of IT in the early 2000 and now brings consistent support for designers. Textile technology is grouped on main techniques to manufacture fabrics, such as: weaving, knitting, clothing/garments, and embroidery. The available software applications are specialized in one of these technologies. The main added value of software is the possibility of virtually testing the properties of the designed textile materials and changing parameters without having to manufacture the products. Moreover, most modern weaving or knitting machines require software to control and manufacture desired fabrics. In the case of clothing, the 2D/3D patterns are of utmost importance when designing a garment on a human model, and software may predict draping and customizing problems. Knitting machines require specialized programming of patterns and can produce seamless garments. Embroidery is usually done on an existing textile substrate, and the software of the embroidery machine may lead to the desired pattern to achieve, e.g., an e-textile product with metallic yarns. Another possible application is using statistics tools, such as the experimental design, to conduct research experiments on smart and technical textiles (Tatu et al., 2012). In such a case, the use of the software is indispensable too. Some textiles software applications are proprietary; others are open-source and can be readily for educational purposes.

2. THE ERASMUS+ OPTIMTEX SOLUTION

The Erasmus+ project "Software tools for textile creatives" aims to offer a solution in this regard by providing educational resources in the e-learning format of software for textile design and modelling. Six European research and education providers have joined forces for tackling this objective: INCDTP-Bucharest, TecMinho / University of Minho – Portugal, Ghent University – Belgium, University of Maribor - Slovenia, Technical University Iași – Romania and University West Bohemia – Czech Republic. Main target group of the educational materials are students of higher education in fashion textile and technical textile fields as well as young professionals from the industry. The project has an implementation period of two years (Dec. 2020 – Nov. 2022). It is an ongoing project, with the creation of educational materials for the first year and the organization of courses and multiplier events for the second year. Courses of Intensive Study Programs are meant for students, and Multiplier events are meant for young professionals. Figures 1 a) and b) show the Erasmus+ and the project's logo.

Figure 1a). ERASMUS+ logo

Figure 1b). PROJECT's logo

More information is available on the project's website (www.optimtex.eu).

3. THE E-LEARNING COURSE

The e-learning course of software for textile design was implemented on a Moodle e-learning platform (www.advan2tex.eu/portal/). This platform includes the OERs of four Erasmus+ projects, implemented during 2014-2022, with INCDTP – Bucharest as coordinator.

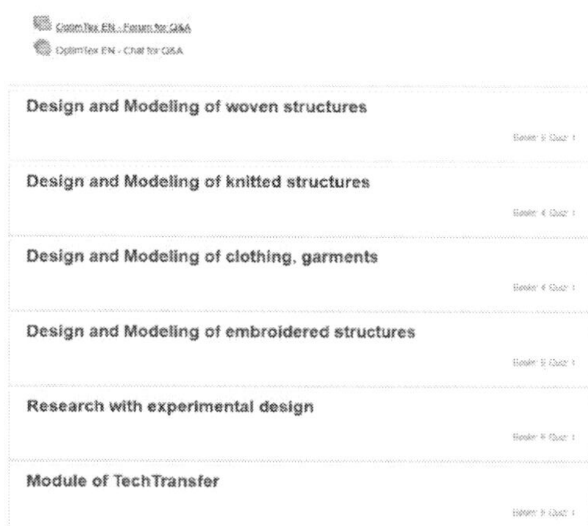

Figure 2. PRINT screen of the six modules - English course

Figure 3. PRINT screen of the first module on weaving software

The OptimTex course has developed six modules in the field of design and modelling software for textiles. Each module tackles a textile technology field (figure 2) and includes 4-5 examples sets (figure 3). One example set includes: description of Example, the corresponding Theory, the available software Application, and the Multiple choice questions. The course is available in English and the five European languages of the partnership: Czech, Dutch, Portuguese, Romanian and Slovenian. A course category for the OptimTex educational resources was created on Moodle, with six courses in topic format for each language. Each course has one topic for the corresponding module. Book resources were implemented for each Example, Theory, and Application. The Books include navigation buttons and table of contents for a rapid selection of the desired element of the course. The Multiple choice questions were implemented as Moodle Quiz activities. The 20 questions per module were uploaded via Aiken format and some of them have images. A Forum and a Chat activity ensure the communication between tutor and trainee. Images and videos were embedded in the courses for the visual understanding of the materials. Figure 2 presents a print screen of the six modules of the English course and figure 3 presents the first module of weaving software and its 5 examples. Table 1 showcases the specific sets of examples.

Table 1. THE EDUCATIONAL examples of the course

Design and Modeling of woven structures	**Design and Modeling of knitted structures**	**Design and Modeling of clothing, garments**
E1: Standard woven structures and Texgen E2: Complex yarns in woven structures E3: 3D Woven Structures E4: Simulation of Woven Structures with Abaqus E5: Complex weaving patterns and coloring	E1: Knitted fabrics with normal loops E2: Knitted fabrics with modified loops E3: Spacer weft knitted fabrics E4: 3D shaped knitted fabrics	E1: 3D human body scanning using the 3D photogrammetry E2: 3D human body modelling and reconstruction E3: Construction of a kinematic 3D body model E4: 3D virtual prototyping of personalized smart garments
Design and Modeling of embroidered structures	**Research with experimental design**	**Technology transfer of textile software solutions into the industry**
E1: Technical computerized embroidery E2: Design and digitizing of technical embroidery E3: Textile Based Heating Element E4: Illuminated fabrics E5: Textile based water leak sensor on fabric	E1: Factorial design of plasma treatment for hydrophobic fabrics E2: Central composite design for optimizing plasma coated electric conductive fabrics E3: Factorial design of plasma treatment for hydrophilic textiles E4: Central composite design and bivariate analysis of process variables for EM shield development E5: Draping Simulation using Tensor Flow E6: FEM Analysis using Python	E1: WeaveEXVBA - Academic software development for weaving E2: Spin-off UMinho TO-BE-GREEN - Screening and Business plan E3: IOTech a driver to Industry 4.0 - Business development E4: Protechdry® - Reusable underwear for urinary incontinence SWOT analysis

In order to tailor the e-learning resources to the specific of these educational materials, the www.optimtex.eu website includes two additional resources:

- The E-learning instrument with a HTML5 button of Example, Theory, Application and Quiz for each set of examples – programmed in JavaScript (TAB Instrument);
- The Glossary of terms and definitions on the key terms within the modules in all languages of the partnership (CZ, NL, PT, RO, SI and EN), meant to support the students during the courses taught in English – programmed in PHP / MySQL (TAB Glossary).

Evaluation of the educational performance of these two e-learning resources will be tackled in future work.

4. DISCUSSION

This project and the created educational resources started from a need of the textile industry: the need of professionals mastering software of knitting machines. Since the recent evolution of textile technology involves software for design and modelling patterns and structures, the OptimTex course is in line with the Digitalization trend of Industry 4.0. The overall need for IT specialists is increasing, since all domains require digitization. There is close compatibility between IT education and e-learning, due to the same technological profile and engineering structure (Radulescu et al., 2017).

The educational resources of OptimTex project will be validated in 2022 by pilot courses organized by each partner with their own students and by three Intensive Study Programs with the mobility of 60 students and 15 lecturers. UGent has already organized a pilot courses with 19 students of the International Master of Science in Textile Engineering, as part of the practical part of the course Computation Sciences and Engineering Principles for Textiles. In all these settings, the OptimTex material was well received.

Several courses were already implemented during 2014-2020, within three Erasmus+ VET partnership projects. The courses were organized either as classroom courses combined with e-learning – the so-called blended courses, or as virtual courses and e-learning - during the pandemic. The courses were organized in the national languages of the partnerships (CZ, IT, NL, PT, RO, SI), and in our experience translation of the educational modules brings a lot of support to the learning process. The organized classroom and virtual courses had as objective a brief presentation of the modules and instructions for e-learning. These courses were followed by one week of e-learning for each module. Our Moodle e-learning platform has at this moment 933 users, including VET trainees and HE students, lecturers, professionals, stakeholders from the industry/associations and the project teams. More than 650 trainees followed one e-learning course.

5. CONCLUSION

An e-learning course in software for design and modelling textiles was created on the Moodle platform www.advan2tex.eu/portal/ . The course derives from the need to prepare textile creatives within the new digitization trend of the industry. The course includes state-of-the-art knowledge, based on three pillars: e-learning, design software, and e-textiles. This course will be validated within the second project's year 2022 by three Intensive Study Programs. Our previous experience with classroom / virtual learning and support of e-learning depicts a viable solution for complementary education during pandemic restrictions. The course content will be adapted to the specific target group of students and professionals in textiles. Limitations are related to the course's relatively high level of knowledge when approaching the target group. Applications of the course are promising, since knowledge of software for textile design offers substantial competitive advantages within the world-of-work. Future work will be related to educational performance evaluation of the additionally tailored e-learning instruments for these specific materials: the e-learning instrument and the glossary of terms – available on www.optimtex.eu .

ACKNOWLEDGEMENT

This project has been funded with support of the European Commission, Erasmus+ KA2 projects "Software tools for textile creatives", acronym OptimTex, grant agreement number 2020-1-RO01-KA203-079823.

REFERENCES

Carames T. and Lamas P., 2018, P, Towards The Internet of Smart Clothing: A Review on IoT Wearables and Garments for Creating Intelligent Connected E-Textiles, *Electronics 2018*, 7, 405; pp 1-36

Ehlers U., 2011, From Open Educational Resources to Open Educational Practices, *eLearning Papers*, 23/2011,

Grosseck, G. et al, 2020, *Ghid pentru aplicarea Practicilor Educaționale Deschise în timpul pandemiei de coronavirus. Utilizarea Resurselor Educaționale Deschise în conformitate cu Recomandările UNESCO*, Smart Learning Institute of Beijing Normal University (SLIBNU)

Grosseck G. and Craciun D., 2020, *Ghid practic de resurse educaționale și digitale pentru instruire online*, Editura Universității de Vest, Timișoara, Romania

Radulescu, IR, et al, 2017, E-learning for innovation in textile enterprises, Proceedings of the 13th International Scientific Conference eLearning and Software for Education, Bucharest, April 27-28, 2017, pp 455-460

Simegnaw A.A. et al, 2021, Review on the integration of microelectronics for e-textile, *Materials 2021*, 14, 5113. https://doi.org/10.3390/ma14175113, pp 1-27

Tatu, M, et al, 2011, *Cercetarea experimentala aplicata in cresterea calitatii produselor si serviciilor*, AGIR Publishing, Romania

Whittle, C. et al. 2020, Emergency remote teaching environment: a conceptual framework for responsive online teaching in crises, *Information and Learning Sciences,* Vol. 121 No. 5/6, 2020, pp. 311-319, Emerald Publishing Limited, UK.

CHILD'S PLAY: TEACHING YOUNG CHILDREN HEBREW MORPHOLOGY USING E-LEARNING TECHNOLOGIES

Nofar Rimon, Iris Melamed Gorodesky, Goren Gordon and Einat Gonen
Tel Aviv University, Tel Aviv, Israel

ABSTRACT

Hebrew words are known to be composed of roots, entities of three or four consonants that are combined in different patterns. Roots form an integral part of Hebrew morphology and the knowledge of extracting them is essential for high-school matriculation exams. Even though these skills are formally taught starting from second-grade, students still exhibit difficulties applying them. Hence, we created an innovative online root instruction program of five short video lessons that teaches 5- to 8-year old children to extract roots. Children significantly improved their root extraction skills after having completed our program. Furthermore, our program helped close the gap between the younger children and the older children who had already been introduced to the notion of the root in school. Using advanced technologies that allow the development of new teaching methods that are not traditionally used in schools, we managed to teach very young children a complex subject in morphology.

KEYWORDS

E-Learning, EduTech, Hebrew Morphology, Root Extraction

1. INTRODUCTION

As a Semitic language, Hebrew is known for its root-and-pattern morphology, which means that words are composed of three or four consonants, referred to as root, combined in a vocalic pattern, sometimes with additional affixes. The root carries the basic meaning of the word, while the pattern classifies the word into a specific category (Ravid and Schiff 2006). For example, the verb *bišel* 'cooked' is composed of the root *b-š-l* in the pattern CiC[C]eC (C stands for consonant), and the noun *nasix* 'prince' is composed of the root *n-s-x* in the pattern CaCiC.

Root extraction is formally taught in schools in Israel from second grade on, and is essential for high-school matriculation exams, where students are required to extract roots of different words (Avinun 1996, Bolozky 1999, 2003; Lipkin 1985, Ravid 1990, 1991, 2003; Ravid and Malenky 2001). However, students seem to demonstrate low achievements in this section. In light of that, we created an innovative online root instruction program that teaches young children to extract roots in only five short video lessons. Unlike school pedagogy which focuses on identifying roots in written words, the program does not require any literacy skills and is suited for young children starting from preschool.

In this paper we present the effects of our program, as demonstrated by the improvement in children's root extraction abilities. In five short online video lessons, the children learned to extract roots from verbs, nouns and even pseudowords of different patterns in Hebrew. The children's prior knowledge was assessed in a pre-test, and after having completed the program, we examined their root extraction abilities in a detailed post-test. The whole experiment was conducted online, using various E-Learning technologies, and has been accessed from computers, tablets and smartphones. This allowed us to reach a large audience, drawing many participants from varied backgrounds. The program was suited for the challenges posed by Covid-19 that necessitated specialized distance education, yet it can be easily implemented in frontal instruction as well.

2. METHODOLOGY

2.1 Technology and Method

We prepared the videos using recorded audio text and avatars from SitePal.com ©, a dedicated commercial website that enables integration of audio files and animated avatars. As shown in figure 2, we used two cartoon-like avatars, which we named Tutty and Fuzzy, to address the appropriate age range. The recorded videos were uploaded to Youtube.

Our new method develops the skill of actively identifying roots using oral instruction only. In the videos, the children are provided with a long series of structured examples of words and their roots. The avatar poses the question "what is the root of the word X?", then, after giving the children a few seconds to answer, the avatar provides the correct answer, adding a compliment after each set. The questions and answers are given in a rhythm that resembles recitation, and the cartoon avatars encourage active participation from the children, as the children decipher the roots alongside the avatars. This way, children learn to extract roots without any theoretical explanations nor literacy skills.

2.2 Participants

96 children took the pre-test and completed the first lesson, 84 completed the second, 73 completed the third, 69 completed the fourth and 68 completed the fifth. The final analysis was performed on 64 children (32 males and 32 females) who completed both the pre- and the post-test and participated in the entire program. The children were preschoolers (n = 29), first-graders (n = 23) and second-graders (n = 12), aged 5;3-8;9 (M = 6;11). All participants were native speakers of Hebrew: 55 monolinguals and 9 bilinguals with dominant Hebrew. Parents were requested to fill in a form of demographic and personal information, which indicated that participants were of different regions and varied backgrounds.
The study was approved by the Institutional Review Board (IRB).

2.3 Procedure

An invitation to participate in the experiment was posted on social media and sent to potential participants individually. Parents who were interested in signing up their children to the experiment had to consent to participate, then fill in a form of demographic and personal information. First, the children had a one-on-one Zoom meeting with an interviewer, where they watched a short introductory video in which they were invited to join 'The root detective club', and provided with a short training of three examples of root extraction. Then, the children were asked to extract the roots of 13 words of different patterns. The interviewers were instructed to always give positive feedback to the children, regardless of the answer they provided. After the pre-test, the children participated in five different lessons, in which they watched five root instruction videos on Youtube in their free time. The duration of each video was between 6 to 10 minutes, and the overall duration of all lessons was approximately 40 minutes. After each lesson, the parents filled in a feedback form in order to get the link for the following lesson. Later, having completed all five lessons, the children were invited to another one-on-one Zoom meeting, in which, after a short video, they took the post-test. In the post-test, the children were requested to extract the roots of 34 words. The post-test contained all pre-test items and 21 additional items. It is important to note that the experimental items did not appear in any of the lessons and the children were not exposed to them prior to the test.

2.4 Results

We first analyzed the percentage of all correct words in the pre- and post-tests. As shown in Figure 1, two-tailed paired t-tests revealed that the percentage of correct answers in the post-test was significantly higher than the pre-test (Pre-test: $M=0.1$, $SD=0.16$, Post-test: $M=0.73$, $SD=0.09$. Pre-Post: $M=0.62$, $SD=0.16$, $t(63)=30.95$, $p<0.01$). Moreover, the percentage of correct answers out of the identical thirteen items of the pre- and post-tests, was significantly higher in the post-test, compared to the pre-test (Pre-test: $M=0.1$, $SD=0.16$, Post-test: $M=0.72$, $SD=0.11$. Pre-Post: $M=0.62$, $SD=0.18$, $t(63)=26.99$, $p<0.01$).

The roots of the extra 21 items that appeared in the post-test, but not in the pre-test were also successfully extracted (M=0.73, SD=0.12). These results were significant with comparison to the pre-test (Pre-Extra: M=0.63, SD=0.17, $t(63)=29.65$, $p<0.01$).

As for demographics, two-tailed paired t-tests revealed no significant difference between boys and girls, bilinguals and monolinguals, and children of Jewish religious and secular education.

In a one-way ANOVA, a significant main effect for grade in the pre-test has been found ($F(2,61)=7.57$, $p<0.01$). As demonstrated in table 1, post hoc tests revealed that second-graders performed significantly better than preschoolers in the pre-test (preschoolers: M=0.04, SD=0.08, second-graders: M=0.23, SD=0.24, difference: M=0.19, SD=0.05, $p<0.01$). However, no such difference was found in the post-test (Preschoolers: M=0.7, SD=0.09, Second-graders: M=0.77, SD=0.09. Difference: M=0.07, SD=0.03, $p=0.08$).

2.5 Figures and Tables

Table 1. Mean normalized scores by grade and standard deviation

Grade	Test	Mean(SD)
Preschool	Pre	0.04(0.08)
	Post	0.7(0.09)
First-grade	Pre	0.12(0.14)
	Post	0.73(0.1)
Second-grade	Pre	0.23(0.24)
	Post	0.77(0.09)

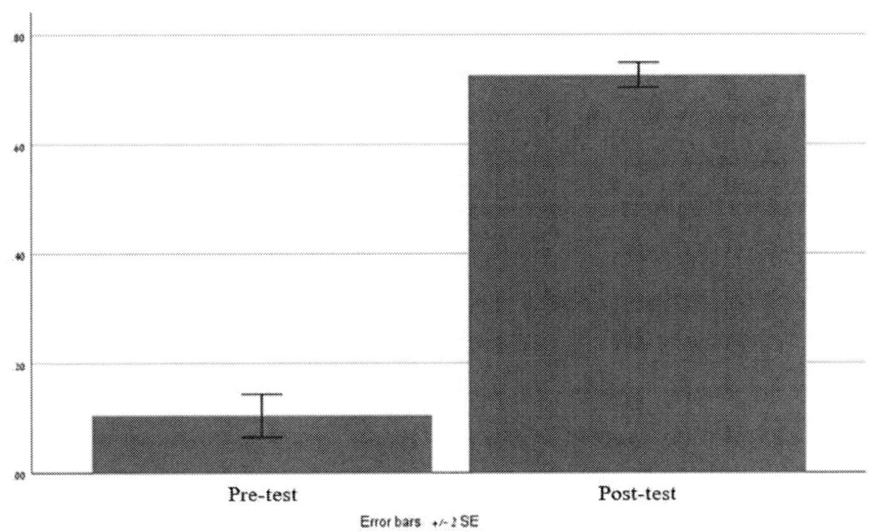

Figure 1. Mean normalized scores

Figure 2. An image of the cartoon-like avatars, Tutty (left) and Fuzzy (right)

3. CONCLUSION

The results of the experiment show that children significantly improved their ability to extract roots of Hebrew words after having completed our program. As the results show, the average score increased drastically between the pre-test and the post-test from 0.1 to 0.73 (out of 1). The same items that appeared in the pre-test got a significantly higher rate of correct answers in the post-test. The extra items that appeared only in the post-test were also successfully extracted. Furthermore, the overall number of correct answers in the post-test was significantly higher than that of the pre-test. It is worth pointing out that not only did children succeed in extracting roots of common verbs, but they also successfully dealt with complex verbal forms, as well as nouns and pseudowords.

Our program helped preschoolers reach the same level as the second-graders in their root extraction skills. The experiment was conducted in June, which is when the school year in Israel is almost over. By this time, second-graders had already been formally introduced to the notion of the root in school, while younger children were not at all familiar with it. Therefore, the second-graders' pre-test served as an ad-hoc control group in the experiment. After participating in our program, the significant difference that was found between preschoolers and second-graders in the pre-test was no longer present.

Although our program is extracurricular, it can be easily implemented in schools in Israel, and with some modifications, also abroad, serving for instruction of Hebrew as a foreign language. As roots are typical of Semitic languages, we are currently working on a parallel research, examining our method on native Arabic speakers as well. The program provides younger children with a deeper understanding of Hebrew morphology. It may also facilitate the process of the acquisition of the lexicon, as children rely on the consonantal skeleton while identifying relationships between lexical entries and interpreting novel words (Bat-El 2017; Berman 1985, 2003; Clark and Berman 1984; Levy 1988; Nespor et al. 2003). This is of high relevance for the education system, as the program improves students' linguistic competence, and teaches skills that are necessary for high-school matriculation exams. Our program is highly accessible to children all over the country, even in times of a global pandemic, and is compatible both for self- and group-learning, inside a classroom and out (see Levinson et al, 2020).

ACKNOWLEDGEMENT

Research was supported by a grant from the Cukier-Goldstein-Goren Center for Mind and Language ([Goren Gordon and Einat Gonen 2019]).

REFERENCES

Avinun, S., 1996. *Hebrew Word-Formation for High School*. Center for Educational Technology, Tel Aviv.

Bat-El, O. 2017. Word-based items-and processes (WoBIP): Evidence from Hebrew morphology. On looking into words (and beyond), 115-135.

Berman, R. A., 1985. The acquisition of Hebrew. *In D. I. Slobin (Ed.), The cross-linguistic study of language acquisition*, Vol. 1, pp. 25–371.

Berman, R. A., 2003. Children's lexical innovations: Developmental perspectives on Hebrew verb structure. *Language processing and acquisition in languages of Semitic, root-based, morphology*, Vol. 28, pp. 243-292.

Bolozky, S., 1999. Measuring Productivity in Word Formation: the Case of Israeli Hebrew. *Studies in Semitic Languages and Linguistics*, Vol. 27. Leiden: Brill.

Bolozky, S., 2003. The 'roots' of denominative Hebrew verbs. *Language processing and acquisition in languages of semitic, root-based morphology*, pp. 131-146.

Clark, E. V. and Berman R. A., 1984. Structure and use in the acquisition of word formation. *Language*, pp. 542-590.

Levinson, L. et al, 2020. Learning in Summer Camp with Social Robots: A Morphological Study. *International Journal of Social Robotics*, pp. 1-14.

Levy, Y., 1988. The nature of early language: Evidence from the development of Hebrew morphology. *Categories and processes in language acquisition*, pp. 73-98.

Lipkin, S., 1985. *Modern Hebrew Phonology for Junior High School*. CET, Tel Aviv.

Nespor, M. et al, 2003. On the different roles of vowels and consonants in speech processing and language acquisition. *Lingue e linguaggio*, Vol. 2, No. 2, pp. 203-230

Ravid, D., 1990. Internal structure constraints on new-word formation devices in modern Hebrew. *Folia Linguistica*, Vol. 24, pp. 289-346.

Ravid, D., 1991. *Modern Hebrew Morphology for High Schoolers*. Educational Television Center (in Hebrew), Tel Aviv.

Ravid, D. and Malenky, A., 2001. Awareness of linear and nonlinear morphology in Hebrew: A developmental study. *First Language*, Vol. 21, No. 61, pp. 25-56.

Ravid, D., 2003. A developmental perspective on root perception in Hebrew and Palestinian Arabic. *Language Acquisition and Language Disorders*, Vol. 28, pp. 293-320.

Ravid, D. and Schiff, R., 2006. Roots and patterns in Hebrew language development: Evidence from written morphological analogies. *Reading and Writing*, Vol. 19, No. 8, pp. 789-818.

IDEAL LEARNING ENVIRONMENT: HOW TO BUILD IT WITH ARTIFICIAL INTELLIGENCE

Elisabetta Crescio
Tecnologico de Monterrey, Escuela de Ingeniería y Ciencias,
Ave. Eugenio Garza Sada 2501, Monterrey 64849, NL, Mexico

ABSTRACT

With the massive use of new learning technologies, such as mobile learning through on-line platforms, or more "traditional" live classes taught through virtual meeting platforms, the interaction between students and teachers can be poor or limited. The professor can monitor the students' reactions and appreciation with the use of polls, forms, and forums, but in general it is very difficult to understand how students feel, what they really like and how to give them an unforgettable learning experience, especially when they are many and in a heterogeneous environment. A method to automatically detect students' needs, based on unsupervised machine learning techniques is proposed.

KEYWORDS

Professional Education, Educational Innovation, Higher Education, Ideal Environment

1. INTRODUCTION

In any kind of classroom environment, the student's experience is fundamental for the degree of learning obtained. In 1975 Mihaly Csiksentmihalyi introduced the concept of "flow" (Csikszentmihalyi, M. ,1975) to describe a particular emotional state of engagement during an activity which produces happiness. In this state, people are so involved in an activity that nothing else seems to matter and people feel strongly motivated. Csiksentmihalyi refers to this situation as "optimal experience" (Csikszentmihalyi, M. ,1990). Thinking to students in the classroom, it is believed that a student can get his optimal learning experience in such an emotional state. Therefore, it is important to create the ideal environment where students can live their "optimal experience". This issue is particularly important in a "virtual" environment as the one we were obliged to use during the COVID-19 pandemic (Liu Y.C., Kuo R.L., Shih S.R., 2020), where engagement during classes is critical to maintain students' attention. In asynchronous mobile learning it is even more difficult to monitor the engagement of students and understand their needs. Due to the complexity of class dynamics and inhomogeneity of students within the same classroom, creating ideal classroom conditions for all the students is a challenging task. The main question is – "How to create the ideal mobile learning environment"? In the following, a method based on sentiment analysis is presented.

2. MOBILE LEARNING EVALUATION WITH SENTIMENT ANALYSIS

2.1 Theoretical Background

Sentiment analysis is a field of Data Science aimed to automatically identify and extract opinions, sentiments, psychological and emotional states from written text. The methods used in this kind of analyses are based on machine learning techniques which are grouped under the name of Natural Language Processing (NLP) algorithms. Sentiment analysis has been used as a powerful tool to improve didactic strategies in on-line platforms as "Coursera" (Rani, S., and Kumar, P., 2017), where the interaction between teacher and student is very limited. By the application of machine learning techniques to comments and answers to polls taken during the course, it is possible to quantify the students' appreciation (Esparza, G.G., et al., 2018) automatically. In general, using NLP techniques it is possible to detect sentiments and emotional states. As described in detail in (Kaur., W., Balakrishnan, V., Singh, B., 2020), the term "sentiment analysis" describes a kind of study where we aim to detect the polarity of a written text, i.e., if it represents a positive or a negative feeling. The analysis of emotions is an extension of sentiment analysis which tries to detect also if the person who wrote the text was happy, sad, frustrated, angry, or in other emotional states. With these kinds of analyses one can classify the opinions of the students and classify their feelings, but it is hard to retrieve what they really would like to receive from a class.

2.2 Objectives

The analysis presented here uses an NLP algorithm called Probabilistic Latent Semantic Analysis (PLSA), which is normally used to extract topics from collections of documents by grouping them by similarity (Hofmann T.,1999). The use of this algorithm was inspired by studies in the field of Social Signal Processing, aimed to automatically detect personality patterns, which make use of statistical and probabilistic algorithms of this kind (Judee K. Burgoon J. K., Magnenat-Thalmann N., Pantic M., Vinciarelli A.,2017). The main idea is to detect latent aspects among the words of the feedback comments written by the students, in order to find common characteristics or sentiments that they would like to experience during the class and sort them by importance. A similar approach has been used recently to analyze comments of hotel customers, as standalone method and in addition to Deep Learning techniques (Khotimah, D. A. K. and Sarno, R., 2018, 2019).

2.3 Data Collection

In the present analysis the data are represented by a sample of 42 written opinions from university students of ages between 18 and 20. Students were asked to write their comments following specific instructions. They were asked to share the aspects that, in their opinion, make a professor the "ideal" professor. Students were asked, also, to describe which sentiments they want to feel during the class that make them feel strongly motivated and which characteristics the ideal class must have. We want to prove whether the algorithm can "extract" from the students' comments these principal aspects which define the ideal learning environment. The data were taken in the period between August and December 2020. The participation was voluntary and a total of 42 comments was collected. The students' comments were firstly collected through the "Padlet" platform (Padlet, n.d) anonymously and successively imported in a csv (comma separated value) file. The comments are written in Spanish.

2.4 Methodology

The PLSA algorithm "counts" the co-occurrence between words and documents (using Bayesian statistics) and divides the documents into groups. Each group is defined by a "latent" aspect (or topic) which is not known "a priori". In the classical application of PLSA aimed to group, for example, articles by similarity, the latent aspects represent the different topics of the articles, such as science, economy, education and so on. In the analysis presented here, in principle, the number of latent topics is also unknown. Since the comments were written following specific instructions, we can guess that the number of topics is 3: one related to the professor's personality, one related on the way of teaching and one related to the feelings the students want to experience. So, the number of topics was set to 3. The dataset, from the point of view of the algorithm, is a set of documents (the comments), each composed by a sequence of words. The full dataset is defined also as "corpus". After running the analysis, one obtains two numerical results. The first is a number (between 0 and 1), for each topic, representing how probable, or frequent, is the topic within the corpus. The second result is a list of numbers (between 0 and 1), for each topic, representing the probability within the topic of all the words of the corpus (i.e., the importance of the word in the topic). The "importance" of a word in the corpus is the frequency of the word in the corpus, i.e., among all documents. Usually, NLP techniques require a big amount of data to perform well, due to statistical implications. In the presented analysis, however, the corpus is composed by only 42 comments and some uncertainties and instabilities of the result have been observed when running the analysis different times. However, the method should provide stable results when applied, as it is intended to, to analyze bigger datasets.

3. RESULTS

The analysis was focused on the lists of probabilities associated to the words, topic by topic. For each topic, this list is a sequence of 312 (the number of words in the corpus) descending values representing the probability of each word in the topic. In Figure 1, on the left, a scatter plot of the list of probabilities for the first topic extracted is shown.

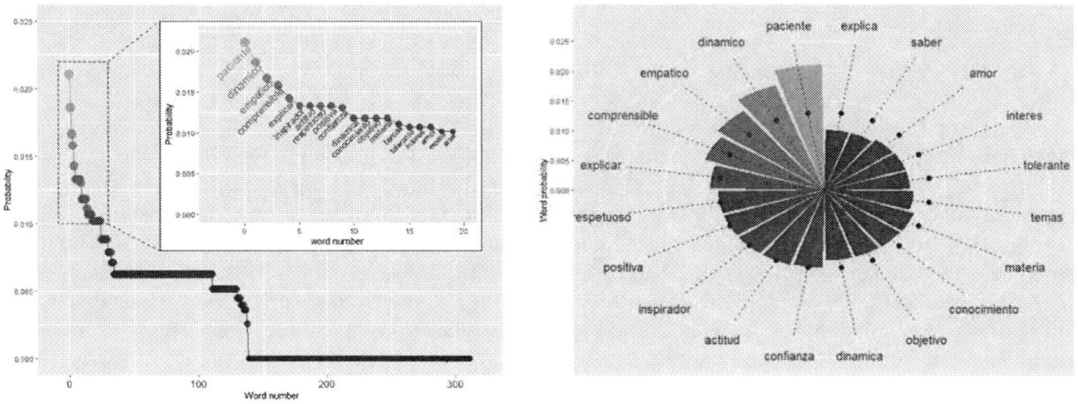

a) b)

Figure 1. a) Probabilities of the 312 words of the first topic extracted. A zoom for the 20 most probable words is shown on the upper right corner. b) First 20 most probable words associated to the first topic. The black circles represent the mean probability of the sample of words

Considering the first 20 most probable words of each topic we can analyze the difference among the three topics detected. Figure 1, on the right, shows the first 20 words for the first extracted topic. The words are: "paciente" (having patience), "dinamico" (dynamic), "empatico" (empathic), "comprensible" (understandable), "explicar" (to explain), "respetuoso" (respectful), "positiva" (positive, feminine), "inspirador" (inspiring), "actitud" (attitude), "confianza" (trust), "dinamica" (dynamic), "objetivo" (objective), "conocimiento" (knowledge), "materia" (subject), "temas" (topics), "tolerante" (tolerant), "interes" (interest), "amor" (love), "saber" (to know), "explica" (to explain). It is possible to infer to which aspect of students' preferences each topic refers to by associating the corresponding words. Even though the interpretation could be somehow subjective, we can identify in this topic words mainly related to the personality of the professor.

Figure 2 a) shows the 20 most probable words collected for the second topic. The words are: "clases" (classes), "dinamicas" (dynamic, plural feminine), "didacticas" (didactic, plural feminine), "tareas" (homeworks), "materia" (subject), "rete" (that challenges you), "actividades" (activities), "todas" (all), "situaciones" (situations), "seguridad" (certainty), "salon" (classroom), "retar" (to challenge), "hacer" (to do), "habilidades" (abilities), "general" (general), "explicaciones" (explications), "bueno" (good), "aprender" (to learn), "apasionada" (passionate, feminine), "flexible" (flexible). The second topic seems to be related to class activities and way of teaching. The two first most probable words are "clases" and "dinamicas", both plural and feminine, suggesting that they could be associated to form the description of the ideal class as a "dynamic class".

Finally, the probabilities of the first 20 words of the third topic are depicted in Figure 2 b). The words are: "area" (area), "sientes" (you feel), "excelente" (excelent), "flexible" (flexible), "pasion" (passion), "bien" (good, noun), "transmitir" (to transmit), "transmite" (he transmits), "nuevas" (new, plural femine), "motivacion" (motivation), "mismos" (same, plural masculine), "humor" (humor), "gusta" (he likes or you like), "experto" (expert), "educado" (educated), "capaz" (able), "temas" (subjects), "manera" (way), "comprensivo" (understandable), "clases" (classes).

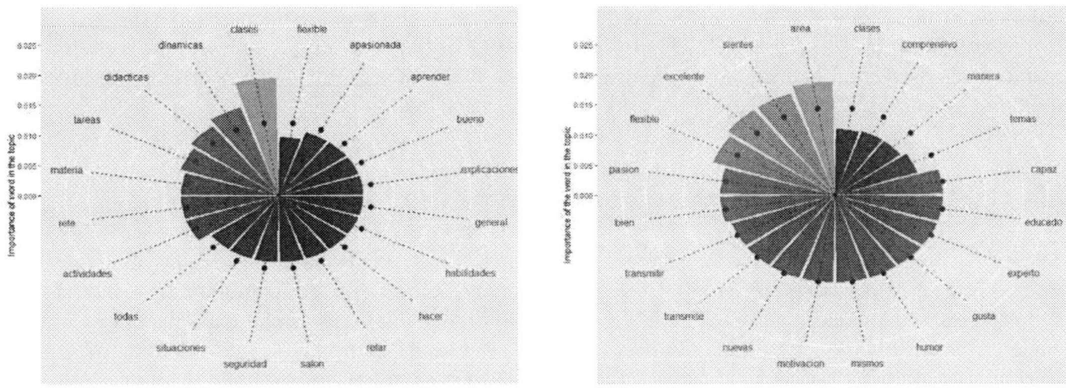

a) b)

Figure 2. a) First 20 most probable words associated to the second topic. b) First 20 most probable words associated to the third topic. The black circles represent the mean probability of the sample of words

Even though in this last topic the words are more mixed, words such as "sientes" (you feel), "pasion" (passion), "transmite" (he transmits) and "motivacion" (motivation) suggest feelings that students want to feel o want the professor to transmit. The difference among topics can be visualized comparing the probabilities of the same word in the three topics. To do so, the first 10 words with highest probabilities of each topic have been chosen, for a total of 30 words. The comparison is shown in Figure 3 a).

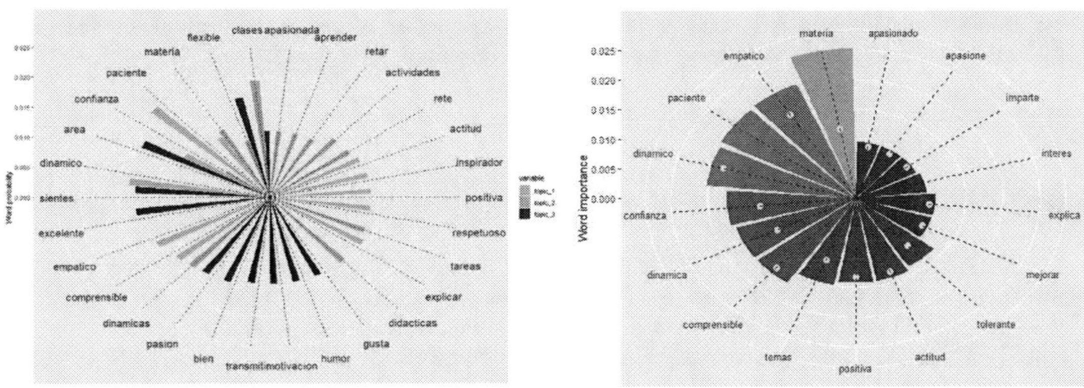

a) b)

Figure 3. a) Word probability of the 30 most common words within the topics. b) Comparison between the probabilities of words belonging to the first topic in two runs of analysis. The bars represent the probabilities of the new run, the yellow circles represent the probabilities of the previous run

Figure 3 a) shows that most words have a high probability in only one topic. Some words appear in two topics, as "clases" (classes), "flexible" (flexible), "materia" (subject) and "dinamico" (dynamic), with different probabilities. The word "confianza" (trust) appears in the three topics, being more probable in the third topic, than in the first and at last in the second topic. From this comparison we can conclude that the three topics are well "separated", i.e., are characterized by different words. Also, one could guess the students' preferred aspects in each topic just looking at the most probable words and interpreting the meanings. Looking at the word corresponding to the highest probability, we could conclude that the most important aspect for the students is "paciente" (having patience). However, due to the uncertainties of the algorithm due to the small statistics, the probability cannot be interpreted as the relevance of the corresponding student requirement, at least for the present dataset. As an example, the analysis was run a second time. Figure 3 b) shows the most probable words of the topic related to the personality of the professor and the probabilities obtained in the two runs of analysis. The bars represent the probabilities obtained in the second run and the yellow circles represent the probabilities obtained in the previous run. It is possible to observe some fluctuations in the probabilities, as for the word "materia" (subject), which appears as most probable word of the topic in the second run while it had a much smaller probability in the first run. Despite these uncertainties, the algorithm was able to detect the three aspects on which students were asked to write about in their comments.

4. CONCLUSIONS AND FUTURE DEVELOPMENTS

The results presented above show the possibility to automatically detect students' needs by analyzing the words written in their feedback comments. The limit of this method is that the interpretation of the results is somehow subjective and that there could be lack of reproducibility when applied to small datasets. On the other hand, since the result is expressed through words, the results are easily interpretable. In the framework of mobile learning, by applying this method on a larger dataset of posts written, for example, by students following a course offered on-line through a smart-phone application, one could guess the students' needs and preferences in real time during the course and change educational strategies to create the ideal learning environment.

A further development of the present analysis could be the application, on a larger dataset, of other algorithms used for topic extraction, as Latent Dirichlet Allocation (Blei D.M., 2003) and more recent techniques based on pre-trained models and Deep Learning (Angelov D., 2020).

ACKNOWLEDGEMENT

The author would like to acknowledge the technical support of Writing Lab, Institute for the Future of Education, Tecnologico de Monterrey, Mexico, in the production of this work.
The author would also acknowledge her friend and thesis supervisor Alessandro Vinciarelli, who introduced her to the Artificial Intelligence world.

REFERENCES

Angelov, D. (2020). Top2Vec: Distributed Representations of Topics. arXiv preprint arXiv:2008.09470.

Blei D.M et al., 2003. Latent dirichlet allocation. *J. Mach. Learn. Res.* Vol. 3, pp. 993–1022.

Burgoon J. K. et al., 2017. *Social signal processing*. Cambridge University Press.

Csikszentmihalyi, M., 1975. *Beyond boredom and anxiety: The experience of play in work and leisure*. San Fr CA: Jossey-Bass.

Csikszentmihalyi, M., 1990. Flow. *The Psychology of Optimal Experience*. HarperPerennial, New York.

Hofmann T., 1999. Probabilistic Latent Semantic Indexing. *Proceedings of the Twenty-Second Annual International SIGIR Conference on Research and Development in Information Retrieval (SIGIR-99).* Pp. 50-57. doi: 10.1145/312624.312649

Kaur, W. et al., 2020. Improving teaching and learning experience in engineering education using sentiment analysis techniques. *IOP Conference Series: Materials Science and Engineering.* Vol. 834, No. 1, p. 012026.

Khotimah D. A. K. and Sarno R., 2018. Sentiment Detection of Comment Titles in Booking.com Using Probabilistic Latent Semantic Analysis. En *2018 6th International Conference on Information and Communication Technology (ICoICT)*. IEEE. doi:10.1109/ICoICT.2018.8528784.

Khotimah D. A. K. and Sarno R., 2019. Sentiment Analysis of Hotel Aspect Using Probabilistic Latent Semantic Analysis, Word Embedding and LSTM. *International Journal of Intelligent Engineering and Systems.* Vol. 12, No. 4, pp. 275-290. doi:10.22266/ijies2019.0831.26

Liu Y.C. et al., 2020. COVID-19: The first documented coronavirus pandemic in history. *Biomedical Journal*, Vol. 43, No. 4, pp. 328-333.

Padlet, https://padlet.com/

Rani S., Kumar P., 2017. A Sentiment Analysis System to Improve Teaching and Learning. *Computer,* Vol. 50, No. 5, pp. 36-43. doi: 10.1109/MC.2017.133.

THE SPOC+ PLATFORM: EVALUATION AND PERSPECTIVES

Hamed Asgari and Georges Antoniadis
Université Grenoble Alpes, Laboratoire LIDILEM, France

ABSTRACT

Mobile artifacts are the objects that increasingly surround us in life. They provide us with the opportunity to engage in activities outside the traditional context and at our own pace. In this article, we present the results of the tests of our mobile application intended for the learning of the French language with the concept of SPOC with a methodology of teaching pedagogy by project founded based on MIRTO by using the NLP tools.

KEYWORDS

SPOC, NLP, MIRTO, mLearning, SPOC+, FLE

1. INTRODUCTION

As part of our research, we have set up a new platform, SPOC+. This platform is a FLE (French language learning) system based on SPOC (Small Private Online Course) integrating NLP (Natural Language Processing) tools and the MIRTO[1] project (Antoniadis and Ponton, 2004) on mobile artifacts with a personalized follow-up for each learner. As described (Asgari and Antoniadis, 2021), our platform, SPOC+, is modular and allows for the incorporation of new features resulting from scientific progress in the field of NLP as well as technological innovations, such as virtual reality and augmented reality. We have developed the SPOC+ learner interface only on smartphones, to enable learning anytime and anywhere. SPOC+ covers all skills of language learning: listening, reading, speaking and writing. SPOC+ is based on the same principles that founded MIRTO (Antoniadis and Ponton, 2004), simplicity, modularity and user-friendliness. Simple, because NLP tools are designed for teachers who have little or no computer skills. Modular to be able to integrate new NLP functionalities as its tools develop. User-friendly because of the users who use our system, the generation of thumbs.

2. CONTEXT

In the test phase of our application, we tested SPOC+ with 25 non-French adult learners inform Iran where French is not an official language. As Wang and his colleagues point out, gender and age variants of learners have no impact on mobile learning (Wang et al., 2009). We do not distinguish gender differences in the selected learners. We limited the number of learners per class to allow the teacher a personalized follow-up, which is one of the significant differences between MOOC and SPOC (Asgari and Antoniadis, 2020). According to the study conducted by Lui and colleagues, prior knowledge in SPOC does not influence SPOC usage and learning performance (Lui et al., 2017) by new learners. The 25 learners had never been used or participated in SPOC courses.

[1] In French Multi-apprentissages Interactifs par des Recherches sur des Textes et l'Oral

We defined two selection criteria. The first criterion for selecting the 25 learners is based on their level of knowledge of French language. The learners in our system, in this phase, have all previously reached level B1 according to the CEFR (Europarat, 2011) global scale. Our second selection criterion concerns the learners' mobile artifact. Our mobile application is available for smartphones with an operating system from Android 5 and IOS 11, our learners all had a smartphone with an Android operating system higher than version 5 with an internet connection.

As presented (Asgari and Antoniadis, 2020), our system consists of two websites and a mobile application. Our survey is formed of 30 questions and sent to all 25 learners who were using our mobile application. They had followed courses for 8 weeks (at a frequency of one session per week). During these 8 weeks, we covered the verbs in the imperfect tense and possessive adjectives for level B2 according to the CEFR (Europarat, 2011) global scale with the main theme, the Louvre Museum. With an interval of two weeks after the last lesson, the learners received a notification on their smartphone to participate in our survey. The questionnaire could only be validated and sent if all questions had been answered. All learners answered our questionnaire. We present our analysis results in detail in the following sections.

3. METHODOLOGY

Our questionnaire is divided into two sections. The first section consists of 10 questions related to learners' subjective views and ease of use of SPOC+. The second section of the survey asks learners 20 questions about their satisfaction with using SPOC+ in their French language learning process. In order to obtain correct answers, we translated the questionnaire into the learners' native language. As Sharples advocates, the assessment of mobile learning is not inherently different from other forms of learning, in that we want to understand the individual and collective processes of knowledge acquisition and the resulting changes in knowledge, skills, and experience. Learning that is both initiated and structured through the use of mobile technologies can be assessed in different ways, including Likert scale questionnaires (Sharples, 2009). Cronbach's alpha test (Cronbach, 1951) was used to assess the reliability of the questionnaire. As recommended by Kline (Kline, 2015), the Cronbach's alpha coefficient of our questionnaire with a threshold of 0.94 confirms sufficient reliability of our questionnaire. Our questionnaire consists of two sections. The first part contains 10 questions to assess the satisfaction and ease of use of SPOC+ and the second part to measure learners' satisfaction with using the SPOC+ app on their smartphones for online French language learning. We present our approach in the following sections. In order to analyze the first section of our questionnaire, we use Brooke's method (Brooke, 1986) and for the analysis of the second section, we use the statistical analysis software SPSS.

3.1 Section One

In order to collect learners' opinions on the usability of our system, we chose the System Usability Scale (SUS) satisfaction questionnaire, as it is practically technology-neutral (Brooke, 2013). This questionnaire is easy to understand, fairly short with easily interpretable scoring. The SUS scale consists of 10 items in the affirmative form, so every other item is reversed (the answer requires answering the opposite of the previous item). The goal is to have learners read each question and make an effort to think about whether they agree or disagree with it (Brooke, 2013). Scoring starts from 1 to 5, with 1 representing "strongly disagree" and 5 representing "strongly agree." As Brooke points out, SUS yields a single number, representing a composite measure of overall satisfaction with the system under study, so the scores of individual items are not significant in themselves (Brooke, 1996) and we cannot analyze them individually. The SUS score for SPOC+ is 79.8 out of 100. Using a 0-100 scoring system typically leads to a percentage interpretation, which is not the case with SUS (Brooke, 2013). We interpret the SPOC+ SUS score in three different forms. First, using the six adjectives proposed by Bangor and colleagues (Bangor et al., 2009), second, with the five grades presented by Sauro in this research (Sauro, 2018), and third using a degree of acceptability consisting of three different levels from the scientific work of Bangor and colleagues (Bangor et al., 2008).

3.2 Section Two

The second section of our questionnaire is based on the work done by Sulaiman and Dashti (Sulaiman and Dashti, 2018), consisting of 19 questions with a yes or no answer and 1 question with the possibility to give us possible feedback from the learners. These 20 questions concern technological aspects (communication and interaction tools, app usability, availability), didactic aspects (content and resources, teaching and tutoring, course organization, clarity of learning objectives, assessment methods), and overall evaluation of the user experience (originality compared to traditional courses and pedagogical methods, learner satisfaction, other positive/negative aspects that we may not have anticipated, as well as suggestions for improvement).

4. RESULTS

According to Bangor and colleagues' classification (Bangor et al., 2009), the score of 79.8 is above "good" but not yet "excellent." According to Sauro's research (Sauro, 2018), with the results we obtained, SPOC+ has a grade of "C". As shown in the work of Bangor and colleagues (Bangor et al., 2008), a score above 70 is "acceptable," which is the case for SPOC+. Figure 1 represents the SPOC+ SUS score in three different forms of interpretation that we have discussed.

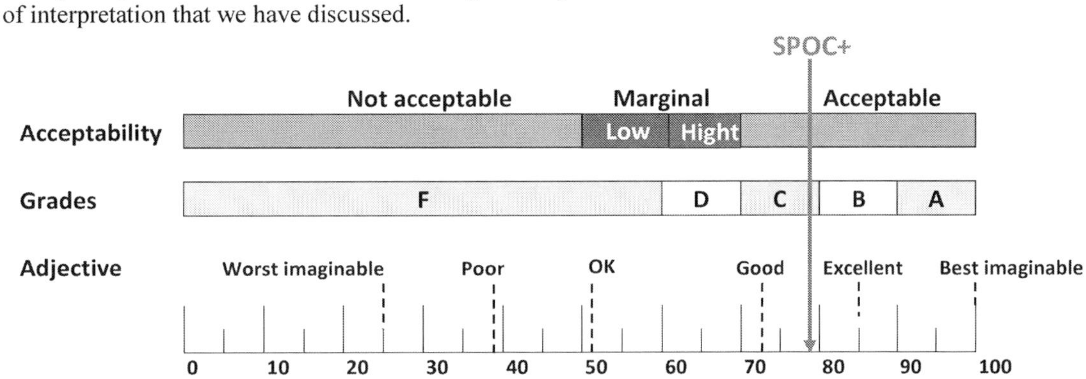

Figure 1. SPOC+ SUS Score rating scale, from (Brooke, 2013)

On the 6 questions of the scope of the tools made available in the SPOC+ application, the distribution of the answers reveals that 30.7% of the learners were dissatisfied, while 69.3% expressed their satisfaction regarding these tools, which may indicate the level of satisfaction of the learners regarding the tools made available in the SPOC+ application. To improve learner satisfaction with our tools, it is important to properly integrate tools that are closer to the tools that the learner's generation are used to using.

According to the learners' responses to the 5 questions about "mobile artifacts", it was found that 30.4% of the learners were not satisfied with the use of mobile artifacts in teaching while 69.6% expressed satisfaction. This shows that mobile artifacts are overall appreciated in the learning process.

According to the learners' answers to the 8 questions, it was found that 29% were not satisfied with this type of training while 71% expressed satisfaction with this type of training. Although SPOC is a new learning method, we found that with a satisfactory percentage, learners enjoyed this new method that we integrated on their smartphones through our SPOC+ application.

As it is previously presented, the last question of the second questionnaire is open-ended. This question allows us to have the learners' opinions, gives them the means to express their opinion about the SPOC+ application and the French language learning process. We did not require a minimum or a maximum number of characters for the comments in this question. All 25 learners responded with different degrees of length.

One answer among the 25 is not usable and we cannot conclude any result. This is the case of learner number 16, his answer "سپاس", which is translated into French as "remerciement" (Parsayar, 2005) does not allow us to clearly rule his point of view towards our system. In Iranian culture, this word does not reflect agreement or disagreement. Learner number 11 states that he has no idea about the SPOC+ application, we consider the response of learner's numbers 11 and 16 as neutral. Among the 25 learners, 19 learners are satisfied with the SPOC+ application and have demonstrated their satisfaction with the use of the SPOC+ application in learning the French language. They described SPOC+ as a practical and interesting application that allowed them to discover a new learning method. According to the answers to this last question and the analysis of the other 19 questions of our 2nd section questionnaire, it was found that in general learners were satisfied with the SPOC+ application in the process of learning the French language on their smartphone.

5. CONCLUSION

We were able to test SPOC+ with a group of 25 French language learners. As the analysis of the results of our questionnaire shows, with a SUS score of 79.8 according to two interpretive scales, learners' satisfaction with SPOC+ is "good" and "acceptable". Using a questionnaire with sufficient reliability, more than 70% of these same learners showed their satisfaction with the use of SPOC+ in the French language learning process. The results of our test showed us that the implementation of an online FLE course on smartphones with the SPOC concept is possible. In order to better analyze the satisfaction of learners with SPOC+ it would be useful to have the results of a larger number of learners in our future tests.

On the technological aspect, we will have to improve our chat and forum tools to allow better collaboration between the teacher-learner and the group of learners. On the didactic side, we can improve our pedagogical content through better cooperation with teachers. To better realize project-based learning, we are considering integrating GeoLearning on our platform.

REFERENCES

Antoniadis, G., Ponton, C., 2004. MIRTO : un système au service de l'enseignement des langues.

Asgari, H., Antoniadis, G., 2021. Mobile Artefacts And Language Teaching, The Example Of The Spoc+ Platform, in: 17th International Conferences Mobile Learning 2021 (ML 2021). Lisbonne (virtual), Portugal.

Asgari, H., Antoniadis, G., 2020. SPOC, Future of M-Learning and Language Learning?, in: 16th International Conference Mobile Learning 2020. Sofia, Bulgaria.

Bangor, A., Kortum, P., Miller, J., 2009. Determining what individual SUS scores mean: Adding an adjective rating scale. Journal of usability studies 4, 114–123.

Bangor, A., Kortum, P.T., Miller, J.T., 2008. An Empirical Evaluation of the System Usability Scale. International Journal of Human–Computer Interaction 24, 574–594. https://doi.org/10.1080/10447310802205776

Brooke, J., 2013. SUS: a retrospective. Journal of usability studies 8, 29–40.

Brooke, J., 1996. SUS-A quick and dirty usability scale. Usability evaluation in industry 189, 4–7.

Brooke, J., 1986. System usability scale (SUS): a quick-and-dirty method of system evaluation user information. Reading, UK: Digital Equipment Co Ltd 43.

Cronbach, L.J., 1951. Coefficient alpha and the internal structure of tests. Psychometrika 16, 297–334. https://doi.org/10.1007/BF02310555

Europarat (Ed.), 2011. Common European framework of reference for languages: learning, teaching, assessment, 12th printing. ed. Cambridge Univ. Press, Cambridge.

Kline, R.B., 2015. Principles and practice of structural equation modeling. Guilford publications.

Lui, R.W., Geng, S., Law, K.M., 2017. Project management SPOC with animation, in: 2017 IEEE 6th International Conference on Teaching, Assessment, and Learning for Engineering (TALE). IEEE, pp. 29–34.

Parsayar, M.R., 2005. Dictionnaire de poche persan français.

Sauro, J., 2018. ways to interpret a SUS score. Measuringu. Com 1–12.

Sharples, M., 2009. Methods for evaluating mobile learning. Researching mobile learning: Frameworks, tools and research designs 17–39.

Sulaiman, A., Dashti, A., 2018. Students' satisfaction and factors in using Mobile learning among college students in Kuwait. EURASIA Journal of Mathematics, Science and Technology Education 14, 3181–3189.

Wang, Y.-S., Wu, M.-C., Wang, H.-Y., 2009. Investigating the determinants and age and gender differences in the acceptance of mobile learning. British journal of educational technology 40, 92–118.

DIGITAL SIMULATION GAMES FOR MEDIA EDUCATION. A DIDACTIC SCENARIO

Jasmin Bastian[1], Christian Toth[2] and Christina Wolf[1]
[1]*University of Mainz, Germany*
[2]*University of Kaiserslautern, Germany*

ABSTRACT

The authors developed, implemented, and evaluated a digital simulation game for media education in teacher training. The aim of the simulation game is to simulate decision-making processes in schools for the implementation of hybrid teaching in the context of the pandemic. The question is whether the participation in a digital simulation games initiates reflection processes that change or deepen students' attitude towards hybrid learning concepts. For this purpose, N=300 students who participated in 12 simulation games were surveyed by means of a questionnaire as part of a pre-post design.

KEYWORDS

Media Education, Simulation Game, Digital Inequality, Hybrid Teaching, Higher Education Teaching

1. INTRODUCTION

In German-speaking countries, simulation games are increasingly used in the context of university teaching (Meßner, Schedelik and Engartner 2018). Due to the COVID19 pandemic, face-to-face formats had to be dropped or converted into digital formats at universities. The authors therefore developed, implemented, and evaluated a digital simulation game format for media educational teacher training. The main purpose of a simulation game is to initiate experiential and action-oriented learning in a constructed situation that is modeled after real processes (Meßner, Schedelik and Engartner 2018). The objective of the developed simulation game is to replicate decision-making processes in schools for implementing hybrid teaching in the context of the pandemic. The pedagogical learning objectives were formulated as: (1) an associative introduction to the design of hybrid teaching and learning formats in schools, as in many cases no own experiences with this format have been made in the school context, (2) the training of professional competencies (planning of hybrid teaching concepts considering digital inequality) as well as (3) the testing of the methodological arrangement digital simulation game. The question arises whether the use of the digital simulation game caused reflection processes among the students that changed or deepened their attitude towards hybrid teaching concepts.

The findings on learning effects through (digital) simulation games are still limited. However, concerning the phases of a simulation game, which are divided into (1) preparation (2) implementation and (3) reflection (Capaul and Ulrich 2010), it is evident that the reflection phase is of great importance with regard to learning success (Kriz and Nöbauer 2015). Therefore, quantitative questioning was used to find out to what extent the perception of multiple perspectives and digital inequality as well as the planning of hybrid teaching caused reflection processes among the students. Methodologically, the conducted simulation games were evaluated by means of questionnaires in a pre-post design. N=300 students who participated in 12 simulation games were surveyed. The aim of this paper is to reflect on the potential of digital simulation games for (hybrid) university teaching.

2. SPECIFICS OF THE SIMULATION GAME

Digital simulation games offer the possibility of action-oriented learning in constructed situations. These situations are modelled on everyday situations in a virtual world (Pappa and Papadima-Sophocleous 2018). In the case of the present media-educational simulation game, for example, a situation from everyday school life is simulated. Of course, the simulation cannot be compared 1:1 with the everyday situation. Rather, it is reduced to certain decision-making situations that the players have to deal with. Nevertheless, the constructed situations still contain the characteristic structures and possibilities for action of the everyday situation (Meßner, Schedelik and Engartner 2018; Von der Weth et al. 2018). Simulation games are characterised by the following dimensions, which are also omnipresent in everyday situations (Imhof and Starker 2020):

(1) Uncertainty and the pressure to act or make decisions.
(2) Openness to the future, in the sense that the players can decide and act in different ways and thus encounter and change situations.
(3) Development options, in the sense that the decisions made have a perceptible effect.
(4) Interconnectedness, in the sense that the actions can also have an effect on the other roles.
(5) Dynamics, in the sense that a spiral of emotions can be set in motion.

The process of simulation games can be described using a certain phase structure (Reinhardt 2016). As part of the introduction, the learners receive materials for preparation, from which a situation description, tasks, rules and role descriptions emerge. In the following phase of information, the focus is on the examination of the materials, the learners prepare for their roles and finally take them. The phase of deciding and planning offers the players space to organise themselves within group structures by analysing needs, wishes and conflicts arising from the role description. In the course of the interaction, the different group structures meet and come together with different, sometimes opposing positions; the exchange and negotiation begins. The final phase of evaluation - also called reflection phase in the following - is connected to the game and allows the learners to reflect on what they have experienced by taking up and discussing procedures, conflicts that have arisen and possible solutions that the learners have experienced within their roles. Likewise, a reference to reality is established and a transfer of what has been learned to this very reality is aimed at (Fischer and Reinhardt 2018). If we condense this fine-grained structure, the phase structure basically always comprises introduction, game and reflection.

The form of simulation games can vary and differs above all in the role-based interaction phase of the game. This can take place, for example, in an analogue learning environment, within the framework of a board game or also in a digital learning environment. There can be methodological overlaps and parallels between the simulation game method and other teaching-learning arrangements. In principle, simulation games are characterised by their reference to institutional mechanisms of function and effect and complex issues, thus distinguishing them from role-playing games. In the context of role-playing games, the focus is much more on dealing with and processing the immediate living environment (Fischer and Reinhardt 2018). Accordingly, differentiations can also be found in the role descriptions: In simulation games, roles of functionaries often appear, whereas in role plays, life-world roles are central (Petrik 2017). Both in a case study and in a simulation game, learners have to deal with a case or a scenario in which abstract and complex contexts are shown on a concrete person-related level, and to understand this case or scenario. However, the scenario of the simulation game provides role-based, partly institutional, guidelines for action and rules that require attention from the players and provide a framework (Fischer and Reinhardt 2018). Thus, the learners experience the interrelationships as well as the complexity from the dynamic model-based game events (Schwägele 2015). Learning in case studies, on the other hand, takes place primarily through the development of questions that should lead to making the complex interrelations visible and understanding them. Only then are action and solution strategies formulated and discussed (Fischer and Reinhardt 2018).

Didactically, the implementation of a simulation game always makes sense if the learning objective is to deal with complexity (Riberio 2019). Digital simulation games make it possible to encounter the complexity of a specific everyday situation in a virtual, protected space and to deal with one's own actions and the available options for action within the framework of playful action and later joint reflection in the group (Adipat et al. 2021; Vasmatzoglou and Ní Chiaráin 2020).

3. SCENARIO OF THE SIMULATION GAME

In the developed simulation game "Hybrid Teaching in Times of Pandemic. Challenges and Possible Solutions", the complexity is reduced to the aspect of planning or designing hybrid teaching during the pandemic, with different levels of digital inequality becoming perceptible during the game (such as unequal equipment, access, user experience or media literacy). Each simulation needs its specific scenario and specific roles. In the present scenario, typical roles were developed for teachers, student representatives, parent representatives and school management and were given to the players digitally in the form of an individual role description for each. Roles can be, for example, the "innovative principal" or the "media-critical teacher". How the media-critical teacher behaves, whether he voices his criticism aloud, tries to boycott digital instructional design or simply does not support media innovations, is a matter of interpretation for the players.

The spatial scenario was chosen so that the simulation begins at a fictive school. School management, teachers, parent and student representatives initially meet in an assembly hall. The vacations are over and the school management informs about new ministerial requirements. Due to the pandemic, purely face-to-face teaching is currently not possible on site and classes must be held hybrid for the time being. First, the homogeneous status groups start planning or exchanging ideas in virtual rooms: the teachers develop concepts under pressure on how they can design their subject lessons hybridly from now on; parent representatives and student representatives exchange ideas on dimensions of digital inequality that make hybrid teaching more difficult. Afterwards, the status groups mix and go into the discussion of the developed concepts in a new composition. In the virtual rooms, for example, discussions take place between teachers and student representatives, different levels of digital inequality are pointed out and their consideration in the concepts is insisted on.

4. EVALUATION

The implementation of the simulation game "Hybrid Teaching in Times of Pandemic. Challenges and possible solutions" was additionally evaluated and the results will be presented in the following. Participation in the pre- and post-survey was completely anonymous and voluntary. The allocation of data from the pre- and post-survey was carried out using personalised complex codes that did not allow any conclusions to be drawn about the individuals. First, the students took part in the pre-survey, then in the simulation game and after the simulation game in the post-survey in the sense of a pre-post design. Of the total of 300 participating students, N = 221 students took part in both the pre- and post-surveys. 23 (10.4%) of the 221 participants had already taken part in a simulation game before. Of these 23, 20 (87%) had participated in a face-to-face simulation, 2 (8.7%) in a digital simulation and 1 (4.3%) in a hybrid simulation. In the simulation, 107 (48.4%) took on the role of teachers, 45 (20.4%) the role of parent representatives, 16 (7.2%) the role of headmasters or vice-principals and 53 (24%) the role of student representatives.

The students went into the simulation in a positive frame of mind, even though most of them were not sure what to expect (see Table 1). They also stated that they were more sceptical about digital simulation games than face-to-face simulation games. In addition, they believed that the simulation game would provide them with both an increase in competence and opportunities for reflection. It was striking that 181 (82.7%) of the 221 students stated that they knew different arguments for and against hybrid teaching, but only 85 (38.5%) had a firm opinion on hybrid teaching. Of these 85 students, 40 (47%) are sceptical about the digitisation of face-to-face teaching. Finally, the pre-survey revealed that the students largely perceived themselves as competent, both critically-reflexively and in the conception and implementation of digital or hybrid teaching lessons.

Table 1. Mean values of items in relation to expectations and attitudes towards digital simulation games

Item	*M*	*SD*
I prefer a digital simulation game over the offline version. (N=221)	**2,71**	**1,31**
I am uncertain about what to expect from a digital simulation game. (N=220)	**3,71**	**1,13**
I'm looking forward to the digital simulation game. (N=218)	**3,67**	**,98**
I expect to learn something by participating in the digital simulation game. (N=220)	**3,90**	**,89**
I expect the digital simulation game to encourage reflection about the topic. (N=221)	**4,02**	**,92**

Notes: M = mean (with 1 = fully disagee, 5 = fully agree); SD = standard deviation.

The simulation game as a whole was predominantly evaluated positively (see table 2), it seems to have been fun for most students. The cooperation with other students was viewed positively for the most part. The reflection phase that followed the simulation was also considered useful for the most part. Although some students stated that their own attitude did not match the attitude of the role they had to play, most stated that they found it easy to play their role. This indicates that the role descriptions and the tasks set were clear and not overwhelming, but at least that the handouts on the simulation and the support can be rated as helpful.

Table 2. Mean values of items describing the effects and evaluation of the digital simulation game

Item (N=221 for all items)	*M*	*SD*
The simulation helped me to better understand arguments for and against hybrid learning.	**4,15**	**,82**
I enjoyed the digital simulation game.	**4,31**	**,75**
The digital simulation game got me thinking about hybrid learning.	**4,19**	**,76**
I learned something through the digital simulation game.	**4,00**	**,86**
My expectations of the digital simulation game were met.	**4,04**	**,83**
My opinion of hybrid learning has become more positive as a result of the digital simulation game.	**2,84**	**,95**
I felt comfortable in my role in the digital simulation game.	**4,11**	**,95**
The attitude of my role also corresponded to my own attitude.	**3,17**	**1,34**
It was easy for me to "play" the attitude of my role.	**4,06**	**1,01**
I made an effort to slip into my role as authentically as possible.	**4,05**	**,90**
I can imagine using a digital simulation game in my classes someday.	**4,14**	**,953**
I would like to play the digital simulation game again.	**3,50**	**1,11**
The reflection period was useful.	**4,03**	**,95**
The cooperation with other players worked well.	**4,52**	**,62**
Things also got a little emotional in the digital simulation game.	**2,03**	**1,07**
I felt activated by the simulation.	**3,90**	**,89**

Notes: M = mean (with 1 = fully disagee, 5 = fully agree); SD = standard deviation.

It is worth mentioning that the simulation obviously stimulated reflection processes about hybrid teaching in the students and they also noticed an increase in learning, but this did not automatically translate into a more positive opinion towards hybrid teaching.

Overall, the feedback was predominantly positive (see table 3). Both gather.town as a platform for the digital simulation and the support provided by the game leaders were predominantly rated positively. Although the students had a certain basic scepticism towards digital simulation games, they stated that their expectations were largely fulfilled and that they perceived an increase in knowledge.

Table 3. Mean values of items describing the students‘ feedback

Item (N=221 for all items)	*M*	*SD*
How do you rate the user interface design in gather.town?	**4,34**	**,65**
How do you rate the support before and after the simulation by the game management?	**4,48**	**,64**
How would you rate the role description/manual for the simulation?	**4,42**	**,66**
How well were your expectations of the simulation met?	**4,12**	**,71**
How has the simulation impacted your growth in knowledge about hybrid teaching and learning?	**3,87**	**,71**
How well is the knowledge acquired through the digital simulation game suited for transfer to reality?	**3,97**	**,67**

Notes: M = mean (with 1 = very bad, 5 = very good); SD = standard deviation.

5. CONCLUSION

There are still few didactic concepts for the implementation of simulation games in the field of media education - although the concept is particularly suitable for this field because it enables to deal with digitality at different levels.

An evaluation of whether the learning objectives of a simulation game have been achieved presents itself as a challenge (Spaude, Starker and Imhof 2016), because there is the difficulty of measuring how the acquired knowledge or competences from the digital simulation game are transferred into practice or how the reflection is to be evaluated. Due to the quantitative data collection carried out in the context of this simulation game, no statement can be made about the quality of any knowledge and competence growth. The results of this evaluation therefore point to the need for further analyses and the addition of qualitative data in order to be able to present and measure the effects of the digital simulation game in a more differentiated way. Based on the quantitative evaluation, it can only be stated that reflections took place and were perceived as enriching. A more in-depth methodological and didactic examination of the simulation game method in the area of teacher training as well as media education appears to offer added value.

REFERENCES

Adipat, S. et al, 2021. Engaging students in the learning process with game-based learning: The fundamental concepts. *International Journal of Technology in Education*, Vol. 4, No. 3, pp. 542-552.

Capaul, R. and Ulrich, M., 2010. *Planspiele. Simulationsspiele für Unterricht und Training*. Altstätten.

Dörner, D., 1987. *Die Logik des Misslingens. Strategisches Denken in komplexen Situationen*. Rororo, Reinbek.

Fischer, C. and Reinhardt, S., 2018, Planspiele in der sozialwissenschaftlichen Hochschullehre. *Das Planspiel als didaktische Methode: Grundlegende Charakteristika und begriffliche Abgrenzungen*. Wiesbaden, Deutschland, pp. 29-42.

Heckhausen, H., 1964. Entwurf einer Psychologie des Spielens. *Psychologische Forschung*, 27, pp. 225–243.

Imhof, M. and Starker, U., 2020. Das psychologische Planspiel als didaktisches Szenario – Anwendung und Nutzen. *Psychologiedidaktik und Evaluation XIII*. Aachen, Deutschland, pp. 161-169.

Kriz, W., 2018. Planspiele als Trainingsmethode in der Hochschuldidaktik: Zur Funktion der Planspielleitung. *Planspiele in der sozialwissenschaftlichen Hochschullehre*. Wiesbaden, Deutschland, pp. 43-56.

Kriz, W. and Nöbauer, B., 2015. *Teamkompetenz. Konzepte, Trainingsmethoden, Praxis*. Göttingen.

Meßner, M. et al, 2018. Zur Relevanz von Planspielen in der sozialwissenschaftlichen Hochschullehre. *Planspiele in der sozialwissenschaftlichen Hochschullehre*. Wiesbaden, Deutschland, pp. 11-26.

Pappa, G., and Papadima-Sophocleous, S., 2018. Creative Muscle: the serious learning game. *Future-proof CALL: language learning as exploration and encounters – short papers from EUROCALL*, pp. 249-254.

Petrik, A., 2017. Raus aus der Alltagswelt! Zur unterschätzten Anforderung der transpersonalen Perspektivenübernahme in Planspielen. *Handbuch Planspiele in der politischen Bildung*. Schwalbach/Taunus, Deutschland, pp. 35–57.

Reich, K., 2012. *Konstruktivistische Didaktik. Das Lehr- und Studienbuch mit Online-Methodenpool*. Beltz, Weinheim.

Reinhardt, S., 2016. *Politik – Didaktik. Praxishandbuch für die Sekundarstufe I und II*. Berlin.

Riberio, M. C., 2019. Analog and digital games as a pedagogical tool in the teacher training context. *Research in Social Sciences and Technology*, Vol. 4, No. 2, pp. 163-73.

Schwägele, S., 2015. *Planspiel – Lernen – Lerntransfer. Eine subjektorientierte Analyse von Einflussfaktoren*. Norderstedt.

Spaude, E. et al, 2016. Unterricht als komplexes Problem erfahren im Planspiel „Schulalltag". *Psychologie in Erziehung und Unterricht*, 63, pp. 193-203.

Vasmatzoglou, A., and Ní Chiaráin, N., 2020. The development of an online game-based simulation for the training of English language teachers in virtual environments. *CALL for widening participation: short papers from EUROCALL 2020*, pp. 334-341.

von der Weth, R. et al, 2018. Das psychologische Planspiel. *Planspiele in der sozialwissenschaftlichen Hochschullehre*. Wiesbaden, Deutschland, pp. 101-114.

DESIGNING A READING COMPREHENSION APP USING DESIGN-BASED RESEARCH FRAMEWORK

Heydy Robles Noriega and Karen Villalba Ramos
Universidad del Norte, Km 5 Antigua Via Puerto, Colombia

ABSTRACT

Microlearning has increased its popularity for course designs in eLearning environments due to short attention spans and time constraints. The objective of this designed-based research is to describe the multiple iterations of design, development, and revision of a general framework for creating a microlearning reading mobile application. First, we present the components from the perspective of users and for the execution of a software architecture that allows a modular approach. Understanding the pedagogical features of mobile learning: personalization, authenticity, and collaboration are included as part of the IPAC framework to create it. This app was developed in different phases: Analysis and exploration, design and construction, evaluation and reflection, redesign and reconstruction and final critical reflections.The findings link design-based research (DBR) as a methodology that allows engaging in theory building and development of reading applications. It also reveals engagement in reading skills, satisfactory usability ratings and a rise in students' awareness towards new types of texts.

KEYWORDS

Microlearning, Usability, Mobile Technology, Design-Based Research, Reading Comprehension

1. INTRODUCTION

Critical reading is necessary for university students to develop skills that will make their academic work easier since reading does not receive enough attention in primary and secondary education. Several studies in Latin American contexts claim that university students lack strategies that allow them to understand a text and cannot organize information into summaries or different texts (Garcia, Nájera & Téllez, 2014).

In Colombia, in recent years, national tests administered to students have revealed significant weaknesses in critical reading in both languages (Spanish & English). Only 1% of students were top performers of levels 5 and 6 in the Programme for International Student Assessment (PISA) reading test. Based on these needs, a framework to develop mobile applications was defined to create a reading comprehension app called *Entrelíneas* due to the unavailability of Spanish/English technological mediations for undergraduate students who pursue this learning outcome (Vásquez et al., 2019).

As a response to this issue, a technique called microlearning in which people learn with small chunks of information during short periods was applied (Hug, 2007; Jomah et al., 2016). Micro-learning has three objectives: 1) reduce the quantity of information the students need to access by organizing it into bite-size pieces, 2) redefine the learning process and the environment in which the students learn, and 3) motivate the students to personalize the way they learn (Trowbridge, Waterbury & Sudbury 2017; Mohammed, Wakil & Nawroly, 2018). The type of text that matched with microlearning characteristics was aphorisms because of the challenges implied based on its concise content and short length, that might involve students in more complex reading comprehension strategies such as inferences. The inference procedures become especially relevant in textual understanding (Shihab, 2011). Aphorisms are defined as "a concise statement of a principle, a short, pointed sentence expressing a wise or clever observation or a general truth" (Morson, 2003, p.409).

The aphorisms help students interpret topics critically, recognizing the relationship with their historical, social, and cultural context (Hui, 2019; Lobo, 2017). Recently, researchers have adapted new eLearning methodologies for new users using microlearning. New generations of students prefer to access information digitally, use visual representations, and receive short chunks of data (Zhang & West, 2020). Some research has found that students can remember content learned using microlearning strategies longer than traditional approaches (Mohammed et al., 2018). The following example illustrates the type of aphorisms that students find in *Entrelíneas* app: *Beauty is worse than wine, it intoxicates both the holder and beholder. (Aldous Huxley.)* Mobile apps are convenient, low-cost, and downloadable global information and communication technology pieces that are innovative (Islam & Mazumder, 2010). Apps suit different purposes, and their characteristics can become tools to mediate in different scenarios, such as learning and teaching critical reading in Spanish and English. To design it, three pedagogical features of mobile learning distinguish from the sociocultural theory perspective were implemented: personalization, authenticity, and collaboration. These are part of the IPAC framework, which gives opportunities for learners to control their learning process. It also provides contextualized tasks in collaborative networked environments (Bano, Zowgui & Kearney, 2017). There are also pedagogical affordances involving planning, imagination, and creativity. This opportunity serves as the basis of usability testing (Burden & Atkinson, 2008) and creating learning objectives.

This paper defines a new view of the dimensions that influence the satisfaction of micro-learning students. From that point, it presents a DBR framework for developing mobile applications that use microlearning in an eLearning environment, focusing on course design and technology dimensions to influence students and try to improve engagement and decrease dropout. It also attempts to answer the following research questions:

1. What are the characteristics of a framework design for a reading comprehension microlearning mobile application?
2. What is the students' performance after using the reading comprehension microlearning mobile application?

1.1 Reading Framework Components

The students' side shows the components that the mobile application should implement. They build from gamification to encourage participation and adherence to the app, which has previously demonstrated effectiveness (Caro-Alvaro et al., 2017). Some strategies include reward systems, use of levels, and immediate feedback such as success messages when challenges are accomplished (Atkins et al., 2017). The components of this side of the architecture are the following:

- -Microlearning activities: this is the core of the mobile application. Activities may include short videos, readings, or any concise bite-sized information the student can learn (Bothe et al., 2019).
- -Players challenging: this is where gamification is shown the most and implements the leaderboards strategy or point systems (Atkins et al., 2017).
- -Discussion: this component has the purpose of engaging interaction between students. Previous research, such as the one presented in (Saade & Huang, 2009), has proven the impact on learning processes when students are encouraged to participate in online forums.
- -New content co-creation: the purpose of this component is to encourage students to create their content to share as a micro lesson. Previous work has also shown the importance of allowing students to develop and design content, as shown in (Nahar & Cross, 2020), who proposed a Student-Staff Partnership (SSP) to encourage students to participate in the process.
- -User progress: it allows the students to see their progress in the points system and can provide feedback about their performance.
- -Tutorials: this component provides users with digital content for help without interacting with educators.
- -Data Analytics services layer: it allows designers to build their own data analytics services or select one of the many services available.

2. METHOD

We followed the design-based research (DBR) methodology which is a flexible and systematized methodology that describes design research as a socially constructed and contextualized process (Bannan-Ritland, 2016; Papavlasopoulou et al., 2019). This approach, characterized by three iterative phases: (1) analysis and exploration, (2) design and construction, and (3) evaluation and reflection, includes software design, professional development, and collaborations between research faculty and active participants (Edelson, 2002; Cochrane et al, 2017). (See Table 1).

2.1 Sample

28 Colombian undergraduate students between 16 to 20 years old participated. They had reading difficulties The group used the app ***Entrelíneas*** for four weeks and they signed the informed consent forms for the study.

3. RESULTS

To answer the research questions, we listed different abstract software components that could be implemented. A microlearning framework and the DBR approach to design the application effectively were demanded since educators´ participation was necessary.

The findings revealed the potential of the tool. It is not intended to prove that through applications, students will have a very marked advance. However, the *Entrelíneas* application might increase the level of engagement towards these activities. Learners are more attracted when they work digitally (Ciampa, 2014; Stephen, 2020). The gamification process is emphasized. It is a recent concept that encourages learners to be active participants. Challenge, competition, and cooperation tasks can enhance motivation (Glover, 2013; Su & Cheng, 2015; Jayalath & Esichaikul, 2020). *Entrelíneas* application was designed taking into consideration, a previous DBR work that has exposed the importance of process of gamified mobile learning and the articulated pedagogical, administrative, and technical intervention in formal higher education (Jong, et al., 2021).

4. CONCLUSION

Teachers and instructional designers may need to consider DBR as a methodology because it has shown to be a helpful tool for building mobile applications for research purposes due to it allows the construction of a technological solution to reading comprehension. Given that the methodology works with cycling phases, we designed several versions of the framework and the mobile application prototype to test with users. Land & Zimmerman (2015) have used several iterations to achieve expected results. Another study (Wong et al., 2011) used what the authors called a micro-cycle (Leinonen et al., 2016), incorporating DBR to design several learning applications. Our work used five phases, which were essential to evaluate how effective it was to develop a framework design for a reading comprehension microlearning mobile application, determine the perception of the usability and measure students' performance after using the app. Some of the implications of this DBR are related to the credibility, confirmability and dependability applications which were crucial to obtain authentic results, triangulate the information from the instruments and organize the qualitative feedback accurately (Pool & Laubscher, 2016).

Table 1. App design phases

Phases	Analysis and exploration	Design and construction of the app	Evaluation and reflection	Redesign and reconstruction of the app	Final evaluation and critical reflections
Purpose	Observation, definition, gap, identify pedagogical features, affordances for reading	Ideate / prototype Apps components and modules selection	Testing /improvement	Implementation of challenge and creative mode	Refining adjustments Socialization and Teacher training
Instrument	iPAC rubric to evaluate 25 apps Pretest to evaluate current reading levels	Framework component design for a demo app 3 levels of reading comprehension selection Selection of aphorisms Categorization of aphorisms per level of complexity	App implementation Usability test 1 Focus group 1	International advisor iPAC framework adoption	Post test Usability test 2 Focus group 2
Credibility	International validity from extensive trials in Australia and the UK		Extensive time of the app implementation		Detailed feedback from students Authentic responses from participants
Dependability		Aphorism's coding			Usability coding
Confirmability			Member checking		Triangulation Member checking

REFERENCES

Atkin, D., Chaudhry, A., Chaudry, S., Khandelwal, A. K., & Verhoogen, E. (2017). Organizational barriers to technology adoption: Evidence from soccer-ball producers in Pakistan. The Quarterly Journal of Economics, 132(3), 1101–1164

Bannan-Ritland, B. (2016). The Role of Design in Research: The Integrative Learning Design Framework: Educational Researcher. https://doi.org/10.3102/0013189X032001021

Bano, M., Zowghi, D., & Kearney, M. (2017, July). Feature based sentiment analysis for evaluating the mobile pedagogical affordances of apps. In IFIP World Conference on Computers in Education (pp. 281-291). Springer, Cham.https://doi.org/10.1007/978-3-319-74310-3_30

Bothe, M., Renz, J., Rohloff, T., & Meinel, C. (2019, April). From MOOCs to Micro Learning Activities. In 2019 IEEE Global Engineering Education Conference (EDUCON) (pp. 280-288). IEEE.

Burden, K., & Atkinson, S. (2008). Evaluating pedagogical affordances of media sharing Web 2.0 technologies: A case study. Proceedings ascilite Melbourne, 121-125.

Caro-Alvaro, S., Garcia-Lopez, E., Garcia-Cabot, A., De-Marcos, L., & Martinez-Herriaz, J.-J. (2017). Development of a Social Gamified Platform for e-Learning. International Conference on Information Systems Development (ISD). https://aisel.aisnet.org/isd2014/proceedings2017/Education/2

Ciampa, K. (2014). Learning in a mobile age: an investigation of student motivation. Journal of Computer Assisted Learning, 30(1), 82-96.https://doi.org/10.1111/jcal.12036

Cochrane, T. D., Cook, S., Aiello, S., Christie, D., Sinfield, D., Steagall, M., & Aguayo, C. (2017). A DBR framework for designing mobile virtual reality learning environments. Australasian Journal of Educational Technology, 33(6).https://doi.org/10.14742/ajet.3613

Edelson, D. C. (2002). Design Research: What We Learn When We Engage in Design. Journal of the Learning Sciences, 11(1), 105–121. https://doi.org/10.1207/S15327809JLS1101_4

García, B., Nájera, N., Téllez, M. (2014). Comprensión lectora en estudiantes universitarios. México DF.

Glover, I. (2013, June). Play as you learn: gamification as a technique for motivating learners. In Edmedia+innovate learning (pp. 1999-2008). Association for the Advancement of Computing in Education (AACE).

Hug, T. (2007). Didactics of Microlearning. Waxmann Verlag.

Islam, R., Islam, R., & Mazumder, T. (2010). Mobile application and its global impact. International Journal of Engineering & Technology (IJEST), 10(6), 72-78.

Jong, M. S. Y., Chan, T., Tam, V., & Jiang, M. Y. C. (2021). Design-based research on gamified outdoor social enquiry learning with context-aware technology: Integration of teacher facilitation for advancing the pedagogical effectiveness. International Journal of Mobile Learning and Organisation, 15(1), 107-126.

Jomah, O., Masoud, A. K., Kishore, X. P., & Aurelia, S. (2016). Micro Learning: A Modernized Education System. BRAIN. Broad Research in Artificial Intelligence and Neuroscience, 7(1), 103–110.

Land, S. M., & Zimmerman, H. T. (2015). Socio-technical dimensions of an outdoor mobile learning environment: A three-phase design-based research investigation. Educational Technology Research and Development, 63(2), 229–255. https://doi.org/10.1007/s11423-015-9369-6

Leinonen, T., Keune, A., Veermans, M., & Toikkanen, T. (2016). Mobile apps for reflection in learning: A design research in K-12 education. British Journal of Educational Technology, 47(1), 184–202. https://doi.org/10.1111/bjet.12224

Morson, G. S. (2003). The aphorism: Fragments from the breakdown of reason. New Literary History, 34(3), 409-429.

Mohammed, G. S., Wakil, K., & Nawroly, S. S. (2018). The effectiveness of microlearning to improve students' learning ability. International Journal of Educational Research Review, 3(3), 32-38.

Papavlasopoulou, S., Giannakos, M. N., & Jaccheri, L. (2019). Exploring children's learning experience in constructionism-based coding activities through design-based research. Computers in Human Behavior, 99, 415–427. https://doi.org/10.1016/j.chb.2019.01.008

Pool, J., & Laubscher, D. (2016). Design-based research: is this a suitable methodology for short-term projects?. Educational Media International, 53(1), 42-52. https://doi.org/10.1080/09523987.2016.1189246

Saade, R. G., & Huang, Q. (2009). Meaningful learning in discussion forums: Towards discourse analysis. Issues in Informing Science & Information Technology, 6, 87-100.

Shihab, I. A. (2011). Reading as critical thinking. Asian Social Science, 7(8), 209.

Su, C. H., & Cheng, C. H. (2015). A mobile gamification learning system for improving the learning motivation and achievements. Journal of Computer Assisted Learning, 31(3), 268-286.

Trowbridge, S., Waterbury, C., & Sudbury, L. (2017). Learning in bursts: Microlearning with social media. Educause Review.

Vásquez, C., Jiménez, J., Guevara, M., Cortés, P., Herrera, M., Pittaluga, E., ... & Peña, M. (2019, March). Interactive System for Language and Communication Stimulation Directed to Young Children. In 2019 9th International IEEE/EMBS Conference on Neural Engineering (NER) (pp. 9-12). IEEE.

Wong, L.-H., Boticki, I., Sun, J., & Looi, C.-K. (2011). Improving the scaffolds of a mobile-assisted Chinese character forming game via a design-based research cycle. Computers in Human Behavior, 27(5), 1783–1793. https://doi.org/10.1016/j.chb.2011.03.005

Zhang, J., & West, R. E. (2020). Designing Microlearning Instruction for Professional Development Through a Competency Based Approach. TechTrends, 64(2), 310-318.

THE INFLUENCE OF MOTIVATION AND SELF-REGULATION ABILITY ON STUDENTS' ONLINE LEARNING SATISFACTION

Zixian Yu[1], Hui Zhang[1], Zhizi Zheng[1], Yuqin Yang[1] and Qi Li[2]
[1]*Faculty of Artificial Intelligence in Education, Central China Normal University, Wuhan 430079, China*
No. 152, Luoyu Road, Hongshan District, Wuhan City, Hubei Province, China
[2]*Primary School Affiliated to Central China Normal University*
No. 152, Luoyu Road, Hongshan District, Wuhan City, Hubei Province, China

ABSTRACT

This study examined the influence of motivation and online self-regulation on students' online learning satisfaction. A sample of 1649 middle school students participated in the study. The findings suggested that online self-regulation and motivation played a driving role in students' online learning satisfaction and that motivation indirectly affected their online learning satisfaction through the three elements of a Community of Inquiry. These findings imply that both teachers and students should be targeted with interventions to improve students' satisfaction with their online learning. Future research should consider the impact of the relationship between motivation and online self-regulation.

KEYWORDS

Online Self-Regulation, Motivation, Community of Inquiry, Satisfaction

1. INTRODUCTION

The use of the Internet is becoming more and more prevalent in many fields. Studies have shown that online self-regulation strategies are the key to successful online learning and that students' motivation levels will have an enormous influence on their learning state. As a significant indicator of online learning performance, online learning satisfaction can directly reflect the learning state of online learners. Studying the factors of online learning satisfaction can help to guide online learning in the post-epidemic era. This study uses structural equation modeling to explore how motivation and self-regulation affect students' online learning satisfaction.

2. LITERATURE REVIEW

2.1 Description of Variables

Many factors influence online learning satisfaction. Learners' academic motivation is reflected in their effort into learning. In online course learning, the influence of students' learning motivation can be summarized into cognitive, behavioral, and environmental aspects. The relationships between learners' cognition, behavior, and environment are not linear. Self-regulated learning is the process of students actively regulating their cognition, motivation, and behavior. Puzziferro (2006) pointed out that meta-cognitive self-regulation is significantly correlated with learning satisfaction. Therefore, we speculate that online self-regulation is also vital to predict online learning satisfaction. The community of inquiry (CoI) framework consists of cognitive presence, teaching presence, and social presence (Kozan & Richardson, 2014). Joo et al. (2010) found that teaching presence and cognitive presence significantly influenced learning satisfaction, and social presence was closely related to learning achievement and satisfaction.

2.2 Hypotheses

Studies have found that motivation and self-regulation ability influence students' satisfaction during online learning and that the CoI elements of cognitive presence, teaching presence, and social presence also impact online learning satisfaction. However, there is still a lack of systematic and comprehensive exploration of the relationship between motivation, self-regulation ability, and satisfaction. Based on these considerations, we propose the hypothetical model shown in Figure 1. H1-H3: motivation has a direct and positive impact on teaching, social, and cognitive presence. H4-H6: online self-regulation has a direct and positive impact on teaching, social, and cognitive presence. H7-H9: teaching presence, social presence, and cognitive presence directly and positively impact satisfaction.

3. METHOD

3.1 Participants

The participants were middle school students from nine schools in the province of Hubei in China. The questionnaires were administered to students online at the end of the school term. There were 1649 student participants, of whom 548 were in Grade 7, 531 in Grade 8, 16 in Grade 9, 530 in Senior 1, 12 in Senior Two, and 12 in Senior 3.

3.2 Instruments

The study used online questionnaires to measure the learning satisfaction of 1649 students during the COVID-19 pandemic. The 78 questionnaire items were adapted from previous studies and measured six constructs: motivation (12 items), self-regulation ability (24 items), cognitive presence (13 items), teaching presence (13 items), social presence (9 items), and online learning satisfaction (7 items), with reliability coefficients are 0.929, 0.985, 0.954, 0.983, 0.985, and 0.930. The responses were given on a 5-point Likert scale ranging from 1 = strongly *disagree* to 5 = *strongly agree*, and SPSS 22.0 and AMOS 23.0 were used in the data analysis.

4. RESULTS

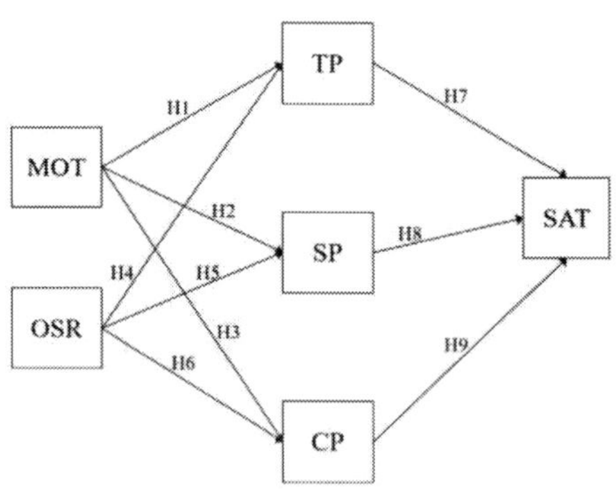

Figure 1. Hypotheses model

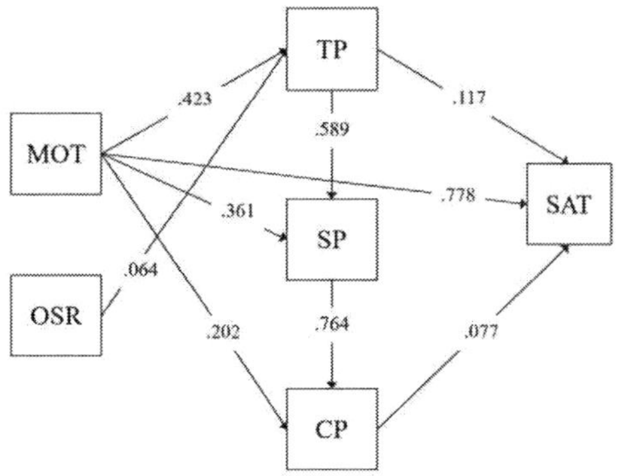

Figure 2. Final model

Table 1. Descriptive statistics and correlation analysis

	Mean	SD	MOT	OSR	TP	SP	CP	SAT
MOT	3.17	.79	1					
OSR	3.55	.85	.10**	1				
TP	4.08	.89	.43**	.10**	1			
SP	3.75	.87	.61**	.11**	.74**	1		
CP	3.65	.92	.67**	.11**	.64**	.89**	1	
SAT	3.37	.92	.88**	.10**	.50**	.64**	.67**	1

**: Correlation significant at the .01 level (two-tailed). MOT: motivation; OSR: online self-regulation; TP: teaching presence; SP: social presence; CP: cognitive presence; SAT: satisfaction.

4.1 Descriptive Statistics

As shown in Table 1, students perceived a high level of motivation, online self-regulation, teaching presence, social presence, and cognitive presence—for example, the mean of motivation values on 4.08, followed by social presence values on 3.75. We conducted a correlation analysis to inquiry if there exist relationships between satisfaction and other variables. The results suggested that all the factors are significantly related. Uncommonly, motivation is most strongly correlated to satisfaction, the value of 0.88, followed by cognitive presence, the value of 0.67, and social presence, the value of 0.64, indicating that motivation may impact students' satisfaction.

4.2 Path Analysis

The final model (Figure 2) shows that students' academic motivation directly influences the satisfaction of students, as well as the teaching, social and cognitive presence, with the estimates respectively are 0.423, 0.361, 0.202, and 0.778. In addition, motivation also has an indirect influence on satisfaction through the meditating of teaching, social and cognitive presences. These results indicted that motivation is a vital factor in this model, as it not only strongly determines the satisfaction of students but also may influence the experiences of students on learning and communication.

However, there exists no direct relationship between online self-regulation and learning satisfaction. Online self-regulation only influences teaching presence, with an estimate of 0.064. Nevertheless, with the mediating of presences, online self-regulation may indirectly influence satisfaction (path A: OSR→TP→SAT and path B: OSR→TP→SP→SAT).

5. DISCUSSION

The results of this study suggest that motivation is a strong affection of students in the online learning context, according to previous studies. Motivation is the most strongly potential predictor of satisfaction, teaching presence, social presence, and cognitive presence. It means that students' motivation, like interest, value, responsibility, and pressure, determined their satisfaction with the courses, which also predicted their intended behaviors. Although online self-regulation has no direct or significant impact on satisfaction, it does directly influence teaching presence, which could directly influence satisfaction or indirectly by having an impact on social presence and cognitive presence. Thus, in our study, we find that online self-regulation plays a regulated role, which revealed the mechanism of regulation—affecting the process of the online learning experience.

There are a few limitations and implications in our study. First, we found that motivation is a very important role in online learning, but in our study, 'motivation' is an element. Therefore, more specific researches should be completed. Then, online self-regulation has a specific relationship with other variables, which need to be investigated deeply with more quantitative and qualitative data. In the future, researchers can focus on improving students' learning motivation and online self-regulation and further explore the three presences of the CoI. As learners' motivation and the dynamics of self-regulated learning processes appear to be more complex than expected, further research should determine the complicated relations between these two factors and the three presences to generate more meaningful instructional implications for educators.

REFERENCES

Hosler, K. A., & Arend, B. D. (2012). The importance of course design, feedback, and facilitation: student perceptions of the relationship between teaching presence and cognitive presence. *Educational Media International*, 49(3), 217-229.

Joo, Y. J. et al (2010). The Structural Relationship among Teaching Presence, Cognitive Presence, Social Presence, and Learning Outcome in Cyber University. *Journal of The Korean Association of Information Education*, 14(2), 175-187.

Kozan, K., & Richardson, J. C. (2014). Interrelationships between and among social, teaching, and cognitive presence. *The Internet and higher education*, 21, 68-73.

Puzziferro, M. (2006). *Online technologies self-efficacy, self-regulated learning, and experiential variables as predictors of final grade and satisfaction in college-level online courses*. New York University.

DE-POLARIZING BY COLORING, REASONING BY CURATING

Tsafrir Goldberg, Alan Wecker, Tal Tabashi, Joel Lanir and Iris Reinhartz-Berger
University of Haifa, Israel

ABSTRACT

This short paper describes an early look at a project aimed at aiding students to understand various viewpoints through the advocacy of a museum visit. It aims to both improve historical reasoning and allow for more open-mindedness. This is done by combining a process of citizen curation with the use of de-polarization techniques.

KEYWORDS

Citizen Curation, Mobile learning, Active OPEN Minded Thinking

1. INTRODUCTION

Political and cultural polarization blights the public arenas in democratic societies posing ongoing threats to the social cohesion and the political process (McAvoy & Hess, 2013). Growing attention is focused on the role of social media and mobile assisted realms in promoting polarization. Algorithms driving social media and mobile information consumption increase individuals' exposure to information enhancing preconceived opinions (Lee, Choi, Kim, & Kim, 2014). This creates "echo chambers" in which self-confirming evidence is adopted uncritically while opposing views are rejected as "fake news" and adversaries are demonized (Gillani, Yuan, Saveski, Vosoughi, & Roy, 2018). History education and heritage sites have also become arenas of polarized politicized debates. Interpretations of the past which shed doubt on a nation's moral image or threaten to harm its esteem are deemed unpatriotic and ostracized while conservative and time accustomed historical symbols are criticized as colonialist and racist (Imperial War Museum, n.d.; T. Linenthal & Engelhardt, 1996).

However, heritage sites may also offer trajectories for dialogue and pluralistic engagement. Thus for example, Dutch museums dealing with controversial heritage such as slave trade or collaboration with Nazism created activities in which visiting students take up the roles of various historical agents, research their lives and engage with other (Savenije, van Boxtel, & Grever, 2014). Mobile learning in museums can also offer visitors the chance of an individualized active engagement with historical artefacts, making meaningful personalized structuring and interpretation of the exhibits according to their opinions (Tselios et al., 2009). Still, it is unclear whether encountering another person's opinion about the past or individualized interpretation of heritage facilitates depolarization (Bail et al., 2018). Debate with peers presenting opposing opinions may actually lead to entrenchment due to confirmation bias and face keeping (G. Lord, Ross, & R. Lepper, 1998). Similarly, tracing a personalized path and interpretation based on a mobile learning system may lead learners to establish their own polarizing echo chamber in the museum.

Our study explores the effects of a project which aims at promoting both engagement with diverse opinions and depolarization or open-mindedness, using the opportunities that mobile learning in museums could offer. We rely on Active Open-minded Thinking (AOT) theory both as a guideline and in tracing and assessing impact on student visitors (Baron, 2002; Stanovich & West, 1997). AOT centers on the ability to appraise evidence and claims regardless of prior opinion. It stresses both evidence based reasoning and considering the other's perspective. Evidence based reasoning should help learners to deliberate controversial issues in a rational manner, allowing them to form an informed independent opinion and to critically appraise opposing claims and their reliance on evidence. In a museum setting the evidence is drawn from the exhibits. In the process the learner-visitor selects, prioritizes, interprets and structures relationships between exhibits; a set of practices which aligns to some degree with a curator's role (Bruni et al 2020) (Mackay & Couldwell 2004). This gives a prominent space for proponents to present their views, acknowledges their voice and affirm self-worth in a way which facilitates acceptance of challenging information or views (Crocker, Niiya,

& Mischkowski, 2008). However, buttressing your own stance or interpretation with evidence may also enhance certainty and entrenchment, impeding open-minded deliberation. Another approach to overcome entrenchment and promote open-minded engagement with differing opinions, derived from Constructive Conflict theory, is taking a turn at defending the opponent's stance or part of it (Johnson & Johnson, 1988).

Following these theoretical approaches, we developed an interactive mobile supported museum learning activity. Mobile learning is first used to engage learners in using exhibits in historical reasoning doing virtual curation. Consequently, the system is used to promote AOT and avoid selective exposure to self-confirming information using recommendations that inverts the common polarizing effect of social media, engaging visitors with opinions opposite to their own, and helping them deconstruct the opposing argument into parts they can accept or reconsider.

2. SYSTEM DESCRIPTION

In this section, we describe two processes based on the theoretical background above: (A) curation through gathering evidence to support opinions and (B) exposure and analysis of others opinions. These processes take place in a three phase activity at different locations: (1) Pre-visit which occurs mainly in a computer classroom, (2) Within visit which consists of activities both in a museum and in a computer classroom; and (3) Post visit which occurs mainly in a computer classroom. We concentrate here on the activities that take place during the second phase, at the museum. The system is a web application so theoretically can take in different venues including mobile phones. The activity took place in the Hecht Museum in Haifa Israel.

2.1 Curation Through Gathering Evidence to Support Opinion

During this process, the users are reminded of their previous opinions (regarding the museum exhibition topic). The users are then requested to take 4 pictures in the museum on their phones with an app which supports their arguments. On each picture they are requested to place **tags** and write a short paragraph (or two) why they chose the particular object to support the argument (Figure 1). In the museum the students discuss the various artifacts (photos, justifications) which they capture in the museum grouped by whether they were for or against the Rebellion.

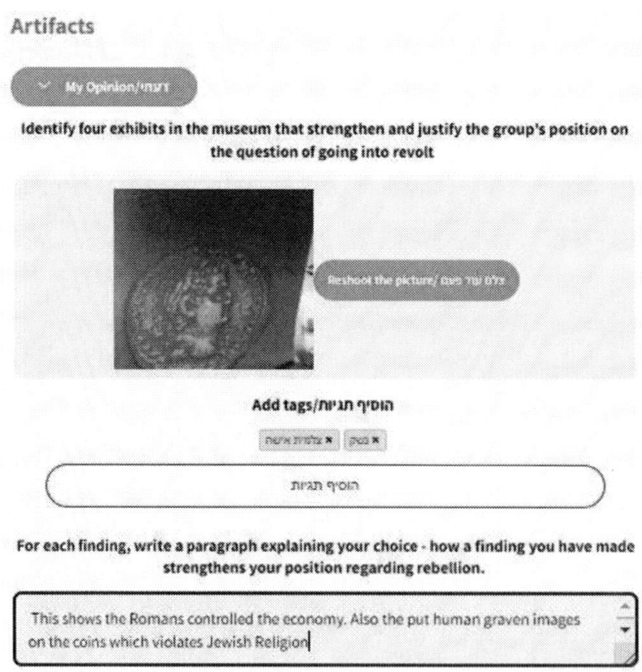

Figure 1. Choosing an artifact by Visitor Employed Photography

2.2 Exposure and Analysis of Other Opinions

In this process the users are first reminded of their own opinions (regarding the museum exhibition topic). They are then given two opinions in a serial order, depending on the experimental condition used. In particular, we examined two experimental conditions. In the first one, the visitors are given first one opinion which is similar to their opinion (based on own tagging of the own opinion[1]) and an opinion which is different from their opinion. The reasoning behind this experimental condition is that the first similar opinion opens the visitor up to future different opinions (inclusion then understanding). The second experimental condition is to expose the visitor to two differing opinions. The reasoning behind this experimental condition is that the more exposure to differing opinions the more likelihood of achieving understanding.

The process itself is supported by three screens. In the first one, the visitors are asked to color the text based on 4 levels of agreement: I agree with the item, I understand the item but disagree, the item caused me to rethink my views and I am still formulating my response, and I totally disagree with the item. The visitors then select what their relationship to the view presented is (see Figure 2;).

In the second screen (not shown in this paper), the visitors see what they colored in the categories of "understand but disagree" and "rethink". They are asked to give reasons for each of these two colorings. In the third and last screen (also not shown here), the visitors see their coloring again and are asked: a) what are the values embedded in the view presented? and b) independent of your individual opinion, what is your evaluation of the historical arguments used?

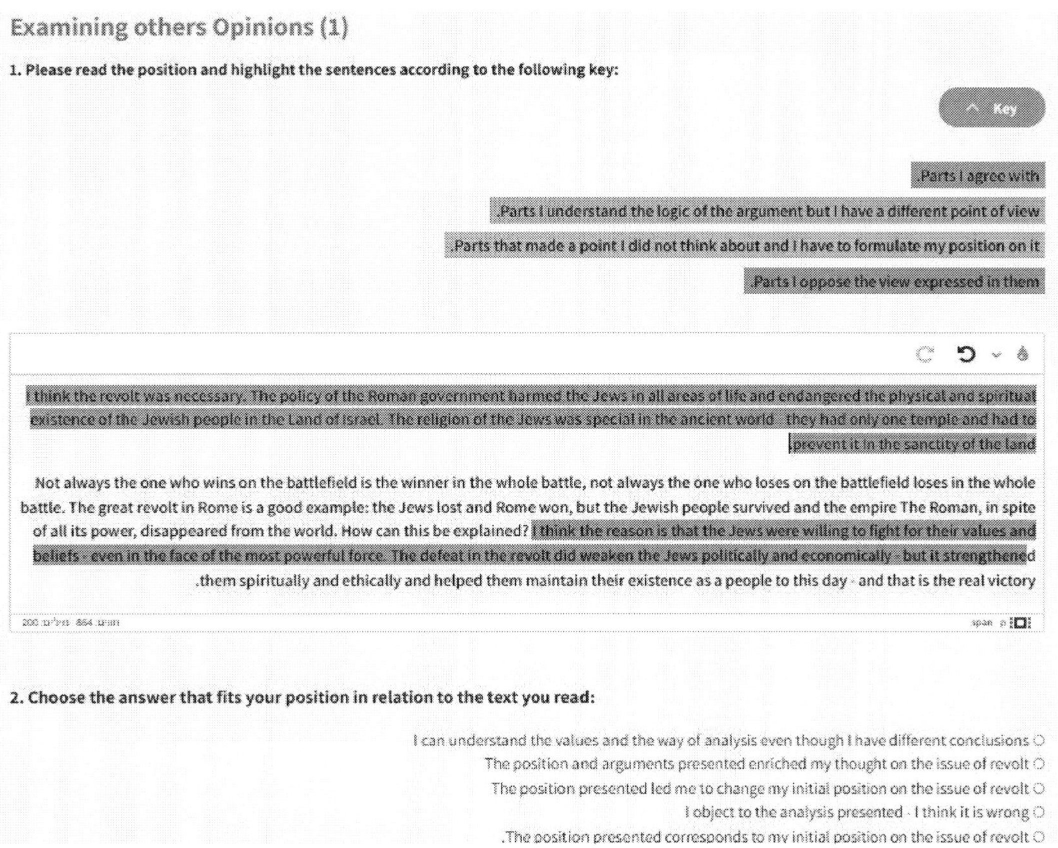

Figure 2. Analyzing others Opinions (first screen)

[1] In the future we intend to explore tagging through semantic analysis.

3. CONCLUSIONS

As we have suggested above, mobile learning in the museum could serve as a meeting point for learner-visitors through citizen curation and exhibit-based debate. We still need to explore whether this engagement would enhance self-confirmation bias and entrenchment or allow for active open-minded thinking, overcoming polarization and echo chambers. We believe mobile learning systems may help counter the tendency for polarization and atomization the mobile supported social media aroused. This paper showed the direction of novel technique aimed at enhancing inclusion and social cohesion by encouraging historical reasoning and open-mindedness. Hopefully the museum atmosphere combined with the techniques mentioned above will contribute to the above goals. We started exploring the use of the system with actual students, measuring the changes they undergo through questionnaires and repeating some of the activities at a later point in school.

ACKNOWLEDGEMENT

This project has received funding from the European Union's Horizon 2020 research and innovation programme under grant agreement SPICE No 870811.

REFERENCES

Bail, C. A., Argyle, L. P., Brown, T. W., Bumpus, J. P., Chen, H., Hunzaker, M. B. F., ... Volfovsky, A. (2018). Exposure to opposing views on social media can increase political polarization. Proceedings of the National Academy of Sciences of the United States of America, 115(37), 9216–9221. doi:10.1073/pnas.1804840115

Baron, J. (2002). Actively open-minded thinking. Unpublished manuscript.

Bruni, L. E., Daga, E., Damiano, R., Diaz, L., Kuflik, T., Lieto, A., . . . Wecker, A. "Towards Advanced Interfaces for Citizen Curation." Proceedings of *AVI2CH* 2020: Workshop on Advanced Visual Interfaces and Interactions in Cultural Heritage (*AVI2CH* 2020). New York: AC

Crocker, J., Niiya, Y., & Mischkowski, D. (2008). Why does writing about important values reduce defensiveness? Self-affirmation and the role of positive other-directed feelings. Psychological science, 19(7), 740-747.

Lord, C.G. , Ross, L., & Lepper, M.R. (1998). Biased assimilation and attitude polarization: The effects of prior theories on subsequently considered evidence. Journal of personality and social psychology, 37.

Gillani, N., Yuan, A., Saveski, M., Vosoughi, S., & Roy, D. (2018). Me, my echo chamber, and I: introspection on social media polarization. In Proceedings of the 2018 World Wide Web Conference on World Wide Web' ' - WWW '18 (pp. 823–831). New York, New York, USA: ACM Press. doi:10.1145/3178876.3186130

Imperial War Museum. (n.d.). Teaching Difficult Histories in Imperial War Museum.

Johnson, D.W., & Johnson, R.T. (1988). Critical thinking through structured controversy. Educational leadership, 45(8), 58–64.

Lee, J. K., Choi, J., Kim, C., & Kim, Y. (2014). Social media,

photography to investigate destination image. Journal network heterogeneity, and opinion polarization. The Journal of communication, 64(4), 702–722. doi:10.1111/jcom.12077

MacKay, K. J., & Couldwell, C. M. (2004). Using visitor-employed of Travel Research, 42(4), 390-396.

McAvoy, P., & Hess, D. (2013). Classroom deliberation in an era of political polarization. Curriculum Inquiry, 43(1), 14–47.

Savenije, G. M., van Boxtel, C., & Grever, M. (2014). Learning about sensitive history: "heritage" of slavery as a resource. Theory & Research in Social Education, 42(4), 516–547. doi:10.1080/00933104.2014.966877

Stanovich, K., & West, R. (1997). Reasoning independently of prior belief and individual differences in actively open-minded thinking. Journal of educational psychology, 89(2), 342–357.

Linenthal, E.T., & Engelhardt, T. (1996). History wars: The Enola Gay and other battles for the American past. New York, NY: Henry Holt and Company.

Tselios, N., Papadimitriou, I., Raptis, D., Yiannoutsou, N., Komis, V., & Avouris, N. (2009). Design for mobile learning in museums. In D. Taniar (ed.), Mobile computing: concepts, methodologies, tools, and applications (pp. 3282–3299). IGI Global. doi:10.4018/978-1-60566-054-7.ch242

REFLECTION

CYBERSTALKING IN INDIA: CHALLENGES ON THE SOCIAL SIDE AND THE UNDERLYING CONTRADICTIONS

Ameema Miftha, Marc Conrad and Marcia Gibson
Institute For Research in Applicable Computing
The University of Bedfordshire, University Square, Luton, Bedfordshire, UK

ABSTRACT

The ordeal of woman victims in India has rightly been given the term – secondary victimization and its outcome in the form of deindividuation. Arguably, the positioning of a cyberstalking victim in the Indian patriarchal society only belittles her existence and leads to deindividuation. The fear of loss of reputation, poor social perception and fragility of her womanhood make her a sitting duck for any cyber stalker; and the case is the same for even a male victim. In view of the contextual realities, the present research sets itself to argue the fact that, 'conservative beliefs, lack of awareness and the patriarchal outlook seem to curtail women's sovereignty and choices; this seemingly engenders a secondary form of social punishment victims endure'. It goes on to argue why the guilt and the blameworthiness are for only the victim to endure and why the victim has to keep quiet and fall prey to negative stereotypes of the society. Most importantly, the research tries to fill the gap on existing work by finding an answer to - what can possibly prevent deindividuation and secondary victimization of Indian women based on regulation, mechanism and enforcements on the social side? The assessment would be based on an integrative contextual analysis of the contemporary realities of cyberstalking in India. A solution is sought with in the domain of behavioral studies based on - neutralization theory, sexual solicitation of the society methods of monitoring and Zero FIR for influencing the motivators of the cyber-stalkers.

KEYWORDS

Secondary Victimization, Loss of Reputation, Routine Activity Theory, Cyberstalking

1. INTRODUCTION

A Contemporary reality on cyberstalking and the notion of a traditional Indian woman are just as aloof entities as the sun and the moon. Practically, cyberstalking is just as big a crime in India as it is for the rest of the world, but it seems to get bigger given the social circumstances of the country. All the prominent authors have identified (or defined) cyberstalking as an obnoxious activity carried out via the digital medium to limit the freedom or privacy and harm the victim by doxing, trolling, abusive messaging and threatening (Mehta, 2012). In fact, the digital medium further acts as its propagating ground where it gives the stalker more opportunities, convenience and anonymity to indulge more in the activity. India, specifically, adds more dimensions to this scandalous behaviour by providing circumstances where the stalkers exploit disproportionately the victim's 'predicament' of being a woman. One can see this with the fact that India ranks 2nd when it comes to sharing of sensitive private information between women on the online medium, but surprisingly it ranks exceptionally low in terms of the registered complaints on cyberstalking (New Delhi Television, 2017). This is despite the fact that the country shows a very high expected prevalence of stalking behavior (Thakur, 2016). The chief consultant of the cyber cell in India admits, 'there is an ambiguity regarding the exact number of cases filed under cyberstalking as there is no stand-alone section under the Indian IT Act that defines online stalking as a crime' (Times of India, 2021). What substantiates it further is the fact that Maharashtra, one of the progressive states in India, showed an exceptionally low conviction rate where only 56 of the 4500 plus detained offenders could be imprisoned (India Today, 2020). 'No surprise that the numbers of cases on cyberstalking have increased by over 500% in the year 2020', as what the chairperson of the National Commission for Women admits (Times of India, 2021). So, to say, there exists an anomaly in terms of the actual number of cases on cyberstalking in India and those which are truly registered. Compared to other countries, the social fabric of India can possibly be the factor which explains this anomaly more precisely than any other factor.

2. CONTRADICTIONS ON THE SOCIAL SIDE

2.1 Secondary Victimization and its Culmination into Deindividuation

Practically, the social and cultural attitudes and normative beliefs affect the way cyberstalking is addressed in India. A big section of the researchers tend to believe that the socio-cultural values have a limiting effect on the way cyberstalking should be approached (Gupta, 2012). In fact, it is the victim who gets to see the bad side of the crime practice and the actual perpetrators go scot-free. Similar assessments have been made by Roy (2015) who claims that most of the cyber-stalkers in India are not brought to book as most often no formal complaint is registered against them. Rozatkar and Gupta (2019) connect this with a flawed imagination of Indian women as 'Maa Durga' where every woman is given the status of a demigod and is credited with all the moral undertakings of the society. The accomplishments lie with her role of a 'giver' who keeps sacrificing herself for the betterment of her family, people, and the society at large. This positioning of a woman in the Indian patriarchal society only belittles her existence as an individual. The fear of loss of reputation, poor social perception and fragility of her womanhood make her a sitting duck for any cyber stalker (Roy, 2015). This ordeal of woman victims has rightly been given the term – secondary victimization. This eventually leads to deindividuation which signifies a state of alienation that comes out of reduced sense of personal identity, inhibition, and lack of self-awareness. In a state of isolation, the victim tends to sunk further into his or her grief and distress. From a social perspective, the lack of sympathy or support from family and friends makes this further shocking.

2.2 Social Constrain

Nothing can be more satirical than a state where the woman victim is asked to marry her stalker just because the society feels that it was the woman herself who instigated the stalker and, owing to the incident, no one else is ready to marry the victim (Joshi, 2013). One can see a similar state of apathy when the parents asked their girl child to leave the college just because the stalker was the son of an influential politician and that he could tarnish the reputation of their family (Kashimiria, 2014). These are the cases which clearly highlight the fact where the liability is very easily placed on the female, and the male behaviour is largely excused. The fear of loss of reputation and social shame are so overriding on people's mind that they tend to succumb to their fears and remain silent. Speaking of social contradictions, 'conservative beliefs, lack of awareness and the patriarchal outlook seem to curtail women's freedom and choices; this seemingly engenders a secondary form of social punishment victims endure' (Kabra, 2013).

2.3 Looking for a Solution

The empirical studies have identified 'habitual internet socialization' as the most prominent factor on the recent rapid swell of cyberstalking (Rozatkar and Gupta, 2019). There are people who use the Routine Activity Theory (RAT) to conclude that minimization of internet socialization habits can possibly reduce the prevalence of this crime (Kalia and Aleem, 2017). However, the question that needs to be answered is why internet socialization should be proscribed among the women when the actual need is to identify the stalker and to convict them. The real action should ideally be to encourage women to use the internet productively and freely without observing any inhibitions on security breach and abuse of privacy. Apparently, the social scenario is to blame for, and one needs to find a solution within this complex mesh of social realities. A possible answer lies with behavioral studies that go deeper into what prompts 'revenge porn'. Here, the elements of neutralization theory have the potential to trim down the rationalization of rule-breaking behaviour. Also, there are possibilities with sexual solicitation of the society towards accepting cyberstalking as a serious crime. Method of monitoring and Zero FIR are few such initiatives which might have its impact on the motivators of the cyber-stalkers.

2.4 Research Methodology to fill the 'Gap'

Studying cyberstalking has already been done widely in the Indian context, but most of it has been on the technological and legal side. The problem is that the social realities are largely untouched or unaddressed. Given the studies, a significant effort has been made in highlighting the social realities that govern the patriarchal makeup of Indian society. There is a frequent mention of terms such as 'reputational loss', 'secondary victimization', 'secondary effects', 'family shame', 'traditional Indian woman' and most importantly, 'social stigma'. This all points towards the 'culpability' of woman and the negative stereotypes in a complex mesh of things. However, there is no effort made in terms of finding a solution to the impending problem of secondary victimization or talking about social reforms so that woman (or the victims of cyberstalking) of the society gets to see some justice on equitable terms. This research tries to fill this gap based on an integrative contextual analysis of the contemporary realities of cyberstalking in India. An effort is being made to develop a classification of cyberstalking theoretically and to use this for predicting cyberstalking behaviour within the society.

The theoretical development of cyberstalking would be based on the theories: (1) rationale choice theory, (2) self-control theory, (3) neutralization theory, (4) self-control theory and (5) social learning theory. Together, the theories would be coupled with Lifestyle Routine Activities Theory (L-RAT) to explain deviant conduct under a sociological perspective. Lawrence E. Cohen and Marcus Felson (1979) talked about repetitive tasks principle based on 3 key factors – a desirable target, driven criminals, and the lack of a competent guardianship. A collision of these 3 factors in time and space lead to crime. Hindelang (1978) explains this with Lifestyle Exposure Theory (LET) where victimization is believed to be an outcome to repetitive behaviours and habits where competent guardianship is very weak and empowered criminals are very strong. The proposed integrative contextual analysis would therefore aim to perform a meta-analysis of the theoretical and empirical data so as to build a comprehensive understanding of the phenomenon (Broome, 1993). The strategy would be to take a step-by-step process: (1) Problem Formulation, (2) Literature Search, (3) Data evaluation, (4) Data analysis and (5) Presentation (Jackson, 1980). The challenge would be combine diverse data sources to address a specific issue.

3. CONCLUSION

This brings the discussion to a very important point – what can possibly prevent secondary victimization of Indian women based on regulation, mechanism and enforcements on the social side? The literature points out clearly that cyberstalking in India has serious secondary effects and it is very important for the country to focus on social reforms just as it did with its technological and legal framework. But the question is – how? Especially in the Indian context, it is very important to realize that it is a patriarchic society by nature and to curb cyberstalking is still a farfetched dream. The country might have all the technological and legal readiness to identify the perpetrators (offenders) and to put them behind the bars, but what if there is no formal complaint of FIR (First Information Report) lodged against the offenders. Most importantly, the notion of 'the traditional Indian woman' is a reality which puts the man of the society in absolute control of the things.

ACKNOWLEDGEMENT

Studying 'cyberstalking' would not be possible without the contribution of the people who have either experienced or studied the social crime in its entire length. The present research is based entirely on the experiences of the victims who have given an exhaustive description to how they felt as a victim and what could have possibly been their guard to protect them in the first place. Similarly, a mention is obligatory about the researchers who have gone a step ahead to understand the social perspective on the problem and have alienated factors which have led to the proliferation of the crime.

REFERENCES

Broome M.E. (1993) *Integrative literature reviews for the development of concepts. In Concept Development in Nursing,* 2nd edn (Rodgers B.L. & Knafl K.A., eds), W.B. Saunders Co., Philadelphia, PA, pp. 231–250.

Cohen, L.E.; Felson, M. *Social Change and Crime Rate Trends: A Routine Activity Approach. Am. Social.* Rev. 1979, 44, 588.

Cooper H. (1998) Synthesizing Research*: A Guide for Literature Reviews*, 3rd edn. Sage Publications, Thousand Oaks, CA.

Gupta N (2012). *The conundrum of emotionally unstable personality disorders*. Indian J Soc Psychiatry 2012; 28:36-42

Hindelang, M.J.; Gottfredson, M.R.; Garofalo, J. Victims of Personal Crime: *An Empirical Foundation for a Theory of Personal Victimization; Ballinger:* Cambridge, MA, USA, 1978.

India Today (2020). Maharashtra: *One woman stalked or bullied on social media every day, says data,* available on https://www.indiatoday.in/india/story/maharashtra-one-woman-stalked-bullied-social-media-every-day-data-1730199-2020-10-10

Jackson G. (1980) *Methods for integrative reviews. Review of Educational Research* 50, 438–460.

Joshi, D. (2013). *India's Criminal Law Amendment to Include Cyber Stalking, Harassment and Voyeurism, Centre for Internet and Society.* (Online) Available at: http://www.medianama.com/2013/04/223-criminal-law-amendment-toinclude-cyber-stalking-harassment-and-voyeurism-cis-india/

Kabra, R (2013). Cyberstalking*: one problem control-alt-delete can't solve*.

Kalia, D. and Aleem, S. (2017). Cyber Victimization Among Adolescents*:* Examining the Role of Routine Activity Theory, *Journal of Psychosocial Research* Vol. 12, No. 1, 2017. pp. 223-232.

Kashmiria, S. (2014), Mapping Cyber Crimes against Women in India*, International Research Journal of Commerce and Law (IRJCL)* Volume -1, Issue -5

New Delhi Television (2017). Over 18,000 Stalking Cases Registered in Last 3 Years: Government. New Delhi. Available from: https://www.ndtv.com/india-news/over-18-000-stalking-cases-registered-in-last-3-years-government-1735109. [available on https://www.ndtv.com/india-news/over-18-000-stalking-cases-registered-in-last-3-years-government-1735109].

Ramona, L. CECIU, (2013), "The Architectonics of Corporeal and Textual Selves: *From Durga via Banalata Sen to the Virtual Indian Woman",* Asia Studies I (XVII), 1(2013), pp. 65–90,

Roy, P.K. (2015), *why online harassment goes unpunished in India*, article Available: http://www.bbc.com/news/worldasia-india-33532706

Rozatkar AR, Gupta N. (2019). The concept of "Stalking" and its relevance to the existing phenomena of internet and social media. *Indian J Soc Psychiatry* 2019; 35:1-3.

Shah, T and Srivastava, T. (2014), "Indian Women at Risk in the Cyber Space: A Conceptual Model of Reasons of Victimization"*, International Journal of Cyber Criminology*, Vol 8 Issue

Times of India (2021). Beware! Cyberstalking is on the rise during the pandemic, Amrita Prasad. Available on https://timesofindia.indiatimes.com/life-style/spotlight/beware-cyberstalking-is-on-the-rise-during-the-pandemic/articleshow/81924158.cms

Thakur, A (2012). Cyberstalking: *A Crime or A Tort, Jun*. 21, 2016. Dr. Swati Mehta, Cyber Forensics & Admissibility of Digital Evidence, (2012).

Zarina, V. et al. (2016*),* Toward the Adaptation of Routine Activity and Lifestyle Exposure Theories to Account for Cyber Abuse Victimization, *Journal of Contemporary Criminal Justice*, Vol. 32(2) 169–188

ROLE OF ONLINE PLATFORMS IN SUSTAINING THE LOCAL MEDIA

Bolormaa Battsogt
Department of Journalism and Media Technology, University of the Humanities, J.Sambuu St. 14200, Ulaanbaatar, Mongolia

ABSTRACT

Local media developed in Mongolia since the 1940s. Today, 126 local media operate normally. However, it is lacking research and study of their sustainability and existence way. This study tries to clarify local media theory based on "good neighbor" journalism norms, participatory journalism, and citizen journalism theory. Therefore, the study clarifies the following: 1) how the local media can simultaneously uphold regionality and cooperativity, and 2) the possibility of local media cooperating with citizen participation and, the method for future establishment and development of the local media in Mongolia through individual online participation.

KEYWORDS

Local Media, Online Platform, Citizen Journalism, Participatory Journalism

1. INTRODUCTION

Local media are "communication media that cover a certain local region," where local region is defined as "an entity that includes characteristics such as regionality, commonality, solidarity and cooperativity of people living there" based on spatial or geographical range (Takeuchi 1989, pp. 3–4). Mass communication, or mass media, closely relates to the "imaginary community," which transcends regional characteristics, and is linked to the cooperative formation of a nation-state (Anderson, 2006). It is certain that the local media, such as newspapers, radio, and television, have played a part as one of the mass media roles of cooperativity.

Moreover, the local media have become widespread in human lives and, by creating relationships between people in the respective areas, they have activated the senses and expanded the realms of individual consciousness and memory. Thus, the local media attempt a national and global expansion of spatiality to transcend regionality; simultaneously, they are deeply involved in the regional reality, thus mediating people's commonality and local characteristics and functioning as social memory (Battsogt 2017). In the concrete regional context of their activity, the ambivalent nature of local media — national, global, and local — is a topic that deserves closer analysis. This study clarifies the following: 1) the ways in which the local media can simultaneously uphold regionality and cooperativity, and 2) the method for future establishment and development of the local media in Mongolia through individual online participation.

2. A SHORT HISTORY OF LOCAL MEDIA IN MONGOLIA

In 1942, the "Jana Omir" newspaper was published in Bayan-Ulgii aimag (Zulkafil, 1997, pp. 13), and the first local newspaper factory was established in Arkhangai aimag in 1947 through a decision of the Politburo of the Socialist Party Central Committee (Norovsuren, 2001, pp. 177). In the 1980s, the establishment of a full-fledged system that included local TV and radio stations was a key event in Mongolian journalism (Norovsuren, 2001, pp. 12,78). Since 1990, following the collapse of the Soviet Union and Mongolia's transition to a market economy, the media — which had previously been under the auspices of the state and directly transmitted party ideology — have faced significant challenges (Norovsuren, 2001, pp. 98). From 1990 to 2000, the local media sector was financially unstable and lacked its own ideology; this phase can be described as a period of transition for the local media (Sharavdorj, 2006). In 2021, there are 126 local media outlets in Mongolia providing information to half of the nation's population.

3. FEATURES AND DEFINITIONS OF THE LOCAL MEDIA

As there is no common understanding of the classification of the theory of journalism, its constituent subjects are often ambiguous (Skinner et al., 2001; Berglez, 2003). For example, Siebert (1956) categorized the constituent subjects of journalism into four categories based on issues of press freedom and press responsibilities. There have also been comparisons between normative ethics and norms as "watchdog" and "good neighbor" journalism (Franklin, 2005). In recent years, not only has a media-based journalism model been seen (Poindexter et al., 2006) but a public journalism model between sender and recipient has also been witnessed (Nip, 2006). Nip's five models have been widely cited since the mid-2000s, when the internet and SNS's were classified based on the current prevalence (Rausch, 2012).

The question arises as to which topics should be given more attention when discussing journalism tailored to the specifics of the local media. Ogawa asserted that the ideas, theories, and practices of "watchdog" journalism are not appropriate in small regions, such as rural areas (Ogawa, 2005). The "watchdog" journalism that has developed in Great Britain and in United States since the mid-18th century has been called the "Fourth Estate." It has traditionally been compared to a "watchdog" for loudly exclaiming to others to control the government and the rule of law. Some researchers have noted that journalism focuses on minorities and lacks tools to make known the interests of the majority in the community. The local media must contribute to the well-being of the people and emphasize whether they influence the region (Richards, 2014). Heider suggested that the local media should help people find solutions to real-life problems, thus promoting "good neighbor" journalism instead of only providing information about one segment (minority) (Heider et al., 2005). Poindexter outlines the reason for high hopes regarding the "good neighbor' local media (Poindexter et al., 2006). A similar conclusion was drawn from a study on the local media in Japan (Etsushi, 2005).

This section focuses on the specifics of the media and the relevance of local people as recipients of media information, as shown in Figure 1. This section attempts to identify appropriate media theories for local media. In Figure 1, the vertical axis represents the level of information dissemination to the public, while the horizontal axis represents the level of citizen participation. The lower areas can be classified as local or citizen media. The upper left corner of the Figure contains the most accessible media. The upper right section contains the main or traditional media.

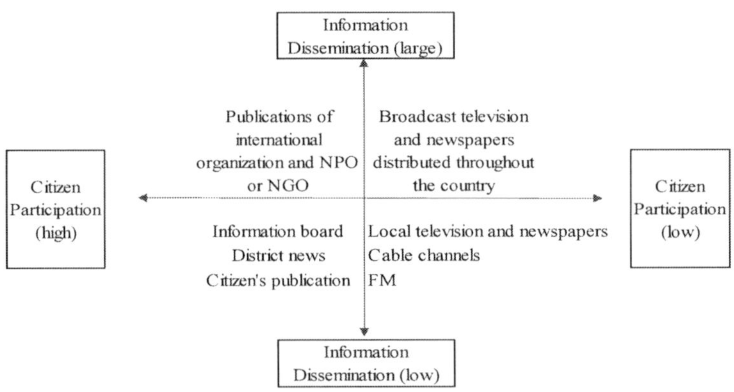

Source: Developed by author

Figure 1. Features of the media and classification of citizen participation

However, Figure 1 is a classification that depends only on specific characteristics of the media, the level of citizen participation, and the means of receiving information. In recent years, with the advent of the internet, the local media have been able to cross not national borders and create global networks. Cooperation with social networks such as *Facebook* and *Twitter* is difficult to describe in Figure 1. Furthermore, the local media cannot be directly interpreted as being separate from the traditional media. Figure 1 is merely an attempt to classify according to the levels of citizen participation and dissemination of information.

Comparing Nipp's five categories of journalism, citizen journalism, and participatory journalism are shown at the bottom of Figure 1. Emphasizing citizen participation in the media is not only a factor in citizen development but also an engine of social progress (Habermas, 1984). The media is required to cooperate with the private sector and government authorities concerning news sources and the economy. Thus, by encouraging citizen participation, it is possible to strengthen independence from external influences and further improve the quality of news (Brown, 2021).

4. VALUE OF LOCAL NEWS

This section discusses the value of local news and its theoretical research approaches, which are the main contents of the local media. Local news often contains values of public goods (Nichols and Robert, 2010; Radu, 2019), necessary goods (Ali, 2016), or public services (Mersereau, 2021).

If local news is a public service, such as electricity, water systems, and postal services, public policy is essential to ensure the stability and development of the local media organizations that distribute it. If local news is considered public goods or necessary goods, it is possible to obtain assistance and support for the variable costs of disseminating and transmitting the news, not only from the government but also from foreign and domestic public organizations. In recent years, a nationwide online platform has been supporting the local media to highlight the value of local news, which will be expanded upon in the following section.

4.1 Local News as Public Goods

The concept of public goods has two basic principles: it is non-excludable and non-rivalrous. Public goods can be used by all consumers, regardless of whether they pay a price, such as a free rider (Holcombe, 1997; Suber, 2009). Examples of this type of goods are the defense sector, police, and public streets. Regarding news, a group of commercial-based channels provides services that can be used at no cost. Most media platforms, such as newspapers and magazines, are unable to distribute public property without unrestricted competition.

However, recently, with the proliferation of false news on SNS, it has become clear that the media should be made public. The Nieman Foundation for Journalism at Harvard University conducted a systematic study on the value of news and produced a sub-report, entitled "News as Public Goods" (Nieman Lab, 2016). The World Bank's report, "The Right to Tell: The Role of Mass Media in Economic Development," states that the media should be responsible for the creation of public goods (Islam, 2002). Nobel Prize-winning economist Joseph Stiglitz has said that the value of news in many areas is reflected in the fact that it becomes a public good (Stiglitz, 2002, pp. 7).

Table 1 classifies the media based on the principle of public goods, those that are non-excludable and non-rivalrous. Researchers have often noted that commercial channels, which generate revenue from advertising, have difficulty delivering accurate information to audiences (Lamarre, 2015). With the support of online platforms, the local media can disseminate local news that is socially owned.

Table 1. The classification of media platforms based on public goods principles

	EXCLUDABLE	NONEXCLUDABLE
RIVALROUS	Newspapers and magazines	Commercial channels
NONRIVALROUS	Public channels	Local media + Online platforms

Source: Developed by author

5. COMMUNITY-BASED MEDIA

Since 1999, the Press Institute in Mongolia has published reports on the quantitative changes in local media types. Local news websites have been included in this report since 2019. Local news websites are among the most powerful local media platforms, as shown in Table 2 (Press Institute, 2021, pp. 99 -100).

Table 2 presents measures of the degree to which local media platforms support citizen participation online. It summarizes the number of local media platforms and the number of local people who participate in media activities, such as news processing, editing, and publication. Some websites have news entry section, where citizens can participate. Such websites attempt to create and develop their own space in the media market by promoting citizen participation, and their numbers are expected to increase. In contrast, however, none of the traditional local media platforms have websites or use *Facebook* pages to interact with citizens and encourage their participation. Eighty-two local media outlets use *Facebook* pages, but only 22 are active and support citizen participation. Most media platforms in Ulaanbaatar, the capital city, have developed their own websites and *Facebook* pages that are open and interdependent (Press Institute, 2021). However, the citizen-participation activities of the local media platforms are insufficient (<50), which reveal both the inequality of digital technology and the huge differences in the development of the online media market nationwide.

Table 2. Local media platforms' citizen participation

LOCAL MEDIA TYPES	NUMBER	SUPPORT CITIZEN PARTICIPATION		NOT-SUPPORT CITIZEN PARTICIPATION
	Year of 2020	Through Websites	Through Facebook	
Newsletter	22	0	5	17
Magazine	1	0	0	1
Radio	19	0	2	17
Of which: FM Radio	17	0	0	17
Television	64	0	15	49
Site	20	8	6	6
Total	126	8	28	90

Source: Developed by author

6. CONCLUSION

The political, social, and cultural contexts created by the local media are complex and multilayered. The local media act simultaneously in local and global information fields. This study clarified 1) the possibility of local media that simultaneously plays the roles of regionality and cooperativity, and 2) the method for establishing and developing in the future through individual online participation in local media in Mongolia.

This study highlights the lack of research, theories, and methodologies for local media development in Mongolia. Today, Mongolia has 126 local media platforms. However, only 30 local media platforms — that is, 25% of all local media platforms — are active through their websites and Facebook pages to ensure citizen participation. Defining the development of local media in line with the specifics of information delivery and the development of internet technology by promoting citizen participation may be the best option for sustaining the local media.

However, this study illustrates only current citizen participation on local media websites and *Facebook*. Further analysis is needed to improve the effectiveness and quality of local media activities and understand other impacts on the local media. For example, we need basic research, including local media affiliation and program relevance and content analysis, and information about local media staff ideologies, such as journalists' perceptions, differences of opinion, and conflicts. Continued study of the image, future direction, and normative concept of phrasings, such as "local media theory" and "local journalism," is needed.

REFERENCES

Ali, C. (2016). The merits of merit goods: Local journalism and public policy in a time of austerity. *Journal of Information Policy*, *6*(1), pp.105-128.

Anderson, B. (2006). *Imagined communities: Reflections on the origin and spread of nationalism*. Verso books.

Battsogt, B. (2017). The Societal and Cultural Background of Individual Support Activities beyond Regional Boundary, *The International Journal of Interdisciplinary Cultural Studies* 12 (2): 1-11. doi:10.18848/2327-008X/CGP/v12i02/1-11.

Berglez, P. (2013). *Global journalism: Theory and practice*. Peter Lang Publishing Group.

Briggs, A. and Burke, P. (2009). *A social history of the media: From Gutenberg to the Internet*. Polity.

Brown, C.L.S. (2021). *Breaking News: Professional Participatory Journalism*, Doctoral dissertation, Clemson University.

Etsushi T. (2005). *Contemporary Media and Politics: Journalism and Politics in Theater Society*. Ichigeisha.

Franklin, B., Hamer, M., Hanna, M., Kinsey, M. and Richardson, J. E. (2005). *Key concepts in journalism studies*. Sage.

Habermas, J. (1984). *The theory of communicative action* (Vol. 2). Beacon press.

Heider, D., McCombs, M. and Poindexter, P.M. (2005). What the public expects of local news: Views on public and traditional journalism. *Journalism and Mass Communication Quarterly*, *82*(4), pp. 952-967.

Holcombe, R.G. (1997). A theory of the theory of public goods. *The Review of Austrian Economics*, *10*(1), pp. 1-22.

Islam, R. (ed.) (2002). *The right to tell: the role of mass media in economic development*. World Bank Publications.

Janowitz, M. (1952). *The Community Press in an Urban Setting*. Glencoe, Ill. The Free Press 14: 73-74.

Mersereau, M. (2021). Universal and non-excludable broadband Internet access: A modest proposal for municipal provisioning of broadband as a basic service. *Canadian Journal of Urban Research*, *30*(1), pp. 30-39.

Milton, J. (1890). *Areopagitica: A speech of Mr. John Milton for the liberty of unlicensed printing, to the Parliament of England*. Grolier club.

Munson, E. S. (1998). *Adobe walls and black-tinted windshields: The press and community identity in Santa Fe, New Mexico*. University of Illinois at Urbana-Champaign.

Nichols, J. and McChesney, R.W. (2010). How to save journalism. *The Nation*, *7*, pp. 2010.

Nieman Foundation. (2016). News is a Public good, *Nieman Reports*, Harvard

Nip, J.Y. (2006). Exploring the second phase of public journalism. *Journalism studies*, *7*(2), pp.212-236.

Norovsuren L. (2001). *Historical Review of Mongolian Journalism*. Sub-volume. Ulaanbaatar: Mukhiin useg.

Norovsuren L. (2003). *Historical Review of Mongolian Journalism*: Volume 3. Ulaanbaatar: National University of Mongolia.

Ostrom, E. (1978). Citizen participation and policing: What do we know? *Journal of Voluntary Action Research* 7, no.1-2: 102-108.

Poindexter, P.M., Heider, D. and McCombs, M. (2006). Watchdog or good neighbor? The public's expectations of local news. *Harvard International Journal of Press/Politics*, *11*(1), pp. 77-88.

Press Institute (2021). Mongolian Media-Today, Ulaanbaatar

Radu, R.N. (2019). Externalities and Journalism. *The International Encyclopedia of Journalism Studies*, pp.1-7.

Rausch, A. (2012). *Japan's local newspapers: Chihōshi and revitalization journalism*. Routledge.

Richards, I. (2014). Differences over difference: journalism beyond the metropolis. *Australian Journalism Review*, 36, no. 1: 5-14.

Sharavdorj, C. (2006). Situation of Local Media in Mongolia. *Journalism Studies*, 268(06), Mongolian National University

Siebert, F., Siebert, F.T., Peterson, T., Peterson, T.B. and Schramm, W. (1956). *Four theories of the press: The authoritarian, libertarian, social responsibility, and Soviet communist concepts of what the press should be and do* (Vol. 10). University of Illinois press.

Skinner, D., Gasher, M.J. and Compton, J., 2001. Putting theory to practice: A critical approach to journalism studies. *Journalism*, *2*(3), pp. 341-360.

Stiglitz, J. (2002). Transparency in government. *The right to tell*, pp. 27.

Suber, P. (2009). Knowledge as a public good. *Sparc open access newsletter*.

Takeuchi, I. (1989). *[New Edition] Regional Media*, Nihon Hyoronsha

Zulkafil, M. (1994). *Reform and Media*, Ulaanbaatar, MNCCI Press.

Zulkafil, M. (1997). *Modern Mongolian Journalism*. Ulaanbaatar: Academy of Arts.

TMOOC IN THE AGE OF MLEARNING. A CASE STUDY OF ECO DIGITAL LEARNING

Sara Osuna-Acedo[1], Roberto Feltrero[1] and Eva Bunbury[2]
[1]*Universidad Nacional de Educación a Distancia (UNED), Spain*
[2]*Universidad de Zaragoza, Spain*

ABSTRACT

A social demand in today's digital society is digital literacy of citizens throughout their lives. That aim has to be done without any discrimination on the grounds of disability. It is necessary to motivate all citizens to participate on such literacy, particularly including the population sector on which we focus and designing educational strategies to include and motivate them.

For this purpose, is proposed a learning methodology through the tMOOC, that is to say, massive online and open courses which prioritize the direct transfer of what has been learned to the working environment. It is needed a research on the real state of the problem and the possible effects and difficulties of the proposed training solution in case of disable students. The methodology to implement this research is presented as the result of a group of experts study, research and discussion.

KEYWORDS

tMOOC, Mobile Learning, Digital Competencies, Citizens, Disability

1. INTRODUCTION

This research focuses on digital literacy and its importance in ensuring access to technology in general, and access to services in particular, for citizens and, in a larger extent, for vulnerable people. The only intention of participating is not enough; one must also know how to participate and acquire the digital skills necessary to do so, responsibly and critically. In this sense, an unknown global scenario has been taking shape regarding media literacy for citizens, structured in a quite decentralized way, where MOOC (Massive Open Online Courses) is one of the main responses, taking into account two-way communication models for the construction of open knowledge (Osuna-Acedo et al., 2018).

According to data from the World Health Organization, approximately one billion people worldwide - 15% of the population - suffer from some form of disability and, for one in five, this limitation has a significant impact on their daily lives. In the coming years, the ageing of the population and the increase in certain chronic diseases such as diabetes, cardiovascular diseases and mental health disorders are expected to increase the prevalence of disability, since those who suffer from it will achieve poorer health and academic outcomes, lower economic participation and higher poverty rates than people without disabilities (OECD, 2019).

In the framework of the VII Framework Program "Elearning Communication Open-Data" the project No: 621127 "ECO" was developed under the research leadership of UNED. The international relations resulting from the cooperation of up to 45 entities finally involved in the development of ECO, and its successful assessment by the European Union (EU), led to the creation of the spin-off ECO DIGITAL LEARNING led by UNED. Thus, a consistent, innovative and qualified digital platform is made available to the project to host the MOOC and to implement the proposed tMOOC methodology for disable people.

2. TOWARDS MOOC ACCESSIBLE AND INCLUSIVE

The social challenge to address with these educational tools, in a particularly critical situation due to the emergence produced by the COVID-19, is the acquisition of digital skills by citizens facing Europe today and, specifically, Spain. Digital skills are key to the construction of a digital economy. In this second dimension, the EU recognizes its importance and measures the capacities of each country to take advantage of the potential that the digital world offers.

Spain's position is worrying, both because it continues to lag behind the European average (position 17 out of 28), and because of its poor performance since 2016. It is behind the most dynamic European economies. Far from narrowing, the gap with the leading countries on this indicator (Finland, Sweden, Luxembourg and Estonia) and with the European average has increased in recent years.

Despite the relentless work of associations and foundations such as the ONCE Foundation, the Spanish Confederation of Physically and Organically Disabled People (COCEMFE) or the Institute of Elderly and Social Services (IMSERSO) and the development of specific plans such as the inclusion of Network, it is essential, under the auspices of Legislative RD 1/2013 approving the revised text of the General Law on the Rights of Persons with Disabilities.

Even the MOOC is a useful tool for tackling the task of a long life learning for teaching digital skills, there is a long way to walk to improve nowdays models to be really useful for teaching digital literacy to people with especial needs. MOOC offer the possibility of acting as a means of training and dissemination because they offer the members of their virtual community a wide range of proposals for interaction and communication, valuing their applications in different ways according to the activities, resources, media, methodology, evaluation processes (Camarero Cano & Cantillo Valero, 2016) and interactivity. From this perspective, Berners-Lee (1996) coined the term inter-creativity to describe people's ability to create original and more productive elements in a virtual environment through citizen participation.

Consequently, an unknown global educational scenario is taking shape, structured in a rather decentralized way, where MOOC (Massive Open Online Courses) are one of the main solutions with two-way communication models for the construction of open knowledge (Osuna-Acedo et al., 2018). The social literacy of the MOOC allows to reach a number of people unknown by the conventional formal education and to extend the existing systems available to the population in terms of educational training. As a result of the digitalisation process, a significant and worrying discrepancy has emerged between technological development and citizens' skills, which reveals a growing digital gap between the training received and the qualifications required to face the labour and social challenges of the digital society (van Laar et al., 2017). As recent research has already shown (Pettersson, 2018), curricula in primary, secondary and higher compulsory education do not respond adequately to the demands of the new context, which are especially evident in the MOOC models.

2.1 MOOC and tMOOC

The evolution of MOOCs over the last decade has been constant and dynamic. They have moved from the first models of c-MOOC and x-MOOC to other post-MOOC modalities that foster digital interaction by means of the social networks (Martínez Pérez, 2016; Pei & Shen, 2017; Yousef et al., 2015; Zancanaro & Domingues, 2017). For the purpose of teaching digital literacy to people with especial needs, a new generation of MOOCs, the tMOOC (Transfer Massive Open Online Courses) seems to be more appropriate.

One of the main conclusions posits that the tMOOC supposes a new generation of MOOC that promotes effective transfer of knowledge and of learning by means of opportunities for personal, professional and collective development. Open and Diversified Participation, everyone with their own skills, functionalities and interests is a very good possibility for the tMOOC framework. It is so because learning and improvement on that model is evaluated on the parameters of measurement used for social networks, not on the traditional academic criteria (where participation is not part of the equation).

Authentic tasks, transfer of knowledge, pedagogic transformation, TRIC, transmediality, opened temporality, intercreative talent, collaborative toil, transnationalism and tolerance are the ten characteristics and values that sustain the inclusive approach fo tMOOC better than classic MOOC. Therefore, the model of tMOOC is proposed for this project Enter the text here.

3. METHODOLOGY

A research project with this philosophy has to be designed to study how to implement it on educational resources. For that purpose the group of experts methodology has been used to establish the required methodological steps. That group has been constituted with researchers belonging to the following entities:

• SMEMIU (UNED Research Group on Social Media, Inclusive and Ubiquitous Media Education) will provide the research staff carrying out the academic training in the tMOOC. PI: Sara Osuna-Acedo.

• GICID (Digital Communication and Information Research Group of the University of Zaragoza) will support the project from the three axes that play a leading role in the communication process (senders, receivers and messages) in virtual and digital environments for the field of science. PI: Carmen Marta-Lazo.

• ECOLEARNING (ECO DIGITAL LEARNING) offers its experience of hosting sMOOC courses in six languages. Research has shown and published in leading scientific journals that the empowerment of participants in their sMOOCs has increased the level of learning, involvement in sMOOC and interaction among participants. CEO: Vicente Montiel-Molina

• UNIDIS (Centro de Atención a la Discapacidad de la UNED) will guide the adaptation of activities

The expert group start the discussion from two big questions, the answers to which will mark the axes of this research:

1. How can MOOCs help to develope digital competences of disabled groups?

2. Why are the educational-communicative and methodological foundations of quality sMOOC and tMOOC necessary for the transfer of knowledge to the working environment of the disabled?

Expert group proposed the following methodology:

Research has to be held in three phases. In the first phase, a study of the accessibility characteristics of the MOOCs available in the target country has to be carried out. In this first phase, a documentary review will be used with natural language processing techniques, based on big data, of the scientific literature and sources that will allow to establish the basis of the state of the art.

In the second phase, a study of the digital competencies of the target population with some kind of disability will be produced. It is also necessary to investigate with natural language processing techniques, based on big data, about the collaboration and interaction of the participants, the processes of co-creation and co-authorship, the social process of creative exchange and the social transfer of knowledge.

In the third and last phase, a tMOOC will be designed and carried out in the ECO DIGITAL LEARNING portal, which will provide training to citizens, without any discrimination on the grounds of disability, on digital literacy.

4. CONCLUSION

As far as this is a big project, experts group suggested the following list of collaborative entities to implement and develop the three phases and three methodological steps. The following figures (figure 1 and figure 2) synthesize the proposed research methodology to study possibilities and conditions to implement tMOOC methodology for mLearning with an inclusive philosophy.

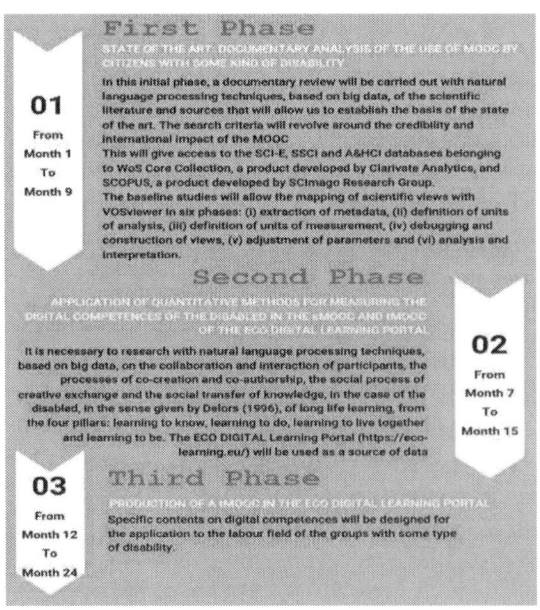

Figure 1. Three phases project to implement mLearning with accessible tMOOC

Objectives	Methods and activities	Resources	Expected outcomes
Learn about the specific needs in digital competences of people with disabilities considering a basic right for this citizenship the access to training plans that prepare them to face the digital challenges	- *Focus group* of people with disabilities who are interested in working in the specific communication market. - Surveys of people with disabilities seeking employment in the communication market. - Applied Neuroscience Experiment Neuroscience: • *Eye tracking* • GSR.	-Our own resources are available to contribute to the design of discussion groups. - Resources are needed in order to: • Hiring companies' support for the processing of focus data, the development of the survey, the realization of the experiment and the development of the WebApp. • Dissemination of results in scientific impact and social outreach formats	- Publication of results in publications of international prestige. - Dissemination of results through participation in conferences. - Outcome reports of interest to society on the digital needs of the disabled - Development of the App to facilitate the labour insertion of the disabled.

Figure 2. Summary of principal project aims

ECO DIGITAL LEARNING project is ready to implement this methodology at any interested educational institution and at any european country. The final result will be the development of a realm of tMOOCs contextualized to the particular citizens, topics and social priorities for digital literacy. Clearly indicate advantages, limitations and possible applications.

ACKNOWLEDGEMENT

This article has been written as part of research works carried out at ECO Project, registered in the Competitiveness and Innovation Framework Programme (CIP-ICT-PSP.2013 Theme 2: Digital content, open data and creativity, Obj 2.3.a: Piloting and showcasing excellence in ICT for learning for all); It is also supported by UNESCO Chair "Self-fulfilment in the era of sustainable digital development", at Sorbonne Nouvelle, Paris (France).

REFERENCES

Berners-Lee, T. (1996). WWW: Past, present, and future. *Computer, 29*(10), 69-77. https://doi.org/10.1109/2.539724

Camarero Cano, L., & Cantillo Valero, C. (2016). La evaluación de los aprendizajes en los sMOOC. Estudio de caso en el Proyecto Europeo ECO. *Revista Mediterránea de Comunicación, 7*(2), 21. https://doi.org/10.14198/MEDCOM2016.7.2.2

Martínez Pérez, J. (2016). El empoderamiento del alumnado desde el modelo sMOOC. *Revista Mediterránea de Comunicación, 7*(2), 69. https://doi.org/10.14198/MEDCOM2016.7.2.6

OECD. (2019). *Education at a Glance 2019: OECD Indicators*. OECD. https://doi.org/10.1787/f8d7880d-en

Osuna-Acedo, S., Marta-Lazo, C., & Frau-Meigs, D. (2018). From sMOOC to tMOOC, learning towards professional transference. ECO European Project. *Comunicar, 26*(55), 105-114. https://doi.org/10.3916/C55-2018-10

Pei, P., & Shen, L.-L. (2017). Design and Implementation for cMOOC-oriented Online Course Learning Community. *DEStech Transactions on Social Science, Education and Human Science, eshd.* https://doi.org/10.12783/dtssehs/eshd2016/5206

Pettersson, F. (2018). On the issues of digital competence in educational contexts – a review of literature. *Education and Information Technologies, 23*(3), 1005-1021. https://doi.org/10.1007/s10639-017-9649-3

van Laar, E., van Deursen, A. J. A. M., van Dijk, J. A. G. M., & de Haan, J. (2017). The relation between 21st-century skills and digital skills: A systematic literature review. *Computers in Human Behavior, 72*, 577-588. https://doi.org/10.1016/j.chb.2017.03.010

Yousef, A. M. F., Chatti, M. A., Wosnitza, M., & Schroeder, U. (2015). A Cluster Analysis of MOOC Stakeholder Perspectives. *RUSC. Universities and Knowledge Society Journal, 12*(1), 74. https://doi.org/10.7238/rusc.v12i1.2253

Zancanaro, A., & Domingues, M. J. (2017). Analysis of the scientific literature on Massive Open Online Courses (MOOCs) / Análisis de la literatura científica sobre los cursos en línea abiertos y masivos (MOOC). *RIED. Revista Iberoamericana de Educación a Distancia, 20*(1), 59. https://doi.org/10.5944/ried.20.1.15910

AUTHOR INDEX